Ireland, Colonialism, and
the Unfinished Revolution

Ireland, Colonialism, and the Unfinished Revolution

Robbie McVeigh
Bill Rolston

Haymarket Books
Chicago, IL

Originally published in 2021 by
Beyond the Pale Books
2 Hannahstown Hill,
Belfast, BT17 0LT

This edition published in 2023 by
Haymarket Books
P.O. Box 180165
Chicago, IL 60618
773-583-7884
www.haymarketbooks.org
info@haymarketbooks.org

ISBN: 978-1-64259-984-8

Distributed to the trade in the US through Consortium Book Sales and Distribution (www.cbsd.com)
and internationally through Ingram Publisher Services International (www.ingramcontent.com).

This book was published with the generous support of Lannan Foundation, Wallace Action Fund,
and the Marguerite Casey Foundation.

Special discounts are available for bulk purchases by organizations and institutions.
Please call 773-583-7884 or email info@haymarketbooks.org for more information.

Cover design by Eric Kerl.

Library of Congress Cataloging-in-Publication data is available.

10 9 8 7 6 5 4 3 2 1

Printed in Canada with union labor.

The front cover photograph shows a bronze statue of Queen Victoria being removed from the forecourt of Leinster House, Dublin, by the Office of Public Works on 22 July 1948. First erected in 1908, the statue survived the first wave of colonial-iconography eradication in the 1920s, even though public calls for its removal began soon after partition. One suggestion was to send the statue to Belfast and to find a suitable location in the grounds of Stormont. Instead, the statue ended up in a museum overflow store at Daingean, Co. Offaly, where it lay behind a wall of a derelict reformatory school, covered in weeds and brambles. In 1986, the statue was given to the city of Sydney, Australia, where it now sits facing the City Hall.

Y. Whelan (2002) 'The construction and destruction of a colonial landscape: monuments to British monarchs in Dublin before and after independence', *Journal of Historical Geography*, 28, 4: 508-533.

Do threascair an saol is shéid an ghaoth mar smál

Alastrann, Caesar, 's an méid sin a bhí 'na bpáirt;

tá an Teamhair 'na féar, is féach an Traoi mar tá,

Is na Sasanaigh féin do b'fhéidir go bhfaighidis bás!

Life has conquered: the wind has blown away

Alexander, Caesar and all their power and sway;

Tara and Troy have made no longer stay;

Maybe the English too will have their day.

Anonymous (18th century)
translated from the Irish by Frank O'Connor

Contents

Acknowledgements

Thanks to Carol Coulter, Margaret Ward, Mike Ritchie and Nalina Eggert for helpful comments as we developed the ideas in this book. And to Mike Ritchie for the many hours of work put into proofreading. Any errors that remain are the responsibility of the authors.

Preface

It is difficult at times to repress the thought that history is about as instructive as an abattoir; that Tacitus was right, and that peace is merely the desolation left behind after the decisive operations of merciless power. —Seamus Heaney

Every political conflict is unique, and yet all political conflicts have shared elements, not least those which involve colonial conquest and anti-colonial resistance. There is a tendency to see the Irish experience as quintessentially unique – the first English colony, the first colonial nation of modern times to seriously attempt to break free from the imperial grip, the role model for so many anti-colonial struggles worldwide. In recent times, that label of uniqueness took a particular turn. The conflict in the North since the 1960s confused many observers. The concept of colonialism was seen to be no longer any help, if it ever had been, in understanding what was happening in Ireland. After all, the Free State gained its independence in 1921. The North was incorporated in a stable state, the United Kingdom, the state which, after all, is said to have given parliamentary democracy to the world. The Northern Ireland conflict came to be judged as some anachronistic outlier, its 'troubles' due to ethnic hatred, terrorism or simply criminality. Before the Balkans exploded in the 1990s, Northern Ireland was seen to have only one European comparator, the Basque Country.

If the concept of colonialism was already judged inadequate, it received a further body blow in the new millennium. The attack on the World Trade Center in New York in September 2001 spelt the death knell for anti-imperialist struggle. Support for such struggle in less developed countries had already waned with the collapse of the Soviet system, but now there was little space for claiming anti-imperialism as one's political motivation. Thankfully some struggles, such as that of the ANC in South Africa, had broken through into mainstream politics by this stage so did not have to suffer global opprobrium. For its part, the Irish republican struggle had made similar progress and reached a newly proclaimed plateau of uniqueness. The Irish peace process was touted worldwide, from Colombia to the Philippines, from the Basque Country to Sri Lanka, as a beacon and indeed a model for conflict transformation. Lost from this ideological representation was any suggestion that the deep roots of 'the troubles' were in colonial conquest.

This silence was further compounded by academic writing. At a time, the Northern Ireland conflict was the most written about conflict globally proportionate to its population. And while there were many interpretations, sophisticated and otherwise, put forward as to the reasons for the conflict, there were few academics who considered the explanatory value of colonialism. Some rejected the paradigm altogether, while others acknowledged its past but not its contemporary relevance. Most did not even consider the concept at all.

Our starting point is that, now more than ever, it is crucial to retrieve that concept. This is a disruptive moment in human history: climate catastrophe is imminent, the rise of the Right, from Brazil to Hungary, from the US and UK to the Philippines, seems inexorable. And, as we write, Brexit threatens the economic, social and political arrangements in Ireland, Britain and further afield. Former Prime Minister Theresa May spoke frequently of 'our precious Union', a catchphrase taken up by the leader of the Democratic Unionist Party, Arlene Foster. May's successor, Boris Johnson, appointed himself 'Minister for the Union' in 2019. Yet in all this there is a whiff of protesting too much, a reluctant acknowledgement that Brexit is the greatest threat to the Union, at least since it settled into its current form a century ago. The rise of narrow-minded, xenophobic English nationalism threatens to do what Irish republican struggle did not manage to do: break up the United Kingdom and lead to the reunification of Ireland.

As this disruptive moment deepens, not a day goes by without colonialism entering the agenda of the mainstream British news – Cecil Rhodes' statue at Oxford, the Windrush generation, criticism of 'white saviours', the plight of the Chagos islanders, Jeremy Corbyn's election pledge to launch an audit of Britain's colonial past. This reveals a fundamental point not always prominent in debates about Brexit, and certainly not in the discourse of the pro-Brexiteers. Brexit represents the death throes of empire (O'Toole 2018). That decline began slowly after the first World War and gained momentum after the second World War. The Commonwealth emerged at a relatively early stage to compensate for this decline, a sort of empire-lite. But what is becoming increasingly clear is that, just as the British empire began with the formation of Great Britain, so it will end there – end of empire, end of Britain, and thereby the circle will be closed.

The existential angst that leaving Europe produces has led to aspirations towards Empire 2.0 (YouGov 2004, Booth 2020). Whether based on economic links with the white former colonies of Canada, Australia and New Zealand, or more widely on a boost to the Commonwealth as an economic and not simply a cultural amalgamation, the bottom line is nostalgia, or what Paul Gilroy (2005) called 'postcolonial melancholia'. The project rests on a myth of a golden age which never really existed and yet its reconstruction is sought. Most empires in the history of humanity have ended with a whimper rather than a bang. They were not militarily defeated but crumbled from within. It is now Britain's turn. And one measure of the misguided millenarianism involved in seeking to reconstruct empire is, as David Olusoga (2017) puts it, that, while some Commonwealth members 'may well be up for a better trade deal or more freedom of movement … they don't want to be part of Empire 2.0, any more than most of them wanted to be part of Empire 1.0'.

Meanwhile in Ireland the end of the 'decade of centenaries' is approaching. The revolutionary decade 1912-22 saw Ireland partitioned and two new states emerge from the ashes of three wars: the 'Great War', the Tan War and the Irish Civil War. Despite the

surfeit of memorializing of the centenaries of both states, contemporary Ireland is in a
fairly grim situation: austerity hegemonic in both states; the southern state still recovering
from its fall from Celtic Tiger self-confidence; the North incapable of sustaining power
sharing or, indeed, contemplating any alternative to the distinctly colonial model of
'direct rule'; the Irish diaspora all but silenced and removed from any positive relationship
with contemporary Irish politics.[1] Economic stagnation, the collapse of the Good Friday
Agreement (GFA) and multiple crises around Brexit all point to significant challenges.
Indeed, the realisation that Brexit was to be made in the image of the DUP finally alerted
many people to the true character – and multiple dangers – of that particular project.
Moreover, despite this late flowering of empire loyalism, the potential disintegration of
the UK promises further crisis as the Irish unionist 'dark eleventh hour'[2] is finally realised.

Between 2016 and 2019 discussions of the 'divorce settlement' between the UK and
the EU focused on three items. The first two were predictable and turned out to be capable
of solution: the €39 million owed by the UK, and the citizenship status of UK nationals in
the EU and EU nationals in the UK. The third agenda item, one not referred to at any point
by any British politician in the lead-up to the referendum, was what the media constantly
referred to as 'the Irish border', more accurately, the British border in Ireland. This proved
to be the rock on which negotiations perished. The proposed solution to the problem of a
land border of the EU within one island was the so-called 'backstop' whereby the whole of
the UK would remain within the customs union until such time as new arrangements were
in place, while Northern Ireland would continue in the single market indefinitely. This was
rejected by many Tories and their DUP allies on the grounds that it would create 'a border
in the Irish Sea', the outcome that the UK eventually agreed with the EU in December
2020. The irony which was not lost on many Irish commentators is that partition, seen as a
solution to Britain's Irish problem, had come back a century later to plague British politics
again – a classic return of the repressed.[3]

At the same time what is from one perspective an ending is also a beginning. The

---

[1] This may change, at least symbolically, as a result of the proposed referendum on allowing all holders of
an Irish passport, whether living in the state or not, to vote in presidential elections from 2025 onwards.

[2] The phrase is from Rudyard Kipling's poem, 'Ulster': 'The dark eleventh hour/ Draws on and sees us sold/
To every evil power/ We fought against of old.'

[3] For Brexiteers the reaction to this has not been to question partition but to blame the Irish for derailing
what was promised to be an effortless Brexit. Witness Boris Johnson wondering why Taoiseach Leo Varadkar,
the son of an Indian father and Irish mother, 'isn't called Murphy like all the rest of them' (Stephens 2019).
Sections of the British media pursued the same ideological line. 'This is tough right now, being a proud and
loyal British subject who has lived in, and loved, Ireland for more than 60 years. What is tough is watching
the ridiculous behaviour of the Taoiseach Leo Varadkar and his foreign minister, Simon Coveney, trying to
destroy, like wilful children, relations with an ancient and friendly neighbour' (Arnold 2019). And it must
not be forgotten that, as with Empire 1.0, ideology in Empire 2.0 is propaganda for and often precursor to
policy. Thus, Tory minister Priti Patel, noting that the Irish Republic was likely to experience food shortages
as a result of Brexit (Coates 2018), urged that this should be more forcefully emphasised in negotiations,
thus revealing a staggering ignorance of Irish-British relations. At least one million Irish subjects of the UK
died from famine between 1848 and 1851.

plate tectonics of Irishness are shifting once again. Walter Benjamin's angel of history[4] is focused intently on contemporary Ireland and we can be sure that another transformation *of some description* is coming. Moreover, behind all the bleakness of the contemporary Irish landscape these significant structural changes suggest that the coming times might finally see the decolonisation project completed– partition ended, the legacies of colonial expropriation and racism and sectarianism finally addressed and excised.

Ireland might finally see the completion of a decolonisation process begun over a century ago – the finishing of the revolution. Seamus Heaney's pessimism can be channelled and represented as an optimism of the will.[5] An interrogation of history is fundamental to leaving the 'abattoir' of colonialism behind; peace – and decolonisation – offers *all* sides of the Irish conflict a future beyond our contemporary desolation.

This book is about putting colonialism back in as a lens, a frame to understand where we came from, where we are now and where we might be going. As stated above, the concept is not popular in academia. It is also likely to be dismissed by political elements who want to 'draw a line under the past' in favour of reconciliation or who are blind to how they have benefited from colonialism. This book is for those who are open to considering the value of the analysis to understanding this disruptive moment as it affects Ireland. Most of all, the book is for us – that is, the people connected to Ireland, whether living on the island or in the diaspora, whether born on the island or arriving from elsewhere, and especially for the people of the North where the unfinished business of decolonisation is painfully apparent and is becoming more so by the day.

Although we the authors have spent a lifetime in academic teaching and research, we do not present this as an academic text. The book, although it deals with some conceptually complex and difficult issues, is not geared specifically towards an academic audience. More precisely, although it considers a lot of historical facts and interpretations, it is not a history book. Similarly, while it considers social classes and trends as well as statistical evidence, it is not a sociology text. Likewise, it discusses political theories and concepts, but it is not a political science primer. It has elements of all of these approaches and more but none of them is its central purpose.

Put simply, its aim is to reclaim the concept of colonialism as the central frame in understanding Ireland past, present and future. To this end, it seeks to situate Ireland's

---

[4]Benjamin (1940) refers to a painting by Klee called Angelus Novus. The angel 'looks as though he were about to distance himself from something which he is staring at. His eyes are opened wide, his mouth stands open and his wings are outstretched. The Angel of History must look just so. His face is turned towards the past. Where we see the appearance of a chain of events, he sees one single catastrophe, which unceasingly piles rubble on top of rubble and hurls it before his feet. He would like to pause for a moment so fair, to awaken the dead and to piece together what has been smashed. But a storm is blowing from Paradise, it has caught itself up in his wings and is so strong that the Angel can no longer close them. The storm drives him irresistibly into the future, to which his back is turned, while the rubble-heap before him grows sky-high. That which we call progress, is this storm.'

[5]'I'm a pessimist because of intelligence, but an optimist because of will.' Antonio Gramsci, letter from prison, 19 December 1929.

experience in a global context. It considers the origins and development of colonial conquest and consolidation in Ireland in the light of these phenomena elsewhere. Likewise, it examines Ireland's experience of decolonisation alongside that of other decolonising societies. Its scope is at once specific and broad.

Above all, the book is not intended to be academic in the more pejorative sense of that word, that is, aloof and disconnected. It is concerned with the past and the present as providing clues to understand a possible future in which decolonisation is completed on the island of Ireland. That possibility is greater now than it has been in a century and so we seek to examine and indeed help expedite that possibility. At the risk of overstating our goal, we have at the centre of our understanding the admonishment of Karl Marx, the epitaph carved on his gravestone: 'The philosophers have only interpreted the world, in various ways. The point, however, is to change it'. That is not to say that we provide a political manifesto or programme to guide the task of decolonisation. Rather, we argue that sound political outcomes depend on robust political analysis. There is, we believe, nothing as practical as a sound theory. In the Irish context the failure to consider the role of colonialism in the past and the legacy of colonialism in the present detracts from the possibility of future progress. Ireland was a colony. Ireland, north and south, continues to bear the scars of that colonial experience. The future development of Ireland depends on settling the unfinished business of colonialism.

The bulk of this analysis was completed before the coronavirus pandemic took hold. And in one obvious way, of course, this might have made much of it instantly redundant. The world that our analysis addressed at the end of 2019 – as well as Ireland's place within it – seems a lifetime away at the start of 2021. A year ago, Ireland, north and south, was particularly absorbed by the challenges facing the future after having been battered by the maelstrom of Brexit. While this crisis is not resolved, much else has obviously changed in the interim. Even the consequences of the two recent elections on the island – including the hegemony of Johnsonism in the British state and the Sinn Féin 'surge' in the 26 county elections of December 2020 – seem some distance away. These new discontents give some cause to pause and reflect on what this focus on Ireland and colonialism means in the context of our post-pandemic world. There are two principal elements to this reflection – first, how much has the pandemic changed our prognosis – how different is the world in which we now engage with the legacy of colonialism? Secondly, the other side of that coin – what does the history of Ireland and colonialism teach us about how we make sense of the contemporary pandemic and its consequences?

Belfast
February 2021

Section I

Situating Ireland within paradigms of colonialism and imperialism

This Deep, Bloody American Tragedy is now concluded, and my Pen choakt up with Indian Blood and Gore. I have no more to say.... —Bartolomé de las Casas, 1552

All these mountains of Irish dead, all these corpses mangled beyond recognition, all these arms, legs, eyes, ears, fingers, toes, hands, all these shivering putrefying bodies and portions of bodies once warm living and tender parts of Irish men and youths – all these horrors in Flanders or the Gallipoli Peninsula, are all items in the price Ireland pays for being part of the British Empire. —James Connolly, 1915

How do we measure the cost of empire to Ireland? The first section of our analysis – comprising chapters one to four – situates Ireland – and the wider Irish experience – within broader analyses of colonialism and imperialism. It offers a schematic overview of both these processes. What were the different forms and stages of colonialism and imperialism? How does the trajectory of the British Empire compare with other empires? What lessons for Ireland can be drawn from these wider histories? We then address the long process of colonisation in Ireland – under first English and then British authority – in more detail. We address the symbiotic development of *Union* and *Empire*, assessing Ireland's specific role within both. Finally, we signal the beginning of the outworking of resistance to – and collapse of – Empire.

The first chapter outlines our broad approach – our theoretical contexts and our methodology and key sources. The second chapter offers a genealogy of colonialism and imperialism – this helps situate British imperialism in comparative context along with Ireland's place within it. The third chapter opens with a discussion of Ireland as England's 'first colony'. It details Irish colonial history from the proto-imperial English engagement with Ireland in 1155 to the Union in 1801. The fourth chapter details the place of Ireland within the expanding British Empire and engages with the complex nexus of Union and Empire over the period 1801-1922. It concludes with the partition of Ireland. This moment marks a key conjuncture not just in Irish history but as, arguably, the first stage in the breakup of the British Empire.

I

Our overview of colonial expansion from the 'age of discovery' to the 'scramble for Africa' situates Ireland – and Irish people – within the broader colonial and imperial story. This history is most obviously revealed in the maelstrom of peoples thrown around the world by the forces of colonialism and imperialism. The Irish diaspora itself is the most obvious and tangible evidence of this context – it witnesses the powerful centrifugal forces of colonisation and empire. In his 2019 St Patrick's Day message, President Michael D Higgins characterised this as our 'extended family across the world'. He suggested, 'Wherever you may be, and in whatever circumstances, you are part of Ireland's global family joining with us as we celebrate our shared Irishness, its culture, heritage and history' (BBC News 2019d). Mary Robinson reconnected this population with her notion of Irishness and the 'fifth province'.[1]

There are Irish populations across the USA – and all of the former white dominions of the British Empire: Canada, Australia, New Zealand and South Africa. This history is widely known and continues to impact each of these societies. But the diaspora is also found in other less well-known contexts. For example, the Irish in Jamaica formed a large part of the island's early population, making up two-thirds of the white population on the island in the late 17th century, twice that of the English population. They were brought in as prisoners, indentured labourers and soldiers after the conquest of Jamaica by Cromwell's forces in 1655.[2] Most Irish were transported by force as political prisoners of war from Ireland as a result of the ongoing *War of the Three Kingdoms* at the time. The migration of large numbers of Irish to the island continued into the 18th century. Likewise, the Irish pop up in such seemingly unlikely places as Montserrat and Barbados.[3] There is also a huge Irish population in Britain – assuming markedly different forms in England, Scotland and Wales. This has great currency not least because of the

---

[1] 'Inaugural Speech Given by Her Excellency Mary Robinson, President of Ireland, in Dublin Castle on Monday, December 3, 1990.'

[2] There has been a tendency in recent years to see the Irish transported to the Caribbean by the likes of Cromwell's son Henry as 'slaves' (O'Callaghan 2000; McCafferty 2002), a trope taken up by white supremacists in the US. Two characteristics ensured that they were not slaves like the Africans alongside whom they often worked: despite often harsh work conditions, their period of imprisonment or indenture could come to an end, and their children were not automatically indentured. The transport of Irish felons continued long after Cromwell's time, with 18,500 transportees during the 18th century. Although some of these were petty criminals and political prisoners, a large number were simply 'vagrants' (Fitzgerald 2001: 117). There were actual Irish slaves in the 17th century, captured by Barbary Corsairs and brought to North Africa. These included hundreds of inhabitants of Baltimore in County Cork who were seized in 1631 (Clissold 1977: 54).

[3] The Irish in the Caribbean were regarded as 'a riotous and unruly lot'. In 1666, the Irish servants and freemen on St. Kitts celebrated the announcement of war between England and France by rising up against the English and aiding the French to take control of the island. The following year, the Irish on Montserrat also helped the French to take the island from the English. In 1689, when word reached the Caribbean of William of Orange's accession to the English throne, the Irish again revolted on St. Kitts and plundered English estates in support of the ousted King James. One leading St. Kitts planter wrote in 1673: 'Scotchmen and Welshmen we esteem the best servants, and the Irish the worst, many of them being good for nothing but mischief' (quoted in Beckles 1990: 511).

number of British people applying for Irish passports in the wake of Brexit. There are also sizeable Irish diaspora populations across other European countries.

Apart from the notable exception of the post-colonial USA, the Irish diaspora developed most obviously *within* the British Empire. Moreover, much of the migration to the US occurred while this was still a British colony. But there was an even wider diaspora which still survives – from Hennessy Cognac in France[4] to McIlhinney Tabasco sauce in Louisiana. Irish people played significant roles in other empires – on 'both sides'; Fitzcarraldo the would-be rubber tycoon in Peru;[5] the San Patricio Brigade switching sides in the Mexican-American War of 1846-48 (Stevens 2005); Antoine Walsh, one of the founders of the first slave trade company in Nantes in 1748 (Stein 1979: 280); John MacBride who formed the Irish Transvaal Brigade to fight with Boers against the British in South Africa, 1899-1902 (Fallon 2015). The most significant legacy of this diaspora was that for many Irish this experience was 'how the Irish became white'. Ignatiev (1995) classically traces the synergy between whiteness and Irishness that developed in the USA. More recently, Cheng has extended Ignatiev's approach in specific reference to Irishness and whiteness in the American South (2018: 93-118). A similar process accompanied Irishness within the other white dominions of the British Empire. But this process also *denied* Irishness to whole sections of the diaspora – the 'Black Irish' and *mestizo* and *mestiza* Irish – not only in places like Barbados and Montserrat but also in the white dominions. This history of Irishness of colour is hardly acknowledged let alone integrated into the wider story of Ireland and colonialism.

The Irish – like many other colonised peoples – also played a significant part in supporting the imperial project – as settlers, soldiers and administrators. For example, Irish people played a key part in establishing Newfoundland – England's first extra-European colony. Some 400 years later, the Gilbert Islands bookended imperial settler colonisation – and this also featured an Irish lead. The *Phoenix Islands Settlement Scheme* was begun in 1938 in the western Pacific Ocean as the 'last attempt at human colonisation within the British Empire' (Maude 1969). The first officer-in-charge for the Colonial Administrative Service of the UK was Gerald Bernard 'Irish' Gallagher. He died in the colony and was buried on the parade ground beneath a union flag (King 2000).

Throughout the former British Empire, there are constant, and sometimes surprising, traces of Irish connections. Even where Irish settlement did not occur, an imperial reference often signals some deeper resonance of colonial commonality. Thus, 'Connaught Place', the epicentre of the Lutyens' imperial New Delhi and the financial and commercial hub of post-colonial India bears the name of an Irish province.[6] Kipling

---

[4] Founded by Irish Jacobite military officer Richard Hennessy in 1765. His son James Hennessy gave the family name to the company in 1813.

[5] Brian Sweeney Fitzgerald, known locally as Fitzcarraldo, was the central character in Werner Herzog's eponymous film from 1982, starring Klaus Kinski in the title role.

[6] It was actually named for Prince Arthur, Duke of Connaught – third son of Queen Victoria – whose only

references this contradictory location of Irishness throughout his work (Nagai 2006). He does this most famously in his novel *Kim* – in which the Irishness of the hero 'Kimball O'Hara' is used to negotiate between the worlds of the white colonisers and the black colonised of the Raj. But it is perhaps most poignantly evoked in one of his *Humorous Tales*. This story portrays a contrasting *mestizo* and *mestiza* Irish experience as a group of red-haired, mixed-race children recite the 'Wearing of the Green' in memory of their absent father (McNally 2016). These kinds of half-remembered colonial connections can also remerge in all sorts of unexpected ways that directly affect Ireland. Most recently, Brexit threatens to the reignite the longstanding controversy around ownership of Rockall.[7]

Thus, right across the reach of empire – from Ireland's dubious distinction as the 'first colony' in 1155 to 'Irish' Gallagher's 'last' attempt at settler colonisation within the British empire – there is a connection between empire and Irishness. This briefest of examinations gives some sense of the extent of the Irish diaspora – and already suggests a connection to colonialism and imperialism. But just how to make sense of this nexus presents a less straightforward and more contested challenge.

Most immediately, despite the longevity of English engagement with Ireland, some analyses insist that Ireland itself was *never colonised* at all. In particular, in his book, *Ireland and Empire: Colonial Legacies in Irish History and Culture* (2002), Stephen Howe complained of 'a growing band of historians, political commentators, and cultural critics' who 'sought to analyse Ireland's past and present in colonial terms'. He signalled the tension between Irish republicans, for whom this was 'the only proper framework for understanding Ireland' and the outrage that the use of the term provoked in Unionists. Unfortunately, his analysis leaves Ireland in a form of imperial limbo – signalling the complexity of Ireland's location without ever committing on whether Ireland was colonised or not: 'The modern conflict in Northern Ireland is a colonial one in the eyes of Irish Republicans and of many international observers, emphatically not so in those of British governments and of Ulster Unionists' (Howe 2002: 32).[8]

---

connection with Connacht was a prodigious appetite for imperial titles. He did have a long career as an army officer across the British Empire, including service in South Africa, Canada, Egypt and India. He was Commander-in-Chief of Ireland from January 1900 to 1904. He also enjoyed a more direct military engagement with Irishness in Canada. There Arthur was an officer with the Rifle Brigade and was involved in defending this white dominion from the Fenian Raids. There were concerns that his involvement might put the Prince in specific danger from Fenian supporters in the United States. In 1870 he was engaged in repulsing Fenian invaders during the Battle of Eccles Hill, for which he received the 'Fenian Medal'.

[7] Rockall is a small uninhabitable granite island 180 miles west of Scotland and 260 miles north-west of Ireland. Britain claimed it in 1955, a claim Ireland rejects.

[8] Howe is by far the most direct in rejecting the concept of colonisation, but it is a motif which runs through much of mainstream history writing on Ireland. Take the doyen of the profession, Roy Foster. Like Howe, he presents a dichotomy but fails to directly come down on one side or another (Foster 1988). That said, through much of what follows it is clear that he finds little mileage in employing colonisation as an explanatory concept.

The simplest and most immediate repudiation of Howe's 'Ireland was (perhaps) never colonised' thesis comes from those who remain broadly sympathetic to the British Empire and its legacy. Thus, we do not need to turn to Marx or Connolly to support the notion that Ireland was indeed colonised but rather to British experts on empire like Ferguson and Morris (1968; 1973; 2004).

For Ferguson (2012: 57):

> Ireland was the experimental laboratory of British colonization and Ulster was the prototype plantation. What it seemed to show was that empire could be built not only by commerce and conquest but by migration and settlement.

Thus, the general conclusion for a range of historians from both pro- and anti-imperialist stances is that we can move swiftly on from the Ireland 'never colonised' or 'too complicated to say' arguments: Ireland *was* colonised.

Others, drawing on their own experience of colonialism, had no difficulty seeing the Irish experience as colonial (McVeigh and Rolston 2009). They took Ireland's resistance to colonialism as an inspiration for their own struggles.[9] This explains why Sivanandan (1983) had no difficulty including the Irish as a constituent part of what was 'politically Black'. Of course, Sivanandan was not suggesting that the experience of Africans and Asians and Irish – or even the experience of African Caribbean and South Asian and Irish migrants in post-war Britain – was identical. Likewise, Ireland's trajectory *within* empire was different from that of India or Jamaica or South Africa. Each one of these colonial situations carried a degree of specificity. Significantly Ireland was unique among all British colonies in that it had *representation* at the imperial parliament – albeit this was emphatically not democratic. It was inside rather than outside the Union. This made Ireland different; not just from India and South Africa but also from Australia and Canada and the other white dominions. There were costs as well as benefits of this location and it makes Ireland's experience atypical; but it does not make it 'not colonial'.

The 'de-imperialising' of Irish history dovetails with a wider process of reconsideration and rehabilitation of empire more generally. There is an overweening need to forgive and to find a positive legacy to the whole process. This is also, of course,

---

[9] For example, newly-freed slaves in the United States offered support to the Fenians and Indian nationalists in Bengal named their military organisation the IRA, Indian Republican Army. However, there was another side to the story. In India, the Connaught Rangers, famous for their mutiny in support of the Easter Rising, were hated by the local people. 'The Connaughts were strong believers in the saying that what had been conquered by the sword must be kept by the sword; but not being issued with swords they used their boots and fists to such purpose that they were more respected and feared by the natives than any other British unit in India' (Richards 2003: 22). In Australia in 1837 a missionary had blankets carefully sewn together as winter clothing for Aborigines. On a later visit he found they 'had unpicked all the stitches and turned them back into blankets, because they thought them "Irish cloaks"'. The Aborigines rejected left-over convict slops with the words, 'No good – all same like croppy', thus turning an Irish badge of honour into a label of disdain (Hughes 1987: 279).

a reminder that none of these battles is ever over. Recent years have revealed a broader recrudescence of pro-colonial analysis across academic and political debates on the subject (Prashad 2017a,b; McQuade 2017).

In Ireland there have been generations of ideological intervention – community relations, good relations, cultural relations – designed to 'balance' perspectives. As Roy Foster declared, 'we are all revisionists now'. Here empire, even in its most grotesque manifestations – from the slaughters of plantation through *An Gorta Mór* to the Somme – is subtly rehabilitated. At this point, this 'cultural war' in Ireland is helpfully reframed by the wider reference. The flipside of imperial revisionism is that the colonised rarely exhibit this need to rework or sanctify the memory of empire. While the coloniser insists on the virtues of empire, the colonised continue to contest and resist.

Colonialism reduced and depleted Ireland in a whole range of ways: from a nation to a province; from something that was equal to England – in size, in population, in culture – to something less. It reduced whole swathes of Irish life and culture: from multilingual Irish speakers to monoglot speakers of English; from earls to refugees; from soldiers to mercenaries; from free people to peasants; from peasants to felons; from the feasts of Tara to the great hunger of Skibbereen. At the nadir of this process of reduction, Ireland itself was to be expunged from the imperial record. In Westminster in 1834, the Unionist MP Thomas Spring Rice insisted that 'I should prefer the name of West Britain to that of Ireland'.[10] This is a reduction from which Ireland has hardly begun to recover – despite all the talk about post-colonialism in Ireland or, indeed, the brief ascent of the Celtic Tiger economy.

Of course, it is important to keep returning to the broader context to emphasise the fact that it was not only Ireland that was diminished in this way. This profound denudation was a much more general consequence of the parasitism of empire. Columbus found Haiti awash with gold; five hundred years later it is the poorest country in the Americas. The English went to Bengal – twenty times the size of England – and reduced it in much the same fashion.[11] This broader referent makes it clear that there is no way to represent this process positively. It is a characteristic of contemporary apologists for imperialism that they do not ignore the bad – they list the piracy, and the opium monopoly, and the enslavement, and the starvation, and the genocide – but they then insist, 'It wasn't all bad'. Ferguson admits that British colonialism didn't always live up to its own high ideals but it still 'more than justified its own existence' in the twentieth century; Paxman lists the wrongdoings of the British empire in considerable detail but then cannot help but conclude his analysis under the banner 'Doing Good'.[12] In the hands of less sophisticated

---

[10] 'Repeal of the Union – Adjourned Debate'. *Hansard House of Commons Debate*, 23 April 1834. Col. 1194.

[11] To take one measure: 2 million people died of starvation in India in 1860, another 2.6 million in 1910. 'India was largely free of famine under the Mogul emperors…' (Jones 2006: 43).

[12] This is the title of the fifth and final episode of Jeremy Paxman's BBC series *Empire* in which he 'tells the extraordinary story of how a desire for conquest became a mission to improve the rest of mankind,

commentators this special pleading is simply reworked as a contemporary imperialism. As Margaret Thatcher opined: 'I believe in the acceptance of personal responsibility, freedom of choice, and the British Empire, which took freedom and the rule of law to countries which would never have known it otherwise'.[13]

This kind of apologism discords horribly, however, with the perspective of the colonised. As with any violation people may learn to live, to cope, to survive, even sometimes to triumph. But that does not make it alright. Indeed, the one simple conclusion regarding colonialism that emerges more or less in unison from the colonised world is that it should not have happened. This may in the end be the prosaic epitaph of empire – *it would have been better if it had not happened* – for you, for us, for the world. Colonialism and imperialism, however, *did happen*. And Irishness *was* part of that process. The rest of our analysis is dedicated to making sense of the place of Ireland and the Irish within that history.

A crucial point in all of this is that it is always something more than *history*. In the second half of the analysis, we turn from history to the present. We examine how our broader analysis of colonialism and imperialism frames the experience of the two contemporary Irish states. Both states – 'the Republic of Ireland' and 'Northern Ireland' – emerged from Ireland's long and bitter struggle against its colonising power. Both are still dealing with the legacies of Ireland's colonial past – a fault line still based on native/ settler divisions that runs through the body politic in the North but also haunts the South. Ireland is not simply a country with a colonial history. Colonialism continues to structure the lived experience of Irish citizens, north and south, in the most profound ways. Finally, we address the question of what all this past might mean for Ireland's future. Put simply, the key issue is therefore not whether Ireland was colonised but when or indeed if it was ever *decolonised*. Did this 'first colony' become 'post-colonial', and if so, when and how?

For some the answer is yes and the 'when' and 'how' are encapsulated in the Act of Union 1801. While it is true that Ireland was in the heart of imperial decision-making in a way that no other colony was, not even the white dominions, we will demonstrate at a later point that this did not constitute decolonisation. A stronger candidate for acceptance is the answer that decolonisation occurred with the Treaty in 1922. There are two problems with this conclusion. First, it would take a particularly perverse kind of denial to fail to see the ways in which Northern Ireland remained colonised over the last century. Those of us who have remained 'British subjects' since partition find it singularly difficult to recognise our particular part of Ireland as decolonised. Equally significant is the long and difficult journey the Free State and later the Republic took to decouple from empire after 1922, a process that arguably may only become

---

especially in Africa, and how that mission shaded into an unquestioning belief that Britain could – and should – rule the world'.

[13] House of Commons, 17 February 1983.

realisable because of Brexit. But, even if one concedes an element of decolonisation on the island, the crucial point is that decolonisation is unfinished business. Here we emphatically reject the O'Leary notion – put forward in his monumental history of Northern Ireland – that the GFA represented the 'final decolonisaton' of Ireland (2019: 131). The unresolved status of the North is the most obvious measure of the unfinished revolution, but there are other elements. They may be as simple as the continuation of the use of 'royal' for institutions in the South – the Royal Dublin Society, the Royal Irish Academy. More fundamentally, there are real and substantial legacies of colonialism in the economy, culture, politics, and the law, which speak clearly of the long shadow of empire North *and* South. There are commentators, English and otherwise, who accuse the Irish of being fixated with history and of having a collective mental disorder which means they continue to fight old battles endlessly. But if history is taken in the simplest sense as an account of the past, that is, of something that is over, then in a sense Ireland does not have a history. Rather, it has an ongoing experience, albeit periodised, whereby the past is not yet over. Consequently, one of the goals of this book is to attempt to indicate how Ireland can come to have a history, and thereby a future. This approach assumes that, whatever futures are possible on the island of Ireland, they cannot be realised without reference to the long shadow cast by colonial history. Making sense of this reality – alongside engaging with the question of what needs to be done to change it – is the core problematic of this book.

Chapter I

Methodologies:
interpreting Ireland in order to change it

We shall reclaim them from their barbarous manners ... populate, plant and make civil all the provinces of that kingdom ... as we are persuaded that it is one of the chief causes for which God hath brought us to the Imperial Crown of these Kingdoms.
—Francis Bacon, 1603

Truth will out. Elgar, who wrote the paean of Empire, lived to compose its elegy.
—Jan Morris, 1968

We prefaced our analysis with Seamus Heaney paraphrasing Tacitus, suggesting that peace is no more than the 'desolation left behind after the decisive operations of merciless power'. In the original speech, this is followed by Tacitus' excoriating characterisation of the Roman Empire.

> Romans, from whose oppression escape is vainly sought by obedience and submission. Robbers of the world, having by their universal plunder exhausted the land, they rifle the deep. If the enemy be rich, they are rapacious; if he be poor, they lust for dominion; neither the east nor the west has been able to satisfy them. Alone among men they covet with equal eagerness poverty and riches. To robbery, slaughter, plunder, they give the lying name of empire; they make a desolation and call it peace. (Tacitus 2010: 20)

The speech is a devastating critique of imperial power and greed and hubris. But in fact the recorded speech involves Tacitus *reporting* Roman General Julius Agricola *quoting* Caledonian chieftain Calgach – the leader of resistance to Agricola's campaign against the Celts in Scotland. It is Calgach not Tacitus – a colonised Celt not a colonising Roman – who provided the withering critique to whom the quote is attributed. Calgach left Scotland after the defeat by Agricola at Mons Graupius and probably went on – as a political refugee from Roman imperialism – to found the city of Derry in Ireland (originally Doire Calgach, later Doire Colmcille). Calgach's voice is mediated through Agricola – a military commander of the very imperial project that is so devastatingly addressed by the speech. If it was made in the form it is presented, it was spoken neither in English nor Latin (the language in which it is recorded) but in Gaelic (or a pre-Gaelic Celtic language). In other words, it is necessary to work fairly hard – or *dig* deep as

Heaney would have it – before even *beginning* to decide whether Tacitus 'was right' about the instructiveness of history.

There is no better allegory for the complexity of the task of making sense of imperial history in general and Irish history in particular. Listening to Calgach's voice gives some sense of the methodological challenge that we have set ourselves in this analysis – to ask how to 'read' colonialism and its enduring influence on Ireland and Irishness. We seek to answer the question of what an anti-imperialist analysis of Ireland means in 2020. It is instructive, therefore, to begin this process by recalling that the imperial project embodied a dense, multi-layered complexity *from the first*. However, the difficulty of this task does not provide an excuse for any retreat into post-truth relativism. We start from the position that the world is knowable. History *matters*; and, for all its complexity, *it can be read*. On the one hand history is continuously reinterpreted. On the other, however, history *happened*, and this provides a kind of Cartesian platform for analysis. History of course can be revised – and even distorted and denied – but it cannot be *undone*.

Nevertheless, in the contemporary world the traditional notion of truth – historical or otherwise – is no longer a given. This idea has been around for some time – it was perhaps never more boldly articulated than by Nietzsche.

> What then is truth? A movable host of metaphors, metonymies, and anthropomorphisms: in short, a sum of human relations which have been poetically and rhetorically intensified, transferred, and embellished, and which, after long usage, seem to a people to be fixed, canonical, and binding. Truths are illusions which we have forgotten are illusions – they are metaphors that have become worn out and have been drained of sensuous force, coins which have lost their embossing and are now considered as metal and no longer as coins. (Nietzsche 2001: 1174)

But this broader challenge is compounded by the post-truth signs of the times. In this regard, the confusion around truth value has achieved epochal proportions in the 21st century – as the notion of 'alternative facts' is no longer risible but has become part of the discourse of the most powerful state in the world. Arguably the scholarly project is the same as it has always been – to work towards truth – but the obstacles are much greater. The process of distortion is reified to new levels.

This twisting of truth is also a strategic intervention – it is often about clouding the waters and deliberate misinformation. States have always been aware of the coercive power of propaganda and disinformation. But this is elevated in the age of the internet. At this point, this confusion can become not just an epistemology but also an ethics. Thus, with Berlusconi it becomes a masterly defence against the abuse of power: 'If all are guilty, none are guilty'. In one deft finesse the abuser's self-excuse – from Bush and Blair to Trump – is evident. It follows, of course, that truth value disappears as part of this most reactionary nihilism – if we are all liars then it doesn't really matter if anyone is lying.

But it is possible to resist this process. Just as those who most vehemently deny the existence of hierarchies are usually found near the top of them, so those who most benefit from the relativizing of knowledge are loudest in their claims of post-truth. Once again it helps to ground the debate in the history of colonialism. As already suggested, Calgach's critique of empire pre-echoes all subsequent analysis. As Calgach and Tacitus implied, from the very start empire was perhaps the biggest lie in history. It was the original progeniture of alternative facts, of propaganda and censorship. This presents no small challenge. But it also grounds our approach in years of anti-imperialist practice. Here we can suggest that history and truth are on our side. As Michael Ignatieff (1996: 113) observed about truth commissions, they may not be able to achieve full truth, but they can work diligently to 'reduce the amount of permissible lies'.

But, how do we know what we know in a post-truth world? There are two problems involved. First is the postmodernist notion that there is no 'regime of truth' (as Foucault would argue), no vantage point to stand on outside of things in order to judge truth. The second problem is the valid critique of truth absolutism coming from societies in the global south, especially in relation to notions of universal human rights (Mutua 2001). But it is undeniable that there are certain bedrocks of a worthwhile society – equality, justice, respect for diversity – which are undermined by colonialism, imperialism and their aftermath. Moreover, a powerful form of anti-colonial practice is to insist on those bedrocks and to seek their full implementation. In the case of Ireland, it could be argued that the insistence of republicans on equality in the North proved to be their most powerful weapon. A state built on inequality finds the demand for equality metaphysically threatening. It may ultimately be impossible to concede, but often the demand has effects long before the ultimate point is reached. The demand for concessions to the marginalised even at the level of respect and acknowledgment can lead to the collapse of structures.

Central to our approach is the notion that interpreting the world *is* a key element in changing it. From this perspective, we seek to understand Irish history not simply for the historical record but because this is part of making Ireland – and the world – a better place, more equal, less violent – less 'desolate' as Heaney would have it.

In other words, the truths addressed in this analysis are existential and dialectical. For example, we are preoccupied by *An Gorta Mór* because millions of Irish people should not have starved and died and emigrated under what Kipling exalted as the 'English flag'. They deserve to be remembered and their treatment by empire foregrounded in any assessment of the legacy of colonialism. Equally importantly, however, this catastrophic episode in Irish history is important because of what it teaches people about the contemporary world – how does it help to prevent this happening again? How does a reflection on the horrors of imperial starvation – alongside all the other brutalities to be found in the 'abattoir' of Irish history – help to make Ireland – and the world – a better place?

Colonialism, imperialism and the state

Beyond this broad epistemological approach, our analysis engages a series of key insights. First, we have to tease out the overlap and differences between the concepts of colonialism and imperialism. These words run through history – as they do our analysis – often conjoined but less often deconstructed. It is difficult to overstate the classical legacy that underpins both notions. Here – in the 'glory that was Greece and the grandeur that was Rome' – was the evidence of the beneficence of empire for all budding imperialists to see. As Gibbon (1996: 93) famously declared:

> If a man were called to fix the period in the history of the world, during which the condition of the human race was most happy and prosperous, he would, without hesitation, name that which elapsed from the death of Domitian [96 AD] to the accession of Commodus [180 AD].

Thus, in the eyes of lovers of empire at least, *Pax Romana* became idealised for eternity.

From this point onwards, however, subtle differences between the two phenomena become discernible. They both invoke the novel idea of a metropolitan state sending out satellite populations as a *strategy* of conquest over other peoples. In this manner, Greek colonisation created a *Magna Graecia* – Greater Greece. But this template for colonialism appears defined by its very banality – transplanting people and ideas from classical Greece to other parts of the Mediterranean. 'Empire' conveys something altogether grander – it evokes imperial arches and statuary and colosseums, suggesting borders bounded by fortified walls that have lasted two millennia. This reflects some of the hubris of empire – something closer to the German notion of *Reich* than any idea of 'commonwealth'.

From the perspective of the colonised, however, the most important lesson from the classical world was Plutarch's account of Spartan Law: that it is not wrong to steal but only to *be caught* stealing. Arguably this method underpinned the whole ideology of western imperialism. The approach was to expropriate wherever and whenever empire deemed desirable – but then to reframe colonial theft as *something else*. This probably gets as close as possible to the difference between colonialism and imperialism: colonialism was the act of theft; imperialism was the act of reframing the theft as a moral rather than an immoral act. For proof of the legacy of this approach, there is no need to go further than the British Museum or the Louvre or the Pergamon or the Prada. How did these imperial institutions acquire their cornucopia of treasures from around the world? How did these great museums across the capitals of Europe acquire such bounty from *outside* the continent? Why do these museums house the Benin bronzes or the treasures of Magdala or, indeed, half the Lane pictures? In short, what was the provenance – skilful curating or colonial looting?[1]

---

[1] In 2015, the British Museum agreed to loan aboriginal artefacts to Australia, which had originally been taken from there, having been guaranteed that traditional owners had no legal basis to take them back. In response the federal government colluded with the former colonial power and enacted the Protection of Cultural Objects on Loan Act 2013 and the exhibition 'Encounters: Revealing Stories of Aboriginal and

Already imbued with religious justification, European colonialism and imperialism quickly assumed other ideological forms. At one level, this was simply functional – reflecting traditional psychological mechanisms of projection and transference. How could you treat humans this badly without somehow transferring the guilt? With this finesse the colonist was able to conclude that 'we treat them horribly because they deserve to be treated this way'.[2] We enslave them because it is their natural condition. But there was a flipside to this process– not only were the colonised to be dehumanised, but the coloniser was to be exalted. The stereotypes from the high colonial period seem almost laughable in their conceit from a contemporary perspective, but there is no doubt that people often internalised the nonsense.

Young's (2001: 17) distinction is also helpful:

> Imperialism ... operated from the centre as a policy of state, driven by the grandiose projects of power. Thus, while imperialism is susceptible to analysis as a concept ... colonialism needs to be analysed primarily as a practice...

However, regarding imperialism as the *theory* and colonialism the *practice*, does not tell the whole story. A similar dichotomy between imperialism as an ideological project and colonialism as a material project is also imperfect. From the classical period to the present the two words overlap and synergise – but never quite become synonyms.

In practical terms, however, imperialism was most transparent when empires acted in concert. Certain key moments at the beginning and end of this process are worth attention. In 1494 Spain and Portugal divided the *whole world* between themselves in the Treaty of Tordesillas; four hundred years later in 1885, the fourteen imperial participants at the Berlin Conference did the same thing to Africa. The Eight-Nation Alliance sacking of Beijing in 1900 was an even cruder example of such multi-imperial cooperation. Eight empires banded together to 'encourage' China to 'open up' to free trade in what became the 'biggest looting expedition since Pizarro' (Lynch 1901: 179).[3] This imperial alliance approach reached its nadir in 1914, however, as two multi-imperial formations vied for global dominion. In the process they dragged almost the entire peoples of the planet into the brutal reality of *imperial world war*. In these moments the reality of imperialism as a European and a western project is laid bare. Nor has this imperial collectivism gone away – we need look no further than the security council of the UN to see the long shadow

---

Torres Strait Islander Objects from the British Museum', went ahead (Daley 2015).

[2] Here are two historical examples, selected at random. At Sand Creek, Colorado, in 1864, Colonel John Chivington ordered his troops to kill all the Indians, including children, the latter on the grounds that 'nits make lice' (quoted in Jones 2006: 73). Douglas Duff had been stationed with the Black and Tans in Galway before moving to Palestine. Referring to the Palestinians of Haifa, he wrote: 'Most of us were so infected by the sense of our own superiority over these "lesser breeds" that we scarcely regarded these people as human' (quoted in Cronin 2017). The phrase 'to duff someone up', meaning to repeatedly hit and injure someone, derives from his surname.

[3] The alliance force consisted of about 18,000 soldiers from Russia, Britain, the US, Japan and France. These included colonial troops from other parts of their empires, including India and Indochina. Austria, Italy and Germany were also largely symbolic partners.

of empire. This institution is controlled by five former empires and a white dominion, all but one predominantly white. Only the Chinese presence offers a fig leaf in terms of both colour and colonial history. More recently the concept of the 'five eyes' has offered an even narrower contemporary perspective – now the whole world is expected to feel reassured by the combined surveillance capacity of these former white dominions.[4]

In other words, then as now, the focus must be on the *structural* reality of empire. Empire was primarily a *practice* with an ideological infrastructure. State power is the base on which ideologies of imperialism are built. This functional reality is manifest in every colonial situation, from the expropriation of land to the collection of taxes. It was always supported by powerful capacity for violence and repression in navies and armies and militias and police forces. For example, the British Empire was not just dependent upon but also defined by the state apparatus that emerged in each of its colonies – both repressive and ideological. In Ireland this embraces the full gamut of colonial models over the course of 900 years: direct rule and indirect rule; lordship, kingship and commonwealth; home rule and dominion.

From the beginning, therefore, our analysis pays close attention to *what the state is doing*. The colonial state mediates different interests and classes across the entire history of imperialism. Ireland provides plenty of examples of the state making these kinds of decisions: deciding who could own land, who could vote, who could bear arms, who could own a horse worth more than £5.[5] Lest this last seem a trivial issue, consider *Caoineadh Airt Uí Laoghaire* – perhaps the greatest of Irish anti-imperialist poems. Art Ó Laoghaire – one of the 'wild geese' and uncle of Daniel O'Connell – was 'legally' murdered for being Catholic and in possession of just such a horse. At its apogee the colonial state could render Ireland and its native population non-existent. As Morris observes (1968: 469):

> Irish Catholics had virtually no rights at all – as was said in an Irish court case in 1759, the law 'does not presume a Papist to exist in the kingdom, nor can they as much as breathe here without the consent of the Government'.

In consequence, there is a constant interest in the state and its institutions through our journey tracing the nexus of Irishness and colonialism. At any given stage it is illuminating to ask: what is the state trying to do with the colonial project? Of course, across an eight-hundred-year journey the state is hardly identifiable as the same phenomenon – this entity changes profoundly over time. There are, of course, a few constants. For example, the institution of the 'Crown' plays a key integrating role for nearly all of this period. But the Dutch and the French and even the English – albeit briefly – found that republics could colonise just as brutally and effectively as monarchies. Likewise, the apparatus of occupation was fairly continuous. For example, Carrickfergus Castle was a colonial

---

[4] The 'five eyes' – the US, UK, Canada, Australia and New Zealand – are countries that share a broad range of intelligence in one of the world's tightest multilateral arrangements.

[5] Penal laws allowed a Protestant to pay five guineas to a magistrate and walk off with an expensive horse owned by a Catholic (Froude 1969: 231).

military garrison from its erection in 1177 during the Anglo-Norman invasion of Ireland until 1928, when ownership transferred from the British Army to the Government of Northern Ireland for preservation as an ancient monument.

None of the many colonial continuities, however, can disguise the dynamic, chimeric nature of the colonial state. In Ireland, for example, even the appropriate adjective is not a given – is it the 'English' or the 'British' or the 'UK' or the 'imperial' state or the 'Irish colonial' state that we need to address? Which element within these overlapping state structures drives the colonial process? Nevertheless, at the heart of the story there is always an identifiable state structure doing something specific in its role of mediating between Englishness and Irishness, institutionalising native/settler difference and using some combination of force and ideology to reproduce those differences. However the character of English rule is formulated, the relationship is defined by English dominance and Irish subordination. In other words, it involves – definitively – a colonial state structure. The core institutions of state – government, parliament, church and crown – all combine to make and keep Ireland institutionally subaltern. Even during the brief legislative independence after 1782, the English privy council could still veto legislation of the Irish parliament and the Irish executive remained headed by the lord lieutenant and the chief secretary – British politicians who were members of the British government and accountable to the British rather than the Irish parliament. This colonial state structure holds across 800 years – it is not until 1922 that any part of Ireland can even pretend to be free.

The ongoing complexity of these questions in Ireland encourages some wider engagement with the more general question of what constitutes a state. It is impossible to fully understand the role of the state in Ireland without some sense of what its role is *elsewhere*. Here, the most referenced definition is Max Weber's notion of the state as a political organisation with a centralised government that maintains a *monopoly of the legitimate use of force* within a certain territory. Within this framework, state institutions typically include administrative bureaucracies, legal systems and military and religious organisations. A less sociological and more legalistic definition of the state is the one given at the Montevideo Convention on Rights and Duties of States in 1933. The state 'should possess the following qualifications: (a) a permanent population; (b) a defined territory; (c) government; and (d) capacity to enter into relations with the other states'. In 1933, Ireland – or at least its 'Southern Ireland' iteration – was just about meeting all four of these criteria. But clearly there was a state in Ireland before this point – so how do we make sense of this colonial state structure?

This immediately raises the question: *in whose interest did this state apparatus work?* Marx provided the classic definition in the context of the European state: 'The executive of the modern state is nothing but a committee for managing the common affairs of the whole bourgeoisie'. He also suggested of the 19th century bourgeoisie that, 'if the aristocracy is their vanishing opponent, the working class is their arising enemy. They prefer to compromise with the vanishing opponent rather than to strengthen the rising enemy, to whom the future belongs'. In other words, even in the nineteenth century, the state apparatus is something more than a simple tool of the ruling class – however that might be constituted. States often embed and reflect a complex mediation of tensions based on class – as well as gender and race.

In this regard, Jon Elster's 'abdication theory' of the state provides useful context. This suggests that in the nineteenth century the ascendant bourgeoisie found that the advantages of wielding direct power were often outweighed by other costs and disadvantages. In consequence, they were willing to tolerate an aristocratic or despotic government so long as it did not act detrimentally to their interests. There are obvious moments where this appears to resonate with the reality of contemporary state power in the twentieth century – most notoriously the rapprochement between capitalism and fascist states in the 1930s. And there is further evidence in the present day – with the toleration by contemporary liberal democracies of any number of reactionary despots in preference to democratically elected governments. As these examples suggest, this approach is particularly characteristic of the formerly colonised world. Time and again – from Spain in 1936 to Chile in 1973 and Egypt in 2013 – the 'democratic' west has often preferred reaction to democracy. More recently, there has also been a despotic shift within established democracies – not least in the form of Trumpism in the USA and Johnsonism in the UK. All this begins to suggest that the state has emergent qualities well beyond the notion that it is simply a tool of the 'ruling class', however that ruling class is constituted.

The crucial issue is how all this state theory might help us understand the role of the state in a *colonial context*. Nearly all the discussions on the nature of the state were crudely Eurocentric. None of the key state theorists – not Poulantzas nor Miliband nor Habermas nor Foucault – said very much about the specificity of the colonial state. They showed little regard for the state structures that emerged in colonial and imperial contexts – even though the states that they were ostensibly describing were themselves inextricably linked to colonialism and imperialism. For example, the UK state that Marx saw 'managing the affairs of the bourgeoisie' was simultaneously embedded in the Raj and managing the affairs of a colonised people five times the size of the UK population at that time. Of course, *some* of the questions around the nature of the state in places like British India – or the Dutch East Indies or the Congo Free State – were much the same as those being asked in Europe or North America. Weber's insightful focus on the issue of the monopoly over the means of coercion is always a determining factor. But different colonial formations – British India, Dutch East Indies, French Africa – also raised questions of their *specificity*. How did these colonial formations connect to any idea of the ruling class? And how much autonomy did they exhibit?

The perspective from the periphery made a further, definitive question unavoidable: what was the connection between the imperial state in the metropole and the colonial state apparatus in the satellite? Was it the same state? And, if it wasn't, how was the connection between the state in the imperial heartland and the colonial periphery to be understood? Any notion of the ruling class begins to deconstruct in this context. Might this mean simply transnational capitalists – the banks and bankers who financed the colonial project across different empires? Or the *nabobs* – the settler colonial elite who also made fortunes from that same project? At a more personal level in what sense were the most celebrated imperialists at the core of a ruling class – any of the infamous 'heroes' of colonialism might be cited: Stanley, Livingstone, Rhodes, Raffles. All of them had careers defined by the pursuit of profit in their colonial project – but this was always accompanied by complex and sometimes contradictory ideological projects only tangentially linked to capital accumulation in the imperial metropoles.[6] Finally, how much space if any exists for any vestigial or new native co-option into this ruling class? Different colonial formations found some 'native' leaders in positions of marked economic and political power – from the Nawabs of Bengal to the House of Saud. But are these figures to be numbered among the colonised or the ruling class?

These are complex questions, and in one sense the answers seem tangential alongside the examination of what the state is doing at any given time. In fact, in relation to the British Empire and its relationship to Ireland the history lends some support to Foucault's observation that the state is 'no more than a composite reality and a mythologised abstraction' (1979: 20). Despite the immensely powerful ideological reference of the notion of the British Empire, it often becomes hard to identify *any* clear structure. Under examination – in the manner of Conrad's 'heart of darkness' – we find a profusion of 'horror' but it is often hard to detect *any method at all*.

Recognising the routine absence of method or theory is, of course, very different from suggesting that there is no systemic injustice or oppression involved. Perhaps the best critique of all came from Johnathan Swift, an early observer of the process of turning 'discovery' into exploitation. Towards the end of *Gulliver's Travels*, the narrator explains his reluctance to identify the location of the countries he has visited.

> I had another reason, which made me less forward to enlarge his majesty's dominions by my discoveries. To say the truth, I had conceived a few scruples with relation to the distributive justice of princes upon those occasions. For instance, a crew of pirates are driven by a storm they know not whither; at length a boy discovers land from the topmast; they go on shore to rob and plunder, they see a harmless people, are entertained with kindness; they give the country a new name; they take formal possession of it for their king; they set up a rotten plank, or a stone, for a memorial; they murder two or three dozen of the natives, bring away a couple more, by force, for a sample; return home, and get their pardon. Here commences a new dominion acquired with a title by divine right. Ships are sent with the first opportunity; the natives driven out or destroyed; their princes tortured to discover their gold; a free license given to all acts of inhumanity and

---

[6] Take, for example, David Livingstone's goal of bringing 'commerce and Christianity' to Africa and the notion that 'trade follows the flag'.

lust, the earth reeking with the blood of its inhabitants: and this execrable crew of butchers, employed in so pious an expedition, is a modern colony, sent to convert and civilize an idolatrous and barbarous people! ... as those countries which I have described do not appear to have any desire of being conquered and enslaved, murdered or driven out by colonies, nor abound either in gold, silver, sugar, or tobacco, I did humbly conceive, they were by no means proper objects of our zeal, our valour, or our interest. (1985: 343-4)

Swift was himself a complex character, sometime proto-Irish anti-imperialist, sometime arch-English Tory.[7] But there is perhaps no better or simpler characterisation of state formation in a modern colony.

Concepts

Beyond a focus on what the state is doing in Ireland at any specific moment, we routinely reference the centrality of the three keystones of any sociological analysis – gender, race and class. The most universal of these – gender – is perhaps the least theorised in the colonial context (*Cultural Studies* 2016; Ghosh 2004, Bueno-Hansen 2015). Often the focus on gender is narrowed to the single question of violence against women. Of course, phenomena like slavery were unambiguously gendered in this sense; wholesale rape was the lot for women slaves, but for fewer men slaves. Similarly, rape was, and is, a weapon of war, directed overwhelmingly at women. But the focus needs to be wider than this; *everything* was gendered under empire. In other words, empire impacted differentially on men and women. Men joined imperial armies or were subject to surveillance as they went about their business; they were more likely to end up in jail and the underdevelopment caused by conquest could lead to massive male unemployment or migration for work elsewhere. Women had the constant struggle of holding families together, in terms of food and support; they cared for the men injured or traumatised by violence and for the children when the male parent was gone to war or in search of work elsewhere. Yet, even when the impact looked identical, it was never experienced as such. Starvation may kill men and women equally but in the lead-up to death, and indeed for the survivors, women had more responsibility for caring for the children, old and ill.

This complexity throws up the question of how it is possible to engage with the specific nexus of gender and imperialism. One illustration may suffice, Maya Lin's

---

[7] Being Swift, it is left to the reader to decide whether his exceptionalism in terms of British colonialism is to be read as satire or national chauvinism: 'But this description, I confess, does by no means affect the British nation, who may be an example to the whole world for their wisdom, care, and justice in planting colonies; their liberal endowments for the advancement of religion and learning; their choice of devout and able pastors to propagate Christianity; their caution in stocking their provinces with people of sober lives and conversations from this the mother kingdom; their strict regard to the distribution of justice, in supplying the civil administration through all their colonies with officers of the greatest abilities, utter strangers to corruption; and, to crown all, by sending the most vigilant and virtuous governors, who have no other views than the happiness of the people over whom they preside, and the honour of the king their master' (Swift 1985: 344). Here Swift anticipates subsequent apologists for British imperialism who employed the same exceptionalism without irony.

powerful memorial to Vietnam dead in Washington – which despite its location and subject sits powerfully on the cusp of imperialism and anti-imperialism. The memorial is immediately gendered – the memorial records the American *men* who died in the US intervention. A separate women's memorial was commissioned – but its immediate reference seems puny in comparison. The official US national archives record 58,212 male against eight female deaths (National Archives 2020). In other words, at first glance Vietnam is represented as something that impacted disproportionately negatively on men. But, of course, this is not anything like the whole story. Across the wider history of imperialist intervention in Vietnam, huge numbers of women died both as combatants and non-combatants. Moreover, the colonial intervention resulted in a whole series of additional negative gendered impacts – from femicide and rape to prostitution and the legacy of a generation of mixed-race children consequent upon the occupation.

The structuring effects of gender across this whole narrative are undeniable, but gender is sometimes lost among the broad generalisation attendant upon this kind of schematic approach which can lead to a form of gender-ignorance. Thus, something as general as 'contact' and colonial invasion both had generic effects on colonised peoples – but also directly gendered forms, specifically, in terms of violence against women and more generally in terms of gendered relations between colonising men and colonised women. The vast series of mixed-race populations across different empires is one obvious legacy of this specifically gendered encounter constructed out of male sexual violence and other forms of patriarchal control. But beyond this obvious reality, colonialism was gendered in a range of other ways, such as the masculinist ideologies of colonialists and their gendered riposte.[8]

Race is usually easier to 'read' across the colonial story because it was so often an explicit logic of empire. It created the ethnic interface – or interfaces – that so obviously defined a colonial situation as a 'plural society' (Furnivall 1948). Whether these new, racialised structures emerged from slavery or genocide or indentured labour or plantation, all are characterised by attendant racisms.

From landfall in Ceuta onwards through a myriad of different colonial iterations there are contemporary racialised discontents rooted in colonial and imperial processes. Racist othering remains the first principle of colonial discourse. The crude, racist naming of the colonised with a host of belittling epithets worldwide simultaneously demarks the assumed superiority of the coloniser. But racial hierarchies have also been embedded in more institutionalised and constitutionalised forms across imperial history. In this regard, the concept of *white dominion* underpins our understanding of race and Irishness. This term appeared first as shorthand for emerging autonomous polities within the British Empire – Newfoundland, Canada, Australia, New Zealand and South Africa. In 1922 the

---

[8] Witness, for example, *The Handbook for Girl Guides or How Girls Can Help to Build Up the Empire* – the first handbook for Girl Guides, published in May 1912 by Thomas Nelson and Sons. The author was Agnes Baden-Powell in conjunction with (then) Lieutenant-General Sir Robert Baden-Powell.

Irish Free State completed the list. At that point, the racism embedded in the concept was transparent. Thus, the very *possibility* of autonomy within empire was explicitly delimited by race – not because of the advance of democracy but simply because of whiteness. But this construction was *doubly* racialised because, of course, none of these former colonies was entirely 'white', however this term is understood. Despite the brutal trajectories of settler colonialism, all had indigenous minorities of colour. Moreover, South Africa had a clear Black majority – the only thing 'white' about it was its economic and political elites. In other words, this notion of dominion has the virtue of declaring that it is explicitly and primarily about race. White dominion delineated a polity committed to the ongoing reproduction of racial hierarchies established by empire.

In this regard we argue that the notion of white dominion powerfully names the *continuity* of colonial racial hierarchies with post-colonial social formations. Crucially we number the USA in the list of contemporary white dominions; but the term arguably names *every* formation that has emerged from formal colonialisation since 1776. In this regard white dominion is not simply an archaic, racist vernacular for historical autonomous polities but also a potent signifier of the survival and reproduction of racist colonial hierarchies within our contemporary world.

It was, of course, impossible to ignore the primacy of race during the colonial period itself. For theorists of empire like Dilke (1868: 405), *everything* was about race.

> In America we have seen the struggle of the dear races against the cheap – the endeavors of the English to hold their own against the Irish and Chinese. In New Zealand, we found the stronger and more energetic race pushing from the earth the shrewd and laborious descendants of the Asian Malays; in Australia, the English triumphant, and the cheaper races excluded from the soil not by distance merely, but by arbitrary legislation; in India, we saw the solution of the problem of the officering of the cheaper by the dearer race. Everywhere we have found that the difficulties which impede the progress to universal dominion of the English people lie in the conflict with the cheaper races.

If gender was immanent, race was usually transcendent: but they were both ever present. The trick is to look for a gendered and racialised impact at every level of Irish colonial history. Sure enough, it is easily found. For example, there is a glimpse of this intersectionality in the speech made by English peer Lord Willoughby de Broke at Dromore in 1912 during the third home rule crisis.

> The Unionists of England were going to help Unionists [in Ireland], not only by making speeches. Peaceable methods would be tried first, but if the last resort was forced on them by the Radical government, the latter would find that they had not only Orangemen against them, but that every white man in the British Empire would be giving support, either moral or active, to one of the most loyal populations that ever fought under the Union Jack. (Cited in Hepburn 1980: 74)

There it is in a nutshell: Irish self-determination was to be resisted by 'every white man in the British Empire'. The categories 'white man' and 'British Empire' were established in a natural and universal synergy. In Ireland, as elsewhere, whiteness and gender were combined effortlessly under the imperial project.

Moreover, we emphasise that the racial codes of empire never simply 'dematerialise' at the end of the formal colonial period. From this perspective, the post-independence US is not an outlier at all but rather the template for every subsequent polity that wanted to recalibrate rather than dismantle the racial algorithms embedded by the colonial process. In this reading the notion of *dominion* is rooted in colonial relations. Furthermore, it is defined by the requisite for race privilege to survive the promise of decolonisation. In the independent US this kind of dominion emerged in an explicitly racialised model of a 'white Republic'. Thus, the notion of 'Jacksonian democracy' extended political power well beyond colonial elites – but it also established the *limits* of enfranchisement.[9] The institution of universal white male suffrage constructed a notion of post-colonial 'democracy' that was profoundly racialised and gendered – and thus in reality profoundly *anti-democratic*.

The enduring implications of this new racially coded power in the US were exemplified by William F. Buckley in 1957. Writing in opposition to the nascent civil rights movement, Buckley argued that, 'the White community in the South is entitled to take such measures as are necessary to prevail, politically and culturally, in areas in which it does not predominate numerically' (Serwer 2019). Crucially, therefore, dominion is defined by its relationship to the principle of democracy in a way that colonialism is not. Once Buckley's 'measures' are elevated to the level of statecraft, there could be no more concise definition of what we understand by 'white dominion'. In this reading, among all the white dominions that emerged from the British Empire only South Africa – after 1994 – could be said to have made a formal journey beyond dominion. (And even there, of course, the multiple racialised legacies of colonisation remain all too tangible.)

Our analysis suggests that different forms of anti-democratic, racialised dominion emerged across the decolonisation process. As this implies, 'white dominion' was a variable feast – it might have been framed as 'Jewish dominion' in Palestine or 'Protestant dominion' in Ireland. In other words, other essentialist identities performed a similar function in polities where whiteness was not the primary indicator of colonial privilege. We also apply the term to many of the post-colonial Latin American polities – although here 'Peninsular dominion' or 'Creole dominion' captures more accurately the legacy of the specific dynamics of Spanish and Portuguese colonial racial hierarchy. The point, however, is that 'white dominion' provides a general theorisation for the phenomenon *across* colonialisms. Dominion is the kind of polity that emerges from the unresolved dialectic between empire and republic. When empires – and crucially their settler

---

[9] Andrew Jackson (1767-1845) was the seventh president of the United States from 1829 to 1837, and his supporters founded the Democratic Party. His parents were Irish Presbyterians from Boneybefore outside Carrickfergus. Despite his reputation as a champion of equality and opponent of elites, he played a significant part in the genocide of Native Americans in his roles as both soldier and politician. He was also a slaveowner and a committed opponent of abolitionism.

colonial populations – are forced towards colonial independence, they turn to the model of white dominion. This strategy was more or less universal. It was tried in colonies with relatively few settlers – like India; in colonies where settlers overwhelmingly dominated an indigenous population depleted by genocide – like Canada; and in colonies where settlers were a dominant, privileged minority population – like South Africa. The British Empire was particularly keen to foist the model more formally on its own decolonising subjects. For example, alongside their white dominions, they tried very hard to reconstitute India as a dominion in the twentieth century.

In our analysis Stormont-era Northern Ireland becomes a paradigmatic example of this notion of dominion. The characterisation of the state by its first Prime Minister as a 'Protestant state for a Protestant people' does not leave much ambiguity around the project. Moreover, the institution of the B Specials – an exclusively Protestant paramilitary force focused solely on the activities of the Catholic minority – made clear what the logic of the repressive apparatus of such a state would be. But the essence of dominion is equally to be found in the prosaic reproduction of sectarian privilege. Thus in 1948, the Unionist MP EC Ferguson encapsulated perfectly the problematic of 'Protestant dominion':

> The Nationalist majority in … Fermanagh, notwithstanding a reduction of 336 in the year, stands at 3,684. We must ultimately reduce and liquidate that majority. This county, I think it can be safely said, is a Unionist county. The atmosphere is Unionist. The Boards and properties are nearly all controlled by Unionists. But there is still this millstone around our necks. (*Irish News*, 13th April, 1948)

This notion of 'atmosphere' captures powerfully the ideology behind the crude machinations of a sectarian state that strove to institutionalise and defend Protestant privilege at every level and resist the ever-present threat of 'Popish democracy'. It also, however, references the elusive sense of privilege and entitlement that underpins the way in which our analysis understands dominion right across Empire. More generally dominion should be understood as both a principle and a methodology. Theory and practice combine to allow colonial racial privilege to prevail politically and culturally and circumvent the millstone of democracy *even after the end of the formal colonial period.*

Arguably, class is less easy to situate within this imperial story. The legacy of Marx meets a singularly challenging obstacle in the colonial context. Traditional notions of class – while they claimed universal application – were worked out in terms of narrowly white and European contexts. To be fair, Marx and Engels were much more aware than most other European socialists of the centrality of Ireland to class relations in England. Marx and particularly Engels, got it half right – they identified the centrality of Irish workers to both English production and English social and political relations.[10] But

---

[10] 'To accelerate the social development in Europe, you must push on the catastrophe of official England. To do so, you must attack her in Ireland. That's her weakest point. Ireland lost, the British "Empire" is gone, and the class war in England, till now somnolent and chronic, will assume acute forms' (Karl Marx to Paul and Laura Lafargue, March 1870; quoted in Slater and McDonough 2008: 171).

the Irish were a relatively minor cog in this great imperial wheel – and the conditions of colonial workers were usually either downplayed or ignored completely. For the European Left the focus of attention was the situation of the English, German and French working classes to the detriment of seeing how this was linked to contemporaneous issues of colonialism and imperialism.

Stuart Hall (2016: 145) made this point famously in terms of the economic embeddedness of the imperial project in Britain: 'It is in the sugar you stir; it is in the sinews of the famous British "sweet tooth"; it is in the tea-leaves at the bottom of the "British" cuppa'. He could have added the European addictions to tobacco or coffee or chocolate or the lust for oil or rubber or grain or mutton or bananas. The list of colonial product goes on and on. All of these were products of empire – and all of them involved relations of production. In other words, they too were embedded in class relations and reflected a white privilege that advantaged workers in the homelands of empire alongside the imperial bourgeoise. Arguably, the notions of class that hold particularly in Ireland have been poorly served by their dependence on white, European models. In reality, class relations are always at least as much *colonial relations* as they are relations between social classes within a given nation state. Any understanding of class in Ireland has to begin with a proper reading of the synergy – or intersectionality – of race and class in the colonial context.

Sectarianism and *mestizaje*

We also need to flag a concept which is less central to the wider colonial story – although not entirely absent. This is the concept of *sectarianism*. This concept is central to colonialism in Ireland but also has wider application. Of course, there is a wider interaction between religious ideas and colonialism that runs right through the whole story of empire –this has obtained ever since the Emperor Theodosius I issued the Edict of Thessalonica in AD 380, making Christianity the state religion of the Roman Empire. No subsequent empire *ever* separated church and state. Consequently, religious faith – and more particularly religious power structures – were central to both the ideology and practice of colonialism. But sectarianism elevated this relationship within the British model. In this sense it became a specific quality of the English state that it sustained across its whole imperial journey. From this perspective, religious difference in Ireland could never be simply a matter of faith. In the English – and later British – model, the idea of the Crown *integrates* religion, state and empire.

This asymmetry holds right across the colonial story. The colonisers always say it is about religion and morality; the colonised say it is about race and dispossession. This operationalisation of religion muddies the waters and redefines the situation. But the institutionalisation of religion was itself a colonial construction – religious institutions became a key element within a wider imperial system of subordination. Thus, the Roman model of Christianity as state religion reappeared in the Spanish and Portuguese empires. This approach was reified further in England with the established church – here was not separation but rather *conjunction* of church and state. Once this fusion of Crown and Church was made, religion itself was never simply 'about religion'. Thus, the terms 'Protestant' and 'Catholic' were and are both ethnic *and* colonial labels – as well as indicating something about faith. This reading of course impacts directly on how to make sense of Irish history. From this perspective, the common English insistence that colonial conflict in Ireland was *not* 'about' race – or indeed about colonialism – but really about religion is itself an imperial intervention. Thus, Irish distance from the 'rudiments of the Faith' becomes a convenient excuse for colonial interference *from the first*.

From Pope Adrian IV's grant of Ireland to Henry II in 1155 onwards, English religious institutions were embedded in the colonial process in Ireland. From this point onwards, sectarianism characterises the long trajectory in which religious power and religious institutions constructed the interface between coloniser and colonised. Across this trajectory, there is no point at which religion is a separate discourse from colonialism. The synergy between established religion and imperialism is crucial at every stage of this process. More specifically, of course, in the English – and later British – model, the Crown integrates state power within an explicitly sectarian Protestant model.

Arguably, this classic imperial fusion of politics, church and state achieved a late flourishing in the person of Ian Paisley as he finally became First Minister of Northern Ireland.[11] Paisley was often subject to ridicule – not least in the Britain to which he routinely and vehemently declared his allegiance. But the notion that a ruler should head their own church, and their own political party, and their own state was not archaic but rather embedded in the British imperial model. The English monarch *still* maintains these roles. In 2018 the bathetic manoeuvring to make the next English monarch head of the Commonwealth was evidence that these things *still matter* – at least to the English ruling class.

We also engage with several less theorised, more ambiguous concepts that interpolate across our story, sometimes synonymously, sometimes meaning quite different things. For example, overlapping entities like 'England' and 'Britain' and 'union' and 'empire' appear throughout our narrative. These are often used in both imperialist and anti-imperialist literatures as if they were synonyms. They are, however, routinely multiply coded and carry meaning that is both ambiguous and yet possesses enormous power. Rather than providing a definition, it is more accurate to suggest that their very ambiguity is part of their ideological force. In the manner of Nelson's 'England expects', this invokes a form of discourse that is inherently antitheoretical.[12] More recently, there has been Theresa

---

[11] Paisley was also associated with the Independent Orange Order. But this presents its own footnote on the tensions between faith and politics in Ireland. His take on the theology of such organisations forbade him becoming a member of – let alone head of – this parallel, and definitively Protestant, power structure. This integrity – so esoteric that a non-believer might addend 'Jesuitical' – led to an even more bizarre contradiction at the 'Siege of Drumcree'. Paisley, cloaked in a faux Orange sash – along with David Trimble – led a parade of a sectarian organisation to which he did not belong through the Catholic community of the Garvaghy Road.

[12] 'England expects that every man will do his duty' was the signal sent by Vice Admiral Nelson from

May's appeal to the concept of '*our precious union*' in an attempt to transcend a host of contradictions around Brexit and minority government. This practice mobilises concepts that not only resist definition but actively preclude it. Perhaps the classic example of this that cuts across the story is the notion of an English/British/imperial constitution that is 'unwritten'. Under examination it is revealed that it is unwritten not simply because it has yet to be written but rather because those who benefit most from its operation insist that it cannot and should not be written. If it were written the privilege of those who benefit most from it would be transparent rather than immanent.

There is one final concept to be introduced: *mestizaje* (pronounced mess-tease-ach-ay). Unusual in the European context, the concept is common in Latin America. Translated as 'mixing', it refers to the 'inter-breeding' of colonial incomers and natives over generations. Although some Latin American societies – such as Paraguay – are more *mestizo* (mixed) than others, the phenomenon holds throughout the region that there was extensive mixing, especially in comparison to some other colonial situations, particularly in Africa and Asia.[13] At the ideological level much is made of this in some Latin American circles where a kind of one-upmanship occurs in relation to its powerful northern neighbour. There is an element of self-satisfaction that as a result of *mestizaje* South America is said to have never descended to the same depths of racism, historically and currently, as the United States. This is an erroneous belief. Genocide against the native populations was widespread in Latin America and the practice echoes to this day in places like Guatemala and Bolivia. Moreover, pride in *mestizaje* serves to mask the reality that, no less than the United States, Latin American states are white settler societies.

We are aware that the concept of *mestizaje* carries negative baggage in the Latin American context. As Latin American nation states emerged and grew in the middle and late 19th century, they did so in a world dominated by European nation states which were economically advanced, imperialist and racist. A Eurocentric ideology was prevalent which stated that populations made up of non-European 'racial stock' were destined to fail to catch up with Europe in the race to progress. The response of Latin American elites was to attempt to turn around the fact of their *mestizo* make-up to claim it as, if not exactly a positive at least a positive in the making. Demographic change in Latin America,

---

his flagship HMS Victory at the start of the Battle of Trafalgar in 1805. Trafalgar was the decisive naval engagement of the Napoleonic Wars. It gave the United Kingdom control of the seas, removing all possibility of a French invasion and conquest of Britain and confirmed British imperial dominance until WWI. The significance of the victory and Nelson's death during the battle meant that the phrase has been constantly referenced ever since.

[13] The Spanish *sistema de castas* – the colonial racial hierarchy – embedded a complex combination of indigenous American, African and European identities. Thus, *mestizos/pardos*, who formed the majority, had fewer rights than the European-born *peninsulares*, and the colonial-born whites, *criollos. Mestizos*, however, had more rights than the minority indio, negro, mulato and zambo populations. The Portuguese *mestiço*, referred to any mixture of Portuguese and indigenous populations in the Portuguese colonies. In Brazil, for example, most of the non-slave population was *mestiço de indio* or mixed white and native Brazilian.

they argued, meant that *mestizaje* ensured that populations were becoming whiter. The Indian was inter-breeding with the *criolla* and the Blacks were destined to rapid decline. At the same time, (white) European emigration shifted the balance even further.

In this scenario, *mestizaje* is less a call to decolonisation and inclusion than an argument underpinning white dominion:

> ... [M]estizaje purportedly favored the "superior" races at the expense of the "inferior" ones. Collectively, mestizaje was presumed to reduce the relative influence of Indianness or Africanness on the nation, while enhancing the influence of Europeanness or native "whiteness" – never the reverse'. (Loveman 2014: 154)

On the road to whiteness, the *mestizo* or *mestiza* could be presented as almost white.

The reason to utilise the concept of *mestizaje* is not to fetishise it but to explore what it might add to the analysis of Ireland's colonial experience and its quest for decolonisation. Unusual as the term might seem, there is no doubt that, as a result of colonisation, Irish history is a definitive example of *mestizaje*. This is patently obvious in the North, where a unionist prime minister can have a Gaelic family name while the founder and leader of the Social and Democratic Labour Party that of Scots planters. The question is what is to be made of this fact. In the eyes of the 'good relations' paradigm which we critique in chapter 8 this can be taken as evidence that in fact the citizens of the North have more in common than they acknowledge and that the acknowledgement of that sharing could be the basis of a peaceful society. Conflict depends on binaries, in this case, native versus settler. But if there is no pure 'native' and no pure 'settler', ultimately there is nothing to fight about. We do not subscribe to this facile and comforting view. At the same time, as will be explained in depth in chapter 11, the concept of *mestizaje* has powerful positive possibilities.

If we are all *mestizos* or *mestizas*, we are an amalgam of both settler and native experience. That is not how people in the North usually approach culture and politics. Political views often run in families; people vote with remarkable consistency on ethnic grounds. It is as if the biological accident of being born Protestant or Catholic is the sole determinant of political identity and action. The recognition of *mestizaje* can deconstruct things. If we are all *mestizos* and *mestazas*, there is the opportunity to explore our mixed past with a view to deciding where each of us stands at the present time. In particular, there are decisions to be made by each of us about reclaiming the parts of our past which support liberation and in particular decolonisation.

To take one example close to home: One of the authors of this book is from a Catholic background and grew up in a Catholic area; on this basis, it might seem no surprise that he espouses the politics expressed in this book. But on both sides of the family, he has a Protestant great-grandfather who married a Catholic, thereby ensuring that the children were raised Catholic. He is by no stretch of the imagination a 'native'; more, to take some absolutist anti-settler political stand would be to deny the settler part of his background. The other author was born a Protestant and grew up in a Protestant area. It would be easy to label him a 'settler'. But in the Irish situation there were, to quote

Memmi (1990), colonisers who accepted colonisation and all the privileges it conferred on them and others in each generation who refused, and there is evidence of each in his family background. The point is that to be Protestant by birth is not necessarily to be unionist. The 'settler' label has not got a single meaning. To put it simply: politics can be a choice. In the context of *mestizaje*, that means that each of us can explore the complexity of our origins with a view to political identity and action: in one case, examining the settler within, in the other examining the settler who refuses within. Ultimately such an examination has profound possibilities for liberation at both the individual and collective political level. Specifically, the task of decolonisation is too important to be left to only one section of Irish society.

What is Irishness?

These, then, are our basic conceptual tools: gender, race, class, sectarianism and *mestizaje*. Starting from this broad methodological approach, we can turn to the question of the specificity of the Irish experience of empire. This, of course, begs the question of whether Irishness itself is an uncontested concept. Conor Cruise O'Brien (1965: 65) famously debunked more traditional accounts of Irishness:

> Irishness is not primarily a question of birth or blood or language; it is the condition of being involved in the Irish situation and usually of being mauled by it. On that definition, Swift is more Irish than Goldsmith or Sheridan, although by the usual tests they are Irish and he is pure English.

O'Brien's characterisation retains the virtue of de-essentialising the subject – it is an invitation to engage with Irishness and Ireland dialectically.

In consequence, it can be suggested that Irishness – or that which has become academicised as 'Irish Studies' – is usefully regarded as a *trichotomy* of relations between north, south and diaspora. In addressing different questions about Ireland and colonialism, this means asking the following: what perspective does the South throw on this? What perspective does the North throw on this? What perspective does the diaspora throw on this?[14]

This approach insists that it is impossible, for example, to study the economy of Ireland by only looking at the Celtic Tiger phenomenon in the 26 counties, or to study violence in Ireland by only looking at the Six Counties. More specifically it makes explicit the notion that in order to understand the nexus of Irishness and colonialism these three dimensions – north, south and diaspora – need to be addressed. Each interface between these three core aspects of Irishness, currently and historically, is a complex mixture of a whole series of dialectical tensions – native/settler, Protestant/Catholic, Black/white – as well as the tensions of gender, race and class and religion highlighted above. To take a tangible example

---

[14] Witness, for example, the organisational structure of the Irish Republican Brotherhood. It had seven sections – the four Irish provinces but also Scotland, North of England and South of England. In this context, the diaspora constituted nearly half the project. This is before factoring in the US and Canadian Fenians who organised separately.

– it is impossible to understand the connection between race and colonialism and Irishness through focusing on any one of these elements in isolation. Any assessment of race in Ireland is diminished without reference to Ignatiev's *How the Irish became White* (1995). While this book focuses on the Irish in America – in this sense it is a classic diaspora text – it remains essential to understand racialisation in Ireland, north and south.

More broadly, therefore, Irishness ought to be regarded as a *trialectic*. Partition has made two elements in this trichotomy inescapable – nobody could suggest that there are not major differences across all key issues north and south of the border, despite the fact that many policymakers and commentators now equate the 26 counties with 'Ireland' as if the six counties can be detached from the very landmass. This amputation fails very quickly – for example, the most committed partitionist in the south would find it difficult to insist that a figure like Seamus Heaney is British rather than Irish, or that Armagh, the Irish ecclesiastical capitol, is not in Ireland.[15] Moreover, the name given the state by empire – 'Northern Ireland' – makes the nexus inescapable for even the most committed of unionists.

This leaves the diaspora as the most undertheorised element of our trichotomy. A key question for Ireland in the coming times is: what role is left for the diaspora? Despite the importance of returnees in 2015 for the successful marriage equality referendum in the South – 'Take the boat to vote' was the powerful mobilising slogan – and the key role of Irish America in the peace process, the diaspora has been less in evidence – and arguably less cherished – in recent years. The annual St Patrick's Day exodus of Irish politicians – from north and south – to participate in various shades of gombeenism across the USA arguably bears little relation to real Irish people in Ireland or elsewhere in the world. If nothing else, however, the diaspora remains singularly important in retaining a notion of Irishness both *without and beyond partition*. In this sense it might be argued that 'pure' Irishness is *only* located in the diaspora.[16] Although there continue to be vestiges of anti-Irish sectarianism and racism in places such as Glasgow and Liverpool, for the Irish abroad there is no partitioned Irishness in New York or London or Sydney or Glasgow or Berlin. In contrast, in Ireland itself, Irishness is only understood in terms of its subjective and objective 'northern' and 'southern' variations. Of course, these still meet fairly routinely – at Croke Park or at the Fleadh or the Oireachtas or in the ecclesiastical capital of Armagh. Moreover, the differences blur almost completely along the border. Nevertheless, most of the time they exist in firmly partitioned worlds. Furthermore, these different worlds have become *increasingly* entrenched in Ireland over the past thirty years, both despite and because of the peace process. Brexit has also, of

---

[15] Heaney had, of course, been forced to make his own position on this issue explicit: 'My passport's green, no glass of ours was raised to toast the Queen'. He wrote this after the *Penguin Book of Contemporary British Poetry* included some of his poems in 1982. Ironically, post-GFA Heaney sat down with the Queen at a formal dinner in Dublin in 2011.

[16] One tangible example of what this means is as follows. It was the diaspora that contested de Valera's Document no. 2 on 'external association' rather than northern republicanism that was more threatened by it. This perspective obtains. In a broad sense the diaspora remains the most 'republican' of the three elements – from its perspective it cannot see a partitioned Ireland.

course, brought the reality of these two Irelands into sharp focus, with profound but unchartered consequences. And recently, Covid-19 sealed the border, temporarily, more effectively than the British army or the B Specials had ever done.

This long tradition of diaspora – forged by both involuntary exile and voluntary migration – also left a profound mark on Irishness in Ireland. This was most obvious in the exile of its indigenous elites following colonial expropriation. First, the Irish nobility left in the Flight of the Earls; next, the Irish bourgeoisie left with the Wild Geese (Murtagh 1996). The vast majority of emigrants were, however, poor. This history radically transformed the character of the Ireland they left behind – not least in terms of anti-imperialist organising. Outside the realm of 'constitutional' parliamentary politics, organising became increasingly resistance from below – by the Irish peasantry and the Irish working class. It is only really in comparison that the fundamental character is seen – Pearse and Connolly were fairly 'ordinary people' – 'street-bred' as Kipling would have it. As the prospect of self-determination began to appear as a possibility to the Irish people, there was no equivalent of an indigenous elite like the Scottish lairds left to provide a leadership role. This contrasts starkly with other anti-imperialist struggles: Nehru went to Harrow and Oxford, Julius Nyerere to Edinburgh University; James Connolly left school in the Little Ireland district of the Cowgate in Edinburgh at the age of ten.

Connolly's great fusion of class and national liberation occurred in the very proletarian ordinariness of the Irish working class and the diaspora. Crucially, it encouraged a healthy disregard for elites – either foreign or indigenous. Of course, this has often been used to denigrate Irish republicanism. Indeed, northern resistance used to be characterised as the 'pseudo-revolution of the lumpen-proletariat' by the more Stalinist members of the Irish Left. The point, however, was that ordinary people were never quite as marginalised by economic and political elites in Irish discourse as they were in the metropole. This resistance to marginalisation prevailed all through the recent troubles – working-class areas like the Lower Falls and the Bogside were central to the struggle. People from these communities formed the backbone of the resistance from below. Their leadership emerged from Ballymurphy, South Armagh and the Creggan and spoke with accents from those communities. In other words, while more heavily theorised leftists often despaired of the absence of expected patterns of class struggle in Ireland, self-determination was always and inescapably about *class*.

Empire or republic, subjects or citizens

Finally, it bears emphasis that there is a need to be sensitive to the dangers of etymological fallacy.[17] There are all sorts of retrospective criticisms of imperialism – and indeed anti-imperialism – based on contemporary standards. In particular, the relentless reciprocity

---

[17] This holds that the present-day meaning of a word or phrase should be necessarily the same as its historical meaning.

of *massacre* committed by 'both sides' is repeated across the entire imperial story. Empire is usually a spectacularly soft target on this – it is all too easy to identify behaviour that would now be unambiguously regarded as genocide or crimes against humanity. But it is also true that contemporary commentators – and not only from the ranks of the colonised – were able to spot the immoral and egregious aspects of colonialism from the first. In other words, historical distance is not in itself an excuse for the scenes from the 'abattoir'.

Still, the etymological fallacy is mobilised time and again when democratic legitimacy is falsely assumed to underpin colonial politics. The colonial governments that governed Ireland were *never* democratic and any assumption of the legitimacy of subsequent readings of political change must be treated duly critically. One classic example is the notion that the Irish people condemned the Rising in 1916.[18] This is assumed to be true because most contemporary reporting suggested that it was. But this reporting was neither neutral nor particularly well informed. One section of the Irish people – predominantly urban, middle class, Protestant and unionist – may well have so condemned the event but this cannot be read as an expression of the attitudes of the 'Irish people'. After 1918, elections provide closer approximations to such views as they become more democratic. Nevertheless, it bears emphasis that the election of 1918 is the only point at which we see a democratic expression of *the will of the Irish people* across the whole colonial story.[19]

The analysis of colonialism and imperialism never happens in a vacuum. This is particularly stark with contemporary readings of conflict in Ireland. Post-GFA, Ireland remains partitioned and fractured and scarred by a bitter conflict. Part of the ideological construction of peace is a hegemony of 'good relations' that resists and represses divisive analysis. To paraphrase Calgach, we are not allowed to describe the 'wasteland' because this might undermine the 'peace'. At its core, this approach mobilises another fallacy – the *argument to moderation*.[20] If there is one epistemological constant that emerges from any engagement with the history of colonialism and imperialism, it is that it forces people towards stark choices – it is quintessentially dialectical in this sense. There is no excluded middle with right or wrong or good and evil. In this context, there is no point looking for a middle ground between disinformation and information, or, indeed, between propaganda and truth. Resolving problems by making compromises and engaging with alternative interpretations – this is very different from committing to the wholesale reinvention of history. But quite often this is precisely what is expected.

Practically, this kind of revisionism manifests itself in the ongoing rehabilitation of empire. This is something that at face value seems entirely counter-intuitive. Why

---

[18] We return to this point in chapter 4.

[19] Even then it is necessary to acknowledge the exclusion of the diaspora and younger women in this relative test of democratic will.

[20] Also known as the golden mean fallacy, this asserts that the truth must be found as a compromise between two opposite positions. An example of how invalid it is would be to take the case of one person saying that the sky is blue, while another claims that the sky is in fact yellow, and concluding that the truth is that the sky is green. Taking the middle ground of two positions does not always lead to the truth.

wouldn't anyone approach those twin evils of colonialism and imperialism in the same way as the Holocaust – recognise both as terrible stains on the human record, learn from them and move on? Take two elements specific to European empire – slavery and genocide. At face value, an institution that routinely supported such crimes against humanity seems to place itself beyond redemption. The 'greatest' empires – Spanish, Portuguese, British, French – fairly unproblematically and incontestably – promoted slavery and genocide. In this context colonial revisionism sounds like a hard sell. Yet people constantly work to re-habilitate these formations – the awarding of honours in the name of empire is only the most obvious manifestation. As the BLM moment helpfully reminded us in 2020, anti-imperialist struggle is never over – confederacy, slavery, genocide, opium wars – all must be refought in the present.

This struggle continues. For many people the crimes of empire can be ignored or downplayed, to the point that it is assumed that imperialism was essentially good. This also constructs a more specific, smaller version of the same thesis – for the British it is especially important to insist that *British imperialism was essentially good*. But this is also the case for the French and the Spanish and the Portuguese. This approach, of course, provides an easier defence – perhaps not all imperialism was good but ours was good, nevertheless. This is not simply about expunging the historical record – contemporary European nationalisms are rooted in colonial history and any delegitimation of empire has profound contemporary as well as historical implications. Ireland and Irishness – alongside the rest of the colonised world – must therefore repeatedly contest this hegemonic force. This is hegemony manifest in a whole range of ways – to even contest the history is often to place oneself once more beyond the pale.

Nevertheless, it is right to continue to contest and resist. History and truth – or perhaps the truth of history – is on our side. There is no need to invent 'alternative facts' because 'ordinary' facts do the work. From an Irish perspective these 'ordinary' facts represent catastrophe rather than civilisation. There are various estimates of the trail of 'anatomies of death' across Irish history. The key point is that thousands upon thousands of real Irish people died – children, women and men – due to the acts and omissions of empire. These deaths have hardly been accounted let alone avenged or restituted. One example from *An Gorta Mór* can speak for all. In the pathetic trail of starving Irish peasants walking to Delphi Lodge in Mayo in 1847 the whole empty conceit of empire is laid bare.[21] At this point – in desperation – we Irish had become supplicants. At one

---

[21] In March 1847, a large group of starving people in Louisburgh, County Mayo, sought assistance from the relieving officer who advised them to apply to the Board of Guardians meeting next day at Delphi Lodge, ten miles away over the mountains. This was a hunting lodge owned by the Marquess of Sligo, a former governor of Jamaica. They walked there through the night but were informed when they arrived that the Board were at lunch and could not be disturbed. When they finally did meet with them, the Board denied them assistance, so they set out on the road home. Many of them perished over the two days (Mayo Ireland 2020). That said, the Marquess himself was much more understanding. At his home in Westport he handed out guns to starving peasants so they could hunt for food.

level the empire had triumphed – we were *subject*. We were prepared to beg empire for survival; and yet we could still be turned away.

This one tragic episode cuts to the quick of the nexus of Ireland and colonialism. The truth of empire was exposed in this moment. If the 'greatest empire there ever was' chose to make a people its subjects – against their express will, mind – then such an empire bore some responsibility for their basic survival. There is no need for Foucault or an understanding of biopolitics to suggest that imperial starvation was a crime against humanity. From an Irish perspective, the 'greatness' of the empire dissolves immediately in the face of *An Gorta Mór*. Moreover, this memory asserts to those who want us to return to subjection in some way – to wear poppies or toast the Crown or accept honours in the name of the British Empire – that we are right to say no. There was no greatness or honour in starving to death under the imperial flag – we could have found a million other ways to die without its imprimatur.

In this context, we continue to have the choice that generations before us have had. This is the choice between empire and republic – there is no excluded middle. Moreover, this choice is not simply about history but rather at the core of what we identify as the 'unfinished revolution'. Contemporary Ireland has a *choice* in terms of whether to stand in solidarity with other victims and survivors of colonialism and imperialism or take its place within white dominion. In 2020, as much as 1800 or 1918, we have to decide whether we should remain subjects or become citizens.

Chapter 2

'Robbers of the world': colonialism and imperialism – a genealogy

A short while ago of our own accord, and out of our certain knowledge, and fullness of our apostolic power, we gave, conveyed, and assigned forever to you and your heirs and successors, kings of Castile and Leon, all islands and mainlands whatsoever, found and to be found, discovered and to be discovered, that are or may be or may seem to be in the route of navigation or travel towards the west or south, whether they be in western parts, or in the regions of the south and east of India. —Pope Alexander VI, *Dudum siquidem*, 1493

Why don't they go back and help fix the totally broken and crime-infested places from which they came. Then come back and show us how it is done. —Donald Trump, 2019

Despite its assumed redundancy, the legacy of empire is everywhere in the modern world. In the conclusion to his review of the subject Niall Ferguson insists, 'like it or not, and deny it who will, empire is as much a reality today as it was throughout the three hundred years when Britain ruled, and made, the modern world' (2012: 381). As metaphor it pervades consciousness from New York as the 'Empire State' to the Star Wars franchise. In the UK its symbols are even more ubiquitous – in biscuits and beer and pubs and cinemas and ballrooms. It endows the honours the UK state invites people to receive – 'Commander of the British Empire', 'Order of the British Empire', 'Member of the British Empire'. Moreover, the flag of the British empire can be found all over the place – in Australia, in New Zealand, in Bermuda, in Fiji and across half of the state flags of Canada. It also pops up in the most incongruous of places: here in the flag of Coquimbo, Chile; there in the state flag of Hawaii; even skeletised within the flag of the otherwise dependably anti-imperialist Basques.

At one level the pervasive nature of imperial iconography implies that there is nothing toxic about the brand; at another it makes what is signified almost impossible to pin down. When empire is put under critical pressure it becomes an elastic concept. When attacked it can flee to the middle of the pack: 'Didn't *everybody* colonise?'. Or it can stand proudly alone: 'Yes, others colonised cruelly but our empire was an exemplar'. Empire is also remarkably selective in memory. Slavery is nearly always referenced in the passive voice – we learn that it was done but not who did it. In consequence the message is that the institution was abominable, but the finger of blame is rarely pointed at any state or culture or class – *or empire*. Agency reappears with alacrity, however, in terms of *abolition*.[1] This is something that 'our' empire can be proud of. The French and British both claim first dibs on this one.[2]

The very ubiquity of empire makes it hard to see. Since much of contemporary culture is steeped in imperialism and colonialism, nothing stands out. In this chapter we offer a genealogy of colonialism and imperialism in order to frame the key elements – to signal what we should look out for in terms of England and Ireland. We then look at these elements more specifically in the British context – to construct a schema of English and British imperialism. There is one profound truth and one profound question running through the whole analysis. First, it would be impossible *not* to accept the notion that these processes have shaped the modern world. On this there is broad consensus: for good or ill, colonialism and imperialism had a definitive influence on the contemporary world. In this sense, empire *has* made the world – and all of us in it. But this, of course, begs the related question – is this a 'good thing'? Once this question is posed, a vast literature follows. There is a prolific continuum of contributions on empire – both celebratory and condemnatory. Britain provides more than its fair share of celebrations of colonialism – from Kipling to Ferguson – extolling the virtues of empire. But there is also an enduring British counter-narrative – from Adam Smith to Wilfred Blunt – excoriating not only the 'blemishes' but the very idea of empire (Newsinger 2013).

While it is unusual to find contemporary celebration of empire in the sense of commitment to any new imperialism, there is a great deal of revisionism and historical celebration. There is a stereotype of post-colonial melancholia of old men sitting in their quietly decaying gentlemen's clubs talking of Churchill and the Raj.[3] But the reality is much more potent than that. It is apparent in different forms of nationalism across Europe – more immediately, its trace can be detected in the forces that argue for Brexit and against reparations. In other words, the valorisation of empire was not

---

[1] Less attention is paid to those who continued to advocate slavery. Alexander H. Stephens, Vice-President of the Confederacy, declared in 1861 that, 'Slavery is the natural and moral condition of the negro ... I cannot permit myself to doubt the ultimate success of a full recognition of this principle throughout the civilized and enlightened world ... negro slavery is in its infancy.' Stephens was re-elected to Congress after the war and went on to become Governor of Georgia. His idea of a re-emboldened slavery was notoriously echoed enthusiastically by the Irish republican John Mitchel – but also supported by influential British intellectuals like John Locke and Thomas Carlyle.

[2] Missing from the self-congratulation evident in the British case is a consideration of the extent to which slave owners benefited from abolition. In 1833 the British government paid out £20m to compensate some 3,000 slave owners for the loss of their 'property'. This represented a staggering 40 per cent of the Treasury's annual spending budget and, in today's terms, equates to around £16.5bn. A total of £10m went to slave-owning families in the Caribbean and Africa, while the other half went to absentee owners living in Britain (*Independent* 24 February 2013). The British Treasury revealed this was not paid off until 2015. In a 'surprising #FridayFact' the government department caused outrage when it announced through its Twitter page: 'Millions of you helped end the slave trade through your taxes' (Olusoga 2018b).

[3] We will consider this at greater length when examining Paul Gilroy's (2005) concept of 'postcolonial melancholia' in chapter 7. See also O'Toole 2018.

simply a product of its time. There has been a contemporary recrudescence of this idea. For example, in 2017, Bruce Gilley's self-explanatory 'The Case for Colonialism' caused widespread outrage (Prashad 2017a,b).[4] Whatever the merits of its arguments, the abstract makes his thesis absolutely clear:

> For the last 100 years, Western colonialism has had a bad name. It is high time to question this orthodoxy. Western colonialism was, as a general rule, both objectively beneficial and subjectively legitimate in most of the places where it was found, using realistic measures of those concepts. The countries that embraced their colonial inheritance, by and large, did better than those that spurned it. Anti-colonial ideology imposed grave harms on subject peoples and continues to thwart sustained development and a fruitful encounter with modernity in many places. Colonialism can be recovered by weak and fragile states today in three ways: by reclaiming colonial modes of governance; by recolonising some areas; and by creating new Western colonies from scratch.

In stark contrast, however, a year later, there appeared as damning an assessment of colonialism as there is likely to be in Dabhoiwala's review of Olusoga's work on 'contact' and 'civilisation' (2018a). Dabhoiwala (2018) characterised

> European civilisation as a slow but inexorable historical plague, which destroys everything it comes into contact with: other cultures, the natural world, and millions upon millions of its own people.

Anyone engaging with the legacy of empire in Ireland – or anywhere else for that matter – must situate their analysis within this essentially contested space. Even if the analysis is confined to Ireland and Irish writers, there is a competing body of imperialist and anti-imperialist readings and interventions – from Carson to Connolly and Lord Meath to Patrick Ford. It is necessary to make sense of this tension in order to situate Ireland's experience within the wider phenomenon. There is a profound contradiction between the notions of British civilisation as the 'greatest instrument for good that the world has seen' and a 'plague that destroys everything that it comes into contact with'. There is also a long continuum of less absolutist assessments between these contrasting analyses. Where Ireland and the Irish should be placed within these diametrically opposed readings of empire is the core problematic of this book.

Europe and Empire

Contemporary notions of imperialism and colonialism developed under the weight of previous iterations of empires and colonies – particularly Rome and Greece. Greece

---

[4] Several members of the editorial board of the *Third World Quarterly* which published the article resigned in protest at its publication. The article was subsequently withdrawn by journal publisher Taylor and Francis and replaced by a withdrawal notice stating: 'This Viewpoint essay has been withdrawn at the request of the academic journal editor, and in agreement with the author of the essay'. The withdrawal notice went on to attribute its removal to 'serious and credible threats of personal violence … linked to the publication of this essay'.

often provides the model of the colony and Rome the model of empire. There is no questioning the ideological reference to both of these formations. Europe has spent the best part of a millennium comparing itself with 'the glory that was Greece, the grandeur that was Rome'.[5] The notion of the Holy Roman Empire directly reclaimed the institution; the imperial titles tsar and kaiser both reference Caesar directly. Whether in reality Charlemagne was much like Augustus Caesar or Queen Victoria much like Emperor Hadrian counts less than the juxtaposition; it is the *emulation* that matters. Whatever the reality, the mythologised power of classical empire and colony continues to inform the model of its modern iteration.

So, the classical world – Greece and Rome – afforded the basic terminology. Moreover, this provided a paradigm for future colonialism and imperialism – or perhaps more accurately, for future colonialists and imperialists. Here was an ideology that could adequately signify the 'greatness' of the project. Alternatively, here was an ideology that could cloak the most brutal acts of expropriation in vainglorious righteousness and supply an apology for the most egregious of crimes. Thus, both positively and negatively, the meter for all succeeding empires was: how does this compare with what the Romans did?[6]

In this vein, many subsequent historians have been inspired by what is perhaps the most influential history ever written – Gibbon's *History of the Decline and Fall of the Roman Empire* (6 vols 1776–1781). As Brendon notes (2008: xv), Gibbon 'became the essential guide for Britons anxious to plot their own imperial trajectory. They found the key to understanding the British Empire in the ruins of Rome'. Moreover, as Peter Greenaway acutely observed, 'Every historian has a vested interest. *The Decline and Fall of the Roman Empire* was not about the Roman but the British empire'.[7] So, when Europeans came to *theorise* their imperialism and colonialism, there is no doubt that their key comparator was the classical model.

This already suggests that there was an elective affinity between Europe and empire. Why exactly this was the case is a complex question but there is no doubt that this was a *European* project. More than three centuries after the fall of the Western Roman Empire in 476, Europe emerged from the Dark Ages with the coronation of Charlemagne in 800. As Pope Leo III crowned the Frankish king as Emperor, the notion of 'Holy Roman Empire' characterised a new fusion of spiritual and temporal power. Across this story can be found a transcendent idea of 'Europe' juxtaposed to the 'rest of the world' – albeit

---

[5] Edgar Allen Poe, 'To Helen', 1845.

[6] Thus, Howard Brenton's play *Romans in Britain* generated huge controversy in 1980 by comparing British policy in Ireland with Roman imperialism – albeit that the play's enacted male rape caused more immediate consternation than the metaphor.

[7] In 1907 Baden-Powell – quoting George Wyndam – makes the comparison very directly: '"The same causes which brought about the downfall of the great Roman Empire are working today in Great Britain." These words were spoken the other day by one of your best-known democratic politicians and their truth is practically admitted by those why have studied and compared the general conditions of both countries' (quoted in Jeal 2001: 382). Wyndham was a conservative MP who established the imperialist review *The Outlook*.

that this also involves a series of European empires that do not always act in concert and often directly confront each other.

The overarching contrast between Europe and the rest of the world was signalled by the Treaty of Alcáçovas of 1478. In what was arguably the first international treaty, the crowns of Spain and Portugal formally outlined the principle that European powers were entitled to divide the rest of the world into 'spheres of influence'. Moreover, they asserted that they might colonise the territories located within these spheres, and that indigenous peoples living there need not provide consent. Alcáçovas was thus the template for a new international order. From the 1494 Treaty of Tordesillas to the resolutions of the 1884 Conference of Berlin, four centuries later, the non-European world is divided into colonial 'spheres of influence'.

Portugal and Spain were the first polities to extend this kind of imperial formation *beyond Europe*. During the 'Age of Discovery' in the 15th and 16th centuries, they pioneered European exploration of the world and established huge overseas empires in the process. Pope Alexander VI's 'Acts of Donation' of 1493 divided the world between the states of the Iberian subcontinent, giving these 'Christian nations' permission to invade 'barbarous nations' and bring their people to Christianity.[8] The Papal bulls were the basis for negotiation between the two powers which resulted in the Treaty of Tordesillas of 1494, apportioning the non-Christian world beyond Europe. This Treaty divided the newly contacted lands outside Europe along a meridian halfway between the 'Portuguese' Cape Verde islands and the islands of Cuba and Hispaniola 'discovered' by Christopher Columbus in 1492. The lands to the east would belong to Portugal and the lands to the west to Spain.

A few decades later in 1529, the other side of the world was similarly divided by the Treaty of Zaragoza, which adopted the antemeridian to the line of demarcation specified in the Treaty of Tordesillas. Even though these treaties omitted other European powers, the division was initially respected by European states. From the late 15th century to the early 19th, Spain controlled a huge swathe of territories across the New World and the Asian archipelago of the Philippines – what they termed 'The Indies'. They also held territories in Europe, Africa and Oceania. For this reason, the Spanish Empire is often characterised as the first 'global empire'. This was the first empire on which, 'the sun

---

[8] The world was divided by way of four bulls in the 'Acts of Donation'. The first bull, *Inter caetera,* recognised Spain's claim to any discovered lands not already held by a Christian prince and protected Portugal's previous rights. The second bull, *Eximiae devotionis,* granted to the kings of Spain and their successors the same privileges in the newly discovered lands that had been granted to the kings of Portugal in the regions of Africa and Guinea. The third bull – also *Inter caetera* – obliged the Spanish monarchs to spread the faith west from a line drawn 'one hundred leagues towards the west and south from any of the islands commonly known as the Azores and Cape Verde'. Finally, *Dudum siquidem* underlined the sense of perpetuity: 'We grant to you and your aforesaid heirs and successors full and free power through your own authority, exercised through yourselves or through another or others, freely to take corporal possession of the said islands and countries and to hold them forever, and to defend them against whosoever may oppose'.

never set'.[9] It was also the world's most powerful empire during the 16th and first half of the 17th centuries, reaching its maximum extension in the 18th century. The Portuguese Empire was, however, arguably the longest lasting of them all. In 1341, a three-ship expedition sponsored by King Afonso IV set out from Lisbon for the Canary Islands. The expedition mapped the islands and claimed them for Portugal. The Portuguese Empire thus existed for almost six centuries, from the capture of Ceuta in North Africa in 1415, to the return of Macau to China in 1999.[10] From the early 16th century it too stretched across the globe, with bases in North and South America, Africa, and various regions of Asia and Oceania. Between them Spain and Portugal colonised nearly all of South and Central America as well as swathes of north America.

Following the Treaty of Alcáçovas, Spain and Portugal continued to observe their imperial carve-up, despite profound ignorance of the geography of the world that had been divided.[11] Increasingly, however, other countries – particularly those that became Protestant after the Reformation – began to ignore the Spanish/Portuguese settlement. Observing the enormous wealth generated within these empires, England, France, and the Netherlands began to establish colonies and trade networks of their own in the Americas and Asia. This initiated a wider sense of a European mission toward occupation and possession of much of the rest of the world. The first wave of European colonisation developed between the 15th and early-19th centuries. European powers conquered and colonised the Americas and Siberia; they then later established further outposts in Africa and Asia. A whole series of European empires emerged: Belgian, British, Danish, Dutch, French, German, Italian, Portuguese, Russian, Spanish and Swedish.[12] Individually and collectively these established colonies spread across *most* of the world. Russia and Austria pursued a model that looks more like internal colonialism in retrospect – creating vast multi-national polities through expanding their borders across neighbouring states and peoples. Nevertheless, they too were very clear that these were 'empires'.

A series of wars in the 17th and 18th centuries with the Netherlands and France left England – and then, following union between England and Scotland in 1707, Great Britain – the dominant colonial power in North America.[13] It also became the dominant

---

[9] The phrase, *'el imperio en el que nunca se pone el sol'* originated with a remark made by Fray Francisco de Ugalde to Charles I of Spain. Spain had many territories in Europe, islands in the Mediterranean and Atlantic, cities in North Africa and vast territories in the Americas. As 'Charles V', the king was also 'Holy Roman Emperor'.

[10] On 1 January 1668, King Afonso VI of Portugal recognised the formal allegiance of Ceuta to Spain and formally ceded Ceuta to Spain by the Treaty of Lisbon. Despite Morocco's objections, Ceuta remains part of Spain and a territory of the EU.

[11] The arbitrariness of these divisions was confirmed for a period between 1580 and 1640 with the Iberian Union – when the Spanish King was also King of Portugal. For this period, there was in effect one combined Spanish and Portuguese empire.

[12] Scotland also tried – and ignominiously failed – to establish its own empire in the Darien Scheme, based in present-day Panama. This led directly to the Act of Union of 1707 and the incorporation of Scotland in both Union and Empire.

[13] The terms are far from exact. As Canny points out, 'The study of the British Empire in the sixteenth

power in the Indian subcontinent after the East India Company's conquest of Mughal Bengal at the Battle of Plassey in 1757. In the 1713 Treaty of Utrecht, Spain ceded Gibraltar to Britain – alongside recognising a British monopoly on the trade in enslaved people. France also ceded Newfoundland, Hudson Bay and Acadie to Britain. In 1763, the First Treaty of Paris marked the beginning of an era of British dominance outside Europe. France ceded all its territories in America to Britain except Saint Pierre and the Miquelon Islands. In compensation, Great Britain agreed to protect Catholicism in the New World.

This hegemony was quickly challenged by the American War of Independence. The Second Treaty of Paris, signed in Paris by representatives of King George III of Great Britain and representatives of the United States of America in 1783, ended the American Revolutionary War.[14] In 1814, with the Third Treaty of Paris, France ceded the Seychelles to Britain and Malta became a British colony.

This process of European colonisation *accelerated* through the 19th century. The 'new imperialism' characterised a period of colonial expansion by European powers, the United States, and Japan during the late 19th and early 20th centuries.[15] This new wave of imperialism reflected a toxic combination of rivalry among the great powers, the economic desire for new resources and markets, and the notion of a 'civilising mission'. The pan-European character of this process was confirmed at the Berlin Conference of 1884-85. The participants were: Austria-Hungary, Belgium, Denmark, France, Germany, Italy, Netherlands, Ottoman Empire, Portugal, Russia, Spain, Sweden-Norway, United Kingdom, and the United States. This established an imperial 'club' which aimed to regulate European colonisation and trade in Africa during the period. The club was now exclusive – any new act of taking possession of any portion of the African coast would have to be notified by the power taking possession, or assuming a protectorate, to the other signatory powers. The Conference was organised by German

---

and seventeenth centuries presents special difficulties because no empire, as the term subsequently came to be understood, then existed, while the adjective "British" meant little to most inhabitants of Britain and Ireland...' (Canny 1998b: 1).

[14] The treaty set the boundaries between the British Empire in North America and the United States – defining what was to become Canada. Details included fishing rights and restoration of property and prisoners of war. Prisoners of war on both sides were to be released; all property of the British army – including enslaved people – now in the United States was to remain and be forfeited.

[15] In 1853, United States Navy Commodore Perry and a fleet of warships was sent by President Fillmore to force the opening of Japanese ports to American trade through the definitive use of 'gunboat diplomacy'. In 1854, the 'Japan and US Treaty of Peace and Amity' or Kanagawa Treaty effectively ended Japan's 220-year-old policy of *sakoku* (national seclusion – prescribing the death penalty for foreigners *entering* or Japanese nationals *leaving* the country). The treaty also precipitated the signing of similar treaties establishing diplomatic relations with other Western powers. This ushered in the 'unequal treaty system' which characterised Asian and western relations during this period and caused profound resentment inside Japan. There were similar agreements with the United Kingdom (1854), Russia (1855), and France (1858). In this sense, even imperial Japan was pushed into colonialism by the pressures of American and European geopolitics. The subsequent Meiji Restoration reimposed imperial rule with the explicit commitment to strengthen Japan against the threat represented by the colonial powers. Japan transformed from feudalism to a market economy with a concomitant increase in Japanese militarism and military capacity.

Chancellor Bismarck and coincided with Germany's emergence as a military, industrial and imperial power. The outcome was the General Act of the Berlin Conference, which marked the formalisation of the scramble for Africa. The conference was followed by a period of intense colonial activity by European powers, which ignored or eliminated existing forms of African self-governance.

The United States was the only one of these parties not styling itself as 'empire'. It bears emphasis, however, that the arch-imperialist Henry Morton Stanley attended Berlin as a US delegate.[16] Cynically the conference framed its objectives with the commitment to end slavery by African and Islamic powers.[17] Thus, European members signed an international prohibition of the slave trade throughout their respected spheres. Alongside this fig leaf, however, there was an unparalleled commitment to exploitation. Most notoriously, the Congo Free State was confirmed as the private property of the Congo Society on the basis that it would open the territory to pan-European investment.

The Berlin Act also included the first reference in an international treaty to the obligations attaching to 'spheres of influence'. This included a definition of regions in which each European power had an exclusive right to pursue the legal ownership of land. It also introduced a Principle of Effectivity (based on 'effective occupation'), to prevent powers setting up colonies in name only. The scramble for Africa accelerated after the conference, since even within areas designated their 'sphere of influence', the European powers still had to take possession under the Principle of Effectivity. In central Africa in particular, expeditions were dispatched to coerce traditional rulers into signing treaties, under the threat of force. Bedouin- and Berber-ruled states in the Sahara and sub-Sahara were overrun by the French by the beginning of World War I. Having defeated the Zulu Kingdom in South Africa in 1879, the British moved north from South Africa and south from Egypt conquering states such as the Mahdist State and the Sultanate of Zanzibar. In the south they dismantled the independent Boer republics of Transvaal and Orange Free State (which were themselves, of course, settler colonial states). These were defeated in the Boer War from 1899 to 1902. Morocco was divided between the French and Spanish in 1911, and Libya was conquered by Italy in 1912. The official British annexation of Egypt in 1914 appeared to complete the colonial division of Africa. This left the Ethiopian Empire as the only free native state. It managed to repulse Italian invasion from Eritrea in what is known as the First Italo-Ethiopian War of 1889–1896. But Italian Fascism renewed the interest in the colonial paradigm. It defeated Ethiopia

---

[16] Moreover, even if the US was not an empire, it began to acquire colonies. These included Hawaii and the Philippines – and another colonial conundrum that obtains to the present – Puerto Rico. Henry Morton Stanley was born John Rowlands in Wales in 1841 but later changed his name in the US. As a journalist for the *New York Herald* he tracked down the missionary David Livingstone. He was subsequently resourced to 'discover' the source of the Nile. Subsequently he was hired by King Leopold of Belgium to map the Congo river region. Leopold's plan was to turn the Congo into a private fiefdom, removing all political power from any native chiefs. The Congo Free State became perhaps the most brutal of colonial regimes.

[17] This supposed 'humanitarian intervention' meshes with George W. Bush's claim a century and a half later that one reason for the invasion of Afghanistan was to save women from the oppressive regime of the Taliban.

in 1936 during the Second Italo-Ethiopian War and integrated it into the Italian Empire. At this point every inch of the continent of Africa had been colonised by one European power or another. Ferguson (2004: 222) concludes: 'Within twenty short years after 1880, ten thousand African tribal kingdoms were transformed into just forty states, of which thirty-six were under direct European control. Never in human history had there been such drastic drawing of the map of a continent.'

This imperial expansion was extended to China and other parts of Asia in the late 19th and early 20th centuries. Thus, Britain, France, Germany, and Russia (and, later, Japan) assumed *de facto* control over large swathes of Chinese territory. These were taken by means of military attacks or threats to force Chinese authorities to sign unequal treaties and long term 'leases'. Germany also acquired a sizeable empire across Africa and beyond: German South West Africa, German East Africa, German New Guinea, German Samoa. Partly in response to this German expansion, France rebuilt a *new* empire after 1850. Concentrating chiefly in Africa, Indochina and the South Pacific, this replaced its first empire which had been lost in the Napoleonic Wars.

As this suggests, individual European empires rose and fell over this period. From Ceuta onwards, there was a degree of swapping and exchanging these colonial possessions. For example, Spain traded Florida to Britain for control of Havana, which had been captured by the British during the Seven Years' War. But Spain regained Florida after Britain's defeat in the American Revolution and the subsequent Treaty of Versailles in 1783. The territory was finally ceded to the US through the Adams–Onís Treaty.

There were, of course, parallel projects outside Europe at different times: such as Imperial Japan, the Ottoman Empire and the United States. These also acquired colonies. But the European mark was distinctive. Most of the world ended up in European hands. Hoffman suggests that in 1800, at the start of the Industrial Revolution, Europeans already controlled at least 35 per cent of the world; by 1914, they had control of 84 per cent (2015: 2-3). By the start of WWI, nearly all of the world outside Europe – North America, South America, the Caribbean, Australasia and much of Asia – had been formally colonised at some point by at least one European state.

Despite its ubiquity, however, the 'age of empire' was relatively brief – although the formations that emerged from this period remained profoundly structured by their colonial origins. Decolonisation began in North America in the 18th century and South America in the 19th century. All Spanish colonies, except Cuba, Puerto Rico, the Philippines and Equatorial Guinea, attained independence by the 1820s.[18] The archetypal European colonial system began to break down even more widely after WWI, and crumbled between 1945 and 1975, when nearly all Europe's colonies gained political independence. But the legacies are palpable – in its former colonies in the

---

[18] Simon Bolivar began an independence movement against the Spanish in 1808. By 1821, after the Battle of Boyacá, the independent state of Venezuela was formed. In the years following Peru, Ecuador and Bolivia also expelled the Spanish and became independent.

Americas, Spanish is the dominant language and Catholicism the main religion, enduring cultural legacies of the Spanish Empire, while Portuguese and Catholicism endure in Brazil courtesy of the Portuguese. In Africa, Protestant forms of Christianity and English came to dominate in most of sub-Saharan Africa.

Even more profoundly, of course, empires were able to shape the polities that would replace them. Arguably, the US precedent indicated the necessity of a different means of resolving the tensions between empire and settler populations. The key lesson that the British Empire drew from US independence was the need to develop a new model of the relationship between empire and settler colonialism. This review evolved into the notion of *responsible government*. The argument went that it was the absence of 'responsible government' – taxation without representation – that had been the key issue in terms of separation of the American colonies. It followed that, had the American colonies been provided with responsible government, then they would have neither demanded nor gained independence.

This issue came to a head once again after the 1837 Lower Canada Rebellion led by Louis-Joseph Papineau, and the 1837–1838 Upper Canada Rebellion led by William Lyon Mackenzie. The imperial parliament appointed Lord Durham as Governor General of British North America with the task of reframing the colonial relationship. Durham argued that 'Canada did not get Home Rule because she was loyal and friendly, but she has become loyal and friendly because she has got Home Rule' (quoted in Ferguson 2004: 253). One of his recommendations was that colonies which were sufficiently 'developed' should be granted 'responsible government'. Crucially, this term implied that henceforth British-appointed colonial governors should reflect the will of elected colonial assemblies.

Nova Scotia became the 'First Responsible Government in the British Empire' in 1848. It had already established a form of representative government within the empire in 1758; but in 1848 it achieved autonomy. This autonomy was still very firmly framed by imperialism and colonialism; there was little anti-imperialist about it. The Mi'kmaq people who inhabited Nova Scotia at the time the first European colonists arrived had been all but wiped out in the preceding two centuries. Neither native rights nor title were recognised. In other words, this was the template for white dominion across the empire. Political power would be ceded almost exclusively to the white settler population – with the indigenous population either minoritised or wiped out completely.

This Nova Scotia development was followed by a broad trajectory towards increasing autonomy/independence across various colonies with either settler majorities or significant white settler populations. Under the British North America Act 1867, Canada received the status of 'dominion' upon the Confederation of several British possessions. At the Colonial Conference of 1907 the self-governing colonies of Canada and Australia were referred to collectively as dominions for the first time. Two other self-governing colonies – New Zealand and Newfoundland – were granted dominion status in the same year. These were followed by the Union of South Africa in 1910 and the Irish Free

State in 1922. At the time of the founding of the League of Nations in 1924, the League Covenant made provision for the admission of any 'fully self-governing state, Dominion, or Colony'. Dominion status was formally defined in the Balfour Declaration of 1926, which recognised these countries as 'autonomous communities within the British Empire', thus beginning to construct them as *political equals* of the United Kingdom. The Statute of Westminster 1931 formalised this status legally, making the dominions independent members of what had become the British *Commonwealth*.[19]

More broadly, the European Union carries with it a significant legacy from this imperial past. Besides Ceuta, there are a host of European colonial outliers around the world, each with an unresolved legacy of European colonialism.[20] Most recently, New Caledonia failed to achieve independence because of the influence of its French settler bloc.[21] This was a striking reminder that the EU inherited the remnants of European empire – and some of the unfinished business of decolonisation. The 'special territories of the European Union' are 31 territories of EU member states which, for historical, geographical, or political reasons, enjoy special status within or outside the European Union. The special territories consist of: nine Outermost Regions (OMR) that form part of the European Union, although they benefit from derogations from some EU laws due to their distance from Europe; and 22 Overseas Countries and Territories (OCT) that do not form part of the European Union, although they cooperate with the EU via the 'Overseas Countries and Territories Association'.

The OMR were recognised in the Maastricht Treaty in 1992 and confirmed by the Treaty of Lisbon in 2007. OMR members are essentially outposts of the former French, Spanish and Portuguese empires: Canary Islands; La Réunion; Guadeloupe; Martinique;

---

[19] After the Balfour Declaration in 1917, whereby the British opened the way for 'a national home for the Jewish people' in Palestine, the *Manchester Guardian* military correspondent, Herbert Sidebotham, suggested that what Britain could end up creating was 'a modern state such as could ultimately, after a period of pupillage, form a self-sufficing state as a British dominion, and not only become responsible for its own government and its local defence, but even, like other dominions, tender voluntary help to the empire in its trials' (Freeman-Molloy 2018: 83). To that end, in 1929 British Zionists founded the Seventh Dominion League. The goal was for Palestine to be converted from a League of Nations trusteeship territory into a Jewish Dominion within the British Empire. See Rose 1971.

[20] All these contradictions are neatly summed up in contemporary Ceuta – which has its origins as the first Portuguese/Spanish colony. Formally part of the EU Schengen Area, Spain performs identity checks on all sea and air passengers leaving Ceuta – and Melilla, the other Spanish enclave in North Africa.

[21] In November 2018, voters in 'New Caledonia' – named as such by British explorer James Cook in 1774 – rejected a bid for independence from France by 56 percent to 44 percent, on a turnout of about 81 percent (BBC News 2018e). The island, some 20,000 kms away from France in the south-west Pacific Ocean, was annexed by France in 1853 and used as a penal colony. It retains around 25 percent of all the nickel deposits in the world. Indigenous Kanaks make up 40 percent of the population and were in favour of independence. But a substantial proportion of New Caledonia's population is descended from some 2,000 Arab-Berber prisoners transported from French Algeria in reprisal for the Mokrani Revolt in 1871. There is also a community of about 2,000 *Pieds Noirs*, descended from European settlers in Algeria who were prominent in anti-independence politics. The rejection of independence means that the territory remains one of the UN's 17 'non-self-governing territories' – in which the UN recognises formally that the process of decolonisation has not been completed.

Madeira; French Guiana; Azores; Mayotte; Saint Martin. The OCT were defined in the Treaty on the Functioning of the European Union 2007. They are dependent territories that have a special relationship with one of the member states of the EU but are not part of the EU or the Single Market. The OCT members trace the outlines of the wider European colonial project across the Americas, the Caribbean and the Pacific.[22]

Beyond these formalised 'special territories', *still further* territories have *ad hoc* arrangements in their relationship with the EU – and many of these too carry a direct colonial legacy. These also bifurcate on EU membership: areas that are part of the EU: Åland Islands, Büsingen am Hochrhein, Campione d'Italia and Livigno, Ceuta and Melilla, UN Buffer Zone in Cyprus, Helgoland, and Mount Athosa (as well as Gibraltar until the UK left the EU); and areas that are not part of the EU: Akrotiri and Dhekelia, Faroe Islands, Channel Islands (Bailiwick of Jersey and Bailiwick of Guernsey), Isle of Man, and 'Northern Cyprus'.

In combination these territories represent a significant colonial legacy. As in New Caledonia, some of them remain sites of anti-colonial struggle; but they most commonly enter popular consciousness as tax havens and tropical retreats for the super-rich.[23] More broadly, these polities still feature in contemporary politics and geopolitics and military intervention – often a base for extraordinary renditions or US and allied airstrikes. Thus, an EU project committed to democracy and human rights needs to focus on completing its own decolonisation process. In addition, it is worth signalling the profound distance between being post-colonial and being decolonised that we return to in our section on decolonisation.

The economics of imperialism

For all its ideological trappings and religious justifications, the early process of European colonialism was usually explicitly economic. The dominant Spanish and Portuguese economic models were nakedly extractive and often piratical – stealing and removing the wealth of the peoples of the Americas and repatriating these to the 'motherlands'. This period of colonisation also introduced the Spanish labour system of the *encomienda*. This system was established during the *Reconquista* and the Christian conquest of Muslim territories. Conquered peoples were considered vassals of the Spanish monarch. It was subsequently applied, however, on a much larger scale during the Spanish colonisation of the Americas and the Philippines. The Crown awarded

---

[22] With the exception of Greenland which 'belongs' to Denmark, they are a combination of French, Dutch and British territories: Anguilla; Aruba; Bermuda; Bonaire; British Virgin Islands; Cayman Islands; Curaçao; Falkland Islands; French Polynesia; French Southern and Antarctic Lands; Greenland; Montserrat; New Caledonia; Pitcairn Islands; Saba; Saint Barthélemy; Sint Eustatius; Saint Helena, Ascension and Tristan da Cunha; Saint Pierre and Miquelon; Sint Maarten; Turks and Caicos Islands; Wallis and Futuna. Nearly half of these territories have lost any association with the EU now that the UK has left the EU.

[23] Perhaps the most absurd of the many contradictions involved in the Brexit debate was when Richard Branson urged UK voters not to leave the EU by satellite from his tax haven in the 'British Virgin Islands' – which is, as an OCT, *not part of the EU*.

an *encomienda* – a grant which entitled the holder or *encomendero* a monopoly on the labour of defined groups of indigenous peoples. This was then held in perpetuity by the *encomendero* and their descendants.

In the colonial context, the *encomiendas* were effectively a form of communal slavery. The Spanish Crown granted a person a specified number of natives from a specific community but did not direct which specific individuals would have to provide their labour. Indigenous leaders were charged with mobilizing the assessed tribute and labour. In turn, *encomenderos* were obliged to provide the *encomienda* natives with instruction in Christianity and the Spanish language and provide them a level of 'protection'. They also had to maintain infrastructure and suppress any rebellion against Spanish rule. In return, the natives would provide tributes in the form of metals – particularly gold – as well and agricultural products. Ultimately, this economic model of slavery and theft was limited in terms of economic development in both metropole and colonies. It was famously characterised as 'turning gold into stone' once repatriated to Europe. Thus, the super-profits of this first adventure in European imperialism were used as much to build ostentatious churches and cathedrals as to capitalise the Spanish and Portuguese economies.

This changed with the Dutch. In their colonial model, private companies capitalised from the Netherlands set up their own colonies as private commercial concerns. Dutch control of international maritime shipping routes allowed them to develop trade through strategically placed outposts rather than large territorial acquisitions. Despite the focus on commerce rather than sovereignty, however, the Dutch Cape Colony (South Africa), Dutch East Indies (Indonesia) and Dutch Guiana (Suriname) expanded to constitute huge colonies under the influence of Dutch settler colonists. The Dutch trading outpost model was quickly followed by similar ventures from England and France. At first, European colonising countries followed policies of mercantilism in order to strengthen the home economy at the expense of rivals. Regulations usually restricted the colonies to trading *only* with the 'mother country'. This was the dominant economic model through most of the early colonial period with high tariffs, especially on manufactured goods, and colonies forbidden to trade with other nations.

For example, the Company of Merchant Adventurers to New Lands was an early joint stock association, which initiated the synergy between private exploration and enterprise. It received its full Royal Charter in 1555 – in a neat confluence of existing and developing European empire this was provided by Mary, Queen of England, and her husband, Phillip of Spain. The purpose of the Company was to seek a new, northern trade route to China and the Spice Islands (the Moluccas). It failed to locate a north-west passage but developed English trade with Russia and became known as the Muscovy Company. The Muscovy Company had a monopoly on trade between England and Muscovy until 1698 and it survived as a trading company until the Russian Revolution of 1917, after which it reinvented itself as a charity. The Company of Merchant Adventurers to New Lands was the first major chartered joint stock company, the precursor of the type of business that would soon flourish in England and become definitive of the economics of colonialism and imperialism. Many of these remain – in different iterations – among the richest and most powerful companies in the world.

This colonial 'trade' was definitively less than equal. From the first, the colonial encounter moved beyond any simple market exchange for the colonised. If the first contact was a trading relationship, this quickly accumulated other differentials of power. As Wahunsenacah, Chief of the Powhatan Confederacy, accused John Smith: 'Your coming hither is not for trade, but to invade my people, and possess my Country' (quoted in Warner and Warner 1997: 109). In this context, a whole series of powerful and immensely wealthy European companies emerged: including the Royal African Company – set up by James II and City of London merchants to trade in gold and slavery; and perhaps the two most famous and influential of all: the Dutch East India Company (VOC) and the British East India Company.[24] Later appeared what was perhaps the most notorious colonial company of all when the vast Congo Free State was confirmed as private property of the Congo Society.

Once again, the Dutch led the way on this corporate imperial model. In 1602 the VOC became the world's first formally listed public company. It was the first corporation to issue bonds and shares of stock to the general public and to be listed on an official stock exchange, thus creating a capital market. This initiative offered an element of democratisation – albeit only for citizens of the colonial power. It opened ownership of companies beyond the ranks of the traditional elites – mostly royalty and aristocracy – that had benefited from mercantile colonialism. The VOC was thus definitive in the rise of corporate-led globalisation through colonialism – the VOC is considered the world's first transnational corporation. This moment also marked a stark juncture in the colonial relations of production – between new publicly owned corporations based in Europe and the colonised who largely generated their wealth.

In this model, the relationship with the 'sending' state remained ambiguous. A complex, symbiotic relationship developed between monarchy, state, parliament and company. The colony usually began with a royal grant which provided a monopoly over trade within a given area. Contemporary politicians were also heavily invested in the companies. The operation also remained dependent on state infrastructure – most obviously the navies which protected trade routes. But the companies also insisted on their independence. In consequence, they often developed into proto-colonial states

---

[24] The Royal African Company (RAC) was an English mercantile company set up in 1660 by the British royal family and City of London merchants to trade along the west coast of Africa. Its first governor and chief shareholder was the Duke of York – the future James II. His brother the king Charles II was also a major shareholder. Edward Colston – whose statue was famously toppled in Bristol during the 2020 BLM protests – was also a major beneficiary. The RAC shipped more enslaved Africans to the Americas than any other institution in the history of the Atlantic slave trade.

– with their own armies and administration.[25] Macauley – the theorist of British imperialism – characterised this in a Westminster debate on reform of the East India Company in 1833:

> It is a mistake to suppose that the Company was a merely commercial body till the middle of the last century. Commerce was its chief object; but in order to enable it to pursue that object, it had been, like the other Companies which were its rivals, like the Dutch India Company, like the French India Company, invested from a very early period with political functions. More than a hundred and twenty years ago, the Company was in miniature precisely what it now is. It was intrusted with the very highest prerogatives of sovereignty. It had its forts, and its white captains, and its black sepoys; it had its civil and criminal tribunals; it was authorised to proclaim martial law; it sent ambassadors to the native governments, and concluded treaties with them; it was Zemindar[26] of several districts, and within those districts, like other Zemindars of the first class, it exercised the powers of a sovereign, even to the infliction of capital punishment on the Hindoos within its jurisdiction. It is incorrect, therefore, to say, that the Company was at first a mere trader, and has since become a sovereign. It was at first a great trader and a petty prince. (Quoted in Young 1935: 117)

In time, however, since the cost of the associated colonial administration was often prohibitive, these companies transferred responsibility to their national governments – particularly in the context of conflict with colonised peoples.[27] This moment was key to the emergence of a fully-fledged colonial state. It happened most famously in India in 1857 following the Indian Uprising (Dalrymple 2019). But the same merger of company and state emerged across the European empires. The Dutch nationalised the VOC in 1796 – with all assets taken over by the government and VOC territories becoming Dutch government colonies. Belgium finally assumed responsibility for the Congo in 1908. Later European empires – like the second French Empire and the German Empire – tended to be state-driven from the start.[28]

Alongside the state assuming responsibility for colonial administration there was a shift of emphasis from mercantilism to free trade. By the mid-19th century, the British Empire gave up trade restrictions and adopted the principle of free trade, with few constraints or tariffs – either inside or outside the empire.[29] Put cynically, it might be observed that

---

[25] For example, at the height of its rule in India, the British East India Company had a private army of about 260,000 – twice the size of the British Army at the time.

[26] A landlord required to pay a land tax to the government.

[27] This reality also produced an influential counter argument to the assumed economic benefits of colonialism. Adam Smith argued against it for this reason. One of the later arguments against colonialism was that it became too expensive as empires expanded for geopolitical rather than economic reasons.

[28] The Spanish conquest of Latin America had earlier followed a similar pattern. Originally little more than a form of plunder, it was reined in by the Spanish Crown, not simply because of the atrocities revealed by clerics such as de las Casas, but also to ensure that the rewards of conquest, in particular gold and silver, would return to the Crown rather than being pocketed by adventurers.

[29] There was also a recrudescence of protectionism specifically in the context of the British empire. *Imperial*

the British used their predominant position to develop competitive advantage and then changed the rule to free trade. Generally, this philosophical principle held sway across 19th century colonialism. In Africa, Livingstone elevated this to a creed – 'Christianity and commerce'. This in turn segued into the model developed by Cecil Rhodes – an unabashed celebration of capitalist colonial greed as synonymous with imperial development. As we have already seen, many colonies also became tradeable quantities themselves. For example, Denmark sold its colonies in India to Britain in 1845 and the Danish Gold Coast in Africa in 1850. The Louisiana Purchase bought that territory from French to the US in 1763; Russia sold Alaska to the US in 1867.

For all the ideological emphasis on trade and commerce, however, colonial economics tended to be inherently parasitic. Thus, it reduced the wealth of the Americas from El Dorado[30] to the contemporary barrios of Latin America. Columbus found a 'land abounding in gold dust' when he arrived in Hispaniola; contemporary Haiti is now the poorest county in the Americas. British India followed the same pattern. When the English arrived in Bengal, it was the richest part of India; three hundred years later, it was the poorest. Shashi Tharoor (2016) drew on this economic history to make the case for reparations:

> Over 200 years of exploitation, depredation, loot and destruction, reduced it to a poster child for third-world poverty; just over three per cent of global GDP, 90 per cent of the population living below the poverty line when the British left in 1947.[31]

In this sense, the colonial process directly instituted the profound inequalities that continue to underpin our contemporary world economic order. Empires did not take over undeveloped places as much as they underdeveloped the places they took over. The colonial and imperial system constituted a world economic order. We saw in chapter 1 how Stuart Hall (2016) illustrated the imperial project through the British taste for tea and sugar. These products were quintessentially 'British' and yet only available in Europe because of the colonial mode of production.[32] They were dependent on colonised Black labour power. Moreover, this labour power was extracted under super-exploitative colonial relations of

---

Preference was proposed as a system of reciprocally enacted tariffs and free trade agreements between the dominions and colonies of the British Empire. Across the first half of the 20th century Imperial Preference was considered a method of promoting unity within the British Empire and sustaining Britain's position as a global power as a response to increased competition from the more protectionist Germany and United States. The system was later revived as a 'Commonwealth Preference'. This was mostly dismantled after WWII in the GATT, but it continued in some forms across the Commonwealth until the UK entry into the EEC in 1973.

[30] See Galeano (2009) for an account of the enormity of the task of mining silver in Bolivia, making the nearby city of Potosi one of the largest in the western world by the 1570s.

[31] Ferguson's (2004: 27) figures confirm the point: 'In 1700 the population of India was twenty times that of the United Kingdom. India's share of total world output at that time has been estimated at 24 per cent ... Britain's share was just 3 per cent'.

[32] Worldwide, restaurants and hotels serve 'English breakfast tea', a beverage called after a country that does not itself have the capacity to grow the product.

production: first by enslaved people; later by indentured people; and, now by various forms of exploited labour across the plantations and sweat shops of the 'Third World'.

The triangular trade that instituted and reproduced the slave trade epitomised this colonial network: enslaved people taken from Africa to the New World; raw materials – like cotton and sugar and tobacco – shipped from slave plantations in the New World to Europe; manufactured goods shipped to Africa and the other colonies. The economic continuities between our contemporary world and the age of empire are immediate. As William Dalrymple (2015a) observes:

> The East India Company no longer exists, and it has, thankfully, no exact modern equivalent. Walmart, which is the world's largest corporation in revenue terms, does not number among its assets a fleet of nuclear submarines; neither Facebook nor Shell possesses regiments of infantry. Yet the East India Company – the first great multinational corporation, and the first to run amok – was the ultimate model for many of today's joint-stock corporations. The most powerful among them do not need their own armies: they can rely on governments to protect their interests and bail them out. The East India Company remains history's most terrifying warning about the potential for the abuse of corporate power – and the insidious means by which the interests of shareholders become those of the state. Three hundred and fifteen years after its founding, its story has never been more current.

In other words, the economics of imperialism established our contemporary world economic order.

The ideology of imperialism

As the Powhatan observed, even if the first contact with Europeans was a trading relationship, this quickly assumed other more exploitative and transformative dimensions. Most obviously colonised spaces were renamed – countries, rivers, towns and cities were retitled in the image of the coloniser.[33] Perhaps the most pathetic example in this renaming was what was to become Papua New Guinea. Here we find a doubly racist European projection: 'Papuan' is cognate with 'Fuzzy Wuzzy' in Portuguese; 'New Guinea' emerged from the similarity that English colonists identified with African 'Guinea' – which was already a racist term.[34] Post-independence from Australia, the name sees colonialism internalised with no reference to native language or culture. This

---

[33] At the same time, there was often remarkable continuity. In New England, Mattapoisett, Waquoit and Mashpee coexist alongside Harwich, Barnstable, Sandwich and Yarmouth. Similarly, in Australia Warnambool, Geelong, Warragol and Traralgon are towns near Melbourne, itself named after the Prime Minister of the UK. Sometimes naming was totally idiosyncratic. Thus, when Cortes asked a cacique the name of the area they were in, the cacique replied that he had no idea what Cortes was talking about. To the Spanish this sounded like 'Yucatan', and thus the area of present-day Mexico was named.

[34] The provenance is colonial. The English term Guinea comes from the Spanish word Guinea, which in turn derives from the Portuguese word Guiné. The Portuguese term emerged in the mid-15th century referring to the 'black' African peoples living south of the Senegal River who contrasted with the 'lighter' Berbers to the north.

bizarre colonial neologism continues to provide a name for an independent state with over 600 indigenous languages and some 7.5 million citizens.

From the first European incursions into the Americas in the 15th century to the height of European imperialism in the late 19th century, a global system of domination wrought havoc on the non-Europeans of the planet. Ideology played a key role in this development. For example, Darwin's observations on evolution were taken to justify genocide: 'At some future period not very distant as measured in centuries, the civilised races of man will almost certainly exterminate and replace throughout the world the savage races' (quoted in Lindqvist 2002: 107). Different colonial nations employed different approaches. The Spanish sought to convert indigenous people in the lands they conquered to Catholicism. While the British seemed less concerned that every subjugated native should be Protestant, they still unleashed centuries of missionary proselytising on the empire.[35]

The rationalisation of colonialism was frequently encapsulated in the notion of the 'civilising mission' of the West. For the British it was summed up in Kipling's notion of 'the white man's burden', the moral obligation to bring to less advanced peoples the economic and social advantages of progress which they were not capable of achieving themselves. For the French, there was a similar sense of superiority where they were obligated to disperse their revolutionary ideals to the inferior peoples of the world (Löytömäki 2013). There was no contradiction between the ideal of a civilising mission on the one hand and the call to extermination on the other; for all its liberal veneer, exporting civilisation was less a process than, in effect, a military offensive. As Van Krieken (1999: 303) concludes: 'The barbarism of colonization did not merely originate in societies which regarded themselves as civilized but was carried out "in the name of civilization".'[36]

Practice swiftly followed ideology. British colonialism justified the takeover of Australia by claiming that it was *terra nullius*, a land where no one lived, relegating the indigenous inhabitants to the level of beasts to be exterminated (Lindqvist 2007).[37] In what became the United States, the presence of an indigenous population was not denied, but their nomadic or semi-nomadic existence and their failure to cultivate the land was anathema to puritan Protestant minds. Their subsequent doctrine of 'manifest destiny' proclaimed that they had a god-given right to take the land from the natives in

---

[35] In India in the late 19th century, proselytizing was deemed to be interfering with state and military priorities. Protestant missionaries were not encouraged, and Queen Victoria reassured Indian leaders that the empire would not interfere with local religious beliefs and customs (Ferguson 2004: 178).

[36] Marx condemned 'the flagrant self-contradiction of the Christianity-canting and civilisation-mongering British government' (Marx 1980: 19). On another occasion he wrote: 'The profound hypocrisy and inherent barbarism of bourgeois civilisation lies unveiled before our eyes, turning from its home, where it assumes respectable forms, to the colonies, where it goes naked' (Marx 1979; 222).

[37] In an interesting twist on this theme, the Cuban government in 1850 declared the 'Indian race' extinct in order to take over the indigenous town of El Caney, thereby expropriating native land.

order to develop it (Pearce 1998). Here, settler colonialism tended to generate an even more brutal experience for the indigenous population than for those in countries where the imperial power sought trade and raw material extraction.

Even when people were not to be physically exterminated, they were to be transformed. Christian missionaries were active in practically all of the European colonies.[38] Later this proselytising project became a *mission civilisatrice* — a fully-fledged mission to 'civilise' the world. For example, in 1884, the leading French proponent of colonialism, Jules Ferry, declared:

> We must say openly that indeed the higher races/Europeans have a right over the lower races/Africans. I repeat, that the superior races have a right because they have a duty. They have the duty to rule, civilize and subjugate the inferior races (Ferry 1884).

This civilising worldview left no question that the colonised were to be *transformed*. Macaulayism framed this project in India:

> We must at present do our best to form a class who may be interpreters between us and the millions whom we govern; a class of persons, Indian in blood and colour, but English in taste, in opinions, in morals, and in intellect. To that class we may leave it to refine the vernacular dialects of the country, to enrich those dialects with terms of science borrowed from the Western nomenclature, and to render them by degrees fit vehicles for conveying knowledge to the great mass of the population.[39]

Strikingly, an explicit colonial hierarchy remained. These 'hybrids' would not be completely English, but nor would they be 'Indian' — their key function was to be 'interpreters of Empire'.

In terms of the status of different territories across colonialism, there was a continuum from British hotchpotch to Portuguese conformity. Britain, as we shall see, presented a contrasting amalgam of many different models — all bundled around the idea of 'Empire'. Indeed, this only really began to take ideological coherence in the second half of the 19th century.[40] In contrast, Portugal developed a uniform approach. Under the ideology of *pluricontinentalism*, the regime renamed its colonies 'overseas provinces'. In this principle, everything was simply 'Portugal'; there was no difference between metropole and satellite. With origins as early as the 14th century, Portugal

---

[38] A key 'Christian' practice which continued well into the 20th century in the US, Canada and Australia, involved indigenous children being stolen from their families and community and placed in 'residential schools' in order to eradicate indigeneity through education and culture. This practice neatly captures the intertwining of the civilizing mission and the thrust to extermination. Done ostensibly for the children's own good, it was, in the case of the United States, summed up in the slogan, 'Kill the Indian, save the man' (Churchill 2004). The genocidal imperative was not simply cultural; mortality rates of children in the 'residential schools' 'matched or exceeded death rates in Nazi concentration camps during the Second World War' (Jones 2006: 76).

[39] Minute on Indian Education.

[40] See, for example, Joseph Chamberlain's *The True Conception of Empire*, published in 1897.

became a pluricontinental formation during the reign of Maria I, with the creation of the United Kingdom of Portugal, Brazil, and the Algarves. Pluricontinentalism was further internalised in the fascist *Estado Novo* regime in 1933. This led to the suggestion that Portugal was not a colonial empire *at all,* but a singular nation state spread across continents. France retains a similar system to this day in some French colonies. Each is regarded as a province of France. All natives are thereby citizens and decolonisation becomes impossible since colonial status is denied.

The apparatus of imperialism

Of course, colonised people did not generally accept the profoundly negative consequences of the colonial process. Nor did they accept or immediately internalise the racist hierarchies implied by different ideologies of empire. It hardly needs said: people did not want to be enslaved; they did not want to be dispossessed; they did not want their culture or language repressed or exterminated. In this context, they resisted both the economic and ideological models characterised above. At this point, imperialism required a further strategy: apparatuses to coerce and control – and sometimes exterminate – the populations they were colonising. In the first phase these were crude – representing a straightforward use of violence and the threat of violence. In later phases, however, this was supplemented by much more extensive and more implicit apparatuses of repression – including an imperial criminal justice system and civil service.

The most striking aspect of this observation about the repressive state apparatus is that institutionalised violence assumed unprecedented proportions under imperialism. Here was Weber's notion of a monopoly over the legitimate means of coercion taken to its logical conclusion: imperialist militarism – and a military mode of production. It was also extremely functional. As we shall see in our chapter on anti-imperialism, chapter 9, the power imbalance meant that victory for the coloniser and defeat for the colonised was (almost) inevitable. Whether this took a matter of days or weeks or years, the outcome was usually a forgone conclusion. So it proved from Magdala to Omdurman and from Plassey to Rorke's Drift. If there was no opportunity to battle then a straightforward army massacre – like Amritsar – would suffice. There was, however, an implicit limitation to this strategy. It works when a maxim gun is used against a people armed with stone age instruments– as in the British massacre of Tibetans at Chumik Shenko in 1904. Such was the key strategy in colonial expropriation. But this dynamic works less well in a fair fight – when a maxim balances a maxim. The colonised were sometimes able to source the same weapons that were being used against them. This shifted the power dynamic considerably.

More significantly, however, the logic of imperialism was such that empire began to square up to empire. By the start of the 20th century, Germany and the United States had begun to challenge British economic dominance. Military and economic tensions between Britain and Germany were major causes of the First World War. While it may have foreshadowed the end of empire, there was no sense of this in terms of the preparedness to support imperial war. Each of these empires subscribed to the notion that the war was in their interest. In this sense they made a terrible miscalculation in terms of both their own futures and the fate of humanity. The conflict also placed enormous strain on the military, financial and human resources of all the European empires. It bears emphasis that this conflict was definitively an *imperial* choice rather than a democratic one. For example, the *whole* British Empire entered the war on the declaration of King George V on 4 August 1914. The white dominions all responded immediately in support of the war. The other colonial armies all delivered the numbers expected in terms of the war effort – for example, some 1.3 million Indian soldiers served. The human cost was, however, enormous – with over one million military deaths across the armies of the British Empire alone and an additional two million wounded.

Lenin made sense of this dynamic in his *Imperialism: the Highest Stage of Capitalism.* He argued that the Great War was 'an annexationist, predatory, plunderous war' among empires. Thus, capitalist imperial competition had provoked global war among the German Empire, the Austro-Hungarian Empire, the British Empire, the French Empire, the Russian Empire and the Japanese Empire – along with their respective allies. In this sense, WWI was the first example of MAD – 'mutually assured destruction' – in operation. From this perspective, it signalled the end of imperialism since it had finally turned against itself. It had no new markets left to penetrate and no new peoples left to colonise – and in consequence began to devour itself. This led to war on an industrial scale – whole economies turned to destruction on an unprecedented scale.

In other words, one of the lessons that empire learned from the ongoing resistance to colonialism was the *limits* of war. This learning had arguably begun with the US war of independence and was brutally confirmed in WWI. In this context, ideology – and the ideological state apparatus – became increasingly important within colonial formations. Now, without any sense of contrition or irony, empire often came to be about 'peace'. Thus, Pax Britannica aped Pax Romana. However, none of this peace came out of anything except the capacity to use force. It was the hegemony of violence rather than the repudiation of violence that created 'peace'. Moreover, the prelude to this state often involved catastrophic violence for the colonised, including ethnic cleansing and genocide. To echo Calgach again, empire creates a desolation and calls it peace.

This ideological state apparatus operated at several levels. First, there was the question of the colonial state itself – what were its boundaries, how was it administered, and what rights were its subjects provided? The notion of dividing up the world was, as we have seen, central to the colonising mission. Thus, four hundred years after Pope Alexander VI divided the world between Spain and Portugal, this was still going on as the Berlin Conference of 1884-85 regulated the competition between the powers by defining 'effective occupation' as the criterion for international recognition of territorial claims.

This division of spoils was particularly problematic in the case of colonialism. The European imperialist scramble for Africa in the late 19th century led to the creation of states where none had existed before. In the Middle East, boundaries were drawn on maps, their clear straight lines either taking little if any cognisance of complex ethnic divisions or dividing groups which had once lived in peaceful coexistence.[41] All were thrown together into the one colonial creation which may have served the administrative, military and economic needs of the colonial power but did little to forge an 'imagined community' (Anderson 1991) among the disparate groups so confined. The roots of later sectarian division and conflict in places as diverse as Ireland, Rwanda and Iraq emerge from these colonial decisions. Decolonisation had further effects on these political structures. Substantial structural problems were imported into the very being of the new states, one consequence of which was that for many, the state was not seen as legitimate. Minority ethnic groups who were marginalised and discriminated against saw themselves trapped within the structures, and were at best sullen and resentful, or determined to resist by all means, including military ones. Arguably, this distortion of space is one of the most profound legacies of colonialism. The acceptance of *uti possidetis*[42] by decolonising states meant that these colonial structures would reproduce in perpetuity with a post-colonial commitment to permanence that matched Pope Alexander's commitments to 'forever' in 1493.

Moreover, this kind of colonial partition had a much wider reference and practice. Imperialism did not simply partition peoples or countries, it partitioned continents – most infamously between Portugal and Spain. This involved imposing borders where they had no clear logic – creating polities that had little organic legitimacy. It left a series of divided peoples in its wake: across America, Vietnam, Ireland, Yemen. Most notoriously of all, the British partition of Bengal established the principle of 'divide and rule' across the politics of Raj. This policy cemented communalism and sectarianism in India and prefigured the later partition of India itself. This led directly to the deaths of approximately two million people and the displacement of some 15 million more (Dalrymple 2015b).

Alongside the imposition of borders where none had existed before, the colonial social formation itself was a key mechanism for coercion and control. Here basic questions of citizenship – measured in terms of civil, political and social rights – became paramount. It bears emphasis, of course, that, most of the time, the colonised were not technically citizens at all but rather subjects.[43] This already hints at the racial

---

[41] For example, the borders of Iraq were drawn in 1918 by Englishwoman Gertrude Bell around three provinces of the former Ottoman empire. 'Bell sketched the boundaries of Iraq on tracing paper after careful consultation with Iraqi tribes, consideration of Britain's need for oil and her own idiosyncratic geopolitical beliefs' (Knickmeyer 2006). See also Howell 2015.

[42] *Uti possidetis juris* is a principle of customary international law that serves to preserve the boundaries of colonies emerging as states.

[43] In 1924, the US Congress conferred citizenship on native Americans. In 1956, a Canadian citizenship act

and gendered hierarchies that structured rights – and more generally the absence of rights – in the colonial context. This impacted directly in terms of the way in which basic services like justice, education and healthcare were provided – and more often *not* provided – in a colonial context. Here the ideological state apparatus took form – in the legal infrastructure and the educational infrastructure – and all the elements of the colonial state apparatus that reproduced generation upon generation of colonial subjects.[44]

Ultimately, however, none of this can be properly understood through the theories of imperialism and colonialism – the toxic combination of propaganda and guidebooks on administrative practice that notionally informed what was done in – and to – the colonies. The reality of actually existing colonialism and imperialism can only really be understood from below. Here we need to turn to the lived experience of colonialism and imperialism.

The lived experience of imperialism

Contrary to what postmodernist postcolonial studies theorists argue, colonialism was not simply a discursive project but involved the real suffering of real people in historical time – land expropriation, settlement, ongoing violence, the use of law as a weapon of submission, skewed wealth distribution, policies of cultural marginalisation or annihilation and ultimately genocide. Extermination was more than a 'blemish' or 'unintended consequence' but rather the inevitable acolyte of colonialism. The first victims of modern imperial expansion were the Guanches, the original inhabitants of the Canary Islands. Their population was estimated at 80,000 before the Spaniards arrived in 1478; by 1541, 'there was one single Guanche left, eighty-one years old and permanently drunk' (Lindqvist 2002: 111). This established the precedent.

Colonisation saw the destruction, in whole or in part, of a chain of national, ethnic, racial and religious groups across the various European colonies. Death by killing, death by disease, death by transportation, death by starvation, death through

---

from 1947 was amended retrospectively to include native Canadians as citizens. It was only in 1967, after a referendum, that aboriginal Australians were granted citizenship.

[44] The commitment to educating the colonised differed from empire to empire, and within each empire. The Spanish opened a college for the education of natives at a very early stage in the conquest of Latin America. A similar college envisaged by early English colonists in Virginia for educating Indians failed to open (Young 2006: 72-73). Charles Trevelyan (1807-1886), sometimes regarded as the 'Eichmann of Ireland' for his role in *An Gorta Mór*, was in favour of the education of young Indian men. He told a House of Lords select committee in 1853: 'The young men educated in this way cease to strive after independence according to the original native model … The natives will not rise against us, because we shall stoop to raise them' (quoted in Boylan 2006:172). In India, he argued that the people were held back by superstitious religion and that a good dose of English rationality, delivered through an education system, would improve them. In the case of Ireland, starvation would act as a purge, getting rid of the inefficiency of the Irish and their agricultural habits, and thereby improving the whole of society.

slave labour.[45] The indigenous population of the Americas was estimated to have fallen by some 90 per cent in the three hundred years after Columbus' arrival. Scholars consider the initial period of the Spanish conquest as marking the most egregious case of genocide in the history of humankind. The death toll may have reached some 70 million indigenous people (out of 80 million) in this period (Todorov 1999: 133).[46] The statistics are endless, and endlessly shocking. The population of Hispaniola may have been as high as 8 million when Columbus arrived. Less than three decades later is was around 200,000 (Jones 2006: 71). Ten million Africans died under Leopold's rule in the Congo alone (Jones 2006: 43).

Transatlantic slavery meant that between 1526 and 1867, almost 11 million slaves were shipped to the Americas; approximately 12 per cent of them died on the journey (Mintz 2019). British imperialist expansion in Australasia was catastrophic for the indigenous people there. The last surviving Tasmanian, Truganini, died in 1876, 73 years after 44 white settlers first landed on the island (Lindqvist 2002: 120).[47] In the scramble for Africa, each European imperial power competed with the others in a race to genocide. The Germans, a late arrival in the imperial contest, massacred 60,000 of the 80,000 population of Herero people and half of the Nama people in south-west Africa in the first years of the twentieth century (Lu 2011: 265). Called 'the first genocide of the 20th century,' the massacre of the people of Namibia is often said to be a precursor for the Holocaust, although the debate was slow in emerging in post-war Germany where amnesia ruled in relation to the events.[48] In 2004, the German Minister for Economic Cooperation and Development finally apologised for the genocide but did not offer compensation; instead he increased development aid to

---

[45] It is estimated that Indians in the Bolivian mines had a life expectancy of three to four months, 'about the same as that of someone working at slave labor in the synthetic rubber manufacturing plant at Auschwitz in the 1940s' (Jones 2006: 71).

[46] Recent research has shown that the effects of this genocide spread far beyond the Americas. Because of the decline in population, 54 million hectares of farmland lay idle and were reclaimed by trees and other vegetation. This stored CO_2 from the atmosphere and led to an overall drop of 0.5 degrees in global temperature. One effect was the 'little ice age' in London in the 16th and 17th centuries, whereby the Thames regularly froze. See Koch et al 2019.

[47] It has been argued that to talk of the last indigenous person in any colonised society can be a form of racism in that it recognises only 'pure blood' individuals as members of the indigenous population (see Perera 1996). The other side of this issue is the space for people of 'mixed blood' to call themselves indigenous. In Australia, the census allows a person to self-identify as aboriginal or from the Torres Strait Islands. However, as far as the aboriginal nations are concerned, the person self-identifying must receive authentication from the nation's elders. Elsewhere the selection process is less rigid. Take the case of possible descendants of the Taíno people of the Caribbean. Many in the Taíno movement propose genetic testing as a means of affirming their ancestry, while others argue that expressing identity is a personal decision that can also make a political statement. Critics of the movement often argue that contemporary Taínos are too racially mixed to be authentic, to which Taínos respond that for many it was through ethnic mixing and cultural adaptation that they survived into the present. (Information from the Museum of the American Indian in New York.)

[48] Some question the claim of a direct link between the Namibian genocide and the later Holocaust, but there is no denying that in some respects the link is both direct and intimate. Goering was the son of the first German governor of colonial Namibia. Eugen Fischer, who supported Mengele at Auschwitz, had conducted 'racial studies' in Namibia (Jones 2006: 81).

Namibia (De Cesari 2012: 324). UN guidelines frown on using development aid – which should be happening anyway – as a substitute for reparation.

This dynamic around 'contact' continues in the present day. In 2018, the killing of a US missionary attempting an unlawful intervention with the Sentinelese people in the Nicobar and Andaman Islands brought this interface squarely up to date. The *Times of India* gave a helpful briefing on the context:

> There are six original tribes in this archipelago of 572 islands spread over the Bay of Bengal from Land Fall island in the north to the Great Nicobar Island in the south.... The first modern settlement of outsiders was established in 1789 by Lt. Blair at Chatham Island, now part of Port Blair. The settlers faced hostility from the start. The most determined effort to push out the British was the 1859 Battle of Aberdeen. But locals with bows and spears were no match for modern British troops. When the Britishers arrived, there were more than 5000 Great Andamanese. After the battle and 'mainstreaming', they number 44 today. The Onges met a similar fate; from 679 in 1900 their population has declined to 101 today. The Jarawas, hostile till 1998, have been relatively successful in maintaining their population. But experts believe their condition has worsened after increased interaction with outsiders. In 1999 and 2006, Jarawas suffered outbreaks of measles, which has wiped out many indigenous tribes worldwide. Tourism also led to exploitation, including sexual abuse of Jarawa women. (*Times of India* 2018)

The article concludes with profound understatement: 'Experts says the Sentinelese could be hostile to outsiders because of similar incidents'.

This pattern was repeated time and again across different colonial formations. Even when it did not lead to immediate genocide, colonialism produced social relations of unmatched horror. It seems inappropriate to look for superlatives in this context, but the Belgian Empire was perhaps the most degenerate of all in this regard. As we have seen, the Berlin Conference of 1884-85 confirmed the Congo Free State as the property of the Congo Society – this effectively made it the personal property of Léopold II of Belgium. The Berlin deal promised to keep the country – nearly equal in size to the whole of Europe – open to all European investment and exploitation. Thus, the territory of today's Democratic Republic of the Congo, some two million square kilometres, was gifted to a single European man.

The provenance of this specific imperial formation is revealing. The Association Internationale Africaine (International African Association) was established by participants at the Brussels Geographic Conference of 1876, an event hosted by King Léopold II of Belgium. The Association was presented by the king as furthering his philanthrophic projects in Central Africa. By this means, he was able to lay claim to most of the Congo basin. Léopold accommodated its headquarters in Brussels. In theory, there were to be national committees of the association set up in all the participating countries and headed by various royal patrons, as well as an international committee. In a trail reminiscent of contemporary corporate ownership, however, the Association was replaced by a succession of increasingly less altruistic iterations. Thus, the Association was succeeded by the Committee for the Study of the Upper Congo. The official stockholders of the Committee were Dutch and British business people and a Belgian banker who was holding shares on behalf of Léopold.

In 1879, this body was replaced in turn with the International Association of the Congo or the Congo Society. Its project was to establish control of the Congo Basin and to exploit its economic resources. The Berlin Conference recognised the society as sovereign over the territories it controlled – albeit that Léopold's philanthropic front was less persuasive to many participants than his commitment not to tax trade across the colony. Léopold finally revealed his less than moral interest in the project and named his colony the 'Congo Free State' in 1885. The Congo Free State operated as a corporate state privately controlled by Léopold through the Congo Society. The state included the entire area of the present Democratic Republic of the Congo and existed from 1885 to 1908. Thus, for over twenty years, it was ruled personally by Léopold II and functioned separately from Belgium. The brutal model of extractive free trade employed attracted widespread international criticism – from, amongst others, Roger Casement.[49] Eventually, Belgian investment companies encouraged the Belgian government to take over the Congo and develop the mining sector. By 1908, public pressure and diplomatic manoeuvres led to the end of Léopold II's rule. Belgium reluctantly annexed the Congo Free State as a colony of Belgium and it became the Belgian Congo. It was this colonial power – reframed as 'Little Belgium' – that was used specifically to recruit thousands of Irish volunteers to fight for the British Empire in the First World War.

There are standard histories of this episode in European venality (Gann and Duignan 1979). But the classic characterisation was provided in Joseph Conrad's *Heart of Darkness*. The book is regarded as racist by many African commentators. But its

---

[49] Roger Casement worked for Henry Morgan Stanley, thus unwittingly opening up the Congo for Belgian exploitation. He shared the ideals of Joseph Conrad, whom he met in 1890, that western intervention could lead to the moral and economic improvement of Africa. Both were disabused of this idealism, as Conrad's *Heart of Darkness* reveals. As for Casement, he returned to the Congo in 1903 at the behest of the British government to examine the ill-treatment of rubber plantation workers. His report on this became in effect the first human rights investigative report of modern times and led to the Belgian government taking over control from King Léopold. In 1906, Casement repeated his investigative work in the Putamayo region of Peru and again revealed brutal treatment of rubber plantation workers. Eventually, having exposed the colonial abuse of two other societies, he turned to continuing colonialism at home and became involved in the Easter Rising. Charged with treason, he was hanged in Pentonville Prison in 1916 (see Mitchell 2007). Casement was charged under the Treason Act of 1351 for attempting to organise Irishmen in the British army held captive in Germany to fight against Britain. The Act defined treason thus: '…if a Man do levy War against our Lord the King in his Realm, or be adherent to the King's Enemies in his Realm, giving to them Aid and Comfort in the Realm, or elsewhere …' Casement's defence was that the comma between 'Realm' and 'or' meant that the comfort given to the King's enemies could be anywhere but that the act of organising war had to take place within the kingdom. The original Norman French in which the Act was written wasn't much help. But the court found that the comma was not in the original Act and Casement's defence collapsed. Hence it was said that he was 'hanged by a comma' (Anderson 2013).

significance is less in the picture it paints of the colonised – which *is* unambiguously racist and one-dimensional – but of the colonisers. Here is all the imperial bombast stripped bare – the reality of imperial 'altruism' is revealed in brutal monochrome. The book captures the sense of what colonialism does to those who engage with it. In this sense it remains a remarkable anti-imperialist text. Here the notion of imperial psychosis is fully exposed: the grandiose claims of altruism and anti-slavery juxtaposed to the brutal horror of colonial exploitation of the Congo. Where else might we find genocide represented as philanthropy?

This is our basic thesis in terms of the broad experience of colonialism. The brutal reality of colonialism in the Congo was repeated across the centuries from 1494 onwards. The grisly calculus of death is almost unthinkable – but those who wish to revise the opinion of the world on colonialism need to think it. Even if it did not end in physical extermination, it ended in cultural extermination. It set itself the task of reconstructing people in its image[50] – of turning heathens into Catholics, Catholics into Protestants, hostiles into a 'civilised tribe', warriors into addicts. In this sense, the cost of imperialism is incalculable – countless genocides since 1478 to the point where, at any one time, a genocide was being prepared or carried out.[51]

White dominion and *mestizaje*

Our brief overview of the arc of colonialisation provides some sense of the complexity of the many different colonial ideologies and formations that appeared in the centuries after 1478. At its heart, however, colonialism comprised two overlapping geopolitical projects: control over people and control over territory. Both projects engaged a defining elective affinity between race and dominion – the right to possess both people and land was assumed to be based on some form of racial entitlement to govern. This notion reached preposterous levels in the work of some of the ideologues of empire. Thus, we find Joseph Chamberlain, speaking in 1895 as Colonial Secretary at the height of the British Empire:

> I venture to claim two qualifications for the great office which I hold, which to my mind, without making invidious distinctions, is one of the most important that can be held by any Englishman; and those qualifications are that in the first place I

---

[50] Sometimes quite literally. For example, in Hobart museum there is an early colonial painting of a local tree that the English artist clearly had never seen at home. Its bunches of leaves face upward, like a cupped hand, to collect water. To the artist, this was impossible, so, despite the evidence of his eyes, he painted the leaves pointing downward.

[51] Thus, in England's 'first colony' of Newfoundland, the indigenous Beothuk who inhabited the island at the time of English settlement had been declared 'extinct' by 1829 (McGregor 1836). This pattern was repeated time and again as a combination of the direct process of colonialism or its attendant ills, native peoples were exterminated. Thus, from *Ikkarumikluak* (Newfoundland) to *Xaymaca* (Jamaica), from *Aotearoa* (New Zealand) to *Lutriwita* (Tasmania), indigenous cultures were eradicated and indigenous peoples either minoritised or subject to genocide. Once cleared of any significant native presence, these spaces could contemplate becoming white dominions.

believe in the British Empire, and in the second place I believe in the British race.
I believe that the British race is the greatest of the governing races that the world
has ever seen. (Cited in Parry 1998: 40)

Colonialism enabled the world to live through the prism of race. As we have seen the
differences – both real and imagined – between the coloniser and colonised were myriad
– European and non-European, Christian and non-Christian, 'civilised' and 'uncivilised'.
But this complexity was generally reduced to an epiphenomenon – it was colour coded
as a binary distinction between whiteness and otherness. This is why we characterise the
overarching colonial formation as *white dominion*.[52]

Despite its reach across empire, however, white dominion was grounded in a
profound contradiction. While the fantasy implied both the possibility and virtue of
segregating whiteness and otherness, the reality of colonialism – what we might regard
as its historical dynamism – was defined by a continuous, furious interfacing and mixing
of peoples. Its leitmotif was the mass movement – both forced and voluntary – of people
around the world in all directions. We characterise this complex process of mixing
by using the Spanish term *mestizaje*. The process of 'combining' – the emergence of
complex forms of *mestizo* societies out of colonialism – is one of the key legacies of
empire (Furnivall 1948).

Moreover, the very act of trying to build colonies in the image of the coloniser could
not but transform that image itself. On the one hand, colonialism aspired to recreate an
idealised fantasy of 'home' within its new colonies – from the Home Counties pastiche
of Simla in India to the French high colonial pomp of Hanoi. Classically, this projection
involved the *plantation* of a colony of settlers from the imperial heartland. This was
supposed to construct a mirror image of the life that these settlers had left behind. But
this process inevitability transformed the world in a whole range of ways – both the
colony and the colonising power. In other words, it failed to generate clones of villages
and towns and cities in England or Spain or the Netherlands or France but instead created
a distorted and dystopian simulacrum. A process that was often intended to *replicate* the
metropole in the colony, instead transfigured both the colony and the colonial power.

At the very heart of this process there was a further conundrum. Those who were
most obviously intended to recreate the metropole – the European settlers that empire
brought to its colonies – were themselves a defining part of the transfiguration. Settler
colonialism, as writers such as Memmi (1990) have pointed out, was a specific form of
colonialism, more intense in certain ways that extractive colonialism and with a system
of violence which, if not more brutal, was frequently more personal. It had several
specific characteristics. From the beginning, settlers were out on a limb. Their declared

---

[52] Specifically in the Latin American case, we suggest that the extent of *mestizaje* in many societies masked
the fact that they were – and remain – white dominions; the veneer of mixing hid the reality that the most
influential citizens, politically and economically, were the whitest, those who could point to purer Spanish
origins.

goal may have been to advance the religious or other beliefs of the colonial power and to contribute to the wealth and glory of the mother country. On the other hand, they were often adventurers, a long way from the colonising centre. They might not live up to the expectations of the rulers who sent them. They might cut corners, saving some of the wealth for themselves. They might get ideas beyond their station and be regarded as a political and perhaps even a military threat to the mother country. The metropolis was frequently wary and suspicious of the settler, and the feelings were mutual. The settlers could resent the metropole as distant, selfish, uncaring and interfering.

As the vanguard of empire in the heart of the colony, the settlers symbolically represented the metropolis. But they quickly came to be something entirely different from simply metropolitans who happened to be living in a different place. The complexity of the settlers' position was that they stood between the metropolis and the natives. As the empire personified on the ground, as it were, they displayed all the characteristics at the heart of imperial conquest – determination, hard work, toughness, practicality and the conviction of an almost divine mission. The problem was that the metropolis was a much more heterogeneous place, not least in relation to ideas. Progress there meant that ideas developed, progress occurred; in particular, liberalism started to replace formerly rigid values. Separated from this heterogeneity, settlers retained the old certainties to the point that they came to believe that they, and only they, continued to represent the real values at the heart of the metropolis.

As Memmi (1990: 128) argues, the colonialist

> may go as far as to threaten – Can such things be! – Secession! Which seems contradictory, in conflict with his so well-advertised and in a certain sense real patriotism. But the colonialist's nationalism is truly of a special nature. He directs his attention essentially to that aspect of his native country which tolerates his colonialist existence. A homeland which became democratic, for example to the point of promoting equality of rights even in the colonies, would also risk abandoning its colonial undertakings. For the colonialist, such a transformation would challenge his way of life and thus become a matter of life and death.

Settlers viewed themselves as loyal to the imperial idea, often more loyal than metropolitan dwellers, who were carrying out a vital and often under-appreciated role for the metropolis. Only they faced directly the threat from the 'natives', which meant that racism was an inherent and inevitable element of the colonial nexus. As Memmi (1990: 128) argued, ' ... every colonial nation carries the seeds of fascist temptation in its bosom. What is fascism, if not a regime of oppression for the benefit of a few? The entire administrative and political machinery of a colony has no other goal.'

The obsession with whiteness became a defining feature of empire. Moreover, the privileging of whiteness was a material reality – often creating more democratic opportunities for white settlers than they ever had in their countries of origin. Thus, as representative government developed in the colonies, suffrage was restricted to 'free white men', usually with property ownership restrictions. Since land ownership was widespread among white settlers, most white men *could* vote. Accordingly, relatively poor white men were afforded political as well as economic power through colonial privilege that had been denied them in the context of the metropole. At the same time, however, this same settler population was relentlessly hybridised in the process; Dutch became Afrikaner; English became Americans; French became *pieds noir*.

Moreover, it wasn't just the settlers who were thus transformed. This notion of *mestizaje* also went well beyond the experience of settler colonists alone. Alongside white settler blocs around the world, colonialism introduced subaltern ethnic blocs. Empire transported millions of colonised people in different directions – as enslaved people, as indentured labourers, as refugees, as migrant workers, as prisoners, as administrators. Novel, ethnically stratified social formations appeared across Empire – from Fiji to Guyana and from Kenya to Singapore – with the widespread ethnic stratification of colonial modes of production.

South Africa is the quintessence of this process. There colonisation involved two distinct white settler blocs – both obsessed with race – and a large indigenous African population. But it also featured a Cape Malay population, enslaved people *brought to* Africa by the Dutch and a large South Asian community brought as indentured labourers by the British. If ever a paradigm case of *mestizaje* were sought, here it is – a melange of different colours, languages, ethnicities, all bearing the legacy of their specific nexus to colonial history.

Thus, South Africa remains the paradigm model for this kind of colonial *mestizaje*. Here too the complex interplay between white settler identity and imperialism assumed its most tragic forms. It bears emphasis that these were directly rooted in the British version of Empire. It was the English arch-imperialist Rhodes who first said of Africans: 'The native is to be treated as a child and denied the franchise. We must adopt a system of despotism in our relations with the barbarians of South Africa' (Liberty Writers Africa 2019). It was under the aegis of the British Empire that the Natives Land Act of 1913 restricted black people from buying or renting land in white South Africa, leading to the forced removals of black people. It was the British parliament that in the 1931 Statute of Westminster allowed South Africa *with a huge Black majority* to follow the 'white dominion' route towards independence. In other words, *it could not but be both racist and anti-democratic to conceive of South Africa as a white dominion*. Thus, colonial South Africa provide the DNA for the apartheid model.[53]

In this sense, South Africa exemplifies the continuity between the genealogy of colonialism that we have traced and the contemporary post-colonial world. More

---

[53] For all the successes of democratic South Africa's 'rainbow nation', it would be difficult to argue that this legacy is not still the defining characteristic of the country. After the end of apartheid in 1994, the ANC government claimed it wanted to return 30 percent of this land to its previous owners by 2014. In 2020 it is estimated that only 10 percent of commercial farmland has been redistributed.

broadly, the notion of white dominion provides the key to the transformation between colonialism and post-colonialism. In this principle, the *continuity* between colonialism and post-colonialism was laid bare. As well as South Africa, the British established white dominions as part of empire that were gradually able to sever their connection to the Empire which had created them: Canada, Australia, New Zealand, and Newfoundland. The US can be added to this list – albeit acknowledging that it severed its connection to the empire in a less gradualist way. One of the key questions for our wider analysis is where Ireland sits in this mix.

There are a number of salient features. Most importantly the Empire first constructed then left behind a polity that it framed as a 'white dominion' – a post-colonial formation strictly and profoundly hierarchised by race. These all have surviving indigenous populations except in Newfoundland where these had been completely removed through genocide. With the notable exception of South Africa, the indigenous populations are now significantly outnumbered by white settler populations. They also included significant numbers of subaltern migrant populations which added further to their plural character – new ethnic migrant communities which must subsequently negotiate their own relationship with 'whiteness'.

As a formal rite of passage, these white dominions could also gain colonies of their own – this happened with Australia (Papua New Guinea) and New Zealand (German Samoa) and South Africa (Namibia) after WWI. The US too had already acquired colonies. These included Hawaii and the Philippines – as well as another colonial conundrum that obtains to the present, Puerto Rico. The US also created Liberia. This state began as a specific settlement of the American Colonization Society (ACS), which supported the repatriation of 'free' African Americans from the United States. The ACS met with sustained objections from many African American leaders who saw this colonisation as a racist strategy for protecting slavery and purging the US of its Black citizens.

At this point, the enduring legacy of empire becomes very clear. While these states were effectively independent, these were all explicitly 'racial states' in their transformation to becoming white dominions. The privilege that had accrued to their settler colonial populations under colonialism was to be retained and codified as they became independent. Thus, they remain racial states with the imprimatur of empire. They have all – including the US, of course – struggled profoundly with tensions connected to race and citizenship. More specifically, they have all struggled with the implications of their privileging of *whiteness*. In 2018 this legacy was raised with poignancy as Australia threatened to deport an aboriginal man to Papua New Guinea (Willacy 2018). That a state created by white European colonial settlers could have the *capacity* – let alone the right – to 'deport' an indigenous person lays bare the profound issues of 'ownership' that continue to underpin equality and inequality in a 'post-colonial' world. This also, of course, captures some sense of the real meaning – and continuing potency – of 'white dominion'.

Thus, our argument is that the central paradox of colonialism was that it was *fantasised as white dominion yet lived as mestizaje*. Despite the aspiration towards white dominion, nothing stands still. Over time people have conspired to mix in a myriad of different ways in even the most racially segregated societies. The ongoing project of constructing justice and equality out of this complex mixture is the defining challenge for anti-imperialism. In Ireland – as elsewhere – settler colonialism constructs a defining question in terms of post-colonial justice – can societies built on *mestizaje* transcend the toxic legacy bequeathed them by setter colonialism and white dominion?

Dudum siquidem

The debate about colonialism shifted following WWII. As decolonisation progressed, the focus shifted from actually existing imperialism to the question of its legacy. For those who want to retain some *positive* notion of empire in general and the British Empire in particular, there is only really one place of refuge. There is a rather risible attempt to map onto US hegemony. Ferguson frames the continuity unambiguously – if offensively – when he reprises Kipling's invocation to the US to 'take up the white man's burden'. He insists that the US *is* an 'empire' and that it needs to self-consciously accept this role. Ever since the height of empire, however, there has been an ongoing attempt to add the 'accomplishments' of Columbia to those of Britannia – they speak English and so they are de facto continuing the work of the British Empire; they are white and so they are de facto continuing the work of the British Empire.[54] Arch-imperialist Cecil Rhodes took this fantasy a stage further:

> Why should we not form a secret society with but one object, the furtherance of the British Empire and the bringing of the whole world under British rule, for the recovery of the United States, for making the Anglo Saxon race but one Empire? What a dream, but yet it is probable; it is possible. (Cecil Rhodes, *Confession of Faith*, 1877, unpublished)

In 2020 the best that an empire loyalist might hope for is that this racist dream might be reframed with the positions reversed: 'making the Anglo Saxon race but one empire under American rule'.

More broadly, as the reality of empire fades, the debate about its significance is only beginning. Here the question of legacy remains essentially contested – it is something much more than an academic debate. From the perspective of the historical record considered above, the notion of colonialism as 'objectively beneficial' and 'subjectively legitimate' appears as a bizarre travesty.[55] The metaphor of 'European civilisation' as an

---

[54] The arbitrariness of this position is contextualised by the vote that was taken in 1774 around whether German or English should be the language of the US.

[55] Comedy may indeed be a way to get to the heart of the issue in ways at least as memorable as academic analysis. To quote Singapore comedian Jinx Yeo: 'If you imagine the world like the human body, then the British are kinda like the large intestine, also known as the colon. And the colon is the part of the body that turns things into shit, which is what the British do to other people's countries. That's why, when the British

'historical plague' is a closer to the mark; this notion resonates with the lived reality of colonialism and imperialism. Whatever the affectations or delusions of the coloniser, this is how it was *experienced* by the colonised. In this sense, whatever the 'white man's burden', imperial revisionism is largely a 'white man's fantasy'.

The last throw of the imperial dice, however, is to dispense with facts entirely. This final attempt to save the empire suggests that any alternative would have been much worse. In this treatise, support for imperialism is now couched in terms of counterfactual assertions – the British were sometimes bad but the Russians/Germans/Japanese – or, indeed, the Africans or the Indians or the Irish[56] – would have been worse. Ferguson juxtaposes the 'British Empire' which 'did the right thing' in the Second World War with the – unquestionably grotesque – alternatives of Nazism and Japanese imperialism. It is, however, a profoundly false dichotomy to set up one moment from the end of empire against Auschwitz or the rape of Nanking – as if all the sins of British imperialism must be forgiven on the basis that they were a preparation for Britain's significant – but still relatively minor – role in the defeat of Nazism.[57]

If there is a need for counterfactual modelling, the juxtaposition should be somewhat different. Across the reality of colonialism and imperialism, the true dichotomy is between history as it was lived by subject peoples and a counterfactual imagining of what life might have been like without that subjugation. There is therefore something profoundly unsettling in the implication of Ferguson and many others that the actuality of colonialism is redeemed because its alternatives would have been worse. Even our brief overview of colonial history suggests that many of those who lived – and died – through the history of colonialism and imperialism in general – and British colonialism and imperialism in particular – might find it hard to imagine something worse. The reality of colonialism and imperialism institutionalised a whole series of crimes against humanity: piracy, enforced addiction, starvation, systemic violence against women, slavery, indenture, ethnic cleansing, apartheid, genocide. How much worse could it get?

It remains an intriguing thought experiment, however, to consider a world that had never been colonised. As we suggested earlier, this was brought into sharp perspective in 2018 in discussions about the future of the 'pre-contact' Sentinelese Islanders (Survival International 2018). What appears little more than an abstract fantasy in our contemporary postcolonial world was 'pre-contact' reality *relatively* recently in the

---

take over a country, it's called colonisation.'

[56] As Akenson (1997) points out, the Caribbean island of Montserrat offers an interesting case study. A large number of the original colonial landowners were Catholic Irish, attracted there by the possibility of land ownership and wealth accumulation denied them by the penal laws in Ireland. They were also owners of Black slaves. His unsurprising conclusion is that the Irish proved to be as effective and as unfeeling colonists as the English, despite their experience of oppression in Ireland. To extrapolate from this one case, as the title implies, that therefore an Irish empire would have been as bad as others which actually existed is a long shot.

[57] Objectively, the war was won by the Soviet/US alliance. It is also useful to remember that Hitler expressed no interest in defeating or reducing the British Empire.

history of humanity. Most of us – peoples, cultures and continents – were 'uncolonised' before the 'age of discovery'. *Dudum siquidem*, indeed: 'a short while ago'. In terms of the practical question of addressing the multifarious legacies of colonialism, however, it is necessary to turn to where most of the world is now – on the other side of colonisation and imperialism. The pre-colonial Japanese policy of *sakoku* is no longer an option. Thus, the future must be faced from the perspective of the *decolonised* rather than the *uncolonised*. Crucially this means that the whole world is characterised by *mestizaje*. This reality frames the challenge for contemporary anti-imperialism: what is to be done?

Chapter 3

Anatomies of death:
the colonisation of Ireland – 1155-1801

England to her misfortune has never been able to persevere long in any one policy towards Ireland. She tries coercion, till impatience with the cost, and a sense of the discredit, produce a hope that coercion is no longer needed, or a belief that it has been a mistake from the beginning. Conciliation follows, and compromise, and concession, and apology. The strain is taken off, the anarchy revives, and again with monotonous uniformity there is a fresh appeal to the sword. —J.A.Froude, 1881

Ireland's misfortune was that she was not colonised enough. —John Biggs-Davison, 1973

England and Ireland: the first colonial nexus?

In chapter 2 we sketched a genealogy of colonialism. We also referenced the commonly held notion that Ireland constituted the 'first' colony. As we have seen other candidates for this dubious honour are sometimes proposed – from Ceuta to Newfoundland. The key issue is that many of the motifs of colonialism sketched in the last chapter characterise the Irish story. Moreover, whether it was Europe's first colony or not, Ireland was central to the development of British colonialism and imperialism. It was palpably among the first polities to be colonised and this experience certainly provided a template for later colonialisms. In other words, the colonisation of Ireland was central to the development of the 'greatest' empire of all. Moreover, Ireland provided paradigm cases of some of the central motifs of imperialism elsewhere – including plantation, crusade and genocide.

In addition, the longevity of this colonial nexus is worthy of comment. For all the later iterations of 'Britain', 'Great Britain' and the 'United Kingdom', it was *England* that first colonised Ireland. This specific English/Irish colonial interface lasted longer – and was arguably of greater intensity – than anything that was to follow. The bare bones are well known and hardly need rehearsing. In 1155 English interference in Ireland was given the imprimatur of Pope Adrian IV through his Bull *Laudabiliter* to Henry II, 'illustrious king of the English' (Aldous and Puirseil 2008: 18-20). Beginning with the arrival of Strongbow in 1169, there was an Anglo-Norman invasion of Ireland. King Henry II of England was declared 'Lord Protector' of Ireland in 1171.

Ireland became a fief of the Holy See under the Lordship of the King of England. The 1175 Treaty of Windsor acknowledged Henry as overlord of the conquered territory and the Irish High King Ruaidrí Ua Conchobair as overlord of the rest of Ireland, with Ua Conchobair also swearing fealty to Henry.[1] However, the Treaty fell apart as Anglo-Norman lords continued to invade Irish kingdoms outside the agreed territory. In 1177, Henry declared his son John to be Lord of Ireland and authorised the Norman lords to conquer the whole country. A period of intense English colonising followed between 1200-50, creating the Pale, the area around Dublin under the control of the English government.

This first informal phase of colonisation culminated in 1494 with Poynings' Parliament. Edward Poynings as Lord Deputy summoned an Irish Parliament with the task of reducing Ireland to 'whole and perfect obedience'. With the enactment of Poynings' Law, meetings and legislation of the Irish parliament were made subject to the control of the English king and council. They also gave statutes of the English Parliament the force of law in Ireland. The English Crown formally claimed Ireland as part of England and made the Irish administration directly dependent on the Crown and privy council.

This first colonisation was consolidated with what became known as the First English conquest of Ireland under Henry VIII from 1536-1541. The title 'King of Ireland' was created by an act of the Irish Parliament, replacing the Lordship of Ireland with the Kingdom of Ireland'.[2] The Crown of Ireland Act 1542 established a 'personal union' between the English and Irish crowns, ensuring that whoever was King of England was to be King of Ireland (Aldous and Puirsiel 2008: 28-9).[3] Initially, the king implemented the policy of 'surrender and regrant' towards the existing Irish aristocracy. All Irish lords

---

[1] Nor did the title 'High King' simply disappear after 1171. Brian Ua Néill claimed the title of High King of Ireland from 1258–60, until his defeat and death in the Battle of Druim Dearg. The Scot, Edward Bruce, Earl of Carrick, declared himself High King of Ireland during the failed rebellion of 1315–18. Along with his brother Robert, he managed to gain control of most of Ireland. However, his forces were defeated at the Battle of Faughart where he himself was killed and buried.

[2] The Parliament of Ireland conferred the crown of Ireland upon King Henry VIII of England during the English Reformation. The monarch of England then held the crowns of England and Ireland in a 'personal union'. The 'Union of the Crowns' under James VI (of Scotland) and I (of England and Ireland) in 1603 expanded the personal union to include Scotland. Despite English opposition, James VI and I unilaterally created a new 'imperial throne' of 'Great Britain'. He assumed the title of King of Great Britain by a 'Proclamation concerning the Kings Majesties Stile' on 20 October 1604 announcing that he did 'assume to Our selfe by the cleerenesse of our Right, The Name and Stile of KING OF GREAT BRITTAINE, FRANCE AND IRELAND, DEFENDER OF THE FAITH'. This monarchy was interrupted by the interregnum in the 1650s – during the republican unitary state of the Commonwealth and the Protectorate – and the Glorious Revolution of 1688, but the titles remained the same. The 'personal union' between England and Scotland became a political union with the enactments of the Acts of Union 1707, which created the Kingdom of Great Britain. The crowns of Great Britain and Ireland remained in personal union until the Acts of Union 1800 united Ireland and Great Britain into the United Kingdom of Great Britain and Ireland from January 1801 until December 1922.

[3] The title of King of Ireland was created after Henry VIII had renounced papal authority, so it was not recognised by the Catholic Church or Catholic monarchs. Following the accession of the Catholic Mary I as Queen of England in 1553 and her marriage to Felipe, Prince of Asturias, (later Phillip II of Spain) in 1554, Pope Paul IV issued the papal bull *Ilius* in 1555, recognising them as Queen and King of Ireland together with her heirs and successors. The plantations of Laois and Offaly were named for them as 'Queen's County' and 'King's County'.

– both Gaelic and Anglo-Norman – were to officially surrender their lands to the Crown, and then have them returned by Royal Charter. The aim was to assimilate the Gaelic and Gaelicised Anglo-Norman elite and cement their loyalty to the new crown.[4] They were granted English titles and the Gaelic chieftains were admitted to the Irish parliament for the first time. In practice, lords around Ireland accepted their new privileges but carried on as they had before. But the ongoing development of the new centralised colonial state brought this English system into increasingly direct conflict with the indigenous Gaelic system. Successive rebellions broke out, first in Leinster and then in Munster. In response, the English moved towards a more direct and radical form of colonisation: plantation.

Thus, the new 'Kingdom of Ireland' was consolidated with a series of plantations or colonies as English planters were sent to Ireland to receive estates as rewards from the king. Lands were granted in the counties of Laois, Offaly, Tipperary, Wexford, Leitrim, and Longford and across most of the provinces of Munster and Ulster. Not surprisingly, this process provoked resistance among the dispossessed Irish – this culminated in the 1641-52 Irish uprising. This was followed by the Second English Conquest of Ireland as Ireland was dragged into the English Civil War (1642-51). (This period also provided England with its first 'Commonwealth' as an alternative to empire.).[5] In 1649, the Lord Protector of the new English Republic Oliver Cromwell crushed the nascent Irish Confederate government and awarded lands to Protestant settlers from England. In the notorious 'hell or Connacht' policy, Catholic landowners who could prove they had not been involved in the uprising were given estates in West Clare. Many Irish prisoners – as well as thousands of children – were sent to North America and the Caribbean planting the first seeds of the Irish Diaspora.[6]

By now – alongside the established colonial nexus – an additional sectarian tension between 'Protestant England' and 'Catholic Ireland' was markedly evident. The Restoration of 1660 and the 'Glorious Revolution' of 1688 further entrenched this difference. This set the context for one hundred years of Protestant Ascendancy – in both England and Ireland. In Ireland the reformation had little purchase among the native population which remained almost entirely Catholic. In consequence, sectarian

---

[4] The king summed up his strategy as 'politic drifts and amiable persuasions'.

[5] In 1649 the English Parliament passed An Act Declaring and Constituting the People of England to be a Commonwealth and Free-State which declared: 'That the People of England, and of *all the Dominions and Territories thereunto belonging*, are and shall be, and are hereby Constituted, Made, Established, and Confirmed to be a Commonwealth and Free-State: And shall from henceforth be Governed as a Commonwealth and Free-State, by the Supreme Authority of this Nation, The Representatives of the People in Parliament, and by such as they shall appoint and constitute as Officers and Ministers under them for the good of the People, and that *without any King or House of Lords*' (emphasis added).

[6] Slavery had existed in Ireland before the Vikings, with slaves regarded as a luxury item who could be given as tributes or gifts. The Vikings added a sophisticated system of slave-trading. Slaves were captured in raids on Scotland and England and were shipped to market in Rouen (Doherty 1980: 84), Iceland, Scandanavia and possibly Arabic Spain (Sheehan 1998: 175). In the 18th and 19th centuries there were some Black slaves in Ireland, as well as Black soldiers, seamen, domestic servants and entertainers. Hart (n.d.: 4) estimates that Dublin had, 'with the exception of London, the largest Black population of any 18th century European city'.

difference now assumed a specifically colonial form with an Anglo-Irish and Protestant settler elite politically and economically dominating a dispossessed native majority that was both Gaelic and Catholic.

Thus, for the first 500 years, the conquest begun in 1155 was both colonial and English. This remains significant because whatever the British state or the UK becomes thereafter, the template for English/Irish relations was set. This English/Irish dynamic was already embedded in the state formation that developed thereafter. Of course, this has been confirmed time and again through the centuries in terms of how people make sense of the conflict: from Froude's overview of Irish colonial history to Tony Blair's 'apology' for the famine on behalf of 'England'; from Morrisey's 'Irish Blood, English Heart' to the riot of English soccer supporters in Dublin in 1995. This focus on Englishness – rather than Britishness or the still less likely UK-ness – is more than a simple anachronism. The recurrent reference to England and Englishness in the colonial project accurately names the central tension in the relationship.

It also bears emphasis that this was confirmed by theorists and documenters of colonialism from the first. Pope Adrian's invitation was to the 'King of the English'. Likewise, Giraldus' work is addressed in his most obsequious style to Henry, 'Illustrious king of the English':[7]

> The Irish people from the first time of its coming ... remained free and unconquered by any attack of foreign peoples, until, invincible king, and your courageous daring in these our days it has at length been subjugated. (Gerald of Wales 1988: 123)

The Statutes of Kilkenny further institutionalised this English/Irish divide:

> Now many English of the said land, forsaking the English language, manners, mode of riding, laws and usages, live and govern themselves according to the manners, fashion, and language of the Irish enemies; and also have made divers marriages and alliances between themselves and the Irish enemies aforesaid; whereby the said land, and the liege people thereof, the English language, the allegiance due to our lord the king, and the English laws there, are put in subjection and decayed. (Cited in Aldous and Puirseil 2008: 22-3)

Edmund Spenser also framed the conquest as 'English' in his own variant of the *Book of Invasions*, *A View of the State of Ireland* (1596):

> The last and the greatest, which was by the English, when the Earle Strangbowe, havinge conquered that Lande, delivered up the same into the handes of Henry the second, then Kinge, who sent over thither great store of gentlemen, and other warlyke people, amongst whom he distributed the Land, and setled such a stronge Colonie therein, as never since could, with all the subtile practices of the Irishe, be rooted out, but abyde still a mightie people, of so many as remayne Englishe of them.

---

[7] His conclusion is equally sycophantic but also introduces the imperial comparator, characterising Henry as 'our western Alexander' (Gerald of Wales 1988: 124).

From first contact onwards accounts make two things clear. First, this new relationship is defined by subjugation: this relationship is about 'conquering' and 'subjugating' and 'colonising' 'Irish enemies'; second, the parties are well defined – this relationship is between the Irish and the English. This confirms a profound and enduring synergy between Englishness and the colonisation of Ireland. This interface was a definitive part of what made the English English. In other words, the colonisation of Ireland created out of the Norman conquest and the complex national, linguistic and ethnic mix within the Kingdom of England, both an English state and an English identity. As the Statutes of Kilkenny made clear, this new English identity was to be routinely understood in juxtaposition to Irish otherness.

Of course, care must be taken not to read too much into this retrospectively. Eight and a half centuries of colonial nexus has produced a host of additional dynamics for the Irish – between Ireland and Wales, and Scotland, and Europe, and the United States, for example. Nevertheless, we can suggest that – stripped bare – the core colonial relationship is a nexus between England and Ireland, between the English and the Irish. The ideological relationship that was instituted in 1155 and the more formal, constitutional relationship that was instituted in 1171 endures to the present. The intervening 850 years may be précised as an attempt by both the English and the Irish to lay the ghost of this fatal coupling to rest. Moreover, the review of this history in this chapter may be prefaced by suggesting that this has been a history of enormous cost to both the English and the Irish. The state formations it generated were characterised by institutionalised violence of the most profound kind – dispossession, starvation, genocide. Of course, these colonial formations evolved and transformed over time. But the remorseless logic of colonialism endured across this history: the English Republic of 1649-60 was hardly more generous to Ireland than the English Crown that preceded and succeeded it; and the repression of the United Irish uprising in 1798 hardly less savage than the response to rebellion in Munster in 1581. This colonisation was defined by institutionalised violence of the most profound kind: a series of anatomies of death, indeed.

Towards 'whole and perfect obedience'

Carty (1999) asks a fundamental question: 'Was Ireland conquered?' The answer is crucial, because 'a country which has not been conquered does not require liberation' (Carty 1999: 11). For some commentators, the answer is straightforward: there was no conquest. There are variations on this reply. One is that as the Anglo-Norman system spread outwards from England in the 12th century it inevitably encountered and influenced its neighbouring island to the west. Ireland can thus be seen merely as part of the border lands 'which stretched from Calais to the Scottish frontier and the marches of Wales' (Canny 1988: 9). But the island was no *terra nullius*: '[T]he Anglo-Normans did not arrive in an exotic backwater of which they knew little. They entered south-east Ireland along well-established lines of commercial, cultural and military communication' (Frame 2012: 7).

A second variant is that one cannot talk of a conquest because there was no nation to conquer. To speak of conquest is to be anachronistic because there was nothing in 12th-century Ireland which came close to the nation as it emerged later. As J.C. Beckett put it starkly, 'in the twelfth century there was no such place as Ireland' (cited in Carty 1999: 17). Ireland, he adds, 'has only existed as a cultural force since the course of the nineteenth century.' What existed instead was a collection of kingdoms and sub-kingdoms, with shifting allegiances and influences and constant rivalry over territory and power. Despite attempts at various points of individuals to establish themselves as High Kings, there was no unitary political system on the island of Ireland.[8]

Third, there was no instant military conquest. Irish chieftains for the most part did not engage in sustained warfare with the incomers but accommodated to the new arrivals. When Henry II arrived in Waterford, most of the Irish chieftains came in person and formally submitted to him. The High King Roderic O'Connor (Ruaidrí Ua Conchobair) was absent but did reluctantly submit later. Only the Ulster chieftains neither appeared nor submitted.

There is an element of truth to each of these positions, but singly or together they do not constitute the complete explanation. Take the question of allegiance. The chieftains did indeed elect to recognise Henry as liege lord, and as such responsible for their protection. They were, as Carty emphasises, vassals, not subjects; what they promised was fealty, to abide by the King's peace and to pay a modest tribute (Carty 1999: 25). The protection they sought was manifold: to some extent, protection from the high king himself, but more immediately from some of Henry's knights who had arrived earlier as adventurers, much to Henry's annoyance. Their move was a rational and tactical one. Under Irish law they could promise no more to Henry than what they promised. Chieftains could not give up the land because it was not theirs; it was the clan, not individuals, which ultimately owned the land. Chieftainships were 'primarily positions of military, not political authority' and as such 'were subordinate to clan law and custom' (Myers 1983: 6). Consequently, 'Henry's treaties with the chieftains could not, in clan law and custom, bind their successors'; the chieftains 'did not enter into hereditary, tenurial relationships' with the English monarch.

Henry was likewise acting tactically. His alignment with the Irish chieftains was a counterweight to the power of the knights. The Norman knights had arrived initially as adventurers rather than direct emissaries of the king. As they began to have military success and to establish a presence in Ireland, Henry came to fear that their increasing power might herald the beginnings of a rival kingdom on his western flank. Consequently in 1170 he

---

[8] This is, however, challenged by none other than Cambrensis. He details at length the numbers of Irish kings from before St Patrick to the Anglo-Norman invasion.

banned anyone in future from venturing to export anything, whether supplies or soldiers, to Ireland, from any pier within his jurisdiction. In the same way, for all the British in Ireland he set a date by which they were to return home; otherwise they would be counted as effectual traitors... (Barry and Morgan 2013: 213)

From the beginning the Anglo-Norman knights found themselves suspect in the eyes not only of the colonised but also of the metropolitan centre. They were aware of their isolation. On one occasion, the Norman commander of Dublin, Fitz-Maurice, is reputed to have addressed his troops before battle thus:

What then are we to look for? Is it for help from our countrymen across the channel? Why, they regard us no less as Irishmen than we do the besiegers you see around our wall. It would be hard to say whether in that island or in this we are held in greater hate. (Quoted in Barnard 1888: 44-5)

A 16th century author, Richard Stanyhurst, attributed identical sentiments to Fitz-Maurice: ' ... that just as we are English to the Irish, so are we Irish to the English. We are hard pressed by the hatred of the latter, by the arms of the former' (quoted in Barry and Morgan 2013: 221).

Justifying conquest: the myth of cultural superiority

As we saw in chapter 2, a core element of colonialism is the denigration of the colonised. The Anglo-Norman justification for the penetration of Ireland was the supposed inferiority of the Irish. Henry's involvement in Ireland was initially justified by the papal bull from 1155, *Laudabiliter*. Adrian, the only English pope, charged Henry VI with waging a crusade against the 'heathen' Irish on the grounds that they were not fit to govern themselves. The Irish church at this point was the only one in western Europe independent of Rome. Adrian sought to rein in the Irish church and clergy. Henry was to be his willing instrument in this task. Adrian instructed Henry in his Bull:

[W]ith a view to enlarging the boundaries of the Church, restraining the downward course of vice, correcting evil customs and planting virtue, and for the increase of the Christian religion, you shall enter that island and execute whatsoever may attend to the honour of God and the welfare of the land; and also that the people of that land shall receive you with honour and revere you as their lord: provided always that the rights of the churches remain whole and inviolate, and saving to the blessed Peter and the Holy Roman Church the annual tribute of one penny from every house. (Cited in Aldous and Puirseil 2008: 20)

This crusade was further endorsed in 1172 by Adrian's successor, Pope Alexander III, who wrote to the Irish bishops confirming that the English king had 'dominion over the Irish people; and since they were grossly ignorant of the rudiments of the faith, further empowered him to mould them by ecclesiastical rules and discipline to a conformity with the usage of the Anglican Church' (quoted in Barnard 1888: 76).

When Henry arrived in Ireland he was accompanied by a monk, Giraldus

Cambrensis, or Gerald of Wales, a member of the De Barri family from Wales, one of the main Norman families involved in the early conquest of Ireland. In two accounts based on visits to Ireland, *Topographia Hiberniae* (c. 1187) and *Expugnatio Hiberniae* (c. 1189), he stressed the religious, social and cultural inferiority of the Irish as a justification for conquest. Cambrensis characterised this encounter in racialised terms from the first: 'This is a filthy people, wallowing in vice' (Gerard of Wales 1988: 106). He condemned their supposed vices, including laziness, treachery, blasphemy, idolatry, ignorance of Christian beliefs, incest and cannibalism.

The incomers were particularly offended by one aspect of Irish society. Ireland may not have been *terra nullius*, but the semi-nomadism of its inhabitants was deemed to result in the wasting of precious resources. As Myers (1983: 15) notes, Cambrensis'

> disdain is based on the confrontation between centralized, agricultural-commercial and feudal England and decentralized, nomadic and tribal Ireland. What marks the Irish out as worthy of rejection is their love of freedom: 'they think that the greatest pleasure is not to work, and the greatest wealth is to enjoy liberty'.

Cambrensis concludes his *Conquest of Ireland* by raising the key question: 'In what manner Ireland is to be completely conquered'. He recommends shock and awe military tactics with cutting-edge military technology, while at the same time noting what many later English generals found in Ireland, the difficulties of military intervention:

> ... a campaign in France is a very different thing from a campaign in Ireland or Wales. In the former case it is carried out in an open country, in the latter in broken country; there we have plains, here woods. There armour is held in esteem, here it is reckoned cumbersome and out of place; there victory is won by weight, here by activity. (Quoted in Barnard 1888: 140)

Despite the fact that Ireland 'was undoubtedly ... more sophisticated ... and infinitely more complex than Gerald's account suggests' (Frame 2012: 5), Cambrensis remained the standard authority consulted by English administrators and militarists for the next 500 years. When English writers came to justify the next major thrust in the colonisation of Ireland, it was to Cambrensis they turned.[9]

During this later colonialisation thrust a contradictory counter-narrative also emerged – despite the stated inferiority of the Irish and Irishness, the English in Ireland are always in danger of 'going native'. Spenser captures this fear in his fictional dialogue:

---

[9] Raphael Holinshed's *The Chronicle of Ireland* in 1586 included translations of both of Cambrensis' publications. And Sir John Davies asserted in 1612: 'The manners of the mere Irish are so little altered since the days of King Henry II, as appeareth by the description made by Giraldus Cambrensis...' (Davies, quoted in Myers 1983: 147). Even without direct references to Cambrensis, the identical ideology is apparent in later British writers. Here is the view of the Scottish philosopher David Hume. 'The Irish from the beginning of time had been buried in the most profound barbarianism and ignorance; and as they were never conquered, even, indeed, by the Romans from whom all the Western world derives its culture, they continued still in the most rude state of society and were distinguished by those vices to which human nature, not tamed by education, nor restrained by laws, is for ever subject.' (See Hume 1773: 1490)

Eudoxus — What is that you say, of so many as remayne English of them? Why are, not they that were once English, abydinge Englishe still?

Irenius — No, for the most parte of them are degenerated and growen almost meare Irishe, yea, and more malicious to the Englishe then the very Irishe themselves.

Ireland was in many ways a laboratory for imperial prejudice. Contemporaneously the colonisation of North America was being carried out: 'The same indictments being brought against the Indians, and later the blacks, in the New World had been brought against the Irish ... Both Indians and blacks, like the Irish, were accused of being idle, dirty and licentious' (Canny 1973). In this, as in many other ways, Ireland became the training ground for growing English – and later British – imperialism (Rolston 1993):

> At the same time that they awakened to the potential of the New World, they began the last stage of the conquest of Ireland. The two enterprises became reciprocal training grounds for English imperial expansion. Personnel moved from one arena to the other; and the ideology that explained English conquest in Ireland supported the establishment of civility in America. (Sheehan 1980: 54)

As Canny observes: 'Their years in Ireland were years of apprenticeship' (1973: 595).

This apprenticeship lasted for centuries. Four hundred years after English involvement in Ireland began with Henry II, English influence on the island was to all intents and purposes still confined to an area around Dublin known as the Pale. Moreover, the descendants of the original Norman English colonists in Ireland, known as the Old English, spoke Irish, intermarried with the Irish, followed Irish customs and got on well with the native clans and chieftains; as such, their loyalty could not be assured. The metropolitan fear was that the colonised and the colonisers would join forces and rebel with help from Spanish or French forces. It was for this reason that the Statutes of Kilkenny were enacted in 1366 to attempt to impose segregation. The Statutes forbade intermarriage between Normans and Irish and decreed that Norman colonists were not allowed to speak Irish, use Irish names, wear Irish dress, live alongside the Irish or ride without saddles as was the native Irish custom (Beckett 1979: 27). In the same vein, a century and a half later, in 1494, King Henry VII sent a deputy, Sir Edward Poynings, to govern his unstable fiefdom of Ireland directly. Poynings enacted a law which severely curtailed the power of the Irish parliament. Poynings' Law decreed that the Irish parliament was not to pass any laws without the express permission of the king of England (Kelly 2001).

As for the native chieftains, they revealed a remarkable resistance to conquest. Their frequent promises of fealty were just as frequently broken. Periodically there were military rebellions, sometimes involving alliances between native chieftains and the Old English. In the northern province of Ulster in particular, the Gaelic chieftains, the O'Neills and O'Donnells, held sway and the old Gaelic system remained intact despite the long centuries of colonialism. John Borlase, a contemporary writer, summed up Britain's Irish problem of the time:

> Though we date the conquest of Ireland from the submission of the kings and natives
> there to King Henry the Second, 1172, yet on a truer estimate we must conclude that
> Ireland was never really subjugated to the crown of England ... (Borlase 1680: 5)

For English commentators at the time,[10] most of the explanation for this problem was said to lie with the Irish themselves. The Irish had odd names by English standards, 'some rather seeming the names of devouring giants than Christian subjects' (Moryson, in Myers 1983: 199). Their diet and table manners were judged to be barbarous. Irish men were condemned for their practice of wearing their hair fringes long over their eyes (known as 'glibs') (Davies, in Myers 1983: 173), as were Irish women for riding side-saddle, but facing the opposite way from that preferred by the English (Moryson, in Myers 1983: 203).[11] The failure of the native Irish to live in 'proper' housing was singled out for particular attention:

> They had no efficient habit of husbandry. Nor could they construct dwellings
> appropriate for city-dwelling, inevitably essential to civilisation. They were, because
> of their unstable laws, lazy and unreliable. Furthermore, their sexual manners were
> undisciplined, repudiating their wives and neglecting their children. They were,
> generally, uncouth. (Davies, quoted in Myers 1983: 34)

The English commentators in fact exaggerated the extent of Irish nomadism and, in addition, failed to see its efficiency and value to the Irish. The Irish custom of transhumance, whereby cattle owners followed their herds around different grazing areas during summer months was entirely practical rather than a sign of backwardness (Kiernan 2007: 177). Nevertheless, nomadism 'came to represent all that was worst in the Irish character' and was heavily legislated against (Elliott 2000: 32). Consequently, laws forbade the custom of mobile dwellings in 1608 and 'house-building was made compulsory in later plantation leases' (Elliott 2000: 31). Ireland was seen as 'a landscape requiring taming, clearing and civilising through building and enclosure' (Elliott 2000: 31), a missed opportunity, a terra if not exactly nullius at least wasted: '... what between the ill-husbandry of that which is inhabited and so much of the country again lying waste for want of inhabitants, there is not the third-part of that profit raised that Ireland would afford...' (Rich, in Myers 1983: 130).[12] This view was underwritten by a reading of Jesus' parable of the talents in the New

---

[10] These commentators wrote pamphlets intended for the Crown and the Court. They included Sir Philip Sidney, John Derricke, Raphael Holinshed, Richard Stanyhurst and John Hooker, Edmund Spenser, John Campion, Sir John Davies, Fynes Moryson and Barnabe Rich. There were also writers such as John Borlase and Edward Borlase who accompanied generals on military campaigns and wrote comprehensive accounts of those campaigns.

[11] Some of the criticisms seem trivial, but a recognition that matters such as behaviour at table were at the heart of debates in the long-drawn European 'history of manners' (Elias 2000: 72-138) reveals that such traits were central to definitions of 'civilisation'.

[12] Similar arguments emerged in relation to the contemporaneous colonisation of North America. For 17th century English colonists in America, the ultimate proof of barbarism was the nomadism of the natives; it was incomprehensible, even offensive on the grounds that they 'range rather than inhabite' the land (Richard Hayklut, quoted in Pearce 1998: 7).

Testament (Matthew 25:14–30). In this respect the aberration of the Irish was not simply economic stupidity but also sinful, and it cried out for English intervention.

Irish habits were one thing, but the problem was said to be compounded by English negligence. Over the course of four centuries Ireland, '... was not in all that space of time, thoroughly subdued and reduced to obedience of the Crown of England, although there hath been almost a continual war between the English and the Irish...' (Davies 1969: 3). And the ultimate reasons: 'the faint prosecution of the war and ... the looseness of the civil government' (Davies 1969: 6).[13]

There were many commentators around the Court who were quick to offer solutions. For example, Campion (in Myers 1983: 32) proposed 'to breed in the rudest of our people resolute English hearts' by setting up grammar schools in Ireland where babes from their cradles should be inured under learned schoolmasters with a purer English tongue, habit, fashion, discipline, and in time utterly forget the affinity of their unbroken borderers...'[14] Little wonder that Irish intellectuals of the time concluded that the intent of English policy was straightforward: to create a 'Sacsa nua darb anim Eire', a new England called Ireland (Kiberd 1991: 15).[15] Others were more committed to repressive, indeed genocidal methods. Moryson (in Myers 1983: 199), for example, argues:

> I do not think, but know, that they will never be reformed in religion, manners, and constant obedience to our laws but by the awe of the sword and by a strong hand, at least for a time bridling them.

Many proposed a dual policy involving both repression and ideology. The absence of a standing army was a major problem for the English. Armies in Ireland were paid for through taxes raised in the Pale and in England, frequently highly resented by the populaces in both places (Canny 1976: 31). There were continuous supply line

---

[13] Davies writes that Henry II did not arrive in Ireland with an army 'so great as might suffice to conquer all Ireland' (Davies 1969: 9). He left five months later 'without striking one blow, or building one castle, or planting one garrison among the Irish...' (Davies 1969: 12). King John arrived in Ireland, 'with a great army... the Irish lords for the most part, submitted themselves to him... his back was no sooner turned, but they returned to their former rebellion...' (Davies 1969: 22). Moreover, '... he left no standing army to prosecute the conquest' (Davies 1969: 23). During the reigns of Edwards I, II and III: 'The standing forces here were seldom or never reinforced out of England, and such as were either sent from thence, or raised here, did commonly do more hurt and damage to the English subject, than to the Irish enemies, by their continual cess and extortion' (Davies 1969: 26-7). In 1400, King Richard II came to Ireland with a large army – according to Moryson (1617: 168), 'four thousand men at arms, and thirty thousand archers' – 'with a full purpose to make a full conquest of Ireland' (Davies 1612: 51). But rebellion in England led him to withdraw before the task was completed. Henry VII sent a mere one thousand troops to suppress the rebellion of Perkin Warbeck, pretender to the English throne (Moryson 1617: 169). During the Geraldine Rebellion in Ireland King Henry VIII, '... sent over Sir William Skevington, with five hundred men only to quench that fire, and not to enlarge the border, or to rectify government' (Davies 1969: 67).

[14] Borderers were colonists who lived on land adjoining that occupied by the 'mere Irish', from the Latin merus, meaning pure, unmixed.

[15] Three centuries later Winston Churchill remarked: 'We have always found the Irish to be a bit odd. They refuse to be English'.

difficulties during military campaigns in Ireland due to the unwelcoming geography and the belligerence of the natives. There was also frequently a profound lack of political will to pursue robust solutions to the Irish problem. These factors combined to produce dire conditions for English soldiers in Ireland. The army was often weak. In cases where there was a competent army, it was often dissolved too soon before conquest was complete. Competent or otherwise, troops were often ill-paid and ill-governed (Davies 1969: 74-5). The lesson taken was that proper military intervention was needed, and sustained military action at that, as John Hooker concluded:

> For withdraw the sword and forbear correction, deal with them in courtesy and entreat them gently, if they can take any advantage, they will surely skip out, and as the dog to his vomit and the sow to the dirt and puddle, they will return to their old and former insolency, rebellion and disobedience. (Quoted in Myers 1983: 58)

State terror was assiduously applied by one English administrator and militarist after another. In Munster, for example, Sir Humphrey Gilbert ordered

> that the heads of all those (of what sort soever they were) which were killed in the day, should be cut off from their bodies and brought to the place where he encamped at night, and should there be laid on the ground by each side of the way leading into his own tent so that none could come into his tent for any cause but commonly he must pass through a lane of heads which he used ad terrorem, the dead feeling nothing the more pains thereby; and yet did it bring great terror to the people when they saw the heads of their dead fathers, brothers, children, kinsfolk and friends lie on the ground before their faces as they came to speak with the said colonel. (Thomas Churchyard, quoted in Canny 1976: 122)

As Canny (1976: 122) concludes:

> The Norman lords were not known to have committed such atrocities in England, and there is no evidence that systematic execution of non-combatants by martial law was practised in any of the Tudor rebellions in England. It is obvious that Gilbert and Essex considered that, in dealing with the native Irish population, they were absolved from all normal ethical restraints.[16]

Charles Blount, Baron Mountjoy, Lord Deputy of Ireland, wrote to the English Lords: '... our only way to ruin the rebels, must be to make all possible waste of the means for life' (Moryson 1617, volume 2: 394). And he delivered on this; he wrote later to the Lords: '... we have left none to give us opposition, nor of late have seen any but dead carcases, merely starved for want of meat, of which kind we found many in divers places we passed' (Moryson 1617, volume 3:184). On another occasion, another letter: '... we found everywhere men dead of famine ... between Tullogh Oge and Toome there lay unburied a thousand dead ... there were above three thousand starved in Tyrone'

---

[16] Foster (1988: 34) agrees: 'Though scorched earth had been advocated since the 1530s, massacres like those perpetuated by Grey and the elder Essex were probably an innovation...'

(Moryson 1617, volume 3: 208).

Nor did they spare the sword:

> In one six-week campaign, Gilbert reportedly captured over twenty castles, and
> slaughtered all the occupants, including women and children, while in 1574 raiders
> led by the great English naval hero, Sir Francis Drake, massacred the entire civilian
> population of Rathlin Island… (Ó Siochrú 2008: 20)

That said, there was widespread agreement that 'a purely military settlement was impossible' (Canny 1976: 70). Rather military action was viewed as part of a wider strategy of conquest which included the establishment of the rule of law. English rule of law did not extend beyond the Pale, and at times was not even fully operational within the Pale. Lord Deputy Henry Sidney envisaged the establishment of provincial presidents throughout the country to vigorously establish the rule of law. In areas where the Gaelic chieftains ruled, this first required the use of force (Canny 1976: 97). Thus, military chiefs would set out in circuits within an area, engaging native forces and establishing castles and forts. Significantly, they also opened up these circuits to judges who would hold assizes, thereby undermining the legitimacy of Gaelic brehon law in these areas. The law was a vital instrument of counterinsurgency, as politicians and commentators clearly understood. There would be no conquest of Ireland unless English law was established throughout the land:

> For, to give laws unto a people, to institute magistrates and officers over them, to
> punish and pardon malefactors, to have the sole authority of making war and peace,
> and the like, are the true marks of sovereignty (Davies 1969: 14-5).

As Davies argues later: 'If the king would not admit them to the condition of subjects, how could they learn to acknowledge and obey him as their sovereign?' (1969: 117). In short, 'to give laws to a conquered people, is the principal mark and effect of a perfect conquest' (Davies 1969: 100).

Popular understandings of law view it as the counter and antidote to violence. But what the experience of Ireland in this period prefigures is the role of law in colonial expansion, what Balint et al (2014: 204) refer to as 'the constitutive violence of law, particularly during the so-called frontier period in settler colonies'. Law is violence during colonial conquest; and it is only with a successful conquest that it can don the mantle of peace.

In 1598 the newly appointed Lord Deputy of Ireland, Mountjoy, set out with the backing of the Crown to break once and for all the power of the northern chieftains, particularly Hugh O'Neill, the Earl of Tyrone. O'Neill's English title derived from the surrender and regrant policy of Henry VIII. To first appearances, the 'conversion' of the Gaelic chieftains seemed authentic. Thus, when almost all of Ulster was in rebellion, O'Neill wrote to Elizabeth and 'protested before God and heaven, that there was no prince nor creature, whom he honoured as he did her majesty; nor any nation of people

that he loved or trusted more, than the English' (Moryson 1617, volume 2: 202).[17]
In reality, the chieftains played a cat and mouse game with the imperial power. A
temporary surrender buys time for regrouping, especially if one realises that the policy
of one's opponents is as changeable as one's own behaviour, swinging between coercion
and conciliation. An occasional grovelling letter or an apology was a small enough price
to pay when compared to the other outcomes on offer, defeat on the battlefield or death
in the Tower of London.

Mountjoy was perfectly happy to use duplicitous tactics also, sometimes seeking
to negotiate, at other times refusing negotiation. But there was no deviation from his
overall purpose: breaking the power of O'Neill and the last remaining bastion of the
Gaelic social order, Ulster.[18] He pursued a ruthless and inexorable campaign against
O'Neill. This involved conventional battles as well as the by now customary scorched
earth policy; he

> resolved, first, to spoil all the country of Tyrone and to banish all the inhabitants
> from thence, enjoining such of them as would become subjects, to live on the
> south-side of Blackwater, so that if Tyrone returned, he should find nothing in the
> country but the Queen's garrisons. (Moryson 1617, volume 3: 202)

The effects of the scorched earth policy were horrifically apparent:

> ... no spectacle was more frequent in the ditches of towns, and especially in wasted
> countries, than to see multitudes of these poor people dead with their mouths all
> coloured green by eating nettles, docks, and all things they could rend up above
> ground. (Moryson 1617, volume 3: 281-3)

To save his reputation if not his head, Mountjoy needed a definitive victory. The
English finally achieved that victory at the Battle of Kinsale in 1601. In support of
the northern rebels, the Spanish sent a fleet to Ireland which landed at the south
coast town of Kinsale. The English emptied their garrisons and forts elsewhere in
Ireland to rush south to take on the Spanish; the total strength of the English army
in Ireland at this point was 1,198 horse and 16,000 foot (Moryson 1617, volume
3: 14). This gave a relatively free passage to the northern clans, led by O'Neill
and O'Donnell to march the length of the island to engage the English who had
the Spanish under siege. The English won. The Spanish were shipped back home
on English ships while O'Neill went back north where he was finally defeated by
Mountjoy's forces. Eventually O'Neill left for continental Europe with a coterie

---

[17] For their part, the English overlords repeatedly granted pardons for even the most egregious acts of
rebellion, including that of O'Neill. Disloyalty by the Old English colonists was treated less leniently. Thus,
while Henry VIII was conceding surrender and regrant to the native Irish, he was confiscating outright the
estates of 'those of the colonists who were unable, or who neglected, to discharge the duties attaching to
their places' (Froude 1969: 40).

[18] Between 1 October 1598 and 31 March 1603 the war in Ireland cost the Crown almost £2 million in the
currency of the time (Moryson 1617, volume 3: 341).

of his clansmen and others, an occurrence known as 'the Flight of the Earls'. Their purpose was to seek military and financial support to continue the rebellion. With the last stronghold of Gaelic power and culture now penetrated, the final conquest of Ireland was within reach.

Plantation: the institution of 'planter' and 'Gael'

The defeat at Kinsale and the Flight of the Earls provided the opportunity for the English state to move to the next stage of colonial conquest by adding one more tactic. The sword and the law had already been employed; now was the time for a further colonial trope – forced population movement. This involved two complementary processes, clearance and plantation: removing the native Irish and replacing them with English and Scots settlers. Where the Irish were to go was often a moot point. There was a suggestion in 1599 'for transferring the Irish population as a whole, to provide a helot class in England...' (Foster 1988: 35). Later, Cromwell proposed moving large numbers of native landowners to the west of Ireland. In his *A Treatise on Ireland* (1687) William Petty, economist and surgeon-general to Cromwell, urged clearances, such as were later enacted in the Scottish Highlands. His 'political arithmetick' approach suggested

> ... there being about 1300 Thousand People in Ireland, that to bring a Million of them into England, and to leave the other 300 Thousand for Herdsmen and Dairy-Women behind, and to quit all other Trades in Ireland, but that of Cattle onely, would effect the Settlement, Improvement, and Union...

But beginning in the mid-sixteenth century, the plantation of British settlers in Ireland became regarded as the key component of a political solution. Lord Deputy Henry Sidney proposed a complex plan for completing the conquest of Ireland. It involved the appointment of a president for each province with overall administrative and military authority. A military campaign against Hugh O'Neill's predecessor, Shane, and the elimination of Scottish settlers would open the way to the planting of soldiers and other colonists in Ulster (Canny 1976: 48-9). Sidney was convinced of the value of settler colonialism as a result of his awareness of Spanish affairs gained while he had previously been an emissary in Spain. He 'knew what conquistadors were up to in South America and this undoubtedly influenced him' (Canny 1976: 66). But he had to convince Queen Elizabeth who, while open to the idea in principle, did not back it in practice. Similarly, when Lord Deputy Perot put forward an ambitious plan for plantation in 1584, the Crown only agreed to finance it if there was matching funding from Irish backers; the plan did not materialise (Morgan 1993: 36).

There had been previous plantations in Ireland, in 1556 in Laois and Offaly and in 1586-98 in Munster. In Munster, after the suppression of rebellion, half a million acres of fertile land were escheated to the Crown and given as reward for service and to undertakers. Ulster too had experienced plantations: between 1542 and 1575, there were plantations in Newry and Mourne, Armagh, mid-Down, Ards and in East Antrim, mainly Islandmagee, as well as the Hamilton and Montgomery settlements in North Down in 1605 (Robinson 1984). Overall, the plantations in Ulster had not proven particularly successful. Sir Thomas Smith established a colony of one hundred English settlers in the Ards peninsula in 1572 but the opposition of Gaelic chieftain Sir Brian McPhelim O'Neill of Clandeboye led to its failure (Canny 1976: 87). In 1575, the Earl of Essex offered to integrate what was left of Smith's colony into his own territory at Clandeboye. But Essex's colony was already facing difficulties. He mortgaged his land in England to enable a loan of £10,000 from Queen Elizabeth, thus bypassing the need for support from private individuals. At the same time, he was involved in a costly war with the Scots and the O'Neills, the main Ulster clan, rather than giving his full attention to the success of his settlement. Elizabeth's government sent him troops and overall expended £21,250 in supporting him, but all there was to show for this expenditure was a series of atrocities, such as the murder of McPhelim O'Neill and his followers at a feast and the slaughter of the entire population, about 600 people, of Rathlin Island by Sir Francis Drake in July 1575. To all intents and purposes, with Essex's death in 1576, attempts at the colonisation of Ulster ceased.

This changed again, however, in the wake of the Flight of the Earls. By 1610, the English had framed their policy for the 'Ulster Plantation' (Aldous and Puirseil 2008: 35-40). This was a complex modern and statist template for settler colonialism. In an early example of colonial planning, the model was framed legally and in some detail in *Conditions to be Observed by the British Undertakers of the Escheated Lands* (1610). Contemporaries regarded this as a completely different scale of intervention:

> ... in the first nine years of his [King James'] reign ... there hath been more done in the work and reformation of this kingdom; than in the 440 years which are past since the conquest was first attempted. (Davies 1969: 259)

The focus now was on Ulster, Ireland's most untamed province, 'the very fostermother and example of all the rebellions of Ireland' (Nicholas Dawtrey, quoted in Morgan 1993: 18). Away from the east coast it remained a no-go area for British administrators:

> No lord deputy, in the sixteenth century, visited the province without the full backing of the army, and even then, they were vulnerable to attacks from the Irish chieftains who were able to select suitable sites for ambush and then disappear into the woods and bogs. (Canny 1976: 2)[19]

---

[19] In similar vein, Sir Walter Scott, in an introduction to the 1883 republication of Dericke's *The Image of Ireland* (1581), writes: 'The Lord-Deputy lived like the general of an invading army in an hostile country, rather than the civil governor of a peaceful and allied province' (Derricke 1883: xiii). Ulster continued to be the most dangerous part of Ireland as far as the English were concerned until after King William's accession

The lesson taken from the failure of earlier attempts at plantation in Ulster was 'the need for a military conquest by government troops before a colony could be introduced' (Canny 1976: 90). The metaphor most commonly used in this regard was a pastoral one. Davies (in Myers 1983: 34) wrote: 'For the husbandman must first break the land before it be made capable of good seed'. The man who turned out to be the architect of this new and successful plantation of Ulster, Arthur Chichester, wrote likewise:

> ...wee must followe the example of good husbandmen who undertakinge the manurance of a land wch hath long layne wast ... doth first inhable hymselfe to cut downe and weede out those hinderers of his profitt. (Chichester and W.P. 1853: 180-1)

Nor was this simply aspirational. On one occasion he reported back to Queen Elizabeth:

> We have burnt and destroyed along the Lough ... in which journeys we have killed above over one hundred people of all sorts, besides such as were burnt, how many I know not. We spare none of what quality or sex soever, and it hath bred much terror in the people. (Cited in Kiernan 2007: 210)

Sir Thomas Blenerhasset, an Englishman who later became one of the new landowners in the north of Ireland, articulated part of the logic of plantation: 'Fayre England, she hath more People then she can well sustaine: goodly Ulster for want of people unmanured, her pleasant fieldes and rich groundes, they remaine if not defliate, worsse' (Blenerhasset 1972: A2). Nevertheless, the land *was* inhabited. In the writings of the English on the proposed plantation of Ulster three positions emerged in relation to the natives. The first was extirpation, the removal of the natives at least from the immediate areas being settled. In this view, the issue of security loomed large. Guaranteeing security for English settlers had proven problematic. Garrisons, fortified farms, bawns and forts existed, but the system was not working. Even a period of peace was no occasion for comfort,

> for although there be no apparent enemy, nor any visible maine force, yet the wood-kerne and many other (who now have put on the smiling countenaunce of contentment) doe threaten every houre, if oportunitie of time and place doth serve, to burne and steale whatsoever... (Blenerhasset 1972: B)

Plantation allowed the creation of a series of towns the inhabitants of which could 'combine to search the country far and wide, capturing or terrorising both wood-kerne and wolf' – each of which is taken to be equally threatening. Without plantation, '... the Irish ... will never otherwise be sufficiently brideled...' (Blenerhasset 1972: B2). With plantation, there would be no need for garrisons and the cost of security could be spread across all the planters who would obviously be motivated to protect their own interests.

This emphasis on security reveals that in the minds of the architects of plantation was not only the desire to develop a land which they saw as being neglected, but ultimately

---

to the throne which led to a new wave of colonisers into the province (Prendergast 1867: 50).

a strategy of counterinsurgency; the planters would be, in the words of the Earl of Salisbury, 'a spear-head in Irish flesh' (quoted in Biggs-Davison 1973: 35). A further advantage was that poor peasant farmers could act as a kind of human shield for more wealthy planters. Thus, a Mr Taylor proposed in his *Proposition for Planting My Lord of Essex's Land* in 1622 that 'the Scotch shall be as a wall betwixt them [the English] and the Irish through which quarter the Irish will not pass to carry any stealths' (quoted in Canny 1998a: 13).[20]

Foster (1988: 59) notes a debate among the advocates of plantation:

> Was it to be a policy of Anglicization or of colonization? 'Anglicization' presupposed a slow process: part of the destabilizing of Gaelic society and practices by introducing English modes of law, tenure and social relations. 'Colonization' indicated a more drastic approach, amounting at least in theory to tearing Gaelicism out by the roots.

For commentators like Spenser there was no doubt that plantation would 'involve the extermination of large sections of the indigenous population' (Spenser, in Myers 1983: 57). He was of the view that settling Ireland could only succeed if its population was removed completely from the land; he wanted to starve the people to the point where they would eat each other.

Carty (1999: 64) quotes an English army officer who had witnessed the effects of such a policy:

> About the year 1653, the plague and famine had so swept away whole counties, that a man might travel twenty or thirty miles and not see a living creature, either man, beast or bird; they being either all dead, or had quit those desolate places.

The second position advocated a form of apartheid, where the natives would be confined to their own bantustans, allowing the colonies to develop separately. Thus, Colonel Richard Lawrence, governor of Waterford, argued that segregation was necessary for the security of the Protestant population. '... the English inhabiting in that Nation should live together in distinct plantations or colonies, separated from the Irish'. He proposed that the number of native servants and tenants should be restricted to one-fifth of the population (quoted in Ó Siochrú 2008: 242).

The third alternative involved a kind of missionary zeal whereby integration would ensure that the natives acquire the civilised customs and manners of the settlers. Sir John Davies supported the establishment of schools where native children could

---

[20] Identical sentiments in a parallel colonial situation were expressed over a century later by James Logan, a Quaker from Lurgan, County Armagh and Colonial Secretary in Pennsylvania: 'I thought it might be prudent to plant a Settlement of those who had so bravely defended Derry and Inniskillen as a frontier in case of any Disturbance' (cited in Fitzpatrick 1989: 73).

learn the English language: so as we may conceive and hope, that the next generation, will in tongue and heart, and every way else, become English; so as there will be no difference or distinction, but the Irish Sea betwixt us... (Davies 1969: 272)

The notion of plantation thus encapsulated a range of contradictory colonial objectives. King James VI & I was a keen supporter of plantation. In the case of Scotland, he offered the Scottish islands to the Marquess of Huntly 'on condition that he wipe out their entire populations' (Lenihan 2008: 43). However, in relation to Ireland, his vision was less apocalyptic; he supported a policy which

did not utterly exclude the natives out of this plantation, with a purpose to root them out, as the Irish were excluded out of the first English colonies; but made a mixed plantation of British and Irish, that they might grow up together in one nation. (Davies 1969: 281)

For James this land seizure offered the opportunity to develop Ulster along English lines:

And now that all Ulster, or the most part, has fallen into His Majesty's power, he intends to order it so as it may redound to his honour and profit.... Rising generations be trayned up to useful industrie, and civilitie, learning, religion and loyalties.[21]

Four million acres were expropriated in Donegal, Fermanagh, Tyrone, Armagh, Cavan and Coleraine. Coleraine was renamed Londonderry and given over to a number of London companies for exploitation (Lenihan 2008: 45). Large tracts were given to 'undertakers' who were required to develop the area through the building of bridges and fortifications and the importation of peasant farmers from England and Scotland. Some land was also given to around 300 'meritorious' natives (Lenihan 2008: 46). The Irish share can be seen for the miniscule amount it was when one considers that the most fertile land, half a million acres in all, was handed over to settlers (Connolly 1915). A key element of the Ulster plantation was that 'the corporate towns and land allotted to undertakers and to the London companies was to be entirely cleared of Irish' (Lenihan 2008: 47).

Lenihan (2008: 81-2) emphasises how radical the plantation of Ulster was:

... institutionalised land confiscation in peacetime would simply not have been seriously considered in England or even in Scotland. The crown ... drove a radical course of colonisation to reshape Irish society as a replica of England, in government, religion, language and culture.

The plan appeared to be realised. By 1641, there were approximately 100,000 settlers in Ireland, 70,000 in Munster and Leinster and 30,000 in Ulster (Lenihan 2008: 54). Davies, as we saw earlier, was convinced that the conquest had succeeded. How according to Davies, did James succeed where previous monarchs had failed? First, by keeping an army there and paying them properly (Davies 1969: 261). Secondly, he passed an Act of Oblivion: 'All offences against the Crown ... were (to all such as would come in to the Justices of Assise by a certain day, and claim the benefit of this Act)

---

[21] Quoted by one tangible contemporary link to the Plantation, The Honourable The Irish Society (2020).

pardoned, remitted, and utterly extinguished ...' (Davies 1969: 263). This legal tactic sent out a powerful message to the Irish about the role of law. Just as they were protected by the rule of law they were also to be regarded, and should regard themselves, as subjects subservient to the law: 'For heretofore, the neglect of the law, made the English degenerate, and become Irish; and now, on the other side, the execution of the law, doth make the Irish grow civil, and become English' (Davies 1969: 272).[22]

There were, however, flaws in the enterprise. 'Pacifying' Ulster continued to cost the English exchequer. It was not such a drain as Elizabeth's military campaign had been, but Ireland continued to cost James £47,000 per year (Lenihan 2008: 72).

Another problem was the quality and commitment of some of the settlers. Previously there had been suggestions of seizing the opportunity of plantation to rid England of some of its social problems.

Richard Beacon, expressing his concern about the increasing agitation among London's lower orders in the turbulent 1590s, recommended that 'the people, poor and seditious, which are a burden to the commonwealth should be removed from the city and sent to colonise Ireland'. A pamphlet of 1619 was even more explicit in advocating Ireland as a 'dumping ground' for the superfluous poor of England. Whilst such practices were recognised as being entirely contradictory to a central tenet of plantation theory – civilising the natives by example – expediency prevailed. During the opening decades of the seventeenth century a sizeable body of vagrants, outlaws and petty criminals were rounded up in the borderlands of northern England and southern Scotland and shipped over to Ireland (Fitzgerald 2001: 118). As the Reverend Andrew Stewart, ministering in Ulster, complained, '... from Scotland came many and from England not a few, yet all of them generally the verie scum of both nations, fleeing from debt or fleeing from justice' (quoted in O'Cahan 1968: 36). Most of the settlers in Ulster 'would have brought few skills with them that were not already widespread among the native population' (Canny 1988a: 95). In addition, there was a great number of disbanded soldiers also settled in Ulster, again, not likely to be skilled craftsmen or farmers. This meant that there was not enough replacement labour among the settlers if all the natives were dispersed. Thus:

> Most British landowners in Ireland were forced to rely on native tenants to occupy at least portions of their lands, and their presence became so vital that the undertakers in the Ulster plantation were forced, in 1628, to negotiate a modification of the regulation that they accept only British tenants on their lands. (Canny 1988: 53-4)[23]

---

[22] This basic English/Irish ethno-national dynamic is further complicated because Scottish involvement in Ireland cuts across the formal colonisation and state formation. Thus, Scots families were part of the earlier plantations. They were also involved in a less formal migration to Antrim and Down. Moreover, after 1603 Scots began settling Ulster which creates a very specific Scots and Presbyterian character to that plantation. But none of this – nor the emergence of the post-union Great Britain state in 1707 – takes away from the specifically Irish/English dynamic of these centuries.

[23] The Ironmongers' Company was required to not let land to any natives, but 'out of 127 undertenants on their estates, all but nine were Irish'. (Foster 1988: 74)

But the greatest problem lay in the ultimate legacy bequeathed by dispossession and settler colonialism. Froude, while unsympathetic towards the native Irish, manages to neatly summarise this legacy:

> Plantations of aliens were in their midst, owning the lands which had once been theirs, and growing rich and powerful. Forays out of the Pale they could defy and smile at. The Saxon bands came and went; crops might be burnt and cattle lifted; but, when the invaders were gone, the air closed behind them, and the losses could be made good by answering raids into the four counties. The colonists, on the other hand, were an ever-present affront, whom, by all the laws of God and man, they were entitled, when they had them at advantage, to destroy. (Froude 1969: 84)

Writing contemporaneously, Irish historian Geoffrey Keating derided the failure of the colonisers to praise the virtues of the Irish, native and Old English alike, in culture, law, military affairs, hospitality and generosity towards the poor. In retrospect, this reads like a swan song for an ancient culture collapsing under the sustained onslaught of plantation:

> For it is the fashion of the beetle, when it lifts its head in the summertime, to go about fluttering, and not to stoop towards any delicate flower that may be in the field, or any blossom in the garden, though they be all roses or lilies, but it keeps bustling about until it meets with dung of horse or cow, and proceeds to roll itself therein. Thus it is with the set above-named; they have displayed no inclination to treat of the virtues or good qualities of the nobles among the old foreigners and the native Irish who then dwelt in Ireland... (Keating 2009: 3)

Crusade and the Cromwellian conquest

Religion had been at the centre of the conquest of Ireland, dating back to Henry II's mission to bring the Irish Catholic Church into the Roman mainstream. The Reformation added a further level to the Protestant English denigration of the Irish who remained obstinately Catholic. Thereafter, Irish rebellion was read by the English in religious rather than anti-colonial terms. A key case in point is the rising which occurred in 1641. We will consider this in full in chapter 10. Suffice it to say here that Irish chieftains and some Anglo-Irish gentry joined together in what was called the Confederacy and engaged in a sustained attempt to overthrow English rule in Ireland. It was in effect the first truly nationalist rebellion in Ireland. It began in Ulster with a sustained campaign against the plantations. The rebels faced the republican government in England which ensued from the success of the Parliamentarians and the execution of King Charles I. The parliamentarian response to the rebellion was headed by the Lord Protector, Oliver Cromwell, who sought not merely to defeat the Confederacy but also to punish the Irish as Catholics for their rebellion.

For the Parliamentarians the Irish troubles were both a burden and an opportunity. The execution of the king had proven deeply unpopular for many in England, so war in Ireland would enable the parliamentary government to represent itself as the defender of the English nation and Protestantism against the dual threats of native Irish barbarism and aggressive international popery (Ó Siochrú 2008: 62).[24] Cromwell claimed that the Irish, if successful at home, would eventually invade England. So, it was up to the Lord Protector to bring the war directly to the Confederacy. He arrived with the New Model Army in August 1649 and left in May 1650. The army remained and fought on until 1653.[25]

Cromwell's view of the Irish campaign was that it was an honourable one. Addressing parliament in September 1660 he spoke glowingly of his army, '… whose sobriety and manners, whose courage and success has made it famous and terrible over the whole world' (Borlase 1675: 256). For many in Ireland 'terrible' was the key adjective. Cromwell quickly gained a reputation as a butcher.

It was the misfortune of many Old English and Irish chieftains to be on the losing side when the execution of the king confirmed Parliament's victory. Having crushed the Confederacy, Cromwell then abolished the Irish parliament. The significance of this cannot be underestimated. This was in effect the first act of union. From the time of King Henry II, the English monarch had been a self-appointed overlord in Ireland. King Henry VIII raised the stakes by having himself declared king of Ireland. The Lord Protector and the parliament confirmed that imposed arrangement by, in effect, establishing an act of union between Ireland and Britain. There had always been a local parliament, albeit highly restricted by Poynings' Law and other obstacles to independence. Now, even that semblance of sovereignty was removed, and direct rule was established.

The intensity of Cromwell's intervention needs to be understood in more than simply strategic and military concerns. To the puritan English mind, religious orthodoxy was also at stake: '… no Protestant state could recognize, without self-condemnation, the exercise of a religion among its subjects which elevates rebellion into a duty' (Froude 1969: 64). For Parliament, and for Cromwell in particular, war in Ireland was as much about destroying the Antichrist as about taking on the Confederate rebellion. That ensured an intensity to the operations of Cromwell and his army in Ireland which was unprecedented in comparison with England and indeed further afield.

In taking the town of Drogheda after a siege, Cromwell had said of his soldiers: 'I forbade them to spare any that were in arms' (Ó Siochrú 2008: 84). The majority of the town's defenders were put to the sword, around 3,000 in all. The next day the dozens of defenders who had held out surrendered. 'Every tenth man was shot; the remainder were sent to the penal settlement at Barbadoes' (Froude 1969: 124). But many inhabitants who

---

[24] The cost of putting down the 1641 rebellion and Cromwell's subsequent campaign was almost £3 million (Foster 1988: 111). The money was raised on the basis of security against two and a half million acres of Irish land. In effect, the enterprise was to be bankrolled through a future massive reallocation of land ownership.

[25] Cromwell faced rebellion from sections of the army influenced by Leveller ideas. One pamphlet circulated among soldiers said: '… what have we to doe with Ireland, to fight, and murther a People and Nation (for indeed they are set upon cruelty, and murthering poore people, which they glory in) which have done us no harme, only deeper to put our hands in bloud with their owne? we have waded too farre in that crimson streame (already) of innocent and Christian bloud' (quoted in Carlin 1987: 280). Thousands of soldiers ordered to go to Ireland refused to do so, to the point where the endeavour was severely threatened. The threat was only dissipated through the military defeat of mutineers at Burford in May 1649.

were not in arms were also killed, including one thousand people, among them clergy, gathered in St Peter's Church. Cromwell justified the massacre as revenge for the killing of Protestants in 1641 and therefore 'the righteous judgement of God upon these barbarous wretches' (Ó Siochrú 2008: 84). Likewise, when he later took the town of Wexford after a siege, he killed at least 2000 defenders and civilians (Ó Siochrú 2008: 97).

Such tactics had not occurred during the bloody war in England between Royalists and Parliamentarians. 'Of all the officers captured at Drogheda, only one was let live ... whereas of the 300 officers who submitted to mercy to Fairfax after the siege of Colchester, the year before, only three were shot' (Lenihan 2008: 128). Ó Siochrú's (2008: 85) conclusion is that 'the sheer scale of the killing was simply unprecedented'. Lenihan (2008: 135) concludes similarly that 'the Protector's war guilt should be judged by his personal commitment to vengefulness at a policy level, rather than what he did or did not do at Drogheda or Wexford'. At the heart of that vengefulness was religious fundamentalism; Cromwell was not simply wiping out a political enemy, but the irreligious followers of the Antichrist.

The effects of the Cromwellian campaign were devastating for the Irish. It was, as Connolly later concluded, 'the final consummation of the conquest of Ireland' (Connolly 1915). In the four years following Cromwell's invasion in 1649, Ireland suffered a demographic catastrophe, with mortality somewhere in the region of 20 per cent, due to a combination of fighting, famine and disease. This compares to an estimated 3 per cent population loss in England during the civil wars of the 1640s (Ó Siochrú 2008: 223).

The Irish were defeated, and Parliament drew up the Act of Settlement 1652. The preamble of the Act stated that there was no intention 'to extirpate the whole nation' and guaranteed mercy and pardon to all who lived 'peaceably and obediently'. Excluded from such mercy was the Catholic clergy (Ó Siochrú 2008: 227). However, the Settlement laid the basis for a shocking and fundamental social upheaval. The Adventurers' Act of 1642 specified that the war in Ireland would be paid for through confiscation of land from the rebels. Consequently, 'given the high costs of the war, the more land seized the better' (Ó Siochrú 2008: 225). So, between two and three million acres were confiscated. One million acres were used to realise bonds paid for in advance and the rest was given to Cromwell's army in lieu of pay (Froude 1969: 132).

The question remained: what was to happen to the Irish who had owned and worked the land in the aftermath of confiscation? Cromwell's plan was 'to make Connaught into a second Wales'. The Irish were to be transported there, leaving the English secure and protected from the age-old infection whereby 'when the English and Irish were intermixed, the distinctive English character in a few generations was lost' (Froude 1969: 133). The realisation of transportation ebbed and flowed. After Cromwell, Ireton was less rigorous, but his successor, Fleetwood, was ruthless in transporting the Irish to Connacht, to the point that Lenihan (2008: 146) accuses him of being 'genocidal' in intention. Things relaxed again when Henry Cromwell took over. Thus, the plans were never fully implemented; for example, the intention to move the entire Presbyterian population of Antrim and Down to Kilkenny, Tipperary and Waterford did not materialise (Lenihan 2008: 36). As regards the transportation of Catholics, there was mixed 'success'. In June 1653, parliament informed Catholic landowners that they had until 1 May 1654 'to remove and transplant themselves into the province of Connacht, and the county of Clare, or one of them, there to inhabit and abide'. They would be 'compensated' by receiving land there one third or two thirds the extent of what had been confiscated (Ó Siochrú 2008: 235). Some landowners obeyed, while others moved to Connacht only to return surreptitiously at a later date; some took to the woods, while others stayed put on their land (Ó Siochrú 2008: 239). Some of these last were hanged for their disobedience (Ó Siochrú 2008: 243).

Any natives on planter estates had to be registered and if not, were classed as 'idle persons'. The Irish could not move from one place to another without a magistrate's certificate. As Burns (1974: 2) points out, these policies pre-date South African pass laws by centuries. There was also a plan to remove all natives from Dublin which was not realised (Lenihan 2008: 145). Many soldiers sold their land on to officers for cash. The result was the emergence of 'not a protestant community but a protestant upper class' (Lenihan 2008: 146).

By June 1657, when the confiscations were declared to be 'duly executed and performed', Ireland was a remarkably different place. The population of the island had dropped from 1.5 million to 850,000, 150,000 of whom were settlers (Burns 1974 2). In addition: 'The Catholic share of land ownership had plummeted from almost 60 per cent to not more than 9 per cent' (Lenihan 2008: 142).

Land ownership throughout Ireland was transformed, but proportionately Ulster was severely affected. Two thousand native landowners were transplanted overall, of whom only 30 were from Ulster. But, while in 1641 there were 58 Gaelic Catholic landowners in Ulster, by 1660 that number was reduced to five (Elliott 2000: 109). In Ulster, outside of Antrim, less than 4 per cent of land remained in Catholic ownership (Elliott 2000: 104). In Ulster 'the Cromwellian land settlement cemented the link between Protestantism and land ownership...' (Elliott 2000: 111). In west Ulster, 'of the dozen Catholics who kept all or part of their estates, half were Scots and one was English' (Lenihan 2008: 140).

By 1662, three quarters of the land in Ireland, five sixths of the housing, nine tenths of housing in walled towns and two thirds of foreign trade were in the hands of the Protestant settlers who comprised three eighths of the population (Burns 1974: 5). In 1641 Catholics were the majority in the Irish parliament; in 1661, there were 260 members of parliament, of whom one was Catholic (Froude 1969: 147).

The scheme for the transportation of Catholics split Protestant opinion. Some were opposed, for economic rather than humanitarian reasons because of the loss of Catholic labourers (Ó Siochrú 2008: 240). Others went further, such as Vincent Gookin, who published a pamphlet condemning the English and Protestant response to the rebellion;

they 'reckoned an Irish man and a rebel tantamount, and on that score forced many into war who desired peace'. Returning to an old trope, he argued that integrated communities would be valuable whereby it could 'be expected that the Irish will turn English' (quoted in Ó Siochrú 2008: 241).

There were other mechanisms which ensured a decline of the Catholic population. Approximately 40,000 sailed to continental Europe where they enlisted in the Spanish and French armies (Ó Siochrú 2008: 230). And possibly 12,000 were sent to the Caribbean through penal servitude and indenture where they lived alongside 50,000 African slaves (Ó Siochrú 2008: 233).

A statue of Oliver Cromwell takes pride of place at the entrance to the British parliament, symbolising his role in establishing the primacy of parliament in the face of the doctrine of the divine right of kings. It has divided opinion in Britain since its erection in 1899. However, the lens through which Cromwell is viewed in Ireland is an entirely different one. Butcher or not? Ó Siochrú (2008: 249) has no hesitation in answering:

> In the mid-seventeenth century, a lethal combination of racial superiority and religious bigotry, reinforced by a genuine sense of outrage at events during the initial months of the Ulster rebellion, created the ideal conditions for Cromwell's campaign of terror against Irish Catholics. His conduct shocked contemporary opinion, not only in Ireland, but also on the Continent, and almost certainly prolonged the war by a number of years.

In May 1660 the British monarchy was restored and Charles II became King. He faced the task of dealing with the changes wrought by the Parliamentarians, the victors in the Civil War. Some of those changes were irreversible; for example, the Parliamentarians had executed his father. He dealt with this by disinterring the corpse of Cromwell and 'executing' him in turn. At the same time, the King was dependent on the military officers who had served the Parliament, and this was crucial when it came to dealing with Cromwell's legacy in Ireland. He managed to square the circle: 'Cromwell was to be disowned with execration; yet his work was to be defended, and the fruit of it secured' (Froude 1969: 149). For the most part, the Cromwellian settlement in Ireland remained intact. English Protestants

> emerged as the clear victors from the wars of the mid-seventeenth century, with Catholics left in possession of only one fifth of the land total, a huge reduction from the 60 per cent they owned prior to the 1641 rebellion. This represented the largest single shift in land ownership anywhere in Europe during the early modern period, and proved to be Cromwell's lasting legacy in Ireland. (Ó Siochrú 2008: 248)

Many Protestant adventurers were given an incredible boost in terms of social mobility as a result of the Irish wars. Take the case of Lord Broghill of Blarney. His father had come from England, 'a barefooted boy, not sixty years before, yet died the possessor of forfeited estates, reaching from the city of Cork eastward, to Youghal, and westward almost to Crookhaven, a length of nearly fifty miles' (Prendergast 1867: 37). Thus, the relentless colonial restructuring of Ireland continued apace.

Charles left the adventurers and soldiers in possession of the estates they had been given. His Gracious Declaration of November 1660 thus 'established the year 1659, not 1641, as the benchmark for all future land claims' (Ó Siochrú 2008: 247). Irish Catholics in the Confederation of Kilkenny had claimed to be fighting for Charles' father; they had joined their Confederate forces with his and had been promised pardon and the restoration of their estates; they had fought Cromwell and some had gone to fight in Europe with 'their return to Ireland constantly in view. They fought and bled to establish a claim to be restored' (Prendergast 1867: 38). Their hopes were high, but it soon became clear that the Gracious Declaration would deliver little to them.

The Gracious Declaration led to the establishment of a Court of Claims where Catholics could seek justice. Prendergast (1867: 40) paints a poignant picture of what ensued:

> Round the doors of the newly opened Court of Claims may be pictured an anxious crowd of impoverished noblemen, tattered gentlemen of old descent, some of English blood, some of pure Irish, many of them soldiers of foreign air ... broken-hearted widows and orphans. These were the 'outs', the dispossessed Irish. Some of them had spent six years in misery in Connaught; some ten years in sieges and battles under perpetual fire in France and Flanders...others in garrets and cellars in Paris or Bruges.

Appeals to the Court meant that none of them got 'so much of their fathers' lands as would serve for a grave' (Prendergast 1867: 43). Many ended up beggars, dying penurious, without enough money for a proper burial. Others relied on the generosity of old acquaintances who had been lucky enough not to have all of their land confiscated until in time even that generosity wore out. And some became Tories, living through robbing rich travellers or collecting protection money from rich, and Protestant, landowners. They were

> too numerous, and the forces at the disposal of the Government too few to cope with them in the wild and difficult countries then frequent in Ireland. It was very rarely that they were taken in any large numbers by means of the many ambushes laid for them. (Prendergast 1867: 52)

This was especially true in Ulster which continued to be the most dangerous province in Ireland until the victory of King William towards the end of the century. 'The condition of the most part of Ulster was such as none dare travel or inhabit there, but as in an enemy's country', wrote Viscount Gosford (quoted in Prendergast 1867: 51). That said, the restoration of the monarchy ushered in a period of relative peace in military terms. The toleration towards Catholics in practice meant that they rapidly revived, helped by a number of decisions of Charles, such as the appointment of a Catholic, Richard Talbot, the Earl of Tyrconnell, as Lord Deputy. Catholics held about nine per cent of land at the Restoration in 1660 and about 22 per cent when Charles died in 1685 (Lenihan 2008: 160). Tyrconnell dismissed countless Protestants from the army, appointed a Catholic chaplain, seemed to be heading towards the disestablishment of the Church of Ireland, packed the Irish House of Commons with Catholics, appointed Catholic sheriffs, all the while, perhaps mischievously, reassuring Protestant landowners that there was no intention of reversing the Cromwellian settlement (Lenihan 2008: 176). Irish Protestants were not reassured, especially when James II followed Charles as monarch. As far as the Protestants of Ireland were concerned, as a papist he was likely to do more than Charles and Tyrconnell combined to undermine their position in Ireland. Archbishop William King published a pamphlet, *The State of the Protestants of Ireland under the Late King James's Government*, in 1691. He argued that the goal of Irish Catholics was to 'out them of their estates and improvements and send them to dig or beg', and that King James supported them (Canny 1988: 117). His solution: 'the final destruction of the Irish Catholic landowners and priests' (Canny 1988: 120). In King William III he may have believed his prayers were to be answered.

Prince William of Orange challenged his father-in-law King James II for the Crown of England and won. One of the decisive battles in his campaign was fought in Ireland at the River Boyne in 1690. William had 36,000 soldiers at his disposal, 'the largest army to tread Irish soil' (Lenihan 2008: 181). The Williamites lost about 800, the Jacobites less than twice that. Despite the fact that it has gone down in Irish (Protestant) folklore as an epic on the scale of Troy, it was 'by contemporary standards ... hardly a battle at all but some half-dozen rear-guard skirmishes' (Lenihan 2008: 182).[26] That said, William's three-year campaign in Ireland cost more than twice the value of all land owned by Catholics on the island (Lenihan 2008: 183).

The Glorious Revolution of 1688 transformed the English state. It was finally established in England that there was a constitutionalist monarchy rather than an absolutist one, that parliament was central in the development of British politics, and that Protestantism was without question the official religion. But this also had implications for Ireland. Irish Catholics had supported James; William's victory over James augured badly for them. William was apparently personally not particularly vindictive. He also needed to avoid alienating his Catholic Austrian allies, and that required reining in the anti-Catholic zeal of Irish Protestants (Canny 1988: 120). The Treaty of Limerick that concluded the war in Ireland in 1691 appeared generous – guaranteeing basic rights for Irish Catholics (Aldous and Puirséil 2008: 48-53). The original draft contained an assurance that 'the Roman Catholics of Ireland should enjoy such privileges, in the exercise of their religion, as were consistent with the laws of Ireland, or as they did enjoy in the reign of Charles the Second' (Froude 1969: 203). At this moment it looked as though the period of crusade was over. Thanks to the power of the High-Church Protestants in the Irish parliament and their supporters in England, however,

---

[26] The Battle of Aughrim one year later was the more decisive battle. The Irish lost and the Treaty of Limerick and the Penal Laws followed. Thousands of Irish soldiers, known as the Wild Geese, were transported to continental Europe where they joined armies and continued to meet English forces in battle, although not in Ireland.

the Treaty was not implemented. When it was finally passed by the Irish Parliament in Dublin in 1697, its commitments on native and Catholic rights were compromised; the draft promise, cited above, was missing from the final document. For the next half-century, colonial administration was not to be characterised by the relative toleration of the Treaty of Limerick but rather by the Penal Laws which formally instituted all the crusading zeal of Cromwell.

Ascendancy and penal laws[27]

As colonisation progressed through the turn of the seventeenth century and into the eighteenth century, power relations in Ireland were codified in a series of Penal Laws. The French lawyer and philosopher Montesquieu concluded: 'This horrid code was conceived by devils, written in human blood, and registered in hell' (quoted in Ford 1915: 21).[28] In effect, 'every Irish Catholic was presumed to be disaffected to the State and was treated as an open or concealed rebel' (Lewis 1977: 37). These laws were sometimes specifically anti-Catholic and sometimes more generally repressive of anyone who was not a member of the established church. While anti-Catholicism was similarly codified in England, the law took on a specifically colonial dynamic in Ireland since they disenfranchised the vast majority of the populace. In England anti-Catholic measures arguably targeted a relatively small section of the aristocracy with a combination of papal and Jacobite sympathies; in Ireland they disenfranchised virtually the whole of the native Irish population.

Moreover, this was more than a symbolic marginalising of the Catholic Church. There was, of course, a specific religious project: Catholic seminarians, lay priests, seminary priests and bishops were banned from preaching; Catholic churches were banned; when subsequently tolerated, Catholic churches were to be built from wood rather than stone, and away from main roads. The Catholic Church was also specifically excluded from education: 'No person of the popish religion shall publicly or in private houses teach school, or instruct youth in learning within this realm'.

But this anti-Catholic regime also extended beyond religious anti-Catholicism to a host of repressive measures that resulted in institutionalised segregation of the most profound kind. First, there was formal sectarian disenfranchisement – banning Catholics from membership of parliament and from voting. Beyond this there was a

---

[27] The last of the Penal Laws was finally repealed in January 2020. The Administration of Justice Act (Irish Language Act) 1737 decreed that only English could be used in judicial proceedings at a time when the vast majority of the population was Irish speaking. As part of the deal to restore the Executive at Stormont there was a proposal to establish a Commissioner for the Irish language in Northern Ireland; along with legal recognition of the language, translation services and speaking through Irish (or Ulster Scots) in court will be permitted. This required the repeal of the 1737 Act. ('Final penal law in Ireland repealed', *Irish Catholic*, January 16, 2020.)

[28] Remarkably, at least one Catholic bishop did not agree. Up to 1793 it was a capital offence for a Catholic priest to conduct a mixed marriage. John Troy, Bishop of Ossory between 1776 and 1782, and later Archbishop of Dublin, believed that 'marriage between Protestants and Catholics is unlawful, wicked, and dangerous. The Penal Laws should not be repealed because they act as a deterrent' (quoted in Dunn 2012).

wider exclusion of Catholics and Presbyterians from public office; there was a ban on Catholic intermarriage with Protestants and the non-recognition of Presbyterian marriages; Catholics were barred from holding firearms or serving in the Crown forces; Catholics were excluded from the legal professions and the judiciary; there was also a ban on foreign education; a bar to Catholics and Dissenters entering Trinity College Dublin; a ban on custody of orphans being granted to Catholics.

Most significantly of all, however, this system also embedded the final process of colonial expropriation in Ireland. Thus, it accompanied an intricate series of mechanisms to redistribute both Irish property and land. This was not simply echoing earlier plantations by stealing land from the Irish and giving to the English. There was now a more complex process of incorporation: some Irish, certainly, could become de facto 'English' but at the cost of colluding in the further immiseration of other Irish people. There was a whole series of mechanisms to achieve this end: there was a ban on Catholics inheriting Protestant land; the legatee of a Catholic could benefit by conversion to the Church of Ireland; Catholic inheritances of land were to be equally subdivided between all an owner's sons with the exception that if the heir converted to Protestantism he would become the only tenant of estate; there was a ban on Catholics buying land under a lease of more than 31 years. There were also a host of associated mechanisms including, perhaps most notoriously, the prohibition on Catholics owning a horse valued at over £5. 'Conversion' was also to be an osmotic process. The costs of movement in the opposite direction were made painfully clear. There was a ban on converting from Protestantism to Catholicism on pain of forfeiting the 'monarch's protection' as well as forfeiture of property, estates and legacy to the monarch and a threat of remaining in prison at the monarch's pleasure.

These laws were not always rigorously enforced. Enforcement depended on the dispositions of local magistrates; moreover, as the eighteenth century progressed their application became more lax. Nevertheless, the symbolic intent was very clear. They were to offer some Irish people the privileges of becoming British subjects. But the inescapable corollary was that they marginalised and impoverished Irish people who refused to follow this path. Edmund Burke characterised this accurately as a 'machine'. To him the Penal Laws were

> a machine of wise and elaborate contrivance, as well fitted for the oppression, impoverishment and degradation of a people, and the debasement in them of human nature itself, as ever proceeded from the perverted ingenuity of man.[29]

Of course, these penal laws also had a wider target than Irish Catholics – Jews and non-conformist Protestants in Ireland were also disenfranchised in different ways. Despite their support for William, as evidenced by such instances as the Siege of Derry when the inhabitants held out for over three months against a Jacobite force and half of them

---

[29] *Letter to Sir Hercules Langrishe relative to [...] the Roman Catholics of Ireland*, 1792; quoted in O'Connor 1979: 371.

died, the Presbyterians of Ulster benefited little from William's victory. The High-Church Protestants of Ireland seized the opportunity to persecute them. Thus, only those who followed Anglican rites could hold a range of civil and military offices (Froude 1969: 313). Consequently, the entire non-conformist corporation of Belfast and the majority of the corporation in Derry were dismissed (Froude 1969: 320). Presbyterians, Unitarians, Quakers and other dissenters were excluded from parliamentary representation. Presbyterians could not be married by their own clergy, and if they were, could be imprisoned and compelled to make public confession of fornication. Marriage between Presbyterians and Episcopalians was illegal. If the heir to a Protestant landowner was a Presbyterian, he would be passed over in favour of a more distant High-Church relative.[30]

Such wealth production as was available for the Irish was restricted to the minority of Anglicans at the pinnacle of society who did not have an independent, sovereign position but rather gained their authority and ability to become wealthy through their incorporation in the English system. As such, they were definitively minor partners in the colonial project, as was shown by efforts which gathered pace shortly after William's victory to stymie economic development in Ireland. Loyalist Ireland's reward for allegiance was economic blockade, as Ford (1915: 21) summarises:

> The manufacturers and merchants of Bristol, jealous of this prosperity presented a petition to King William in which they begged His Majesty to put a stop to that industry in Ireland 'by legislative enactment', declaring that if that were not done 'that country (Ireland) would possess itself of the chief trade of the Empire.' This was in 1696. On June 9, 1698, both houses of the English Parliament addressed the king to the same effect. What was William's answer to this outrageous demand? Hear it: 'Gentlemen, I shall do all in my power to promote the trade of England, and to discourage the woolen manufacture of Ireland!'

As O'Brien (1919: 223) concludes, a political priority in eighteenth century Britain was 'that the political status of Ireland should be reduced from that of a kingdom to that of a colony', no more clearly summed up than in the instructions of Lord Robartes, Viceroy of Ireland: 'You shall in all things endeavour to advance and improve that trade of that our kingdom [Ireland] so far as it shall not be a prejudice to this our kingdom of England' (cited in Truxes, 1988: 8). The Cattle Act of 1663, which prohibited the export of Irish cattle to Britain, and the Navigation Acts of 1663, 1670, 1685 and 1696 which sought to establish an English monopoly on trade with the Caribbean, were at the core of the British project to hinder the economic development of Ireland.

During the 1650s there had been an unprecedented wave of British settlement in Ireland with consequent effects on the natives. For example, in 1655 the town of Galway was said to be 'cleared of Irish' and was given 'to the corporations of Liverpool and Gloucester, for debts, to plant with English' (Ford 1915: 20). Rivalry between

---

[30] Froude (1969: 323) incisively concludes that for the established church 'a Catholic was but an erring brother, while a Calvinist was a detested enemy'.

settlers and natives often ensured that the former, with state backing, won out over the latter. Thus in 1657 the Protestant coopers in Dublin organised to push out the Catholic coopers (Lenihan 2008: 137). Twenty years before William's Glorious Revolution, Presbyterians constituted about one third of the number of Irish Protestants; half a century later, they were over 50 per cent. 'Eighty thousand small Scotch Adventurers came in between 1690 and 1698, into different parts of Ireland, but chiefly into Ulster' (Prendergast 1867: 50). The Presbyterians dominated Ulster, not just, as before, the eastern part of the province but increasingly the west also. 'Between 1663 and 1740 there was a fourfold jump in the number of people of settler (and mostly Scottish) extraction in north-west County Londonderry and an eightfold explosion in the south-east of the county' (Lenihan 2008: 200).

This generated a whole series of novel ethnic encounters that often left neither of these blocs particularly happy. As Connolly (1972) suggested, it left 'the Catholic dispossessed by force, the Protestant dispossessed by fraud. Each hating and blaming the other'. The experience of restriction and persecution meant that by the middle of the 18th century many Protestant settlers decided to leave for more welcoming conditions. As Ford (1915: 35) colorfully puts it:

> The Protestants of the North, when their industries were crushed by the villainous enactments of your Parliament, crossed the Atlantic, bearing in their hearts the fires of indignation; and when the day of vengeance came, down flashed their thunderbolts on the power that had ruined them in Ireland!

In 1718 five ships brought 750 Protestants from Ulster to Boston, Massachusetts. Soon after, the destination shifted to Philadelphia. Around 250,000 emigrated between 1726 and 1776, and a further 100,000 between then and the end of the 18th century (Jones, 1969: 49), by which point it was estimated that one-sixth of the European population of the new nation was of Scots-Irish birth or descent (Evans 1969: 75). In other words, while this episode of Irish history was characterised as one of 'Protestant ascendancy',[31] this is a phenomenon that is immediately deconstructed in the context of the dynamics of race, class and gender signalled in our introduction. Of course, most Catholics and most women were excluded by this model of colonial power in Ireland. But ascendancy also subordinated most Protestants – including Presbyterians who were now the most 'Protestant' element of the Irish population of all.

The notion of 'Protestant Ascendancy' was a characterisation of the culmination of English colonial policy. In combination, the conquests, the plantations, the penal laws resulted in the colonial domination of Ireland by a small minority of landowners, politicians, clergy, and members of the professions – defined by their membership of the Churches of England and Ireland. Indeed, the establishment of both these churches

---

[31] On the origins and evolution of the term, 'Protestant Ascendancy', see McCormack 1989: 159-181. In Irish, the term was *An Chinsealacht*, meaning 'those in dominance'.

– their status as state religions, constitutionally established with the English monarch as Supreme Governor – was a key element in this Ascendancy. As well as Catholics, the Ascendancy excluded other Protestant denominations such as Presbyterians and other 'dissenters' as well as non-Christians such as Jews. Those that were not members of the Ascendancy were formally excluded from positions of power within the state and, more informally, from the upper echelons of society.

From the 1780s onwards, the word *Ascendancy* became used widely in Ireland both positively and negatively: for supporters, it captured a sense of both their privilege and the need to defend it; for opponents, it provided a useful thumbnail of their profound inequality. It assumed a general currency after 1782 in the context of Irish parliamentary reform and the threat to some and promise to others of Catholic emancipation. In that year, a resolution passed by the resolutely reactionary Dublin Corporation to George III included the term: 'We feel ourselves peculiarly called upon to stand forward in the crisis to pray your majesty to preserve the Protestant ascendancy in Ireland inviolate'. Edmund Burke traced this genealogy with a heavy irony:

> A word has been lately struck in the mint of the castle of Dublin; thence it was conveyed to the ... city-hall, where, having passed the touch of the corporation, so respectably stamped and vouched, it soon became current in parliament, and was carried back by the Speaker of the House of Commons in great pomp as an offering of homage from whence it came. The word is Ascendancy. (Burke 1834: 430)

Ironically, the Ascendancy only really came to recognise itself at the point at which it entered its final crisis. But the term reflected the order that had been put in place in Ireland in the series of conquests and colonisations of the seventeenth century, characterised by crusade and institutionalised as the penal laws.

The century of Ascendancy was finally ended by two related developments – the United Irish uprising of 1798 and the Acts of Union. We address the politics of the Society of United Irishmen in chapter 10, but there is no underestimating the profound consequences of the uprising – and its defeat. The noted Irish writer Hubert Butler summed up the dire aftermath of the failure of the United Irishmen:

> Tone's rebellion, as we know, was an utter calamity and ushered in one of the worst of Irish centuries. The Irish Parliament, corrupt and unrepresentative but at least Irish, was dissolved; the Orange Order, seeing no tyranny but Popish tyranny, swept away the last traces of that Protestant Republicanism of the north on which Tone had based his hopes of a United Ireland. The Catholic Church in Ireland became increasingly segregationist and it was considered godless for a Catholic Irishman to be educated alongside his Protestant compatriots. The Irish people, whose distinctive character the eighteenth century had taken for granted, lost its language and, after the Famine, many of its traditions. A period of industrial expansion was followed by one of poverty and emigration. Finally, the partition of Ireland in the twenties of our century set an official seal on all the historical divisions of our country, racial and cultural and religious, which Tone had striven to abolish. (Butler 1985: 10)

The immediate punishment for failure in this, the first uprising in a century, was the decision to incorporate Ireland fully in the British empire via the constructed anew 'united kingdom'. The Irish parliament, weak and subservient as it was, voted for its own demise. That said, the outcome was not guaranteed in advance. The Catholic bishops of Ireland supported Union on the basis of the delivery of Catholic emancipation as promised by British Prime Minister Pitt. But industrial and commercial interests in Ulster were hostile, as was the Orange Order; three lodges in Dublin alone passed resolutions against it (Dudley Edwards 2000: 242). The Newtownbutler Lodge in County Fermanagh declared that all supporters of the Union 'should be execrated by their fellow subjects and by posterity' (quoted in Biggs-Davison 1973: 52).

Conclusions 1155-1801

If Ireland was the first colony, other places and peoples around the world rapidly shared the experience of colonisation. From 1155 onwards, there were obvious resonances between Ireland and other parts of the world that experienced the synergy between colonialism and imperialism sketched in chapter 2. This was especially true of shared experiences within the expanding English – and later British – Empire. Across centuries, we can observe a broad similarity between the Irish experience and that of other British colonies: the differences between coloniser and colonised were hierarchised and institutionalised; there were settlers, plantations and reservations; there were attempts at native incorporation yet the equivalent of the genocidal imperative 'To Hell or Connacht' was repeated in many different contexts.

As we shall discuss in more detail later, native and settler resistance to colonialism was also similar across these colonies. Grattan's Parliament looked to North America as a model of settler anti-colonialism; the United Irish movement presented a more radical and political anti-colonialism foreshadowing the methods and ideals of the great anti-imperialist movements of South America, Asia and Africa. Towards the end of the eighteenth century, these two tendencies of Irish anti-imperialism ensured a crisis in the Irish colonial state – and what was arguably another 'first': the earliest 'modern' anti-colonial uprising anywhere. Infused with the democratic ideals of the French Revolution, the United Irish movement advanced beyond the narrow concept of self-determination for settler colonists and offered a new, radical vision of inclusive, postcolonial self-determination rooted expressly in *mestizaje*. The colonial political and military response to the Rising was also profound and long-lasting – most obviously emblemised by the Union of 1801. Here was yet another first. This moment foreshadowed two centuries of colonial disengagement by all the European empires. They had to begin to frame a post-colonial solution – since self-determination for the colonised was unthinkable. They had to imagine a form of dominion that would replace the colony and yet leave most of the race, class and gender privileges of colonialism *in situ*.

Arguably, the resonance between Ireland and other colonies ends abruptly at this point. From 1801 onwards, Ireland was incorporated into a new, expanded UK state. From the first it was a core constituent of this novel state formation – now designated the United Kingdom of Great Britain and Ireland. Since Scotland was now absorbed into the notion of 'Great Britain', it was the Irish nexus specifically that made this formation 'united'. What this new union meant – and how it connected to the wider processes of British colonialism and imperialism – is the focus of our next chapter. It bears emphasis, however, that this development should be read in the context of the colonial paradigm. Despite the exceptional nature of this union, we insist that this was a colonial rather than an anti-colonial intervention. Rather than an alternative to colonisation, the Union was the culmination of over six hundred years of first English and then British colonisation of Ireland. The text confirmed the imperial logic of union. It was intended 'to promote and secure the essential interests of Great Britain and Ireland, and to consolidate the strength, power, and resources of the British empire'.

Union was deliberately and consciously a mechanism to prevent self-determination for Ireland. In this sense it constituted the defining act of colonisation. The period we have traced from 1155-1801 through all the multifarious strategies of conquest provides the two bookends for the process of colonisation. It frames the period from first 'contact' in 1169 to the point at which Ireland appears truly conquered in 'whole and perfect obedience' with the institution of the Union. Across 650 years can be traced a slow but inexorable transition from an Ireland independent of England to an Ireland integrated into the very heart of the British Empire.

By 1801, colonisation was completed and Ireland was colonised: the demography of settler colonialism – albeit markedly different north and south – was in place; the apparatus of colonial administration was in place; most importantly, the constitutional context was now fixed – with Ireland subordinated in the double lock of union and empire. In other words, the colonising process was over, and the colonial condition was now a state. Now the most relevant question vis-à-vis Ireland and colonialism was what this new constitutional status meant in terms of the lived experience of Ireland and Irishness. What did it mean economically and politically and sociologically to be locked within the colonial synergy of union and empire? Behind this there was a further question implicit. This was hardly even a straw in the wind in 1801, evident nowhere except in the minds of a small number of revolutionaries like Robert Emmet. Nevertheless, the embryonic problematic was there: could Ireland now *ever* be decolonised? Did the 'united for ever' commitment in the Acts of Union really mean *forever*?

Chapter 4

Acts of Union:
Ireland, England and Empire – 1801-1922

*My occupation is now of the most unpleasant nature, negotiating and jobbing with
the most corrupt people under heaven. I despise and hate myself every hour for engaging in such dirty work, and am supported only by the reflection that without an
Union the British Empire must be dissolved.* —Lord Cornwallis, 1798

*Unless we are much deceived, posterity will trace up to that famine the commencement
of a salutary revolution in the habits of a nation long singularly unfortunate, and
will acknowledge that on this, as on many other occasions, SupremeWisdom has educed
permanent good out of transient evil.* —Sir Charles Trevelyan, 1st Baronet, 1848

The Acts of Union 1800 were parallel acts of the separate parliaments of Great Britain
and Ireland which united the Kingdom of Great Britain and the Kingdom of Ireland.
This created the *United Kingdom of Great Britain and Ireland,* a multinational but – more
or less – unitary state. (This kingship had previously only represented a 'personal union'
of two monarchies in one person.) Both acts were passed with the same long title, An
Act for the Union of Great Britain and Ireland, and came into force on 1 January 1801.[1]
The merged Parliament of the United Kingdom met on 22 January 1801. Both acts,
with amendments, remain *statutes in force* in the United Kingdom of Great Britain and
Northern Ireland. They were finally repealed in the 26 counties in 1962.

Arguably the principal agent in this process was not named at all, remaining a
veritable ghost in the machine. In 1801 'England' was nominally a vestigial organ
inside Great Britain.[2] Yet England continued to wield enormous ideological power
at the heart of the Union – despite the fact it did not bear its name. Arguably,
England was *never* concretised in any kind of state formation.[3] Rather, it is best

---

[1] The short title of the act of the British Parliament is Union with Ireland Act 1800, assigned by the Short
Titles Act 1896. The short title of the act of the Irish Parliament is Act of Union (Ireland) 1800.

[2] The term 'British empire' was first used by an Elizabethan, John Dee. It seems to have been simply a
synonym for England and Wales. From the 18th century it was used to describe the British Isles and overseas
dependencies. Prior to this, the term Greater Britain entered the lexicon to incorporate white settlers in
the colonies. In the late 19th century the term 'Great Britain' was used to explicitly divide the empire along
racial grounds (see Jones 2006: 26, 35 and 36).

[3] The state was known as the 'Kingdom of England' before the Act of Union in 1707 – but was already a

located in terms of its otherness – the bit of Britain that is 'not Wales', the bit of Great Britain than is 'not Scotland'; and after 1801, the bit of the UK that is 'not Ireland'. Like Cosimo il Vecchio in Renaissance Florence, it exercises its power discretely, without ever assuming political office, *primus inter pares* in the Union. It was also, of course, at the heart of Empire. Yet, as Kipling was to observe, it is only clearly visible from the *imperial periphery*: 'What should they know of England, who only England know?'[4]

This Union of 1801 went on to assume enormous political and ideological power. With the – not insignificant – loss of the 26 counties in 1922 excepted, it has proved remarkably resilient. It survived the rise and fall of the British Empire – and still provokes less of the soul-searching that accompanies contemporary assessments of the virtues of imperialism. In 2018 British Prime Minister Theresa May was still waxing lyrical about 'our precious union' without qualm.[5] If patriotism is the last refuge of the scoundrel, unionism is usually the first resort in the English case. Thus in 2018 – amid Brexit crises and a gathering leadership challenge – May assuaged a hostile Tory conference with the promise of a Festival of Great Britain and Northern Ireland. This was anticipated as a 'nationwide festival in celebration of the creativity and innovation of the United Kingdom' (Devenport 2018b). Downing Street said it would mark the occasion with a number of events. Ironically, however, given the 'preciousness' of the continuing union, the centenary of the creation of Northern Ireland in 2021 – the imperial finesse that *salvaged* in part the union created in 1801 – was not specified on their list. May's successor, Boris Johnson, was even more aggressively unionist. He assumed power with a pledge to be 'prime minister of the whole United Kingdom' and set off on a tour of what he called the 'awesome foursome' UK nations. He insisted that union was 'stronger than ever', creating for himself the new title of 'minister for the union'.

Despite the persistence of the social formation it created, however, the immediate context of the Union was war and emergency. It sought to bring a new constitutional fix to the vexed colonial relationship between the English and Ireland detailed in the previous chapter. In 1801, Great Britain was still dealing with the aftermath of the United Irish rising and in the middle of a war against revolutionary France. The response to the rising

---

'multinational' formation, including Wales following its conquest by Edward I in 1284. Over much of this period, the Kingdom of England was in possession of substantial areas of France – as well as laying claim to the crown of France.

[4] 'The English Flag'. Despite the title, Kipling's poem was responding to the immolation of the union flag in Cork. This further confirms our observation about the oddly privileged status of 'England' within the Union.

[5] This was in the specific circumstances of Brexit where May was dependent on Northern Ireland unionist politicians in Westminster to stay in power. That said, the claims of preciousness sometimes reeked of protesting too much. For example, the threat of Scottish independence led not only to trying to buy off nationalism through 'devolution max' but also loudly proclaiming the importance of maintaining the Union.

was to incorporate Ireland fully in the British state, a clear act of counterinsurgency. The Union was therefore an early form of emergency legislation – an embryonic defence of the realm act. This was, perhaps, apt given the way in which coercion and emergency legislation characterised the polity thereafter.

In addition, as Cornwallis, tasked with delivering Irish support for the Union, so astutely observed, the Union was also designed to save the Empire.[6] In the shadow of the loss of British America in 1781, the Union was intended to stabilise what was left of its still extensive empire. Thus, whatever else it involved, the Union marked a new phase in the outworking of *both* the colonial history of Ireland and the wider dynamics of the British Empire. Even in 1801, this new formation was sufficiently different to encourage pause for thought on this question: Was the Act of Union the formal end of colonialism in Ireland? As an even more powerful and self-conscious empire was forged around this new UK state and its imperial parliament through the nineteenth century, the question became more pressing. Had Ireland *become* an imperial power through its incorporation in the union?

Certainly, the union in 1801 tried to do more than simply replicate the eighteenth-century Protestant Ascendancy in a new – or 'unified' – form. It also involved an inchoate attempt to incorporate elements of the native Irish population. In this – over a century before such political calculus came to dominate around partition – there was an obsession with *demographics*. Long before the concept of 'gerrymandering' achieved currency in Northern Ireland, the UK state was being constructed around a sectarian calculus.[7] Moreover, the computation involved *balancing fine margins*: Irish Catholics would undoubtedly dominate any broadly representative Irish parliament, but they would be minoritised again by incorporation into a UK parliament. The outworking of these dynamics within the union – and their relationship to wider developments in imperialism and colonialism – is the problematic of this chapter.

---

[6] Cornwallis was not liked by many of his contemporaries. He was said to have a 'mental constitution ... of the highest order of commonplace [and was] entirely destitute of originality' (Seton-Karr. W.S. (1890), *The Marquis of Cornwallis*. Oxford: Clarendon Press, p. 193; quoted in Dix 2006: 200). But he was astute about the Ireland he was sent to govern after the United Irish rising. He judged that the causes of the rebellion were not local nor sectarian but were due to the 'infection' of French Jacobinism. He blamed Irish Protestants for labelling it instead as a Catholic rebellion. He argued that 'their prejudice ... prevented Protestants from understanding the true causes of the Rebellion' ... and that they 'exaggerated the strength and importance of the Rebellion in order to justify their demands for "violent measures" by way of response...' (207), measures he abhorred. He concluded of the Protestant militia and yeomanry that 'murder appears to be their favourite pastime' (208). He believed Catholics would prove loyal subjects if Protestants could be prevented from provoking them and that the Act of Union would curtail Protestant power, but that ultimately stability could only be assured through Catholic emancipation.

[7] Thus, Fitzgibbon, Lord Chancellor, 'became convinced that nothing but union could save Ireland from a "popish democracy"' (quoted in Bolton 1966: 13).

Emancipation

The implications of Catholic emancipation were already exercising minds across the Protestant ascendancies of *both* Great Britain and Ireland in the run-up to the Union. On the Irish side, the Ascendancy class – already laagered insecurely within a hostile mass of native, Catholic Gaels – had been further unnerved by the United Irish rising. On the British side there were well-grounded fears that a newly enfranchised Catholic majority in Ireland would transform the character of the Irish parliament and government – indeed, such a revolution had been the core objective of the United Irish movement. There were also more astute countervailing arguments. As early as November 1792, Pitt suggested joining Catholic suffrage to union:

> The idea has long been in my mind ... The admission of Catholics to a share of the suffrage could not then be dangerous – the Protestant interest in point of power, property and Church establishment would be secure because the decided majority of the supreme legislature would necessarily be Protestant... (Quoted in Bolton 1966: 12)

The Irish parliament was already ahead of Westminster in this matter – in 1793 Catholics in Ireland had regained the right to vote if they owned or rented property worth 40 shillings – i.e. they were 'men of property'. The franchise was limited to a small fraction of the Irish population, but the relief of 1793 meant that Irish Catholics who were otherwise qualified in terms of gender and wealth were enfranchised 35 years before their equivalents in England and Scotland. The Irish Parliament also passed the Maynooth College Act in 1795 which established St Patrick's College as Ireland's Catholic seminary. One reading of these developments is that Union happened not because the Irish Parliament was too reactionary for Westminster but rather that it was too progressive on the specific issue of emancipation. Thus, *before the Union*, the Irish colonial state and the Irish Parliament appeared to be reforming – and emancipating – much more quickly than the British one. In this context, there is a clear *minoritisation* argument. As Pitt had observed, the only way to prevent 'popish democracy' in Ireland was to absorb the native Irish Catholic population in Union. It was also true, however, that there was a clear separation between colonial sectarianism and the sectarianism of the British state. For example, toleration of Catholics was instituted in places across the British Empire – like Canada and Newfoundland – long before it was ever contemplated in Great Britain itself. In this regard, the Union brought Irish Catholics into a hyper-sectarian state formation and minoritised them in the process. Their defining status transformed from constituting the majority of the population in Ireland to becoming a minority (albeit sizeable) of the whole UK population.

One immediately pressing issue was the question of how many Irish MPs should sit in Westminster. This too involved a careful attention to demographics. If the actual population was taken as the measure, this would entail 108 Irish peers and 223 commoners. However, if Scotland were the measure, which had 16 peers and 45 commoners, that would work out at 45 Irish peers and 120 commoners. Even that was thought of as too much, so the decision was taken to have 32 Irish peers and 100 commoners. Lord Sheffield voiced the logic involved; he was opposed to the 'admission of 100 wild Irish. The intrusion of eighty is rather too much, 75 would be sufficient... I do not think any of our country gentlemen would venture into parliament if they were to meet 100 Paddies' (quoted in Bolton 1966: 86). It bears emphasis in this context that these abhorrent 'Paddies' were to be drawn exclusively from the settler colonial Ascendancy class – meeting native Irish in this context was still precluded by the surviving Penal Laws disenfranchising Catholics.

British concerns about the potential disloyalty of Catholic Ireland dovetailed with a new opportunity to recalibrate the relationship between the British state and the Catholic Church. In 1766, Pope Clement VIII had recognised the legitimacy of the Hanoverian dynasty and initiated a process of rapprochement between the Catholic Church and the British.[8] This process was hastened by the French Revolution. France was no longer the bastion of Catholic reaction but rather the centre of anti-clericaliam.[9] In this context the Catholic hierarchy in Britain and Rome was keen to reframe its relationship with the – still anti-Catholic but helpfully counterrevolutionary – British state. The British approach had already moved toward reconciliation and incorporation with the Catholic hierarchy in the establishment of Maynooth. But the threat remained that, if the Irish Parliament were to adopt a fuller version of Catholic emancipation, a Catholic parliament might secede from Great Britain and align with the French. In contrast, the same measure of emancipation within a united kingdom – with a clear Protestant majority – would pre-empt this possibility. These considerations led the British state to engineer the merger of the two kingdoms and their parliaments.[10]

---

[8] Following the death of James III on 1 January 1766, Clement refused to recognise his son – the Catholic Charles Edward Stuart – as King of Great Britain.

[9] The Catholic Church had good reason to fear the revolution. In 1789, the Gallican Church model – which had placed the French Church under the joint control of the pope and the monarch – was suppressed. The Church's land holdings were confiscated, and monastic orders were banned. An effigy of the pope was burnt at the Palais Royal. Pius VI condemned both the Declaration of the Rights of Man and the Civil Constitution of the Clergy and supported a league against the revolution. In 1796 French Republican troops under the command of Napoleon invaded Italy and defeated the papal troops. General Berthier marched to Rome in 1798, and, proclaiming a Roman Republic, demanded of the pope the renunciation of his temporal authority. Upon refusal, Pius was taken prisoner and he died in French custody in 1799. His successor Pius VII took a more cautious approach in dealing with Napoleon, signing the Concordat of 1801. In 1809, however, Napoleon invaded the Papal States again, resulting in his excommunication. Pius VII was taken prisoner and transported to France. He remained there until the fall of Napoleon in 1814.

[10] There were also less profound tensions within the operation of the 'personal union' of the Crown. For example, the Irish and British parliaments gave the Prince Regent different powers when they established a regency during King George III's 'madness'.

The Catholic hierarchy across Britain and Ireland was also strongly in favour of union – seeking Catholic emancipation in Great Britain and the right of Catholic MPs to sit in any unified Parliament.[11] In other words, this broad Catholic approach already carried a pan-UK vision which regarded Irish Catholics as a key tool for re-Catholicising – or at least de-sectarianising – the whole of the post-Union state. As such it formalised the logic of a long-term Catholic strategy – emancipation for Catholics across the UK on the back of a very specific Irish mobilisation toward that end. This pre-Union commitment took some time. After a long period of sectarian mobilisation and reaction in the UK, Catholic emancipation was finally achieved in 1829.[12] It bears emphasis that the sectarianism of the Irish state within the Union was unambiguous – Catholics remained legally excluded from many public offices and there was a virtual exclusion from many additional offices to which they had become eligible under the Catholic Relief Act of 1793.[13] Most significantly in political terms, only members of the established church were permitted to become MPs, though the great majority of the Irish population was Catholic, and even in Ulster the majority of Protestants was Presbyterian.[14]

---

[11] Archbishop of Dublin, John Troy (1739-1823), was in the vanguard of this process. In 1798 he issued a sentence of excommunication against Catholics joining the uprising. In a pastoral, he characterised the priests who joined the rebellion as 'vile prevaricators and apostates from religion, loyalty, honour, and decorum, degrading their sacred character, and the most criminal and detestable of rebellious and seditious culprits'. He argued that Catholic emancipation would never be conceded by the Irish parliament and was one of the most determined supporters of the Union. In 1799 he agreed to accept the veto of the British government on the appointment of Irish bishops and continued to support it even when the other Irish bishops, feeling they had been tricked by Pitt and Castlereagh, repudiated it. He listed the qualities that had delivered the series of gains for Catholics in the run-up to the Union: 'Your loyalty, your submission to the constituted authorities, your peaceable demeanour, your patience under long sufferings.... [S]ome legal disabilities still exclude the most loyal and peaceable Roman Catholics from a seat or a vote in Parliament, from the privy council, from the higher and confidential civil and military departments of the State. I grant it. But is it by rebellion, insurrection, tumult, or seditious clamour on your part that these incapacities are to be removed? Most certainly not...' (quoted in Hepburn 1980:14).

[12] Catholics continued to be barred from sitting in the UK Parliament until the Roman Catholic Relief Act 1829 made it lawful for any – otherwise qualifying – Catholic to sit and vote in either House of Parliament (except for Catholic priests who were prevented from standing for election to the House of Commons).

[13] Thomas Wyse documents the reality of this sectarian exclusion in an appendix to his *History of the Catholic Association* (1829). He lists in detail the thousands of Irish 'state offices' – from the Lord Chancellor downwards – from which Catholics experienced either *de jure* or *de facto* exclusion.

[14] The Parliamentary franchise was specifically withheld from Catholics by statute from 1727 to 1793. This barred about 80 percent of the male adult population from exercising the vote in Parliamentary elections. Restrictions on Catholics voting in Parliamentary elections had also been in place before 1727 under local by-laws. Earlier restrictions had been placed on Catholic voters, requiring that they should take discriminatory oaths of allegiance and abjuration before being allowed to vote. Other restrictions were designed to prevent Catholics taking public office, including Catholic peers and MPs in the Irish Parliament. In order to take their seats, MPs and peers had to take an oath abrogating the supremacy of the Pope and make a declaration that transubstantiation did not occur at the Last Supper. Bizarrely, Catholic peers continued to be summoned to the Irish Parliament but could not make such a declaration. In combination these measures ensured that, from 1692 until its abolition in 1800, the Irish Parliament was an exclusively Protestant assembly. Interestingly, 68 years later, only 37 of the 105 Irish MPs were Catholics (Lee 2008: 64).

In Ireland, this wider pan-UK Catholic strategy also had a countervailing, anti-democratic consequence in the context of the union. As UK emancipation approached, the Irish Franchise Act of 1829 *raised* the threshold for eligibility for the county franchise from 40 shillings to £10. The result was that the registered county electorate across Ireland *fell* by about 80 per cent as the franchise dropped from around 215,000 to under 40,000. Thus Catholic emancipation in the UK was bundled with the *disenfranchisement* of some 80 per cent of Irish Catholics. When the Irish Reform Act followed the English Great Reform Act in 1832, it was more modest than the English equivalent in terms of both the franchise and the redistribution of seats.[15] The electorate in Ireland was increased by about 19 per cent from the position in 1929. This remained a fraction of the number entitled to vote *before* the abolition of the 40-shilling county franchise in 1829 – the franchise that had persisted from the pre-Union Irish Parliament.[16]

In other words, the practical consequence of the Union for most Irish Catholics who had been enfranchised by the Irish Parliament in 1793 was that they were disenfranchised by the British Parliament in exchange for the right of a small number of elite Catholics to sit as MPs in Westminster. The impact in Ireland was a contradictory form of relief. The implications of this new reality in which Irish and Catholic interests overlap but do not combine echoes down the nineteenth century. The Catholic bourgeoisie was promised emancipation in return for Union – which is why the Catholic Church backed the process. The failure to deliver on that promise was what activated Daniel O'Connell and his successful – although, as we have seen, contradictory – emancipation campaign. Emancipation in turn started to give the Catholic bourgeoisie the incorporation across the UK (and therefore Irish) state that they pursued from the establishment of Maynooth onwards.

These cross-cutting strategic calculations are a reminder that the Acts of Union were anything but democratic. In 1800, power in Ireland was restricted to a tiny minority – the Anglo-Irish landed gentry of the Protestant Ascendancy.[17] A small section of this totally unrepresentative minority conspired to end Irish legislative independence and create 'our precious union'. The process was telling. Complementary acts had to be passed in the Parliament of Great Britain and the Parliament of Ireland because the

---

[15] Five additional MPs were created: one each for Belfast, Limerick, Waterford, Galway and the University of Dublin, but no boroughs were disfranchised.

[16] Nor was the process in any sense a modernising one. Westminster processes were often even more archaic and anti-democratic than those of the Irish parliament. For example, registration of parliamentary electors was not required until after 1832 at Westminster – except for the Irish counties following the inclusion of Irish seats in the post-Union Parliament.

[17] Behan's characterisation of 'a Protestant with a horse' is probably the best shorthand for the class position of this group. He also observed: 'An Anglo-Irishman only works at riding horses, drinking whiskey, and reading double-meaning books in Irish at Trinity College'. But the notion of a people who were only really at home on the ferry between Holyhead and Kingstown captures some sense of their otherness within both their Anglo and their Irish worlds.

Irish Parliament had recently gained a large measure of legislative independence under the Constitution of 1782. Many members of the Irish Parliament wanted to retain this autonomy and a motion for union was legally rejected in 1799.

The final passage of the Act in the Irish Parliament was achieved with substantial majorities through bribery in the forms of peerages and honours as well as straightforward payments, to secure a pro-union vote. The British government expended a great deal of effort, and money, to ensure the acquiescence of the Irish Ascendancy class. They paid out over one million pounds (about £32 million at current rates) in bribes to buy votes at a cost of £8,000 per vote (Mitchel 1876: 10). As one example, look at the case of Mr. John Bingham who owned the pocket borough of Tuam. 'He offered to sell its two votes … for £8000 to the opponents of the Union. Lord Castlereagh's party raised the price to £15,000. This settled the bargain. He was likewise made a peer and became Lord Clanmorris' (Davitt 1979: 29). Whereas the first attempt had been defeated in the Irish House of Commons by 109 votes against to 104 for, the second vote in 1800 produced a result of 158 for to 115 against. Echoing Burns' characterisation of the Act of Union between Britain and Scotland one hundred years earlier, a 'parcel of rogues' 'sold their country' for 'English gold'. As O'Connell put it to the UK parliament, 'the Union was achieved by crimes the most unparalleled'.[18] A tiny and palpably corrupt minority of the Ascendancy was responsible for ending the legislative independence of Ireland.

In summary, there was nothing democratic or virtuous about the Acts of Union – or the polity they created. The Union was a cynically anti-democratic and counter-revolutionary intervention.[19] This reactionary quality of the Union acknowledged, we want to address the more complex question of whether it *ended colonialism in Ireland*? We maintain that the answer to this question is *no* – and we detail our reasons below. However, we also recognise that this new state formation put Ireland – uniquely among countries colonised by the British – *within* the colonial metropole. There is no question that the Union profoundly *transformed* Ireland's relationship to colonialism.

The end of colonialism in Ireland?

While there was an *Irish* Parliament before the Union, there was now only a *British* government and administration in Ireland. Despite this momentous change, however, British executive authority in Ireland was characterised by *continuity* rather than change

---

[18] House of Commons, 'Repeal of the Union', 22 May 1834, p. 1158.

[19] For all the hyperbole that accompanies the notion of 'British democracy', this moment only arrives in 1948 with the Representation of the People Act. This abolished the last of the multi-member seats and the university constituencies. Thus, for the first time, each parliamentary election would apply the basic democratic principle of 'one person, one vote'. Of course, any recognition of 'British democracy' at this point must ignore the anti-democratic practice that was institutionalised in that part of the 'precious union' that constituted Northern Ireland. One measure of this was that Queen's University in Belfast continued to elect four MPs to the Stormont parliament until 1969.

following the Union. The dominant position of the Lord Lieutenant at Dublin Castle was central to the administration of the Kingdom of Ireland for much of its history. (Poynings' Law meant that the Irish Parliament lacked legislative independence and the Crown kept control of executive authority in the hands of the Lord Lieutenant and its own appointees rather than in the hands of ministers responsible to the Irish parliament.) Over time, the post of Chief Secretary increased in importance because of its role in managing legislative business for the British government in the Irish House of Commons.[20] While the Irish administration was not responsible to the parliament, it needed to ensure the passage of key legislative measures. The role of Chief Secretary became crucial in the negotiations before the Union when Castlereagh held the post.[21] The Chief Secretary's exercise of patronage and bribery were central to delivering the parliamentary majority for the Union.

This existing colonial system of British government and administration in Ireland continued broadly unchanged following the Union, with the offices of Lord Lieutenant and Chief Secretary retaining their respective roles. As the century progressed, however, the *Chief Secretary for Ireland* became the key political office in the British administration. Nominally subordinate to the Lord Lieutenant, the Chief Secretary to the Lord Lieutenant was effectively the British government minister with responsibility for governing Ireland from the Union until partition. The Chief Secretary, rather than the Lord Lieutenant, sat in the British Cabinet.[22] Meanwhile the Lord Lieutenant doubled as the more symbolic 'Viceroy' – with an associated imperial 'court' in Dublin's Phoenix Park. (These posts disappeared with partition. Executive responsibility was transferred to the President of the Executive Council in the Free State and the Prime Minister of Northern Ireland in the Six Counties.)[23] In terms of executive authority, therefore, there was a *broad colonial continuity from before the Union right up to partition*. While Ireland – like India – was administered separately from the British colonial office which administered most British colonies, it retained all the trappings of a colonial, *viceregal* administration.

Despite these administrative continuities, however, the new Union state sat in a complex relationship to wider British colonialism and imperialism. On the one hand, it was now at the epicentre of empire. The Union framed Westminster as the 'mother parliament' which now began to take on a complex duality – it was both

---

[20] The Chief Secretary sat as an MP in the Irish Parliament.

[21] Robert Stewart, Viscount Castlereagh, was the most reviled reactionary of his day. As well as repressing the United Irish rising and engineering the Union, he was responsible for the Peterloo Massacre in 1819. In response to the latter, Shelley wrote 'The Mask of Anarchy', including the lines: 'I met with murder on the way, he had a mask like Castlereagh'.

[22] The Chief Secretary was also *ex officio* President of the Local Government Board for Ireland from its creation in 1872.

[23] The Crown functions of the Lord Lieutenant were transferred to the offices of the 'Governor General' in the Free State – which was abolished by Fianna Fáil in 1936 – and the 'Governor of Northern Ireland' – which was abolished after the collapse of Stormont in 1973.

a representative British parliament – albeit one dominated by England – and an imperial parliament. In other words, it embedded two profoundly distinct functions – representative government for the UK and colonial *imperium*. In short, the Union was proto-democratic while the Empire was anti-democratic. While the Union did not really become formally democratic – or indeed emancipate most Irish Catholics – until 1918, the potentiality for democracy was there. It was a social formation that could – if necessary – function democratically – hence the calculations around absorbing Irish Catholics in the run-up to Union. The Empire on the other hand could not countenance democracy – even in the white dominions democratisation led inexorably towards separation. The very ridiculousness of the idea of seeking democratic legitimacy for a polity such as the Raj confirms this point.

The representative element within this duality is *relatively* easy to track. It bears emphasis that the population that this parliament represented was not emancipated. For almost the entire period under consideration the UK was *absolutely not a democracy*; a *majority* of adult citizens only got the vote in consequence of the suffragist victory after WWI. Moreover, there was no full adult suffrage until after WWII. From 1801 onwards, however, Westminster was a representative assembly for the UK across constituencies comprising the whole jurisdiction. It was characterised by a political debate between representative political parties and associated changes in policy and government. These broadly reflected the interests of the (minority) British electorate they represented in this parliament. Furthermore, this representative aspect broadly democratised across the century and a half that followed the Union.[24] By 1884 the polity had to pay some attention to securing its legitimacy across a new working-class constituency:

> The Third Reform Act [1884] was the first UK-wide reform. It introduced a uniform Parliamentary franchise qualification across all parts of the UK and equalised the franchise between county and borough voters. This change benefited working class county voters the most and led to a 70% increase in those eligible to register to vote. Although this was a significant advance still only about one quarter of the adult population (those 21 years or over) could register to vote. (House of Commons Library 2013)

This democratic deficit bears emphasis – even at this stage the franchise only represented *one quarter of the electorate that would have voted in a democracy*. Its reforming and emancipating character was not that it had instituted democracy, only that it was *less unrepresentative* than that which had preceded it. It had developed a broad propertied franchise alongside elections and elected members who went on to constitute governments. (This also ignores the continuing constitutional power of the House of Lords and the Monarch – both institutions were, of course, formally anti-democratic.)

---

[24] It would also be a mistake to overemphasise this notion of democratising representation; as late as 1910 nearly a quarter of MPs were returned unopposed. Moreover, the Great Reform Act 1832 was the first to explicitly state that registered voters had to be male.

The Irish dimension to this evolving representative element of the parliament is also relatively easy to track in terms of the Union. After 1801, the Irish Houses of Parliament were abrogated and Irish constituencies added to the Westminster process.[25] There was now Irish representation in both the House of Commons and the House of Lords at Westminster. Correspondingly, as the UK state homogenised its franchise, a greater proportion of the Irish population achieved some degree of political power. But it was not until 1884 that the franchise in Ireland returned to the level it had been in 1793 under the Irish Parliament. Moreover, it was not until over 100 years *after* the Union that even a *majority* of adults in the UK (and thus Ireland) were given the vote with the post-WWI Representation of the People Act 1918.[26] In Ireland, of course, this provided the franchise that elected the First Dáil. *This was the first time that the Irish people had been presented with an opportunity to express their democratic will.* Of course, younger women were still excluded from the franchise and the anti-democratic power of the House of Lords and the Crown remained *in situ*, but this was the closest we ever got to emancipation in Ireland.[27] Here was 'popish democracy' realised. This was the first – and last – democratic election in a 32-county Ireland.

Imperium

As argued earlier, Westminster embedded two profoundly distinct functions – colonial *imperium* as well as representative government for the UK. Thus, alongside its 'representative' function, Westminster also embodied the imperial parliament. While the British monarch partially personified the Emperor/Empress at the apogee of this system, the Parliament was the *de facto* imperial authority.[28] This imperium was often amorphous and contradictory. But the key element is that it had *no* representative quality. It was not simply undemocratic, it was profoundly *anti-democratic* in the sense that it neither pretended nor sought legitimacy from the peoples it governed. From Canada through Africa and India to Australia – across all the peoples it governed – its

---

[25] The Articles of Union provided for 32 Irish Members of the House of Lords and 100 Irish Members of the House of Commons of the new United Kingdom Parliament. The Irish seats in the House of Commons were to comprise two Members each from the 32 counties, two each from Dublin and Cork and one Member from Trinity College, Dublin. The remaining 31 MPs were to come from the largest 31 boroughs, based on taxable wealth. This meant that many parliamentary boroughs that had representation in the Irish Parliament were merged into their respective counties.

[26] This legislation repealed most previous voting qualifications and universal male suffrage based on residence, rather than property ownership, was established. Women over 30 years of age who qualified for a local government vote – or married women whose husband qualified for a local government vote – were able to register to vote in Parliamentary elections for the first time.

[27] The Irish electorate increased from some 700,000 in 1910 to around two million in 1918 (Jackson 2010: 210). In the UK, younger women were only enfranchised on the same basis as men with the 'Flapper Act', the Representation of the People Act 1928. In contrast, the 1922 Constitution of the Irish Free state reduced the voting age for women in elections for Dáil Éireann from 30 to 21, the same as for men.

[28] Thus, the British sovereign did not assume the title Emperor/Empress of the British Empire. This remained true even after the incorporation of India and the declaration of Victoria Saxe-Coburg as 'Empress of India'.

writ was characterised by the fact that its subjects were *not* represented in the imperial parliament at Westminster. Given this absence of representation, emancipation was not simply difficult or challenging, it was *impossible*.

Thus, the Westminster Parliament – in parallel with the British Colonial Office – was the political nucleus of the *whole* British colonial and imperial system. This duality was further complicated by the fact that this imperial role evolved significantly over time. Something that was largely implicit in 1801 became much more significant in the context of the nineteenth century as it came to administer 'the greatest empire the world has ever seen'. It also subsequently *receded* in importance through the twentieth century as this empire was reduced by decolonisation.[29]

The key point is that the Irish – or at least a significant proportion of the Irish political class – were incorporated in this imperial role through the Union after 1801. This began to complicate the Irish relationship with empire. In this sense, the Union situated Ireland *inside* the mothership of empire – Ireland had an entrée denied to even the whitest of white dominions. The Irish could through expression of representative democracy in the UK Parliament both influence and be held accountable for the politics – and administration – of empire. In turn, this constitutional anomaly facilitated an Irish nationalist imperialism.[30]

At this juncture, it is sometimes difficult to remember how embedded notions of empire were in all aspects of Irish politics in the lead-up to partition. There was an incongruous cocktail of Irish nationalism, monarchism and imperialism. Take, for example, Daniel O'Connell's response to the visit of George IV to Dublin in August 1821. It would subsequently become apparent that George IV was a staunch *opponent* of Catholic emancipation, but O'Connell got caught up in the enthusiasm of the time. He decorated his home in Dublin and displayed a bright transparency on the drawing room window inscribed: 'George IV, the only king that declared the Crown was held in trust for the good of the people. Erin go Bragh' (Dwyer 2011).

After the Irish Parliamentary Party was formed in 1874 it also initially organised on this principle. Its first leader, Isaac Butt, suggested that a Home Rule Ireland would become the ideal collaborative partner for the expanding British Empire. The Empire

---

[29] For all its proclaimed 'greatness', it was also relatively short. As Morris reminds us, the man who wrote its paean lived to write its epitaph. She was juxtaposing here Elgar's arch-imperialist 'Pomp and Circumstance March' with his sombre 'Cello Concerto' written after the First World War (Morris 1968: 342). Elgar also made a contribution to the Celtic revival – his other work includes incidental music for the play *Grania and Diarmid* by George Moore and WB Yeats (1901).

[30] Irish representation in the imperial parliament also provided a unique opportunity to reject imperialism. Michael Davitt campaigned unsuccessfully to have Dadabhai Naoroji, an Indian resident in London, returned to the British parliament from an Irish constituency in order 'to give a direct voice in the house of commons to Indian nationalism…' (Moody 1981: 549). We address this dynamic in much greater depth in chapter 10. It implies a significant wider symbolism to the Sinn Féin vote in 1918 – it was the first democratic repudiation of the imperial parliament. No other colony had been provided the opportunity to repudiate its imperial role in this way but the Irish people – more through accident than design – were provided a voice to reject empire.

offered a better framework than the Anglo-Irish Union for equal trading rights for Irish merchants and manufacturers, while continued Irish participation in the imperial system opened doors for migrants, merchants, civil servants and entrepreneurs. Butt's Home Rule campaign therefore acknowledged the 'practical benefits' of imperial partnership and of a shared imperial culture, with Ireland supporting in the co-management of the world's 'greatest empire'. He also argued that the colonies 'belonged to Ireland as much as England – we paid dearly enough for them' (Townend 2007: 165).

Examples abound of this kind of synergy between Irish nationalism and imperialism. T.W. Rolleston, a committed Home Ruler, stated in a lecture in the United States in 1908: 'Personally, I am a Home Ruler and I no more want to see my country cut loose from the British Empire than a citizen of New York wants to cut loose from the United States' (quoted in *Facts of Radical Misgovernment* 1909: 10). Even Erskine Childers, before his conversion to the republican cause, wrote in *The Round Table* that Ireland had nothing to gain by separation from England. 'The truth is that Ireland has taken her full share in winning and populating the Empire. The results are hers as much as Britain' (quoted in Murphy 2007: 78).

From this distance, the other startling observation is that, despite Arthur Griffith's – and the pre-1917 Sinn Féin's – fixation with Austro-Hungary and the notion of 'dual monarchy', the Union had to some extent already anticipated this model. Of course, neither Ireland nor Irishness had anything approaching a formal equality with either Englishness or Britishness in the construction of the state. But it *was* a 'united kingdom' and it did formally name 'Ireland' as a co-partner of this structure. If India was the 'jewel in the crown' of Empire, Ireland was the *named* junior partner of the UK – and none of the other national partners (England, Scotland, Wales) even got a mention. Those who wanted 'dual monarchy' might have advocated an imperialist reformism that would have delivered a kind of equal ownership of empire. Put crudely, if it had been renamed the 'British and Irish Empire' this might have been sufficient for Irish proponents of Kossuth and the Hungarian model.[31] Moreover, Ireland broadly followed this trajectory towards imperial dominion through the 19th century. As stated above, most Irish political leaders took the benefits of Empire as a given while Dublin continued to fashion itself – albeit alongside many other contenders – as 'the second city of Empire'.[32]

Irish political influence grew at Westminster through the nineteenth century in the context of the widening franchise. Over time the 'constitutional nationalist' Irish Parliamentary Party – with some 20 per cent of Westminster seats – became a key powerbroker. Its core demand of Home Rule was eventually supported by the

---

[31] Curiously, this formation is echoed recently by the 'British and Irish Lions' rugby team – this was characterised as the 'British Lions' up until 2001. A belated sensitivity to Irish history was resolved by the addition of the 'and Irish' element.

[32] From this distance, the more remarkable aspect of this was the survival of republicanism and Irish anti-imperialism in the context of all the explicit enticements of Empire. We address this in more depth in chapter 10.

British Prime Minister, William Gladstone, who suggested that Ireland would follow in Canada's footsteps as a dominion within the empire. The 1886 Home Rule bill was, however, defeated in Parliament through the electoral alliance between the Tory Party and Liberal Unionists. Although the bill, if passed, would have granted Ireland less autonomy within the UK than the Canadian *provinces* had within their own federation, many MPs feared that a partially independent Ireland would mark the beginning of the break-up of the empire.

A second Home Rule bill was also defeated for similar reasons in 1893. A third bill was passed by Parliament in 1914, but not implemented because of the outbreak of WWI. This was the first to introduce the idea of partition – although initially this was to be allowable on a county by county basis and it was assumed that only four – those with Protestant majorities – would be excluded. This principle was conceded by the British government – and by the Irish Party – in the face of unionist organisation and the Curragh mutiny.[33]

Most significantly, the duality of the union project was finally exposed by this process. Westminster could not in the end resolve the contradictions between its representative and imperial roles. As unionist historian Hugh Shearman (1952: 117) put it, 'Irish policy now entered deeply into the rivalries of the two main British parties in a way in which no other similar Imperial question, such as Indian policy, has ever done'. This contradiction was centred on the limits of emancipation embedded in the union. It would lead – ultimately – to the break-up of both the union and the Empire. However, there is a more profound implication to all of this: the union and Empire were not *ever* separate projects and thus the breakup of the UK would indeed mark the final break-up of the Empire.

Catastrophe

Any simplistic reading of Irish integration within a gradually reforming and democratising post-Union UK state is cleaved grotesquely by *An Gorta Mór*, the Great Hunger (Woodham-Smith 1962). Whatever its causes, there is broad agreement about the profound impact of what the English constructed as 'the famine' as 'the greatest social disaster to occur in any one country in nineteenth-century Europe' (Crowley et al. 2012: xvi). In this one episode the Union saw a literal *decimation* of the population of the UK 'cleared' by starvation and related disease and emigration.[34] The scale was, of

---

[33] In March 1914, with Home Rule inevitable, British army regiments stationed in the Curragh, County Kildare, were instructed to prepare for action against northern unionists organising militarily and politically against Home Rule. A substantial number of officers responded that they would resign if ordered to move against the Ulster unionists. The British government backtracked, stating that there had never been any intention of acting against the Ulster Volunteer Force.

[34] The 1841 UK Census counted the population of England and Wales to be 15.9 million. Ireland's population was 8.2 million in 1841 – with widespread under-recording recognised. The population of Scotland was 2.6 million. Even after recent unparalleled immigration the population of the island of Ireland only reached 6.6 million in 2018.

course, even more destructive in Irish terms: a population of some 9 million on the eve of *An Gorta Mór* was halved over a generation – and has never reached that level again. But the 'UK' locus of this episode bears emphasis – it was not something that 'happened in Ireland' – rather it was subjects of the Union that died. It took place not just within the Empire but *within the Union, within the UK state*. A population which had been offered no choice in the Act of Union and which had been substantially further disenfranchised within that new formation, was exterminated. The imperial logic behind this genocide was hard to fathom. As Daniel O'Connell observed poignantly of the British: 'You have not made Ireland prosperous and her misery has been of no advantage to you'.[35]

An Gorta Mór was a catastrophe – an Irish Holocaust or Nakba. The experience was so huge and so terrible that, arguably, the Irish people have never been able to address it properly. Thus, almost every Irish village maintains a war memorial to those who died fighting in support of the survival of the British Empire, but the mass graves of *An Gorta Mór* are still referenced *sotto voce*. There are few memorials to the millions who died – and most of these have only appeared in the last twenty years.[36] The Union created a situation that could at least tolerate – and perhaps engineer – a catastrophe that has frequently been referred to as genocide (McVeigh 2008; Coogan 2012).[37] Of course, there are debates about this term as intentionality is taken to be a central element, at least in international law terms, in classing actions as genocidal. The point is a moot one, however; even if nothing more was involved than an act of omission, 'the greatest empire the world has ever seen' was able to govern and administer a decimation *of the population of the Union itself*. The Union promised emancipation, but it delivered catastrophe.

The political economy of the Union created both this mass starvation and the refusal to provide adequate relief. From the moment of union, it was clear that a newly liberated Irish economy could never catch up with that of its stronger neighbour, the same neighbour which kept it subordinate for so long. One peculiar example was the attempt by merchants in Belfast and Galway to establish slave-trading companies in the 1780s (Rolston and Shannon 2002: 17-18). In Belfast the inaugural meeting was

---

[35] House of Commons, 'Repeal of the Union' 22 May 1834, p. 1158.

[36] The Lá Cuimhneacháin Náisiúnta an Ghorta Mhóir or National Famine Commemoration Day is an annual observance in Southern Ireland. A week-long programme of events leads up to the day, usually a Sunday in May. It has been organised officially by the Irish state since 2008. The British state has, however, been conspicuous by its absence. In 1996 British Prime Minister John Major blocked a proposed ecumenical service in Liverpool to mark the 150th anniversary of *An Gorta Mór*. See Phoenix 2020.

[37] In 1846 the Duke of Cambridge stated: 'Ireland is not in so bad a state as has been represented. I understand that rotten potatoes, and even grass properly mixed, afford a very wholesome and nutritious food. We all know that Irishmen can live upon anything, and there is plenty of grass in the fields, even if the potato crop should fail' (quoted in Dunlop 2015: 320). This was no Swiftean parody but a callousness that speaks to genocide. The UN Convention on the Prevention and Punishment of the Crime of Genocide (1951), Article II is clear that the term does not simply refer to specific actions – such as killing members of a group or causing them serious bodily or mental harm, and deliberately inflicting on the group conditions of life calculated to bring about its physical destruction in whole or in part – but insists that these acts are 'committed with intent to destroy, in whole or in part, a national, ethnical, racial or religious group'.

interrupted by Thomas McCabe, a future United Irishman: 'May God eternally damn the soul of the man who subscribes the first guinea'. Opposition to slavery was strong in Belfast, as Oloudah Equiano, a former slave, found in 1791 (Equiano 1789). A slave trading company would have faced fierce opposition had it materialised. However, Belfast, like Galway, was unable to break into this global industry and paradoxically, imperial domination meant that Ireland avoided direct participation in the slave trade. Like the corner store trying to break into a market dominated by transnational companies, the odds were loaded completely against success.

In practice, being a minor partner in the imperial project meant that the Irish economy was held back in many ways. Cottage industries, such as wool and linen production, suffered; by 1830 the whole of Ireland exported less linen than Dundee in Scotland (Biggs-Davison 1973: 54). In 1800 the Irish national debt was over £32 million; fifteen years later it was £112.5 million (Shearman 1952: 65). But there was no denying the value of the Union to the imperial project in Britain. To cite one example: with poverty and famine at home, many Irish people joined British military forces where they became a crucial part of the imperial project. Irish Catholics in the nineteenth century enrolled in British military forces disproportionately to their numbers in the UK population. By 1830 the Irish constituted 42 per cent of the British Army at a point when they made up 32 per cent of the United Kingdom population overall (Jeffery 1996b: 94). In 1771, half of the private army of the East India Company was Catholic (Karsten 1983: 56-7).[38] One quarter of the seamen with Nelson at Trafalgar were Irish (McDowell 1974: 58). 8,500 of the 28,000 British troops under Wellington at the Battle of Waterloo were Irish (Harvey 2015).

In military terms there is no doubt that Irish soldiers in Britain's empire were frequently highly efficient. Dublin-born Private Thomas Byrne won the Victoria Cross for his actions at the Battle of Omdurman in 1885 when a British force under General Kitchener killed 13,000 Sudanese Mahdists with only 47 British casualties. Byrne went on to fight in the Boer War. As the arch-imperialist Henry Stanley recounts, the Irish were very active at the Battle of Magdala in 1868 when British forces defeated the ruler of Abyssinia:

> First came an Irish regiment, each soldier bearded like a pard, and bronzed by the tropic sun, all veterans inured to campaigns in India, Himalaya snows, and fervid days in Scinde. Above their heads waved the regimental banner which was tossed several times on the deadly fields of the Iberian Peninsula, and had received reverence from Wellington. (Stanley 1896: 60)

Stanley breathlessly recounts their exploits in descriptions which would not be out of place in *Boys' Own*: 'No obstacle could stop the excited Irishmen. They prised up the fence; they leaped forward and fired volleys into the very faces of the Abyssinians.'

---

[38] Theobald Wolfe Tone had at one point half-heartedly applied to join the East India military service. His brother, William Henry, did enlist and was killed in battle in India in 1802.

While Catholics were the foot soldiers throughout the empire in the 19th century, their officers were usually either English or Anglo-Irish. One sure outlet for many Anglo-Irish men was through the imperial civil service where they acquired steady jobs in India and elsewhere. They also became civil administrators or police chiefs in various countries. Lord Dufferin from County Down was Viceroy of India in 1885 when the Indian National Congress was formed. He immediately drew parallels with Home Rule agitation in Ireland and warned that some decisive action was necessary if India was to avoid Irish-style political unrest (Kapur, 1997: 14). Sir Charles Tegart, police commissioner of Calcutta, was born in County Meath. He was known for his ruthless suppression of Bengali revolutionary nationalists at the beginning of the 20th century (who incidentally drew their inspiration from Irish nationalists). When Tegart was honoured by the Caledonian Society of Calcutta in 1924, one speaker summed up succinctly the imperial value of such Anglo-Irish functionaries: 'I always think an Irishman is specially suited to be a policeman. Being by instinct "agin the government" he knows exactly what people who want to make trouble feel like and is able to forestall their action' (quoted in Silvestri 2000: 40).[39]

Rural Ireland in the 19th century was dominated by a class of rich landlords, many of whom were absentees, living well in England off the rents from their Irish land. Daniel O'Connell estimated that 'surplus revenue and absentee rents spent in England ensured that £9 million of Irish money was annually spent in England' (Mitchel 1876: 38). The collection of these rents was in the hands of Irish middlemen who were often noted for their ruthless determination to extract as much as possible from the impoverished people who worked the land, endlessly subdividing plots in the process. The average rural smallholder paid £7-17s-11d in taxes and tithes per annum, but earned £5-16s-7d, a shortfall of £2-0s-6d (Lewis 1977: 21). In Munster a rural small holder had to work 240 days to pay a year's rent (Burns 1974: 12). The Irish peasantry was left almost entirely dependent on the potato as their staple diet.

When the potato crop failed because of blight, as it did frequently not only in Ireland but elsewhere in western Europe, the peasants' prospects were grim. Elsewhere the peasantry was not so dependent on a single food source. Because of the small size of Irish holdings, there was little scope for small peasant farmers to diversify crops or produce large surpluses. Moreover, sovereign states elsewhere could intervene to control exports of other food sources if one failed. Given Ireland's incorporation into the British political and economic system, there was no scope for such intervention. In Britain a *laissez faire* philosophy was in the ascendant. Ireland would have to care for its own impoverished masses: '… the maxim was that "the property of Ireland must support the poverty of Ireland;" without the least consideration of the fact that the property of Ireland was all this time supporting the luxury of England' (Mitchel 1876: 213).

---

[39] Later, Tegart was active with the Black and Tans in Palestine (see Cronin 2017).

The political economy of *An Gorta Mór* is most clearly illustrated by the work of the colonial administrator Charles Trevelyan. Trevelyan described the famine as an 'effective mechanism for reducing surplus population' as well as 'the judgement of God'. He insisted: 'The real evil with which we have to contend is not the physical evil of the Famine, but the moral evil of the selfish, perverse and turbulent character of the people'. In his book *The Irish Crisis*, published in 1848, Trevelyan described the famine as 'a direct stroke of an all-wise and all-merciful Providence', one which exposed 'the deep and inveterate root of social evil'. Trevelyan was also influential in persuading the government to do nothing to restrain mass evictions. It bears emphasis that this strategy *was a conscious political act*. Historians like Lyons broadly agree that the initial response of the British government to the outbreak of the famine was 'prompt and relatively successful'. But the Peelite Relief Programmes that were in operation during the first year of the Famine were shut down in July 1846 by the new Chancellor Sir Charles Wood on Trevelyan's orders.[40] Trevelyan insisted that they were creating dependency and reframed the British response from the perspective that 'God sent the calamity to teach the Irish a lesson, that calamity must not be too much mitigated'.[41] And he signalled the positive consequences of such an approach to those that raised concerns:

> We must not complain of what we really want to obtain. If small farmers go, and their landlords are reduced to sell portions of their estates to persons who will invest capital we shall at last arrive at something like a satisfactory settlement of the country.[42]

Agriculture was actually booming in Ireland. But the bulk of what was produced was exported to feed the expanding proletariat and others in England as the industrial revolution took off. Between 10 October 1845 and 5 January 1846, over 30,000 oxen, bulls and cows, over 30,000 sheep and lambs, over 100,000 pigs, and large quantities of wheat, barley and oats were exported to England (Curtis 1994: 41). 'In 1847 alone food to the value of £44,958,000 sterling was grown in Ireland, according to the statistical returns for that year. But a million of people died for want of food all the same' (Davitt 1979: 66). As Mitchel (1876: 112) concluded, '… a government ship sailing into any harbour with Indian corn was sure to meet half a dozen sailing out with Irish wheat and cattle'. For him, the consequence was clear: '… the exact correlative of a Sunday dinner in England is a coroner's inquest in Ireland' (Mitchel 1876: 125).

---

[40] Wood stated on one occasion: '… except through a purgatory of misery and starvation, I cannot see how Ireland is to emerge into anything approaching either to quiet or prosperity' (quoted in Boylan 2006: 175).

[41] For example, the British government response institutionalised famine-related clearances. The 'Gregory clause' of the Poor Law, named after William H. Gregory, MP – future husband of Lady Gregory of the Irish Literary Revival – prohibited anyone who held at least one quarter of an acre from receiving relief. The effect was that no starving tenant could receive public outdoor relief, without first relinquishing all their land to their landlord. Mitchel's observation was characteristically acerbic: 'It is the able-bodied idler only who is to be fed – if he attempted to till but one rood of ground, he dies'.

[42] Letter to Edward Twisleton, Chief Poor Law Commissioner in Ireland.

Those who could emigrated in vast numbers, sometimes with the financial support of sympathetic landlords, to England and North America. *An Gorta Mór* created upwards of two million Irish refugees. Starved and sick, many of them failed to make it to a promised land. More than 100,000 emigrated to North America in 1847 alone; 17,000 died, usually from typhus, during the journey and another 21,000 on arrival (Curtis 1994: 49). 'Ireland, perhaps, was the only country in the world which had both surplus produce for export and surplus population for export; – too much food for her people, and too many people for her food' (Mitchel 1876: 82).

Thus the key fact about *An Gorta Mór* is that there was sufficient food *within Ireland* to feed the Irish people who were allowed to starve throughout the 'famine' (Ó Tuathaigh 1990: 220). Moreover, in terms of the *intent* of the imperial government at Westminster, the passing of the Poor Law Amendment Act 1847 at the very height of the starvation was an act of supreme abnegation by both the UK and the empire. The implications were presented for all to see during the parliamentary debates on the Act. For example, Lord Courtenay – himself an absentee landlord and supporter of the Act – made the contemporary situation brutally clear:

> One question, however, did not seem to him to have been answered—it was, what was to be done with the existing state of things in Ireland?... No answer had been given; but the fact remained, that there were two or three millions of people in Ireland, who if not employed or relieved must starve. (HC Deb 15 March 1847 vol 90 c1377)

In the event, people were neither employed nor relieved and millions did starve. In these circumstances, the notion that 'the relief of extreme poverty in Ireland should be placed upon the property of Ireland' inevitably condemned millions to death. This was unambiguously an intentional act. And the wider policy is framed in some detail by its principal architect Charles Trevelyan in his *The Irish Crisis*. It bears emphasis that this analysis was published in 1848, right in the middle of the starvation.

Indignation at the situation managed to unite otherwise opposed sections of public opinion. Archbishop John Hughes, the Tyrone-born, conservative and frequently racist Catholic bishop of New York, and John Mitchel, son of a Presbyterian clergyman, and a radical republican, were in agreement in assessing the British state's role in the famine:

> Let us be careful, then, not to blaspheme Providence by calling this God's famine. The state, that great civil corporation which we call the state, is bound, so long as it has power to do so, to guard the life of its members from being sacrificed by famine from within as much as from their being slaughtered by the enemy from without. (Archbishop Hughes, quoted in Davitt 1979: 51)[43]

---

[43] Hughes was later used to add some – much needed – community balance to the odd construction that is the 'Ulster American Folk Park' in Tyrone. His childhood cottage was added to the park to include a Catholic 'Ulster American' – regardless of the reality that Hughes own identity would have been unambiguously 'Irish' or 'Irish American'. His initial employment as an 'overseer of slaves' in Maryland and his opposition to abolition (Cheng 2018: 134-5) remain unacknowledged.

Mitchel takes up the same theme of blasphemy:

> The English, indeed, call that famine a 'dispensation of Providence' and ascribe it
> entirely to the blight of the potatoes. But potatoes failed in like manner all over
> Europe; yet there was no famine save in Ireland. The British account of the matter,
> then, is first, a fraud – second, a blasphemy. The Almighty, indeed, sent the potato
> blight, but the English created the famine. (Mitchel 1876: 219)[44]

Indignation about the Famine and Britain's role in it fed into the political project
of Mitchel and those gathered round the newspaper *The Nation*, the Young Irelanders.
They took a firm republican stance in terms of Britain's involvement in Ireland. Their
willingness to propose violent rebellion led to one brief and fruitless military encounter
which resulted in the transportation of Mitchel and others to Van Diemen's Land.
Their espousal of rebellion was often rhetorical, sometimes even tongue in cheek, but
nonetheless striking. Mitchel wrote an article for *The Nation*,

> in reply to a London Ministerial journal, which, in advocating Coercion for Ireland,
> had pointed out that the railroads then in progress on construction would soon
> bring every part of the island within six hours of the garrison of Dublin. The Nation
> showed how effectually railroads could be made impassable to troops – how easily
> troops could be destroyed upon them, and how useful the iron of them would be
> in making pikes. (Mitchel 1876: 111)

In response the government closed down the newspaper, a not insignificant blow to a
paper with a readership of 250,000 (Foster 1988: 311).

Their support for violence put them at loggerheads with 'the Liberator', Daniel
O'Connell, lawyer, orator and organiser of mass campaigns. His skill was undeniable,
in terms of oratory and popular mobilisation. At heart, his goal involved achieving for
the emergent Catholic bourgeoisie the benefits which had accrued to the Protestant
bourgeoisie as a result of the Act of Union. He succeeded in his campaign for Catholic
emancipation and then moved on to a campaign to repeal the Act of Union. His
opposition was not to England *per se* but to the economic and political obstacles in
the path of Irish development as a result of British influence. He was a royalist, on
one occasion presenting King George IV with a laurel crown and pledging to donate
money to build him a palace in Ireland (Curtis 1994: 25), and on another referring
to Queen Victoria as someone, 'who has ever shown us favour, and whose conduct
has ever been full of sympathy and emotion for our sufferings' (Mitchel 1876: 29).
This was the same monarch whom many in Ireland had dubbed 'the famine queen'.
John Mitchel astutely judged the successful campaign of Daniel O'Connell for
Catholic emancipation as, 'a measure for the consolidation of the "British Empire";
it opened high official position to the wealthier Catholics and educated Catholic

---

[44]There was a potato blight across northern Europe at the time (phytophthora infestans) which led to famine
and death in Belgium, Denmark, Sweden, France, Prussia, Spain and the Netherlands. Scotland was badly
hit. But nowhere did the famine reach the horrific proportions that it did in Ireland.

gentlemen; and thus separated their interest from that of the peasantry' (Mitchel 1876: 15-16).

Mitchel, among others, was well aware of O'Connell's limited political aspirations and saw his 'monster meetings' as theatrics in the face of state power:

> What care the government how many thousands of people may meet peacefully and legally, or in what trappings they dress themselves, or to what tunes they march, or what banners they may flaunt – while there are fifty thousand bayonets in all our garrisons, beside the Orange Yeomanry? (Mitchel 1876: 56)

Ultimately Mitchel blamed O'Connell for the failure to achieve revolutionary change:

> To him and to his teaching, then, without scruple, I ascribe our utter failure to make, I do not say a revolution, but so much as an insurrection, two years after, when all the nations were in revolt, from Sicily to Prussia, and when a successful uprising in Ireland would have certainly destroyed the British Empire, and every monarchy in Europe along with it. O'Connell was, therefore, next to the British Government, the worst enemy that Ireland ever had, – or rather the most fatal friend. (Mitchel 1876: 136)

The key question, however, related to the nature of that hoped for revolution. The central question was land, the impoverishment of the small farmers and the criminal levels of exploitation by landlords. Yet the Young Irelanders gathered around Mitchel and *The Nation* newspaper were also limited in terms of confronting this issue. They differed with O'Connell on many counts, not least the question of the use of violence. But as Lalor complained, the Young Irelanders failed to confront the question of land ownership. They failed to see that what was necessary was a class revolution:

> They wanted an alliance with the landowners. They chose to consider them as Irishmen and imagined they could induce them to hoist the green flag. They wished to preserve an Aristocracy. They desired, not a democratic, but a merely national revolution. (Quoted in Curtis 1994: 54)

From this perspective Lalor provided the definitive political economy of *An Gorta Mór*:

> Had the people of Ireland been the landlords of Ireland, not a single human creature would have died of hunger, nor the failure of the potato been considered a matter of any consequence... It is a mere question between a people and a class – between a people of eight millions and a class of eight thousand. They or we must quit this island. (*The Irish Felon* 24 June 1848, in Lalor n.d.: 71)

And who 'quit the island'? In 1911, the last census before partition, the Irish population was 4,390,219 – less than half of what it had been on the eve of *An Gorta Mór*. This was more than a decimation and arguably a genocide of British subjects – *within* the precious union and the 'greatest empire that ever was'.

Coercion

If *An Gorta Mór* was the acute consequence of Ireland's ongoing colonial status within the Union, the infrastructure of coercion needed to maintain order was its chronic attendant. Throughout the entire period from 1801-1921, force and coercion were at the heart of British control in Ireland. The British philosopher Thomas Carlyle stated: 'Ireland is like a half-starved rat, that crosses the path of an elephant. What must the elephant do? Squelch it – by heavens – squelch it' (quoted in Lalor 1895: 95). Others commented on the effects of such an approach. Engels wrote to Marx during a visit to Ireland in May 1856: '... one can already notice here that the so-called liberty of English citizens is based on the oppression of the colonies. I have never seen so many gendarmes in any country...' (quoted in Curtis 1994: 62). Little wonder that Jenny Marx (1981) concluded in 1870:

> Theoretical fiction has it that constitutional liberty is the rule and its suspension an exception, but the whole history of English rule in Ireland shows that a state of emergency is the rule and that the application of the constitution is the exception.

The coercion was relentless: '... in the first half-century after the Act of Union, Ireland was ruled by the ordinary law of the land for only five years' (Mulloy 1986: 8). Thus: 'Between 1800 and 1921, the British government brought in 105 separate Coercion Acts dealing with Ireland' (Farrell 1986: 5). The extent of repression was obvious in the proliferation of armed representatives of the British state, police and soldiers, throughout the country. A key task they had was that of aiding in the exploitation and repression of the peasantry:

> The process of exterminating the Irish people from their homes had progressed so far by 1908 that 60 per cent of the total acreage of Ireland was in grass lands. Fat cattle were grazing where homes had once stood. An army of 10,000 police to keep the peace in a country where there was not the shadow of crime. A yearly sum of $6,680,000 was wrested from a depopulated land to pay the salaries of 'Peelers', as they are contemptuously termed by the people. (Ford 1915: 81)

Between 1846 and 1849, 190,000 families, over 950,000 people, were evicted (Davitt 1979: 68). A further 98,723 families, 504,707 persons, were evicted between 1849 and 1882 (Davitt 1979: 100). Sixty thousand troops were acting as process servers in the summer of 1881 in Ireland (Ford 1915: 74). The plight of the Catholic rural population on the eve of the union was acutely summed up by Arthur Young when he travelled in Ireland in 1776:

> ... speaking a language that is despised, professing a religion that is abhorred, and, being disarmed, the poor find themselves in many cases slaves even in the bosom of written liberty... A landlord in Ireland can scarcely invent an order which a servant, labourer, or cottar dares to refuse to execute. Nothing satisfies him but unlimited submission. Disrespect, or anything tending towards sauciness, he may

punish with his cane or his horsewhip with the most perfect security. (Quoted in
Lewis 1977: 42)

Lewis himself concurs with this assessment:

> ... nearly all the occupying tenants were Catholic, the landlord exercised over his
> tenant not only the influence which a creditor necessarily exercises over his debtor,
> but also that power which the law gave to the Protestant over the Catholic, to the
> magistrate and grand juror over the suspected rebel. (Lewis 1977: 39)

It is little surprise, then, that the nineteenth century saw an upsurge of rural revolt
in Ireland. It was widespread and systematic, although not revolutionary in the sense of
being a coherent, articulate and well-organised movement to abolish the political and
economic system. The methods employed involved attacks on landlords' property, such
as hobbling of cattle and burning of barns, and on occasion the murder of landlords
and their agents. All of this could be dismissed as mindless, but there was a clear and
sometimes clever logic involved. On occasion, small farmers would arrive in their
hundreds with spades and in a short time turn over grassland, so it was no longer fit for
grazing. The owner was then required to let the land for planting (Lewis 1977: 184).

Frequently the homes of landlords were raided. The object was usually to steal guns.
Ignoring the fact that Catholic peasants, unlike Protestant landlords, were forbidden to
possess arms, the position adopted by the government and police was that the motivation
was sectarian. In his comprehensive account of the phenomenon, first published in 1836,
Lewis is at pains to reject this interpretation: 'It is not the creed of the Protestants but
their guns and pistols which are the real objects of attack' (Lewis 1977: 111). He quotes
others who agree with his conclusions, such as Lord Charlemont:

> As the insurgents were all of the Catholic religion, an almost universal idea was
> entertained among the more zealous Protestants, and encouraged by interested
> men, that French gold and French intrigue were at the bottom of this insurrection;
> the real causes were indeed not difficult to be ascertained. Exorbitant rents,
> low wages, want of employment in a country destitute of manufacturers, where
> desolation and famine were the effects of fertility... (Quoted in Lewis 1977: 47)

Sectarian conflict between agrarian groups was in fact most apparent in the
north, where there was often a fine balance between Catholic and Protestant and
frequent competition for work. In County Armagh Protestant agrarian groups such
as the Peep o' Day Boys[45] clashed with Catholic groups such as the Defenders. But
some people giving evidence at an inquiry into rural disturbances in 1825 were at pains
to explain that there was not an equal allocation of blame:

> Does it not appear that the outrages that have taken place in the north of Ireland
> have generally taken place in consequence of conflict between the Ribbonmen
> and Orangemen? No; a great many of them ... have originated with the mere

---

[45]So called because of their strategy of raiding homes of Catholics at daybreak to search for illegal arms.

> insolence of triumph of the Orangemen... In their lodges they work themselves
> up into a great hatred of popery; they go out; they are armed with musket and ball
> cartridges; and at the slightest sign of disrespect of them, they fire at the peasants.
> (Quoted in Lewis 1977: 127)

The impoverished Catholic peasantry had no political power, no national leaders or formal association, but they had the power of numbers. Inchoate as their actions may have appeared, they constituted a popular rebellion. The proof of this is apparent in the reception accorded to the agrarian groups in their local communities:

> The persons who commit these crimes do not, like the bandits of Italy, or the
> London thieves, follow crime as a profession; they are merely called out by their
> brethren for the occasion, and when their task has been done, they resume their
> ordinary habits of life. (Lewis 1977: 183)

They benefited from an 'already existing general and settled hatred of the law among the great body of the Peasantry' (Lewis 1977: 203).

In short, what was true of the Whiteboys could be said to be true of the bulk of the agrarian groups; they

> may be considered a vast trades' union for the protection of the Irish peasantry: the
> object being, not to regulate the rate of wages or the hours of work, but to keep the
> actual occupant in possession of his land, and in general to regulate the relation of
> landlord and tenant for the benefit of the latter. (Lewis 1977: 80)

Neither *An Gorta Mór* nor the Young Ireland uprising of 1848 marked the end of this dynasty of coercion. The second half of the century did not herald any more peaceful, less coercive period of British administration. Rather, spontaneous and nihilistic resistance was now joined in a broader political resistance that became a 'land war'. What the Land War at the end of the nineteenth century did was add leadership and structure to peasant revolt. Land ownership became the central political cause in the country, which required a head-on confrontation with the landlord class. Leadership in this confrontation came from two sources: Michael Davitt, labour leader, socialist, republican, MP and fiery agrarian activist, and Charles Stewart Parnell, Anglo-Irish Protestant landowner and leader of the Irish Parliamentary Party in Westminster.

Davitt (1979: 40) pointed out that: 'For the first twenty-nine years of the Union with England no measure for the protection of the Irish tenant was even introduced into the British House of Commons by any minister or member'. Parnell was to change that, linking the popular struggle in Ireland to a parliamentary campaign. But although he 'spoke of snapping "the last link with England" ... he was no social revolutionary' (Biggs-Davison 1973: 62). Davitt, on the other hand, was. At age four he and his family were evicted from their home in County Mayo over arrears of rent and he was raised in England. He knew directly what the peasantry was experiencing in ways Parnell never could.

Together they organised an impressive agrarian revolution. Tactics included peasants blockading and ostracising, among others, a landlord in County Mayo, Captain Charles Boycott, thereby introducing a new word into the English language. Although mainly peaceful, the Land War confronted a powerful landlord class backed by the British state: at this point, there were 137,000 British soldiers in Ireland for a population of five million. Both Parnell and Davitt were jailed, at which point the campaign flourished with the Ladies' Land League, led by Parnell's sisters, Anna and Fanny. Seen initially as merely caretakers, they quickly developed a mass, efficient and radical organisation, much to the displeasure of the imprisoned male leaders who seized back control on their release. Anna Parnell made clear her disdain at the failure of the male leaders to capitalise on the radical potential of the organisation in her book, *The Tale of a Great Sham* (Parnell 1986. See also Ward 1995).

Previously the Ulster Tenant Right Association had organised in the north. There the so-called 'Ulster Custom' had allowed mainly Protestant small holders more security on the land. The Tenant Right Association persuaded British Prime Minister Gladstone in 1870 to consolidate that custom, therefore ensuring the Ulster was for the most part excluded from the Land War (Biggs-Davison 1973: 60-61). In the rest of Ireland, the Land League demanded the 'three Fs', fair rent, fixity of tenure and free sale. Such was the success of the combined parliamentary and popular campaign that the British government finally conceded land reform in advance of similar developments closer to home in England. Grants were provided by the British government to allow small farmers to buy their previously rented land. At the same time, landowners were not disadvantaged: the Wyndham Act of 1903, one of five land acts, consolidated the reforms by offering 12 per cent on top of the agreed price to landlords to encourage them to sell entire estates (Curtis 1994: 184).[46] Through one act, the land issue was removed from the centre of Irish politics and agitation.

At the same time, the basis for the transfer of land was the current distribution of land. No attempt was made to unravel the various periods of dispossession, the 'unjust enrichment' (Moyo 2015: 72) resulting from various waves of conquest. Land reform was never going to be a mechanism to unpick the conquest.

Constructive unionism? The limits of kindness

From its inception, the Union was characterised by its facility to present itself as an act of generosity towards Ireland and the Irish. Thus, from the promise of emancipation onwards – and despite the manifest genocide and coercion – British involvement

---

[46] This phenomenon of the oppressor rather than the oppressed being compensated is not unusual. On the abolition of slavery, the British government paid slave-owners £20 million. This was the biggest bailout in Britain prior to the banking crisis of 2008 and the debt was not cleared by the Treasury until 2015. Similarly, Haiti had to pay compensation to the French after its revolution to the tune of £21 billion in current money. The payments were finally completed in 1947.

with Ireland was presented as an act of imperial selflessness. In this regard, unionists demonstrated a remarkable capacity to distance themselves from the 'despotism of fact'. This process moved up a gear towards the end of the century. As British politics became increasingly dominated by the 'Irish Question', both British parties were able to see their relationship with Ireland through only the most rose-tinted spectacles. Thus, the Liberal Party would give the Irish what they wanted and deliver the demand for Home Rule. But Conservative opposition to Home Rule assumed an equally selfless character. This was to be a period of 'constructive unionism' and Home Rule was to be 'killed by kindness'.

In this regard, it appeared that a modernising, democratising 'constructive unionism' might have a chance. By the end of the nineteenth century, it was clear that the land question had been 'solved', albeit within the confines of colonial conquest. The economic question had been 'settled' through incorporation in empire. This left one outstanding issue: political emancipation. By now the Irish Parliamentary Party constituted a significant bloc of some 60 MPs in the British parliament. Their paramount commitment was to home rule for Ireland and they were in the strategic position of being able to offer or withhold support for various British administrations in return for a commitment to bringing in a Home Rule bill. This was the nub of the 'Irish Question' which came increasingly to dominate the whole of British parliamentary politics. Three attempts at such a Bill occurred, in 1886, 1893 and 1914; the last of these was successful.

But *opposition* to Home Rule was becoming constructed in a similarly reformist manner. For example, when a Conservative–Liberal Unionist government was returned to power at the 1895 British general election, Gerald Balfour, nephew of the new prime minister, Lord Salisbury (and brother of future prime minister, Arthur) was appointed Chief Secretary for Ireland. He summarised the Irish policy of the new government as 'killing home rule with kindness'. This approach was accompanied by three signature pieces of legislation: the Local Government (Ireland) Act 1898, the Land Law (Ireland) Act 1896 and the Agriculture and Technical Instruction (Ireland) Act 1899. These measures saw a level of local democracy introduced across Ireland for the first time.

But such 'kindness' had very limited effect – and democratisation produced its own contradictions. Profound confrontations within Irish politics remained. Irish unionists were, by definition, bitterly opposed to Home Rule. Thus, on November 14, 1888, an address of the Non-Conformists of Ireland to Lords Salisbury and Hartington stated: 'We do not believe that any guarantees, moral or material, could be devised which would safeguard the rights of minorities scattered throughout Ireland against the encroachments of a majority vested with legislative and executive functions' (quoted in *Facts of Radical Misgovernment* 1909: 6). This kind of pronouncement emphasised the gulf between unionism and 'constitutional' nationalism. The latter was not averse to a bit of sabre rattling from time to time. For example, the leader of the Irish Parliamentary Party John Redmond, commemorating the 1798 Rising, stated:

> We, to-day, from this county of Wexford, send therefore this message to England. We tell her that we, Wexfordmen, to-day, hate her rule just as bitterly as our forefathers did when they shed their blood on this spot. We tell her that we are as much rebels to her rule to-day as our fathers were in '98. (Quoted in *Facts of Radical Misgovernment* 1909: 4)

On another occasion during a tour in the United States, Redmond said: 'There is not an Irishman in America to-day, in whose veins good red blood is flowing, who would not rejoice to hear that a German Army was marching in triumph across England from Yarmouth to Milford Haven' (quoted in Colvin 1934: 31). To unionist ears this was nothing less than treasonable. Thus, even disregarding the growing politics of republican separatism, the limits of 'kindness' were being relentlessly exposed by the widening gulf between parliamentary nationalism and unionism.

British Prime Minister Asquith, set to support a third Home Rule bill, made it clear that the issue of Irish independence was not up for debate. 'There is not and cannot be any question of separation. There is not, and there cannot be, any question of rival or competing supremacies...' (quoted in Colvin 1934: 20). What was on offer was in a form of dominion, such as that conceded to Canada, wherein Ireland would remain part of what was soon to be termed the British Commonwealth. Many Home Rulers were satisfied with this. Others, however, such as Tom Kettle, MP, let the cat out of the bag as far as unionists were concerned: 'I don't accept Home Rule, I go beyond it ... These are our tactics – if you are to take a fortress, first take the outer works' (quoted in *Facts of Radical Misgovernment* 1909: 16).

By 1911, it was clear that the next attempt at a Home Rule bill at Westminster would succeed. James Craig, Northern unionist leader and later Prime Minister of Northern Ireland, echoed John Redmond's previous 'treasonable' statement and concluded that 'Germany and the German Emperor would be preferred to the rule of John Redmond, Patrick Ford and the Molly Maguires' (quoted in Curtis 1994: 213). A volunteer army, the Ulster Volunteer Force, comprising 84,000 men, was raised and guns were brought in from Germany. At the same time a provisional government in waiting was selected. In effect, the unionists indicated that they were prepared to fight the British in order to remain British.[47]

Despite this challenge to the metropolitan power, the unionists had ample support in Britain. Bonar Law, leader of the Conservative Party, stated in July 1912: 'I can imagine no length of resistance to which Ulster will go which I shall not be ready to support, and in which they will not be supported by the overwhelming majority of the British people' (quoted in Colvin 1934: 129). To underline this, leading British military officers based in the Curragh camp in effect mutinied, pointing out that they would not engage in military action against the unionists.

On Saturday 28 September 1912, a *Solemn Oath and Covenant* was presented for male

---

[47] This phenomenon of the descendants of settlers turning on the colonial power was later evidenced also in Algeria in the 1950s.

signatures, along with a separate document for women to sign. 216,206 men in Ulster, 19,162 men elsewhere, 228,991 women in Ulster and 5,055 women elsewhere signed on that day (Colvin 1934: 151). The men's document was worded thus:

> Being convinced in our consciences that Home Rule would be disastrous to the material well-being of Ulster as well as of the whole of Ireland, subversive of our civil and religious freedom, destructive of our citizenship, and perilous to the unity of the Empire, we, whose names are underwritten, men of Ulster, loyal subjects of His Gracious Majesty King George V., humbly relying on the God whom our fathers in days of stress and trial confidently trusted, do hereby pledge ourselves in solemn Covenant, throughout this our time of threatened calamity, to stand by one another in defending, for ourselves and our children, our cherished position of equal citizenship in the United Kingdom, and in using all means which may be found necessary to defeat the present conspiracy to set up a Home Rule Parliament in Ireland. And in the event of such a Parliament being forced upon us, we further solemnly and mutually pledge ourselves to refuse to recognise its authority. In sure confidence that God will defend the right, we hereto subscribe our names.[48]

In response 80,000 Irish Volunteers, also armed with guns smuggled from Germany, supported the Home Rule cause. When World War I broke out and Redmond promised the support of the Volunteers against Germany, the movement split. Most followed Redmond's lead as the National Volunteers while a radical republican group broke away, retaining the name the Irish Volunteers. Along with the Irish Citizen Army, formed by trade unionists after the Dublin Lock-Out of 1913, the Irish Volunteers, recalling the old republican adage that 'England's difficulty is Ireland's opportunity', planned an uprising during the war.

Many outside commentators noted the significance of this rebellion, the Easter Rising in 1916. Du Bois observed: 'The recent Irish revolt may have been foolish, but would to God some of us had sense enough to be fools' (quoted in Guterl 2016). Lenin stated that a blow against the British Empire in Ireland was of 'a hundred times more significance than a blow of equal weight in Asia or in Africa'. He concluded: 'The misfortune of the Irish is that they rose prematurely, when the European revolt of the proletariat had not yet matured' (quoted in Kiberd 1991: 197). Emma Goldman was more effusive:

> The Irish revolution may grow in significance and importance in the near future. The rebels of Dublin may become the advance guard of an international social revolution, which will shake the very foundations of all governments and privileged classes, who have thrown humanity into the hell-fire of this war. The bold spirit of the Irish rebels, their hopes, sufferings and martyrdom will certainly arouse the masses of European and American peoples. It will be realized that they fought and died for more than a mere national issue, that their noble example and sacrifice worked like a trumpet call and storm signal to all the oppressed of the earth. (*Mother Earth*, Vol. XI No. 3, June 1916)

---

[48] Lee (2008: 139) comments wittily that the Covenant represented 'the traditional Presbyterian technique for reminding God whose side he was on'.

The official British reaction was, unsurprisingly, negative. Many commentators, then and since, depicted the rebels as filled with hatred for England. Kiberd (1991: 199) takes exception to this representation:

> There is remarkably little anti-English sentiment in the writings of the Easter rebels... What they rejected was not England but the British imperial system, which denied expressive freedom to its colonial subjects... The 1916 leaders have often been accused of glorifying violence but, apart from one notorious speech by Pearse, they must have been the gentlest revolutionaries in modern history.

After the Rising, one British army officer quipped: 'The Irish ought to be grateful to us. With a minimum of casualties to the civilian population, we have succeeded in removing some third-rate poets' (quoted in Kiberd 1991: 225).

There is a standard view in popular historical accounts of the Rising that Dubliners were initially dismissive of the Rising and its protagonists and only changed their minds once the British began to execute the rebel leaders. But Canadian journalist F.A. MacKenzie, author of an eyewitness account which was published soon after the Rising, concludes differently (1916: 105):

> I have read many accounts of public feeling in Dublin in these days. They are all agreed that the open and strong sympathy of the mass of the population was with the British troops. That this was so in the better parts of the city, I have no doubt, but certainly what I myself saw in the poorer districts did not confirm this. It rather indicated that there was a vast amount of sympathy with the rebels, particularly after the rebels were defeated.

He recounts one specific incident:

> As I was passing through a street near the Castle cheer after cheer could be heard. I looked ahead. A regiment was approaching. People were leaning from their windows waving triangular flags and handkerchiefs. 'They are cheering the soldiers.' I said to my companion... As the main body approached I could see that the soldiers were escorting a large number of prisoners, men and women, several hundreds in all. The people were cheering not the soldiers but the rebels ... I spoke to a little group of men and women at the street corner. 'Shure, we cheer them,' said one woman. 'Why shouldn't we? Aren't they our own flesh and blood?' (MacKenzie 1916: 278)

A captured insurgent tells a similar story:

> We marched along the road and with every yard there were indications of the changed attitude of the people. The open trams passing by always brought a cheer from somebody, even though rifles were pointed at the offender on every occasion, and old men stood at the street corner and saluted despite being pushed around. (Quoted in Barton 2002: 309)

This popular support was galvanised around the 1918 general election. The *Manifesto to the Irish People* on which Sinn Féin stood was uncomprising in both its republicanism and its anti-imperialism:

The coming General Election is fraught with vital possibilities for the future of our nation. Ireland is faced with the question whether this generation wills it that she is to march out into the full sunlight of freedom, or is to remain in the shadow of a base imperialism that has brought and ever will bring in its train naught but evil for our race. Sinn Féin gives Ireland the opportunity of vindicating her honour and pursuing with renewed confidence the path of national salvation by rallying to the flag of the Irish Republic.

There were four key elements to the platform: 1) withdrawal from Westminster; 2) the 'use of any and every means available to render impotent the power of England to hold Ireland in subjection'; 3) the establishment of a constituent assembly of persons elected from the Irish constituencies; 4) an appeal to the Peace Conference for recognition of the 'establishment of Ireland as an independent nation'. In the event, Sinn Féin took over 46 per cent of the votes and 69.5 per cent of the seats across the island of Ireland.[49] It set up its alternative parliament as the Dáil.[50] A war against British forces began on the same day and led eventually to Treaty talks between the Irish and British.

This conflict had profound implications for both union and empire. The war of independence proved a severe strain on the British exchequer. In 1919, approximately half of the British army throughout the empire was tied up in Ireland at a time when the empire constituted 'an area 357 times larger than Ireland, and with 90 times its population' (Curtis 1994: 311). In 1916 Chief Secretary Augustine Birrell wrote to Asquith: 'Nobody can govern Ireland from England save in a state of siege' (quoted in Curtis 1994: 284). And a few years later Joseph Chamberlain concurred: 'The [English] system in Ireland is founded on the bayonets of 30,000 soldiers, encamped permanently in a hostile country' (quoted in Carty 1999: 40). For these and many other reasons there was an urgency on the British side to seek a political solution.

There was an even more pressing need on the Irish side, as revealed in a statement from Michael Collins, the Irish military commander and one of six Irish emissaries to the Treaty talks, to British Chief Secretary Hamar Greenwood in June 1921: 'You had us deadbeat. We could not have lasted another three weeks. When we were told of the

---

[49] This vote would have been considerably higher except that some seats were uncontested while in others in Ulster there was a pact between Sinn Féin and the Irish Parliamentary Party to avoid losing seats to the Irish Unionist Alliance.

[50] One of the women elected to the Dáil was Con Markievicz (1868-1927) – aka Countess Markievicz and Constance Georgine Gore-Booth. She was born in London, the eldest daughter of the Anglo-Irish Gore-Booth family whose Irish seat was Lisadell in Sligo. She was a politician, revolutionary, suffragist, socialist and sometime muse for WB Yeats. A founder member of Fianna Éireann, Cumann na mBan and the Irish Citizen Army, she was second-in-command at St Stephen's Green in the Easter Rising in 1916. She was sentenced to death, but this was reduced to life imprisonment on account of her gender. In 1918 she was the first woman elected to Westminster (for Dublin St Patrick's) but took her seat instead in the First Dáil. She was appointed Minister for Labour, becoming the first woman cabinet minister in Europe and one of the first in the world. She served as TD for the Dublin South constituency from 1921 to 1927. In 1926, she left Sinn Féin and was instrumental in forming Fianna Fáil, chairing its inaugural meeting. In the June 1927 general election, she was re-elected to the Fifth Dáil for Fianna Fáil, but died before she could take her seat.

offer of a truce we were astounded. We thought you must have gone mad' (quoted in Biggs-Davison 1973: 102).

Many republicans were bitterly opposed to the Treaty with its oath of allegiance and other signs of subservience, but especially because of partition. This was not the full independence and sovereignty of the nation for which they had struggled and fought. For their part, Irish republican supporters of the Treaty viewed it as a necessary evil, a stopgap, as Michael Collins put it, 'a stepping stone'. On 19 December 1921, during charged debates in the Dáil, he elaborated: 'It gives us freedom, not the ultimate freedom that all nations desire and develop to but the freedom to achieve it' (Dáil Éireann 1921). The Dáil deputies voted 64 to 57 in favour of the Treaty, and a civil war ensued, in many ways more vicious than the war of independence beforehand. The pro-Treaty forces won. Partition was a central plank of the Treaty: the creation not simply of a Free State government, but the option for the North, henceforth to be known officially as 'Northern Ireland', to opt out and acquire its own devolved government within the Union. It was apparent that the revolution was unfinished at this point. What was less certain was the trajectory that this newly partitioned Ireland would follow within a reconstituted Union and Empire.

Conclusion

The United Kingdom created in 1801 ended with the Treaty of 1922. After the Treaty, the Free State remained in the British Empire but left the union. This departure from the union was, perhaps, its only truly radical achievement. If nothing else, this Irish exceptionalism helped deconstruct the complex synergy between the conjoined projects of union and empire. To date, 'Southern Ireland' has been the only polity ever to leave the union. This opened a whole series of possibilities for the colonised – could you leave the union and stay in the Empire? Could you leave the Empire and stay in the union? Was it possible to quit both simultaneously? Were the white dominions on a journey towards independence or were they moving towards some form of expanded union or 'Greater Britain' – the point at which their whiteness and autonomy would make them equal partners with England in the imperial project?

All these theoretical futures crashed against the despotism of fact when in 1922 the union was left clinging to the gerrymandered rump of Northern Ireland in order to survive at all. This United Kingdom mark 2 was a shadow of its predecessor but, with Northern Ireland on board, it was still possible to refer to a United Kingdom as it is, a century later, to point to a 'precious Union'. Of course, if Ireland had left the Union completely, it would still be possible to refer to the union which existed from 1707, that between Scotland and England (and Wales). But this would not have the legitimacy and prowess that the post-1800 United Kingdom claimed. Without Ireland there would have been no United Kingdom, and with only Northern Ireland a United Kingdom which eventually revealed itself – albeit it took a century and Brexit to fully reveal this – as lacking in legitimacy and prowess.

This helps to frame the understanding of Ireland's relationship to both Union and Empire. Clearly the UK state – created by the Union in 1801 – and the British Empire were and are different things. The Empire was often an amorphous mass – of colonies, dominions, protectorates, mandates and other territories – that is overlapping and contradictory and hard to define. At one level, if the Raj is removed, it is not there at all. In contrast, the UK was – and is – a state formation with borders and a parliament and a civil service and a (famously unwritten) constitution. The curious thing about the symbiosis between these distinct phenomena, however, is that they often appear as synonyms. Even more intriguingly the spectre of England and Englishness interpolates both, although this time as synecdoche. As we have argued, these entities were conjoined in one complex, reactionary project. This reaction had many different dimensions but in terms of our focus, the key issue was that it denied Irish self-determination.

The inherent contradictions between these various phenomena – England/Union/Empire – were finally exposed in the Home Rule crisis. Of course, the crisis was immediately relevant in terms of the Irish demand for self-determination, but it had profound implications for the whole 'imperial family'. The notion that Home Rule would mark the break-up of empire reveals this broader duality. If Ireland was not still colonised, if Ireland was not an imperialised space, then the prospect of its leaving the UK would never have been constructed in such portentous terms. In retrospect we might expect that the reading of pro-imperialist contemporary commentators would be that, at worst, Home Rule for Ireland marked the break-up of the UK, and, at best, perhaps the *strengthening* of Empire. This is precisely the way in which most of Irish MPs were anticipating Home Rule at the time.

In contrast, the outworking of Britain's 'Irish Question' reveals the Union as the 'mothership' of empire for the first time. (At the risk of stretching the metaphor, it also signals that the shipowners were always English.) From this perspective, the imperialist reading was correct – the break-up of the Union *would* represent a fundamental crisis of empire. In contradistinction to the notion of capitalism breaking at its weakest link in Russia, here was empire breaking first at its strongest link. Like the British Constitution, the nexus between England and Union and Empire is mostly unwritten. It is immanent – just like the imperial parliament which inhabits the UK parliament as if there is – and could be – no contradiction between the two. As the Home Rule crisis developed, however, it disclosed the essence of colonisation and Ireland's relationship to it.

As we have seen, the traditional reading of the Union was of a gradually democratising polity – capable of delivering Catholic emancipation, capable of integrating the Celtic fringe into the management of empire, capable of 'killing Home Rule with kindness'. Even more radically, after WWII it appeared capable of delivering social democracy in its most advanced manifestation in the form of the post-war Labour government. This episode suggested that it might turn its imperial subjects into citizens in the process. In reality, however, the imperial dynamic cuts across this claim of democratisation and inclusion. The Union also contained a genocidal tendency. For the nineteenth century Irish peasant eating grass while ships of beef are exported, earning less per annum than is needed to pay rent to an absentee landlord, dying on board a famine ship to America or Canada, debates around intentionality are moot. The UK state was tolerant of – if not actively pursuing – the diminution of the entire indigenous/native population. As Mitchel and others eloquently revealed, it *felt* like genocide. The Union appeared less interested in making citizens of the UK out of its unrepentant Irish natives than erasing them from its borders by any means necessary.

This begs the question of whether this was the entire 'logic' of union. The genealogy of the UK – and the place of Scotland and Wales in it – connects at this point. While the focus tends to be on the Irish and Scots and Welsh contribution to empire and the ways in which they benefited from it,[51] there is a parallel narrative, the clearance of the Celtic Fringe. In this reading 'North Britain' and 'West Britain' are not simply internal colonial ideological spaces but also determinedly *material* projects of Union. Over its 220 years of existence, the Union certainly attempted to clear this fringe of native language and thought and politics and agency – but it also often removed any physical native presence. Thus, hollowed out, the empty shell of Britishness would be English by default – since this would be the only identity left.

The question of conquest and clearance, therefore, begins to overlap with the broader problematic of when – *or did* – colonialisation end in Ireland? Of course, this question runs through our whole analysis. The role of the Union features heavily in this problematic. As we have seen, there is an argument that the incorporation through the Act of Union was that point. Another suggests – *à la* Carty – that it was, at least for the South, with partition and the emergence of a Free State. Alternatively, a sanguine reading of the Good Friday Agreement (GFA) might suggest that this was the point that the conquest ended – or at least that it had the potential for it (O'Leary 2019: 131). Indeed, this was precisely the spin that SDLP leader John Hume embedded in the GFA – the palpably false notion that it was an act of self-determination by the Irish people as a whole.

As this chapter has suggested, it is profoundly misguided to characterise the Union as a post-colonial formation. Here, as we have seen, the historical narrative is crucial. When we begin to ask what the Union state was trying to do with Catholic Ireland – the 'native population' – and whether this was colonial, the wheels begin to come off any simple notion of emancipation or decolonisation. Moreover, when we confront the reality – and legacy – of *An Gorta Mór* we are forced towards the conclusion that this

---

[51] Thus, the adage regarding the British empire: 'The Irish fought for it, the Scottish and Welsh ran it, but the English kept the profits'.

dynamic could only be colonial. What other name would serve for government that administers such a catastrophe at the heart of the richest and most powerful of empires?

This logic was embedded in the Union from the first. If Home Rule for Ireland would presage the break-up of the Empire for the imperialist, then how could the Union *not* be a function of Empire? The Irish experience under the Union might be characterised as 'hypercolonialism' or 'hyperimperialism' as a way of helping to frame the Irish location within the UK state that emerges from our analysis. The Union did not free Ireland from Empire *but rather locked the Irish people within it.*[52] The beast transformed as time went on but stayed true to its nature while doing so. This points towards a simple conclusion – since there was no formal decolonisation, the whole island of Ireland and its people remained colonised throughout the entire 1801-1921 period. This presages the conundrum that faced the two new Irish states that emerged from partition – what exactly was their relationship with the British Empire to be?

---

[52] There is an obvious comparison to be made with Native Americans or Native Canadians or Native Australians with this notion of being locked into empire. In these settler colonial dominated formations, how might any native free themselves from the imperial dynamics? Thus, whether the colonised are denied citizenship, or have it foisted upon them, they remain trapped in a racist, colonial construction. These white dominions also await decolonisation.

Section II

Carnivals of reaction: partition and the emergence of the 26- and 6-county states

The partition of Ireland would mean a carnival of reaction both North and South, would set back the wheels of progress, would destroy the oncoming unity of the Irish labour movement and paralyse all advanced movements while it endured. —James Connolly, 1914

Notwithstanding the establishment of the Parliaments of Southern and Northern Ireland, or the Parliament of Ireland, or anything contained in this Act, the supreme authority of the Parliament of the United Kingdom shall remain unaffected and undiminished over all persons, matters, and things in Ireland and every part thereof. —Section 75, Government of Ireland Act, 1920

Partition was the key conjuncture in the outworking of the dialectic between empire and republic in Ireland. One hundred years later, it is instructive to remember just how deeply notions of empire were embedded in all aspects of Irish politics in the lead-up to partition. In 2020 it is unusual to see anything other than the most reactionary of interpretations framed by the politics of empire. In the hundred years before partition, however, the survival and prosperity of the British Empire was the *sine qua non* of most political discourse in Ireland. Thus, most of the politics of unionism *and nationalism* in nineteenth- and early-twentieth-century Ireland was regarded through the prism of empire.

As late as its 1917 Ard Fhéis (Party Conference), even Sinn Féin was still struggling with the question of support for monarchism or republicanism. From this perspective, the relationship between Irishness and Britishness was not to be measured in solidarity with the rest of the colonised world but rather in a unique capacity to share responsibility for colonising. In other words, the paradigm shift to anti-imperialism – which will be considered in chapter 10 – did not emerge simply or unproblematically out of Irish nationalism.

Even after all was changed utterly by the Easter Rising, this paradigm continued to dominate unionist and nationalist political thought. Witness John Redmond – as leader of the Irish Party at Westminster – pleading for clemency for rank-and-file republicans involved in the Easter Rising and hoping

> that out of the ashes of this miserable tragedy there may spring up something
> which will redound to the future happiness of Ireland and the future complete and
> absolute unity of this Empire. (House of Commons 1916)

For this Parnellite leader of constitutional nationalism, the future of Ireland and the future of empire were inextricably and positively bound together even after 1916. Arguably, however, there was nothing odd or contradictory about native or Catholic or indeed nationalist Ireland and an unequivocal commitment to empire. The Union had ostensibly created a political context to resolve any sense of contradiction between these two dynamics.

Unsurprisingly, this support for empire was true with greater logic on the unionist side. The elective affinity of unionism and empire made the virtue of imperialism a self-evident truth for most unionists. Speaking as Prime Minister in 1885, Salisbury epitomised opposition to Home Rule and support for Irish unionists in precisely these terms:

> The integrity of the Empire is more precious to us than any possession we can have.
> We are bound by motives, not only of expediency, not only of legal principle, but
> by motives of honour, to protect the minority. (Cited in Bentley 2001)

The First World War and the 1916 Rising, however, both reflected and generated an inexorable rise in anti-imperialist politics in Ireland. The response to the Rising and its aftermath left little space for nationalist imperialism. As Connolly made clear in his statement to his court martial in Dublin Castle on 9 May 1916:

> We went out to break the connection between this country and the British Empire,
> and to establish an Irish Republic. (Connolly 1916)

This stark juxtaposition between empire and republic echoed through the following five years of political and military conflict.

When Sinn Féin won a huge majority of Irish seats in the 1918 election, these 'Republican members of the Irish constituencies' reconstituted themselves as Dáil Éireann. At its first meeting on 21 January 1919, Dáil Éireann was presented with its three foundation documents. First, *An Fhaisnéis Neamhspleádhchuis* – the Declaration of Independence, then the 'Message to the Free Nations of the World' and then the 'Democratic Programme of Dáil Éireann'. The first two were presented in Irish first, then in French and English; the Democratic Programme only in Irish and English. The Declaration made the context clear:

> Whereas at the threshold of a new era in history the Irish electorate has in the
> General Election of December, 1918, seized the first occasion to declare by an
> overwhelming majority its firm allegiance to the Irish Republic: Now, therefore,
> we, the elected Representatives of the ancient Irish people in National Parliament
> assembled, do, in the name of the Irish nation, ratify the establishment of the Irish
> Republic and pledge ourselves and our people to make this declaration effective by
> every means at our command.

It looked as if the republic had triumphed. There is a retrospective poignancy to the insistence in the Declaration that this was the 'last stage of the struggle'.

Under international law, the declaration satisfied the principle of the 'declarative theory of statehood'.[1] In 1919, however, most states – particularly those with colonial empires, of course – followed the 'constitutive theory of statehood' and therefore did not recognise the Irish Republic. The political path to independence blocked, key republicans now re-assumed the military logic of a war of independence.

Simultaneously – although it appears without much strategic coordination – what became known as the Tan War[2] or war of independence had also begun. The same day as the Declaration of Independence, Volunteers ambushed a delivery of dynamite at Soloheadbeg Quarry in Tipperary. Two RIC officers were killed in the action. The British Empire responded in traditional fashion with the apparatus of coercion in Ireland. The legislation used was the Criminal Law and Procedure (Ireland) Act, 1887 – this had first been introduced in the context of the Land War. This had the foreboding – or propitious – quality of being permanent – rather than emergency – legislation.[3] On 2 July 2018 several organisations – including Sinn Féin, the Irish Volunteers, Cumann na mBan and the Gaelic League – were declared to be 'dangerous'. On 9 September 1919 Dáil Éireann was 'prohibited' and 'supressed'. On 10 December French, Lord Lieutenant-General and General Governor of Ireland, declared martial law. After two years of brutal guerrilla war and reprisals, this conflict ended with the Anglo-Irish Treaty of December 1921. This emerged from a stalemate in the Tan War – neither British Crown forces nor the IRA was able to inflict sufficient damage on the other side to secure military victory. In the interim, however, Ireland had been partitioned by the Government of Ireland Act 1920 and it was not Ireland but rather the 26 counties of Southern Ireland that would reinvent itself as a 'Free State'.

Our second section engages with the two states created by the Government of Ireland Act 1920. This was an act of the British parliament 'to provide for the better

---

[1] The constitutive theory is the model of statehood by which a state exists through recognition by other states. This was standard in the nineteenth century. In contrast, the declarative theory defines an entity's statehood is independent of its recognition by other states, providing its sovereignty was not gained by military force. The declarative model was classically expressed in the 1933 Montevideo Convention which became a key moment in the decolonisation process: 'The state as a person of international law should possess the following qualifications: (a) a permanent population; (b) a defined territory; (c) government; and (d) capacity to enter into relations with the other states'. The delegations at this convention represented states that had emerged from former colonies. Their own independence had been opposed by European colonial empires. They identified criteria that made it easier for other dependent states with limited sovereignty to gain international recognition. The European Union, in the principal statement of its Badinter Committee, follows the Montevideo Convention.

[2] Named after the Black and Tans, a reserve force of the RIC, brought in to counter the republican military campaign. They were mainly former British soldiers and were notorious for their brutality.

[3] The act was repealed in the Republic of Ireland by the Statute Law Revision Act 1983. The act was partially repealed in Britain by the Northern Ireland (Emergency Provisions) Act 1973 but it remains a statute in force.

Government of Ireland'. The crucial legacy of this legislation was that – for the first time – it delineated two polities and thereby created a political border in Ireland:

> For the purposes of this Act, Northern Ireland shall consist of the parliamentary counties of Antrim, Armagh, Down, Fermanagh, Londonderry and Tyrone, and the parliamentary boroughs of Belfast and Londonderry, and Southern Ireland shall consist of so much of Ireland as is not comprised within the said parliamentary counties and boroughs.

It is not without irony that only Northern Ireland was defined geographically – Southern Ireland was the residue of the former Union. The defining point for us, however, is that *both* these proto-states were colonial and imperial formations – they emerged from the efforts of the British Empire to prevent Irish self-determination and to reconstitute imperial authority across the island of Ireland.[4]

Despite the huge political and constitutional changes in the interim, these two formations – 'Northern Ireland' and 'Southern Ireland' – continue to frame the state in Ireland to the present. Of course, one of these states did not assume the political forms envisaged by the 1920 Act. While Northern Ireland continued to be framed by the Act, Southern Ireland acquired further autonomy following the Treaty of 1922. Now styled a 'Free State', it became a white dominion of the British Empire – like Australia, Canada and South Africa. Despite this enhanced autonomy, however, it was a far remove from the Republic proclaimed in 1916 and endorsed by the Irish electorate in 1918. Northern Ireland was of course left even more unambiguously locked within a colonial context – still in the double bind of union and empire.

As we have seen, the 26-county state was an odd elision – its definition by the British was effectively 'not Northern Ireland'. This bears emphasis in terms of the trajectory of the 26-county state thereafter. This state might have been regarded both by itself and by others as an interim measure since the Act had promised as much in the Council of Ireland:

> With a view to the eventual establishment of a Parliament for the whole of Ireland, and to bringing about harmonious action between the parliaments and governments of Southern Ireland and Northern Ireland, and to the promotion of mutual intercourse and uniformity in relation to matters affecting the whole of Ireland, and to providing for the administration of services which the two parliaments mutually agree should be administered uniformly throughout the whole of Ireland, or which by virtue of this Act are to be so administered, there shall be constituted, as soon as may be after the appointed day, a Council to be called the Council of Ireland.

---

[4] The partition of Ireland was first raised as a possibility by Joseph Chamberlain during the parliamentary debate on the First Home Rule Bill in 1886, but no one paid much attention at the time. By 1913, Lloyd George was proposing a vote in each Ulster county for exclusion for up to six years from Home Rule. This 'county option' was backed by Asquith and others but rejected by Carson as a 'stay of execution'. In 1916, a Cabinet Committee proposed that the six counties be excluded temporarily without county votes. This was the basis of the final British legislation.

Thus, partition – along with the 26- and 6-county states it created – was framed as a temporary measure; this constitutional innovation was in theory a prelude to reunification. Later both states *might* have had their boundaries redrawn by the Boundary Commission – but this did not happen either. The Boundary Commission was set up in 1924 to renegotiate the border between Northern Ireland and the Irish Free State; Minister for Education Eoin MacNeill represented the Free State. On 7 November 1925 *The Morning Post* published a leaked map revealing that a substantial part of eastern County Donegal was to be transferred to Northern Ireland. MacNeill resigned from the Commission and as Minister for Education. On 3 December 1925 the Free State government agreed with the governments in London and Belfast to end its Treaty requirement to pay its share of the United Kingdom's imperial debt, and in exchange it agreed that the 1920 boundary would remain as it was, superseding the Commission. The intergovernmental boundary deal was approved by a Dáil vote of 71–20 on 10 December 1925 that formally legitimated partition.

Thus, the Government of Ireland Act situates the genealogy of the 26-county state within this British neology of 'Southern Ireland'. This state had it borders imposed by the British imperial parliament. From this distance, it bears emphasis that this partition border had neither democratic nor ethnic legitimacy. The state proposed as 'Northern Ireland' was a land grab of the crudest kind. It represented the largest area that could be held for Britain in the context of the war in Ireland. The northern unionist reading of the conflict was explicitly sectarianised. Unionist MP Captain Charles Craig symbolised this response to partition with the observation that 'the overwhelming majority of the Roman Catholic population of Ireland is in practically open rebellion against this country'. He went on to provide the definitive justification for the boundary of the new state – it was to be an area that they could hold as Protestant 'in perpetuity':

> I come now to ... the most distressing of the problems we had to face, and I refer to that of the area. As hon. Members know, the area over which the North of Ireland Parliament is to have jurisdiction is the six counties of Antrim, Down, Armagh, Londonderry, Tyrone and Fermanagh. The three Ulster counties of Monaghan, Cavan and Donegal are to be handed over to the South of Ireland Parliament. How the position of affairs in a Parliament of nine counties and in a Parliament of six counties would be is shortly this. If we had a nine counties' Parliament, with 64 Members, the Unionist majority would be about three or four, but in a six counties' Parliament, with 52 Members, the Unionist majority would be about 10. The three excluded counties contain some 70,000 Unionists and 260,000 Sinn Féiners and Nationalists, and the addition of that large block of Sinn Féiners and Nationalists would reduce our majority to such a level that no sane man would undertake to carry on a Parliament with it.... Obviously, when we set ourselves to safeguard Ulster and to prevent Home Rule from being imposed upon us, the best way to carry that pledge into effect was to save as much of Ulster as we knew we could hold. To try to hold more than we could hold would seem an act of gross folly on our part, and in the difficult circumstances, I have no hesitation in saying

we took the only commonsense business decision we could possibly take. On that matter I leave those who come after us to judge whether we took a right or a wrong decision. (House of Commons 1920)

Thus, the 'six counties' included two counties that had Catholic and nationalist majorities – Tyrone and Fermanagh. Moreover, the land mass to be 'held' was actually majority Catholic since it included the less populated nationalist and republican rural areas of south Down, South Armagh, Fermanagh, Tyrone and Derry. It anticipated the notion of 'Protestant dominion' – a political space in which Protestant privilege would be institutionalised in every corner of the new state.

Partition was a catastrophe for northern Catholics, nationalists and republicans. But it also had negative implications for both *Irish* and *Ulster* unionists. This sense of betrayal by six-county unionists was particularly acute among unionists from Cavan, Donegal and Monaghan who had signed the Ulster Covenant in 1912 as the foundation principle of a partitioned state:

If it is now open to one portion of the Province for its own safety to desert the rest, there was never any meaning in the Covenant at all. If we were not all 'to stand by one another' what was the object of the Covenant? The facts about the three Counties were as clear when the Covenant was signed as they are today, and they have not altered. The position of Ulster as a whole remains the same. Why were we asked to come in and sign if, when the emergency comes, we are to be thrown over?[5]

Thus, partition did not only partition Ireland, it partitioned Ulster. Moreover, it did not only partition Irish nationalists and Irish republicans and Irish unionists, it partitioned Ulster unionists as well. It partitioned Irish Protestants just as inhumanely as it partitioned Irish Catholics. An expressly sectarian anti-democratic land grab created two state formations without any organic political or ethnic *raison d'etre*. Yet, these formations continue to structure the whole of life across the contemporary 32 counties. For this reason, we continue to use the terms 'Northern Ireland' and 'Southern Ireland' throughout this analysis. This reflects the reality of these two entities – specifically this roots the contemporary 26-county state (which now styles itself simply as 'Ireland') in the 'Parliament of Southern Ireland' defined by the Government of Ireland Act.

Even though this southern parliament never functioned, since most of its members were republicans and sat instead in the First Dáil, it was this shadow parliament – and the partitioned state formation that framed it – that ultimately made its peace with the UK. Within two years of Soloheadbeg, the Treaty was signed to end the British/Irish conflict. Rather than bring peace, however, it caused further conflict as the forces that had combined on an explicitly republican agenda to fight an anti-imperialist guerrilla war against the British Empire were split in the negotiations that led to the Treaty. When the Article of Agreement for a Treaty between Great Britain and Ireland was signed on 6

5 'Ulster and Home Rule. No Partition of Ulster.' Statement by the Delegates for Cavan, Donegal and Monaghan 1920 (cited in Mitchell and Ó Snodaigh 1985: 73).

December 1921, partition was concretised. The 26 counties were given dominion status, but the Parliament of Northern Ireland was given the power to withdraw from this new Irish Free State dominion.

Saorstát Éireann emerged, therefore, less a culmination of anti-imperialist struggle than the tawdry compromise of empire and a profoundly divided Irish population. Ireland had white dominion status thrust upon it not as an act of volition but as the least bad model in terms of the interests of the British Empire. This had profound long-term implications in terms of Irishness and whiteness. Noel Ignatiev famously traced 'how the Irish became white' in the process of migration to the US and their Janus-like interface with African Americans and WASPs. But in Ireland, this deferred decolonisation was 'how the Irish became white'. In this sense the Irish of the 26-county state had whiteness thrust upon them.

With remarkable prescience, James Connolly had anticipated a 'carnival of reaction' on *both sides* of the border in any partitioned Ireland. Of course, there was already a surfeit of reaction in the *pre-partition* Ireland in which Connolly lived and worked and organised. This was the state formation examined in chapter 4 – the United Kingdom of Great Britain and Ireland – that lasted from 1801-1921. In other words, Connolly was not underestimating the *depth of reaction* in pre-partition Ireland; how could he since he spent his entire life struggling against its consequences in many different forms? Nevertheless, while the incorporation of Ireland within the UK had been conceived of *and remained* a repressive, sectarian and anti-democratic state project, the broad trajectory of nineteenth century Ireland within the Union was liberalizing and democractising and de-sectarianising in the context of a widening franchise, the development of the Irish Party and the influence of that party in Westminster politics. It was tellingly a pre-echo of the combination of repression and reform that characterised the later direct rule intervention in Northern Ireland after 1972, albeit that much of this liberalisation ended abruptly with the levels of repression in the 1914-21 period. After *An Gorta Mór*, this state moved away from its legacy of formal 'Protestant Ascendancy' and towards an incorporation of the majority Catholic population. In consequence, much of the Irish state was comprehensively Catholicised by 1900 – here the make-up of the RIC and criminal justice system were paradigmatic. In other words, when Connolly anticipated the reaction that would follow partition, he correctly predicted a *specific* symbiosis of reactionary projects consequent upon partition. The reaction associated with partition did indeed take very different paths in the states that emerged: one 'Catholic', the other 'Protestant'. These states remain in place today albeit in hugely transformed ways.

We have already suggested that the nexus between England and Ireland and Englishness and Irishness repeatedly raises profound questions of state theory. This next section – chapters 5 to 8 – raises a further question in this context. Arguably there is a uniquely insightful moment with evolution/revolution of the colonial state as it becomes a post-colonial state. Here it seems reasonable to assume that something definitive about the state *should* be revealed at the spectacularly disrupted moment of 'independence'. It might be expected that the relationship between phenomena like capitalism and the ruling class and the state would be laid bare, because at this moment – arguably more starkly than even France in 1798 or Russia in 1917 – both state and ruling class are – or appear to be – apparently *utterly transformed*. This power shift assumes acute proportions at the point of transformation during decolonisation – in theory at least. The independence handover ceremony appears to symbolise a definitive transfer of power that is – or is expected to be – much more profound than any change of government in an ordinary democracy. The ostensible message is that the state is about to be completely reconfigured – from an agent of colonisation to one of decolonisation (or, less radically perhaps, post-colonialism).

Since most of the world has followed this path over the last century – the transition from *colonial* to *post-colonial* – there is plenty of evidence to engage with. In other words, this is as much an empirical as a theoretical question. Did these state transformations transform other social relations? Or is there a sense in which Yeats' cynicism about the 'great day' was routinely realised?

> Hurrah for revolution and more cannon-shot!
> A beggar upon horseback lashes a beggar on foot.
> Hurrah for revolution and cannon come again!
> The beggars have changed places, but the lash goes on.[6]

This decolonising moment is the starkest juncture in the development of the state – and it arguably raises the profoundest questions of state theory. At this point does a structure that evolved directly in response to the needs of colonialism *volte face* and serve anti-colonialism? Or is there a degree of relative autonomy whereby this state formation continues to serve the power matrix embedded by colonialism? If and how this transformation is possible is the problematic in the next section of our book.

While the problematic is broadly theoretical, the focus of our analysis is intensely practical and empirical. It focuses on the two novel state structures that emerged in Ireland after partition in 1920 and that were solidified by the Treaty of 1922. Over the next four chapters, we focus on the ways in which both have changed – often quite profoundly – over the following 100 years. In this regard, Ireland offers a unique perspective on this colonial/post-colonial process because the transformation did not happen in a single ceremony. Rather the journey from empire towards republic was eked out over many years. Some of us stopped celebrating 100 years ago while others of us are still waiting for our Independence Day. From our perspective, the journey remains incomplete – the revolution is palpably unfinished. But there is little question that it

---

[6] Again, Connolly's prescience is remarkable. In a talk given to the Irish Citizen Army the night before the Rising he said: 'The odds against us are a thousand to one, but if we should win, hold on to your rifles, for the goal of the Volunteers may not be the same as our own. Remember, we are out not just for political freedom, but for economic freedom as well. So, hold on to your rifles' (quoted in Coffey 1970: 33).

started on 16 January 1922. The most die-hard republican would have to admit that *something* in British/Irish relations was transformed at that moment. While the Republic may not have been born then, with the benefit of hindsight it is possible to situate the approaching death of both the Empire and the Union at that juncture.

Unsurprisingly, many of contradictions of that moment remain unresolved. Not least of these, of course, was the parallel creation of 'Northern Ireland'. This new phenomenon was the polar opposite of an anti-imperialist state – a formation determinedly committed to reinforcing its location *inside* both union and empire. It was in this sense an unusual formation – a truly reactionary, hyper-imperial offshoot symbolising the antithesis of independence. On the one hand it was to be numbered alongside apartheid South Africa and Rhodesia under UDI in a list of polities that managed to successfully reverse decolonisation; on the other, unlike these insalubrious comparators, it managed to keep its connection to the UK. Because of this it was often characterised as a 'statelet' rather than a state. This use of the diminutive was not simply a cheap dismissal by those who regarded it as inherently sectarian and anti-democratic. The term also captured its liminal existence – dependent upon the UK state and Westminster and yet largely ignored by both. It was born out of opposition to Home Rule and yet protected its right to 'self-determination' and autonomous structures with remarkable vigour. So, if it wasn't a state or a statelet, what was it? And has it managed to distance itself from these deeply unfashionable antecedents one hundred years later? These questions can only be answered in comparative context. Both new Irish states were often comically antithetical. At the same time, however, the one cannot be understood without the other. Moreover, both were in very different ways the alternative to the Republic. They were what the Empire was prepared to concede in order to obviate the Republic that was declared in 1916 and democratically sanctioned in 1918.

The next four chapters follow the trajectories of these two states and schematise their different constitutional, political and economic characteristics over the last 100 years. Their economic journey alone hints at some of the complexity of this history. In the south, this saw the 'balanced books' approach of Saorstát Éireann, the economic protectionism of Fianna Fáil's economic war and the free market industrial development under the banner of the 'Republic' which culminated in the Celtic Tiger and continues – albeit slightly chastened – to the present. In the north, the heavy industry that had underpinned the politics of unionism has all but disappeared. The temporary success of replacement by new transnational corporations has also declined and contemporary Northern Ireland is characterised by an economy that is both sluggish and heavily state-dependent.

The emergence of these two unusual state formations presaged a turbulent and often violent century in Ireland as they both negotiated their relationship to the British state. One that did not want to be a dominion had that status enforced upon it, the other that craved dominion status in the context of its continued loyalty to empire had that privilege denied. As the six counties lurched from emergency to emergency, the 26 counties anticipated a peculiarly Irish road to republicanism over the next thirty years. This trajectory from 'dominion' to 'republic' was bridged by the 1937 Constitution. This is – or at least *was* – explicitly anti-colonial in the respect that the revolution was recognised as unfinished given the reality of partition.

None of the key blocs in the Irish political landscape of 1914 – republicans, nationalists or unionists – achieved their favoured outcome in 1922. Ironically, and in very different ways, partition was imposed upon all of them and they all had to live with its toxic consequences. The compromise of 1922 produced two state formations in Ireland – neither of which anyone wanted or voted for – yet these were to determine the lives of their citizens for the next hundred years. James Craig famously invited historians to reflect on which state had been more successful – his 'Protestant' state in Northern Ireland or its 'Catholic' alternative in Southern Ireland. Our next four chapters offer some perspective on that question.

Certainly, the compromise – or stalemate – of the 1920-23 period marked a key juncture in the dialectics of empire and republic. Out of the stand-off emerged partition and its two unhappy, dysfunctional states – one a pale shade of the Republic, the other a last hurrah for imperial continuity. Both descended immediately into emergency and civil war, despoiling both the imperial and anti-imperial mythologies that had inspired their creation. The crises and transformations in both states over the next hundred years are testament to the unfinished revolution. Through the century that followed partition, the dialectic between empire and republic endured.

Chapter 5

Southern Ireland 1922-73:
from republic to 'white dominion'

Now as one of the signatories of the document I naturally recommend its acceptance. I do not recommend it for more than it is. Equally I do not recommend it for less than it is. In my opinion it gives us freedom, not the ultimate freedom that all nations desire and develop to, but the freedom to achieve it. —Michael Collins, 1921

This matter has been put to us as the Treaty or war. I say now if it were war, I would take it gladly and gleefully, not flippantly, but gladly, because I realise that there are evils worse than war, and no physical victory can compensate for a spiritual surrender. —Mary MacSwiney, 1921

The Irish Free State was established on 6 December 1922 following the terms of the Anglo-Irish Treaty signed on 6 December 1921. The Treaty created a new state with dominion status within the British Empire. Crucially, it allowed the parliament of Northern Ireland to opt not to be included in the Free State, in which case a Boundary Commission would be established to determine the border between the two states. Thus, the state comprised *32-county Ireland* for one day before the parliament of Northern Ireland resolved to opt out. The template for this new state was, however, colonial rather than anti-colonial. The area that partition had defined as 'Southern Ireland' was to become a self-governing dominion of the British Empire, a status shared by Australia, Canada, Newfoundland, New Zealand and the Union of South Africa. Members of the parliament of the Free State would be required to take an oath of allegiance to the 'King-Emperor'. This new formation was, of course, no mean concession by the British Empire – none of these former colonies achieved dominion status without a struggle against imperial direct rule. Despite its recent bitter anti-imperialist war, this part of Ireland could be forgiven too and readmitted to the British imperial club. These dominions were all explicitly racial formations – power had been devolved to their settler colonial rather than their native populations. In other words, their self-governing status was predicated on their *whiteness* – this quality was captured in their colloquial characterisation as *white dominions*. Moreover, it was this quality that was reasoned to qualify them for this specific position in the imperial hierarchy. From this perspective, Ireland had white imperial privilege foisted upon it unasked. Rather than taking the form of an anti-imperial, revolutionary Irish state, the Free State was an explicitly British – and white – imperial construction.

145

The main clauses of the Treaty were: Crown forces would withdraw from most of Ireland; the King would be the Head of State and would be represented by a Governor General; members of the new parliament would be required to take an oath of allegiance to the Irish Free State with a secondary part of the oath to 'be faithful to His Majesty King George V, His heirs and successors by law, in virtue of the common citizenship'; Northern Ireland (which had been manufactured earlier by the Government of Ireland Act) would have the option of withdrawing from the Irish Free State within one month of the Treaty coming into effect; if Northern Ireland chose to withdraw, a Boundary Commission would be constituted to draw the boundary between it and the Irish Free State; Britain would continue to control the Treaty Ports (Berehaven, Cóbh and Lough Swilly) for the Royal Navy;[1] the Irish Free State would assume responsibility for a proportionate part of the United Kingdom's debt, as it stood on the date of signature. Crucially, the Treaty would have superior status in Irish law. In the event of a conflict between it and the new 1922 Constitution of the Irish Free State, the Treaty would take precedence. In summary, this new 26-county state was significantly *unfree* for a 'free state'.

From the first it was clear that the British Empire would continue to intervene very directly in the life of this state: supplying ordnance to the Free State forces; insisting that the new constitution could not be republican and thus precipitating the main split in Sinn Féin in the Dáil and the IRA in the country; at one point, Churchill even planned to intervene militarily against the anti-Treaty IRA elements in the Four Courts. In other words, the continuing British interest in the politics of Ireland remained selfish, and strategic rather than symbolic. Crucially, the spiritual and physical break with England and empire that had been so central to the ethos of 1916 and the Tan war was replaced with a new imperial nexus. Ireland had become a white dominion of the British Empire by default.[2] Neither side in the Tan war had campaigned for this status; unionists wanted the union, and republicans wanted the republic. With hindsight the Free State also carried an ominous new – if hardly recognised – quality: in this new imperial formation, Ireland and the Irish were defined by whiteness for the first time.

Civil War 1922-3: 'a madness from within'

From this distance it is instructive to remember that when the Treaty was signed in 1921 the 'Free State' was even less tangible than the Republic declared in 1916. The Tan war or 'war of independence' ended with a truce in July 1921. British troops were confined to barracks but negotiations on a settlement were delayed because of the – ultimately unmet – British demand that the IRA decommission its weapons. These negotiations

---

[1] The Treaty Ports Annex to the Treaty also included reference to Belfast Lough because Northern Ireland was included within the original territory of the Irish Free State.

[2] Maxwell observes this continuity: '1922 was the annus mirabilis – the "wonderful year" of modernist literature in English. James Joyce's *Ulysses*, the novel that changed everything *but the Ireland it dissected*, was published in Paris' (Maxwell 2015, emphasis added).

resulted in the Anglo-Irish Treaty signed in London under the threat from Lloyd George of 'immediate and terrible war'. Article One made the constitutional status starkly clear – it was not to be a republic but rather to join the white dominions of the British Empire:

> Ireland shall have the same constitutional status in the Community of Nations known as the British Empire as the Dominion of Canada, the Commonwealth of Australia, the Dominion of New Zealand, and the Union of South Africa, with a Parliament having powers to make laws for the peace, order and good government of Ireland and an Executive responsible to that Parliament, and shall be styled and known as the Irish Free State.

The ratification of the Treaty gives some sense of constitutional contortions employed on both sides to lend legitimacy to this process. It had to be ratified in *triplicate*: by Dáil Éireann, by both Houses at Westminster, and by the House of Commons of Southern Ireland. By far the most contentious and divisive of these processes was the endorsement by the Dáil. After nine days of debate it was passed on 7 January 1922, by a vote of 64 to 57. For opponents, this was the end of the Republic declared in 1916 and endorsed in the 1918 election. Moreover, from this perspective it represented an even more profound disavowal of Irish identity. As Cathal Brugha characterised it, the Treaty signified 'committing national suicide':[3]

> [B]reaking the national tradition that has been handed down through centuries... doing for the first time a thing that no generation thought of doing before – wilfully, voluntarily admitting ourselves to be British subjects, and taking the oath of allegiance voluntarily to an English king... (Dáil Éireann, 'Debate on Treaty', Saturday, 7 January 1922)

For all the bitterness of the divisions in the Dáil, this process was not specified in the Treaty which required instead a meeting of the House of Commons of the Parliament of Southern Ireland. This body had been established by the Government of Ireland Act but had never met since all but four of its elected members were in Sinn Féin and constituted the Second Dáil instead. Yet, it duly formally approved the Treaty on 14 January 1922. The meeting itself had a bizarre liminal status, since it was neither convened or conducted in accordance with the procedures established for the Parliament of Southern Ireland nor declared a session of Dáil Éireann. Anti-Treaty members of the Dáil absented themselves, meaning only pro-Treaty members as well as the four elected unionists for Trinity College (who had never sat in Dáil Éireann) attended the meeting. Thus 'Southern Ireland' approved the Treaty, nominated Michael Collins as chairman of the Provisional Government and then dispersed. This was the only time the House

---

[3] Cathal Brugha (1874-1922) was Chief of Staff of the IRA from 1917 to 1919. He was a TD from 1918 to 1922. Brugha was elected *Ceann Comhairle* of the First Dáil at its first meeting on 21 January 1919. He read out the Declaration of Independence that ratified the establishment of the Irish Republic. He was also appointed first president of the Dáil on a temporary basis until 1 April 1919, when Eamon de Valera took his place. He was mortally wounded as commandant of republican forces on O'Connell Street at the start of the Civil War.

of Commons of Southern Ireland ever functioned. But it was this partitionist rump of the Government of Ireland Act that formally created the Free State. On 16 January 1922 there was a formal transfer of Dublin Castle from the UK to the 'Provisional Government' established by the Treaty – but those opposed to the Treaty refused to recognise the legitimacy of this new formation. When the Free State took command of Beggars Bush Barracks on 31 January, a new 'National Army' emerged out of the pro-Treaty elements of the IRA.

The legislation required to establish the Free State was enacted by the Parliament of the United Kingdom – the Irish Free State (Agreement) Act which became law on 31 March 1922. This new, partitioned state then called a general election on 18 June 1922. Pro- and anti-Treaty factions went into the election, still both calling themselves Sinn Féin.[4] Pro-Treaty Sinn Féin won the election with 239,193 votes to 133,864 for Anti-Treaty Sinn Féin. A greater number voted for other parties, including the Irish Labour Party, most of whom supported the Treaty. Since anti-Treaty TDs now boycotted the self-identified 'Third Dáil', the state-building continued apace without them. This body reconstituted itself as a constituent assembly. The Constitution of the Irish Free State (*Bunreacht Shaorstát Eireann*) was adopted by this Dáil Éireann sitting as a constituent assembly in October 1922. In response the UK parliament enacted the Irish Free State Constitution Act 1922. Thus, the Irish Free State came into existence formally by a royal proclamation when its constitution became law on 6 December 1922.

In tandem with the political divisions in Sinn Féin, the IRA, which regarded itself as the guarantor of the Irish Republic, was also fundamentally split by the Treaty. These tensions came to the fore as British institutions began to be transferred to the Provisional government. On 14 April 1922, anti-Treaty IRA militants, led by Rory O'Connor, occupied the Four Courts and several other buildings in central Dublin. The British Government put pressure on the Free State government to resolve this situation. This pressure increased following the assassination of Field Marshal Henry Hughes Wilson in London in June 1922, even though it appeared that this action had been the responsibility of pro-Treaty volunteers. Lloyd George informed Michael Collins:

> The ambiguous position of the Irish Republican Army can no longer be ignored by the British Government. Still less can Mr. Rory O'Connor be permitted to remain with his followers and his arsenal in open rebellion in the heart of Dublin in possession of the Courts of Justice, organising and sending out from the centre enterprises of

---

[4] There was an election pact between Collins and de Valera before the election: 'We are agreed that a National Coalition Panel for this third Dáil, representing both parties in the Dáil, and in the Sinn Féin organisation, be sent forward on the ground that the national position requires the entrusting of the Government of the country into the joint hands of those who have been the strength of the national situation during the last few years, without prejudice to their respective positions [and] that this Coalition Panel be sent forward as from the Sinn Féin organisation, the number from each party being their present strength in the Dáil' (cited in Mitchell and Ó Snodaigh 1985: 134-5). This balance was also supposed to constitute a 'Coalition Government' after the election. But the participation of the Irish Labour Party and other parties undermined the delicate balance between pro- and anti-Treaty TDs.

murder not only in the area of your Government but also in the six Northern Counties
and in Great Britain. His Majesty's Government cannot consent to a continuance of
this state of things, and they feel entitled to ask you formally to bring it to an end
forthwith. Assistance has on various occasions been given to Dominions of the Empire
in cases where their authority was challenged by rebellion on their soil; and His
Majesty's Government are prepared to place at your disposal the necessary pieces of
artillery which may be required, or otherwise to assist you as may be arranged. I am
to inform you that they regard the continued toleration of this rebellious defiance of
principles of the Treaty as incompatible with its faithful execution. They feel that now
you are supported by the declared will of the Irish people in favour of the Treaty, they
have a right to expect that the necessary action will be taken by your Government
without delay. (Cited Mitchell and Ó Snodaigh 1985: 137)

The Provisional Government finally acted when the anti-Treaty forces occupying the
Four Courts kidnapped their former IRA comrade and now National Army Lieutenant-
General Ginger O'Connell. Collins gave the Four Courts garrison an ultimatum to leave
the building on 27 June. The Provisional Government appointed Collins Commander-in-
Chief of the National Army. Collins accepted the British offer of artillery from Richmond
barracks in Inchicore. This was used to bombard the Four Courts and the Civil War
officially began. Richard Mulcahy, Minister for Defence, characterised the conflict to the
new National Army on 28 June:

> Your efforts have brought our county into the mid-stream of the world – brought
> it here with our national morale raised by the tempering effects of your struggle
> against our nation's oppressors, with our national prestige raised by the brilliance
> of that struggle... Today having driven the tyranny of the stranger from our land,
> instead of having the opportunity to turn to these services of construction which
> must develop and crown the strength of our county, you are called upon to serve
> her still in arms, to protect her from a madness from within, from men who seek to
> inflict injury and injustice upon particular individuals and upon particular sections
> of their countrymen, and who conceive the mad purpose of driving our county by
> such actions back into a war which can be avoided for her, and by taunt and threat
> and forced disorder drive our gallant people hopelessly into a struggle that their
> strength cannot stand. (Cited Mitchell and Ó Snodaigh 1985: 137)

Similarly, the IRA framed its struggle with a proclamation issued at the start of the
Civil War:

> Fellow Citizens of the Irish Republic: The fateful hour has come. At the dictation of
> our hereditary enemy our rightful cause is being treacherously assailed by recreant
> Irishmen... We ... appeal to all citizens who have withstood unflinchingly the
> oppression of the enemy during the past six years, to rally to the support of the
> Republic and recognise that the resistance now being offered is but the continuance
> of the struggle that was suspended with the British. We especially appeal to our
> former comrades of the Irish Republic to return to that allegiance and thus guard the
> Nation's honour from the infamous stigma that their sons aided her foes in retaining a
> hateful domination over her. (Cited Mitchell and Ó Snodaigh 1985: 139-140)

The anti-Treaty forces in the Four Courts surrendered after three days of bombardment and the storming of the building by Provisional Government troops. Pitched battles continued in Dublin until 5 July, as anti-Treaty IRA units from the Dublin Brigade occupied O'Connell Street. After a week of fighting, leaving 65 people dead – including Cathal Brugha, the Ceann Comhairle of the First Dáil who had read out the Declaration of Independence – the Free State government was firmly in control of Dublin and anti-Treaty forces dispersed around the country. Anti-Treaty forces still held Cork, Limerick, and Waterford as part of what they termed the 'Munster Republic'. However, government victories in the cities soon forced a return to guerrilla warfare. IRA Chief-of-Staff Liam Lynch ordered anti-Treaty IRA units to disperse and form flying columns as they had when fighting the British.

Michael Collins – Chairman of the Provisional Government and Commander-in-Chief of the National Army – was killed in an ambush by anti-Treaty Republicans at *Béal na mBláth*, near his home in Cork, in August 1922. Arthur Griffith, the Free State president, had also died naturally of a brain haemorrhage ten days before. This left the Free State government in the hands of W.T. Cosgrave and the Free State army under the command of General Richard Mulcahy. For a brief period, with rising casualties among its troops and its two principal leaders dead, it looked as if the state might collapse before it was legally proclaimed. Instead it ratcheted up the war. On 27 September 1922, the Free State Provisional Government introduced an Army Emergency Powers Resolution extending the legislation for setting up military tribunals and transferring judicial powers to the Army Council. This 'Public Safety Bill' empowered military tribunals to impose life imprisonment, as well as the death penalty, for 'aiding or abetting attacks' on state forces, possession of arms and ammunition or explosives 'without the proper authority' and 'looting destruction or arson'. The list of punishments available to the Military Courts as a result of the Free State 'Proclamation' of 10 October 1922 warned of the implications of continued 'insurrection' and reprised the coercive methodologies of Ireland's colonial past: 'Death, Penal Servitude, Imprisonment, Deportation, Internment, Fine'. Anti-Treaty forces were also losing political support across the 26 counties. Crucially, on 11 October 1922 the Irish Catholic hierarchy issued a pastoral letter approved by the Provisional Government which condemned the anti-Treaty forces and appealed to them to 'recognise the lawful government' (Aldous and Puirseil 2008: 141-5). This intervention directly denied the sacraments and a Catholic burial to volunteers who had died on active service or hunger strike. But it also *de facto* sanctioned the extra-judicial killings by the state. With this singularly ignominious alliance of Christ and Caesar, the 26-county area was stabilised.

On the republican side the commitment to 'very drastic measures' by Chief of Staff Liam Lynch hinted at some reciprocal brutality as it attempted to prevent this state building. Quite apart from its ruthlessness, the Civil War bloodletting removed some of the most able and influential political actors on both sides. The Free State side lost Collins and Sean Hayes – and later Kevin O'Higgins; on the republican side a whole generation of republican leaders was singled out for summary execution: including Erskine Childers (for possession of a handgun given him by Michael Collins), Rory O'Connor, Harry Boland and Liam Mellows. The intimacy of this conflict was personified by the Minister of Justice Kevin O'Higgins signing the execution order for Rory O'Connor who had been best man at his wedding only a year previously. Further key figures were killed in action in fighting between pro- and anti-Treaty forces, including Liam Lynch and Cathal Brugha.

Lynch's death was perceived to facilitate the end of conflict. He was regarded as an unreconstructed militarist having declared: 'We have declared for an Irish Republic. We will live by no other law'. His replacement as IRA Chief-of-Staff, Frank Aiken, believed the war could not be won by anti-Treaty forces and ordered the 'suspension of offensive' from 30 April, 1923. Eamon de Valera[5] – who had remained sidelined as an 'ordinary volunteer' during the conflict – supported the order and issued a statement to Anti-Treaty volunteers:

> Soldiers of the Republic! Legion of the Rearguard! The Republic can no longer be defended successfully by your arms. Further sacrifice of life would now be in vain, and the continuance of the struggle in arms unwise in the National interest. Military victory must be allowed to rest for the moment with those who have destroyed the Republic. Other means must be sought to safeguard the nation's right. (Cited in Hepburn 1980: 129)

Within three years this commitment to 'other means' was confirmed when Sinn Féin split again over the issue of abstentionism from the Free State Dáil. In March 1926, the majority – led by Mary MacSwiney and Father Michael O'Flanagan – stayed with Sinn Féin when Fianna Fáil under de Valera split from the organisation.[6] The broad republican

---

[5] Éamon de Valera (1882-1975). Born in New York city to a Spanish father and Irish mother. His name was a *mestizo* journey in itself, first registered as George de Valero and changed to Edward de Valera before he assumed the Irish form. Returning to Ireland aged two, he was raised by his maternal grandmother and became a maths teacher. He was a member of the IRB and the Irish Volunteers and was involved in the Howth gun-running in 1914. In 1916 he was commandant at Boland's Mill during the Rising. He was arrested and sentenced to death, but the sentence was commuted largely because of his US connection. After imprisonment, he was released in the amnesty of June 1917. In July 1917, he was elected MP for East Clare; he was elected President of Sinn Féin in the same year. In May 1918, he and 72 other leading republicans were arrested for the spurious 'German Plot' used to intern Sinn Féin leaders but he escaped from Lincoln Jail. He became president of the First and Second Dáilaí but resigned after the Anglo-Irish Treaty. He led anti-Treaty Sinn Féin until 1926, when he and his supporters left the party to set up Fianna Fáil which he led for the next 33 years. He took over as President of the Executive Council from W.T. Cosgrave in 1932. He served as Taoiseach from 1937 to 1948, from 1951 to 1954 and from 1957 to 1959. He was elected President of Ireland in 1959 and served two full terms.

[6] Mary MacSwiney (1872-1942). Born in London, her mother was English and her father Irish. She studied for a teaching diploma at Cambridge University. She was a suffragist and became a founder member and Vice President of *Cumann na mBan* in 1914. She was imprisoned following the Easter Rising and dismissed from her teaching post. Upon release, she and her sister Annie founded *Scoil Íte*, sister school in Cork to Pearse's *Scoil Eanna*. After the death of her brother Terence on hunger strike in October 1920, she was elected for Sinn Féin in Cork and took her seat in the Second Dáil. She was excluded from the Treaty delegation to London as de Valera regarded her as 'too extreme'. She vociferously opposed the Treaty. During the Civil War, she was arrested and interned in Mountjoy. She went on hunger strike, and the Women Prisoner's Defence League was formed in August 1922 in support of her and other republican women internees. She

movement which had established the First Dáil continued to fracture. The IRA – which in its first iteration had created the Republic – was finally outlawed by the state through the Constitution (Declaration of Unlawful Associations) Order 1931, alongside other republican organisations such as *Fianna Éireann* and *Cumann na mBan*. Yet it continued to hold to the principle that the Republic declared in 1916 could not be liquidated by any other party.

Meanwhile, from 1923 onwards the Free State became an exercise in fact creation, whatever the principle involved. Pro-Treaty Sinn Féin reconstituted itself as *Cumann na nGaedheal* and entrenched its position in government with a further election in 1923 although abstentionist 'Republicans' under de Valera (they did not stand for election as Sinn Féin) continued to attract nearly 30 per cent of the vote. While it struggled with ongoing instability – not least in the 1924 Army mutiny[7] and the failure of the Boundary Commission[8] – the legitimacy of the state was now recognised by most Irish people and most governments around the world. Arguably, the Civil War ended with the assassination in 1927 of the Minister of Justice, Kevin O'Higgins. He had been personally responsible for the summary executions of some 81 republican prisoners during the Civil War.[9] At one level the killing of the Minister of Justice suggested a profound crisis in the new state. In retrospect, however, this death marked the end of the primacy of revolutionary militarism. The biographies of the three-person assassination squad offer a telling thumbnail sketch of the splintering of the IRA after 1922. Tim Coughlan was a member of Fianna Fáil as well as the IRA (rendering clear the notion of 'slightly constitutional'). He was subsequently killed in 1928 in disputed circumstances by former IRA member and undercover agent Sean Harling. Bill Gannon joined the Communist Party of Ireland

---

retained her seat at the 1923 general election but along with other Sinn Féin members refused to enter the Free State Dáil. She lost her seat at the 1927 general election. She remained a committed republican and unrepentant opponent of the Free State until her death (Fallon 1986).

[7] In March 1924, senior Irish Army officers presented in the name of the 'IRA Organisation' an ultimatum to the government demanding the removal of the Army Council and an end to demobilisations and reorganisation. The context was the transition from the Civil War 'National Army' to the smaller peacetime 'Defence Forces' which continue to the present. Invoking the spirit of Michael Collins, the episode spoke to those pro-Treaty forces who had expected the Free State to be a stepping-stone to the Republic rather than an end in itself. Lee suggests, 'the "army mutiny" was an unedifying episode as much for the opportunist cynicism it exposed among the civilian politicians as for the militarist threat to civilian government' (1989: 101).

[8] It had been argued by pro-Treaty southerners that the Boundary Commission would transfer significant nationalist areas of the north – including Derry City – to the south and therefore make Northern Ireland unviable and reunification inevitable. Outrage was, however, greatest in the north. Cahir Healy suggested: 'The Nationalists of Fermanagh are overwhelmed with amazement that any men representing the county can sign such a document. It is a betrayal of the Nationalists of the North and a denial of every statement put forward by the Free State in their alleged support of our case since 1921' (cited in Mitchell and Ó Snodaigh 1985: 170).

[9] Kevin O'Higgins (1892-1927) was a leading member of Sinn Féin, the IRA and *Cumann na nGaedheal*. Alongside Griffith and Collins, O'Higgins was the key architect of the Free State. In his capacity as Minister for Justice, he established the Gardaí and made Eoin O'Duffy commissioner. When the Civil War broke out in June 1922, O'Higgins introduced emergency and extrajudicial measures, and he confirmed the death sentences of 81 republican prisoners during the conflict. In reprisal, the anti-Treaty IRA murdered his father and burned his family home in Stradbally, Co Laois. He was assassinated by an IRA unit in Booterstown Avenue while on his way to mass.

and played a central role in organising Irish *brigadistas* to fight on the Republican side in the Spanish Civil War. Archie Doyle remained a prominent IRA volunteer. Up to his death in 1980 he remained unrepentant for having executed O'Higgins. Although it did not seem like it at the time, the O'Higgins execution marked the end of a phase of Free State politics framed by militarism on all sides. In response to his killing – which followed the 1927 election – *Cumann na nGaedheal* introduced a further Public Safety Act which introduced the death penalty and an Electoral Amendment Act which forced elected TDs to take the oath of allegiance or lose their seats. Thus, the murder further encouraged Fianna Fáil entry to the Dáil. Within five years Fianna Fáil would win the 1932 election and form the government of the Free State.

This transfer of power was the final confirmation of state legitimacy. There were many actors who believed that the state belonged to the pro-Treaty forces that had created it and supported the notion of a coup. These included Garda chief (and future Blueshirt and leader of Fine Gael) Eoin O'Duffy. The IRA was similarly convinced that a coup was likely in the event of a Fianna Fáil victory. In the end, however, power transferred peacefully and 'constitutionally'. In some ways this was the greatest achievement of this state. It managed to construct a functioning democracy out of a bitter civil war and a dishonest disavowal of republican principle. No doubt a profound denial around the exclusion of the north was part of that process – arguably this elision was simply too hard to address for anyone who had committed themselves to the Proclamation in 1916 or the Declaration of Independence in 1919. Nevertheless, in comparative context, and in a significant way, the political forces in the state managed to function despite the brutal legacies of civil war. In this regard, perhaps the greatest achievement of the state was the way in which it dealt with – or did not deal with – the legacy of the past. This appears striking from a contemporary perspective – no truth and reconciliation commission, no restorative or transitional justice, and Freudian denial of epic proportions. Nevertheless, the Free State managed to contain these tensions within democratic structures. A state that had been born out of the internecine brutality of a 'madness within' managed to move forward very quickly. There is no denying the ruthlessness of the approach – most obviously symbolised by the summary execution of republicans, including many democratically elected officials, by the new state. Yet, despite all the atrocities and reprisals, there could be a transfer of power between the two sides in the Civil War within ten years. And the surviving IRA volunteers who had assassinated the first Minister for Justice could live unhindered in the state. No doubt at one level there was a common reference point that made this possible – these enemies had once been comrades. Many key figures on all sides – including WT Cosgrove and Richard Mulcahy and Gerald Boland and Brian O'Higgins – had been internees in Frongoch under a sentence of penal servitude after the Easter Rising.[10] Moreover, the key

---

[10] Brian O'Higgins (1882-1963) – aka *Brian Ó hUiginn* and *Brian na Banban* – was a poet and Irish language activist who fought in the GPO in 1916. He was elected as a Sinn Féin TD to the First, Second and Third Dáilaí. He resigned from Sinn Féin in 1934 along with Mary MacSwiney in protest at the election of Father Michael O'Flanagan as President on the basis that he had a state job and was therefore 'on the payroll of

combatants in the Civil War had all been Sinn Féin republicans in 1918. And the parties to the split in 1926 remained self-identified republicans. Nevertheless, and especially from the perspective of the bitterness and brutality of later republican – and loyalist – splits and feuds, this moment of transcendence appears remarkable.

Saorstát Éireann 1922-37

Acceptance of the Treaty in 1922 represented – fairly unambiguously – a repudiation of 'the Republic' which most (non-unionist) political and military forces had fought for since 1916. More specifically, this idea of the Republic was something that the entire leadership of the pro-Treaty elements of Sinn Féin had endorsed. In other words, this new governing elite had to move very quickly to divest itself of the trappings of traditional republican anti-imperialism. It cannot have been easy for many of these leaders – schooled in the politics of the IRB and Gaelic League – to accept the *volte face* in their political aspirations.

Nevertheless, the new state embraced its dominion status. The first Imperial Conference attended by the new Irish Free State met in London in October and November 1923. (It was to attend another in 1926 and then in 1930 – the last that any Irish government ever participated in.) [11] Here was the clear symbol of the Republic abolished – the Irish Free State had joined the imperial family – indeed it now numbered among the white dominions. [12] The decolonisation project – begun through the Gaelic League and IRB – and emblemised by the 1916 Proclamation – was clearly and abruptly deferred. At best, the Treaty could be presented as an historical compromise: inevitable given the balance of military and political forces in Ireland in 1922 and thus a stage on the path to decolonisation. This was famously characterised by Michael Collins – who was, of course, himself a convinced republican – as the 'freedom to achieve freedom'.

The intense ideological debates of the First and Second Dáil and the Treaty were part of a more nuanced and prolonged ideological journey away from the Republic and

---

a usurping government'. Along with MacSwiney, O'Higgins was one of the seven who had been elected to the Second Dáil, who met with the IRA Army Council in 1938 and signed over what they regarded as the authority of the Government of Dáil Éireann. This was the link whereby different iterations of the IRA continued to present the Army Council as the legitimate government of the Irish Republic.

[11] The Irish Free State was still regarded as a Commonwealth member at the time of the 1937 Imperial Conference – and later again in 1944 – but chose not to participate. De Valera said it was 'not in the interests of the state' (Dáil Éireann 1937).

[12] Ireland was initially invited to attend the 1948 Commonwealth Prime Ministers Conference – the first imperial conference to include newly liberated Black commonwealth countries like India and Pakistan. After Ireland announced the pending repeal of its last connection to the British crown, this invitation was revoked. At the time, the British Commonwealth still regarded Ireland as one of its members even though Ireland had not participated in any equivalent conferences since 1932. Irish foreign minister Sean MacBride and finance minister Patrick McGilligan attended one day of the conference as observers. Four days before the 1949 Conference met, Ireland formally declared itself a republic. The other members of the Commonwealth regarded this declaration as terminating Ireland's membership.

towards dominion status. Both sides in the Civil War and in subsequent southern Irish politics made some reference to the 1916 Proclamation of the Irish Republic and the 1919 Irish Declaration of Independence. For many Free Staters, the connection to the *idea* of the Republic remained important. It was imperative that their leadership had been 'out' in 1916. Of course, for many their connection to the IRA and the military leadership *was* unambiguous – from Collins and Cosgrave to Mulcahy and Kevin O'Higgins. In other words, while they had committed to a historic compromise that clearly fell far short of the Republic, they did not repudiate the principle. It was pragmatism – in the face of Lloyd George's threat of 'immediate and terrible war' – that justified the change of heart. Many of the shibboleths of Irish republicanism remained genuinely important to them. The Irish language project remained central to the new state as did many of the cultural manifestations of republicanism – including the national flag.[13]

For anti-Treaty republicans, of course, this issue of the repudiation of the Republic was even more central than partition – it was the core reason for the rejection of the Treaty. Thus, while the Republic was never recognised by the UK or the Treaty, it retained a symbolic reference for all the key parties in nationalist politics. Ironically in retrospect, the formerly anti-Treaty Fianna Fáil worked hardest to make Collins' prescription of the 'freedom to obtain freedom' work in the context of the new state. Once they decided to end abstentionism and enter the Dáil in 1926, Fianna Fáil engaged within the Free State structures in precisely this reformist way in order to distance the state from the UK, the Crown and the British Empire. From the 1932 Irish election – when Fianna Fáil took power for the first time – successive Irish governments unilaterally amended the state's status: the *Constitution (Removal of Oath) Act 1933* implicitly abrogated the 1921 Anglo-Irish Treaty; the 27th amendment and External Relations Act 1936 attenuated the role of the monarchy; the enactment of the Constitution in 1937 established the office of President. The state also disengaged with Commonwealth structures – albeit it was not until the 1949 Republic of Ireland Act that Ireland formally left the British Commonwealth. While the UK actively campaigned against these changes, it subsequently ratified the changed relationship in the Éire (Confirmation of Agreements) Act 1938 and the Ireland Act 1949.

The economic programme of the Free State also saw a protracted process of attempted separation from economic dependency. Once again, the more radical aspirations of the

---

[13] These tensions produced contradictory figures like Earnán de Blaghd or Ernest Blythe. He was variously an Orangeman and an IRB member who missed the Easter Rising because he was already imprisoned by the British for his republican activism. He was elected Sinn Féin TD for North Monaghan in 1918. As a pro-Treaty minister, he repressed republican opposition with all the commitment of a northern unionist. He was a financial conservative and ended up supporting Irish fascism. But his commitment to the Irish language and the cultural revival never faltered. He was a key supporter of the Abbey Theatre and his aggressive approach to language issues kept the revival in a preeminent position. He wrote *Briseadh na Teorann* (The smashing of the border) – in Irish – in 1955. He also published three volumes of autobiography: *Trasna na Bóinne* (1957), *Slán le hUltaibh* (1969) and *Gaeil á Múscailt* (1973).

Republic – from Connolly to the *Clár Oibre Poblacánaighe*, the Democratic Programme of the First Dáil – were summarily shelved. Kevin O'Higgins infamously derided the quasi-socialist Democratic Programme as 'mostly poetry'. Thus, the Free State economic project began in fairly unambitious fashion with the commitment to 'balanced books' by Minister of Finance Earnán de Blaghd (Ernest Blythe). In 1924 Blythe infamously cut the old age pension. Patrick McGilligan – another northerner from Coleraine and *Cumann na nGaedheal* Minister of Industry and Commerce, took this approach a disturbing step further in the Dáil in the same year: 'There are certain limited funds are our disposal. People may have to die in this country and may have to die of starvation' (Dáil Éireann, October 30, 1924).

In five years, things had moved a long way from the aspirations of the Democratic Programme. Here was the new state playing to a conservative economic agenda – there was no question of repudiating the British imperial debt. No doubt a more radical approach would have ended any possibility of further borrowing and would have been framed as fiscal irresponsibility. Although some discussion of reparations in a formal decolonisation context might have been expected, in contrast, in the Treaty the Free State had committed itself explicitly to sharing the debts of Empire.

This ongoing dependency can be traced – symbolically and economically – through the trajectory of the Irish currency. Sterling continued to be used after independence until the Irish Free State introduced its own currency in 1928. The Currency Act 1927 pegged the new Saorstat punt at 1:1 with sterling. *De facto* parity with sterling was maintained for another fifty years. As with sterling, the £sd system was used, albeit with the Irish names *punt*, *scilling* and *pingin*. The aesthetics of this new currency – envisioned by a committee chaired by WB Yeats – symbolised the Irishness of the new Free State powerfully. But it equally powerfully emphasised the practical dependency of the state – the link to sterling remained absolute.[14] Even as late as the 1970s, when the British government decimalised its currency, the Irish government felt obliged to follow suit. For this whole period, the Free State kept its currency in a form of quasi-monetary union with its currency pegged to sterling. This continued from 1926 – through periods of profound UK economic shock – right up to 1978 when Ireland joined the EU Monetary Union and the European Exchange Rate Mechanism, and the UK did not.

Nevertheless, the economic relationship did inevitably change even in the context of

---

[14] After the new Constitution changed the name of the state in 1938, the means of tender was referred to as the 'Irish pound' through The Currency Act 1927 Adaptation Order, 1938. In 1926 a committee was appointed to design the coinage for the new state. There were five people on the committee with WB Yeats as its chair. They took the decision to have a harp on the back of each coin and an animal on the front. Several sculptors, most of them from abroad, were invited to submit designs. In the end the designs of an Englishman, Percy Metcalfe, were chosen. The animals featured on the coins were a horse, a salmon, a bull, a wolfhound, a hare, a hen, a pig and a woodcock (Old Currency Exchange 2014). Some critics suggested that the designs indicated that the mission of the new state was to be a farmyard. Maude Gonne McBride's criticism was more scathing: 'The coins were entirely suitable for the Free State: designed by an Englishman, minted in England, representative of English values, paid for by the Irish people' (quoted in Morris 2004).

pro-Treaty fiscal conservatism. Part of this dynamic was the commitment of the British state to make its new white dominion work. Concerns about stability, and about possible losses to its own subjects post-'independence', led the UK state to agree to continue to share the currency and to support the new state in the form of debt relief and sovereign debt guarantees.[15] Under the London Agreement, the Free State was relieved from its Treaty obligation to pay its share of the public debt of the United Kingdom (Fitzgerald 2017; Fitzgerald and Kenny 2017). This deal was done amid tensions around the Boundary Commission and the treatment of northern Catholics. In other words, it represented a shabby compromise in which finally and explicitly 32-county concerns were traded for 26-county stability. As Fitzgerald (2017) starkly concludes: 'The end results were a solvent Irish economy but continuing discrimination in the North for the following 50 years'. The Financial Settlement between the British government and the government of the Irish Free State – signed by de Blaghd and Churchill in March 1926 – copper-fastened this deal but also recommitted to paying annuities associated with the Irish Land Acts.[16] These originated from the UK government loans granted to Irish tenant farmers by the Land Commission from the 1880s onwards, which had enabled them to purchase their land from their former landlords. This did not signal any radical decoupling of the Free State economy from the UK.

The issue of annuities came to the fore again in the context of the 'economic war' of the 1930s – which invites the question of how much this episode was part of an anti-colonial/post-colonial struggle. Certainly, de Valera framed it in these terms. In 1932 he suggested to the British government that:

> During these ten years [since the establishment of the state] there has been extracted from us, though in part only as a consequence of the agreement [Treaty], a financial tribute which, relative to population, puts a greater burden on the people of the Irish Free State that the burden of the war reparation payments on the people of Germany... (De Valera 1932)

The economic war also reflected the wider tensions surrounding the Fianna Fáil commitment to changing the constitutional status of the Free State *vis-á-vis* Britain and the Empire. On assuming power in 1932, the Fianna Fáil government under Éamon de Valera embarked upon a protectionist policy and tariffs were introduced for a wide range of imported goods. These were mainly from Britain, which remained by far the Free State's largest trading partner. This approach was supposed to accentuate the measures brought in by the previous *Cumann na nGaedheal* government to boost tillage farming and industry and to encourage the population to avoid British imports and 'Buy Irish Goods'. Protectionism – led by Minister for Industry and Commerce Seán Lemass – was

---

[15] See further, Foley-Fisher and McLaughlin 2015, on UK post-independence sovereign debt guarantees to Ireland.

[16] 'Heads of the Ultimate Financial Settlement between the British government and the government of the Irish Free State' (Royal Irish Academy 2000).

regarded as a necessary condition to develop Irish industry and remove the economic dependence on Britain. It was also intended to compensate for the impact of the Great Depression in 1929, which saw a marked fall in demand for Irish agricultural products in international markets. This contributed to a profound imbalance of trade and a mounting national debt. In theory, protectionism would lead to the Free State becoming both agriculturally and industrially self-sufficient.

The Trade War lasted from 1932 to 1938. The trigger was the Fianna Fáil government refusal to continue reimbursing Britain with land annuities.[17] In 1923, Cosgrave's *Cumann na nGaedheal* government assured Britain that the Free State would honour its debts and transfer the land annuities as well as meeting other financial liabilities. But Fianna Fáil wanted to end the repayment. Discussion of the Free State's liability to administer land annuities payments led to a debate as to whether these were private or public debts. Less technically, they were debt incurred against land which had been expropriated from the Irish people by the colonial state – put simply it was Irish people compensating British landlords for land which had been stolen from them through colonial land grabbing in the first place. In 1932, de Valera insisted that the annuities were part of the public debt from which the Free State had been exempted by the 1925 London Agreement and declared that the Free State would no longer pay them to Britain. His government passed the Land Act of 1933. This reduced the annuities to be paid and allowed the remainder to be spent on local government projects in the 26 counties.

British/Irish negotiations broke down in October 1932 over whether the liability to pay the land annuities should be adjudicated by a panel chosen from experts from the British Empire – as the British suggested – or from the wider international community – as the Irish suggested. In a counterclaim to the British, de Valera demanded that the British should pay back the £30 million already paid in Land Commission annuities and pay the Irish Free State £400 million in respect of Britain's overtaxation of Ireland between 1801 and 1922. In other words, this framing of the issue did begin to look more like reparations. The British Prime Minister Ramsay MacDonald responded with the imposition of 20 per cent import duty on Free State agricultural products into the UK. These constituted 90 per cent of all Free State exports and demand for Irish goods fell starkly. The Free State responded by placing a similar duty on British imports and on coal from the UK. However, the asymmetric relationship between the two economies ensured that the UK economy was much less affected than the Irish economy.

The Irish government continued to collect the annuities at a reduced rate. The government also urged people to support the confrontation with Britain as a national sacrifice to be shared by every citizen. Farmers were urged to turn to tillage to produce enough food for the domestic market. The Economic War impacted particularly on farmers and exacerbated class and political tensions in the rural Free State. As the

---

[17] The Stormont government was also keeping its portion of these annuities and not returning these to the British Exchequer, but this disparity did not enter the debate (House of Commons 1937).

cattle industry declined, the government purchased most of the surplus beef. Bounties were paid for cattle slaughtered because they could not be exported. The Fianna Fáil government also introduced a 'free beef for the poor' scheme. The associated agricultural depression had disastrous consequences for many farmers, especially the larger cattle breeders. With echoes of the Land War of the previous century, they refused to pay property rates or pay their land annuities. To recover payments due, the government counteracted by impounding livestock which was then auctioned off for less than its value. Farmers campaigned to have these sales boycotted, and blocked roads and railways. Gardaí were mobilised to protect buyers of the impounded goods and, in the process, people were killed and injured by the 'Broy Harriers'.[18] These developments began to create serious legitimacy problems for Fianna Fáil.

Lemass also introduced the Control of Manufactures Act 1932, whereby the majority ownership of Free State companies was to be limited to Irish citizens. While the introduction of new import tariffs helped some Irish industries to expand, this also encouraged larger Irish companies with foreign investors, such as Guinness, to relocate their headquarters – and consequently their corporate taxes – abroad. The recession in the farming economy also led to a decline in the demand for manufactured goods, so that Irish industries were also affected. Some British exporters were critical of their government due to the loss of business they suffered in Ireland. Their pressure, allied to the discontent of Irish farmers with the Fianna Fáil government, encouraged both sides to seek settlement. Tensions began to ease in 1935 when Britain and Ireland signed the Coal-Cattle pact – which removed tariffs from both crucial commodities. The pact signalled a desire on both sides to end the Economic War and the Anglo-Irish Trade Agreement – including a final resolution of the land annuities issue – was reached in April 1938 (Lee 2008: 214).

Alongside this economic conflict, there was an intense period of constitutional and political transformation throughout the 1930s. At the heart of this was the dual process whereby the formerly anti-Treaty Fianna Fáil first came to terms with the reality of the 26-county state and then became the dominant political force within that state. Seán Lemass famously outlined the beginning of this process in the Dáil in 1928:

> Fianna Fáil is a slightly constitutional party. We are perhaps open to the definition of a constitutional party, but before anything we are a Republican party. We have adopted the method of political agitation to achieve our end, because we believe, in the present circumstances, that method is best in the interests of the nation and of the Republican movement, and for no other reason.... Five years ago the methods

---

[18] Colonel Eamon 'Ned' Broy (1887–1972) was, in succession, a member of the Dublin Metropolitan Police, the Irish Republican Army, the National Army, and An Garda Síochána. He was Michael Collins' principal agent inside the police during the Tan War. He served as Commissioner of Gardaí from 1933 to 1938 after Fianna Fáil replaced Cumann na nGaedheal in government. In 1934 Broy formed the Auxiliary Special Branch – or 'Broy Harriers' – of the Gardaí, mainly with anti-Treaty IRA veterans. It was used first against the fascist Blueshirts, and later against the IRA. It engaged in several controversial fatal shootings, including farmers protesting against the Land War.

we adopted were not the methods we have adopted now. Five years ago we were on the defensive, and perhaps in time we may recoup our strength sufficiently to go on the offensive. Our object is to establish a Republican Government in Ireland. If that can be done by the present methods we have we will be very pleased, but if not we would not confine ourselves to them. (Dáil Éireann 1928)

Over the next decade, Fianna Fáil moved from being a 'slightly constitutional party' to becoming the natural party of government in the state. De Valera's Fianna Fáil government initially decriminalised the IRA and freed prisoners who had been interned by *Cumann na nGaedhael*. But Fianna Fáil reintroduced the ban with the Constitution (Declaration of Unlawful Association) Order 1936. These developments were of course profoundly interdependent. This in turn created a new context for contestation in British/Irish relations within wider imperial developments.

This British/Irish tension was also affected by changes in the wider dynamic of empire. In 1931, the Statute of Westminster granted parliamentary autonomy to the six British 'dominions' (now known as 'Commonwealth realms') within a British 'Commonwealth of Nations'. (The whole Statute applied to the Irish Free State without the need for any acts of ratification.) This had the effect of making the dominions *de facto* sovereign nations. In the 26 counties this created a new context for constitutional change. Since the Irish Free State constitution of 1922 was a direct consequence of the Anglo-Irish Treaty, anti-Treaty forces – notably Fianna Fáil– were committed to removing this key Treaty institution. After 1932, under the provisions of the Statute of Westminster, some of the articles of the original Constitution which were required by the Anglo-Irish Treaty were dismantled by acts of the *Oireachtas* of the Irish Free State. Such amendments removed references to the oath of allegiance, appeals to the United Kingdom's Judicial Committee of the Privy Council, and reframed the relationship to the British Crown and the Governor-General. The abdication of Edward VIII in 1936 provided a further opportunity to redefine the connection to the British Crown. Nevertheless, Fianna Fáil remained keen to completely replace the Treaty Constitution that had been framed by the British government in 1922. In consequence they introduced a new Constitution in 1937 that formally dismantled the 'Irish Free State' and instituted 'Éire' as the framing constitutional status of the 26 counties.

Éire 1937-48: 'pending the re-integration of the national territory'

The formal transition from the Saorstát to Éire was marked by *Bunreacht na hÉireann*, or the Constitution of Ireland. This asserts the national sovereignty of the Irish people. It guarantees certain fundamental rights, along with a popularly elected non-executive president, a bicameral parliament and the separation of powers. An aspect of direct democracy is retained in terms of the Constitution – it may be amended solely by a national referendum. *Bunreacht na hÉireann* continues to be the defining constitutional document of the southern Irish state.

The *Bunreacht* replaced the 1922 Constitution of the Irish Free State. While the transition may have been largely symbolic, it marked the appearance of a new and formally distinct state formation. This came into force on 29 December 1937 following a 26-county-wide referendum held in July 1937. The new Constitution was approved by 56.5 per cent of those voting – but a high number of abstentions meant this comprised just 38.6 per cent of the whole electorate. Since this franchise already excluded one third of the Irish population in the 6 counties, it was a less than auspicious legitimation of a document that continues to frame Irish constitutional life. The 1937 Constitution exemplified all the tensions of an anti-Treaty government trying to transform a state based on the Treaty. It was, therefore, in many ways the embodiment of the ethos of Fianna Fáil. It exemplified all the contradictions of the unfinished revolution, of partition and the continued link to the UK; but it also represented a 'slightly constitutional' party becoming fully constitutional, if not hegemonic. With this finesse, Fianna Fáil finally made peace with the 26-county state through rebranding it in its own image.

At the core of this project was Fianna Fáil embracing pragmatism over principle. This involved coming to terms with a whole bundle of *realpolitik* in terms of the 26-county state formation: the acceptance that the partitioned state existed and that it carried legitimacy for most of its citizens; that it was relatively stable and was, more or less, able to exercise 'a monopoly over the legitimate means of coercion'. This allowed Fianna Fáil – and its core constituency which by now represented the dominant political force within the 26 counties – to begin to progress its project on both the core elements of the unfinished revolution. This meant an end to partition and the restoration of the Republic. It was clear that it could not do much beyond rhetoric on partition since it was now committed to repressing the republican militarism that threatened its own legitimacy from the Left. This aspect of the transition to 'fully constitutional' status was confirmed when Fianna Fáil finally declared the IRA an illegal organisation in 1936.[19]

Fianna Fáil could, however, progress the notional, symbolic republicanism of the 26-county state – the oath and the relationship to the monarch. All of this was concretised in the Constitution of 1937. It saw all the contradictions of unfinished revolution manifest – most significantly, the symbolic commitment to reunification juxtaposed with the *de facto* acceptance of partition. Alongside this, the Catholicism of the 26-county state was made explicit.[20] It bears emphasis that this was only possible in a partitioned state and was arguably the negation of all Irish republican tradition on this issue – from Tone's 'unity of Catholic, Protestant and Dissenter' to the commitment to

---

[19] Constitution (Declaration of Unlawful Association) Order 1936. The anti-imperialist politics of the non-Fianna Fáil, anti-Treaty republican movement in the 1920s is examined in detail in chapter 10.

[20] In 1951, the Taoiseach, John Costello, stated: 'I am an Irishman second, I am a Catholic first, and I accept without qualification in all respects the teaching of the hierarchy and the church to which I belong' (quoted in Maher and O'Brien 2017: 26). Like Craigavon's 'Protestant parliament for a Protestant people', such developments only became possible when partition removed the ability of the minority to curtail the confessional 'enthusiasm' of the majority.

'cherishing all the children of the nation equally' from 1916. Rather than the reality of 'Ireland' in 1937, it reflected the reality of part of Ireland – the partitioned, southern state. It also embodied the 'unfinished revolution'. Article 2 made clear that:

> The national territory consists of the whole island of Ireland, its islands and the territorial seas.

Meanwhile Article 3 addressed the question of how this anti-partitionist principle would function in the context of the practical reality of partition:

> Pending the re-integration of the national territory, and without prejudice to the right of the Parliament and Government established by this Constitution to exercise jurisdiction of the whole of that territory, the law enacted by that parliament should have the like area and extent of application as the law of Saorstát Éireann and the extra-territorial effect.

As discussed further in chapter 6, however, articles 2 and 3 were transformed by the peace negotiations and the Good Friday Agreement. This process quietly transformed the national all-Ireland aspects of the Constitution and reframed them as only referent to the partitioned state. The other motive for replacing the Free State constitution was primarily symbolic with another decolonisation matter close to de Valera's heart. While the Free State had seen a degree of Irish nomenclature and symbolism, this decolonising motif was reinforced in the new Constitution. *An Ghaeilge* was now the first language of the state and embedded across the institutions of government.

The Constitution of Ireland also consolidated a form of Catholic Church hegemony across the new state which could be characterised as 'National Catholicism'. It had many similarities with *Nacionalcatolicismo* in Fascist Spain under Franco.[21] It included a constitutional ban on divorce and confirmed that Catholic social values would be imposed on non-Catholics. The prohibition reflected the Catholic reaction that had come to constitute the social programme of the 26 counties. Ever since the Civil War, the pro- and anti-Treaty blocs had engaged in a Dutch auction on this form of Catholic conservatism. Fianna Fáil – many of whose leaders had been denied the sacraments based on their commitment to the Republic – rehabilitated itself with a renewed commitment to institutionalised Catholicism. This was a core part of its project to become the dominant political force within the 26 counties. Thus Article 44 recognised the 'special position of the Holy Catholic Apostolic and Roman Church as the guardian of the faith professed by the vast majority of its citizens'.

The reality of 'National Catholicism' was, however, even more profound in terms of the *informal* influence of the Catholic Church over the government. From partition onwards, the state made a series of interventions in support of the notion that the Catholic Church was – and should be – hegemonic in most aspects of life in the state. Thus, it was consulted on government policy and the Constitution. From the operation of religious-based censorship to the 'Mother and Child Scheme' controversy (Lee

---

[21] See 'National Catholicism' in Payne 1984: 171-191.

2008: 313-21), the Catholic Church exercised profound control over the politics and administration of the state. The outworking of this 'special position' further confirmed national stereotypes – the first time the state took a position *against* the wishes of the Church hierarchy was when it introduced Sunday opening with the 1959 Intoxicating Liquour Act. The legacy of this fusion of 26-county nationalism and Catholicism was profound and long-lasting. It characterised the social programme of the 26-county state for generations and remained in place at least until the 2018 amendment on abortion.[22]

In many ways the young state was a cold house for liberals, socialists, republicans, feminists and, in particular ways, for Protestants. When the Free State came into being, Protestants constituted approximately 11 per cent of the population. Their numbers were already in decline in the decades before because of factors such as deindustrialisation in Dublin which led skilled Protestant workers to seek employment in England. 'Independence' helped speed up Protestant decline; most obviously British troops left, along with their families. More significantly, this decolonial moment delivered a blow to the Protestant ascendancy of the previous century. 'Big house' unionists opted to regroup back in metropolitan circles and an IRA campaign of destruction of some of their mansions undoubtedly encouraged their departure. By 1926 Protestants were 7 per cent of the population of the Free State. At the same time, they accounted for 40 per cent of lawyers, over 50 per cent of bankers and the majority of large farmers, indicating that privilege was far from totally eradicated.[23]

Surprisingly, despite the rhetoric on Catholicism, the Constitution remained relatively tolerant and inclusive of other religious traditions. In other words, it encouraged a pluralist religious conservativism. While much was made of the privileged position of the Catholic Church, the Constitution also institutionalised the position of other faiths – including the first explicit recognition of a Jewish population being part of the nation *anywhere*. It was in this sense a pluralist theocracy. One of the enduring themes of the southern carnival of reaction was that it would – in a perverse corruption of the United Irish mission – succeed in uniting the most conservative elements of *all* denominations to its cause.

These contradictions were symbolised with powerful force in the person of Dúbhghlas de hÍde (Douglas Hyde) – the first president of this new state.[24] Hyde was inaugurated as President of Ireland in June 1938. Moreover, he became president as much *because* of being a Protestant as despite it. Ironically – much more than the Constitution itself which was far from universally approved – his appointment was an attempt to transcend

---

[22] The profoundly patriarchal constitutional reference to the place of women in the home remains a piece of unfinished business (RTÉ 2018).

[23] Currently Protestants constitute 5 percent of the population in the south, with that percentage rising slightly in recent years.

[24] Dubhghlas de hÍde; (1860 –1949), known as An Craoibhín Aoibhinn ('the beautiful little branch'), was an Irish academic, linguist, Irish language scholar, politician and diplomat who served as the first President of Ireland from June 1938 to June 1945. He was a leading figure in the Gaelic revival, and first President of the Gaelic League.

pro- and anti-Treaty elements to unify the new state. This was particularly significant since the new 1937 Constitution left it unclear whether the President or the British monarch was the official head of state. Thus, Hyde was chosen as the first President of Ireland after inter-party negotiations and was elected unopposed. The cross-party consensus was explained by several factors. He was not strongly associated with either side in the Civil War but had sound pre-Treaty credentials, including his involvement in the Howth gunrunning in 1914. His record on promoting the Irish language and culture were impeccable. In 1893, he was a co-founder of *Conradh na Gaeilge* (the Gaelic League) and he had written what was in effect the early 'manifesto' of cultural anti-imperialism *The Necessity for De-Anglicising the Irish Nation*. A whole generation of Irish republicans including Pádraig Pearse – as well as almost the entire pro- and anti-Treaty leaderships (including Éamon de Valera, Michael Collins and Ernest Blythe) – had been politicised through involvement in the League (although Hyde himself had resigned in 1915 after the League committed itself to the 'national movement').[25] Alongside these attributes, both sides were also keen to choose a Protestant to disprove the assertion that the 26-county state was a 'confessional state'. This gesture would undermine any notion of endemic sectarianism and repudiate attempts to paint the 26 counties as a mirror of the institutionalised sectarianism of the northern state. All these elements were captured powerfully with his installation and its representation of the 'new order':

> In the morning [Dr Hyde] attended a service in St. Patrick's Cathedral presided over by the Archbishop of Dublin, Dr. Gregg. Mr. de Valera and his Ministerial colleagues attended a solemn Votive Mass in the Pro-Cathedral, and there were services in the principal Presbyterian and Methodist churches, as well as in the synagogue. Dr. Hyde was installed formally in Dublin Castle, where the seals of office were handed over by the Chief Justice. Some 200 persons were present, including the heads of the Judiciary and the chief dignitaries of the Churches. After the ceremony President Hyde drove in procession through the beflagged streets. The procession halted for two minutes outside the General Post Office to pay homage to the memory of the men who fell in the Easter Week rebellion of 1916. Large crowds lined the streets from the Castle to the Vice-Regal Lodge and the President was welcomed with bursts of cheering.... In the evening there was a ceremony in Dublin Castle which was without precedent in Irish history... It was the most colourful event that has been held in Dublin since the inauguration of the new order in Ireland, and the gathering, representing as it did every shade of political, religious, and social opinion in Eire, might be regarded as a microcosm of the new Ireland. (*Irish Times*, 27 June 1938)

The inherent contradictions in this symbolism became manifest a decade later at Hyde's funeral in Dublin in 1949. The same generation of the Free State/Éire

---

[25] In 2008 *Conradh na Gaeilge* adopted a new constitution reverting to its (and Hyde's) pre-1915 non-political stance, dropping any reference to Irish freedom, and restating its aim as that of an Irish-speaking Ireland. 'Is í aidhm na hEagraíochta an Ghaeilge a athréimniú mar ghnáththeanga na hÉireann'.

establishment that had courted excommunication by the Catholic Church because of its support for the Republic – and transcended their differences in choosing him to personify the new state – proved incapable of summoning sufficient courage to attend Hyde's funeral. He was accorded a state funeral given his status as former president and the service took place at St. Patrick's Cathedral – not unreasonably since he was a member of the Church of Ireland. However, the Catholic Church in Ireland prohibited Catholics from attending services in non-Catholic churches. As a result, all but one member of the cabinet, Noël Browne, remained *outside* the cathedral grounds for the duration of Hyde's funeral. There could be no more poignant – nor pathetic – example of the sectarian contradictions of the 26-county state.

The new state formation did, however, herald an end of sorts to the economic war. The resolution of the crisis came after a series of talks in London between British Prime Minister Neville Chamberlain and de Valera and Lemass. A settlement was agreed in 1938 and enacted in Britain as the Éire (Confirmation of Agreements) Act. Under the terms of the three-year Anglo-Irish Trade Agreement all duties imposed during the previous five years were lifted. Although the period of the Economic War had resulted in a deal of economic difficulty for the 26 counties, its outcome was presented as a Fianna Fáil victory. Under the agreement, Éire was still entitled to impose tariffs on British imports to protect new Irish industries. The Treaty also settled the potential £3 million-per-annum land annuities liability by a one-off payment to Britain of £10 million, and a waiver by both sides of all similar claims and counterclaims. More importantly it also included the return to the 26 counties of the Treaty Ports which had been retained by Britain. The profound implications of this revision of the Treaty were revealed a year later with the outbreak of World War II. The return of the ports allowed Éire to remain neutral and prevented the south of Ireland becoming a theatre of war.

In broad terms, therefore, the coming of Éire marked a significant transformation of the 26-county state. It symbolised the assumption of control of the Treaty state by anti-Treaty forces and their remoulding of the state in their own image. The – relatively short – ten years duration of the Éire state marked a key transformation in the nature of the 26-county state formation. It also, of course, spanned World War II or what in Ireland was characterised as 'the Emergency'. In less momentous circumstances there might have been more focus on this process in terms of constitutional and international law. Two remarkable things happened. First, the 'Southern Ireland' 26-county state became – literally and symbolically – 'Ireland'. Second, this 'Ireland' changed its status away from dominion towards independence. In this sense Ireland left the Empire just in time for there to be something left to leave. A constitutional process that would have provoked intense political and legal argument around the constitutional status of the successor state in less unusual circumstances attracted relatively little attention.

Ironically, Fianna Fáil – the key architects of this finesse – received none of the final plaudits for the 26-county state 'breaking the connection with England'. Their surviving commitments on the egregious nature of partition prevented them from formally naming the Éire state as 'a republic'. Since the Republic that they had organised and fought for could only be represented by a re-unified Ireland, it remained accepted that it would be wrong to name the 26 counties a 'republic' with any sense of triumph or celebration. In consequence it was left to the 'Free Staters' to go the final furlong and lend the name to this fiction. Despite the protests of politicians committed to Irish membership of the Commonwealth, like Garret Fitzgerald, it was Fine Gael – formerly architects of partition and dominion status – that would name the 26 counties a republic, albeit with more a whimper than a bang.

Republic of Ireland 1948-1973: 'not a foreign country'

In 1948 the 26 counties became a republic in bizarre circumstances. The 1948 election saw power change again as a coalition government of Fine Gael, Labour and Clann na Poblachta replaced Fianna Fáil. The new Taoiseach John A. Costello announced that Éire was to be declared a republic unexpectedly – and apparently unplanned – during a visit to Canada. The connection between the 26-county state and the British Empire had been hollowed out by Fianna Fáil. By 1948 the only functions remaining to the Crown were the accreditation of Irish ambassadors to other states and the signing of international treaties. Thus by 1945 Éamon de Valera in reply to the question in the Dáil as to whether he planned to declare Ireland a republic could reply that 'we are a republic'. But the contrast between the gravitas of the Proclamation of Easter Week and this understated aside was lost on no-one. Whatever their perspective on the 'Republic' of 1916, it was clear to most observers that the 26-county Treaty state was not it.

Costello's unexpected move made this notional transition tangible. This chaotic policy shift was given legislative effect by the Republic of Ireland Act 1948. This abolished the last remaining functions of the British monarch in relation to Ireland and provided that the President of Ireland would exercise these functions in place of the Crown. The Act also made clear that 'the description of the State shall be the Republic of Ireland'. Moving the Bill, An Taoiseach suggested:

> This Bill will end, and end forever, in a simple, clear and unequivocal way this country's long and tragic associations with the institution of the British Crown, and will make it manifest beyond equivocation or subtlety that the national and international status of this country is that of an independent republic. (Dáil Éireann 'The Republic of Ireland Bill' 24 November 1948)

When the Act came into force on 18 April 1949, it ended Southern Ireland's status as a British dominion. But 'this country' was now very clearly limited to the 26 counties. Costello did, however, speak directly to the issue of partition and recognised the existence of 'fellow Irishmen' outside the new state, albeit only in the confessional form of 'masses of our Catholic people':

There have been sometimes smug, sometimes fearsome declarations by British Ministers or British Governments that the problem of Partition is an Irish problem that must be settled between Irishmen. That Pilate-like attitude can no longer be held by statesmen with the courage and decency to look facts in the face. This problem was created by an Act of the British Parliament, the Government of Ireland Act, 1920. It may be insisting on the obvious, but I have had occasion to insist very strongly on the obvious in recent months. That Act of 1920 was passed before the Treaty of 1921 and it is surprising how many people think that the Partition of our country was effected by the Treaty of 1921. The problem was created by the British Government and the British Parliament and it is for them to solve the problem. They cannot wash their hands of it and clear themselves of responsibility for it. The Act of 1920 is a very poor title for a claim which is not based upon morality and justice. The Government of the six north-eastern counties claim that and assert it by virtue of a majority, a statutorily created majority, a majority created deliberately under the Act of 1920 to coerce and keep within the bounds of their so-called State masses of our Catholic people and fellow Irishmen who do not want to be there. (Dáil Éireann 'The Republic of Ireland Bill' 24 November 1948)

More generally, however, partition hardly featured in the public discussions around the declaration of the republic. The notion that the Six Counties had somehow disconnected from its 'long and tragic associations with the Crown' was too ridiculous to bear scrutiny.

That said, at a meeting with the British government at Chequers, Séan MacBride complained that United Kingdom governments had 'never found any occasion appropriate for discussing partition', but that some occasion for discussing how it might best be ended would have to be found 'in the not too distant future'. The British government took this as meaning (as was made clear at a cabinet meeting on 28 October 1948) that the ultimate goal of the Irish in declaring the Republic was a 'determination to end partition'. They would be helped in this regard by being admitted to the United Nations where they could raise the question of partition in the General Assembly with the assurance of substantial support. It would be embarrassing for the United Kingdom government to be put in the position of having to support the continuance of partition (Fanning 1982: 100).

In addition, the British government was aware of the disquiet the declaration of the Republic would cause for northern unionists. Ernest Bevin reminded his colleagues:

Northern Ireland had stood in with us against Hitler when the South was neutral. Without the help of the North Hitler would unquestionably have won the submarine war and the United Kingdom would have been defeated. That would have brought Hitler at once to Dublin and they would have made the Irish become as slaves. (Quoted in Fanning 1982: 114).

Consequently, the British moved to further institutionalise partition through the Ireland Act 1949. This intended to deal with the consequences of the Irish Republic of Ireland Act 1948 and was:

> An Act to recognise and declare the constitutional position as to the part of Ireland
> heretofore known as Eire, and to make provision as to the name by which it may be
> known and the manner in which the law is to apply in relation to it; to declare and
> affirm the constitutional position and the territorial integrity of Northern Ireland...

Inter alia, the Act declared that the country known in British law as 'Éire' ceased to
be 'part of His Majesty's dominions' (i.e. a member of the Commonwealth) on 18 April
1949 (the date that the Irish Republic of Ireland Act 1948 came into force). The reasons
for including this declaration were described in a *Working Party Report* to the British
Cabinet. The Report suggested such a declaration was desirable firstly because 'as a
matter of law, it [was] arguable, on the terms of the [Statute of Westminster], that some
provision by the Parliament at Westminster is required in order to complete the process
by which a country ceases to be a member of the Commonwealth' and that inclusion of
the declaration would 'forestall any such legal argument'. In addition, the Report said
the declaration would have the

> additional advantage of excluding, for all purposes of United Kingdom law, any
> future argument that Éire ceased to be a member of the Commonwealth, not
> merely from the date of commencement of the Republic of Ireland Act, but from
> the entry into force of the new Éire Constitution of 1937.

But the complex nature of British/Irish relationships were as much compounded as
resolved by the text of the Ireland Act. Although it was never characterised in this way,
here was the constitutional proof of a very 'special relationship'. For example, s. 2(1)
declared that, even though the Republic of Ireland was no longer a British dominion, it
would *not be treated as a foreign country for the purposes of British law*. Moreover, the legislation
also made blanket provision for how certain wording in existing British legislation should
be understood. For example, references to 'His Majesty's dominions' were to be construed
as *including* a reference to the 'Republic of Ireland' despite its actual change of status. In
this sense, the British legislation represented the last working out of an imperial power
game – a country could not 'take' freedom; it was required that it be 'given'.

More significantly, however, in practical terms was a re-enforced commitment to
partition. The Act declared that *all of Northern Ireland* would continue as part of the
United Kingdom, and would remain within the Commonwealth, unless the *Parliament* of
Northern Ireland consented otherwise.[26] The *Working Party Report* reported that 'it [had]
become a matter of first-class strategic importance ... that the North should continue to
form part of His Majesty's dominions'. The Report also suggested that it was 'unlikely

---

[26] This put paid to any notion that there remained any unfinished business from the Treaty commitments on
the Boundary Commission and re-partition. At the same time, it is worth emphasising that an element of
conditionality was involved. At a meeting with Northern Ireland Prime Minister Basil Brooke on 6 January
1949, Clement Atlee confirmed that the new Bill would involve an 'affirmation by parliament that in no
event would Northern Ireland cease to be part of the United Kingdom except with the consent of the
parliament of Northern Ireland.' He went on to state that 'a subsequent [Westminster] parliament could
revoke such a declaration' (quoted in Fanning 1982: 107).

that Great Britain would *ever* be able to agree to [Northern Ireland secession] even if the people of Northern Ireland desired it'.

The British Ireland Act of 1949 provoked widespread anger in Ireland because its provisions copper-fastened the unionist veto in British law.[27] The Dáil called for a *Protest Against Partition* as a result. There was little ambiguity in the principle of the Dáil position:

> PLEDGING the determination of the Irish people to continue the struggle against the unjust and unnatural partition of our country until it is brought to a successful conclusion;
>
> PLACES ON RECORD its indignant protest against the introduction in the British Parliament of legislation purporting to endorse and continue the existing partition of Ireland, and
>
> CALLS UPON the British Government and people to end the present occupation of our six north-eastern counties, and thereby enable the unity of Ireland to be restored and the age-long differences between the two nations brought to an end. (Dáil Éireann 1949)

Captain Cowan of *Clann na Poblachta* offered an even more unreconstructed republican version which *inter alia* denied 'the right of British armed forces to occupy any part of Ireland'. This, however, failed to find a seconder – an indication perhaps of the limits on rhetoric in the context of the new state. This also proved the high-water mark of anti-partitionism in the Dáil. This was the first – and last – cross-party declaration against partition by the Dáil (Dáil Éireann 1949).

Moreover, this episode brought the transitional phase of the 26-counties state formation to an end. In terms of the 26-county state, the 'unfinished revolution' was now finished. It was now a republic – even if it was not *the* Republic. The endgame on Empire was not entirely finished, however. In the 1960s on the instructions of the Taoiseach, Seán Lemass, Brian Lenihan as Minister for Justice suggested that Ireland should join the British Commonwealth. (Nehru and India had by this time established that it was possible to be a republic within the British Commonwealth.) Reaction from the Irish public was hostile, and the plan was abandoned with Lemass claiming that Lenihan had been speaking 'theoretically' and in a personal capacity and not for the government.[28]

The complexity of this ongoing relationship was evidenced by the issues this raised in terms of British nationality and its connections to Irishness that reprised some of

---

[27] Before the final Act was published, there was also discussion as to whether the legislation should change the name of 'Northern Ireland' to 'Ulster'. This generated adverse reaction from Irish nationalist politicians in Northern Ireland as well as the Minister for Foreign Affairs. When Brooke suggested this renaming to Atlee, the latter astutely replied that the use of 'Ulster' 'would undoubtedly give offence in the Republic, 'since Northern Ireland did not include three counties which had formerly made part of the province of Ulster' (quoted in Fanning 1982: 108).

[28] The idea was to reappear in the context of contemporary discussions on Brexit and reunification.

the complexities and paradoxes of the Treaty. The Ireland Act was used by the United Kingdom to 'repair an omission in the British Nationality Act, 1948'. The British Nationality Act included provisions dealing specifically with the position of 'a person who was a British subject and a citizen of Éire on 31st December 1948'. Because of this, the application of British nationality law was dependent on a question of Irish law, namely, who was a 'citizen of Éire'. The UK Government had profoundly misunderstood the position.

Under Irish law the question of who was a 'citizen of Éire' was, in part, dependent on whether a person was 'domiciled in the Irish Free State on 6th December 1922'. The UK Secretary of State for the Home Department explained:

> The important date to bear in mind there is 6th December, 1922, for that was the date ... the Irish Free State was constituted, and as constituted on 6th December, 1922, it consisted of the 32 counties with the six counties which now form Northern Ireland having the right to vote themselves out. They did so vote themselves out on 7th December, but on 6th December, 1922, the whole of Ireland, the 32 counties, was the Irish Free State and it was not until 7th December, the next day, the six counties having voted themselves out, that the Irish Free State became confined to the 26 counties. Therefore, the Eire law, by inserting the date 6th December, 1922, and attaching to that the domicile, meant that anybody domiciled inside the island of Ireland on 6th December, 1922, was a citizen of Eire.

The impact of this was that many people in Northern Ireland were in theory deprived of British nationality. As this episode illustrated, the complex interconnectedness of the two states made any simplistic implications of nationality ridiculous. (There was, of course, a pre-echo of Brexit in all of this.) The UK had millions of Irish residents, the 26 counties had thousands of British residents and the six counties formed a grey zone of overlapping contested and competing formal and informal British and Irish national identities. It was, therefore, a most intimate separation – an intimacy that has, of course, endured ever since.

Towards Europe: fifteen minutes later...

The 'Republic' declared' in 1948, the state hobbled into the post-war period and the second half of the twentieth century. Southern Ireland had not failed but it was hardly a roaring success either. When John Anthony O'Brien's *The Vanishing Irish: the enigma of the modern world* appeared in 1953, it captured the mood of national despondency. Here was the notion that a combination of abstinence and emigration represented a kind of 'race suicide'. While undoubtedly hyperbolic, the book represented a sense of defeat and hopelessness in post-war Ireland that went well beyond a sense of disappointment at the achievements of the 26-county state. Using this most basic of meters, the state had failed a fundamental test: it could not sustain its own citizens. While it contrasted with the starvation policies of the empire in the nineteenth century, the consequence was not dissimilar; Ireland could not reproduce itself. The population of the 26-county area, which was 3.14 million in 1911 in the last census before partition, had fallen to its lowest ever in 1961 with only 2.82 million citizens remaining.

There were many reasons for this sense of national failure. The broader national project appeared over – partition had been copper-fastened.[29] The economy was stagnant. Protectionism remained a key element of Irish economic policy into the 1950s, arguably stifling trade and prolonging emigration. There was a general sense that this policy had failed – not least because the Irish population was literally disappearing. Ironically, the chief architect of protectionism, Seán Lemass, is now best remembered for dismantling and reversing the policy in the 1960s. The new approach – along with its attendant dangers – was presaged as Shannon became the first Free Trade zone in the world in 1955. Protectionism and dependence on agriculture were to be replaced by a new industrial economy almost completely committed to the attraction of low/no taxation companies. The key moment for this transition was TK Whitaker's 1958 report *Economic Development* for the Department of Finance.[30] This provided the blueprint for Fianna Fáil's First Programme for Economic Expansion. The state would now have a much more planned and interventionist role in the economy. In addition, the Irish economy would be opened to international trade and competition.

Ireland's possible entry into the European Economic Community (EEC) became a signature element in this economic *volte-face*. The 26-county state first applied for full membership of the EEC in 1961. (Associate membership was ruled out as it suggested that Ireland was economically underdeveloped.) The application was made in tandem with a parallel one from the UK. The European Commission response was predicated on the belief that Ireland was not sufficiently developed economically for EEC membership.

---

[29] Thus, the Irish Anti-Partition League (APL) which campaigned for a united Ireland from 1945 to 1958 was based and organised in Northern Ireland. In 1948 the League organised a rally in Dublin challenging de Valera to confront the British government on partition. His subsequent world tour speaking in favour of a united Ireland was regarded as a response to the League intervention. Generally, however, southern anti-partitionism carried little political traction. There was a brief hint of another viewpoint with the establishment of the Inter-departmental Committee on the Implications of Irish Unity in 1972, just about the time of the disastrous Northern Ireland Border Poll of 1973. The brief of the Committee was as follows: 'With a view to contributing to a peaceful settlement of the Northern Ireland situation it has been agreed to set up an inter-party Committee to establish the common ground between the parties represented on the committee on the constitutional, legal, economic, cultural, social and other relevant implications of a united Ireland to make recommendations as to the steps now required to create conditions conducive to a united Ireland' (Dáil Éireann 1972a). There is, however, no record of the Committee producing such recommendations and it swiftly transitioned to the less contentious subject of 'Irish Relations' (Dáil Éireann 1972b).

[30] TK Whitaker (1916-2017) was a northern-born Catholic who became Secretary at the Department of Finance in 1956. His vision for economic development, for good or ill, is credited with the model which the state has followed ever since. He later served as a Senator and on various public bodies. When he died, President Higgins recognised him as the 'most influential Irish person of the 20th century'. He had a less well-known love of Irish. The collection of Irish poetry *An Duanaire: Poems of the Dispossessed 1600–1900*, edited by Seán Ó Tuama and Thomas Kinsella was dedicated to Whitaker. An epigram from this collection prefaces this book.

Irish neutrality and non-membership of NATO were also regarded as problematic in the context of the commitment to further European political integration in the 1961 Bonn Declaration. Lemass visited the capitals of the EEC to emphasise that Ireland was sufficiently economically developed to join the EEC and that Ireland's military neutrality and non-membership of NATO should not be obstacles to entry. In October 1962, the EEC Council of Ministers agreed to open entry negotiations with the Irish government on the basis of full membership. Britain's entry negotiations took priority, however, and in 1963 De Gaulle raised doubts over UK EEC membership and vetoed its application. France did not veto Ireland's application, but with its main trading partner remaining outside the EEC, it was accepted that Ireland could not join alone.

Despite this setback, Lemass continued to promote economic modernisation. The 26-county economy began to grow significantly. Further trade barriers were removed. In 1966 the advent of the Anglo-Irish Free Trade Area was regarded as creating the conditions in Ireland for successful EEC membership. In a further suggestion of optimism, the population of the 26 counties rose in the late 1960s for the first time since the formation of the Free State.

When a new British application for EEC membership was submitted in May 1967, the Irish state followed fifteen minutes later. In response, however, General de Gaulle's 'velvet veto' insisted that conditions were still not right for Britain to join. Irish hopes of membership were dashed again. As this process suggested, the intimacy of the connection to Britain was still a defining aspect of the 26-counties economic and foreign policy. For example, as Britain decided to decimalise its currency in the late 1960s, the south inevitably followed suit.[31] At the time it looked as if the UK and Ireland were as tightly bound as ever.

Following De Gaulle's resignation in 1969, however, the possibility of EEC enlargement re-emerged. Patrick Hillery became Minister for External Affairs after the June 1969 Dáil election, replacing Frank Aiken, whose diplomacy had been focused on the UN. The appointment of Hillery signalled Dublin's determination to achieve EEC membership and was followed by a campaign promoting Ireland across the EEC. Crucially, since it would have separated Ireland from its main export market, Hillery managed to stop a proposal that the UK application be dealt with before that of the Irish state. Negotiations between the Irish state and the Commission recommenced in September 1970. The European Community (EC) was by now a grander project than the nascent Common Market that the Irish had tried to join a decade earlier. As a result of the Hague Summit, the EC was committed to completing the Common Market, moving towards a European Monetary System and integrating foreign policy. In 1970, the Irish Ambassador to the European Communities, Seán Kennan, attempted to allay fears around Irish neutrality, insisting that, 'with regard to foreign affairs and defence,

---

[31] The Decimal Currency Act 1969 provided the legislative basis for decimalisation. The changeover occurred on Decimal Day, 15 February 1971 – the same day as the UK.

the evolution of common policies in the Community is for the future and we would participate in their shaping as members'. Kennan endorsed the commitment to peace as the primary political goal of European integration:

> The EEC has been such a success in this regard that war between its members is no longer conceived as possible. As a European country with no less an interest in stability and peace on the Continent we would be serving a fundamental political interest of our own by joining and further promoting this endeavour.

Hillery also made clear to EC members that Ireland would accept the political and economic obligations of membership.[32] The White Paper *Membership of the European Communities – Implications for Ireland* was published. At this point, the main concerns were protecting Irish interests during the entry negotiations and the transitional period following entry, particularly in trade, agriculture, industry and fisheries. Once again, the British nexus remained paramount: 'The most important objective for us in these negotiations will be protection during the transitional period of our interests in the British market, particularly as regards agriculture'. These entry negotiations coincided with the most brutal phase of the Northern Ireland troubles. Despite this, Hillery worked closely with his UK counterparts to ensure that they cooperated on matters of joint concern through the entry negotiations. The most significant concerns facing Ireland through 1971 were the five-year transitional measures for industry and agriculture, and the question of the Common Fisheries Policy. What was presented as a kind of liberation, however – joining the EU as an alternative to British dependency – was also arguably a function of continued dependency. There was no viable project to join the EU *independent* of the UK.

The signing ceremony for Irish EC accession followed in Brussels in January 1972. The Third Amendment of the Constitution Act allowed the state to join the European Community and provided that European law would take precedence over the Constitution. It was introduced by the Fianna Fáil government but also supported by Fine Gael and by employers' and farmers' organisations. It was, however, opposed by the Irish Labour Party, Sinn Féin, the Workers' Party and the trade unions:

> A principal aim of the 'No' vote was to protect Irish sovereignty. Here the Common Market Study Group, a broad coalition of the Irish Left including future President of Ireland Michael D. Higgins, Raymond Crotty, Anthony Coughlan and John B. Keane, was the most vocal anti-EC grouping. It was effective in raising the profile of the 'No' vote in the Dublin area. It suggested that the supranationalism of the Common Market was the opposite of genuine internationalism and that the EC demanded the suppression of national sovereignty and the independence of small states. Citing Iceland, Switzerland, Finland, Austria, Sweden, Spain and Portugal, the CMSG argued that the problems of staying out were less than the dangers of entry. Arguments were also made that by joining the EC Ireland would open

---

[32] For example, the Cabinet agreed that the negotiators were 'to signify the acceptance, without reservation, of the principle of equal pay for men and women'.

itself to future defence commitments. A further CMSG argument was that the
CAP would result in such changes to Irish agriculture as to reduce the number
of farms, create resulting widespread unemployment, greater emigration and the
destruction of the social fabric of Irish society. (National Archives of Ireland and
the Royal Irish Academy 2018)

There were also echoes of more traditional concerns. President Éamon de Valera
opposed the state's entry based on the loss of sovereignty. This issue – which concerned
both the Left and traditional republicanism – was real. Membership of the European
Community granted powers to European institutions which the 1937 Constitution had
vested exclusively in the *Oireachtas* and the government. It was also clear that many
provisions of the Constitution might be found to be incompatible with European law.
For these reasons, the Third Amendment introduced a provision expressly permitting
the state to join the Community and stating in broad terms that European law had
supremacy over the Constitution.

Despite these different strands of opposition, the majority in support of membership
was overwhelming. In May 1972, the 26-county referendum on EC entry passed by a
large majority. Turnout was 70.9 per cent with 1,041,890 (83.1 per cent) in favour and
211,891 (16.9 per cent) against. Marking a symbolic new phase in the constitutional
history of the state, this was the *first* amendment to the Constitution to be successfully
approved by Irish voters in a referendum. The European Communities Act 1972 was
signed into law on 6 December 1972 providing the legislative basis for the primacy and
direct effect of European Community law.

This was also, of course, a further profound change taken by the 26- rather than
32-county Ireland. The north of Ireland had no say in the 26-county vote. It was only
provided a voice later – and on British rather than Irish membership – when the UK
voted on membership in 1975. By default as much as design, 26-county Ireland had
ended up where the whole of Ireland wanted to be in 1918 – no longer tied to the UK
or British Empire. With the benefit of hindsight, we can identity 1973 as the key juncture
in the history of the 26-county state. Here – via the ambiguous attractions of the EC –
was the 'freedom to obtain freedom', albeit in a much less exalted form than Michael
Collins had ever imagined it. It might be swapping one dependency for another but here,
finally, was the opportunity to cut the umbilical cord of colonialism – the connection
with England.

Chapter 6

Southern Ireland 1973-2020: Europeanisation, 'leprechaun economics' and the price of peace

The question is: what are we doing in Europe? Building or destroying sovereignty?
—Etienne Balibar, 2004

[The citizenship referendum] is not a debate on racism, interculturalism, asylum seeking or immigration. It is about one issue only – what it is to be a citizen of Ireland. Does it mean more than being born in Ireland and handed a passport? —Mary Hanafin

On the 1st of January, 1973, the Republic of Ireland – along with the UK and Denmark – joined the European Communities (EC), later the European Union (EU).[1] At that time there was little sense of any epochal change in the 26 counties:

> There was neither ceremony nor flourish in Dublin or Brussels. RTE radio and television broadcast no programming reflecting the greatest change in Ireland's sovereignty and international relations since independence. The Italian President, in his New Year's message welcomed Ireland, Britain and Denmark, with their 'glorious traditions' into the EC. Norway had rejected accession earlier in 1972, and already almost half the population of Britain were unhappy with EC membership. A small number of low-key events were held to mark Ireland's accession. Minister for Foreign Affairs Brian Lenihan spoke at an Irish Management Institute celebratory lunch, and tree planting ceremonies were held in every county. Children born on New Year's Day 1973 were presented with a special medal. Opponents of Ireland's entry into the European Communities still maintained that entry would begin a period of great threat to the social, economic and political fabric of Irish society.[2]

Despite this low-key initiation, our analysis contends that Ireland joining the EC was the key disjuncture in the history of the 26-county state.

---

[1] Ireland became a member of three Communities on 1 January 1973: the European Coal and Steel Community (established by Treaty signed at Paris on 18 April, 1951); the European Economic Community (established by Treaty signed at Rome on 25 March, 1957); and the European Atomic Energy Community (established by Treaty signed at Rome on 25 March, 1957).

[2] National Archives EU Accession 40th Anniversary Exhibition – joint project of the National Archives of Ireland and the Royal Irish Academy, funded by the Department of Arts, Heritage and the Gaeltacht.

The contemporary argument around Brexit has become a key measure of how far things have changed. Most southern politicians were deeply unhappy with the decision of the UK to leave the EU in 2016. Moreover, the border in Ireland became one of the crucial issues in Brexit negotiations and threatened to unravel the whole process. At the same time, however, nobody suggested that Ireland would *have* to leave the EU because the UK was leaving.[3] This epoch-defining nature of EU accession was not so evident in 1973. As with the declaration of a Republic in 1948, a key transformation in the constitutional status of Ireland occurred without anybody much noticing. Moreover, for those who did notice, the move inspired at least as much trepidation as hope.

Of course, Irish accession to the EC still can be read very negatively – as simply swapping UK clientlism/dependency for a more modern, European version. From this perspective the 26-county state simply traded dependence on a declining imperial economy for an ascendant post-war European model of contemporary capitalism. This was indeed the reading made by most contemporary Left analysis at the point of accession. Nevertheless, EU accession also marked a key moment in the break in the dependent relationship with the UK. This change *was* epochal in nature. While the 26-county state could not join the EC without the UK, as we have detailed in the previous chapter, the act of joining set in motion a process of political and economic development that meant it could remain in the EU when the UK left some fifty years later. In this sense accession to the EC was the beginning of the end of Southern Ireland's formal economic and ideological dependence on its colonial power.

Equally importantly, since the UK joined the EC at the same time, the 1973 accession also marked a key disjuncture for the broader structures and legacies of late British colonialism. This looked like the final repudiation of empire – both economically and ideologically – by the UK state. In consequence, Ireland remained more integrated with the British polity and economy through the new regime of the EC than the other former colonies in the British Commonwealth. In other words, integration with the EC meant that the 26 counties remained *more* intimately connected to the UK than all other former British colonies – despite its position outside the Commonwealth. This was precisely because both states were part of an expanding and integrating EU project. In this context, it took some time for the separation of the 26 counties from the UK to become apparent. At first, it looked as if membership of the EU had integrated Ireland more firmly into the regimen of post-imperial Britain than any of its other former colonies (bar Northern Ireland, of course).

For example, the Common Travel Area (CTA) is an odd construction (McGuinness and Gower 2017). The CTA is a special travel zone between the Republic of Ireland and the UK (as well as the Isle of Man and Channel Islands). It dates to the establishment of the Irish Free State. Nationals of CTA countries can travel freely within the CTA without

---

[3] There were still dissenting voices, of course, supporting 'Irexit' (see, for example, Kinsella 2017). But there was 'little evidence of any emerging popular support' (*The Journal* 2018).

being subject to passport controls. The arrangements for non-CTA nationals are more complex. Although there are minimal immigration checks for journeys started within the CTA, non-CTA nationals must have the relevant immigration permission for the country they are seeking to enter. (Until the UK exited the EU, citizens of EEA member states retained prevailing rights of entry and residence in both the UK and Ireland under EU 'free movement' law. All of this changed, of course, in the aftermath of Brexit, but the consequent recalibrating of citizenship and residency rights remains an unresolved matter of negotiation between the UK, Ireland and the EU.)

Although the Republic of Ireland and the UK maintain their own visa and immigration policies, there has been a significant degree of practical cooperation and policy coordination to ensure the security of the CTA. Controls on the border are generally regarded as impractical as well as politically toxic. The freedom of movement implicit in the CTA is reinforced by the special status of Irish citizens in UK law. As we have seen, this is separate from and pre-dates the rights they have as EU citizens. The Republic of Ireland is not considered to be a 'foreign country' and Irish citizens are not considered to be 'aliens'. Furthermore, Irish citizens are treated as if they have permanent immigration permission to remain in the UK from the date they take up 'ordinary residence' there. This special status affects Irish nationals' rights across a number of areas, including eligibility for British citizenship, eligibility to vote and stand for election, and eligibility for certain welfare benefits. As a result, Irish nationals have more rights than other EU/EEA nationals resident in the UK – and, of course, far more rights than most citizens of the British Commonwealth.[4] How profoundly this changes after Brexit remains, of course, a moot point.

Brexit has brought this continuing relationship between the Irish and UK states into sharp focus. This is because the post-1973 recalibration of relations between the UK and Ireland, and the 26- and 6-county states took place within the wider European project. In other words, a clear if unintended consequence of the dual accession of the UK and the 26-county state was that the partition of Ireland and the border in Ireland now sat in a very different constitutional framework. At the time, any suggestion to this end would have seemed faintly ridiculous. EC accession coincided with the height of the troubles: the UK government – and to lesser extent the 26-county state – was simultaneously erecting a heavily militarised security border between the north and south of Ireland. This reinforced physical border resembled more closely the Iron Curtain dividing eastern and western Europe, rather than anything that might prefigure a supposedly frictionless border.

Crucially, however, the constitutional paradigm had changed. Whatever it looked like on the ground, the partition border was no longer simply a matter for the UK government and the 26- and 6-county states. While partition remained the dominating

---

[4] Interestingly, in an earlier era, the Military Service Act of January 1918 exempted not only Ireland from conscription but also Irishmen working in Britain (Grant 2012: 77).

feature of the constitutional status of Ireland, this reality was reframed utterly in the context of the EC and later EU. The Irish story featured two enduring themes over the next fifty years: in the south, there was the 'economic miracle' of the Celtic Tiger; in the north, it was the peace process. Both experiences were perceived as partitioned: the Celtic Tiger happened in the south, 'the troubles' and then the peace process in the north. But these were far from being separated phenomena.

Here again, the EU played a crucial integrating role. Just as the EU provided the framework for the 'economic miracle' of the Celtic Tiger in the south, so it also came to provide the framework for the peace process in the north. Most famously and persistently pushed by John Hume, the notion of 'pooling' sovereignty via the EU created a context for a reinvention of the border and the politics of partition and reunification. The strong version of this was that the border would 'wither away' in the context of the 'ever closer union' so despised by Europhobes. Even if this was hyperbole, the EU at least provided a fig leaf for both national projects – British and Irish – in the six counties. What did it matter now that all our passports – British and Irish – were burgundy and signified EU citizenship? While flags remained a contested issue across Ireland, the union flag and the Tricolour could fly relatively untroubled beside – and under the protection of – the European flag.

The Northern Ireland peace process was equally important to the EU. To this end it funded four special peace programmes (on top of all the normal funds). Even though this was primarily funding to a region of the UK rather than the 26 counties, it rarely featured in British discussions of 'What has the EU done for us?' (Cohn 2019). Thus, the EU actively supported peace building projects on both sides of the border in Ireland since 1995 and most of this funding went north of the border. The most recent programme – Peace IV – ran to 2020. An estimated €1.6 billion has been committed to peace in Ireland by the EU over the 25-year period. In this context it is little wonder the EU prioritised defence of the Good Friday Agreement in negotiating the Withdrawal Agreement. (Thus, ignorance of the significance of the 'backstop' among many Westminster politicians was underlined by their ignorance of the EU's investment in peace and what the EU has done for them.)

The peace process in the north became a European process with the 26-county state playing a very specific role. In time this was to transform the 26-county state from a revanchist ally of northern nationalism to a junior partner of the UK state in the management of the six counties. In this respect, the peace process changed the 26-county state just as profoundly as the six-county state. Ironically, the characterisation by the British state of its own relationship to the north – 'no selfish or strategic interest' – might apply *a fortiori* to the conclusion of this element of the 'Southern Ireland' project over the last 50 years. This was only possible because of the Europeanisation of partition.

Accession: 'wholehearted members at the heart of the European Union'

As we have suggested, Europe – or more accurately the developing structures of the EEC/EC/EU project – provided an alternative paradigm for the 26 counties to postcolonial dependency on the UK. Ireland had formally repudiated Empire and Commonwealth, but it now could be *for* something – we would become 'good Europeans'. This ideological commitment to Europeanness was also supported by a less cerebral commitment to the immediate economic benefits. Thus, a contemporary (2018) review of the 'Benefits of EU membership to Ireland' by the European Commission accentuates this more prosaic dimension to the project, alongside larger issues of peace and identity:

- Irish businesses have unhindered access to a market of over 510 million people.
- An estimated 978,000 jobs have been created in Ireland during the years of membership and trade has increased 150-fold.
- Foreign Direct Investment in to Ireland has increased dramatically from just €16 million in 1972 to more than €30 billion.
- Irish citizens have the right to move, work and reside freely within the territory of other member states.
- Between 1973 and 2015, Ireland received over €74.3 billion from the EU. During the same time, it contributed approximately €32 billion to the EU budget (Department of Finance figures).
- Between 1973 and 2014 Irish farmers received €54 billion from the Common Agricultural Policy.
- Irish views and interests are reflected in the policies of the EU towards the rest of the world.
- EU membership has helped bring peace and political agreement in Northern Ireland through support and investment in cross-border programmes.
- The Irish language is an official working language in the EU, which helps to protect the country's native mother tongue for future generations.

There, in crude simplicity, is the thumbnail sketch of the European journey of the 26-county state over the past 50 years.

Whatever spin is put on the process, it involved a discrete but inexorable movement of the centre of gravity of southern Irish external affairs away from London towards Brussels.[5] Despite the relentless use of the term 'Ireland' by both the 26-county state and the EU to describe the state, it was also clear that this process was leaving a large part of Ireland behind. Roughly one third of its population and one fifth of its land mass had dematerialised.[6] In other words, one of the consequences of the decoupling of the

---

[55] One consequence of this was the Republic's inexorable move away from the more non-aligned stance it had assumed previously in forums such as the United Nations, supporting Cuba, Palestine and other 'small nations'.

[66] For example, one map from an official EU source on 'Ireland in the EU' shows the 26 counties with the six counties removed completely and the border presented as a coastline.

26 counties from the UK was a reinforcement of partition and further separation of the people, north and the south.

This ongoing separation of the 26-county state from the UK state was neatly evidenced by breaking the link with sterling that had obtained since the formation of Southern Ireland. When the European Monetary System (EMS) was established in 1979, most EC members linked their currencies to prevent large fluctuations relative to one another. At this crucial juncture, Ireland joined the EMS but the UK remained outside. To participate in the European Exchange Rate Mechanism (ERM), Southern Ireland was required to break the parity of the punt with the pound sterling in 1979. The UK subsequently entered the ERM in October 1990 but exited again within two years following the 'Black Wednesday' crash of 16 September 1992. With further symbolism, this period also saw the creation of the Currency Centre at Sandyford so that banknotes and coinage could be manufactured within the Irish state. Up to this point, banknotes were printed by specialist printers in England, and coins by the British Royal Mint.

This divergence between the currencies and the economies of the UK and Ireland continued as the euro project developed. The exchange rates between the European Currency Unit (ECU) and the punt and ten other EMS currencies (all but the pound sterling, the Swedish krona and the Danish krone) were fixed. The euro became the currency of the eurozone countries including the 26 counties on 1 January 1999. On 1 January 2002 the physical euro was introduced, and the Irish state began to withdraw Irish coins and notes, replacing them with euros and cents. Similarly, all other eurozone countries withdrew their currencies from that date. Irish pound coins and notes ceased to be legal tender on 9 February 2002. Yeats' key symbolism for the independent Irish state in the 1920s had disappeared in the context of European integration.

Europeanisation also proceeded in a host of other ways. From 1973 onwards, a whole infrastructure was constructed funded by European Structural and Investment Funds. The 26-county state proved to have a healthy appetite for European capital, and this encouraged an ever-closer union. Until the expansion of the EU in 2004, the 26 counties remained a net receiving country of the EU. Despite Ireland becoming a net donor, significant financial support continues to the present.

The legacies of history still threw up contradictions. The Irish Constitution and the Irish commitment to neutrality made the 26 counties sometimes a less than helpful partner in the European project. Since the Constitution's commitment to direct democracy required a popular mandate for any constitutional reform, EU Treaty changes had to be agreed in popular referendums. This reality was confirmed by the 1987 *Crotty v. An Taoiseach* decision. This landmark judgement by the Irish Supreme Court ruled that were the 26 counties to ratify Part III of the Single European Act,[7] it would amount to

---

[7] The Single European Act proposed the establishment of a Single Market by 31 December 1992. It also established the basis for the Common Foreign and Security Policy.

unconstitutional delegation of the state's external sovereignty. The court rejected the argument that the constitutionality of a treaty could only be questioned when it was incorporated into law by a statute. It ruled that the courts had the power to interfere in the government's exercise of foreign affairs in the case of there being a 'clear disregard by the government of the powers and duties conferred on it by the Constitution'.

The Supreme Court decision meant that Ireland could not ratify the Single European Act unless the Irish Constitution was first changed to permit its ratification. The case led directly to the Tenth Amendment of the Constitution of Ireland which authorised the ratification of the Single European Act. It also established that significant changes to European Union treaties required an amendment to the Irish Constitution *before* they could be ratified by the 26-county state. In consequence, the Republic of Ireland, uniquely in the EU, requires a referendum for every new or substantive change to a European Union Treaty.

This created new opportunities for populist disruption of the European project long before Brexit. First, the Treaty of Nice was signed by the member states of the European Union in February 2001, amending the Treaties of the European Union. Following the Crotty decision, an amendment to the Constitution was required before it could be ratified by the 26-county state. Southern Ireland was the only one of the then 15 EU member states to put the Treaty to its people in a referendum. In response, the Twenty-fourth Amendment of the Constitution Bill 2001 proposed an amendment to the Constitution to allow the state to ratify the Treaty of Nice. The proposal was rejected in the first Nice referendum.

This was no simple anti-Irish government or anti-European intervention. The referendum was held on the same day as referendums on the prohibition of the death penalty and on the ratification of the Rome Statute of the International Criminal Court, which were both approved. The key element on the No side was the argument that it would undermine Irish neutrality which remained valued by citizens of the 26 counties. The Treaty of Nice contained several optional discretionary provisions that member states could activate later following adoption. This creeping military logic was distrusted by a sceptical Irish public and the amendment was rejected by voters in the 26 counties in June 2001 by a margin of 53.9 per cent to 46.1 per cent, with a turnout of 34.8 per cent.

Both the 26-county state and the EU moved swiftly to address this unhelpful expression of sovereignty. The Irish government and the European Council jointly made the Seville Declarations on the Treaty of Nice in June 2002 to recommit themselves to shared interests ahead of a second vote. When the Nice Treaty was put to a second vote, the wording of the constitutional amendment excluded participation in common defence. The Twenty-sixth Amendment permitted the Republic to choose to exercise these options, provided its decision was approved by the Oireachtas. The Nice Treaty was subsequently approved by Irish voters in the second Nice referendum in October 2002.

Despite the EU celebration of its 'democratic heritage', this unedifying process of disregard for popular sovereignty was repeated six years later. The Treaty of Lisbon was signed by the member states of the European Union in December 2007. It was in large part a revision of the text of the Treaty establishing a Constitution for Europe after its rejection in referendums in France in May 2005 and in the Netherlands in June 2005. The Treaty of Lisbon preserved most of the content of the rejected Constitution, especially the new rules on the functioning of the European institutions, but it removed the symbolic reference to a Constitution. Once again, an amendment to the Irish Constitution was required before it could be ratified by the 26-county state. Again, Southern Ireland was the only one of the then 15 EU member states to put the Treaty to the people in a referendum. (The Treaty was ratified by national parliaments in all other EU member states.) Thus, the Twenty-eighth Amendment of the Constitution Bill 2008 was put to a referendum. This amendment too was rejected by voters in the 26 counties on 12 June 2008 by a margin of 53.4 per cent to 46.6 per cent, with a turnout of 53.1 per cent.

Once again, rejection of the Treaty was not simply a problem for Ireland; it undermined the whole European project since this required support from all the member states. In this context, it looked as if the Irish had become particularly *bad* Europeans. The Treaty had been intended to enter into force across the EU on 1 January 2009 but was delayed following the Irish rejection. At a meeting of the European Council (the meeting of the heads of government of all European Union member states) in December 2008, Taoiseach Brian Cowen conveyed the concerns of the Irish people relating to taxation policy, family, social and ethical issues, and Irish neutrality. Ireland's position was renegotiated, and the revised package was put before the electorate in 2009.

In the interim, the Irish financial crisis had left the country in a much weaker negotiating position since it was clear that the Irish government required substantial financial support from the European Union. The Lisbon Treaty was duly approved by Irish voters when the Twenty-eighth Amendment of the constitution was accepted in the second Lisbon referendum in October 2009. President of the European Commission José Manuel Barroso said the vote made it 'a great day' for both Ireland and Europe:

> I see the Yes vote as a sign of confidence by the Irish electorate in the European Union, as a sign of their desire to be wholehearted members at the heart of the European Union, as a sign that Ireland recognises the role that the European Union has played in responding to the economic crisis. (RTÉ News 2009)

The Treaty of Lisbon entered into force across the EU on 1 December 2009. Finally, it seemed, the Irish had become 'wholehearted members' of the EU project. More generally it looked as if the entire EU project was back on track – until it was unceremoniously derailed with much more devastating effect by the UK Brexit vote. As the EU confronts an existential crisis in the face of Brexit and the Covid-19 pandemic, it remains to be seen how the Irish state will situate itself in the context of a project which looks much less resilient than it did only a decade ago.

The 26-county state and the peace process

In the run-up to EU accession in 1973, Ireland appeared to be on the brink of war. In the context of widespread anti-Catholic violence across the north, Taoiseach Jack Lynch made a statement on 13 August 1969 which reiterated the traditional anti-partitionist solution:

> It is clear … the Irish Government can no longer stand by and see innocent people injured and perhaps worse… Recognising, however, that the reunification of the national territory can provide the only permanent solution for the problem, it is our intention to request the British Government to enter into early negotiations with the Irish Government to review the present constitutional position of the 6 Counties of Northern Ireland. (National Archives 2000)

As the conflict escalated in the north, however, the 26-county state proved completely ineffective in defending innocent people – all of whom were Irish citizens by dint of the Constitution and many of whom were Irish passport holders.

Instead it began to renegotiate its relationship with both its own anti-partitionist base and the British state. In the process the 26-county state was forced to distance itself from the north. It had to sever finally the lingering commitment of the 26-county state – that had obtained from Collins onwards – to defending northern nationalists. Moreover, it had to repudiate absolutely the territorial claim on the six counties. This shift took place over a remarkably short period of time. Thus, in the course of a decade the state moved from 'not standing idly by' with members of its government involved in covertly supplying arms to the IRA[8] to a novel partnership with the British state. This shift was perhaps most emblemised by two events surrounding the British Embassy in Dublin. The burning of the British Embassy in 1972 in the aftermath of Bloody Sunday was an unprecedented event in western democracy. A decade later, however, in the context of the Hunger Strikes in 1981 – as a mass mobilisation moved on the British Embassy again – the repressive forces of the 26-county state made sure that this would not be repeated. The intervening ten years transformed the Irish state and its relationship to the north.

This was, of course, a complex process. It was tied to the state's own ambiguous relationship to revolutionary violence in Ireland. On the one hand, the Free State and its subsequent iterations had, as we have seen, developed its own repressive state apparatus specifically around the threat of republican violence. But it had a more ambiguous relationship to the efforts of the British state in this regard. Moreover, no state is homogenous. Thus, until at least the late 1980s, it appeared that elements in the southern apparatus were more sympathetic to the Irish republican project than British 'anti-terrorism'.[9]

---

[8] In 1970 cabinet ministers Charlie Haughey and Neil Blaney were dismissed for allegedly conspiring to smuggle weapons to the IRA. At a subsequent trial, charges against Blaney were dropped and Haughey was acquitted. It was Blaney's contention that the government knew all about the plan.

[9] For example, Maurice Gibson, Lord Justice of Appeal in Northern Ireland, was killed in a roadside bomb, along with his wife Cecily, by the IRA in 1987. Judge Gibson's most controversial judgement was his 1977

All of this made for a difficult and ambiguous relationship with the British 'war effort' in Ireland. Nevertheless, there was a gradual alignment of the repressive state forces north and south. In the early days of the northern 'troubles', British soldiers who had 'inadvertently' crossed the border into the south were arrested by the Garda Siochana and returned north after suitable criticism by the 26-county government. Now cooperation increased incrementally on politically contentious issues such as flyover agreements for the British Army along the border, the use of special criminal court and extradition. Perhaps more than anything, the Dublin Monaghan bombings exposed the inherent weakness of the southern state in this regard. In aggregate this was the worst atrocity in the whole of the troubles.[10] Yet the state continues to resist any effective investigation of the terrorist murder of its own citizens in which the British state was heavily implicated. It refused even to have a national day of mourning. The most sympathetic reading was that the 26-county state was simply too weak to resist the repressive logic of its more powerful, formal colonial neighbour.

Broadly, we can trace a tension between the organic solidarity of most southern Irish citizens to the situation of northern nationalists alongside a more complex rejection of the penetration of the northern crisis into the politics – and everyday life – of Southern Ireland. There were specific moments at which the northern crisis undermined the everyday politics of the south. This had happened to some extent with the election of anti-partitionist and republican candidates in the 1950s. This dynamic, however, re-emerged with full force during the Hunger Strikes. In the 26-county elections of 1981 two anti-H-block candidates were elected, Paddy Agnew and Kieran Doherty. Once more, northern republicanism – which had been symbolically excluded along with Sean O'Mahoney[11] – had re-entered the partitionist Dáil.[12] The two seats gained by these anti-H-block candidates denied Charles Haughey the chance to form a Fianna Fáil government. Instead, the 22nd Dáil saw Fine Gael and the Labour Party forming a coalition government with Garret Fitzgerald as Taoiseach.

---

acquittal of the soldier who killed 12-year-old Majella O'Hare. The UK government subsequently apologised for the killing (Bowcott 2011). The deahs of Gibson and his wife were investigated by the Cory Collusion Inquiry in 2003 after allegations that Gardaí had alerted the IRA to Gibson's travel arrangements. Cory found insufficient evidence to warrant a public inquiry. The later Irish Government Smithwick Tribunal concluded that there had been collusion in the deaths of the Gibsons and of RUC Chief Superintendent Harry Breen and Superintendent Robert Buchanan in an IRA ambush near the border in 1989.

[10] The Dublin and Monaghan bombings of 17 May 1974 were a series of co-ordinated bombings by loyalist paramilitaries and British agents. Three bombs exploded in Dublin during the evening rush hour and a fourth exploded in Monaghan ninety minutes later. They killed 33 civilians and an unborn child and injured 300 people. The bombings were the deadliest incident in the troubles and the deadliest incident in the history of Southern Ireland.

[11] Séan O'Mahoney (1872-1934) was elected for Sinn Féin in Fermanagh South in the First Dáil and Fermanagh in the Second Dáil. He was the *only* attendee elected exclusively from a constituency in the six counties and thus his status in the partitionist Third Dáil of 1922 was unclear. An anti-Treaty republican, O'Mahoney was not invited to attend the opening of this new parliament. This confirmed that the assembly was not an all-Ireland Dáil and that the succession from the Republic through the First and Second dáilaí had been formally severed.

[12] This re-entry was metaphorical rather than literal. The two TDs were unable to take their seats since they were in prison in Long Kesh. They were in any case abstentionist.

This broad process of southern Irish disengagement proceeded with even greater haste as the peace process gathered momentum in the wake of the Hunger Strikes. Before 1999, Articles 2 and 3 of the Constitution made the claim that the whole island formed one 'national territory'. The Irish government had committed in the 1998 Good Friday Agreement to submit Articles 2 and 3 to amendment by referendum. To this end, the Nineteenth Amendment of the Constitution was adopted in June of the same year by 94 per cent of those voting. Article 2 and Article 3 of the Constitution were completely revised by this amendment which took effect on 2 December 1999. The new wording describes the Irish nation as a community of individuals with a common identity rather than as a territory. This was intended to reassure unionists that a united Ireland could not come about without a majority of the Northern Ireland electorate declaring in favour of such a move:

> Article 2 It is the entitlement and birthright of every person born in the island of Ireland, which includes its islands and seas, to be part of the Irish Nation. That is also the entitlement of all persons otherwise qualified in accordance with law to be citizens of Ireland. Furthermore, the Irish nation cherishes its special affinity with people of Irish ancestry living abroad who share its cultural identity and heritage.

> Article 3.1 It is the firm will of the Irish Nation, in harmony and friendship, to unite all the people who share the territory of the island of Ireland, in all the diversity of their identities and traditions, recognising that a united Ireland shall be brought about only by peaceful means with the consent of a majority of the people, democratically expressed, in both jurisdictions in the island. Until then, the laws enacted by the Parliament established by this Constitution shall have the like area and extent of application as the laws enacted by the Parliament that existed immediately before the coming into operation of this Constitution.

As amended, Article 2 provides that everyone born on the island of Ireland has the right to be a part of the 'Irish Nation'. The stated intention was to allow the people of Northern Ireland to feel included in the 'nation' while repudiating the traditional revanchist claim to the Six Counties. However, it was argued by both unionist and republican commentators that in reality the 'the new Article 2 of the Irish constitution gave northern nationalists nothing' (Morgan 2011: 8). Article 9 of the Constitution of Ireland already established Irish citizenship. It provides only that the 'future loss and acquisition of Irish nationality and citizenship shall be determined in accordance with law'.

Since it was further amended in 2004 (as detailed below), Article 9 now also provides that '[n]otwithstanding any other provision of this Constitution, a person born in the island of Ireland, which includes its islands and seas, who does not have, at the time of the birth of that person, at least one parent who is an Irish citizen or entitled to be an Irish citizen is not entitled to Irish citizenship or nationality, unless provided for by law.' Citizenship rights created by Article 2 of the Constitution have therefore since been severely diluted. All of this cut across the suggestion that Article 2 confers the right to citizenship on all persons born in Northern Ireland.

The changes to Article 2 reflected a qualified provision in the Good Friday Agreement (GFA) recognising the birthright of all the people of Northern Ireland to identify themselves and be accepted as Irish or British, or both, as they may so choose. This confirmed that the right to hold both British and Irish citizenship was accepted by both governments and would not be affected by any future change in the status of Northern Ireland. This qualification to that provision of the GFA is contained in Annex 2. That Annex clarifies that the reference to 'the people of Northern Ireland' only means 'all persons born in Northern Ireland and having, at the time of their birth, at least one parent who is a British citizen, an Irish citizen or is otherwise entitled to reside in Northern Ireland without any restriction on their period of residence.' Accordingly, the GFA did not bind either state to provide for any unqualified entitlement to birthright citizenship. In a further vague reference to traditional republican notions of Irishness, Article 2 further recognises the 'special affinity' between the people of Ireland and the Irish diaspora. In effect the logic of the constitution was undermined by the new Articles 2 and 3 as Article 9 already dealt with citizenship. The references to the 'Irish nation' in the new Articles have no meaning in practical articles of the Constitution.

Nor was the commitment to reunification any less nebulous. As amended, Article 3, Section 1 expresses the 'firm will' of the Irish nation to create a united Irish people, though not, explicitly, a united country or any end to partition. It emphasises that a united Ireland should respect the distinct cultural identity of unionists and that it should only come about with the separate 'democratically expressed' consent of the peoples of both parts of the island. This provision was expressly intended to diminish the concerns of unionists that their rights would be ignored – or suppressed – in a united Ireland. Under the GFA, the people of Northern Ireland's 'democratically expressed' consent must be secured in a referendum. Despite the expressed 'desire for unity', this adds an additional legal requirement for a referendum to be held not only in Northern Ireland but also in the Republic of Ireland before reunification. This is the ultimate confirmation of the hegemony of partitionism embedded in the GFA. In effect this measure is 'doubly-partitionist' since it creates a further barrier to reunification. This contrasts starkly with the constitutional dynamics around the 1973 border poll in Northern Ireland. This referendum posed the choice between Northern Ireland remaining part of the UK and reuniting with the Republic of Ireland. (Pro-Irish unity voters almost completely boycotted the border poll in Northern Ireland in 1973, which unsurprisingly affirmed the *status quo*.) The key point, however, is that there was no negotiation by the UK state with the Southern Irish state around what would have happened in the event of a vote for unity – it was a given that the 26 counties would 'accept' the six counties without issue.

When we juxtapose this to the Proclamation or the First Dáil – or even the 'motion on partition' of 1949 – the position of the 26-county state in 2020 looks remarkable. It unilaterally repudiated its claim on the north and it is now a junior partner in the management of the northern conflict – alongside its erstwhile colonial power. Moreover, despite the lurching of the post-GFA state from crisis to crisis, no-one nowadays in the political establishment of the 26 counties is suggesting that the reunification of the national territory 'could provide the only permanent solution to the problem'.

In retrospect, it is remarkable to observe how cheaply the 26-county state could sell these constitutional principles. Alternatively, however, it might be argued that what it got was exactly what it had wanted – the final disconnect from the six counties, from anti-partitionism and from 32-county republicanism. In other words, the territorial claim was to be reformulated as good neighbourliness. This profoundly disempowered Catholics, nationalists and republicans in the six counties. Bizarrely – just as the symbiosis of politics and demographic transition threatened the existence of the six-county state – the 26 counties assumed a key role in bolstering the northern state and its commitment to unionist majoritarianism.

This was not, of course, an accident; it overlapped neatly with European concerns. Once again, the peculiar dynamics of Irish nationalism that we traced earlier emerged to take control of the situation. In particular, the fingerprints of John Hume – MP, MEP and quintessential northern nationalist – were all over this.[13] Here in effect, if not intent, was another classic nationalist intervention that would reinforce partition and undermine the republic. All the elements were there: the post-nationalism idea itself; the belief that European membership would enhance that post-national compromise; Hume's unparalleled influence with the Americans as underwriters for any partitionist settlement. Of course, in Irish terms these issues are rarely ever 'resolved'. Moreover, we now observe a wider Europe that threatens to become post-post-nationalist in response to the combined impacts of Brexit and the pandemic. The contemporary backlash associated with Brexit has seen several colonial legacies 'dealt with' by the EU – not least Ireland and Gibraltar – threaten to unravel once again. Meanwhile borders which had 'disappeared' are reappearing across the EU and beyond as national security becomes the paradigm for managing the pandemic.

Leprechaun economics: 'the largest tax avoidance structure in history'

All of these political developments took place against a backdrop of profound economic change. Integration into the EU certainly reflected a changed economic base in the 26 counties. On the one hand the story across the fifty years since 1973 has been a sweep from bust to boom and back again. This rollercoaster ride can be tracked in a series of headlines from the *Economist* magazine – from the 'poorest of the rich' to 'Europe's Shining Light'

---

[13] John Hume (1937-2020) was one of the chief architects of the peace process and the GFA. He was awarded the Nobel Peace Prize in response (alongside David Trimble). Hume was SDLP party leader for twenty years from 1979 to 2001. He was both an MP for Foyle and MEP. His broader appeal was recognised when he topped a 2010 RTÉ poll to select the 'greatest person' in Irish history. His role in bringing weapons manufacturers Raytheon to Derry exposed some of the contradictions of his nationalism and commitment to peace. His most significant legacy – that of 'Europeanising' conflict in Ireland through a 'pooling of sovereignty' – has been put under profound threat by Brexit.

to 'the bursting of the Irish property bubble' – much of this explained, in distinctly anti-microeconomic terms, in terms of the 'luck of the Irish' (*Economist* 1988, 1997, 2015; Peet 2004). For a brief moment, Ireland's 'economic miracle' did not only surprise Ireland but the rest of the world. In 2006, this unexpected turn of events found British Chancellor of the Exchequer George Osborne in Dublin fawning over the Celtic Tiger:

> A generation ago, the very idea that a British politician would go to Ireland to see how to run an economy would have been laughable... Today things are different. Ireland stands as a shining example of the art of the possible in long-term economic policymaking, and that is why I am in Dublin: to listen and to learn.

The 'shining example' did not last long, however. In September 2008, the Irish government – a Fianna Fáil-Green coalition at the time – officially acknowledged that the Celtic Tiger economy had entered recession. It thus became the first state in the eurozone to do so. Within two years the Celtic Tiger hype was a distant memory and the reality of the new economic order in the 26 counties was made clear. Now George Osborne was bailing the Irish state out of its financial crisis and defending his bilateral loan as being in the UK national interest. With the banks 'guaranteed' and the National Asset Management Agency (NAMA) established, Taoiseach Brian Cowen confirmed on live television that the EU/ECB/IMF troika would be involving itself in managing Ireland's financial affairs. The state had managed to put its citizens in hock to transnational capital for two generations.

Despite this, another two years later Irish recovery was again flavour of the month. Now the Irish had become particularly good Europeans since – unlike the Greeks – we accepted this state of affairs with hardly a word. Sure enough, this passivity was rewarded. In another two years, without any sense of irony, the Celtic Tiger had re-emerged as the Celtic Phoenix.

It was tempting to suggest that the only constant across these fifty years of boom and bust was journalistic hyperbole. At the same time, however, there was a broad continuity to the economic policy of the 26-county state after 1973 – the refusal to tax big business in the hopes that it might regard Ireland as an appropriate tax haven. It was a simple enough macroeconomic approach – create an environment so conducive to transnational corporations that they will regard this in itself as competitive advantage. This provides a certain level of low- and medium-wage employment – albeit something that the state has no control over. The added advantage is that it provides almost limitless opportunities for graft – for politicians and developers and for anyone else prepared to get their trotters in the trough.

Thus, from its inception in the Shannon Free Trade Zone in 1959[14] through 'Ansbacher Man'[15] to the 'Double Irish' and 'Green Jersey' approach of recent years,

---

[14] The Shannon Free Zone was established in 1959 as the first modern free trade zone. It was a response to the advent of new aircraft technology that permitted transatlantic flights to skip refueling stops at Shannon. It was an attempt by the Irish government to maintain employment around the airport and for the airport to continue generating revenue for the Irish economy. On its own terms, it was hugely successful and is still in operation today.

[15] Socialist TD Joe Higgins memorably charted 'a day in the life of Ansbacher man' in the Dáil in 1999. His speech summarised the synergy between power and corruption revealed by the 200 Irish citizens holding offshore accounts with the eponymous bank. The scandal was first disclosed during the McCracken tribunal

the economy of Southern Ireland was premised on the commitment not to tax, not to interfere, not to monitor and not to criticise. By 2018 it was being identified as 'the world's biggest tax haven' (O'Dwyer 2018). This whole approach has been characterised as 'leprechaun economics' – the economics of a state which panders to economic nationalism but simultaneously does nothing to support – let alone 'cherish' – its people. This kind of empty economic nationalist rhetoric reached its nadir in the notion of 'putting on the green jersey' – this started as a glib appeal to uncritical support for Irish tax arrangements – no matter how corrupt.[16] But it has now become a metaphor for the whole approach of the Irish state to taxation of transnational capital (Smyth 2019; European United Left/Nordic Green Left 2018: 6).

This leprechaun economics characterisation of the 26-county state was first made by US economist Paul Krugman in July 2016 following the publication of growth figures by the Central Statistics Office (Brennan 2016). The CSO – in the spirit of new Celtic Phoenix optimism – had revised Ireland's growth up to 26 per cent for 2015. This prompted Krugman to respond:

> Leprechaun economics: Ireland reports 26 per cent growth! But it doesn't make sense. Why are these in GDP? The figures appeared to have been affected by various one-off factors including activity in the aircraft leasing sector and restructuring by multinationals involving the movement of patents. (Cited in Brennan 2016)

The notion of 'leprechaun economics' carried echoes of the way that the term 'gombeenism' had been used in the past. It signified the toxic cocktail of *laissez faire* and corruption with a shamrock topping that characterised the economic climate cultivated by the 26-county state since 1973. This leaves the free market only mediated by corruption, and the corruption only mediated by the free market – the realisation that too much graft can encourage the goose to take its golden eggs elsewhere. The end product is an economic policy in thrall to transnational corporations – the very definition of an 'unfree state'. The approach was not only not to tax but also to avoid any kind of corporate accountability to the state or government whatsoever (RTÉ 2013).

What does this Irish version of the free market entail? There was an extraordinary moment in 2016 when the Irish government – still strapped for cash following its humbling in the crash of 2008 – fought the EU for the right *not* to claim taxes from

---

in 1997, which investigated corrupt payments to former Taoiseach Charles Haughey and former minister Michael Lowry. As Higgins observed, 'the system is rotten to the core and it is time these people were exposed' (Dáil Éireann 1999).

[16] Witness Pearse Doherty, TD: 'It was interesting that when Matt Carthy put that to the Minister's predecessor, his response was that this was very unpatriotic and he should wear the green jersey. That was the former Minister's response to the fact there is a major loophole, whether intentional or unintentional, in our tax code that has allowed large companies to continue to use the double Irish. The Minister's predecessor has acknowledged the reputational damage this has done to Ireland. He was not really concerned about losing tax revenue and all the rest, but about the reputational damage. Let there be no doubt that, as we close one loophole and create another door, or do not close the door, this reputational damage is going to continue' (Dáil Éireann 2017).

Apple.[17] At this moment, the three tendencies of contemporary Irish state engaged – good Europeanness, platform capitalism and supine non-intervention by the 26-county state. Once again, the defence of this refusal to tax was a folksy, hibernicised one. This would be like 'eating the seed potatoes' – if the metaphor from history had not so clearly referenced *An Gorta Mór*, it would have been simply funny.

This was only one manifestation of 21st-century Irish economic management. All the contradictions of this state formation were exemplified by the 'Double Irish' arrangement. This was a tax scheme used by some US corporations in Ireland (including Apple, Google and Facebook) to shield non-US income from both the US worldwide 35 per cent tax system – and almost all Irish taxation. (This was before Donald Trump's Tax Cuts and Jobs Act of 2017 removed US companies from these obligations.) It had the shameful distinction of being characterised as, 'the largest corporate tax avoidance structure in history'. It became a conduit by which US corporations built up offshore reserves of around $1 trillion. Alongside a myriad of other Irish tax avoidance tools, it has contributed to Ireland's rise to the top in many global lists of corporate tax havens and 'offshore financial centres' (Mark 2018; Ferriter 2018; Fowler 2018).

The Irish players in this game were strikingly familiar too. The 'grand architect' of the scheme was Feargal O'Rourke of the International Financial Services Centre and a partner in PwC (Pricewaterhouse Coopers). He was 'close to the thinking' of Fianna Fáil – son of former Minister Mary O'Rourke, nephew of Presidential candidate Brian Lenihan (he who had celebrated EU accession quietly back in 1973) and cousin of the 2008-2011 Irish Finance Minister Brian Lenihan Jr. Here was the modern version of Joyce's take on the Irish state – if God and Caesar were no longer hand in glove, Mammon and Caesar were as intimate as it was possible to be.

Of course, this episode also offers a counterfactual impression of what the 26-county state might look like *without* the EU. For all the anti-democratic tendencies, the EU imposed some level of corporate responsibility on the 26-county state. It was the EU that put the brake on some of this activity. Without this, the postcolonial path might have been even more alarming – somewhere between the Isle of Man and the Virgin Islands on an economic model completely framed by corporate tax haven status.

The supreme irony in all of this is when the froth was removed, there was little explanation for why the Celtic Tiger had happened at all. At one level, it was little more than a property bubble based on greed and the anticipation of ever-increasing house prices. In the middle of it, however, there was one substantive explanation for the Irish competitive advantage that was so ruthlessly exploited by those who profited

---

[17] The European Competition Commissioner found that Apple had been given 'up to €13bn (£10.8bn) in illegal state aid via a secret, sweetheart tax deal spanning many years' and ruled that Apple must pay it back. The 'trick' was that Apple's base in Ireland was where profits from all its European sales were registered and then taxed at 0.005 percent (*Guardian* 2016). The Irish government appealed this decision and in July 2020, the European Union's General Court overturned the European Competition Commission's decision (BBC News 2020d).

from Tiger economics. Across the history of the 26-county state, there had been a long-term investment in education across the whole population. This was the key to Ireland's economic success, yet it was not informed by economic logic at all. It was the unintended consequence of broad Catholic social policy in relation to education, a policy based on educating all of the children. This remained far from the 'cherishing all the children of the nation equally' promised in the Proclamation since the 26 counties retained both elite private schools and brutal reform schools outside of the mainstream system. It was, however, less unequal than the private/state, grammar/secondary model adopted in the six counties and the UK. Cruel irony indeed that this consequence of Catholic social democracy should reap such reward with such little credit.

White Europe and Irishness

If the trajectory in Southern Ireland since 1973 has signalled some of the contradictions of economic development, this is true *a fortiori* in terms of constitutional and political developments. The 'Europeanisation' of the 26 counties over the past fifty years raises the most profound issues in terms of where the whole island is going. These have obviously been brought sharply and brutally into focus by Brexit. While this poses a serious threat to the peace process in the north, it also raises wider issues of race and Europeanness and the question of how the 26 counties sits in relation to these basic issues of national identity. The legacies of colonialism – and its racial signifiers – were reframed in the context of contemporary Ireland. In turn, the specific experience of Irishness in the EU also illuminates broader questions around 'race' and its relationship to 'Europeanness' and the EU project. Arguably the very weakness of the contemporary 26-county state – it has a doubly subaltern position vis-à-vis the European Union and the British state – makes it easier to trace the tension between Irish state openness to Europeans and closure to (almost) everyone else.

We can illustrate this point with two Irish case studies – one part of a general trend, the other the consequence of a very specifically Irish dynamic. Both of these impacted profoundly on the 26-county state over the past fifty years. The first is the way in which Irish migration policy has been changed by its relationship with the European Union and its employment and migrant labour strategies. The second is the Chen case and the profound change this forced in notions of Irish citizenship and nationality. As we shall see, this change was consequent upon the unique nature of Irish nationality and citizenship in the context of the EU.

In terms of the broader shifts in 26-county migration policy, the telescoping of changes in Irish citizenship, nationality, migration and refugee law over recent years provide a unique perspective. Changes that took more than sixty years in other European countries have happened in Ireland over two decades. From its inception, the 26 counties was a state defined by emigration. Neither asylum nor immigration nor nationality nor citizenship issues were particularly high on the political agenda of any of the iterations of the Southern Ireland state before the 1990s. Immigration only became a live issue because of the pull factor of Ireland's resurgent Celtic Tiger economy:

> [T]he number of work permits issued to non-EEA nationals rose dramatically from 5,750 in 1999 to 47,707 in 2003. Furthermore, it is known that approximately three out of every four permits issued in 2002 were for relatively low-skilled and/ or low-wage occupations, especially in the service sector. There was also great diversity in the composition of the migrant workforce employed on work permits at that time; in 2000-2003, work permits were issued to nationals from more than 150 countries, with workers from the ten new EU member states accounting for about one-third of all permits issued during that period. (IOM 2006: 30)

For a moment, therefore, Ireland became a country of high in-migration with migrants of colour drawn from around the world. Over a short period of time, Southern Ireland became conscious of its own whiteness, discovered 'diversity' and began to manage migration and integration. A generation later, the dependency on migrant labour remains as apparent but the source of migrant labour has changed remarkably over the last fifteen years. This key shift in the 26 counties came with changes in migration policy in the context of the EU. In 2003, after ten years of unprecedented economic growth and a remarkable multi-ethnicizing of the Irish labour market and Irish society, the shutters of Fortress Europe came down on non-EEA nationals. The Department of Enterprise, Trade and Employment made it clear that:

> Employers are obliged to have demonstrated that they have made every effort to employ an EEA national before a work permit will be issued. (Department of Enterprise, Trade and Employment 2003: 6-7)

By 2004, the National Employment Action Plan had internalised this shift:

> It is expected that employers will be able to fill the majority of their labour needs from the extended EEA (European Economic Area) going forward. Consequently, work permits are now only being granted for non-EEA nationals in respect of highly skilled positions where no suitable personnel could be sourced within the enlarged EEA. (Department of Enterprise, Trade and Employment 2004: 39-40)

The low-skilled jobs which had generated the multi-ethnicising of Ireland for the previous decade were now closed to non-EEA nationals. These priorities were made clear by the Lisbon Agenda Report:

> Economic migration policy is based on firstly, increasing participation and upskilling the resident population; secondly, maximising the potential of European Economic Area (EEA) nationals to fill skills deficits; and thirdly, using employment permits to meet skill needs which cannot otherwise be addressed. (Department of the Taoiseach 2006: 36-7)

This process was confirmed by the Labour Market Needs Test (Department of Enterprise, Trade and Employment 2007: 2). Henceforth, legally defined employment routes to the Republic of Ireland for low-skilled workers from outside the EU were effectively ended by the introduction of a green card system. This system was introduced for highly skilled occupations identified by the Expert Group on Future Skills Needs (Department of the Taoiseach 2006: 37; Department of Enterprise, Trade and Employment 2007: 1).

A hierarchy of migrant labour was very clearly established and the colour-coding of this hierarchy was stark. Thus, in 1996 migrants were overwhelmingly people of colour from outside the EU. By 2003 there were migrants from 150 counties, with around one third coming from the EU (IOM 2006: 30). By 2006 seven out of eight immigrants were from within the EU (Fahy 2007: 28). The IOM (International Organisation for Migration) characterises this transition:

> The publication of the Employment Permits Act in April 2003, which facilitated the access for workers from the ten EU accession countries to the Irish labour markets immediately upon EU enlargement, marked the beginning of a more interventionist work permit system in Ireland. The government felt that its liberal policy toward workers from the EU accession countries required a more managed approach to regulate the number and selection of migrant workers to Ireland from outside the enlarged European Union. This was primarily based on the expectation that local employers would be able to fill most of their vacancies after 1 May 2004, from within the enlarged European Union. (IOM 2006: 30)

This bears some emphasis. The situation is now one in which all the non-EU nationals who had been meeting labour market needs of the Celtic Tiger were effectively excluded while EU member migrant workers were privileged. This is itself clearly racially coded. But it is even more problematic than this. There is privileged access to the Irish labour market not only for EU citizens but also for non-EU citizens who are members of the EEA and Switzerland. In the absence of any other logic, the most obvious 'sufficient connection' with Ireland in these cases was whiteness. Again, this logic is not spelt out – only the reference to the 'mistakes' of other countries hints at the real policy objective. Boucher characterises this in his review of the NESC (2006) and IOM (2006) interventions on 'managing migration':

> [T]he policy recommendations in the NESC report ratify what the government had already done or planned to do: use EU nationals from the new member states for low-skilled work; severely reduce work permits for low-skilled work for non-EEA nationals; create high-skilled green cards for non-EEA nationals; and attempt 'to avoid the mistakes of other countries in operating policies to attract low-skilled workers on a (supposed) temporary basis' *who could become the socially excluded, ethnic minorities of the future* (our emphasis). (2007)

In this sense, the EU has been part of a process of forcing the Irish to become white all over again. Through the particular Irish prism of that process, we also come to a wider appreciation of what is happening to Europeanness.

This broad tendency towards a *de facto* 'White Europe' policy was brought into sharp focus by the Chen case. While others tended to cloak the racial politics of this case, the

Taoiseach framed these more directly in his summary of the episode:

> We also need to protect our laws from being used to abuse European citizenship. We know from the Chen case currently before the European Court of Justice that the acquisition of Irish citizenship by children of non-nationals – with no sufficient connection to Ireland – has implications for other member states. That case concerns the birth in Belfast of a child to a Chinese woman who is claiming a right to reside in Britain by virtue of the Irish citizenship of her child. It is common ground in that case that the reason Ms Chen went to Belfast was to ensure her child, when born, would acquire Irish nationality, thereby enabling her mother to raise a possible claim to remain in the United Kingdom. This situation illustrates an unacceptable consequence of Article 2 of the Constitution. This abuse is not what the Governments and the Irish people expected would occur, but it has occurred and we need to take corrective measures. Hence the proposed referendum. (Dáil Éireann 2004a)

The case did indeed have profound EU-wide implications. The issue was only possible because of the specific character of the construction of Irish nationality in the Constitution.[18] Irish nationality law had allowed migrants access to EU citizenship through its application to the whole island of Ireland – thus transcending the formal sovereignty of the two EU member states on the island. This harked back to the formation of the state – the brief 24 hours when the Free State had jurisdiction over the whole island. As we have seen this caused significant problems for the UK state in its efforts to include and exclude the 'right' people. But this 32-county citizenship was reinforced and formalised by the 1937 Constitution. Moreover, it was protected by the GFA changes to nationality as an outcome of the peace process, something central to the EU project.

In the event, the Chen case resulted in fundamental changes in Irish citizenship and nationality – most obviously emblemised by the citizenship referendum. The referendum – and consequent legislation and practice – was indeed a direct consequence of European sensitivities over the openness of Irish citizenship law following the GFA. The nuances and silences associated with this case – which profoundly changed the nature of Irishness and undermined the GFA – provide a unique example of the racially-coded European project in action.

Despite this context, the Irish government, through its Justice Minister at the time, Michael McDowell, insisted that the changes were not made in the context of pressure from the EU: 'No formal representations have been made to me by my EU ministerial counterparts concerning our citizenship laws' (Dáil Éireann 2004b). McDowell also made the astonishing claim that, 'between 40% and 50% of non-EU nationals who give birth in Ireland do so to gain Irish citizenship for their children' (RTÉ 2004).

There was, however, constant reference to the EU context: 'the Chen case ... could seriously affect the standing of our citizenship law within the European Union if we did not take an early opportunity to amend our Constitution to prevent continuing abuse of

---

[18] Case C-200/02 – Zhu & Chen v Secretary of State for the Home Department.

the jus soli entitlement to citizenship for any person born in the island of Ireland' (Dáil Éireann 2004c). Frequent reference was also made to the Chen case throughout and after the citizenship referendum (Dáil Éireann 2004d,e,f; Seanad Éireann 2004). Thus, Fianna Fáil Chief Whip Mary Hanafin notoriously argued:

> I consider myself to be a citizen of Ireland as does everybody in the House, not just because I was born here. I am a citizen of Ireland because my parents and grandparents lived and worked here and contributed to society. I too continue to make a contribution to society. Citizenship does not imply any cultural or ethnic uniformity but it implies that contribution....It is an incredible distortion of what it means to be Irish to have a constitutional framework which confers citizenship and all of the legal and political rights which go with it on people with no tangible connection with the country. It gives all those rights to people whose parents came here purely to obtain an Irish birth certificate and an EU passport before flying back to the EU country of their choice, where they can avail of their rights as an Irish citizen. By conferring Irish citizenship on the future children of these estranged Irish-born citizens we are not just creating one generation but a couple of generations of Irish people who have no connection with Ireland. (Dáil Éireann 2004g)

On 11 June 2004 the referendum was held on the proposal to remove the constitutional entitlement to citizenship by birth. The wording of the citizenship referendum 2004 was as follows:

> Notwithstanding any other provision of this Constitution, a person born in the island of Ireland, which includes its islands and seas, who does not have, at the time of the birth of that person, at least one parent who is an Irish citizen or entitled to be an Irish citizen is not entitled to Irish citizenship or nationality, unless provided for by law.

This change was supported by the two Irish government parties Fianna Fáil and the Progressive Democrats as well as Fine Gael, the largest opposition party. It was opposed by the Irish Labour Party, Sinn Féin and the Green Party. In the event, voters elected by four to one to change the *jus soli* basis of Irish citizenship. On a turnout of 59.9 per cent of the electorate (1,823,434) 79.2 per cent (1,427,520) voted Yes and 20.8 per cent (375,695) voted No.

In effect, therefore, Irish citizenship law had become completely determined by the implications that it was deemed to have for EU citizenship. The outcome of the case *was* potentially a 'problem' for the UK and the EU *but not for the Irish state*. Yet changes driven through by the Irish government and almost completely justified in terms of concerns about the 'abuse' of EU citizenship had profound implications for both the GFA and Irish citizenship and nationality.

Once again this supine acceptance of the logic of being 'good Europeans' had a clear racial undertow. For all the government disclaimers, the population was quite clear that the referendum was about race and migration. The RTÉ Exit Poll following the referendum made clear the 'spontaneous reasons for voting Yes': 'Country being exploited by immigrants' – 36 per cent; 'Too many immigrants' – 27 per cent; 'Bring in line with other EU countries' – 20 per cent; 'Children should not be automatically Irish citizens' – 14 per cent. Aggregating the first, second and fourth of these, we can suggest that the Hanafin insistence that the referendum had 'nothing to do with racism or immigration' rang more than a little hollow. Southern Ireland – in the middle of the Celtic Tiger boom, mind – was defining its politics by race for the first time.

The politics of 'sufficient connection' evolved in a more technical and legalistic way in the Irish Nationality and Citizenship Act 2004 which enshrined the referendum decision in law. Most cruelly and bizarrely of all, some children of the Irish nation without 'sufficient connection' became 'non-people' – they were no longer 'persons' in the context of the Act:

> (6) In this section 'person' does not include a person born in the island of Ireland on or after the commencement of the Irish Nationality and Citizenship Act 2004 – (a) neither of whose parents was at the time of the person's birth – (i) an Irish citizen or entitled to be an Irish citizen, (ii) a British citizen, (iii) a person entitled to reside in the State without any restriction on his or her period of residence (including in accordance with a permission granted under section 4 of the Act of 2004), or (iv) a person entitled to reside in Northern Ireland without any restriction on his or her period of residence.[19]

These Irish-born 'non-persons' were still provided with Irish nationality by virtue of the GFA and Article 2 but Irish citizenship was denied them. Even more strangely, it was left to another state to decide whether someone might qualify for Irish citizenship. The question of whether someone is a 'British' citizen' or 'a person entitled to reside in Northern Ireland without any restriction on his or her period of residence' are matters entirely beyond the control of the Irish state. A state which had been so concerned about the 'abuse of European citizenship' offers a route to Irish citizenship (and therefore European citizenship) which is entirely out of its control. (This takes on an even greater significance post-Brexit as it provides a route to European Union citizenship for *any* 'British citizen'; they only have to move to Northern Ireland.) It denies citizenship to children with Irish nationality as a birthright, yet offers it to any child born in Northern Ireland whose parents' right to be there is determined by the British state. Arguably after 80 years of formal independence the Irish government had handed a definitive element of its sovereignty back to the British state.

Thus, the referendum saw an embryonic racial and ethnic pluralism to southern Irishness brought swiftly to an end. The possibility of Irishness of colour had become real for a brief period before it was closed by the citizenship referendum and the European Employment Strategy.[20] There is no suggestion in all of this that many white Europeans

---

[19] In contrast, the Irish Nationality and Citizenship Act 1956 read 'Every person born in Ireland is an Irish citizen from birth' and the Irish Nationality and Citizenship Act 2001 read 'Every person born in the island of Ireland is entitled to be an Irish citizen.'

[20] By 2005, asylum was effectively no longer a route to Irishness. Only 455 applicants were given refugee status; 4,787 were refused (ORAC 2006). If any of these refugees had children in Ireland, these children

do not experience racism in contemporary Ireland. They do, of course, north and south of the border. Moreover, there is no question that a zero migration policy is the preferred option of both Irish and European racism. However, the EU position, the institutionalised capital logic position, is that white European migrants – whether from inside or outside the EU or EEA – are preferable to third-country nationals or 'former colonials'. This policy of 'avoiding the mistakes of the past' is explicitly racialised and explicitly racist: first, try not to let people of colour in at all; second, if you do let them in, do not provide them with avenues to citizenship. In this reading, whiteness trumps language and historical connectedness and any attempt to acknowledge the legacy of European colonialism. Despite all the window-dressing, this is a *de facto* antithesis of diversity policy. In this sense, current Irish and EU migration policy prevents diversity rather than encouraging it.

Here the specific complexity of contemporary Irishness was crucial in the outworking of this citizenship struggle in the context of the EU. Irish citizenship only became an issue because of the post-GFA resolution to Irish nationality. In turn, the fundamental change to citizenship forced through in the referendum only became a 'solution' because of the ability of the two governments to ignore the GFA.[21] Thus, the recent experience of Irish migration and migration policy provides a particular perspective on European citizenship and the largely hidden white Europe policy this embraces. This in turn repudiates and prevents other more inclusive notions of Irishness.[22] The 26-county state insisted that the 'integrity of European citizenship' would take precedence over the peace process and the birthright of people born in Ireland. Undermining the Good Friday Agreement and stripping children with Irish nationality of their citizenship had become less problematic than 'affecting the standing of our citizenship law within the European Union'. For all that the EU presents as 'united in diversity', it is defined by the commonality of whiteness and exclusion. The intentions of this approach are a moot point; no doubt the EU commitment to European humanism would be outraged at the idea that this might involve exclusion on racial grounds. Nevertheless, the consequences are a white Europe policy (Rankin 2018).

---

would become part of the Irish nation as their birthright, but they could also be denied Irish citizenship.

[21] In 2015 Northern Ireland-born Emma De Souza applied for a residence card for her US-born husband. She applied using her Irish passport. The UK Home Office rejected the application on the grounds that she was British. She has never held a British passport and argued that, under the terms of the GFA, she could identify as British, Irish, or both. The Home Office advised her either to reapply as a British citizen or renounce her British citizenship; she could then pay a fee to apply as an Irish citizen. A court in 2017 agreed with Emma De Souza, but in October 2019, an appeal against this decision by the Home Office was successful (BBC News 2019a). Finally in September 2020, the Home Office abandoned its appeal and conceded that anyone born in Northern Ireland would henceforth be regarded as an EU citizen for immigration purposes (McClements 2020).

[22] A similar process also undermines pluralism in other state identities like 'Spanishness' or 'Portugeseness' or 'Britishness' or 'Frenchness' – where older colonial constructions of multi-ethnicity and multiculturalism are renounced in favour of new forms of white Europeanness.

European traditions are of course multifarious and complex. In terms of non-Europeans, these traditions include both repression and refuge. They have both excluded peoples and permitted them access with varying degrees of generosity. However, 'Fortress Europe' not 'Sanctuary Europe' remains the correct metaphor for the contemporary European project. Brexit may have represented the nadir of racist nationalism for the European project but there is now a series of similar challenges: Orbán in Hungary, Salvini in Italy, Petri in Germany, Wilders in Holland, Le Pen in France. Rather than united in diversity, there is a popular and rising tide of support for the EU uniting in whiteness.[23] As this implies, European whiteness is not a state but a process – the EU is still becoming white. It is perhaps needless to add that this process is both institutionally racist and profoundly anti-humanist. It is also the very antithesis of becoming 'united in diversity'.

Thus, the 26-county state played a small but highly significant role in the construction of Fortress Europe. In the process it reframed its own sense of nationhood as well as its formal citizenship laws in order to secure the vision of this Fortress Europe. In consequence, race and Irishness had been reframed in the context of the EU and the peace process in a quite remarkable way.

This begins to signal the need for a wider process of questioning the ongoing implications of EU membership for Irishness. We have suggested, of course, that this should be framed by our juxtaposition of Empire and Republic. Arguably, this question of the nature of the EU and Ireland's relationship to it remains the single most important challenge for the 26-county state – and it will become the single most important challenge following reunification. What is to be done about the EU? As Balibar asked, are we building or destroying sovereignty? And what does this mean for a small, relatively peripheral European island still struggling with complex legacies of imperialism and colonialism? Put simply in the terms of the Proclamation, is it possible to cherish the children of the nation equally in a state that will not allow a portion of the 'children of the nation' to even become citizens?

The outworking of this ongoing tension between whiteness, Europeanness and Irish citizenship has been quite bizarre in terms of notions of Irishness. The most recent Irish census captures this process.[24] It at least conveys the possibility of Irish people of colour – but the sense of confusion remains as the state attempts to shoehorn its citizens into their appropriate 'ethnic or cultural group'. Whiteness frames the construction

---

[23] Despite the general argument we are making here, it is noteworthy that the presence of right-wing political groupings in the south of Ireland has been minimal. A right-wing, anti-immigration party, Identity Ireland, was formed in 2015, but apart from joining with others in public protests over such issues as the rehousing of Syrian refugees, it has had almost no impact. However, in the 2020 election Verona Murphy – who had been deselected by Fine Gael because of her racist anti-refugee stance – was elected as an independent TD in Wexford (Halpin 2020).

[24] See 'Table 1A Persons usually resident in each Province and County, and present in the State on Census Night, classified by ethnic or cultural background'.

of ethnicity and 'White Irish' remains the default setting. Travellers – who had their ethnicity actively denied by the state for decades and who used to be constructed in the vernacular as 'yellow tinkers' – now have whiteness thrust upon them. But there is no equivalent default of Black Irish. The implication remains that it is not possible to be unproblematically Black and Irish. Thus, the Irishness of a host of quintessentially Irish people – from Phil Lynott and Paul McGrath through Samantha Mumba and Ruth Negga – remains ambiguous in this formulation.[25] Perhaps most weirdly of all, Taoiseach Varadkar himself must have struggled to locate his appropriate 'ethnic or cultural group' within this construction of Irishness. This is, of course, about much more than a census form. The broader analysis should properly reflect the complexity of contemporary ethnicity in Ireland grounded in the complex ethnicised colonial history we have already detailed. Getting this 'right' remains an immediate challenge for the 26 counties as it passes its centenary. More widely, however, it signals the necessity for integrating a proper reading of the place of Black Irishness – Irishness of colour – across both states on the island and the diaspora. From this perspective, the citizenship referendum marked a definitive moment in the evolution of the southern Irish state. It was a conscious and deliberate intervention to summarily halt the development of Black Irishness and Irishness of colour. In terms of our wider analysis, it was a depressing and profoundly reactionary undermining of the possibility of Irish *mestizaje*.

Before this, the defining quality of Irishness has been something other than skin colour. This very different sense of race in the habitus of ordinary Irish people is captured in the diary of Amhlaoibh Ui Shuilleabhain from 1831. The complex positioning of Irishness and race is reflected perfectly in his response – *written In Irish* – to hearing that Irish was spoken in the Caribbean:

> I hear that Irish is the mother tongue in 'Montserrat in the West Indies' since the days of Oliver Cromwell, who transported numbers of the Children of the Gael to that island. And now Irish is spoken there by people, black and white. Well, the poor Irish exiles are very dear to this heart of mine, whether they are black or white. The Children of the Gael are ever dear to me! (Irish Texts Society 1936: 33)

This bears some emphasis. Rural, Catholic, Gaelic Ireland was able to accept – and cherish – the reality of Irishness of colour *two hundred years ago* without any sense of crisis at all. Whenever the British Empire reinvented Southern Ireland as a white dominion, this identification with whiteness was far removed from the experience of most Irish people. And whenever the citizenship referendum constituted a further elective affinity between whiteness and Irish, there was nothing inevitable – nor indeed 'Irish' – about this process.

---

[25] The English census does this even more crudely – there whiteness and Irishness are mutually exclusive categories, thus precluding *any* possibility of Black Irishness.

Moreover, despite the framing racial homogenisation of white dominion status, the Free State itself was obviously a state defined by ethnoreligious *difference* – between Protestants and Catholics – rather than uniformity *from the first*.

Jedward and the triumph of bathos

It would, of course, be silly to suggest that nothing has changed for the better in the 26 counties since 1973. By 2018 – with the election of Leo Varadkar – the polity had successfully modernised in a whole range of ways (*Economist* 2017). Not only had it – without almost any sense of angst – elected a Taoiseach who was openly gay and of colour, but it had become the first country in the world to legalise gay marriage through a popular vote. Even the most sanguine of us might have found this turn of events hard to imagine back in 1982 after the defeat of the first divorce referendum. The 26 counties went from being a state that could not countenance divorce – even for its non-Catholic citizens – to being one that enthusiastically paraded its gay-friendly credentials around the world.

Moreover, this tide of liberalism just kept coming. On 25 May 2018 Ireland voted overwhelmingly in support of access to abortion. The scale of the victory shocked its most ardent supporters.[26] Even more than the marriage equality vote, this moment signalled the end of national Catholicism. A combination of push and pull factors – liberalism, economic development, the ever-deepening mire of abuse associated with institutionalised Catholicism in all its forms – had helped. Put alongside the personal stories of thousands of women who had been victims and survivors of this particularly virulent theme within national Catholicism,[27] these trends ensured a stark break with the past. It did not mean that the 26-county state had transformed overnight – but it did suggest that the version of the carnival of reaction carefully constructed on the back of partition had not endured. While it was hardly a portent of either the Republic or reunification, it made the possibility of a radical, progressive reunification of the island a great deal easier.[28]

The 26 counties – albeit with a difference sequencing – had followed the path of a bundle of western European democracies from Catholic conservatism to secular

---

[26] The result was: For 1,429,981; Against 723,632; Majority 706,349. The percentage result was Yes 66.4, No 33.6 on a turnout of 64.1 percent.

[27] A major element in the success of the campaign was the creation of a Facebook platform to allow women to tell their stories: 'In Her Shoes'. The humanity of the women from every aspect of Irish society came across powerfully, convincing many wavering voters to come down on the side of reform.

[28] This new liberalism was doubly ironic since it further exposed the reactionary heart of unionism in the north. The DUP's committed opposition to gay marriage and abortion in the north was left looking like a throwback to mainstream Catholic Ireland in the 1970s. Moreover, in the interim both issues had become a touchstone for the supposedly 'British values' of diversity and tolerance. Indeed, one of the most striking features of contemporary politics in the Six Counties is the way in which it begins to look like a throwback to the worst manifestations of 'gombeen' politics in the 26 counties. With the DUP in government, we find a politicised form of religious bigotry that echoes the worst of the Oliver J Flanagan/Alice Glenn wing of Fine Gael alongside a simultaneous – and no doubt related – institutionalisation of graft that rivals the endemic corruption of the 'cute hoor' era of Fianna Fáil.

democracy – Italy, Spain, Portugal, and Belgium. In each the aegis of the EU had at least facilitated a variant of national Catholicism to be replaced with a broad commitment to European social democracy. A genuine sense of Europeanness had framed the idea of a different politics and a different polity from their specific variants of national Catholicism. Moreover, there was no doubt that this did in ways offer a vision – a sense of a future instead of a past. For all its limitations, the 26-county state had made this journey – not so much away from Irishness but towards an Irishness that could offer some sense of a future for the island – as well as a more self-confident sense of its place in Europe and the world.

This sense of self also framed an odd adventure in post-colonial economics across the history of the state. Of course, this was far from perfect – the economic reality of the southern state looks dreadfully tarnished when compared with the 'poetry' of the democratic programme. By 2020, Ireland's economy looks very different to what it did in 1850 or 1920 or 1973. It features routinely in the top ten of the Human Development Index of the United Nations – some distance ahead of the UK. The journey from 'poorest of the rich' to 'Celtic Tiger' and beyond signified something in the relative confidence of Southern Ireland. In other words, if it unambiguously failed to meet the expectations of the Republic, it was also far from being a 'failed state'. There is a danger in turning an anti-imperialist gaze on a post-colonial project. Southern Ireland in 2020 hardly matched the aspirations of the Democratic Programme of the First Dáil. But it compared favourably with the 'defeated, colonial city' that was Joyce's Dublin. There is a danger in colluding with the imperialist defence – that anything that followed colonialism was poorer, less grand and generally tawdrier than life under the colonial regime. This was palpably untrue. If nothing else, Southern Ireland had negotiated a space in which Irishness could be viewed through something other than a colonial stereotype.

We might argue that there was a moment when this new perception of Irishness became real. In 1994, Riverdance was performed during the interval of the Eurovision Song Contest at the Point Theatre in Dublin to an estimated 300 million viewers across Europe and beyond. Albeit helped by being framed by the shallowness of Eurovision itself, here was Irishness presented in novel, exciting – nay, sexy – ways. It looked like something new and different. It looked like Irishness might be becoming rather than vanishing. Here was a palpable reinvention of tradition that had the whole of Europe standing in ovation. We had – in this quintessentially European moment – become good Europeans. Not only were we proud of ourselves but the whole of Europe was proud of us. Perhaps this was what Irish postcolonialism looked like?[29]

For all that Riverdance presaged something about the possibilities of 21st-century

---

[29] The irony is that the Riverdance phenomenon owed much to the diaspora in the US rather than solely to the Irish from the 26 counties. Although the brains behind it was Irish production team Moya Doherty and John McColgan, a number of the key performers were Irish American. Lead male dancer and choreographer Michael Flatley was born in Chicago; his father was from County Sligo and his mother from County Carlow. Lead female dancer Jean Butler was born in Mineola, New York; her mother was from County Mayo. The fiddle player on the world tour which followed was Eileen Ivers, born in New York of Irish parents.

Irishness, the 26 counties was better emblemised a generation later by another, shallower musical phenomenon, Jedward. This Irishness had an odd flavour. It had lost its sense of threat to the English. (Anti-Irish racism through the 70s and 80s and 90s remained conditioned by the threat of violence but this had largely cleared by the millennium in the wake of the GFA.) Irishness could be tolerated – even feted on occasion. But it was in effect a millennial West Britonism. Ireland had found a face that made it acceptable – even popular –to a British audience. As Fintan O'Toole (2009) observed in his evocation of the 'unbearably poignant last gasp of Celtic Tiger culture':

> Often, the most poignant and potent moment of a culture is its dying gasp....
> Step forward John and Edward Grimes, aka Jedward, aka the terrible twins of the [British] X-Factor TV show who have no discernible talent but who got enough public votes on Sunday night to stay in the competition yet again. Jedward are the pure essence of a culture we have inhabited for 15 years and that is now functionally extinct. As Simon Cowell, one of the talent show judges, puts it: 'They are completely deluded and they live in a fantasy world, but they're lovely... And Jedward do capture the essence of Tiger culture with stunning precision. Born and raised within its brassy ambit, they embody its ruling values to perfection. They have boundless ambition and no talent; phenomenal energy and no point; hyper-confidence and no substance. They are completely immune to useless emotions like embarrassment and shame. With their American accents and plastic appearance (they look like they're actually designed as models from which toy manufacturers will make Jedward dolls), they are supremely vacuous.

This variant of southern Irishness had lost any sense of danger and its otherness was reduced to a contemporary form of stage Irishry – characterised by 'loveliness'. Still refusing to surrender to the despotism of fact, the 26 counties could throw up a succession of stage Irish *amadáin* from this mould to take their place within British society. Brexit, however, soon forced the 26-county state towards a more realistic self-evaluation.

It was clear from the first that Brexit – whatever its nihilistic impact on British economy and society – could cause severe collateral damage for the southern Irish state. In this context, the entire 26-county political class was forced to engage with the border – and the politics of partition – for the first time in a generation. There was an associated recrudescence of unionist antipathy to southern politicians that brought memories of Peter Barry and the Anglo-Irish Agreement. The supreme irony was, of course, that few of these politicians had an iota of republican or anti-partitionist commitment – they were looking at the interests of the partitionist capitalist state rather than furthering any broader or more radical agenda. Such are the contradictions of Irish politics: it was the little Englandism of the Brexiteers rather than any mainstream or 'dissident' republican intervention – north or south – that had brought partition back to the centre of 26-county politics.

This meant that the Irish state was forced to engage critically with unionism and Britishness again. Nevertheless, this remained processed through the self-interest of its governing classes rather than any residual commitment to anti-partitionism. Indeed, the Sinn Féin surge in the February 2020 election appeared to make the Irish government parties even less likely to rock the boat. Fine Gael and Fianna Fáil attempts to organise politically in the north have stalled while junior partners the Greens – who have played a contrasting radical pro-independence role in Scotland – have failed even to integrate their party across the island. The crude reality was that in terms of the political logic of the 26 counties, the DUP presented no threat whatsoever to Fine Gael or Fianna Fáil. Rather Sinn Féin – potential partners in the reunification project – presented the real threat. Sinn Féin's new position as the most popular party in the state – one hundred years after its victory in 1918 – exposed the limitations of 26-county 'republicanism'. Despite Fine Gael looking to a new Republic Day and Fianna Fáil characterising itself as the 'Republican Party', Irish republicanism threatens as much as it promises to Irish nationalism. In the venal calculus of 26-county politics, it is Sinn Féin rather than the DUP that now presents a very clear risk from the north: immediately in terms of Dáil seats and the possibility of majorities in the Dáil, and in the longer term to the southern state itself. In this context, opposition to partition takes on an entirely different complexion.

The 26-county state finds itself at an odd moment on its centenary. It is undoubtedly very different to the Treaty state of 1922; it is also very different to the state that joined the EU in 1973. But it is also much further removed from the promise of the Republic of 1916. It was a sign of the times that Taoiseach Varadkar could – without any sense of irony – announce that he was prepared to instate a Republic Day. Any cursory review of the history of his own state might have suggested that a Republic Day or an Independence Day could only follow the end of partition – unless they were preparing to celebrate the bathetic moment in Canada in 1948 when the 26 counties became a republic 'by accident'. This core difficulty obtains: partition continues to structure everything else. In this sense the national project appears some distance from even the 1949 26-county cross-party consensus solemnly asserting 'the indefeasible right of the Irish nation to the unity and integrity of the national territory'.

In many ways, therefore – one hundred years after the Declaration of Independence – the Irish state remains as dependent as it ever was. It broke free from a classical colonial form of dependence only to embrace others, including the EU and transnational capital. Brexit added a final irony to this in terms of 'what it means to be a citizen' of this state. Following the UK Brexit vote in 2016, there was a surge in applications for Irish passports from the UK (Scully 2018; Heffernan 2019). Yet, in direct contrast to the Chen case, this inspired no agonised soul searching south of the border. There were no Dáil debates on the nature of Irish citizenship; nobody suggested these people did not have 'sufficient connection' to the 26 counties; there was no covert instruction from the

EU to close this loophole in EU citizenship law; there were no strident appeals on the 'need to protect our laws from being used to abuse European citizenship' from any of the 26-county political class. To paraphrase Mary Hanafin, there appeared no issue at all with these people being born *outside* Ireland and being handed an Irish passport.

Of course, there was an element of this which was an important recognition of the diaspora. But it was tempting to observe that most of the diaspora whose Irishness mattered to them had got their Irish passports already – in the pre-Jedward generations when it was not easy to be Irish in Britain. The recent stampede for Irish citizenship represented little more than a post-Brexit guarantee to some of the continuing benefits of EU citizenship (Mullally 2019a).[30] It was therefore, definitively, in Bertie Ahern's phrase 'the use of Irish law to abuse European citizenship'. To rehearse Mary Hanafin, it was creating a whole new 'generation of Irish people who have no connection with Ireland'. Yet this was of no concern to the 26-county state. In combination the Britishness and whiteness of these applicants was 'sufficient connection' for them to become citizens. In this moment, a hundred years after the foundation of the state, the 26 counties had finally made peace with the twin challenges of the Treaty. It had come to terms with both Britishness and whiteness. From this perspective, for all the hyperbole about post-colonial identity, the 26 counties was to be found securely locked in a colonial paradigm. This was a perfect reflection of the zeitgeist of post-Celtic Tiger, post-Brexit Southern Ireland. Finally, the 26 counties had come to accept itself – via the good offices of the EU – as a white dominion.

---

[30] Former British ambassador to the 26 counties, Sir Ivor Roberts, obtained an Irish passport on the grounds that his father had been born in the six counties. He did so to retain his EU citizenship. 'I don't want to find myself queuing to get through Rome airport every time I go there' (Mortimer 2017).

Chapter 7

'A Protestant state and a Protestant parliament':
Northern Ireland 1920-72

A Protestant government for a Protestant people. —Viscount Craigavon, Prime Minister of Northern Ireland, 1934

If Catholics have no revolvers to protect themselves they are murdered. If they have revolvers they are flogged or sentenced to death. —Joe Devlin, MP, 1922

The template for the 'Northern Ireland' state emerged in the middle of the revolutionary period in Ireland; but it was completely framed by the British government and unionist 'empire loyalists'. The six-county area delineated by the Government of Ireland Act 1920 had two defining characteristics: it was a 'temporary' state and it was an 'emergency' state. Its anticipated transience was embedded in the Act itself. The text anticipated the establishment of a Council of Ireland, 'with a view to the eventual establishment of a parliament for the whole of Ireland'. The Council of Ireland was envisaged to coordinate matters of common concern to the two parliaments, with each parliament possessing the ability, in identical motions, to vote powers to the Council. Ostensibly the British intended this to evolve into a single Irish parliament:

> The Parliaments of Southern Ireland and Northern Ireland may subsequently by identical Acts transfer any of those powers and duties to the Government and Parliament of Ireland, and, in the event of all such powers and duties being so transferred, the Parliaments and Governments of Southern Ireland and Northern Ireland shall cease to exist.

Ireland also remained, in theory, integrated in other ways: both parts of Ireland would share the same viceroy; they would also continue to send MPs to the Westminster Parliament.[1]

---

[1] Elections for both lower houses took place in May 1921 for 128 seats in Southern Ireland and 52 seats in Northern Ireland. No seats were contested in Southern Ireland. 124 members were elected for Sinn Féin unopposed and constituted themselves as the Second Dáil. (Four independent unionists were also elected unopposed for TCD.) Six people were elected for Sinn Féin in Northern Ireland: Michael Collins, Éamon de Valera, Arthur Griffith, Seán Milroy and Eoin MacNeill were elected for constituencies in both Southern and Northern Ireland; only Seán O'Mahoney was elected solely in Northern Ireland. The six Nationalist MPs elected in Northern Ireland also refused to recognise the Parliament and did not take their seats in either Northern Ireland or the Dáil. Forty unionists were returned in the north and constituted a *de facto* one-party state until 1972.

There was, however, a major impediment to this British-framed path to reconciliation and eventual reunification. The Act also embedded the principle of *partition*. In consequence, it removed from Ireland the right to self-determine and delivered it *de facto* to a small and unrepresentative bloc within the north east of the island. It carved a new border across both Ireland and Ulster which had no historical or cultural legitimacy – its only logic was that this was the largest area following existing county boundaries that might be secured on a basis of *Protestant majoritarianism*. In 1910, the Protestant percentage of the population in each of the nine counties of the geographical province of Ulster was as follows: Antrim 79.5, Down 68, Armagh 55, Derry 54, Tyrone 45, Fermanagh 44, Monaghan 25, Donegal 21, Cavan 18.5 (Curtis 1994: 212). Consequently, the unionists determined to draw the border of their new state, not around geographical Ulster, but by excluding the three counties with the smallest unionist minorities – Cavan, Monaghan and Donegal. This created a six-county state which they would informally continue to call 'Ulster'. A nine-country state would have been 56.3 per cent Protestant, while a six-county state would be 66 per cent Protestant (Farrell 1980: 24). The die was thus cast; by abandoning their compatriots in three of Ulster's traditional nine counties, unionists assumed to guarantee a Protestant majority in perpetuity in their new state. This innovation ignored the democratic will of the Irish people in the 1918 election. It also ignored the expressed will of unionists outside of 'Northern Ireland'. Even more dangerously, it provided no voice whatsoever to those Catholics and nationalists who were now trapped inside the artificial entity. In other words, it denied not only the Irish right to self-determination but the same right even to the whole of *Ulster* – in effect *two-thirds* of *two-thirds* of Ulster now held the whole destiny of Ireland in its hands.

The Parliament of Northern Ireland came into being in June 1921. At its inauguration, in Belfast City Hall, King George V made a famous appeal for reconciliation.[2] But the state practice was already one in which sectarian division was normalised across every aspect of the new state formation. The temporary nature of the Government of Ireland Act fix was confirmed as it was quickly superseded by the Anglo-Irish Treaty of December 1921. The Treaty notionally re-integrated the six counties into 'Ireland' again but allowed for the withdrawal of the Six County area from the Irish Free State.

The Treaty was given legal effect in the United Kingdom through the Irish Free State Constitution Act 1922. This Act allowed Northern Ireland to opt out of the newly established Free State. Under Article 12 of the Treaty, Northern Ireland could exercise its option by presenting an address to the King requesting not to be part of the Free

---

[2] The colonial context remained immediate. The speech was drafted by the government of Lloyd George on recommendations from Jan Smuts, the Prime Minister of the Union of South Africa. Smuts had a similar challenge in terms of reconciliation after the Boer War. He also shared a disregard for any democratic implications of 'responsible government' for a 'native' population.

State. Once the Act was passed on 5 December 1922, the Houses of Parliament of Northern Ireland had one month – the 'Ulster month' – to exercise this option during which the Government of Ireland Act continued to apply in Northern Ireland.

On 7 December 1922, the Parliament of Northern Ireland resolved to opt out of the Irish Free State:

> MOST GRACIOUS SOVEREIGN, We, your Majesty's most dutiful and loyal subjects, the Senators and Commons of Northern Ireland in Parliament assembled, having learnt of the passing of the Irish Free State Constitution Act, 1922, being the Act of Parliament for the ratification of the Articles of Agreement for a Treaty between Great Britain and Ireland, do, by this humble Address, pray your Majesty that the powers of the Parliament and Government of the Irish Free State shall no longer extend to Northern Ireland.

Had the Parliament of Northern Ireland not made such a declaration, under Article 14 of the Treaty Northern Ireland, its Parliament and government would have continued but the *Oireachtas* would have had jurisdiction to legislate for Northern Ireland in matters not delegated to Northern Ireland under the Government of Ireland Act. But this even more complex set of arrangements was never activated.

On 13 December 1922 Prime Minister Craig informed Stormont that the King had responded to its address:

> I have received the Address presented to me by both Houses of the Parliament of Northern Ireland in pursuance of Article 12 of the Articles of Agreement set forth in the Schedule to the Irish Free State (Agreement) Act, 1922, and of Section 5 of the Irish Free State Constitution Act, 1922, and I have caused my Ministers and the Irish Free State Government to be so informed.

In simple terms, therefore, Ireland was partitioned by the British state, but this was then legitimised by the Treaty – which included the support of pro-Treaty nationalists, of course – and copper-fastened by the partitioned northern parliament. At this point something that had been sold as a temporary measure began to look more permanent. Its survival now became less an issue of theory than practice – could the new state secure the borders it had arbitrarily set for itself?

Northern Ireland – constructing a state

Once in existence, the task before the Northern Ireland state was relatively simple. The sectarian demography of partition had already put the logic of the state in place – the two-thirds Protestant population would provide democratic legitimacy in perpetuity and prevent any possibility of Irish reunification. This was the simple calculus behind the formation. But the practice of minoritisation would also be vigorously pursued. Crucially an enhanced infrastructure of emergency would put this into practice. The legal infrastructure of emergency in the new Northern Ireland was well rehearsed. In 1920 the whole of Ireland was already being administered with a brutal emergency regime. Martial law was declared by Lord French in December 1920.[3] This approach was further internalised by the emergent Northern Ireland state.

In terms of our colonial overview, this new state structure marked a *volte-face* in British imperial policy. Instead of the native incorporation that had been progressing since the Act of Union, Northern Ireland reverted to settler 'responsibility' mode. There had been plenty of Catholics 'about the place' – at every level of the state apparatus – in *fin de siècle* Ireland. The northern state reversed this situation remarkably quickly. In this sense, unionists might have been forgiven for reminding the world that this was no more than a return to *more traditional* modes of colonial government in Ireland. The unionist characterisation of a 'Protestant state and a Protestant parliament' was precisely the model of the state that had been provided in Ireland for 350 years from the reformation until 1830 – so it was hardly untested. The 1921 iteration – essentially reactionary and essentially racist – was, however, being constructed in a world in which democracy was beginning to undermine more archaic forms of legitimacy. Even in terms of the British Empire, responsible government – the transfer of power from the imperial parliament to the dominions – was the order of the day.[4] In that regard, Northern Ireland was not an anomaly. With the Government of Ireland Act, Westminster devolved to this newly manufactured responsible government a free hand to do more or less what it wanted over the next fifty years.[5]

Arguably the most challenging task before the state was to generate a *raison d'être*. From this distance this seems a strange observation – love it or loathe it, Northern Ireland is an entity that we all recognise. In 1920, however, it was yet to become *anything*: it wasn't Ulster; it wasn't *northern* Ireland (Inishowen in 'Southern Ireland' extended much further north than any part of the six counties); it wasn't even the 'Protestant' bits of Ulster since one third of the counties and more than 50 per cent of the land mass retained a Catholic majority.[6] Of course, it did have a practical boundary logic – it represented a calculated land grab for the most extensive territory in Ireland that might be brought under unionist control. But this was hardly the stuff of a successful origin myth. So, what might define – and justify – this new entity?

---

[3] Sir John French, Lord Lieutenant of Ireland. He had been Commander-in-Chief of the British army on the western front in WW1 but was removed from his post when he held back reserves at the Battle of Loos in September 1915, the biggest offensive of the war.

[4] In chapter 2 we noted how this came about as a result of the Earl of Durham's intervention in Canadian affairs in 1837. He concluded that 'those who governed the white colonies should be accountable to representative assemblies of the colonists, and not simply to the agents of a distant royal authority…' (Durham 1912).

[5] Lest, however, there be any question that Northern Ireland had been cut adrift from the responsibility of the UK State, the Act made clear that, 'executive power in South Ireland and in Northern Ireland shall continue to be vested in His Majesty the King, and nothing in this Act shall effect the exercise of that power'.

[6] Thus, it reflected no real effort at self-determination from any perspective – it *excluded* some 90,000 Protestants and unionists who had signed the 'Ulster Covenant' – the document that continued to be held up as the *magna carta* of the new state.

It took the new state over a decade to come up with a definitive answer. In 1934 Craigavon – Prime Minister and chief architect of the state – provided his memorable characterisation of the Northern Ireland state:

> I have always said that I am an Orangeman first and a politician and Member of this Parliament afterwards ... in the South they boasted of a Catholic State. They still boast of Southern Ireland being a Catholic State. All I can boast is that we are a Protestant Parliament and a Protestant State.

Later in the same year, speaking at Stormont in response to an accusation that all government appointments in Northern Ireland were carried out on a religious basis, he confirmed this approach:

> It is undoubtedly our duty and our privilege, and always will be, to see that those appointed by us possess the most unimpeachable loyalty to the King and Constitution. That is my whole object in carrying on a Protestant Government for a Protestant people. I repeat it in this House.[7]

Thus, the Prime Minister confirmed the overdetermination of the sectarianism of Northern Ireland. While this exchange also encapsulated the 'relentless reciprocity'[8] that drove the southern and northern states to mimic each other's insularity, it hardly addressed the specificity and intensity of the sectarian project in the north. Its Orange quality trumped any more complex political philosophy. Its Protestantness was as remorseless as the rhythm of a Lambeg drum: Protestant government, Protestant state, Protestant parliament, Protestant people. If a template were ever wanted for the notion of 'Protestant privilege', here it was.

But this very insistence on such Protestant character invites deconstruction. This identity was not a given – arguably the state had to *make* people Protestant. Certainly, it had to create a context in which the categories 'Protestant' and 'Catholic' were principal determinants of identity within the state. This is not as silly as it sounds. In 1920, Protestants in Ireland were Irish. The unionist party and the Orange Order were both Irish. Even in more formal religion terms, the term 'Protestant' was less than precise in 1920. Most non-Catholics in Ireland were members of the Church of Ireland – self-defined as a 'reformed Catholic' organisation.[9] Even those unambiguously 'Protestant' churches were themselves explicitly Irish institutions – including the largest (non-Catholic) denomination in the north – the Presbyterian Church in Ireland. In other words, while the term 'Protestant' became an ethnic label with real and immediate meaning in the context of the Northern Ireland state, it was never a simple reflection

---

[7] Parliamentary Debates, Northern Ireland House of Commons, Vol. XVII, Cols. 72-73.

[8] The phrase is used by Sartre in his introduction to Memmi (1990: xxviii): 'A relentless reciprocity binds the colonizer to the colonized'.

[9] This point also provides some sense of the transience of the term. A century and a half before, in Tone's day, the term 'Protestant' *only* meant Church of Ireland – cognate with membership of the established church. In consequence, Tone had to addend 'and Dissenters' to the term to integrate Presbyterians and other non-conformists within his vision of an inclusive Irishness.

of religious, political or cultural identity. The new state made people 'Protestant' in an entirely new way. In this sense, the closest parallel is with the function of 'whiteness' in apartheid South Africa: in both cases unifying identities were constructed in novel form in order to transcend all the tensions and contradictions within the settler polity. Thus, while Northern Ireland never succeeded in achieving dominion status within the Empire, here was what Protestant dominion looked like.

The notion of 'Protestant' was constructed out of a complex matrix of identities. Most importantly, however, it was reinforced by the otherness of the native population. In other words, it was clear what it was not: 'not-Catholic', 'not-Irish', 'not-Gaelic', 'not-native'.[10] As this focus on negation suggests, there is an existential angst at the heart of unionism. This unease is caught by the titles of some published works which have closely considered their identity, such as Susan McKay's *Northern Protestants: An Unsettled People* (2000) and former Presbyterian Moderator John Dunlop's *A Precarious Belonging* (1995). There was a deep well of insecurity to draw on here: from *Ulster's Uncertain Defenders* (Nelson 1984) to *The Contested Identities of Ulster Protestants* (Burgess and Mulvenna 2015). It is most graphically characterised as a siege mentality within which potential enemies are everywhere and every change is interpreted as a potential threat rather than an opportunity.[11]

The origins of this angst are, of course, found across the colonial history we traced in earlier chapters. Ultimately the roots are in the plantations of the early 17th century. But between 1912 and 1920, the north rediscovered – or invented – its roots as a settler society. This insight informed the work of Clayton (1996). Her analysis echoes the insight of one of the key writers on colonialism, Albert Memmi (1990). As the vanguard of empire in the heart of the colony, the setters symbolically, and in other ways, represent the metropolis. But the complexity of their position is that they stand between the metropolis and the natives. As the empire personified on the ground, as it were, they display all the characteristics at the heart of imperial conquest – determination, hard work, toughness, practicality and the conviction of an almost divine mission. The problem is that the metropolis is a much more heterogeneous place, not least in relation to ideas. Progress there means that ideas develop; in particular, liberalism can start to replace formerly rigid values. Separated from this heterogeneity, settlers retain the old certainties to the point that they can believe that they, and only they, continue to represent the real values at the heart of the metropolis. In the Irish case, they are more British than the British themselves, the last bastion of the greatness of empire. In this context, Northern Ireland came to assume many of the trappings of anti-democratic states in the inter-war era. For example, an NCCL Commission

---

[10] This was emblemised by the comment of John Taylor, Lord Kilcloney, former Minister of Home Affairs at Stormont: 'We in Northern Ireland are not Irish. We do not jig at crossroads...' (quoted in Cathcart 1993). Incidentally, the Irish peasant custom of dancing at crossroads was long defunct by this stage.

[11] As a mural in the loyalist Fountain area of Derry states, 'West Bank loyalists, still under siege', the implication being that little has changed since the city was besieged by Jacobite soldiers in 1688.

to the North in 1936 concluded that unionists had created 'under the shadow of the British constitution a permanent machine of dictatorship' (NCCL 1936). Their point was that it was like fascist regimes growing elsewhere in Europe, where there was a total identification of party and state. The state constructed in 1921 remained rooted in the semiotics of settler colonialism. This remains the key to understanding the culture and politics of 'Northern Ireland'.

Of course, none of this means that people in Northern Ireland are now 'settler' or 'native' in any straightforward genealogical – or 'racial' – sense. Four centuries of interrelations, including mixed marriages, have meant that hybridity – or to use the term we have been using throughout, *mestizaje* – is the norm. Even if most Catholics in the north are descendants of native Irish, most Protestants are not descendants of settlers or planters. This population was much more composite – obviously bifurcated in terms of English and Scots identities but also including Huguenots, Mennonites, and later migrants from across Europe and beyond. From the first there were the migrant 'others' – people who could not be shoehorned into either category: Jews for centuries; more recently a proliferation of people of colour and EU migrants. At the same time, however, it is essential to realise that what started out as a settler society bears the marks and scars of its origins. In a mirror of the function of 'whiteness' across other settler societies, 'Protestantness' constructed a clear and largely impermeable boundary between those who were 'Protestant' and a native other. This ethnic boundary can be seen in cultural displays and social attitudes, in patterns of land ownership and the distribution of resources, and above all in the political choices and aspirations of different sections of the population.

Following partition, this was the principal truth left to Protestants. Northern Ireland became a state of permanent emergency and ritual dominance undermined by a territorial pissing extended to every stony acre of the new state. Conor Cruise O'Brien – no great friend of republicanism and, later, in 1985, elected to the Northern Ireland Forum for the United Kingdom Unionist Party – summed up the semiotics powerfully in 1969:

> When the Orange Order and the Apprentice Boys commemorate the victories of 1690, as they do each year in elaborate ceremonies, the message they are conveying is that of their determination to hold for Protestants in Northern Ireland as much as possible of the privileged status which their ancestors won under William of Orange. These are not, as outside observers so easily suppose, comically archaic occasions. The symbols are historical, the iconography old-fashioned, but the message is for the here and now. The ritual is one of annual renewal of a stylized act of dominance: 'We are your superiors: we know you hate this demonstration of that fact: we dare you to say something about it: If you don't you ratify your own inferior status'. That is what the drums say. (O'Brien 1969: 11)

In this regard the Northern Ireland state became – ironically – more like Francoist Spain than anything else (albeit bonded by anti-Catholicism rather than Catholicism). In a similar manner to Spain, it institutionalised untheorised, anti-democratic reaction in which loyalty to the state – rather than political ideology – became the key determinant. In another sense, however, the operationalisation of the principle of Protestant majoritarianism made Northern Ireland more like a 'Herrenvolk democracy' – in the manner of apartheid South Africa. In other words, the state was always vulnerable to democratic and populist pressures from different elements *within* the Protestant community. Conversely, it was almost completely impervious to *any* demands from the Catholic community. Rather, the best that Catholics might hope for was indifference. More often, however, what they came to expect was terror. The state was defined *from the first* by its emergency nature. In this regard, there was no break *at all* from the all-Ireland state that preceded it – the new 'Northern Ireland' took its *modus operandi* from the martial law of the imperial parliament through which it emerged.

Policing the citadel

If the partitioned state took some time to confirm its ideological foundation, it had no such luxury in terms of its commitment to coercion. Northern unionists had vehemently opposed Home Rule and yet paradoxically what they had achieved through partition was a form of Home Rule for themselves. Second best it may have been, but it was a solution which they embraced with enthusiasm. That they would do so was already clear in 1912 when Sir Edward Carson, leading unionist ideologue, insisted that the unionists 'must be prepared, in the event of a Home Rule bill passing, with such measures as will carry on for ourselves the government of those districts of which we have control' (quoted in Colvin 1934: 78-79). A decade later the task facing unionism was to do the political arithmetic to determine the extent of 'those districts'. The imperative was to determine an area for the state which was not so small as to be unviable and yet not too large as to be uncontrollable. Lord Cushendun, a leading unionist, explained how they finally did the sums:

> … the inexorable index of statistics demonstrated that, although Unionists were in a majority when geographical Ulster was considered as a unit, yet the distribution of population made it certain that a separate Parliament for the whole Province would have a precarious existence, while its administration of purely Nationalist districts would mean unending conflict. (McNeill 1922: 182)

The template was set on a crude sectarian calculus: the state could do or say whatever it wanted to its Catholic minority, but it had to secure the support of *all* of its Protestant majority. This entailed a singular obsession with 'loyalty' and a reciprocal paranoia with regard to 'disloyalty'. At its heart there was a class compromise that demanded an economic policy that could and would secure the continued support of the Protestant working class. Any threat to Protestant unity – from liberalism, from feminism, from socialism, and, latterly from 1960s radicalism – was correctly judged to threaten the fine margins of sectarian majoritarianism within the state.

Although partition had apparently solved the mathematical/geographical problem, dominance could never be guaranteed through this one-off event. Control also had to become an everyday reality in the operation of the state. Various mechanisms were employed, most of which entailed keeping down the numbers of the minority and keeping them 'in their place' – on the margins of society. Unionism was helped by several factors. The uneven economic development of Ireland since the industrial revolution meant that industrialisation was more or less confined to the north-east of the country where the unionists were in the majority. That meant that, by the time of partition, they had wealth and power, an advantage *vis-à-vis* northern nationalists. The task ahead was to, at minimum, maintain that advantage if not actually increase it.

Industrialisation had also produced a working class divided not only on the basis of religious affiliation but also of skill and gender, and these divisions mapped onto each other. The skilled jobs in the main industries which were the backbone of the economy and the basis of unionist wealth and power – shipbuilding and heavy engineering – were disproportionately occupied by Protestant men. Meanwhile Catholics were massively over-represented in the ranks of unskilled labour. Maintaining that differential could ensure political unionism two benefits: the loyalty of a section of the working class in support of a political union that provided them with better and more secure jobs, and the economic marginalisation and by extension political marginalisation of the other section of the working class. Poverty and its concomitant effects – from infant mortality to pressure towards emigration – were expected to work in favour of unionist power by keeping down the numbers of the minority.[12]

Partition enabled the state under unionist control to revert to the default position on controlling Irish Catholics – repression and hyper-sectarianism. There were two mechanisms involved. The formal mechanism involved the state's quest for total domination of the means of coercion. In the first few years of the state, the unionist government could call upon a garrison of thousands of British soldiers as well as the newly formed Royal Ulster Constabulary (RUC) which rose from the disbandment of the Royal Irish Constabulary (RIC). They also had Special Constables: A Specials, full-time; B Specials, part-time; and a massive reserve of C Specials who could be mobilised when needed. In 1922, there were 16 battalions of the British army in the North, 5,500 A Specials, 19,000 B Specials and an unknown number of C Specials. Almost one in five Protestant males was in one or other of the Special forces (Farrell 1980: 49-50).

All these police organisations were armed, not simply with side arms, but with submachine guns and armoured cars boasting heavy machine guns. Military force was backed up by so-called 'emergency' law which remained on the books even during periods of political calm. Thus, the Civil Authorities (Special Powers) Act, enacted for a year in March 1922, was renewed annually, then in 1928, when politically there was no immediate threat to the state, renewed for five years, and finally was made permanent

---

[12] Between 1937 and 1961, 90,000 of the 159,000 emigrants from the North were Catholic (56.6 percent) in a situation where one-third of the population was Catholic. Despite that, Catholic numbers increased, from 33.5 percent of the population in 1926 to 35 percent in 1961 (Farrell 1980: 92 and 214).

in 1933. Among other interventions it allowed search, arrest and detention without warrant, flogging and the death penalty for arms and explosives offences, and the total suspension of civil liberties if judged necessary by the Minister of Home Affairs. As one MP, George Hanna, responded (seriously rather than sarcastically): 'One section would have been sufficient: "The Home Secretary shall have the power to do whatever he likes, or let somebody else do whatever he likes for him"' (quoted in Bardon 2001: 490).

There was also a further mechanism, an informal layer of control. The Ulster Volunteer Force (UVF) had been formed in 1912 as part of the unionists' preparation to oppose Home Rule through force. Many of its members had, at the outbreak of World War I, joined the British army in the 36th Ulster Division and other regiments. There was a brief revival of the organisation during the early violent days of the creation of the state. The UVF viewed its role as being the equivalent of the regular police and army forces, controlling republican insurgents and indeed the whole nationalist community. Other loyalist paramilitary groups also emerged in the early 1920s with the same purpose. There was a close affinity between these ostensibly illegal groups and the legal state forces. Personnel moved back and forward between them, intelligence and weaponry were shared, joint operations occurred, and the formal forces made no effort to curtail the informal nor to arrest any of their members. Moreover, the tactics of both groups were frequently indistinguishable. For example, reprisals were common in response to republican acts of insurgency and such reprisals were as likely to be carried out by formal forces as by informal.

With its large army of defenders guarding the fortress walls, as it were, the unionist politicians could get on with the job of ensuring total control within the fortress. Technically, they were not absolute masters, however. The Government of Ireland Act 1920, Section 75, made it crystal clear that they were subordinate to the Westminster parliament: 'Notwithstanding the establishment of the Parliament of Northern Ireland … the supreme authority of the Parliament of the United Kingdom shall remain unaffected and undiminished over all persons, matter and things in Northern Ireland'. However, from an early stage there was irrefutable evidence of the tail wagging the dog. In fact, that evidence precedes partition. Unionists had in effect been guilty of treason during the Home Rule crisis, setting up a provisional government in waiting and arming an illegal army with weapons purchased from a country with which, within two years, the United Kingdom would be at war.

They did this with impunity. No arrests of the politicians planning to fight the British to stay British were made and none were removed from office. On the contrary, some of the plotters were rewarded with promotion; Sir Edward Carson was appointed as Attorney-General in the UK government in 1915; Sir James Craig was a junior minister in the UK government in 1920-21, Parliamentary Secretary to the Minister for Pensions[13]

---

[13] His brother Charles, another plotter, succeeded him in that post.

and then Parliamentary Secretary to the Admiralty, resigning to take up the position of first Prime Minister of Northern Ireland. During the Home Rule crisis, British army officers in Ireland revealed their intention to mutiny if ordered to act against the unionists, and British politicians provided uncritical support. Andrew Bonar Law, leader of the Conservative opposition, stated in 1912 that he could 'imagine no length of resistance to which Ulster can go in which I should not be prepared to support them' (quoted in Biggs-Davison 1973: 77).

With the creation of their new state, that support continued. The unionists were able to determine the boundaries of that state and the British government acquiesced. The British government may have claimed that they were in an impossible situation when faced with diametrically opposed positions between Irish nationalists and unionists, but they made massive concessions to the unionists in terms of agreeing to the contours of the new state. To the nationalists they offered the flimsy olive branch of a Boundary Commission, which, given unionist opposition, was unlikely to redraw the border to allow nationalist areas to remain with the Free State. The Unionists established organisations of Special Constables in September 1919, before the Government of Ireland Act was passed, that is, before the state of Northern Ireland officially existed.[14] At James Craig's request the British government, rather than reminding the unionists that they had no authority to make decisions in relation to defence, agreed. Eventually the British paid £6.78 million of the £7.5 million required for the Specials (Farrell 1980: 79).

The 'Irish question' was rarely off the agenda of 19th century British politics – whether in terms of republican bombing campaigns in Britain, the conditions of Irish prisoners in English jails or repressive legislation to suppress 'outrages' in Ireland. During the Home Rule crisis, the politics of Ireland threatened to make and break successive British administrations. Partition solved Britain's problem by containing it on the island of Ireland. The institution of the Free State allowed a substantial section of Irish politicians to accept a measure of self-rule and to busy itself with the apparent tasks of nation-building (albeit with a part of 'the nation' not included) in the face of economic difficulties and a brutal civil war. In the North, the victory of the unionists enabled a similar form of hermetic sealing. As far as British politicians were concerned, Ireland, North and South, was out of sight and mind and there was no appetite during the next half century to threaten that arrangement. It also provided a degree of protection from command responsibility. At various times, different external actors from the NCCL (which produced a scathing report on the Special Powers Act in 1936) to Alan Whicker,[15]

---

[14] Churchill was the first to suggest the Specials as a way of ensuring that no British troops would be tied up in the north but would be freed for the war against republicans in the south. Craig was said to have jumped at this suggestion (Fraser 1984: 41).

[15] In January 1959 broadcaster Alan Whicker made a programme in the 'Tonight' series for the BBC. In it he happened to remark how unusual it was for him to see armed police officers, the RUC, in one part of the UK. The Stormont government was furious, and the BBC issued a grovelling apology (Curtis 1984a: 20-1).

would shine a light on activities of 'responsible' government in Northern Ireland. But for most of the duration of the state, it was possible to suggest that this was nothing to do with Westminster.

In the early most violent days of the formation of the northern state, a major British army force remained. But once violence receded and the minority was corralled in its ghettos, the British withdrew and left the unionists to get on with policing the fortress by themselves. British troops did return to the streets occasionally when particularly heavy violence erupted, as during the sectarian riots of 1935. But this exception served only to highlight the norm that the Unionist Party had its own army in the form of the RUC and the B Specials. When British politicians did display any interest in how the Unionist Party was carrying on its business, that derived from groups of politicians, usually on the Left.

Such was the case of the Friends of Ireland Group, formed in 1945, and the Campaign for Democracy in Ulster, formed in 1964; both consisted of backbench Labour MPs. Appeals to the British government by the minority in the North were ignored. In 1935 nationalist politicians demanded an inquiry from the Unionist government into the sectarian violence of that summer and were, unsurprisingly, rebuffed. They then appealed to the British government which likewise rejected their request. Despite their position as the ultimate power-holders, the British deferred to the supposedly subordinate administration: 'This matter is entirely within the discretion and responsibility of the government of Northern Ireland, and for fundamental constitutional reasons the possibility of holding an enquiry by the imperial government is entirely ruled out' (quoted in Farrell 1980: 142).

The one occasion when the British government made a gesture of intervention was in 1956. Prime Minister Anthony Eden stated in Westminster:

> In the Ireland Act 1949 the Parliament of Westminster declared Northern Ireland to be an integral part of the United Kingdom. This is a declaration which all parties in this House are pledged to support. The safety of Northern Ireland and its inhabitants is therefore a direct responsibility of Her Majesty's Government which they will, of course, discharge. (Quoted in Farrell 1980: 215)

This statement was not in relation to any aspect of unionist misrule, nor was it intended as support for the minority. Rather it was in response to the IRA military campaign in the North; Eden weighed in to protect the state run by the majority. In reality, even then it meant little; the words were not followed up by substantial deeds.

The unionists were given a free hand to manipulate matters in the North to guarantee their rule. A priority was to ensure, if not increase, their majority position. The demarcation of the border was the first major decision in the state in terms of gerrymandering. This was replicated throughout the life of the unionist monopoly government through a series of local government reforms over the next fifty years, each of which benefited unionists. More immediately, several nationalist areas were gerrymandered in such a way that they would return a majority of unionists in elections. The most blatant case was in Derry where the ward boundaries were drawn in such a way that a population, two-thirds of whom were nationalists, elected 20 councillors, 12 of whom were unionist. This was far from a unique occurrence. As Government Chief Whip, Major Curran suggested: 'The best way to prevent the overthrow of the government by people who had no stake in the country and had not the welfare of the people of Ulster at heart was to disenfranchise them' (quoted in Farrell 1980: 86).

This model even managed to trump the arrival of the Welfare State in the post-war period. With the Social Services Agreement Act 1949, the British state agreed to finance welfare provision in theory to the same standards as in Britain but allowed unionists control of the process:

> Unionist governments moulded the post-war welfare state, not into a replica of labourist universalism, but into a somewhat precarious 'Orange state'. This was based largely on the marginalisation of the nationalist minority and the policy areas most affected were economic development (including industrial location), housing and public sector employment. Private sector employment was also highly segmented. With the agreement of the Catholic Church (which at the time was hostile to state-based social provision), the education system was divided on the basis of religion and differentially funded. The absence of universal suffrage and the presence of draconian special powers to deal with political dissent provided the final ingredients to this exclusivist policy culture. (Tomlinson 2002)

The unionist monopoly of political power was impressive. Their one-party state lasted longer than any of the one-party states in Eastern Europe in the aftermath of World War II. With almost no exceptions, government ministers were Protestant males, members of both the Unionist Party and the Orange Order, and most were members of the *haute bourgeoisie* or landed gentry (O'Dowd 1980: 13).

Corralling the minority

In the final years of the 20th century the redrawing of borders in the Balkans led to the creation of a neologism – 'ethnic cleansing'. The word did not exist in Ireland in the early decades of that century, but no less a phenomenon was obvious. Between July 1920 and July 1922, 453 civilians were killed in Belfast and a further 61 outside the city but within the new state of Northern Ireland. In Belfast, 257 of the civilians killed were Catholic and 196 Protestant. Outside of Belfast, 46 of the civilians killed were Catholic and 15 Protestants (Farrell 1980: 62). Of themselves, these figures do not display the uneven balance of victimhood. Catholics represented about a third of the population but two-thirds of the civilian victims. While many of the Protestants killed were caught up in IRA operations or directly targeted in reprisal attacks, a number died at the hands of state forces. And beyond the deaths are other figures which display the sectarian imbalance. There were 93,000 Catholics in Belfast at the time. Almost 11,000 were expelled from mainly Protestant workplaces and 23,000 were forced out of homes. It was not only

Northern nationalists who referred to the experience as a 'pogrom'; the *London Daily News* concluded that the violence was 'probably unmatched outside the area of Russian or Polish pogroms' (quoted in Farrell 1980: 31).

One particular atrocity shocked many people in Ireland and beyond. On 23 March 1922, two Specials – Thomas Cunningham and William Cairnside – were shot dead by the IRA in Great Victoria Street, Belfast. Reprisals soon followed. Two Catholics were shot dead in Short Strand, Peter Murphy and Sarah McShane (aged 15). At 1am on the morning of the 24th, during an all-night curfew, a group of men, some dressed in police uniforms, used a sledgehammer to burst into the home of Owen McMahon in Kinnaird Terrace, off the Antrim Road in North Belfast. The 50-year-old publican was there along with his family and one of his employees, Edward McKinney. The gang shot Owen, his six sons and the employee. Owen, three of his sons – Frank, Patrick and Gerard (aged 12) – and Edward McKinney died instantly. A fourth brother, John, died later. Bernard McMahon was seriously wounded but survived. The youngest son, Michael (aged 11), hid and was not harmed. Owen's wife, Eliza, her daughter and niece were kept in another room while this was happening. So, there were witnesses to the event who were able to report that when Owen asked why he was being targeted, the reply was 'because you are a respected papist'. The witnesses also reported that one of the gang was in civilian clothes and the four others in police uniforms; the opinion was that they were Specials. The nationalist MP Joe Devlin – who knew the family personally – made a specific intervention in Westminster after the murders:

> I intend tonight to take advantage of this opportunity to raise the whole question of the appalling conditions in Belfast, the massacre of innocent and unoffending Catholic citizens, the continued bombing of women and children, the establishment of a system of wholesale terrorism amongst the Catholic minority in the city, culminating in the cold-blooded assassination of Mr. McMahon and his family, which has shocked almost the entire world.... if Catholics have no revolvers to protect themselves they are murdered. If they have revolvers they are flogged or sentenced to death. (House of Commons 1922a)

The response from the Speaker and the British Government – represented by Secretary of State for the Colonies, Winston Churchill – confirmed the new framing of the relationship between Westminster and the Stormont regime. As the Speaker ruled: 'The hon. Member is now going into details of the evidence – matters which are really under the control of the Government of Northern Ireland... I must ask him not to trench on what is really within the province of the Government of Northern Ireland' (House of Commons 1922b).

Frequently in the years following the blame for these and other reprisal killings was laid at the door of the Cromwell Club led by District Inspector John Nixon, an unofficial force within the RIC/RUC set up precisely for this purpose.[16] The McMahon murders

---

[16] John William Nixon (1880-1949), Orangeman and District Inspector in the RIC and RUC member

horrified opinion both in Belfast and further afield, but there were many other atrocities which were more quickly forgotten as the death toll mounted. For example, six children were killed in Weaver Street, off the Shore Road, on 23 February 1922 when a bomb was thrown at them. And two children were killed when a bomb was thrown into a house in Brown Street on 24 March, in all likelihood a reprisal for the McMahon murders. Meanwhile the convention of non-intervention by Westminster that was confirmed by this notorious sectarian execution by uniformed state forces continued for the next fifty years.

In this situation the IRA played a role that was both defensive and offensive. In relation to the former, the need to defend the nationalist community was such that pro- and anti-Treaty republicans in the North did not initially split. Moreover, they were supported by Michael Collins despite his signing the Treaty which brought about partition (McDermott 2001). But they also engaged in offensive operations. Northern nationalists had been horrified to be included within the confines of the unionist state. Many were of the opinion that the arrangement could not last. Either the Boundary Commission, with representatives from the North, the South and Britain, would agree by 1925 to redraw the border in order for nationalist strongholds such as Newry, South Armagh and Derry to be excluded from Northern Ireland, or a sustained campaign of armed opposition would lead to the collapse of the fragile state. But the IRA was isolated, geographically and politically, and faced major armed opposition from state forces. Eighty-two members of the police and British army were killed, but overall little dent was made in the structures of the new state. The political isolation increased when the Free State consolidated itself, wiping out republican opposition and starting down the long road which led eventually to jettisoning claims on the North.[17]

In the initial days of the northern state, many nationalists refused to give their allegiance in any way. Catholic teachers refused to recognise the state and their salaries were paid for by the Free State administration until such time as it proved financially unviable to do so. 25 of the 80 councils in the North after the 1920 elections were in nationalist hands. They submitted minutes of meetings to the Free State government. The Unionist government ruled that any council not fulfilling its duties would be disbanded and replaced by a commissioner. Around a dozen councils were dissolved.

As time progressed, the initial shock of inclusion for the northern minority was replaced by a sense of isolation and disempowerment. Military resistance and non-

---

from Cavan. Nixon was suspected of having orchestrated the McMahon family killings and other sectarian murders such as the Arnon Street massacre. He was never charged and successfully sued the *Derry Journal* on one occasion for repeating the allegation. On the contrary, in 1923, he was awarded an MBE for 'valuable service' 'during the troubled period'. He was dismissed from the RUC in 1924 for addressing an Orange rally, something serving police officers were not allowed to do. At that point he entered politics. He was elected on five occasions as independent unionist MP for Woodvale.

[17] Partition was accepted as a reality by the Free State government from the start. It was conceded by the Irish side at the Treaty talks, albeit on the grounds that it would be temporary and that the northern state was not viable in the long run. It is also significant that in the Dáil debates on the Treaty most of the heat was over the Empire and the oath of allegiance. The issue of partition was raised relatively little.

cooperation had failed; the northern state had embedded its institutions of administration and military control; neither the Southern nor British governments was going to act as a saviour. If any thought that northern nationalist political representatives would succeed in ameliorating conditions, they were soon dissuaded. After the republican landslide in the 1918 General Election in Ireland the British had introduced proportional representation in an attempt to bolster the position of non-republican parties. In a situation of unionist majority rule in the North, this had worked the other way, to bolster the position of republican and other non-unionist groups. So, in July 1922, the unionists introduced a Bill to abolish proportional representation.[18] For the only time ever in the history of the Unionist Party government, royal assent was withheld, albeit temporarily (Farrell 1980: 83). When it was finally passed, the number of nationalist-controlled councils was reduced from 25 to 2.

Six nationalist MPs were elected to the Northern Ireland parliament in 1921 alongside six abstentionist republicans for Sinn Féin; they refused to take their seats claiming that to do so would be to recognise the legitimacy of the new state. But as that state embedded itself successfully, the dilemma for elected nationalists was whether to continue with a policy of abstentionism. This dilemma was solved in different ways at different times. Some nationalists continued to absent themselves while others in the same party did not. Some absented themselves from the Northern Parliament but not from Westminster. What they did not do, however, was put themselves forward as the official opposition, this role being taken from time to time by the Northern Ireland Labour Party. It was February 1965, in the wake of the thaw which saw Prime Minister Terence O'Neill meet with Taoiseach Sean Lemass, before the Nationalist Party agreed to be the official opposition for the first time. It was short-lived. The emerging civil rights campaign was met with virulent state repression and on 15 October 1969, the Nationalist Party opted out of the role of official opposition.

Through the years, nationalists elected to Stormont made little impression through constitutional and non-violent methods. Working from within the system had not produced any notable results in terms of ameliorating conditions for the voters they represented. Frequently they withdrew from participation in politics, but this was evidence of frustration rather than of having an alternative strategy. They were trapped in a system which left them mostly powerless and the support which came from outside – through, for example, the Campaign for Democracy in Ulster – was intermittent and ineffectual. Occasionally, the unionists' failure to give any space to nationalist politics produced what they claimed to abhor, namely IRA activity. The IRA campaign between 1956 and 1962 was the most sustained example, but it was not the only one.

---

[18] History turned full circle when in 1973 the British direct rule administration reintroduced proportional representation in a bid to bolster the electoral outcomes for small, middle-of-the-road parties such as the Alliance Party.

Sectarian divide and rule

The hallmark of the Northern Ireland state was hyper-sectarianism. Sectarian divisions and attitudes have deep roots in Ireland. We have seen that in the 17th century the violent reaction of natives to dispossession by settlers had been represented by pamphleteers and politicians as motivated by Catholic hatred of Protestants rather than by anti-colonial sentiments.[19] For a century or more afterwards anti-colonial resistance was not confined to one religious grouping, as the United Irish aspiration of uniting Protestant, Catholic and dissenter indicates. But as Protestant resistance was suppressed or co-opted by Union and empire, anti-colonial struggle was increasingly confined to Catholics. The power of the conservative Catholic Church as a result of the 'devotional revolution' (Larkin 1972) after the Famine was an added factor in the increasing trend for nationalism and Catholicism to be coterminous on the one hand, and unionism and Protestantism on the other.

Sectarian rivalry between the Protestant and Catholic sections of the working class had arisen with the early industrialisation of the linen trade in County Armagh, specifically around Lurgan and Portadown (Gibbon 1975). It had migrated to Belfast along with the rural workers moving to the city in search of employment (Boyd 1969). Competition over jobs, wages and housing more often than not resulted in the 'class-in-itself' failing to come together as a 'class-for-itself', to use Marx's terminology. Workers frequently fought workers, with occasions such as Orange parades, particularly those each July celebrating King William's victory at the Battle of the Boyne in 1690, proving to be the epicentre of the trouble whose deeper roots were in competition over such necessities as jobs and housing.[20] This rivalry proved beneficial to the unionist ruling class and was exploited by them on many occasions. Catholic militia from Monaghan were transported to Belfast to suppress the United Irish rebellion, most of whose leaders and participants were Presbyterian. Sectarianism could add a frisson to the enthusiasm of state force. Similarly, when the state of Northern Ireland was formed, unionist politicians could conjure a 'green' scare (and often also a 'red' one) to break up any signs of working-class unity. It had happened during the major strikes of 1907 and 1919

---

[19] It is worth remembering that sectarianism is a form of racism and that it did not die out in the 17th century. In 1919, a book was published by Herbert Moore Pim, a Quaker and later convert to Catholicism. He was for a time a committed nationalist and served time in Crumlin Road Jail in 1915 for his activities. However, within a few years he became an arch-imperialist and remained so until his death in 1950. He suggested: 'The Loyalist type in Ireland is a well set-up individual, with clear, straight, honest eyes, a clear skin, and well-formed features such as are found in the case of human beings of the highest type. His hair is usually fair, or if dark, it has a fine texture… Every Loyalist knows the Nationalist type – a person with thick, black hair, or hair of a pale mouse colour, with shifty or dreamy eyes, a complexion – among the men – which is curiously dull or very red; and features which proclaim it as belonging to a low order among civilized peoples' (Pim 1919: 92-3). The book could be dismissed as some archaic aberration for the times, except that the foreword was written by Edward Carson, the architect of the new state of Northern Ireland.

[20] In 1864, seven people were killed and 150 wounded. Between 1872 and 1880, which were regarded as quiet years, ten people were killed and 375 wounded. In 1886, it was 32 dead and over 400 wounded. As Lee (2008: 136) concludes: 'Belfast riots alone accounted for more fatalities than all the nationalist risings of the nineteenth century'.

and happened again in 1932 during a brief but significant labour struggle over outdoor relief (Munck and Rolston 1987).

Ruling class exploitation and encouragement of sectarian division was not confined to such key events. It was an everyday element in the operations of the state. The unionist government had a level of control over the direct allocation of resources through the devolved government and local authorities. The government was ruled for its entire existence by one party and local government was skewed towards that same party, not least by the practice of gerrymandering. The opportunities for the sectarian allocation of jobs and resources such as housing were numerous.

The evidence is there from the beginning. Take, for example, the case of the civil service. There were very few Catholics in the civil service in the North initially and few of them reached the top. Before 1969 there was only one Catholic ever to hold the post of permanent secretary in a government ministry, Andrew Bonaparte Wyse. As his name indicates, he was not a working-class Catholic from west Belfast, but a Limerick-born grandson of an MP who had been knighted. On the creation of the Northern Ireland state, he had transferred from the all-Ireland to the northern civil service. In 1927 he became Permanent Secretary in the Ministry of Education. In similar vein, the first Lord Chief Justice of Northern Ireland was a Catholic, Sir Denis Henry. Previously as the MP for South Derry, he had been the only Catholic Unionist MP at Westminster *ever*.

Discrimination was not confined to the upper echelons but permeated to ground level. Thus in 1933, J.M. Andrews, Minister for Labour – and future Prime Minister – responded to sectarian criticism of employment practices at the seat of government in Stormont by being even more sectarian:

> Another allegation made against the government, which is untrue, is that of 31 porters at Stormont 28 are Roman Catholic. I have investigated the matter and I have found that there are 30 Protestants and only one Roman Catholic, there only temporarily. (Quoted in Farrell 1980: 136)

Historically perhaps the most notorious speech act in the history of Northern Ireland was made by Basil Brooke, later to become Lord Brookeborough and Northern Ireland Prime Minister. On 12 July 1933, Brooke, then junior Unionist government whip, spoke at an Orange rally.[21] The speech was subsequently reported:

> There was a great number of Protestants and Orangemen who employed Roman Catholics. He felt he could speak freely on this subject as he had not a Roman Catholic about his own place (Cheers). He appreciated the great difficulty experienced by some of them in procuring suitable Protestant labour, but he would point out that the Roman Catholics were endeavouring to get in everywhere and

---

[21] This intervention also had a local and personal context. Brooke could only say that he didn't employ any Catholics because he had sacked his Catholic employees the previous year. According to his account at Stormont, this followed an attempt by the IRA to kidnap his son. It is interesting given the wider framing of Catholic disloyalty that his most notorious speech made no reference to this episode. (Northern Ireland House of Commons Official Report, Vol 34 Col 1116.)

were out with all their force and might to destroy the power and constitution of Ulster ... He would appeal to loyalists, therefore, wherever possible to employ good Protestant lads and lassies.[22]

A year later speaking as Minister of Agriculture on 19 March 1934 Brooke said: 'When I made that declaration last "twelfth" I did so after careful consideration. What I said was justified. I recommended people not to employ Roman Catholics, who were 99 per cent disloyal'.[23] In response to these statements, Sir James Craig, as Prime Minister of Northern Ireland, was asked the government's policy in relation to the employment of Catholics. He responded: '[Sir Basil Brooke] spoke [on 12 July 1933 and 19 March 1934] as a Member of His Majesty's Government. He spoke entirely on his own when he made the speech ... but there is not one of my colleagues who does not entirely agree with him, and I would not ask him to withdraw one word he said'.[24]

The sectarian pattern of job allocation at Stormont was repeated at local government level. For example, in 1942 an Englishman was appointed as Town Clerk of Belfast. It was then discovered that, although he was Protestant, his wife was Catholic. The job offer was withdrawn (Farrell 1980: 87). In 1969, there were 77 school bus drivers in Fermanagh, a majority Catholic county; three of them were Catholic (Farrell 1980: 87). Overall in Fermanagh, local government employed 370 people over a range of departments, from housing to welfare: 8.6 per cent of employees were Catholic. Protestants constituted 100 per cent of employees in the housing department and 98.6 per cent in welfare. The best that Catholics could do was reach 22.2 per cent of employees in the health department (figures from De Paor 1970: 147).

Fermanagh fared no better in relation to the record of unionist-controlled councils in building new houses. The problem was that, in a majority Catholic county, where the need for social housing was more likely to be felt in the Catholic community, the 'danger' from a unionist point of view was to facilitate an increased minority population with voting rights which might threaten the sectarian balance of electoral politics. Thus, Fermanagh council built no houses between 1921 and 1945. By that point the nationalist majority in the county was 3,604. So, in 1948, E.C. Ferguson, the Unionist MP for Enniskillen, when addressing the annual Unionist Convention, stated: 'I would ask the meeting to authorise their executive to adopt whatever plans and take whatever steps, however drastic, to wipe out this nationalist majority' (quoted in Darby 1976: 70). At the same time, Fermanagh alderman George Eliot stated: 'We are not going to build houses in the south ward and cut a rod to beat ourselves later on. We are going to see that the right people are put into these houses and we are not making any apology for it' (quoted in Darby 1976: 249). Who these 'right people' were was evident from

---

[22] *Fermanagh Times*, 13 July 1933; quoted in Hepburn 1980: 164.

[23] *Belfast News Letter*, 20 March 1934; quoted in Commentary upon The White Paper (Cmd.558) entitled 'A Record of Constructive Change' (1971).

[24] Parliamentary Debates, Northern Ireland House of Commons, Vol. XVI, Cols. 617-618.

subsequent statistics; Fermanagh council built 1,048 new houses between 1945 and 1967. Four fifths of these houses were allocated to Protestants (Farrell 1980: 87). There was a certain inevitability to the fact that when the civil rights campaign took off in the 1960s, it did so primarily over the issue of the sectarian allocation of state housing.

In 1967 there was a severe housing need in the Dungannon area. As elsewhere, that need was greater for Catholic families. The local council agreed to build 15 houses, not where the need was greatest, but in the mainly unionist village of Caledon. These houses were to be allocated equally to Protestant and Catholic families. As it turned out, all the houses but one were allocated to Protestants. The one exception was a Catholic ex-serviceman. One of the houses was allocated to a 19-year-old single Protestant. Protests over housing allocation had been building in the late 1960s, not least in Derry where the Derry Housing Action Committee was highly active (see McCann 1974). In Caledon, a number of locals decided on direct action. They included the Goodfellow family, a Catholic family which, by any fair means of decision making about allocation, ought to have been housed in one of the new properties. The occupation began in October 1967. Despite the fact that the houses were disconnected from facilities, the Goodfellow family remained through the winter. In May 1968 the state finally reacted and forcibly evicted the family. In protest a civil rights march was organised from Coalisland to Dungannon in August 1968, and the civil rights campaign started in earnest.

Beyond the direct control of the state was a hyper-sectarian society in which, ultimately, nowhere was safe from the inexorable pressure towards sectarianisation. The industry which was the backbone of the economy was in the hands of employers who pursued sectarian hiring practices no less enthusiastically than the politicians. As late as 1970, only 400 of the 10,000 workers in Harland and Wolff shipyard were Catholic (Farrell 1980: 91). In fact, if truth be told, hiring practices in both venues were frequently controlled by the same personnel wearing different hats as businessmen and politicians. In the first cabinet of Northern Ireland the Prime Minister was a landowner and owned a whiskey business; the Minister of Finance owned a flour importing company; the Minister of Education was a landowner and one of the largest coal owners in England;[25] the Minister of Labour was a linen manufacturer (Farrell 1980: 68). Between 1921 and 1974, 94 per cent of unionist MPs at Westminster were professionals,

---

[25] Charles Stewart Henry Vane-Tempest-Stewart, 7th Marquess of Londonderry (1878-1949) was the personification of the 'fur coat brigade' that ruled Northern Ireland between 1921-72. Educated at Eton and Sandhurst, he was a member of both the British and Northern Ireland cabinets. He was appointed to the Northern Ireland cabinet in 1921 as Leader of the Senate and Minister for Education. His educational reforms were presented as an attempt at secularisation but were largely informed by a desire to exclude any Catholic or Irish element from the new educational system. He left Stormont in 1929 and resumed his career in UK politics as Lord Privy Seal and Leader of the House of Lords. In the 1930s he was openly pro-Nazi and antisemitic. His attempts to build links with Nazi Germany included inviting German ambassador Von Ribbentrop – later executed at Nuremberg – to the family home at Mount Stewart on the banks of Strangford Loch in 1936. Without apparent irony given his opposition to any Irish language element in the Northern Ireland education system, he was buried in the family plot *Tír na nÓg* at Mount Stewart – now owned by the National Trust.

managers, executives and large landowners and farmers; 86 per cent of the MPs at Stormont between 1921 and 1969 were from the same class (O'Dowd 1980: 13). Class and ethnicity interwove to produce a tight coterie of people who had deep interests in preserving the class and state structures which existed.

These economic and political arrangements were designed to benefit an elite defined by both ethnicity and class; and yet the instances where that class met specifically with class antagonism were few and for the most part ineffectual. Ethnicity trumped class. Belief in Union and empire allowed for an alliance between the classes on the Protestant side which was tight. And when that unity wobbled, the Protestant ruling class could remind Protestant labour of the benefits of the system. Protestant workers were much more likely to be in skilled employment (in state employment and Protestant owned firms) than Catholic workers. Their wages were higher and their likelihood of unemployment less. For most of the existence of the state, Catholic male unemployment rates were around two and a half times those of Protestant males, no matter the actual level of unemployment overall. When labour came to organise for its own interests, it often separated out along sectarian lines. There were separate trade unions for Catholic and Protestant teachers; deep sea dockers belonged to a Catholic union while cross-channel dockers to a Protestant one. And the ruling class was adept at donning a veneer of labour-friendliness when required. The Ulster Unionist Labour Association was established by Sir Edward Carson in 1918 as a counterweight to the influence of the mainstream labour movement on Protestant workers. In 1942 Harry Midgley formed the Unionist Commonwealth Labour Party and was selected by Brooke to be Minister of Public Security during World War II.

Midgley had previously been a member of the Independent Labour Party, and the ease with which he could switch from this British-based socialist organisation to a Northern Ireland-based unionist one speaks volumes of the difficulty organised labour had in running the sectarian gauntlet. There were periods when the Northern Ireland Labour Party, formed in 1924 and based in the trade union movement, polled well. The fact that it was neutral on the constitutional position of the North and contained a number of key members who were anti-partitionist meant that Catholics were willing to vote for its candidates in elections. In fact, what became clear was that for most of its existence, despite having many Protestant leaders and members, its only substantial base electorally speaking was in nationalist areas. This became palpable in 1949 when it changed its position to accept partition and the constitutional position of Northern Ireland. Its electoral support plummeted. It made a brief comeback in the 1960s, this time having some success among unionist voters, but the civil rights struggle quickly side-lined it again.

Republicans too were squeezed by the reality of the northern state. The northern IRA after partition, focused for the most part on defence and sheer survival, had little time for anti-sectarianism or left-wing politics. In the 1930s, the Republican Congress sought to unite republicans, trade unionists and socialists in an anti-imperialist front. In the North they had some success in attracting a number of Protestants. But a fracas at the annual Wolfe Tone commemoration in Bodenstown in 1934 between Congress members and more traditional IRA members led the northern Protestants to withdraw. A number of them afterwards left for Spain to fight for the republic there. Peadar O'Donnell, a key organiser of the Republican Congress, concluded: 'I always maintained and repeatedly said to the Army Council, "We haven't a battalion of IRA men in Belfast; we just have a battalion of armed Catholics"' (quoted in Munck and Rolston 1987: 184).

Every aspect of society in the North was permeated by sectarian division. There were two separate school systems as a result of the Protestant churches' insistence on 'bible education' (code for Protestant doctrine), the Catholic Church's insistence on maintaining its central importance, built up since the Famine, in the nationalist community, and a state that, despite some early liberal leanings, sided with the former rather than the latter.[26]

Sometimes the division derived from choice: nationalists read the *Irish News*, holidayed in Donegal and attended Gaelic football games, while unionists read the *Belfast Newsletter*, holidayed in Millisle and preferred soccer or rugby. But sometimes the differentials were enforced. Thus, unionists had in effect a civic duty to parade on July 12th in celebration of the victory of Protestant King William over Catholic King James at the Battle of the Boyne in 1690, and whole towns were shut down to enable their passage.[27] The same provisions did not exist for nationalist expressions of culture. The 1954 Flags and Emblems Act enabled the RUC to remove any flag or emblem on public or private property which they thought might cause a breach of the peace. This meant only nationalist and republican flags and emblems were targeted. Thus, a large force of police was used to force an Orange parade along the Longstone Road in Annalong in July 1955, when exactly one year earlier nationalists had been refused permission for a parade during a non-political festival in the village of Newtownbutler. The combined actions of the RUC and loyalists under the Reverend Ian Paisley to remove an Irish tricolour from the West Belfast offices of Sinn Féin during elections in 1964 led to one of the first major street confrontations of what was soon to become 'the troubles'.

It hardly needs to be emphasised which of the competing cultures was dominant. There was a vibrant nationalist culture which involved music, dancing, sport and the Gaelic language. But it took place in nationalist ghettos, in Gaelic Athletic Association sports grounds and assembly halls of Catholic schools, all far away from sensitive

---

[26] Because they had opted out of the state (Protestant) system, Catholic schools received no support for teachers' salaries. In 1967, the state agreed to pay 80 percent of the capital costs and 100 percent of the maintenance, equipment and salary costs of Catholic schools in return for having a minority state representation – two members out of six – on the management committees of Catholic schools. It was 1992 before the state agreed to pay all costs of Catholic schools, putting them on an equal financial footing with state schools.

[27] Indeed, up until the 1970s most major firms, public and private, shut down for two weeks over 'the Twelfth', requiring all employees, Catholics included, to take their annual holidays at that time.

unionist eyes and ears.[28] The most that BBC Northern Ireland radio could do was present programmes by the Irish Rhythms Orchestra, anodyne arrangements of Irish dance music. It was the 1970s before BBC television in the North would broadcast the results of Gaelic games; as all the main fixtures were on Sundays, reporting the results would have offended unionist sabbatarianism. Yet, regular programming was abandoned each July 12th for full live coverage of the Orange parades. Up until the 1980s, BBC television's weather map in the North displayed the six-county state amputated from the rest of the island, entirely surrounded in blue.

House of cards

Despite the apparent impregnability of unionist control, the northern state faced two major problems – economic viability and popular reaction. For the unionist state a major difficulty would have been if economic decline encouraged labour militance, especially among Protestant workers. In a sense, the unionists did not really fear republican violence or nationalist frustration. The former could be controlled militarily and the latter politically. Moreover, unionists expected no better of nationalists than backlash and violence. Labour was a different matter. Labour organisation among Protestant workers, especially if it managed to bridge the sectarian divide to link up with Catholic labour agitation, threatened the core of unionism's power.

The whole house of cards was built on the myth of unionist – Protestant – loyalist unity.[29] Managing that myth was crucial to the survival of the state and of unionist monopoly control. Raising the spectre of republican infiltration could often be enough to spook the loyalist working class into line. There was the regular reinforcement of the purported unity through Orange parades and reminders of military prowess on behalf of empire. And of course, loyalty clearly brought tangible rewards in terms of employment and job security. Even if the unionist working class did not quite constitute a 'labour aristocracy', that was the position they were promised by the system and to which they aspired.

Economic decline had the potential to wreck this compact between the ruling class and labour. The Northern Ireland state could never be a vibrant economy. With a

---

[28] This signals some of the obsessive micro-sectarianism of the Northern Ireland state – but also the limitations of such an approach in a colonial context. For example, on 6 July 1965, it was announced that Northern Ireland's new town would be named Craigavon after the first Prime Minister – he of 'Protestant Parliament and Protestant State' infamy. A nationalist MP, Joseph Connellan, interrupted the announcement with the acerbic comment, 'A Protestant city for a Protestant people'. The existing local townland name Knockmena (from the Irish townland name, Cnoc Meadhnach) had been suggested as attracting broader acceptance. But 'Craigavon' is itself a corruption of two Gaelic words 'carraig' and 'abhainn', meaning, respectively, 'rock' and 'river' – even this explicitly sectarian imposition could not escape the return of the repressed amidst all the contradictions of unionist genealogy.

[29] We can observe that this desperate desire for an exclusive homogeneity still obtains. Thus, 'good relations' discourse has provided us with the acronym PUL – Protestant, Unionist, Loyalist – to designate this 'community'. Its antonym 'CNR' – Catholic, Nationalist, Republican – is less common and generally resisted by those it attempts to describe.

population of 1.5 million it was never going to provide the critical mass necessary for highly profitable production and consumption in its own right. The economy of the north-east of Ireland had developed as an adjunct of the British industrial revolution. That was both its strength and its potential weakness. At the beginning of the Northern Ireland state's existence that weakness was not apparent. The Harland and Wolff shipyard was the largest in the world; the North was responsible for around one quarter of the linen produced globally. But the economy was a subordinate and peripheral one. It could both soar and plummet with the British economy. In fact, coming late to the British industrial revolution and being on the edge of central decision making in the south-east of England, any recession was likely to be more pronounced in the North than in Britain overall.

This was most evident during the economic slump of the 1930s. The northern economy suffered disproportionately compared to the UK overall. No ships were launched in 1933 in either Harland and Wolff or Workman Clark's, 'the wee yard'. The latter did not reopen when the immediate crisis had passed. In 1938 unemployment in the North stood at 28 per cent; 56 per cent of all linen workers were unemployed. War helped the situation; in 1944 unemployment dropped to 3.8 per cent, the lowest ever in the history of the state. But post-war, that trend was reversed. Between 1946 and 1954, average unemployment for males stood at 8.0 per cent in the North and 1.5 per cent in Britain; female average unemployment was 5.7 per cent in the North and 1.4 per cent in Britain (Isles and Cuthbert 1957: 162). The arrival of the welfare state after the war helped to ameliorate the situation to some extent. Conservative to the core, Northern Ireland MPs at Westminster had voted unanimously against the introduction of the National Health Service and social insurance. But, to avoid straining support from their working-class supporters, they adopted a policy of parity with Britain. They enacted social reform bills at Stormont to match those at Westminster and 'quickly claimed credit for what they had initially opposed...' (Farrell 1980: 189).

The economy continued to decline inexorably. Agriculture employed 21,400 people in 1950 and 13,100 in 1961, a drop of 39 per cent. Employment in textiles fell from 72,800 in 1950 to 56,300 in 1961, a 23 per cent decline. Shipbuilding employment was reduced from 24,200 in 1950 to 20,200 in 1961, a decline of 17 per cent (Farrell 1980: 227). The collapse of the linen industry was perhaps the most spectacular, from an output of 226.4 million square yards in 1912 to 59.8 in 1961, a whopping 74 per cent decline (Driver 1975: 42).

The shortcomings of protectionism in the South and dependency in the North led to a similar conclusion: the need to pursue foreign direct capital investment. The case for the North was made cogently by two economists charged by the government with drawing up a programme for economic development, Isles and Cuthbert (1957). In time policies were put in place to attract foreign capital, including grants towards construction, machinery, labour and training costs as well as generous tax deduction schemes. The incentives worked. By 1966 there were 217 foreign firms newly established in the North, and the trend continued through the 1970s.

Where there was a preponderance of capital from pharmaceutical and IT firms in the South, the concentration in the North was synthetic fibres – with firms like Courtaulds, British Enkalon and ICI. Capital from Britain, the US, Germany, Holland and elsewhere arrived. Some of the key firms at the heart of the North's industrial take-off were saved: Gallaher's Tobacco Company was bought over by the American Tobacco Company, Harland and Wolff was Norwegian-owned. Now, however, the magnates of the northern economy were not local capitalists but local managers for international capital. This was arguably one of the key contradictions of the late Orange State. While these companies and their management were quite capable of responding to local demands of replicating the traditional sectarian division of labour,[30] they did not have the same ideological commitment to the model. And, if and when traditional sectarian practices cut across their more basic commitment to capital accumulation, they were not so accommodating to this aspect of loyalist tradition.

Moreover, even as this new industrial strategy was supposed to shore up the economic base of the Northern Ireland state, the meltdown of the northern state was well advanced in other respects. The trigger was a political campaign of direct action for full civil rights. In the 1960s a number of groups emerged which focused on the anti-Catholic discrimination of the state. In Dungannon, the Campaign for Social Justice documented the details of discrimination. In Derry, groups such as the Derry Housing Action Committee engaged in direct action. Eventually the trade unions, political parties such as the Communist Party, the Northern Ireland Labour Party, the Northern Ireland Liberal Party, the Young Socialists and others coalesced around a series of ostensibly reasonable demands. The Northern Ireland Civil Rights Association (NICRA) and Peoples Democracy (PD) were formed and the civil rights movement was in full flow. The movement's demands were articulated by NICRA as follows:

> 'One man, one vote': the removal of multiple votes (up to six) for business owners and the extension of the vote to those over 18 who did not own or rent their own property.
> The end of gerrymandering.
> The end of discrimination in the allocation of public jobs.
> The end of discrimination in the allocation of public housing.
> The abolition of the Special Powers Act.
> The disbanding of the B Specials.

The strategy managed to locate the Achilles heel of the unionist body politic. The unionist state had learned that it could survive whatever militant republicanism could

---

[30] Indeed, international capital and local prejudice could happily coexist. Take the case of Tom Wilson, chief economic planner for Northern Ireland. He wrote that 'Presbyterians and Jews are probably endowed with more business acumen than Irish Catholics'. As for the latter: 'They have less to complain about than the U.S. negroes, and their lot is a very pleasant one as compared with the nationalists in, say, the Ukraine... For generations they were the underdogs... They were made to feel inferior, and to make matters worse they often were inferior, if only in those personal qualities that make for success in competitive economic life' (Wilson 1955: 208-9).

throw at it. The 1956-62 IRA campaign had perished because of military might in the North, isolation from the South and ultimately lack of popular support as it became clearer that the campaign was destined to failure. The Nationalist Party had by this point settled down into the role of being an ineffectual and ultimately non-threatening sideshow. The communists and socialists in the civil rights movement could easily be dismissed by the unionist state as 'usual suspects' who in the past had sometimes been tinged with republicanism. PD members, who saw themselves as part of the radicalism of the time which involved opposition to the war in Vietnam and apartheid in South Africa, and struggles against imperialism and racism generally, could likewise be rejected on the grounds of their idealistic commitment to class struggle and revolution. But there were at least three elements of the campaign with which unionism had no previous experience and in the face of which found difficulty responding.

First, the movement was making no direct or immediate demands in relation to the constitutional position of the North. Some of the student placards read 'British rights for British citizens' – hardly an openly subversive demand. In this respect, the involvement of Catholic students was particularly significant. As a result of the education reforms established through the welfare state after World War II, working class Catholics had access for the first time to free third-level education. They were different from the standard university student in the North prior to this who believed in their entitlement to third-level education. The Catholic students got a taste of opportunity through access to university but found that the system was still entirely weighted against them. It is impossible to know what would have become of them if the state had been able to concede; would equal citizenship have been enough for them to forget the nationalism and republicanism of their parents? But what was clear was that for many, equal citizenship was as far as their aspirations went at that point in time.

Second, the radical youth in PD were not like the republican militants with whom the state was familiar. They may have aspired to the overthrow of the state, but they were not arming themselves or otherwise preparing for an armed struggle. Moreover, their socialist vision was behind their desire to see both sections of the working class united in a common struggle.

Third, although individual republicans were involved in many of the organisations, the civil rights movement was not a republican campaign. Unionist slogans may have read 'CRA=IRA', but the mass organising and direct action were a million miles away from the rural shootings and bombings of a decade previously.

A state founded on inequality could carry on in the face of insurgency. One of the advantages of a permanent state of emergency was that it took an awful lot of resistance to suggest any level of crisis since the state was defined by being permanently in crisis. But it could not so easily survive the sustained demand for equality. This demand was coming from unexpected quarters which unionism had little experience of controlling militarily or ideologically. There is an argument that the challenge was containable had the unionists had the wit to make more concessions at an early stage. But a state built on inequality was never going to be able to concede equality.

One unionist retort at the time, frequently reiterated since, is that there was no justification for protest because there was no substance to the claims of discrimination. Protestants, it is said, were as badly off as Catholics. Yet the statistics of the time indicate clearly that, even if a number of working-class Protestants, like their Catholic neighbours, lived in 'ghastly hovels' with no indoor toilets, the structures of the society were skewed to the benefit of Protestants. Gerrymandering, discrimination in allocation of public jobs and in large unionist-owned private firms, statistics on poverty and unemployment rates, etc. all indicated that while – *as a class* – Protestants did not always do well, Catholics – *as a class* – did worse. The evidence is there, albeit incomplete, in the report of the government inquiry set up to examine the reasons for the outbreak of violence in 1968, the Cameron Report. If there had been no substance to claims of discrimination, there would have been no need for the British government to push the unionist government to institute reforms. As people marched on the streets singing the US civil rights anthem 'We Shall Overcome', they came face to face with the repressive might of the state. Police and loyalists – the latter urged on by a fiery preacher, the Reverend Ian Paisley – harried and attacked the marchers, sorely testing their intention to restrict themselves to non-violent civil disobedience.

The Prime Minister from 1963, Terence O'Neill, was an aristocratic northerner, educated in English public schools and later an army officer. He was aloof and unemotional, but he tried to persuade the Unionist Party to take on a slightly more liberal veneer. He engaged in some symbolic actions which, slight as they were, were unique in the context of the northern state: visiting Catholic schools, engaging with the Taoiseach Seán Lemass. At the same time, he displayed an embarrassing paternalism which was deeply sectarian:

> It is frightfully hard to explain to Protestants that if you give Roman Catholics a good job and a good house they will live like Protestants, because they will see neighbours with cars and television sets. They will refuse to have eighteen children, but if a Roman Catholic is jobless and lives in the most ghastly hovel, he will rear eighteen children on National Assistance. If you treat Roman Catholics with due consideration and kindness, they will live like Protestants in spite of the authoritative nature of their church. (*Belfast Telegraph* 5 May 1969)

By November 1968, O'Neill faced such pressure from the civil rights movement as well as the now-awakened British government that he conceded some reforms: the introduction of a points system for housing allocation, the abolition of business multiple votes and the promise to consider suspending sections of the Special Powers Act. Nothing was said about disbanding the B Specials. For many of the civil rights activists it was too little, too late. At the same time, it was too much for Paisley and indeed for a substantial element of O'Neill's own party, led by Brian Faulkner.[31] O'Neill was forced out of office in 1969.

By demanding equality of citizenship, the civil rights movement managed to split the Unionist Party into its constituent parts. The modernisers and professionals, connected to international capital, saw O'Neill as their champion despite his aristocratic origins. For the more traditional wing of the Party, the beacon was carried by Faulkner who represented local capital; his father had owned the largest shirt-making factory in the world. Like an instance of political nuclear fission, the unionist split had violent repercussions. Violence erupted on a scale not seen since 1921 and 1932. The British army was deployed 'in support of the civil authorities', but quickly came to act as one more arm of the repressive unionist state. The civil rights campaign died in Derry on Bloody Sunday, 30 January, 1972, along with the 14 peaceful marchers gunned down by British paratroopers. By this point all three protagonists – state forces, republicans and loyalists – were engaged in military action.

The nationalist population had come to conclude that, as often before, it was on its own. Westminster had finally broken its long purdah in relation to Northern Ireland affairs, forcing through reforms, disbanding the B Specials, removing the powers of discriminatory local councils, introducing fair employment legislation[32] and eventually proroguing the local parliament and imposing direct rule. But it was clear that their fundamental purpose was to restore the unionist state in a situation where the unionists proved incapable of doing so themselves. Nor was there any indication that the southern state was going to rescue the beleaguered nationalist population. As nationalist working-class areas were torched by loyalists and refugees streamed over the border in 1969, Taoiseach Jack Lynch moved Irish troops to the border. Northern nationalists believed that they were going to intervene, but instead they merely set up refugee camps. A pattern was thus confirmed. Southern politicians could issue apparently authentic republican statements, such as Taoiseach Charles Haughey's construction in 1982 of Northern Ireland as 'a failed political entity' (Kelly 2017). But this did not prefigure any sustained attempt to end partition and thereby guarantee the rights and security of northern nationalists.

Conclusions

The new, artificial state that emerged in 1921 was characterised by both continuity and change. In terms of its core logic of coercion, it both replicated and intensified the model employed by the British in the Tan war. While it is striking how racist and how

---

[31] Faulkner, despite his later reputation as a liberal unionist, was equally capable of patronising sectarianism: '… the real problem with the Catholics of Northern Ireland is one of education … Catholics produced too many children and sent them to inferior schools; they were not fit for key jobs' (quoted in *Sunday Times* 27 February 1972).

[32] The fair employment legislation was a very limited reform when introduced in 1976, outlawing direct discrimination only. The 1989 Act was much stronger and more important. Also, a religion question was included in the 1971 Census for the first time since 1911. This was significant in making discriminatory patterns more observable.

violent the Northern Ireland state was from its inception, this was not significantly different from what the British state was already doing across the whole of Ireland at that point – including martial law. There *was* a stark contrast, however, between Northern Ireland and the pre-partition Ireland under British rule in terms of its relations with the native population – Irish Catholics. The pre-partition UK state had softened its anti-Catholicism over its duration. It had attempted to secure legitimacy through *incorporating* rather than repressing the Catholic majority. The significance of this is that the new state in the north assumed a form that was less a continuation of the Irish state within the Union (1801-1920) than a radically new social formation which had to summarily and brutally re-subalternise and re-ghettoise northern Catholics. It bears repetition that this reality was enabled by the UK state. This policy was also – as so often in Irish colonial history – improvising on earlier themes. This aspect of minoritisation recycled Pitt's logic for the Union from 120 years before. In this regard there is a core logic of the union state from 1800 to the present – 'our precious union': its key function is to minoritise Irish Catholics *within* a British state apparatus.

There was, of course, a cost to all of this – particularly for the Catholic 'subjects' locked inside both Northern Ireland and the Union reconstituted in 1920. The eventual acceptance by some unionists that Northern Ireland 1920-72 was a 'cold house for Catholics' only exposes their capacity for understatement of epic proportions. Post-partition Northern Ireland entered a *permanent* state of emergency. Moreover, its apparatus of coercion was not directed simply against the IRA or republicans or nationalists; it targeted the *whole* Catholic community. Following partition, Stormont reversed the pre-partition Catholicisation project and re-sectarianised with immediate effect. As we have seen, the core logic behind the creation of Northern Ireland was a land grab for the maximum area of Ireland that could be legitimised through Protestant majoritarianism. If we disregard the morality and politics of this approach, the chief mistake in the statecraft was the assumption that this majority would be permanent. In retrospect, the unionist mistake in 1920 was that they took 'too much' of Ulster and incorporated 'too many' Catholics.

The new state had been legitimised by the imperial parliament to do whatever it deemed necessary to stabilise itself. A documentary film emerged in 2018 of a *Radharc* investigation of sectarian inequality in Derry in 1964. It served as a timely reminder of what one of the Derry residents interviewed characterised as 'the backwash of Britain's first colonial effort'. The programme serves as a fitting footnote to our Protestant state analysis. (It is also striking that it was made for – and buried by – RTÉ.)[33] While the various facets of sectarian discrimination – across employment, housing and the gerrymandered council itself – are well detailed, perhaps the most

---

[33] 'Radharc in Derry 1964': Although completed in 1964, the film was regarded by RTÉ as too sensitive for transmission and was not broadcast until 1970 (Radharc 1964).

poignant element is the reminder that Derry nationalists had made a submission to the UK privy council. In this sense, they had attempted to address their situation by appealing to the Crown as 'British subjects'. Asked about possible redress on gerrymandering, Eddie McAteer said:

> I think not. We have even lowered ourselves to a petition to the privy council in England and we had the strange phenomenon that the matter was referred back to the guilty parties, the guilty men at Stormont themselves. I'm afraid there is no normal redress to this problem. It will take a blast of public inquiry and informed public opinion in order to sweep away this rotten system. (Radharc 1964)

From this distance, the levels of discrimination outlined in the programme are shocking. But the state also looks relatively stable – hardly bucolic but neither on the edge of revolution. Yet within a couple of years, Derry was the epicentre of the civil rights campaign and eight years later Northern Ireland – in its 50-year-long 'Stormont' iteration at least – had collapsed.

Partition effectively removed Ireland from the British political itinerary when previously it had rarely been off that agenda. Once administration was handed over to the unionists, the issue of Northern Ireland was barely discussed in Westminster for the next half century. When it appeared at all, it was often by way of exclusion. For example, the 1967 Abortion Act passed in Westminster has a final line: 'This Act shall not apply to Northern Ireland'. The unionists were left to get along with devolved administration within the general confines of the United Kingdom system. Certain matters were not devolved – most notably taxation and defence.[34] Beyond these, the northern government employed – and was permitted to employ – a step-by-step policy in relation to UK-wide legislation. On occasions, this meant mirroring British legislation by introducing its own acts and policies; this was the case in relation to many of the welfare state reforms in the aftermath of World War II.

On other occasions, it meant that legislative change occurred on the same issue but was markedly different from the British model. Thus, when the British government introduced universal suffrage for local government elections, the Stormont government introduced its own Representation of the People Bill 1946, restricting the franchise even further (Farrell 1980: 85). Finally, the unionists refused to follow UK legislation occasionally, especially in relation to 'moral'[35] matters such as abortion and homosexuality. Homosexuality was decriminalised in Britain in 1967, with the North excluded; it was only in 1982, after a successful appeal to the European Court of Human Rights by a gay man from the North, that the law was changed. Abortion was decriminalised in Britain

---

[34] One could have been forgiven for thinking that the latter was a devolved matter when viewing the only armed police force in the UK on the streets of Belfast; the RUC had machine-gun-carrying Shoreland armoured cars as 'the troubles' escalated in the late 1960s. Nine-year-old Patrick Rooney was shot dead in his home in Divis Flats, Belfast, with rounds fired from a Shoreland in August 1969.

[35] Almost without exception, 'morality' related solely to matters of sex and reproduction. Concerns about morality were rarely expressed in relation to issues such as the sectarian allocation of resources, poverty or corruption.

also in 1967, but Northern Ireland continued to criminalise it under legislation from 1886 up until 2019. In the interim, appeals to the British government to extend the 1967 Abortion Act were met with the reply that the British government deferred to the sensitivities of Northern Ireland politicians.[36]

The civil rights campaign broke this seal around the North. When the unionist state responded with repression and minor reforms, the British government was forced to abandon the 50-year-old protocol and once more focus on Irish affairs. Suddenly politicians were faced with the issues in relation to Ireland – upheaval, outrages, repression, emergency law – that their predecessors once faced. Their response was frequently similar – a mixture of shock and distaste. At the same time, the British did set out with some gusto to attempt the Herculean task of cleaning the Augean stables. The first task was to send in troops 'in aid of the civil power'. In mid-August 1969 they were deployed in Belfast for the first time in over 30 years,[37] protecting nationalist areas which had been attacked by loyalists. They also engaged in speeding up the timid reform programme which had been forced on the unionist government by popular protest; this meant in effect recognising many of the civil rights demands and acting accordingly. Some sectarian local councils had their powers taken over by commissioners, most spectacularly Derry City Council. Public housing allocation was taken from councils and given to a non-elected body, the Northern Ireland Housing Executive, which had a strict points system in terms of assessing need. The British disbanded the B Specials and disarmed the RUC, the latter, as it turned out, temporarily.[38]

These were momentous changes, but they were overdue and as such represented a stopgap policy on the part of the British. Between 1969 and 1972 there was an interregnum, a policy arrangement which was neither fully devolution nor fully direct rule. Thus, the British could introduce policing reforms over the heads and objections of local unionist politicians. At the same time, the unionist Prime Minister, Brian Faulkner, could introduce internment without trial in August 1971 against the advice of British army chiefs in the North. This administrative imprecision ended with the prorogation of Stormont in March 1972.[39]

---

[36] When in 2018 a referendum in the South to liberalise abortion law and policy was passed, a spokesperson for Theresa May stated: 'The prime minister said on Sunday that the Irish referendum was an impressive show of democracy, which delivered a clear result, and she congratulated the Irish people on the decision. But it's important to recognise that the people of Northern Ireland are entitled to their own process, which is run by locally elected politicians' (Walker 2018). Ironically, when the law did change, it was a result of intervention by British politicians in Westminster. An amendment to the Northern Ireland (Executive Formation) Act 2019, intended to extend the length of time during which the Executive, inactive since 2016, could be re-established, specified that if the Executive was not up and running by 21 October 2019, abortion would be decriminalised in Northern Ireland and proper legal policies would have to be introduced by March 2020. This occurred.

[37] The previous occasion had been during the sectarian violence of July 1935.

[38] The common observation was that 'civil rights disarmed the RUC and the IRA re-armed them'.

[39] Thus, Northern Ireland became an archetypal example of what Agamben (2005) characterised as a 'state of exception' – when a 'state of emergency' becomes a 'paradigm of government'. From its inception,

Why the Northern Ireland state collapsed is a complex question. Various answers have been provided: the contradiction between the social democratic evolution of the British state and sectarian logic of the northern state; the changing logic of the economic base; the radicalisation of the population in the north around civil rights and equality; the emergence of an educated, articulate Catholic middle class, to some extent a direct product of the UK welfare state.

Ultimately, however, the levels of repression that Stormont required to function produced their own contradictions – as well as different modes of resistance. Perhaps, in the algorithm of oppression, the ratio built into the artificial state was too great – it is simply impossible to permanently elevate two-thirds of a population on the backs of one third. Nevertheless, this was the crude quotient of Protestant privilege that survived for fifty years. In any event, the state did collapse spectacularly in 1972. Having lurched through the first years of 'the troubles', it just managed to mark its half-centenary in the appropriately miserable and militarised 'celebration' of *Ulster '71*.[40] Its government was prorogued by the British government in 1972 and finally abrogated in 1974. This brought an end to one of the most inglorious offshoots of the British Empire. Whether what replaced it would be any better was, of course, the question now preoccupying both the Protestant and Catholic blocs that had been generated by this now redundant exercise in 'Protestant dominion'.

Northern Ireland provided a template for what this might mean to the world (McVeigh 2006).

[40] Despite the depressing debacle that was Ulster '71, in 2017, former Tourism Minister Simon Hamilton, DUP, heralded an Expo 100 festival to celebrate the centenary of the formation of the state. 'Any celebration of Northern Ireland's 100th birthday should reflect on its great strengths and on what makes Northern Ireland a great place to live, work, visit and invest in. Sometimes we forget this, but we have a wonderful, rich and vibrant industrial heritage in this part of the world. We should be immensely proud, if we are not already, particularly of the engineering prowess of people from this part of the world, and the entrepreneurial spirit' (*Belfast Telegraph*, 28 January 2017). Expo 100 never happened. However, in December 2020, the Northern Ireland Office launched 'Our Story in the Making: NI Beyond 100'. As of the time of writing this consists solely of an online endeavour involving Facebook and Twitter, and seems more akin to a branding campaign than anything more substantial.

Chapter 8

Northern Ireland 1972-2020:
direct rule, peace, and the emergence
of a 'good relations' state

It may be of interest to recall that when the regular army was first raised in the 17th century, 'suppression of the Irish' was coupled with 'defence of the Protestant religion' as one of the two main reasons for its existence. —Brigadier Kitson, *Low Intensity Operations*, 1971

Nobody talks like that anymore.[1] —Ivan Lewis, Labour Shadow Secretary of State for Northern Ireland, 2014

Westminster's imposition of direct rule in 1972 provoked an existential crisis for unionists as they lost control of their 'Protestant Sstate'. But this moment also served to remind everyone where real power lay within the Union. Northern Ireland – and 'our precious union' – is a project framed in London rather Belfast. The new formation launched almost immediately into two constitutional referendums that continue to define its status. First, the Northern Ireland border poll was held in Northern Ireland on 8 March 1973. This was a referendum on whether Northern Ireland should remain part of the United Kingdom or join with the Republic of Ireland to form a united Ireland. This was the first time that a major referendum had been held in any region of the United Kingdom. The referendum was boycotted by both nationalists and republicans and resulted in a conclusive unionist victory. On the face of it, the logic of the gerrymander of 1920 appeared to be secure. Northern Ireland seemed set to continue to deliver a unionist majority in perpetuity: on a voter turnout of 59 per cent, 99 per cent voted to remain in the UK.

Second, the UK-wide referendum on membership of the European Communities was held in 1975. This confirmed the position of the UK – and *ipso facto* Northern Ireland – within the wider EC project. At the time, the UK-wide support for continued membership seemed much more important than any Northern Ireland-specific

---

[1] Comment made in response to a delegation of homeless Catholic mothers from North Belfast who asked him to address sectarian inequality in housing (Bell and McVeigh 2016: 42-3).

implications. Nevertheless, the groundbreaking Europeanisation of the partition border was confirmed by this vote. Strikingly in contrast to the 2016 vote, Scotland and Northern Ireland gave *less* support to remaining in the EC than the British mean. In Northern Ireland, 53 per cent voted Yes and 48 per cent No on a turnout of 47 per cent. Turnout was also much lower in NI than other UK regions.[2] Nevertheless, the majority support for membership across NI anticipated a similar – and much more significant – pro-European majority in the 2016 Brexit referendum.

With the constitutional status of Northern Ireland now firmly embedded in both the UK and the EC, the British government could proceed with its direct rule project. Despite the momentous transformations since – including, of course, the peace process and the Good Friday Agreement (GFA) – there is an obvious series of continuities across the last fifty years. It was clear from the first that the British did not want direct rule – they preferred a 'responsible government' model based on an 'internal solution'. White papers, Sunningdale, rolling devolution, various assemblies and finally the GFA Assembly signalled the desire of Westminster to distance itself from this 'god-awful country'. Despite this, however, direct rule became the default mode of government both before – and more tellingly after – the GFA. (Although the years since the failure to establish an executive in 2017 were technically a deadlock, Westminster resisted the reintroduction of formal direct rule.) Like the previous Stormont regime, this too was a state in search of a soul. Since it was no longer a 'Protestant state' – and it was without a parliament for much of this period, both before and after the GFA – it became increasingly reliant on the notion of first 'community relations' and then 'good relations' to provide ideological coherence. This ideology was unlikely to ever gird the loins of a new Northern Ireland nationalism. Nevertheless, it provided a lowest common denominator approach to state legitimacy: any opposition appeared singularly perverse since it implied a preference for 'bad relations'.

The British approach to direct rule after 1972 involved a complex balancing of more repression/more reform (O'Dowd, Rolston and Tomlinson 1980). Although everyday matters under direct rule were handled by government departments within Northern Ireland itself, major policy was determined by the Northern Ireland Office (NIO), under the direction of the Secretary of State for Northern Ireland. In addition, legislation was introduced, amended, or repealed by means of Orders in Council – a return to more straightforwardly colonial law-making.[3] Direct rule also forced Westminster back towards an incorporation model. There was now no question that control of the state could be left to unionists – power sharing with some element of the Catholic community

[2] Held on 5 June 1975, the combined UK electorate expressed significant support for EC membership, with 67 percent in favour on a UK turnout of 64 percent.

[3] In the UK the Order in Council is formally made in the name of the Queen by and with the advice and consent of the Privy Council. Under direct rule in Northern Ireland this is done under the various Northern Ireland Acts 1974 to 2000, and not by virtue of the Royal Prerogative. This prerogative continues to be the mechanism employed across what is left of the British Empire. Notoriously, the mechanism was used to overturn the court finding that the exile of the Chagossians was unlawful; see chapter 2.

was the *sine qua non* of any devolution. This new reality involved an ever-widening embrace of potential allies in the cause of shoring up the state. Both the Irish state and sections of the formerly ostracised Catholic community – most importantly the Catholic Church and SDLP – were courted by the UK/NIO in order to widen the legitimacy of the state. External actors like the EU and the USA were also increasingly involved. For nearly thirty years, these efforts were undermined by the continuing brutal conflict involving sustained political violence from three sources – republicans, loyalists and state forces. This dynamic only changed significantly with the ceasefires of 1994.

Following the peace process and GFA, most republicans were also drawn into this process of detoxifying the Northern Ireland state. For a while at least, the political landscape appeared reconfigured. At this juncture a new 70 per cent pro-Agreement coalition faced an apparently defeated 30 per cent anti-Agreement constituency. In addition to its significant majority, the pro-Agreement side looked the more formidable political force. It included all 'constitutional nationalism', nearly all of republicanism, the centrist unionist Alliance Party, at least half of the Unionist Party and the political leadership of loyalism. It also had the support of the entire international community. The anti-Agreement position was left with the DUP – and splinter sections of republican and loyalist votes – along with the other half of the Unionist Party. Perhaps tellingly, however, the DUP's was the only significant movement that was not split by the peace process. If this caused little sense of foreboding at the time, it seems more ominous in retrospect. Moreover, while support for the GFA looked solid, this did not reflect the equivocal support of many unionists – including unionist leader David Trimble. Before long, it emerged that the majority of unionist grassroots were supportive of the DUP and its unambiguously anti-Agreement position. In this context, most of the anti-Agreement faction of the UUP was gradually integrated into an expanded DUP.

Despite these gathering clouds, Northern Ireland looked a very different place in the aftermath of the Agreement. It was both more peaceful and more stable. There was no doubt that the state that emerged from the GFA was very different to the 'Protestant state' characterised in the last chapter. Two key structural changes from Stormont were instituted: first the Irish government would help the British manage the north; second, Catholics, nationalists and perhaps even republicans were to be provided with some sense of ownership of/belonging in the state. Furthermore, with the St Andrews Agreement of 2006, the DUP belatedly signed up to the process. While this brought the DUP into GFA structures – and created the possibility of a DUP/Sinn Féin power-sharing government – it also signalled a dilution of some of the more progressive potential of the GFA.[4] The Assembly met on 8 May 2007 and elected Ian Paisley of the DUP and

---

[4] For example, the St Andrews Agreement prevented ministers from implementing decisions without support from the other parties in the executive. Sinn Féin Education Minister Martin McGuinness had done away with the 11-plus examination under the GFA; he could not have done so under the terms of the St Andrews Agreement.

Martin McGuinness of Sinn Féin as First Minister and deputy First Minister respectively. The Sinn Féin Ard Chomhairle (national executive) agreed that republicans would take their places on the Policing Board. Reviewing these developments, Martin McGuinness said: 'Up until the 26 March this year, Ian Paisley and I never had a conversation about anything – not even about the weather – and now we have worked very closely together over the last seven months and there's been no angry words between us … This shows we are set for a new course' (Graham 2017).

As this model bedded down over the next decade, however, this new course ran anything but smoothly. Northern Ireland became a fully-fledged 'good relations' state because this was the only ideology that could underpin such a disparate amalgam of interests and identities. Partly in consequence, it has struggled to secure sufficient legitimacy across the political spectrum – with both political blocs finding it difficult to sell the historic compromise to their own base. It could no longer offer undiluted Protestant ascendancy, but neither could it deliver anything approaching equality for Catholics, let alone resolve the paradox of how a growing Irish republican constituency might reconcile itself to what remained a British imperial formation. For a moment, however, it looked as if this unlikely coupling could work as the 'Chuckle Brothers' double act of Paisley and McGuinness symbolised an unlikely late flowering of peace (Purdy 2007). Certainly – to widespread disbelief – Paisley proved much more committed to selling the compromise than Trimble had ever been. Unionist unease with this rapprochement with republicans saw Paisley toppled, however, and a return to the *status quo ante*. There has been a dearth of unionist chuckling since under the dour stewardship of, first, Peter Robinson and then Arlene Foster. The worldwide economic crash of 2008 and the spectacular end of the Celtic Tiger also undermined the NI economy. In this context the historic compromise that informed the GFA began to look increasingly vulnerable. When the Executive collapsed in 2016, the state survived but it looked as if any concomitant politics of reconciliation had been exhausted.

We characterise the post-GFA state as a 'good relations' state. First 'community relations' and then 'good relations' became the *only* paradigms that could offer anything like a coherent ideology for the post-1972 iteration of 'Northern Ireland'. While the state looked to have achieved a degree of legitimacy in the wake of the ceasefires and the GFA, this did not denote a radical transformation. Neither 'side' is particularly sold on the virtues of the GFA – unionists felt that they gave more than they wanted, and nationalists felt they got much less than they deserved. So, over the following years, much of the genuine good will – and hyperbole – associated with the peace process and the GFA has dissipated. It is increasingly difficult to find either unionist or nationalist commitment to make this state work. While this task is more likely to be couched in terms of 'defending the peace process' than 'shoring up the state', the consequence is much the same. The incapacity of the power-sharing executive to function effectively, even before the additional shocks of Brexit and Covid-19, suggests that the Agreement

– and the state – is unlikely to last. How Northern Ireland got to its present chronic dysfunctionality is the subject of this chapter.

Back to the future – direct rule 1972-1998

On 28 March 1972 the Stormont parliament was prorogued, and the 50-year long devolution experiment mothballed. This was also the worst year of 'the troubles'. As the three-way war involving republicans, loyalists and British forces raged, 496 people lost their lives. This represented 14 per cent of the 3,696 people killed between 1966 and 1998. Both factors are connected. As the death toll mounted and as Stormont proved its inability to hold on to the reins, Britain for the first time in half a century became centrally involved in the running of Irish affairs. This was not through choice. British Home Secretary Reginald Maudling spoke for many in the British establishment in July 1970 when he said: 'For God's sake bring me a large scotch. What a bloody awful country!' (quoted in *Sunday Times* Insight Team 1972: 213). For others, of course, the union remained 'precious'. As Margaret Thatcher told the House of Commons in 1981, 'Northern Ireland is part of the United Kingdom; as much as my constituency is'.[5] This was to prove another one of the continuities – the idea of union retained immense emotional and political capital for the English even as they declared their dislike of Northern Ireland and its unionists.

Direct rule had many of the characteristics of a second Act of Union, albeit this time for only part of Ireland. The local parliament and executive were no longer operational. Day-to-day administration of the local state was in the hands of a Secretary of State and other Ministers of State, all of whom were British politicians exercising authority in the North without any direct local mandate.[6] For a substantial period, 1972 until 1999, the Secretary of State was effectively the chief arm of British government in the North. That was also the case on four occasions when the Northern Ireland Assembly which resulted from the Good Friday Agreement was suspended by the Secretary of State: 11 February to 30 May 2000, 10 August 2001 (24-hour suspension), 22 September 2001 (24-hour suspension), and 14 October 2002 to 7 May 2007. Following the withdrawal of Deputy First Minister Martin McGuinness in January 2017, it was suspended for a further three years until it was restored in January 2020. During the rest of the period considered, including the power-sharing executive between January and May 1974, the role of the British Secretary of State for Northern Ireland was a less direct, hands-on matter.

---

[5] As her constituency was Finchley, this is often misquoted as 'Northern Ireland is as British as Finchley'.

[6] All of the Secretaries and Ministers of State during the direct rule phase were British, the partial exception being Brian Mawhinney, born in Belfast but an MP for a British constituency, Peterborough (September 1986-November 1990). Some direct rule ministers were not even elected in Britain. The titles of such ministers would not look out of place in an account of 19th century British administrations in Ireland. Between June 1970 and May 1997, they included: Lord Windlesham, Lord Belstead, Lord Melchett, Lord Donaldson of Kingsbridge, the Earl of Gowrie, the Earl of Mansfield, Lord Elton, Lord Lyell, the Earl of Kilmorey, Lord Skelmersdale, the Earl of Arran and Baroness Denton.

The British intervention in 1972 seemed to present not simply the arrival of a new broom but also the possibility that the 'Protestant state' was about to be dealt a severe blow. The extent of reforms was unprecedented, to the point that it seemed like sectarianism no longer had a role in policy making and implementation. The social democratic model which had emerged and developed in Britain, but which had only partially penetrated the North to date, now arrived in earnest. Take the case of employment equality. British ministers, it was said, had not been socialised in the sectarian patterns of the North and therefore had no axe to grind in relation to sectarianism. The effects of this were to be felt first in relation to those matters which they directly controlled – in particular, the allocation of public jobs. But it went further than this. At an early stage, British administrators began a debate on job allocation more widely, both private and public sector, leading eventually to fair employment legislation. By the 1980s the North had come to have policies and protections in relation to the allocation of jobs which matched or bettered the best practices globally. Told this way, the story of the reform process appears positive and heartwarming. But there are deeper layers to it which do not fit that script.

The presumption was that British politicians, not raised and schooled in the nuances and intricacies of sectarian divisions and attitudes, would hasten a post-sectarian polity in the North. But in fact, there was nothing to prevent direct rule ministers pandering to sectarianism even though they had not been socialised into its Irish version. After all, we have seen how, in post-Reformation Britain, sectarian interpretations had frequently been attached to Irish matters. The 1641 rising against the settlers had been interpreted as anti-Protestant rather than anti-colonial. Cromwell judged that the Irish needed to be suppressed because of their Catholicism rather than their resistance to conquest. A central element in the British government's move towards union was to thwart the rise of a 'popish democracy'. Even after the Act of Union, agrarian agitation by peasants in the 19th century was judged to be anti-Protestant rather than anti-landlord. And above all, the Act of Settlement 1701 stipulated that the British monarch must not be Catholic.[7] There was enough past experience to ensure that, however muted, sectarianism was deep in the DNA of the British body politic.[8]

The positive outlook had its equivalent in relation to capital. Where before the close alignment between unionist politicians and local business ensured that sectarian decision making could affect investment decisions and employment practices in both the

---

[7] In 2013 the Act of Settlement was amended such that marrying a Catholic no longer bars a royal from becoming monarch. However, as the person still holds the position of head of the Church of England, in effect, the monarch has to be a Protestant.

[8] This often slips under the 'hate' radar – for example, on Guy Fawkes night 2018 there was widespread condemnation of a tasteless bonfire which incinerated a model of Grenfell Tower (BBC News 2018a). However, the same evening an effigy of the pope was incinerated in Lewes – as it is every year. This very traditional festival of English nationalism and sectarianism is attended by thousands of people and reported as a 'folk' event (BBC News 2018b).

public and the private sphere, now, it was said, international capital had no particular connection to sectarianism. Like the British government, international capital could be judged to be one of the sources for the emergence of a new, post-sectarian society.[9]

There were two main flaws in this presumption. First, while government departments may not have been in the hands of sectarian ministers and capital investment not in the hands of sectarian owners and CEOs (in the past, often the same people), the day-to-day administration of government and capital was in the hands of local managers. They had been fully socialised in the local rules of sectarianism and were capable of ensuring the continuation of the sectarian *status quo*. Employment differentials in the civil service and in skilled engineering remained relatively undented as a result of the supposed arrival of modernity. This is why the issue of fair employment became so fraught in the 1980s. The direct rule administration had introduced a Fair Employment Agency (FEA), tasked to monitor the effectiveness of new fair employment law to end discrimination in employment. Despite some initial claims to success in relation to the most blatant of sectarian hiring practices, it quickly came up against the reality that law and persuasion were not fundamentally changing the employment structures of various sectors of the workforce. More was needed; but there was a limit to what the FEA could do. Reverse or positive discrimination was forbidden by law, thus shutting off the possibilities of quotas or preferential treatment to less advantaged minorities in the workforce. In the days before such innovations as BEE in South Africa,[10] the most the FEA could do was advise firms to try harder to recruit less represented workers.

It took the example of another South African intervention to eventually change matters in the North of Ireland. In 1977, African American preacher Rev. Leon Sullivan initiated a boycott of investment in South Africa. The simple but effective core of the campaign was to persuade US firms and investors to sign up to a set of principles stating they would not invest in South African firms or initiatives without guarantees that there was a distinct local programme to employ more Black workers. This was taken up by a number of activists in relation to the North. The MacBride Principles were produced in 1984, named after Sean MacBride,[11] and had major success in the US. Their purpose was to ensure no US investment in firms in the North of Ireland without guarantees of correcting the sectarian imbalance in the workforce of those firms. As the level of US

---

[9] At the same time, there was little sense of a clean break. We should not overestimate the desire for multinational capital to dispense with custom and practice. As Mulholland records: 'When the American-owned chemicals plant, Du Pont, was sited in Derry in 1957, it was arranged that the Unionist Party would nominate the personnel manager in charge of recruitment for the first two years of operation' (2004).

[10] Black Economic Empowerment – a policy of affirmative action which went beyond improving the opportunities of underrepresented Black people for employment through, for example, targeted training, and improving outcomes through such policies as employment preference.

[11] Sean MacBride, son of Maud Gonne, had a varied career which involved at different times being Chief of Staff of the IRA, a founder member of Clann na Poblachta and a government minister in the South, and a founder member of Amnesty International. He had also been awarded both the Nobel Peace Prize and the Lenin Peace Prize.

investment in the North increased, this was an effective rider on the decisions of not only the central offices of companies in the US but also the investment funds of a substantial number of US states and cities when decisions were being considered about investment. Eventually 18 US states and 40 cities voted to implement the Principles. To take one example: the Comptroller of New York City managed an investment portfolio of pension funds totalling $100 million. Once New York City signed up to the MacBride Principles, firms such as Gallaher in Ballymena, Du Pont in Derry, Hughes Tool Company in East Belfast and Warne Surgical in Craigavon, all US-owned, could not avail of investment through the Comptroller's office without clear plans to employ more Catholic workers. In short, the painstaking but successful action of dismantling sectarian employment practices owes much to the efforts of activists rather than the supposedly non-sectarian direct rule politicians and administrators. In fact, during the late 1980s, the British state was investing more on preventing US states and cities signing up to the MacBride Principles than advancing fair employment in the North (McNamara 2010).

This draws attention to the second flaw in the presumption that British social democracy would lead to a new dawn in the North of Ireland. The personal attitudes of local managers for direct rule or foreign capital notwithstanding, as well as the possible lack of enthusiasm for pushing reform to its limits, the issue was ultimately not one of personnel but of structures.[12] The legacies of centuries of colonialism and conquest were embedded in material reality − such as the distribution of land, the distribution of wealth and power, the make-up of the skilled engineering sector, the geographical segmentation of the population, the policies and structures in relation to everything from the nature of the education system to the planning decisions regarding new roads, new towns and new universities. It was on and through this material reality that sectarian attitudes were built. A programme of reform could begin to affect change in some of these areas, and a highly robust programme of reform could undoubtedly bring about substantial transformation. But ultimately no programme of reform was ever going to alter the deep foundations of the nature of the state. That would require a more radical intervention than was intended through direct rule; in fact, arguably such a radical intervention on behalf of the metropolitan state would be impossible. The British state's programme, by design and default, was thus not one of anti-sectarianism but rather was about managing sectarianism. The British were not bent on dismantling the Northern state but in returning it to the *status quo ante*, albeit with the rougher edges of unionist discrimination removed.

Nothing spoke more eloquently of the lack of fundamental change than the issue of 'security'. In the years following 1972, the machinery of repression was perfected in many ways. A policy of 'Ulsterisation' (that is, local state forces rather than British

---

[12] One CEO of a US company turned up in Garvaghy Road, Portadown, in the late 1990s in support of local nationalists objecting to Orange parades through their area. At the same time the local branch of his firm employed fewer than 10 percent Catholics.

troops taking the lead role in policing and security) ensured that the police were to take the front line in terms of combating insurrection. Suspects had confessions extracted from them under duress during interrogation (Taylor 1980). For a sustained period, people were imprisoned on the word of supergrasses, former colleagues who had been persuaded to name names, sometimes very unreliably (Gifford 1984). A shoot-to-kill policy was in the ascendant for some time, leading John Stalker, the Deputy Chief Constable of Manchester, to proclaim:

> ...if a police force of the United Kingdom could, in cold blood, kill a seventeen-year-old youth with no terrorist or criminal convictions, and then plot to hide the evidence from a senior policeman deputed to investigate it, then the shame belonged to us all. This is the act of a Central American assassination squad... (Stalker 1989: 67)

Collusion between state forces and loyalist paramilitaries was crucial in allowing the latter to target both republican activists and nationalist civilians; according to a British government commissioned report, 85 per cent of the intelligence used by the loyalist Ulster Freedom Fighters in the 1980s to target nationalist and republican victims came from state forces (De Silva 2012; see also McGovern 2019). The Special Powers Act was erased, and along with it the possibility of internment without trial, but the Emergency Provisions Act 1973 and the Prevention of Terrorism Act 1974 ensured derogation from the full protections provided by law in a democratic society. The government-appointed Diplock Commission recommended the abolition of jury trials in 1974 and the British government complied. And so, it continued.

For some observers there seemed to be a profound contradiction involved. On the one hand a reform programme was making radical changes while on the other hand the apparatus of repression was being inexorably expanded. How was this contradiction to be solved?[13] For some, an over-emphasis on reform allowed them to ignore the repression or alternatively to see it as a reaction to the unnecessary and despicable violence emanating from illegal loyalist and republican military groups. The army were merely 'piggy in the middle' (Hamill 1986), the police were 'holding the line' (see the autobiography of a former Chief Constable of the RUC, Hermon 1997). Admittedly sometimes there were bad apples, excessive reactions or bad decisions, but if the 'terrorists' would simply disappear, the reform programme could be freed to work its

---

[13] The contradiction seemed to be neatly represented by the two direct rule ministers. Secretary of State Roy Mason (1976-1979) came to the job determined that 'Ulster has had enough of initiatives.' He increased security and managed the process of Ulsterisation. He brought in the SAS. And he set out to remove special category status from politically motivated prisoners which led to a lengthy 'blanket protest' and eventually the republican prisoner hunger strikes of 1980 and 1981 in which ten prisoners starved to death. Mason's deputy, Robert Henry Mond, 4th Baron Melchett, had responsibility for health and social services, education, sports and the arts. He increased teacher numbers, leaving the North with the best pupil/teacher ratio in the UK. Additionally, he saw through a Bill which allowed for the beginning of the integrated sector in education. Where Mason was so unpopular with republicans that he had strict security until his dying day, Melchett had no problem later confronting and even breaking the law as an environmentalist campaigner, being arrested on one occasion for helping destroy GM crops.

magic. For others, the reform agenda was at best destined to failure, at worst a cynical mask for the real and unchanged nature of the state, namely, an institution built on violence and the repression of the nationalist community.

In reality, there was no contradiction between reform and repression; both were strategies of the same state, ultimately designed for the same outcome: the management of conflict, division and violence within Northern Ireland (O'Dowd, Rolston and Tomlinson 1980). The value of this analysis is that it does not downplay the substance of either reform or repression. No matter the convolutions of reform, the fact was that reform was real. As the eyes of the world were watching the North in the late 1960s and early 1970s, it became increasingly difficult for Britain to ignore or condone the discriminatory nature of its client state. More tellingly, in as far as the reform programme worked, it would win the hearts and minds of nationalists. As with the Act of Union, the hope was that direct rule would curtail the excesses of the local administrators and politicians, thereby convincing nationalists that it was worth having a stake in the system; this would avert more cataclysmic changes which could lead to the total alienation of the nationalist population with the possibility of the emergence of a 'popish democracy' antagonistic to the Union.

Overall, the reforms brought about as a result of the British intervention should not be dismissed. The Orange state may not have been dealt a fatal blow, but it would assuredly never manage to be the same again. At the core of the project was the double-edged policy of both wooing and controlling Catholics; or, more to the point, wooing one class while controlling the other.[14] For the Catholic middle class this was a remarkable opportunity. What was on offer for them was something which had never been on offer before, namely citizenship. It is noteworthy that from the time of civil rights, the struggles engaged in by this class were over reforming the state; that is, theirs was a politics which, for all that it may have been couched in terms of the possibility of a reunified Ireland at some distant future point, was confined within the borders of the Northern Ireland state. At the same time, it should not be presumed that this pragmatism constituted a recognition of those borders once and for all or indeed identification with union. Their loyalty to the British-sponsored social democratic state was not guaranteed; it was highly dependent on substance. As with the struggle for Black civil rights in the US, as long as the Catholic middle class benefited from a foothold in the system, their more or less enthusiastic participation could be counted on. But if their incorporation

---

[14] In the mid-1980s the Northern Ireland Office began to withhold money from community schemes on the grounds that they had, in the words of Secretary of State Douglas Hurd, 'sufficiently close links with paramilitary organisations to ... have the effect of improving the standing and furthering the aims of a paramilitary organisation'. This included a creche in West Belfast! At the same time funding was increasingly targeted towards groups in the same, mainly nationalist areas which had close links with the SDLP or the Catholic Church. This revealed the true counter-insurgency purpose of the policy which became known as political vetting, attempting to stem the inexorable rise of Sinn Féin in the aftermath of the hunger strikes (see Rolston 1990).

was stunted, denied or disrespected, there was the chance that they would once again feel alienated.

As for the Catholic working class, it is doubtful if they ever felt anything else but alienated during this whole reform period. The most blatant edges of sectarian discrimination had been blunted, but the exercise of security managed to impact on their lives in significant ways. The fact that, for example, they would be stopped and searched on the way to a Gaelic football match by the Ulster Defence Regiment[15] rather than the B Specials did not seem like a radical reform. Increasingly many of them voted for the republican party, Sinn Féin, some despite the party's links to the IRA and some because of those links. The initial Act of Union had differential meanings for different sections of Irish Catholics: introducing ways in which many could be incorporated into the Union while letting a million others die. The Act of Union 2.0, less dramatically but no less surely, settled down into a joint policy of incorporation and coercion. And as with the first Act of Union, the dynamic now involved an infinitely stronger, more powerful state formation. Anyone engaging critically with this formation was now directly confronting the British state.

The evil of banality: the community relations/good relations paradigm

The Northern Ireland Community Relations Commission (CRC) was established on 29 August 1969 to advise government on ways to improve community relations and to encourage better community relations with groups across the sectarian divide. The Commission was modelled on an existing British intervention on race and suffered from the same shortcomings of that intervention in Britain. In the Northern Ireland scenario, there was an initial confusion as to what might be involved in the face of what looked like the meltdown of unionist governance. Bringing Protestants and Catholics together seemed elusive in a situation where the most likely encounters would be between people who needed them least. At an early stage, therefore, a more oblique strategy was begun, that of community development. The logic was that if working class groups could gain confidence through what came to be called single identity work, organising on their immediate social concerns – such as housing conditions or local amenities – they might eventually see the value of cooperating with working class groups on the other side organising on similar issues. The logic was similar to that of the trade unions in the North, seeking to unite workers by focusing on common concerns. The vibrant community sector which had emerged owed its vitality to several factors, not least the need to fill the hiatus left by the failure of statutory agencies to deliver in working

---

[15] The Ulster Defence Regiment was the largest infantry regiment in the British Army. It was formed in 1970 and in effect replaced the B Specials as a force raised solely in the North for duties solely in the North. It had a strongly colonial character; while the rank and file were local, most officers were British. Initially 20 percent of the membership was Catholic, but by 1979, that had slipped to 2 percent, leaving the Regiment even more like the B Specials. It was disbanded in 1992.

class areas. The Catholic working class was particularly adept at such organising. The community development programme of the CRC played some part in encouraging and supporting that sector.

The CRC lasted from December 1969 until March 1974. It was disbanded by Ivan Cooper, Minister of Community Relations, in the power-sharing executive which emerged from the Sunningdale talks the previous year. Cooper's logic was that such a commission was necessary in 1969 when the nationalist population and the government were alienated from each other, but that now that the 'mainly Catholic' SDLP[16] was sharing power with Brian Faulkner's Unionist Party of Northern Ireland: 'There is no longer any need for any section of the community to feel excluded from government or to fear that government may be unsympathetic to them.'[17] The least that could be concluded is that his enthusiasm was premature.

The significant development indicated by his ministerial role and his logic was that some nationalists had been persuaded to participate in the system. As it turned out, the power-sharing executive did not long outlast the CRC; it was brought down by a loyalist-enforced general work stoppage in May 1974 and direct rule was reinstated. Brief as it was, this experiment went far beyond anything prior in the history of the unionist state. Nationalists had only taken on the role of official opposition in the unionist state late in the day and only for a very brief period. Now nationalists were in government under a premier who, as Minister of Home Affairs, had overseen the introduction of the disastrous policy of internment without trial only two and a half years previously.[18] The bubble of nationalist political exclusion had been burst. The SDLP went on to play the role of official opposition to the unionists in the various political arenas of the direct rule state. Their incorporation was not final and beyond doubt, however. Technically the party still supported the goal of a united Ireland – or as party leader John Hume came to call it, 'a unified Ireland', a phrase which neatly sidesteps constitutional questions such as partition and the legitimacy of the Northern Ireland state. The British had tried something which unionism had never attempted – inviting nationalists in from the cold. The nationalist acceptance indicated that they would acknowledge the parameters of the state and by extension the Union, at least for the foreseeable future.[19]

---

[16] Ivan Cooper was the only Protestant of significance in the SDLP; he had previously been a liberalising member of the Young Unionists. His presence was enough to justify the 'mainly Catholic' qualifier. It was destined never to be the social democratic party it set out to be but rather the latest version of a nationalist party in the North.

[17] Northern Ireland Assembly Reports, 4 April 1974

[18] Internment without trial was announced by the arrest of over 300 men in the early morning of 9 August 1971. All but one of those arrested were from the nationalist community, even though the loyalist Ulster Volunteer Force had been militarily active from 1966, two years before the Provisional IRA appeared. The one non-nationalist arrested originally was an anarchist who later wrote two books on the subject, one of which detailed the torture of 11 men (the 'hooded men') in the days after the initial round-up. It was February 1973 before any loyalists were interned. See McGuffin 1973 and 1974.

[19] After Bloody Sunday, Hume caused a stir when he allegedly said, 'It's a united Ireland now or nothing.'

This was in many ways a logical outcome of the civil rights campaign which had produced nationalist leaders such as Hume and Cooper. They may not have been demanding 'British rights for British citizens', but their quest for citizenship was confined within the boundaries of the Union. In terms of British management of its volatile client state, this was a major success. The reform programme was about ameliorating the state, not dismantling it, and it had found willing partners in the 'constitutional nationalism' of the SDLP.

That the CRC should have been thought of as one of the first vehicles of reform and that it survived through the first few deadly years of the conflict gives the clue to the fundamental premise of British policy. This was to contain the conflict within the North, and within the working class ghettos in particular through whatever repressive means necessary, while at the same time encouraging better community relations (O'Dowd, Rolston and Tomlinson 1982). It was the long-term reform-repression dyad that came to dominate right up to the GFA. The bottom line was that it was a policy to shore up the state, not dismantle it.

This community relations paradigm was modelled on the race relations approach which had been developed in the mid to late 1960s in Britain. Numerous criticisms have been made of this approach (Sivanandan 1985), the most damning being that it places the onus on the subaltern to accommodate to an unjust system and therefore does not ultimately challenge the structures of inequality and injustice. While some activists urged a more radical approach of confronting the deeply racialised structures of capital and state in Britain, this was beyond the brief and indeed capability of the state. Audre Lorde (2018) made the broader philosophical point to those tempted to engage with such compromise: 'The master's tools will never dismantle the master's house'. The similarity with sectarian structures in the North of Ireland is clear, as is the impossibility of the state confronting those structures – a state founded on sectarian principles cannot be the primary agent for dismantling sectarianism. The state therefore chose the easier option: to persuade people to put up with each other and to work together where possible. There was an arena of tolerance, the confines of which were the state and the Union. The colonial nexus between England and Ireland was to be ignored or denied.

The strategy requires a dyadic relationship between opposing groups now willing to accept the parameters and contribute accordingly. This was epitomised by the power-sharing executive of 1974. The problem is that, while the reformist institutions can display adequate evidence of incorporation and acceptance, there is always the risk of the deeper structures making their relevance felt. The epicentres of such convulsions can appear relatively simple: the killing of one more Black teenager such as Stephen

---

What had occurred was that he gave an interview to a reporter on the walls of Derry and, pointing down to the nationalist Bogside area, said: 'Many people down there feel now that it's a united Ireland or nothing'. He then went on to criticise the British army and to point out how more difficult the task of working within the system would be for nationalists. See McLaughlin 2006: 163.

Lawrence which reveals the institutional racism of the police and thereby the state;[20] the killing of one more nationalist such as Robert Hamill which indicates similarly the nature of the RUC and the sectarian structures they protect;[21] the killing by police of George Floyd in Minneapolis in May 2020 which catalysed the ongoing BLM intervention against systemic racism around the world.

The other striking feature of the 'community relations' paradigm was that, although it was clearly modelled on UK and US state interventions on race, sectarianism was to be understood as something different to racism. Despite the obvious resonances, under direct rule community relations practitioners proved reluctant to address the racism experienced by BAME (Black, Asian and minority ethnic) communities in Northern Ireland.[22] The sector played little part in the efforts to extend some form of British anti-racism legislation to Northern Ireland and it was made clear that racism and sectarianism were to be understood as separated discourses.

This all changed, however, in the wake of the GFA – even though neither community relations nor good relations had featured in the GFA negotiations. Now 'good relations' quickly began to define the emerging post-GFA state formation. There were three key stages in the evolution of this good relations paradigm. First, the concept of 'good relations' appeared from nowhere in legislation in Section 75(2) of the Northern Ireland Act 1998 which gave effect to the GFA. Section 75 committed public authorities to promote equality of opportunity across a range of constituencies: gender, disability, religious belief, political opinion, racial group, age, marital status or sexual orientation. But it went further to state that, 'a public authority shall in carrying out its functions relating to Northern Ireland have regard to the desirability of promoting good relations between persons of different religious belief, political opinion or racial group'. Ostensibly this commitment to good relations replaced the notion of 'parity of esteem' coined by the Agreement and without any grounding in existing practice or law. In short, this new phase in 'relations' interventions did two key things. First, it signalled that 'good relations' rather than 'community relations' was to be the key concept in this new statutory approach. Second, it made clear that this notion of good relations was to *include* race and *exclude* other equality grounds.

By 2004 the racism/sectarianism synthesis within good relations was complete (McVeigh and Rolston 2007). When the Community Relations Council launched its *A*

---

[20] Nineteen-year-old Stephen Lawrence died after a racist attack in London in 1993. An inquiry led by Sir William Macpherson found that the Metropolitan Police had viewed the incident as a fight rather than an attack and had therefore not robustly pursued evidence to prosecute the main suspects. He termed this 'institutional racism'; see Macpherson 1999.

[21] 25-year-old nationalist Robert Hamill was kicked unconscious by a large group of loyalists in Portadown in April 1997 while members of the RUC watched from a nearby vehicle. He died twelve days later. Police initially treated the incident as a sectarian fight rather than an assault and some of the perpetrators were given advice by one police officer as to how to avoid detection. See Rolston 2000: 275-284.

[22] Thus, the definitive CRC publication *Approaches to Community Relations Work* made no reference to race or racism (Fitzduff 1991).

Good Relations Framework: An Approach to the Development of Good Relations, 'dealing with' racism had been unambiguously integrated into the community relations/good relations paradigm (2004: 5). In 2005, the NIO centred this approach in the philosophy of the new state with *A Shared Future: Policy and Strategic Framework for Good Relations*. Finally, in 2013 this approach was endorsed by the post-St Andrews power-sharing executive with the appearance of *Together: Building a United Community Strategy* (T:BUC). This strategy reflected, 'the Executive's commitment to improving community relations and continuing the journey towards a more united and shared society … where cultural expression is celebrated and embraced and where everyone can live, learn, work and socialise together, free from prejudice, hate and intolerance'.

The contradictions of 'good relations' are at their most extreme when they overlap with issues that *should* be more central to criminal justice. Since hate crime might be regarded as the quintessential example of 'bad relations', it is unclear why some equality constituencies should be addressed by good relations while others – such as lesbian, gay, bisexual and transgender rights – should not. Overall, the T:BUC document collapsed the difference between racism and sectarianism in Northern Ireland almost completely (OFMDFM 2014). The new paradigm of 'good relations' was used to integrate racism and sectarianism and separate them from other rights issues. They had become 'twin blights' to be addressed together. Just as importantly, however, they were presented as something to be addressed separately from other forms of violence or discrimination or hate.

Why does it matter that all this ideological effort goes into this nebulous concept of 'good relations'? It might seem at worst a victimless crime. The good relations state is characterised by the blandness of neutralism. Its quintessence is banality – since this representation can offend nobody and must include everybody, it is both shallow and inane. We find this everywhere in manifestations of the new state. For example, the new PSNI emblem offered a veritable cornucopia of competing and contradictory elements – at least the crown dominant above the harp on the badge of the RIC and RUC left no ambiguity with its symbolism.[23] The most troubling aspect of this approach is that it assumes that it cannot be offensive since its defining quality is that it should not offend. Sadly, however, this is not true. Thus, the semiotics of good relations becomes a key part of a process of *not* naming the real issues: of silencing that which needs to be said and repressing that which needs to be confronted.

This is evident in a sustained state policy in recent years of transforming public space in the name of 'shared space' – creating shopping malls, peace bridges and public art in prominent places. But what is there to be shared in this shared space? All too often it is

---

[23] Around the St. Andrew's saltire – itself a British invention – there are six symbols representing 'different and shared traditions': the Scales of Justice; a crown (but *not* the St Edward's Crown worn by or representing the British Sovereign); a harp (but *not* the Brian Boru harp used as the emblem of the Irish Republic); a torch; an olive branch; and a shamrock.

nothing more than shopping. Consumerism is the most facile of interactions and yet it is at the core of the rebranding of the city centres of Belfast and Derry as well as a number of out-of-town malls. In the new Northern Ireland these places become temples not simply of consumerism but of social transformation.

If the claims for consumerism are fragile, those for a lot of public art are threadbare. For example, approaching Belfast on the motorway from the west is a large structure of two geodesic domes, one inside the other. It is titled 'Rise'. The claims for 'Rise' are particularly grand. It stands in a large area of empty space where motorway and roads converge. On one side is a Catholic working class area and on the other a Protestant working class area; it is what is known in Belfast as an interface zone where stone-throwing between teenagers is not uncommon. So, what is the point of 'Rise'? According to the promotional literature, 'it says confidence, it says outward-looking, it says international'. The hidden message is more definitive. The sculpture says: don't look at the local economic and social conditions either side of the roundabout, don't look at the political tensions between communities, don't look at massive youth unemployment and high youth suicide rates nearby, don't mention the war and don't dwell on the past. 'Rise' is supposed to aid reconciliation by looking to the future and seeking to bring about local economic transformation through tourism. But the tourists don't come to this spot; the most they see is a brief glimpse of the sculpture as their bus passes. More to the point, the tourists will never spend any money in these adjoining communities which might be a vehicle for some sort of economic transformation, however slight. And as for reconciliation: there is no evidence that the sculpture speaks to local people. This alienation is evident in this and other public art in the most fundamental of ways; the artists are not local; the forms are generic with the slight gloss of a name which seems to speak to local history and concerns but could quite easily exist elsewhere under a different name. They are supposed to be unique to the place but are in fact global, an exercise in 'staged authenticity' (Hocking 2015) where all the complexity, ambiguity and contradiction of the local has been removed.

In consequence, the hegemony of 'good relations' creates a profound and terrible doublethink in contemporary Northern Ireland. On the one hand, the whole social formation signals its commitment to 'good relations'. A DUP first minister and Sinn Féin deputy first minister – both ex-prisoners – can introduce T:BUC as 'a clear choice to move away from division, and instead establish a new, reconciled and shared society'. *Everybody* 'unites against hate' – the British and Irish governments, Sinn Féin and the DUP, the PSNI and the loyalist paramilitaries and everybody else in between. At the same time, the genocidal imperative decorates a gable end in almost every working class community. The instruction – KILL ALL TAIGS or KILL ALL HUNS[24] – sits festering, untouched – except by wind and weather – for decades. In a good relations state, everybody has united against hate and yet nobody bears any responsibility for removing graffiti that

---

[24] 'Taig' is a derogatory, racist term for a Catholic.

encourage people to commit genocide against their neighbours. That, in essence, is the problem with 'good relations'.

The peace process

The Direct Rule interregnum appeared to come to a definitive end as the Good Friday Agreement (GFA) emerged from the Irish peace process of the 1990s. A combination of war-weariness and a growing recognition that no side could win the ongoing war meant that all parties had some interest in a peace settlement. Northern Ireland's present devolved system of government is based on the GFA. The GFA also created several transnational institutions between Northern Ireland and the Republic of Ireland, and between the Republic of Ireland and the United Kingdom. The Agreement is made up of two inter-related documents:

> the *British-Irish Agreement* – an international agreement between the British and Irish governments; and
>
> the *Multi-Party Agreement* – involving eight political parties from across the political spectrum in Northern Ireland. (Crucially, this excluded the DUP and the UUP was profoundly split on the issue.)

The Agreement set out a complex series of provisions relating to a number of areas including:

> The status and system of government of Northern Ireland within the United Kingdom. (Strand 1)
>
> The relationship between Northern Ireland and the Republic of Ireland. (Strand 2)
>
> The relationship between the Republic of Ireland and the United Kingdom. (Strand 3)

There were a number of novel, indeed radical aspects of the Agreement. First, it committed the Irish government (and the northern nationalist parties) to accepting the current constitutional status of the North as a part of the UK. This required the Irish government to amend its constitution to remove Articles 2 and 3 which claimed jurisdiction over the North. Second, it situated the British government as technically neutral on the long-term constitutional position of Northern Ireland – there was no mention of 'our precious union' here. Third, it committed all parties in the North, including republicans, to non-violent means of political change, acknowledging that constitutional change could only be by consent. Fourth, it recognised that Northern Ireland would remain a part of the UK for as long as a majority of its citizens agreed, while at the same time allowing for a border poll to be held at an unspecified future date on the issue of leaving the UK.

The Agreement was approved by voters across the island of Ireland in two referendums held on 22 May 1998. In Northern Ireland, voters were asked whether they supported the multi-party Agreement. In the Republic of Ireland, voters were asked whether they would allow the state to sign the Agreement and allow necessary constitutional changes to facilitate it. The people of both jurisdictions needed to approve the Agreement to give effect to it. This was not, however, an expression of all-Ireland democracy in action. The two parts of Ireland did not vote on the same issue and there was little exploration of what might be implied if either part had voted the 'wrong way'.[25] Even more basically of course the votes were not aggregated. Thus, this was not an expression of self-determination by the Irish people; at best, it might be regarded as a simultaneous self-determination by the peoples of Northern Ireland and Southern Ireland. Either way, the British-Irish Agreement came into force on 2 December 1999.

The DUP was the only major political group in Northern Ireland to oppose the GFA. It was, however, subsequently integrated into the process through the St Andrew's Agreement of 2006 – thus belatedly accepting the legitimacy of the GFA. At this point the two major parties in Northern Ireland, the DUP and Sinn Féin – which represented widely different constituencies – entered the power-sharing government together. It looked for a period as if the GFA state was secure and functioning relatively successfully.

This was no small achievement. The post-GFA Northern Ireland state emerged from 80 years of a permanent state of emergency and 30 years of 'the troubles'. The state was newly legitimised in the process – the repudiation of political violence by (most) republicans and the acceptance of partition – whether on a temporary or a permanent basis – by all parties to the Agreement meant that it emerged as a much more stable formation. The mopping up of the vestiges of anti-state violence that has continued through the intervening period has seen a consolidation of that process. This contemporary normality, however, looks very different to what was promised by the GFA.

The Agreement reads as a sophisticated version of a very simple negotiation: peace in exchange for human rights and equality; an end to non-state political violence in exchange for guarantees of an end to state injustice and inequality. In other words, *de facto* recognition for the state – and more specifically acceptance of the state monopoly on the use of legitimate force – was conceded on the basis that the equality and human rights agendas would remove the most egregious inequalities and abuses that led to the support for political violence in the first place. Again, the implications of this are pretty clear – republicans would stop using political violence against the state – and the reformed state would reform the institutionalised sectarianism that had characterised the state as well as dismantle the repressive apparatus – itself profoundly sectarianised – that kept the state in place. The GFA deal held the promise that the state would (and could) become 'post-sectarian'.

Essentially, therefore, the GFA was about a reconfiguration of the dynamics of

---

[25] In the North, the question on the ballot was: 'Do you support the Agreement reached at the multi-party talks on Northern Ireland and set out in Command Paper 3883?' In the South the wording was: 'Do you approve of the proposal to amend the Constitution contained in the undermentioned Bill, Nineteenth Amendment of the Constitution Bill, 1998?' There was an 81.1 per cent turnout in the North, with 71.1 per cent voting Yes and 28.9 per cent voting No. In the South the turnout was 55.6 per cent – 94.4 per cent Yes and 5.6 per cent No.

sectarianism in the Northern Ireland state. On the one hand, it recognised the 'right to freedom from sectarian harassment' – even if, for all the genuine changes associated with the peace process, neither sectarian violence nor sectarian incitement had disappeared. However, the GFA and, more particularly, the new state formation that emerged from it, was a reworking rather than a transcending of sectarianism. It engendered not so much a society free from sectarianism as one in which sectarianism was institutionalised in new forms. It achieved this in an unprecedented way with the creation of an Assembly legitimised through the necessity for cross-community support for its decisions. This means: (a) the support of a majority of the members voting, a majority of the designated nationalists voting and a majority of the designated unionists voting; or (b) the support of 60 per cent of the members voting, 40 per cent of the designated nationalists voting and 40 per cent of the designated unionists voting.

In other words, there was an absolute privileging of 'sectarian' nationalist/unionist politics to the exclusion of all other possible forms of political expression or affiliation. The sectarian self-designation and the consequences of that for voting do nothing to encourage a middle ground. Rather they reward parties which can build deeper and more secure bunkers. There was a logic to such structures in terms of protecting minority rights, something that majoritarianism in the unionist state had never succeeded in doing. But the downside was that from this point onwards sectarianism was embedded in the institutions of the new state. The post-GFA state reconfigured sectarianism – constitutionalizing and institutionalizing it in new forms. Underlying all of this, the state required some degree of ideological legitimacy and found it in the notion of 'good relations'. Its troika remains 'interdependence' 'diversity' and 'equity' – a commitment to 'equality' still proved to be a bridge too far for the NI state.

At the same time, it would be wrong to suggest that nothing had changed. Social relations across Northern Ireland are very different now to what they were in 1921 or 1972 or 1998. By the 1980s, bastions of Protestant employment, such as the civil service, were witnessing an inflow of Catholics, albeit in the first instance at the lower and middle ranks. Basil Brooke may have once boasted of not having a Catholic about the place, but now the corridors of state administration were full of them. Other formerly 'Protestant' strongholds such as Queen's University were similarly transformed, with previously unionist faculties such as Law now teaching a majority of nationalist students. Eventually some of these students would become Catholic magistrates, judges and other key people across the justice system.[26] Some Catholics were offered knighthoods and British honours and, unlike in previous eras, happily accepted them. Where before loyalists would insist on referring to the region as 'Ulster' and republicans as 'the North of Ireland', never 'Northern Ireland', now a new term entered the lexicon of identity

---

[26] By 2015, the Attorney General, the Lord Chief Justice, the Director of Public Prosecutions and the Police Ombudsman were all Northern Ireland-born Catholics.

consciousness: 'Northern Irish'.[27] In the 1980s, southern-born boxer Barry McGuigan used his family connections to the North to take British citizenship in order to fight at the Commonwealth Games, thereby incurring the wrath of many nationalists.[28] But in 2017 Catholic-born golfer Rory McIlroy said he was unlikely to compete in the 2020 Olympic Games because he viewed himself as Northern Irish rather than Irish or British. He subsequently suggested that he would most likely represent Ireland at the Olympics (BBC News 2019b).

The issue of identity is a nebulous one. Specifically, it raises the question of how identity might translate into political behaviour. A Northern Ireland Life and Times Survey in 2017 found that 33 per cent of those surveyed self-identified as unionist, 25 per cent as nationalist, and 40 per cent as neither (Wilson 2017: 23). The evidence is that support for a united Ireland is three times greater among people who identify as Irish Catholics (59 per cent) than among those who identify as Northern Irish Catholics (21 per cent) (Garry and McNicholl 2015). Protestants who identify as British Protestants are 'unionist' by a proportion of 2 to 1 while those who identify as Northern Irish Protestants are almost evenly divided between 'unionists' and 'neither unionist nor nationalist'. Fewer people in Northern Ireland think of themselves as British than in any other UK region, with 82 per cent seeing themselves as 'strongly British' in England, 79 per cent in Wales, 59 per cent in Scotland and only 47 per cent in Northern Ireland (Devenport 2018a). The percentage seeing themselves as British was less than those who described themselves as Irish (58.6 per cent), Northern Irish (57.9 per cent), or European (56.7 per cent).

Twenty-nine per cent of those from a Protestant background defined themselves as Irish, but only 4 per cent of those from a Catholic background identified as British. More than eight out of ten Protestants described themselves as British or Northern Irish. More than nine out of ten Catholics said they were Irish and more than eight out of ten Catholics described themselves as European. Finally, support for a united Ireland is stronger amongst younger voters. Amongst those surveyed under the age of 45, 49 per cent backed a united Ireland and 38 per cent preferred staying in the UK.

There is some evidence here of the rise of a 'Northern Irish' identity challenging the traditional identities of British and Irish. However, it is not enough to conclude that the GFA has worked some sort of magic or to lend credence to John Hume's view that people in the North were moving towards post-nationalism, in some Irish version of the 'end of history' thesis. There are at least two reasons for caution. First, even if acquiescence in the good relations strategy, or embracing a new identity of 'Northern Irishness', can be judged as post-nationalist, it cannot thereby be presumed to be pro-unionist. Northern Catholics

---

[27] One interesting element of this is that the term contained a reference to Ireland; people were not seeing themselves as 'West British' for example. This could lead to the question whether, when the chips are down, the Irish part of the identity might come to the fore.

[28] He had the advantage that he could also use his 'Irish' origins to fight for the South when he wanted.

are not demanding equality of citizenship as British. They are not rushing to join unionist parties, not least because there is little sign that they would be welcomed.[29] What they may therefore be expressing is a neo-nationalism rather than a post-nationalism; beneath the surface important elements of nationalist culture and identity remain which can easily be persuaded to surface in the face of unionist posturing, disrespect or denial.

This signals the second flaw in Hume's argument: post-nationalism requires its mirror image in post-unionism, and there is frequent evidence of the failure of the other supposed partner in the community relations dyad to play its full part. Neo-unionism, even liberal unionism, is an endangered species. Unionist leaders occasionally point to the need for unionism to modernise in order to attract Catholics,[30] but, as we shall see, the actual phenomenon of post-sectarian unionism is as rare as hen's teeth.

The most important development of all from the peace process was peace itself – arguably this was the 'peace dividend'. Of course, widespread political violence continued at various points and political killings also occurred.[31] The response of some politicians was less than might have been expected during a peace process. For example, on 8 May 2006, a 15-year-old Catholic boy, Michael McIlveen, died in hospital after having been beaten with baseball bats when cornered by a group of Protestant youths in his home town of Ballymena the previous evening. Roy Gillespie, a local DUP councillor, offered the following opinion: 'As a Catholic, he won't be going to heaven unless he has been saved. If he did not repent before he died and asked the Lord into his heart, he will not get to heaven. Catholics are not accepted into heaven' (*Irish News* 2006). Some politicians at least remained as far away from post-sectarianism as it was possible to be.

Nevertheless, the GFA still represents a watershed on the levels of political violence and conflict across the state. Northern Ireland is certainly – for most people at least – a more peaceful and less frightening place to live in than it was before 1998. But it has also unambiguously continued along the trajectory of more repression/more reform. At the very dawn of the new iteration of the state – in the aftermath of the Omagh Bomb – draconian *new* emergency legislation was passed to further supplement the infrastructure of coercion that had been assembled since 1920. This surpassed anything that had been used by either Stormont or the direct rule state. The potential for repression had been ratcheted up another gear in the context of the state's increased legitimacy. There was an

---

[29] Prior to the GFA there was only one Catholic who had served as a minister in the Northern Ireland government, Gerard Benedict Newe, Minister of State from 1971 to 1972. In 1996 John Gorman, a lieutenant in the Irish Guards during WWII and later an RUC District Inspector stood successfully as an Ulster Unionist Party MLA for North Down. More recently, Stephen McCarthy was coopted as an Ulster Unionist Party councillor onto Antrim and Newtownabbey Council in 2017. He is a working class Catholic West Belfast man whose grandfather was killed by loyalists in 1991.

[30] See, for example, DUP leader Peter Robinson's admonition that, 'Unionism must reach far beyond its traditional base if it is to maximise its potential. That means forming a pro-Union consensus with people from different religious and community backgrounds' (*Belfast Telegraph*, 30 March 2012).

[31] The PSNI recorded 158 'security-related' killings since the signing of the Agreement. See Nolan 2018.

often-quoted trope at the time of the peace process – 'peace is not the absence of conflict but rather the presence of justice'. If this is true, Northern Ireland still has a way to go before it might be regarded as being 'at peace'.

A good relations economy?

The political collapse of the Stormont state in 1972 overlapped with the less dramatic crumbling of its economic base. The rapid success of Stormont's 1960s industrialisation policy had hidden for a time a twofold flaw at its heart. Firstly, the over-reliance on one production sector could be disastrous if that sector were to decline. This is precisely what happened in the 1980s as most of the big synthetic fibre producers closed operations. This was a particular problem for the Protestant working class. Many of the firms had been established in places like East Antrim, the area of the North with the largest proportion of Protestants. The loss of jobs – over 80,000 in East Antrim in 1982 alone – was a devastating blow. However, the blow was somewhat cushioned as a result of the violent conflict. Employment opportunities opened up for Protestant men in particular in security and defence. At the height of the conflict, one in ten Protestant males was employed in this sector (Rowthorn and Wayne 1988: 112).

The second problem was that the incentives were almost too good to be true. They were touted internationally along with breathless claims about the productivity and low wages of labour in the North. This pitch managed to attract relatively footloose international capital which had no organic connections to the locality and was content to move on when higher productivity, lower wages or more enticing incentives were available elsewhere, in Asia or Eastern Europe. Some dubious endeavours were also attracted to the North. For example, in the late 1970s the North's Industrial Development Board competed ruthlessly with the Republic and Puerto Rico to attract the De Lorean Motor Company. Four years and £80 million of investment later, the firm folded.

Since then, there has been little strategic success in altering the Northern Ireland economic base. The long, slow decline of the old industrial base continued while none of the international capital that came offered any sense of longevity or security. For much of the conflict it survived as a war economy – a militaristic Keynesianism that increased dependency on the public sector and the security sector in particular. During this period, it was famously characterised as 'more like an eastern European economy than eastern Europe'. In addition, it was referred to as a 'workhouse economy':

> A large part of its population is unemployed. Those who are not are chiefly engaged in servicing or controlling each other – through the provision of health, education, retail distribution, construction, security and social services. Relatively few people within the province are engaged in the production of tradeable goods and services which can be sold outside. (Rowthorn and Wayne 1988: 98)

This changed somewhat with the peace process. Throughout the 1990s, the Northern Ireland economy grew significantly as a result of a peace dividend alongside the knock-on benefits of the Celtic Tiger growth south of the border. By 2005, the economy was growing almost twice as fast as that of the UK as a whole. This period of growth was, however, undermined in the wider economic crash of 2008 and it has subsequently failed to recover. Most reviews of the Northern Ireland economy underline the general sense of underperformance and vulnerability. Concerns are generally expressed regarding productivity and the dependence on the public sector.[32] It would be stretching a point to characterise this as an 'economy of good relations' but the fetishizing of success of the *Game of Thrones* TV series (partially filmed in Northern Ireland, thereby leading to a major boost to the tourist industry) serves to highlight the dearth of less fantastic, more long-term economic initiative (Meredith 2018). This model was not without foundation – by 2019 a tapestry of *Game of Thrones* at Belfast's Ulster Museum had become the largest visitor attraction in Northern Ireland (Discover Northern Ireland 2019) – but in essence it remains a fantasy of a fantasy. In so far as the Executive had any less fantastical economic strategy this was emblemised by the commitment in the Stormont House Agreement (SHA) to reduce corporation tax in order to compete with the 26 counties. This – alongside a commitment to balance the public/private sector divide – was a key element in the SHA. This policy was not implemented because of the Executive collapse and looks unlikely in the aftermath of Covid-19.[33] So, what does the current economic base of the good relations state look like?

Overall, the Northern Ireland economy is in poor shape. It contrasts negatively with obvious comparators like Scotland and the south of Ireland (NISRA 2019a: 8). The *Belfast Telegraph* Top 100 Northern Ireland Companies provides a general profile. The list is dominated by banks and utilities companies, with only Bombardier, Moy Park and Schrader Electronics suggesting any wider economic base. The profile of the largest private sector employers is similarly limited – dominated as it is by companies servicing local demand. The contemporary profile confirms the significance of the public sector in terms of both employment and the wider economy. Thus, by far the largest employers are 'Public Authorities'. The NHS and the education sector – including the two universities – and the civil service remain crucial to the Northern Ireland economy.

---

[32] 'The Republic's economy is four times larger [than the North's], generated by a workforce that is only two and a half times bigger. The south's industrial output today is ten times that of the north. Exports from the Republic are 17 times greater than those from Northern Ireland...' (David McWilliams, *Irish Times*, December 2017; quoted in Gosling and McArt 2018: 9).

[33] The assumption that the lower rate of corporation tax was primarily responsible for the Celtic Tiger phenomenon in the Republic in the 1990s is challenged by the evidence, as PwC pointed out: 'it came nearly four decades after the initial opening to FDI, when the tax rate was zero... A comparison of 19 OECD countries found that tax policy had no discernible impact on foreign-direct-investment flows (Jensen, 2012, quoted in Wilson 2017: 21).

Overall, the contemporary profile contains few remnants of either the 'old' shipbuilding and heavy engineering or the 'new' artificial fibres industrial base – although Shorts/Bombardier remains the second largest private employer in the north. Northern Ireland's economy remains characterised by low investment, low productivity, low employment and low incomes. Even though the UK recovery has been the slowest on record, Northern Ireland has lagged behind even that – and is still further behind the recovery in the 26 counties – with only a modest upturn since 2013 (Wilson 2017: 17). Northern Ireland remains the poorest of the UK devolved jurisdictions in terms of living standards (Wilson 2017: 19).

The employment rate in Northern Ireland has remained below the pre-recession level. Moreover, skilled, well-paid jobs have been lost in recent high-profile closures and cutbacks – with Michelin and JTI Gallaher announcing shutdowns in Ballymena and ongoing cuts in the key east Belfast engineering hub of Bombardier and Harland & Wolff.[34] Such recovery as there has been is characterised as overly dependent on private consumption. This consumption is in turn heavily dependent, directly and indirectly, on the Westminster subvention balancing the excess of public expenditure over revenue in Northern Ireland (Wilson 2017: 18).

In short, the economic performance of the good relations state remains underwhelming – and heavily dependent on the public sector. In this context, the shifting dynamics of the labour market within the state have been at least as interesting as the changes in the economic base itself. Here the changes since 1972 have seen a more significant transformation. Catholic self-confidence has followed a (partial) reversal of traditional Protestant advantage – with the collapse of almost exclusively 'Protestant' male industries mirroring the growth of predominately 'Catholic' knowledge industries. This has further tipped the Protestant/Catholic imbalance alongside the vast reduction in state discrimination in most sectors. Significant migrant worker immigration followed post-GFA growth and contributed further to this demographic transition within the labour market.

In short, there is a distinctive emerging economic base to the new 'good relations' state formation. Moreover, it is markedly different to the economic base of Northern Ireland in 1921 or 1972. For example, Moy Park Ltd is now often regarded as Northern Ireland's largest company. Indeed, according to *Ulster Business*, Moy Park has been Northern Ireland's 'most successful company' for nearly a decade (Mulgrew 2019). Moy Park is hardly a blue riband company – it is a poultry processor – but it is a major employer. The story of Moy Park illustrates just how 'open' the economy has become. It is owned by the US-based Pilgrim's Pride Corporation which in turn is 79 per cent owned by a Brazilian company which itself bought Moy Park from another Brazilian

---

[34] In October 2019, the Northern Ireland section of Canadian-owned Bombardier, facing severe financial difficulties, was sold to the US firm Spirit AeroSystems. In the same month, Harland and Wolff was saved from closure at the last minute when bought by Infrastrata, a UK firm better known for energy 'prospecting'.

company in 2015 before selling it on to Pilgrim's Pride in 2017. Tellingly, Moy Park was also at the centre of the RHI story in terms of the 'corporate welfare' angle. Its disproportionately 'Catholic' workforce also contrasts starkly with earlier patterns. It also employs large numbers of migrant workers – indeed the company itself is a major pull factor in migrant worker migration to Northern Ireland. This reality begins to expose some of the limitations of the binary approach to labour market equality issues in contemporary Northern Ireland. While the headline totals give some sense of the disproportionate Protestant/Catholic ratio, they exclude migrant workers (here designated as 'N.D.' or 'non-determined'). At Moy Park, however, this migrant worker population is one third of the workforce and is larger than the Protestant proportion.

The actual breakdown of the workforce is Catholic (50 per cent), migrant worker/'other' (30 per cent), and Protestant (20 per cent). Moreover, among new appointees the migrant worker proportion is larger than the Protestant and Catholic totals combined.[35] Whatever their background, most of these workers are employed in a low-wage, low-skill employment – but the company might be characterised as both stable and successful. This example of one company is, of course, no more than a snapshot. Nevertheless, it might be regarded as an ideal type of the 'good relations' economy. It hardly needs emphasis that this iteration of Northern Ireland's 'most successful company' is a long way removed from Harland and Wolff in 1920 or Shorts in 1972 – or even Wrightbus in 2019.[36]

Separate but equal?

There may be a defining motif for the good relations state amid these structural changes. If Northern Ireland – in line with its economic base – is becoming *separate but equal,* this would undoubtedly mark a significant shift from its 'Protestant state' iteration. Contemporary Northern Ireland *is* indisputably a place in which representation and allocation is much more 'balanced' than it was before 1972. The post-GFA state has further evolved from Protestant majoritarianism towards institutionalising a form of sectarian balance across its structures – but this is very different from suggesting that the categories 'Protestant' and 'Catholic' no longer matter. In this regard, the comparison

---

[35] Because of the arcane contortions of the equality monitoring process under a 'good relations' regime, these NDs must be assumed to have no experience of – or potential to experience – 'religious or political' discrimination. They are thus removed from the percentage breakdown of the workforce. This category is reserved for 'Protestants' and 'Roman Catholics' (ECNI 2020a: 2). But the really striking thing about the Moy Park workforce is that it is now one-third migrant worker/people of colour – the first question on any equality agenda should be, 'What are the fair employment issues for this new group'?

[36] Based in Ballymena, Wrightbus is the largest bus manufacturer in the UK, employing 1,200 workers. It came close to closure in October 2019, being bought at the last moment by the English-based Bamford Bus Company. Its most recent fair employment returns indicate only 14 per cent Catholic employees with a similar proportion of 'other' (ECNI 2020c).

with pillarisation in the Netherlands and Belgium bears emphasis.[37] It is possible that the post-GFA state has achieved stability at the point at which the labour market – alongside the housing and education sectors – is segregated but broadly equal.

Historically the Northern Ireland labour market was one of the most contested arenas of all in terms of discrimination. This issue produced the first interventions of the reform aspects of direct rule in 1972. In 1976 the Fair Employment Act was established as well as an associated administrative intervention through the Fair Employment Agency. By 1989, the now Fair Employment Commission, FEC, Fair Employment Tribunal system and other policy interventions represented a fairly robust attempt to combat employment discrimination and inequality. While this did not end discrimination or inequality overnight, it marked a crucial corrective intervention in the existing sectarianised labour market. By and large, this intervention was successful (Muttarak et al. 2012). There is now a contemporary labour market that looks very different from that of 1921 – or indeed 1972. The traditional Protestant/Catholic dual labour market that characterised the 'Protestant state' for its entire duration has now largely gone.

The Northern Ireland Civil Service (NICS) is a paradigm case.[38] The Civil Service was one of the key institutions for complaint of sectarian bias under the old Stormont. Direct rule saw strenuous attempts by the British government to improve its record on the employment of Catholics and the grades and contexts in which they were employed. This involved not only the application of new fair employment legislation but also proactive policy engagement *within* the Civil Service itself. For example, at one time the Equal Opportunities Unit which was driving change within the Civil Service had more staff than the FEC which had responsibility for equality across the entire labour market. These efforts undoubtedly led to a radically changed workforce. By 2019, it was suggested that fair employment had been achieved: 'Overall the community background composition of the NICS is similar to that of its comparator population (1.8 percentage points difference)' (NISRA 2019b: 8).

The contrast between the civil service under Stormont – which had fetishised the project of ensuring that there was 'not a Catholic about the place' – and the current iteration is extraordinary. This 'exclude all Catholics' model was also replicated at local government level – as late as 1964, the Guildhall (City Hall) in Derry employed *no Catholics at all* at any grade in the centre of a majority Catholic city (Radharc 1964). By any standards, the convergence over the past 50 years has been remarkable.

There is, however, one contemporary state sector in which fair employment convergence is far from complete: policing and the wider security apparatus (Tomlinson

---

[37] Pillarisation is a form of social stratification whereby the sectors of the society are not arranged horizontally (as in class societies) but vertically, thereby taking in a range of classes within the same 'pillar'. As a concept it has also been applied to Christians and Muslims in Lebanon.

[38] In this case, monitoring its performance is helped by the existence of periodic equality statistics. The provision of such data was itself a crucial part of the fair employment intervention.

2012). At the point of its disbandment the RUC was only 8 per cent Catholic (Patten 1999: 82).[39] The Patten Commission was tasked with creating 'a new beginning to policing in Northern Ireland with a police service capable of attracting and sustaining support from the community as a whole' – and increasing Catholic participation was one of its key challenges. In 2001, Catholics made up fewer than one in ten officers and women a little more. After a decade of the new PSNI, the Catholic proportion of police officers had risen close to the critical mass (30 per cent) identified by Patten as the threshold for the '50-50' (Catholic / non-Catholic) recruitment quotas he recommended to come to an end.[40] They were duly removed by the Alliance Party justice minister David Ford in 2011.

In the intervening years, however, there has been little advance in the Catholic proportion. Today, Catholics comprise around three in ten, women a little less. In other words, in this sector convergence has stopped. Of course, since that period has been marked by austerity, the opportunities offered via new recruitment have been limited to less than the rate of natural wastage. Yet the proportion of Catholic applicants remains stuck at around 30 per cent, *despite the Catholic plurality among the relevant age cohort for recruits.* It remains equally problematic that the proportion of Catholic employees among other Northern Ireland Policing Board staff remains stubbornly stuck around *one in five.* With a plurality of people of working age Catholic, Catholics remain even more significantly under-represented among support staff (Wilson 2017: 51). Prison officers are now integrated within civil service figures, but these too reflect a profound imbalance across prison grades staff, with 77 per cent Protestant, 14 per cent Catholic and 9 per cent 'Non-determined'.

Thus, a significant sectarian imbalance obtains across the whole of the 'security sector'. In consequence, the state repressive apparatus now appears 'stuck' in a limbo somewhere between the 'Protestant state' model and 'fair employment'. Moreover, this sector is a defining element in the good relations state: first because it remains a key economic sector – it employs a significant number of people in relatively secure and well-paid employment; more importantly, it is symbolic of the whole state. This is precisely why the Patten Commission was established and why the state went to such extraordinary lengths to de-sectarianise policing. If the good relations model had worked, we would expect fair employment outcomes across the sector. This is not the case – in 2020 less than a third of police officers is Catholic and only one fifth of police staff (PSNI 2020). So the key issue is whether this is an ongoing transition – or whether

---

[39] The RUC always had a Catholic component – it was never 'Catholic-free' in the manner of the civil service or the B Specials even at the height of the 'Protestant state'. It was originally envisioned as being one third Catholic – although this was more to ensure that it was two-thirds Protestants than to secure Catholic representation. This was possible since the RUC inherited personnel from the RIC which had been an overwhelmingly Catholic force. The last RUC officer killed in 'the troubles' was a Catholic. Francis O'Reilly was killed in September 1998 by a loyalist bomb during the Drumcree conflict.

[40] 50-50 recruitment to the police was the only occasion where otherwise forbidden reverse discrimination was permitted in the pursuit of fair employment.

the new state has now embedded a model in which a disproportionately Protestant repressive state apparatus polices and incarcerates a *majority* Catholic population. This latter scenario would – if only from the perspective of Patten – be a recipe for disaster for the state.

Wider Protestant/Catholic convergence took place in the context of a *demographic transition* in the Northern Ireland labour market. The 2011 census suggested that the point at which Catholics form the majority of the working age population had already been reached. The 2019 *LFS Religion Report* confirms this trajectory:

> In 2017, the religious composition of the working age population was 38% Protestant, 43% Catholic and 18% 'other/non-determined'. In 1990, the corresponding figures were 54% Protestant, 41% Catholic and 6% 'other/ non-determined'…. Over this period, the number of Protestants of working age decreased by 10% (from 495,000 to 446,000), the number of working age Catholics increased by 36% (from 375,000 to 509,000), and the number of those classified as 'other/non-determined' more than quadrupled (from 53,000 to 216,000). (Executive Office 2019: 13)

There are thus two key structural trends: first, the Catholic and 'other' proportions of the workforce are growing as the Protestant proportion shrinks; second, there has been a general dovetailing of the profile of Protestants and Catholics over time. This dovetailing – characterised as 'convergence' by the LFS – holds across most but not all indicators (McVeigh 2019).

In the GFA, the British government explicitly committed to 'measures on employment equality … a range of measures aimed at combating unemployment and progressively eliminating the differential in unemployment rates between the two communities by targeting objective need'. This differential has gradually reduced. The numbers of unemployed for both communities have also fallen over this period although Catholics remain more likely to be long-term unemployed. Likewise, significant differences remain within the economically inactive population: Protestants are more likely to be retired than Catholics; Catholics are more likely to be students or permanently sick or disabled. Put simply, Northern Ireland remains some way away from the point at which there are no significant differences between Protestants and Catholics across the labour market.

Marked labour market imbalances and disproportions remain. Employers with less than 30 per cent of Protestants or Catholics in their workforce continue to present a *prima facie* case for concern (bearing in mind that travel-to-work areas and qualifications also play a key part in this process).[41] In the public sector there are only three such employers with more than 1,000 employees – the aforementioned NIPB and PSNI, both disproportionately Protestant, alongside the Western Health and Social Care

---

[41] This 30 percent is arbitrary, but it is the threshold that Patten used to trigger extraordinary additional equality mechanisms in the PSNI. In this sense it offers the most appropriate indicator.

Trust which is disproportionately Catholic. Local councils also perform poorly on this measure – with nationalist councils employing low proportions of Protestants and unionist councils employing low proportions of Catholics (ECNI 2020b). Generally, however, public sector employers have relatively minor disproportions between Catholics and Protestants – while this process is far from finished, again the trajectory remains towards fair employment.

The private sector exhibits more profound evidence of 'unfair employment'. Using the 30 per cent indicator again, there are around 240 firms with less than 30 per cent Catholic employees and around 160 firms with less than 30 per cent Protestant employees (ECNI 2020c). Many of these are significant employers recognised for their 'outstanding success' despite their palpable failures in terms of employment equality. For example, Shorts Brothers PLC is Northern Ireland's second largest employer and characterised by the BBC as 'a jewel in the crown of the Northern Ireland economy'. Shorts has a workforce that is only 18 per cent Catholic despite being situated in Belfast which – excluding the 'other' category – has a working age population that is 55 per cent Catholic. Several other large employers have less than 10 per cent Catholic employees. In contrast, Norbrook Laboratories – characterised by the BBC as 'the holy grail for economic development in Northern Ireland ... locally owned, hi-tech, export-focused firms which employ lots of skilled people' – has only 17 per cent Protestant employees (ECNI 2020c).

As these examples suggest, there is some evidence of a post-GFA balancing of unfair employment, with more employers with disproportionate numbers of Catholic employees matching employers with continuing disproportionate numbers of Protestant employees. However, this balancing of inequality provides no easy or principled calculus for fair employment. Until all employers employ fairly, there is every danger that a strategy focused on private sector growth will lead to further sectarian disproportion. Nevertheless, in terms of the history of the Northern Ireland state, this represents a significant shift from the days of a dual Protestant/Catholic labour market with an effective division between skilled working-class Protestants and unskilled working-class Catholics alongside a state sector that was hugely disproportionately Protestant. In contrast, the economic base of the GFA state is now something akin to pillarisation in the Netherlands and Belgium in which labour markets are segregated but broadly equal.

In the longer term, there may also be a countervailing tendency. The long-term decline of shipbuilding and heavy engineering has had a disproportionate impact on the Protestant working class – not least because historical discrimination had favoured their employment in this sector. As this continues it may well be that the most vulnerable sectors of the Northern Ireland economy are for the first time 'Protestant' rather than 'Catholic'. This could, of course, have political implications well beyond the surviving industrial heartland of East Belfast. For example, if Shorts/Bombardier were to close completely – as is periodically forewarned in the press (BBC News 2018d) – this would to all intents and purposes symbolise the end of the Protestant 'aristocracy of labour' which underpinned the existence of the Northern Ireland state.

It hardly requires emphasis that such equality of misery would not be welcomed by any section of the Northern Ireland populace. Moreover, just because things are less unequal does not mean that they are resolved. For example, in 2020 the ECNI quietly informed us:

> Over time, the increase in the Roman Catholic community share of the monitored workforce has been close to estimates of Roman Catholics available for work. Since, 2016, the Roman Catholic community composition of those in monitored employment has ceased to approximate estimates of Roman Catholics available for work (see Chart 11). In 2017 and 2018, the gaps were 2.8 pp and 3.1 pp respectively. (ECNI 2020a: 1)

This trend contradicts the convergence argument. Other things being equal Catholics would expect to form the majority of every workforce since they now form the majority of those available for work. Moreover, the fact that they now form the majority of *leavers* (ECNI 2020a: 6) as well as appointees within the monitoring data might suggest that the limits of 'good relations' fair employment have been reached.

Nevertheless, recent data confirms a profound transition *towards* equality since 1972. Broadly state fair employment intervention – with its resolve stiffened by activism such as the MacBride Principles campaigning – *worked*. The Northern Ireland state is moving towards the point at which there is no statistical significance in terms of the correlation between being Protestant or Catholic and labour market status – whether someone is employed or unemployed, economically active or inactive. In this sense, the labour intervention started with direct rule and confirmed in the GFA has addressed one of the root causes of the conflict – and the notion of 'separate but equal' *could* be held to broadly characterise the current labour market.[42]

Of course, the specific focus on employment inequality under Stormont was part of a much wider concern around discrimination in housing and health and education. The debate focused almost entirely on Protestant/Catholic differentials within these sectors too. In other words, the focus was on *Catholic inequality* – not on gender or race or any other constituency. As with the labour market, these inequalities were addressed with varying degrees of success in the context of the reform agenda of

---

[42] There is, however, nothing that would justify any reduction in equality safeguards. In terms of the differentials it is worth emphasizing that they remain greater in the private than the public sector – this leads NERI to conclude: 'If the aim of the voluntary redundancy policy [of the SHA] is to "re-balance" the Northern Ireland economy, policies would be more efficiently focused on the gaps between outcomes in the private sector in Northern Ireland rather than the public sector' (2015: 4). Certainly, any change in the balance between the two sectors will have to address the reality that sectarian differentials are greater in the private sector than the public sector with particular imbalances in particular workforces (ECNI 2020a,b,c). This too has specific implications in terms of sectarian inequality – the areas that rely most on public sector employment are places like West Belfast and Derry which are also disproportionately Catholic.

direct rule. Here too there was a general tendency towards convergence in terms of Protestant/Catholic difference across housing and education and access to other goods, facilities and services.

Thus, by 2007 the ECNI – itself a creature of the GFA – could issue a *Statement on Key Inequalities in Northern Ireland* that paid little regard to the concept of Catholic inequality *at all*. That *Catholic inequality* now features so little in these key inequalities reflects how much the debate had been redefined post-GFA as much as any objective reduction in Catholic disadvantage. The oddly positioned 'prejudice' – harder to measure than the absence of a house or a job – also hinted at the increasing dominance of good relations approaches. Of course, this issue is complex. On the one hand this broadening of the equality agenda was necessary. For example, gender is now a much more significant indicator of labour market differences than sectarian identity. Being a woman or a man is more likely to determine location within the labour market than being a Protestant or a Catholic. It was also true that women *qua* women were just as disadvantaged under the 'Protestant state' as Catholics *qua* Catholics – yet this gendered reality invited a pale shadow of the fair employment intervention. This truth signals the importance of intersectionality in the reality of discrimination and oppression – Catholic women were doubly disadvantaged by sectarianism and sexism, yet very little time was spent addressing *their* specific economic location within the state. Likewise, the continued focus on Protestant/Catholic differentials in the fair employment debate now excludes a growing people of colour/migrant worker population in a way that is straightforwardly racist.

At the same time, however, the ever-widening reach of equality discourse (and related hate discourse) could soon lose sight of the specificity of Protestant/Catholic dynamic in the context of Northern Ireland. The 'Protestant state' was a profoundly unequal place in many ways but it did not collapse because of the way it treated women or Travellers or gay people; neither was there a brutal conflict in Northern Ireland because of any of these inequalities. Likewise, the good relations state will neither survive nor collapse based on the way that it treats any of its equality constituencies *other than Catholics*. This does not make Catholic equality – or inclusion – any more important that any of the other issues. But it does make it central to the functioning and survival of the state formation. It remains the crux of the Northern Ireland state in a way that none of the other oppressions are.

In this regard the key structural shift in equality in Northern Ireland is not really addressed at all by the current equality framework. Northern Ireland was traditionally a social formation cleaved on a two-thirds to one-third Protestant/Catholic split – indeed the state was constructed around this very specific sectarian ratio. In this context, Catholics were both unequal and discriminated against across a whole range of indicators. The direct rule reform interventions outlined above intended to correct this equality imbalance *not to change the ratio*. In other words, the project was to deliver a semblance of equality to a Catholic *minority*. While many issues remain, this intervention was broadly successful – in this sense it did change the nature of the state.

However, the demographic contours are now considerably different and the trajectory is unambiguously towards a Catholic majority. In addition, more than 10 per cent of the population is now 'other' – a migrant worker and BAME population. This changing demographic requires a considerable recalibration in equality intervention. In other words, it is no longer the experience of the Catholic minority that provides a metre of performance but rather that of a developing Catholic plurality/majority. In the contemporary good relations state, the equality dynamic is now more like South Africa or indeed like Ireland before partition – the key issue is one of a *disadvantaged majority*.

This transforms the whole debate on equality. The change is most obviously expressed in terms of education – here there is a clear Catholic majority across the whole sector. There was a collective unionist shudder when in 1999 Martin McGuinness opted to become Minister of Education – unexpectedly since the brief was regarded as a poisoned chalice. This offered a striking sense of history being made as this former IRA commander assumed responsibility for the education of Protestant children (along with all the other children in Northern Ireland, of course). However, the sectarian imbalance was much more marked when the DUP assumed control of the brief in 2016. Now a DUP minister with a track record of gratuitous anti-Catholicism was in control of an education sector which was unambiguously majority Catholic.

Another consequence in terms of the Catholic/Protestant dynamic is that the demographic transition makes equality – or the lack of it – much easier to read. Now – *other things being equal* – over half of any resource allocation across Northern Ireland should go to Catholics. If there are more Protestants than Catholics – in a firm or in a housing estate or in parliament – this indicates an inequality and signals a *prima facie* case of discrimination. The onus should therefore be on the firm or institution involved to prove that the imbalance is *not* due to discrimination. This approach offers a slightly less rosy take on the convergence phenomenon discussed earlier. For example, of the 20 leading public authority employers, only four employ more Catholics than Protestants – this in a labour market in which Catholics now clearly make up the plurality of people of working age. This rule of thumb also applies more broadly. Take for example housing policy – the current demography means that half of public housing should be Catholic – but it is not because of the continued segregation of public housing stock. Conversely, in 1972 the fact that people from the Catholic third of the workforce formed a majority of the unemployed signalled profound inequality. Nowadays, however, since the plurality of the labour market is Catholic, this same fact might signal a tendency toward equality – in this context it would be 'normal' for more Catholics than Protestants to be unemployed.

It bears emphasis that this kind of balance – even when it is 'fair' – is far removed from the 'cherishing all of the children equally' that was promised by the Republic. The institutionalisation of sectarian categories in the post-GFA state is the very antithesis of liberation from sectarianism. The grubby deal-making that has characterised consociationalism in practice – an equal allocation of spoils, as it were – is anything but post-sectarian. In truth, the present state formation reinforces rather than undermines what the Proclamation characterised as 'the differences carefully fostered under an alien government'. There is no hint of the colonial categories 'Protestant' or 'Catholic' becoming less relevant in the good relations state. Where it has become 'fairer', this has largely been on a 'separate but equal' basis. Over twenty years after the GFA Northern Ireland remains characterised by a segregated and sectarian dual market in employment and housing and education.

This begs, of course, a broader moral and philosophical point. Even if Northern Ireland has become 'separate but equal' this would be neither desirable nor make the state particularly stable. Elsewhere, it has been generally accepted since the US *Brown versus the Board of Education* decision in 1955 that 'separate but equal' cannot be regarded as equality. The centrality of 'separate development' to apartheid provides further evidence of the dangers of institutionalising separateness as a proxy for – or an alternative to – equality. This core contradiction in the logic of the good relations state is the crux of why this formation cannot survive. Here the irreconcilability of *two* structural factors fatally undermines the legitimacy of the post-GFA formation: Protestant majoritarianism and the demographic transition.

Protestant majoritarianism and 'La Revanche du berceau'

The defining quality of the Northern Ireland social formation is the continued primacy of the categories 'Protestant' and 'Catholic'. These categories were embedded in the state at its foundation and were at the base of its sectarian ratio – this was the 'original sin' of Protestant majoritarianism. Arguably there is no escape from this position. Once the state had been defined thus it could never offer equality to Catholics. The GFA made a pretty good stab at a historical compromise between unionism and nationalism. If, however, the GFA had genuinely delivered a post-sectarian state, the proportion of Catholics to Protestants would have had as little relevance as the proportion of left-handed to right-handed people. This is not the case. The colonial binaries continue to carry as much weight as they ever did: Protestant/Catholic; settler/native; planter/Gael. Moreover, the material, lived experience of Northern Ireland reproduces this fundamental division daily in concrete form – literally so in peace walls for example.[43] For all the platitudes around 'peace' and 'sharing', the binary opposites of Protestant and Catholic continue to define identity across contemporary Northern Ireland.

---

[43] There are 54 interface structures, 41 walls or fences and 13 gates, throughout the North, nine of which have been erected since 1998. Four are in East Belfast, 18 in West Belfast, 20 in North Belfast, and six each in Derry City and Craigavon (Executive Office 2013: 20-21).

As pointed out in chapter 7, the commitment to Protestant majoritarianism underpinned a permanent crisis of legitimacy in the state – this was the reason it could never be a 'normal', democratic polity. But the new prospect of a Catholic majority in Northern Ireland profoundly undermines even this dysfunctional form of legitimacy. It threatens to provide the final nail in the coffin of Northern Ireland. This process – and its political outworking – might even be termed as 'la revanche du berceau'.[44] At the same time, it is dangerous to presume that there are biopolitical solutions to the 'Northern Ireland problem'. Moreover, the tectonic shifts in the politics of Northern Ireland have been equally significant, especially in the twenty years following the GFA. The DUP has come from the political margins to supplant the Unionist Party which had operated Northern Ireland as a one-party state since 1921; it then delivered unionist support for the GFA. Operationalising a remarkable mix of populism, sectarianism and corruption, the DUP became hegemonic within unionism. While Sinn Féin was less successful at completely neutralising the SDLP, it did overtake them to become the dominant republican/nationalist party.[45] The crucial question is how this political landscape responds to the new reality of a demographic transition. This transition, depending on perspective, either promises or threatens to replace the 2:1 Protestant/Catholic sectarian ratio on which Northern Ireland was founded with, first, a Catholic plurality and then a Catholic majority. This unexpected endpoint could see the establishment of 'popish democracy' in the Six Counties – something that has been the bogeyman of British imperialism for over two hundred years. But the process is likely to be slightly more complex than the swapping of ascendancies. As we have already suggested, there are *two* elements in the demographic transition. *First* Catholics are overtaking Protestants as the plurality/majority. *Second*, the growing 'other'/BAME/migrant worker category promises to remove the possibility of *any* ethnic majority or ascendancy. This latter development compounds the difficulty in shoehorning people into the traditional Protestant/Catholic categories.

It bears emphasis that this demographic transition is an *ethnic* phenomenon – any associated political transformation is uncertain. The implications are neither inevitably nationalist or republican. In terms of the Protestant/Catholic interface that has defined the Northern Ireland state since its inception, however, this is still a transformative

---

[44] La Revanche du Berceau ('the revenge of the cradle') is a term for a demographic transition promised by high birth rates among particular ethnic groups. It was specifically associated with French Canadians – who were traditionally mostly Catholic. The phrase originated in Québec before the First World War, suggesting that – although Anglo-Canadians dominated Canada in the 19th century – the higher birth rate in Québec (and other francophone areas of Canada) would enable French-Canadians to transform their situation. The phrase implicitly suggests that the Québécoise might through this means reverse the Conquest of 'New France' by Great Britain in 1759. We should note, of course, this was a settler colonial construct – the First Nations of Canada were excluded from any promise of 'revenge'.

[45] As this polarisation unfolded, the centrist Alliance Party remained fairly constant, although its share of the vote has increased over recent years. The loyalist political parties which had been significant actors in the peace process failed to make any inroads within the unionist electorate.

moment. The emergence of a clear Catholic plurality transforms the nature of the state. Take just one example – the issue of policing the state. The question of how to police a Catholic minority obsessed the state from day one – but this is now being reframed as the question of how to police a Catholic majority. In this context, the failure to finish the Patten project and deliver a representative police force for Northern Ireland assumes an even greater significance than it did in the past. (Sooner or later, a further concomitant challenge will arise – *how to police a Protestant minority?*) With the demographic transition, the rules of the game have changed absolutely. The outworking of this new dynamic will inevitably transform the state. This transformation is more than speculation – it is already a cold, hard fact.[46] The key milestones are all being passed – a majority of school children has been Catholic for years; a majority of Belfast is now Catholic; a majority of the workforce has been Catholic since 2011. A majority of the population will be Catholic in 2021, just in time for the centenary of the formation of the state; a majority of voters will be Catholic sometime after that.[47]

Crucially, this has also begun to take political effect. In the 2016 Assembly election, Sinn Féin had only one MLA less than the DUP. For the first time in the history of the state, unionists were in the minority in the parliament.[48] Moreover, the UK Brexit referendum saw a loose alliance of Sinn Féin/nationalists/others in a Northern Ireland majority (against Brexit).[49] Tellingly – in terms of the long view – the coming legitimation crisis begins to look more like Ireland between the 1880s and partition. The British state is being forced to consider once again the question of how it might reconcile an Irish Catholic majority to the Union within the confines of formal democracy. The answer– as we saw in 1918 – is that this is almost impossible. So Northern Ireland – as well as the whole of Ireland – is back at a 1912-22 juncture.

The post-GFA dynamics are slightly different with the concomitant rise in the 'other'/BAME population. This new population – neither 'Catholic' nor 'Protestant'

---

[46] Thus, before the start of the peace process, the NIO was already addressing the question of how to respond to the possibility of a Catholic majority (BBC News 2018c).

[47] The most recent census in 2011 showed that 45 percent of the population was Catholic and 48 percent Protestant. However, the balance shifts noticeably when working age people only are tallied: 44 percent Catholic and 40 percent Protestant. Finally, when the focus is solely on schoolchildren, the imbalance is highly significant: 51 percent Catholic and 35 percent Protestant. It is only among the 60+ group that Protestants maintain a distinct majority: 57 percent Protestant and 35 percent Catholic, which is more or less the balance when unionists opted to draw the border of the new state around six counties. (Gordon 2018).

[48] In the subsequent Assembly election of March 2017, the DUP, UUP and Traditional Unionist Voice gained 39 of the 90 Assembly seats. Sinn Féin and the SDLP together also had 39 seats. The other 12 seats are taken by the Green Party, Alliance Party and People Before Profit, and one independent.

[49] This trend was further consolidated when the Unionist Party lost its MEP position in the European election of May 2019, a post that it had held since 1979. The DUP held its seat, while the other two seats went to Sinn Féin and the Alliance Party. In the 2019 British general election unionist representation fell from three seats to one seat in Belfast as the city delivered a plurality of nationalist/republican MPs for the first time (two Sinn Féin, one SDLP).

– presents a different challenge to majoritarianism, either 'Orange' or 'Green'.[50] While there had always been a smaller 'other' community in Northern Ireland, it grew exponentially in the wake of the GFA. The most recent statistics suggest some ten per cent of the population born to a mother from neither Ireland nor Britain (about half of this population is Eastern European and half from the rest of the world). So, this 'other' population is not going to somehow 'go away', and it is likely to be rooted in BAME categories rather than the traditional ethno-religious labels.[51]

In combination, therefore, this demographic pincer effect presents a profound challenge to the basis of Northern Ireland's legitimacy. Moreover, the state has a linked instability embedded in its very foundation with the commitment to deliver a border poll at the point at which there is evidence that a majority might support reunification. In this context, unionism/British nationalism needs to speak beyond its traditional base and offer something to both Catholics and BAME if it wants them to support 'our precious Union'. It has, however, illustrated very little capacity to do so. Every time unionists join in a pro-Union front with loyalist paramilitary organisations directly involved in anti-migrant and anti-Catholic violence, they further reduce even the possibility of any more liberal Catholic- or BAME-friendly unionism.

The demographic transition means that the traditional pan-'PUL' legitimacy of the 'Protestant state' can no longer hold. It must secure Catholic buy-in and therefore must mediate the Orangeist tendencies of unionism – unreconstructed anti-Catholicism of the crudest, most traditional kinds. This mediation assumes all kinds of forms and it would be wrong to suggest that it has not happened at all in the context of the good relations state. We find a whole series of thresholds being crossed – quite literally – in ways that would have been unthinkable in the 'Protestant state': unionists visiting Catholic schools; unionists attending Catholic churches; perhaps most remarkably Arlene Foster attending the funeral of Martin McGuinness.[52] We also find some Catholics engaging with unionist structures – like the honours system and engagement with British royalty. And we find some evidence of the emerging 'Northern Ireland' identity considered earlier. Thus, there is a sense in which something that was formerly unambiguously sectarian in reference – like the NI soccer team – becomes emblematic of the 'new' post-sectarian NI. There is no doubt a stark contrast between *A Night in*

---

[50] The local government elections saw many voters turn away from the main parties over issues such as Brexit and the continuing suspension of government at Stormont. 14 percent of the votes went to parties which do not categorise themselves as nationalist or unionist. Whether this trend will continue in later elections remains to be seen.

[51] There have been some noteworthy exceptions, for example, the Shoukri brothers in the UDA, whose father was Egyptian. Tim Brannigan, whose mother was from Belfast and father from Ghana, served time for republican activity; see Brannigan 2010.

[52] There are other examples. Arlene Foster and Christopher Stalford of the DUP attended the GAA final in Dublin in June 2018. Taoiseach Leo Varadkar paid a formal visit to the Orange Order headquarters in East Belfast in the same month. Tánaiste Simon Coveney laid a wreath in November 2018 at the Belfast Cenotaph on Remembrance Sunday.

November and the presentation of the Northern Ireland participation in the European Championships in 2016.[53] This has happened with support for other sports too like boxing and Ulster rugby and Irish hockey – there was something remarkable about seeing Gerry Adams at an Ulster rugby match.[54] But there is also a hint of desperation about all of this – an attempt to find new legitimacy for this space but very little evidence of its emerging.[55]

Nevertheless, at face value a Union-saving, Catholic-friendly unionism *seems* possible. Arguably the Alliance Party already occupies this space, but it has become less sure about its unionism over recent years.[56] The UUP – under former journalist Mike Nesbitt – tried a similar approach in the run-up to the Assembly elections in 2017. This involved an unprecedented cross-sectarian alliance.[57] As Mike Nesbitt characterised it as his party conference:

> 'Vote me, you get Colum [leader of the SDLP]. Vote Colum, you get me,' he said. 'Vote Colum and me, and you get a whole new middle ground politics, dedicated to making Northern Ireland work, whatever our motivations.' (*News Letter*, 22 October 2016)

---

[53] *A Night in November* is a play written by Marie Jones. It follows the personal and political journey of a Protestant dole clerk from Belfast, whose life is transformed after his attendance at the 1994 FIFA World Cup qualifying between Northern Ireland and the Republic of Ireland. His crisis of identity is sparked by the vitriolic sectarianism he witnesses at Windsor Park as the Northern Ireland team – who cannot qualify themselves – are incited to prevent the southern team reaching the World Cup. By the end of the play he travels to New York to support the Republic of Ireland at the 1994 FIFA World Cup, his identity transformed: 'I am a free man, I am a Protestant man, I am an Irish man'. By the 2016 Championships, the team and its supporters were the toast of the tournament. Former captain Neil Lennon suggested: 'The fans have been incredible. They have been starved of these big occasions and Northern Ireland have covered themselves in glory both on and off the pitch.' This is only remarkable when it is remembered that its supporters used to boo their own Catholic players – particularly those associated with Celtic. Lennon himself retired from the captaincy of the Northern Ireland team after receiving sectarian death-threats.

[54] Given rugby's traditional association with the unionist side of the community in the North, Gerry Adams' attendance in Dublin at the final between Ulster and Colomiers in 1999 was seen as a symbolically significant moment. It may not have been on a par with Nelson Mandela wearing a Springboks shirt and cap at the 1995 Rugby World Cup, but it was significant nonetheless.

[55] One other example is the claim to the reconciliatory potential of punk. 'Politicians, journalists and academics continually use the phrase "two traditions" to describe everyone living in Northern Ireland… there is a third tradition, an alternative community that rejects the tribal placards placed around their necks at birth. It is a tradition that is undogmatically left, anarchistic, disparate and tolerant. During the darkest days of the Troubles, it brought together kids from the Falls and Shankill, the Markets and Donegall Pass, the Short Strand and the Newtonards [sic] Road' (McDonald 2002).

[56] The Party is 'neutral' on the constitutional question. This allowed former MLA Anna Lo to state in an interview with the *Belfast Telegraph* on 24 October 2016 that she would vote for a united Ireland. The fact that the Alliance Party has managed to hold its position suggests some remaining space for centre-ground politics. Arguably it should have been wiped out at the last Assembly election which abolished the sixth seat in constituencies that had traditionally gone to Alliance candidates. However, Alliance managed to hold all its seats in an election in which every other major party – including DUP and SF – lost seats. Moreover, its popular leader, Naomi Long, took one of the three European MEP seats in May 2019 and it secured the North Down parliamentary seat in the December 2019 UK general election.

[57] Pre-echoed only by the equally unsuccessful proposal for 'voluntary coalition' with nationalists from Bill Craig of Vanguard back in the 1970s.

There is no question that it was a bold intervention. This kind of radical reinvention is precisely the kind of initiative that would be needed to create any kind of Catholic-friendly unionism. But it was undermined by the realpolitik of the Six Counties. The strategy did not revive the fortunes of either party. Ultimately it suggested that Nesbitt had gone too far beyond both his party membership and his electoral base. He resigned the leadership after the failure of his 'Vote Colum, get me' strategy in the election and the party returned to its more traditional conservative unionist roots.

Meanwhile the DUP continued to plough a furrow that seemed closer to its roots as the 'Protestant Unionist Party' than to any politics that might appeal to a Catholic constituency. Thus, not uncharacteristically, Ian Paisley entered the process leading to the St Andrew's Agreement accommodation insisting that republicans should 'wear sackcloth and ashes … until the sackcloth and ashes wear out' for all they did during the 30 years of 'the troubles' in the province (Oliver and White 2004). Three years before he shared the leadership of the Northern Ireland Executive with Martin McGuinness, he stated that McGuinness 'needs to be converted to democracy' and that Sinn Féin 'need to repent and turn from their evil ways' (*Irish Times*, 9 March 2007). Later, DUP leader Arlene Foster infamously managed to undo all her best efforts to extend an olive branch to Catholics in the run-up to the 2017 election with her observation in relation to the demand for an Irish Language Act that: 'If you feed a crocodile it will keep coming back and looking for more' (*Belfast Telegraph*, 7 February 2017). Nor has suspension of the Executive led to any great reduction in this kind of intervention. For example, an Ulster unionist MLA was ridiculed and criticised by his DUP counterparts for attending a civic reception for Pope Francis and reminded that 'the pope is the antichrist' (Manley 2018).[58]

None of this catalogue of offence suggests any fundamental rethink on unionism and sectarianism. This begins to beg the question of what any Catholic – or Muslim – might need to qualify. Notoriously, Ulster unionist leader Tom Elliott was reported to the Orange Order to which he belongs for attending a Catholic funeral. Not just any Catholic funeral, but that of Catholic Constable Ronan Kerr, 25, killed in a republican booby trap car bomb at his home in Omagh on his way to work. In the end, no action was taken but the incident might have caused even the most loyal 'non-Protestant' to wonder what they would need to do to be regarded as an equal citizen in Northern Ireland (BBC News 2011).

There are severe limits to any Catholic-friendly unionist strategy, even if unionists were more committed to the project than they currently are. While a quarter of Catholics questioned are happy with living in Northern Ireland 'the way it is', that doesn't mean they are unionists. That step of voting unionist is one too far for most. Arguably Sinn

[58] Lest there be any doubt that the gratuitous offensiveness of the DUP would be limited to Catholics, consider DUP leader and First Minister Peter Robinson on Muslims. 'I'll be quite honest, I wouldn't trust them in terms of those who have been involved in terrorist activities. I wouldn't trust them if they are devoted to Sharia Law. I wouldn't trust them for spiritual guidance. Would I trust them to go down to the shops for me, yes I would, would I trust them to do day-to-day activities … there is no reason why you wouldn't' (*Belfast Telegraph* 29 May 2014).

Féin have a better chance with their mirror policy of persuading some unionists to vote for Sinn Féin.[59]

Emblematic of the DUP's seeming inability to change its ways to appeal to nationalists is the straw that broke the camel's back for many nationalists and collapsed the Executive in 2017 – not the RHI scandal,[60] but the decision of DUP Minister Paul Givan to withdraw £50,000 from the Líofa Gaeltacht Bursary Scheme on the basis of 'cost-cutting'.[61] (When he managed to subsequently find the money in the face of widespread criticism, it was too late.) To begrudge such a piddling amount was the ultimate measure of disdain. This is an example of the impossible contradictions of the good relations state. In reality, the politics of the Irish language should be an easy unionist concession given that the UK state had provided without any controversy in Scotland and Wales – on Gàidhlig and Welsh – what Sinn Féin demanded in Northern Ireland. Moreover, the equality implications of this existing intervention are far from revolutionary. The DUP could have conceded the £50,000 for Líofa – and thrown in an Irish Language Act – and preserved the absence of an anti-poverty strategy. With one symbolic concession, they could have kept RHI and all the ongoing structural discrimination around investment in East Belfast. In other words, even post-GFA and despite its hegemony within unionism, the DUP has proven incapable of concession even when this is in its own interests.[62]

Unionist intransigence places severe strains on the ability of the Northern Ireland state to survive. Beyond the specific limitations of the DUP, the changes, demographic, economic and social, in the North will undoubtedly have a range of political consequences which are neither unitary nor easily predictable. For example,

---

[59] Sinn Féin's Máirtín Ó Muilleor topped the poll in the Assembly elections in South Belfast in 2017. In many ways, the constituency of South Belfast represents the possibilities of political change in the 'new' Northern Ireland. Between 1922 and 2005 it was a safe unionist constituency in Westminster elections but the current MP is from the SDLP. The current Stormont MLAs for South Belfast are as follows: Sinn Féin, SDLP, Alliance Party, Green Party and DUP. The constituency contains many BAME residents who might be expected to vote for candidates on other than Orange/Green issues, and many of them immigrants familiar with issues of colonialism and indeed British colonialism elsewhere. It also contains young unionist professionals who might be persuaded to vote in non-traditional terms out of dissatisfaction with unionist policies overall, whether in relation to abortion and equal marriage, or with the restriction of opportunities for business, education, career, etc. represented by the DUP's support of Brexit.

[60] As Minister for Enterprise Arlene Foster oversaw the introduction of the Renewable Heating Incentive which provided payback for people installing heating systems which ran on wood pellets. Although partially modeled on the English equivalent, the Northern Ireland scheme was notable for reimbursing users much more than the cost of running the systems, thus leading to evidence of some large farmers running multiple boilers in empty barns. The estimated cost to the Northern Ireland exchequer was somewhere in the region of £500m. By January 2017 Foster was First Minister in the Stormont executive. Her Deputy, Martin McGuinness, resigned over this and other scandals, thus bringing down the executive (see McBride 2019).

[61] The Líofa scheme was a yearly programme that allowed 100 school-age children to travel to the Donegal Gaeltacht to improve their Irish (BBC News 2017).

[62] A 2017 survey revealed that two-thirds of DUP voters were opposed to an Irish Language Act and that fewer than half would support one in order to restore devolution (Nolan 2017). By this measure, they would be more willing to accept an Executive committed to abortion law reform than to providing an Irish Language Act.

between the repeal of the Eighth Amendment in May 2018 in the South and the decriminalisation of abortion in the North in October 2019, the flip side of the attraction of the South to liberal unionists in the North was the fact that Northern Ireland became more appealing for many Catholic reactionaries than the newly liberal 26 counties. Likewise, Brexit saw the odd phenomenon of both Protestant and Catholic racism framed by notions of its implications for migrants. A tentative white Northern Ireland commonality emerged – whoever Northern Ireland belonged to, it didn't want migrants and people of colour.

Social conservativism offers the prospect of odd new alliances alongside different forms of progressive politics. The changing landscape can provide new opportunities to improvise on the theme of a 'carnival of reaction'. Thus, some Protestants and Catholics share equally reactionary views on gay marriage and abortion.[63] While such pan-sectarian reaction may seem unlikely in the context of Irish history, it is not so ridiculous in the context of contemporary politics.[64] The key point is that Northern Ireland with a Catholic majority is not necessarily a more progressive place than it has been with a Protestant majority.[65] This version of 'popish democracy' might well fall significantly short of the ideals of the Proclamation and the Democratic Programme. We suggest in our assessment of 'what is to be done' (chapter 11) that we need to focus minds on a more progressive, inclusive politics to transform the Six Counties. This reading adds extra urgency to the notion that the Northern Ireland state needs dismantling rather than further reinvention.

The endgame begins

The 'good relations' state looked to have achieved a degree of legitimacy in the wake of the ceasefires and the GFA. But this historic compromise now appears doomed as it steers between the Scylla of Protestant majoritarianism and the Charybdis of a growing Catholic and 'other' plurality/majority. In this context, unionism has proved incapable of making the necessary concessions to deliver anything that might be understood as 'good

---

[63] A 2017 survey revealed that 72 percent of Catholics, 84 percent of Protestants and 93 percent of those with no religion said that it should definitely or probably be legal to have an abortion if the foetus has a fatal abnormality and the baby will not survive beyond the birth. For a woman who has become pregnant because of rape or incest, 69 percent of Catholics, 81 percent of Protestants and 93 percent with no religion stated it should be definitely/probably legal to have an abortion (University of Ulster 2017).

[64] For example, much of Irish America has recently gone on such a journey. It had its whiteness confirmed in the changing dynamics of race in America and its politics transformed in the process. The specific 'Catholic' stance on abortion opened the door to new alliances with (traditionally anti-Catholic) Protestant fundamentalists. Thus, committed Democrats – raised in the context of traditional GOP and KKK anti-Catholicism – could become Trump supporters.

[65] A new all-Ireland party, Aontú, was formed in January 2019 by Peadar Tóibín, who resigned from Sinn Féin over its support for abortion reform in the 26 counties. The party faces an uphill struggle to convince republicans to abandon Sinn Féin while at the same time attracting Protestant fundamentalists to vote for a republican party.

relations' – let alone equality. Ironically perhaps, in its most recent form this intransigence has taken the form of a commitment to corruption as much as racism and sectarianism.

Advancing equality, however, remains the ultimate red line in this context. The question of equality has, in different ways, been the irresolvable contradiction at every point in the state's existence. Contemporary Northern Ireland suggests that there is a simple calculus in this – a state that denies equality to one third of its citizens might just function– as Northern Ireland did 1921-72; but a state that denies equality to *most* of its citizens cannot but be temporary – like apartheid South Africa. This notion of equality is not just about the key indicators of discrimination that so exercised the civil rights movement – employment, housing, education – but also about a less tangible but even deeper sense of identity: to whom does Northern Ireland belong? In this sense – as loyalists have insisted over the past ten years – it *is* about flags and emblems and statues, at least by way of metonym.

The Executive collapse marked the start of the endgame for Northern Ireland. More immediately, the collapse resulted from two factors – both facilitated by the good relations state – corruption and political sectarianism. The level of corruption – which had been endemic and long-lasting – was finally exposed by RHI. But RHI had been preceded by NAMA,[66] Red Sky,[67] and other scandals. There was a finding of incompetence rather than corruption by the Inquiry. But that only applies to RHI, as the others were not subject to inquiry. The Iris Robinson saga was perhaps most emblematic of all. As a government minister married to the First Minister, she presumably had many legitimate avenues to accrue additional income. Yet she remained wedded to the model of DUP graft in power: she insisted on taking a cut of £5000 pounds out of a larger corrupt payment to her lover. Nor, of course, did this kind of activity end with the collapse of the Assembly. In 2018 it was revealed that Ian Paisley Jr, MP, had lobbied on behalf of the genocidal Sri Lankan regime in exchange for two luxury holidays (BBC News 2018f). It genuinely beggars belief.

This is an odd state of affairs – even in Northern Ireland. While we cannot imagine a unionism without sectarianism, it should be possible to imagine one without endemic corruption. This surely cannot be a 'normal civic society' in action. There is something shocking about the scale of the practice; but even more shocking is continued support for a party which is so tied to it. There was some anticipation that under leader Mike Nesbitt, centrist unionism would get some traction in the Assembly election given the series of scandals that had dogged the DUP. The UUP – running on an anti-corruption ticket – got a 0.3 per cent bounce on the back of RHI and managed to lose seats in the process – as well as losing Mike Nesbitt. There were, ironically, echoes of the scale of political corruption in the 26 counties. Here was an uncomfortable resonance with

---

[66] A scandal in 2014 involving the sale of a portfolio of loans by the National Asset Management Agency where then First Minister Peter Robinson of the DUP allegedly benefited to the tune of £7.5 million.

[67] A scandal in 2010 where Minister of Social Development Nelson McCausland DUP was alleged to have influenced the allocation of a large amount of money for public housing to a company called Red Sky.

the success of CJ Haughey and the 'cute hoor' syndrome – the populist approach to corruption of 'wouldn't we all do it if we had the chance?'

Arguably, unionism has been at this for one hundred years – using the Northern Ireland state to advantage unionists as part of a process of disadvantaging Catholics. Indeed, the further back we go, into the colonial history of the entire island, the more formalised it becomes – what was the payment of tithes in Ireland other than the transfer of wealth from poor Catholics to rich Protestants? Or the massive handouts to rich Protestants to bribe them into supporting the Act of Union? Or, the massive compensation to Protestant landowners following the transfer of land ownership to Irish Catholics through the land acts? Using the state in this way is not an aberration but rather a key tenet of political philosophy – accepted by most of the unionist electorate.

The second factor in the collapse was the DUP's arrogance toward Sinn Féin – and more significantly the Sinn Féin electoral base. Sinn Féin was demonstrably committed to the institutions of the GFA. Arguably this had become the party's Achilles heel. The DUP was at best ambivalent about them – it had repudiated the GFA in the first place and was pushed into St Andrews. In this context the DUP felt it could ignore or disrespect Sinn Féin in the knowledge that they were unlikely to walk away from the institutions. Meanwhile Sinn Féin was the target of mounting criticism from its base since it appeared to be losing every battle in government. As we have seen, the final straw for grassroots republicans was not RHI (a scheme that transferred millions from the state to advantage – overwhelmingly – businesspeople who were friends of unionist politicians) but rather the removal of the Líofa Scheme (a grant that transferred £50,000 to mostly working-class Catholics).

Sinn Féin could simply observe that they had to share power with whatever political representation the unionist electorate generated for them. Not unreasonably they might have observed that this is the essence of power-sharing. This approach inevitably led, however, to a more difficult engagement with the limitations of the peace process and the GFA. Republicans had to subscribe to the notion that the 'Protestant state' was transformed – or at least transforming. The alternative was to move towards the inescapable conclusion that the GFA itself was a profound failure – that it had created the dysfunctional government of Northern Ireland as well as unreconstructed sectarianism presented as 'a normal civic society'. This further confirms the irreformability/crisis point issues that we have framed here. If republicans are unable to make the institutions work, it is the state rather than the GFA that is the problem.

The quintessential truth remains that the sole legitimacy for the 'Northern Ireland' constructed in 1920 was Protestant majoritarianism. As we have emphasised, the demography underpinning this state legitimacy has already gone. This does not mean that a united Ireland is inevitable; but it does mean that a legitimacy crisis for post-GFA Northern Ireland is inevitable. The wagons are already being circled within unionism – the increasing calls for 'one party' and 'no split vote' – with depressing echoes of earlier unionist formations. Crucially, however, they cannot achieve this traditional ethnic laager given the demographic transition. It would take a gerrymander surpassing anything that was done in Derry between 1921 and 72 to create a democratic fig leaf for the state as it is currently constituted. The point is now approaching where *every* Protestant in Northern Ireland voting for the DUP will not be enough.

For anyone clinging to the notion of 'saving' Northern Ireland, this leaves the unhappy prospect of repartition. This is hardly a new idea – a boundary commission to reconfigure the border on more sectarian lines had been central to the Anglo-Irish Treaty and this was rejected by Southern Ireland rather than Northern Ireland. This idea was raised again in 1972, by Conservative MP Julian Critchley. In the same year the British government published a discussion paper on *The Future of Northern Ireland*. It proposed,

> that consideration might be given to a partial or incomplete transfer of sovereignty either in geographical terms (i.e. by transferring to the Irish Republic those parts of Northern Ireland where a majority in favour exists) or in jurisdictional terms (e.g. by adopting a pattern of joint sovereign responsibility for Northern Ireland as recommended by the SDLP) or by a scheme of condominium for which there are such precedents as the New Hebrides and Andorra. (Critchley 1972)

In the 1970s, British Prime Minister Ted Heath had considered the possibility, in the event of the government losing control, of redrawing the border and transferring large sections of the population (Ferriter 2019: 83). In 1984, the British Cabinet discussed moving a number of border areas with Catholic majorities into the Republic 'to produce a more homogenous population in Northern Ireland' (Ferriter 2019: 105). Margaret Thatcher was reported (by Sir David Goodall) as saying that if Northern Catholics wanted to be in the South, 'well, why don't they move over there?' (quoted in Ferriter 2019: 105). And in 1984, in a conversation with Taoiseach Garrett Fitzgerald, she 'wondered if a possible answer to the problem might not simply be a redrawing of boundaries' (BBC News 2014). So, when in 1986 Professor Liam Kennedy (1986) produced three maps to show three different possibilities for repartition he was following a minor but already trodden path. Finally, the UDA took up his suggestion in 1994 (see Wood 2006: 184–185).

In the context of the developing crisis of legitimacy, there will no doubt be some people who will want to look at Kennedy's infamous maps again. In reality, however, this kind of talk seems more akin to the dystopian 'Afrikaner homeland' maps of democratic transition South Africa than anything else. Given that, as we have argued, sectarianism is a form of racism, and the original boundaries of the state were derived on the basis of a sectarian/racist majoritarian logic, arguments for redrawing the boundaries of the state are certainly racist. But they are also constructed on the verge of political insanity. It bears repetition: in 2021, Belfast – the capital of Northern Ireland – is a majority Catholic city. Moreover, as became clear during the protracted Brexit negotiations post-2016, the EU will take more than passing interest in any attempt to reconfigure its borders. While it remains true that a nihilist approach to transition by loyalists could be terrifying, it looks like having little capacity to construct any kind of social formation that the British state – or anyone else for that matter – would want to be in union with.

Unionist unease at the transition certainly signals some of the dangers in the coming period. It would be difficult to over-emphasise the capacity of unionism to mobilise violence and destruction rather than reconcile to its historical fate.[68] Despite the fears of unionist nihilism, however, neither repartition nor a detoxified unionism is making any great traction in the current political constellation. Which again leaves collapse as the most likely outcome of the current dysfunctionality. This in turns begs the question of what interventions help to make a further legitimacy crisis in the six counties more positive and less violent than the similar crisis of 1969-72.

This juncture represents the endgame for the state. This is because the 'Northern Ireland problem' is the state itself – not Protestants or Catholics, not 'terrorists' or 'ugly mindsets', not even settlers and natives. We have posited two inescapable – and intimately related – antinomies that mean the current state formation cannot survive. The first is existential – a state defined by Protestant majoritarianism cannot reinvent itself as a 'normal, civic society'. The second is situational – a state that is based on Protestant majoritarianism cannot survive a demographic transition to a Catholic plurality/majority. Thus, centennial Northern Ireland finds itself at a spectacularly disrupted juncture. This post-Brexit, post-Covid moment represents the beginning of the end for Northern Ireland and it is not an entity that is worth saving. The energies of all parties – British and Irish and European, Catholic and Protestant and 'other', native and migrant – should now turn to constructing something better and more democratic in its place.

---

[68] In October 2019, loyalists from a broad range of organisations met in East Belfast to oppose Boris Johnson's Brexit Bill. Spokesman Jamie Bryson stated: 'No sensible person wants to see violence, loyalism has spent three years reaffirming a commitment to peace, but ultimately loyalism's support for the peace process and the Belfast Agreement was predicated upon one very simple thing, the union is safe and the threat of violence has been used to undermine the union and drive us into an economic united Ireland and people can read into that whatever way they want' (*Belfast Telegraph,* 21 October 2019).

Section III

Situating Ireland within paradigms of anti-colonialism and anti-imperialism

The coming General Election is fraught with vital possibilities for the future of our nation. Ireland is faced with the question whether this generation wills it that she is to march out into the full sunlight of freedom, or is to remain in the shadow of a base imperialism that has brought and ever will bring in its train naught but evil for our race. Sinn Féin gives Ireland the opportunity of vindicating her honour and pursuing with renewed confidence the path of national salvation by rallying to the flag of the Irish Republic. —Sinn Féin election manifesto, 1918

The Irish have... shown a marked aversion to the idea of the state, which levies taxes and asks for other sacrifices.... The problem is that the ideal nation can only achieve concrete form through the medium of the state, whose apparatus ever since the colonial phase of their experience, many of them have learned to hate or fear. A true republic – a happy embodiment of the idea of the nation in a state – is something that all Irish people ... have yet to know. —Declan Kiberd, 1991

The final section of our book turns to the other side of the colonial story – anti-imperialism and decolonisation. This tradition comprises some of the greatest texts of world literature and political philosophy (Cabral 1974; Césaire 1955; Fanon 1952, 1961; Memmi 1990; Said 1979; Spivak 1988) – and in the Irish context, Tone, Lalor, and Connolly. Just as we have situated Ireland and Irishness within the broader process of colonialism, we now turn to examine the ways in which the Irish story is framed within broader developments in anti-colonial resistance and self-determination. This notion that Ireland remains colonised is, of course, a bold assertion. It is counterintuitive for many people. It also runs against the grain in much of the historiography that we referenced in our introduction.[1] This is true, of course, for those like Howe who insist that Ireland was 'never colonised'. But it also holds for those who accept that colonisation was part of Irish history at some point

---

[1] For a devastating critique of revisionist historians in this regard, see O'Leary (2019).

but no longer applies. Thus, utilising an anti-colonial paradigm is equally problematic for those who indicate an arbitrary date – for example, 1800 with the Union or 1922 with the establishment of the Free State or 1998 with the Good Friday Agreement – marking the end of colonialism in Ireland.

There is an immediate problem with this 'end of colonialism' thesis, however. Most shallowly, it is well known that the English like to mark these occasions with appropriate pomp and circumstance (Brendon 2008; Morris 2004). Whether in Delhi in 1947 or Hong Kong in 1997 they usually leave no ambiguity around the end of empire. It seems odd that Ireland transitioned so stealthily towards what O'Leary characterised as the 'final decolonization of Ireland' (2019: 131). Is it really possible that neither the English nor the Irish appear to have noticed? In truth, the only thing approaching such a decolonisation ceremony took place in Dublin Castle on 16 January 1922 with the transfer of power to the new Provisional Government by the last Lord Lieutenant and 'Viceroy of Ireland'. As we have seen, however, this transition was framed explicitly as the 26-county state taking its due place within empire rather than outwith it. In the north, of course, the imperial flag has never been lowered at all.[2]

More deeply, however, the circuits of colonialism and imperialism remain embedded in both Irish polities. This organic colonial dynamic is most obviously manifest in the partition border which has recently become so contentious – and portentous – once again. In other words, anyone interested in understanding the Irish present or constructing the Irish future, must begin with a reading of this reality – and not as a colonial history but rather as a colonial present. As we argue in chapter 9, globally there is an arc of decolonisation which begins with the resistance of the colonised to conquest, travels through struggle against the established colonial state, and ends with the process of decolonisation. This final phase involves the disengagement of the colonial power and the long journey of the former colony to establish its relationship anew with its former colonisers as well as the rest of the world. Arguably almost every former colony is located somewhere on this final stage of the arc, with few able to point to completed decolonisation. Ireland is certainly situated somewhere along this final stage of the arc.

Our review of the two Irish states that emerged from partition clearly signals that the Irish anti-imperial revolution remains unfinished. This notion might have seemed faintly ridiculous even ten years ago. Despite economic challenges, it looked as though both states would edge tentatively towards a muted celebration of their centenaries. In the north, the Good Friday Agreement for all its fragility looked to have generated a

---

[2] Most bizarrely, it was suggested that the flag be flown from public buildings to celebrate the birthday of the disgraced Prince Andrew in early 2020 – somebody from whom English royalists, let alone Irish nationalists or unionists, had sensibly distanced themselves.

more inclusive polity; in the south, it seemed as if Shaw's solution might finally have been realised: 'If only we could forget that we are Irish and become really Catholic Europeans, there would be some hope for us' (cited in Kiberd 1991: 315). On 23 June 2016, however, the unexpected English endorsement of Brexit brought the enduring, colonial border that separated the two states in Ireland back to the centre of world attention. Once again, the partition of Ireland became a toxic, divisive issue across Irish, British and European politics. Much was made, of course, of this potential new external border of the EU. What was acknowledged less often was that it also constituted an equally divisive border for union and empire. Thus, Brexit saw the return of the colonial repressed with remarkable intensity. The colonial history that both states had – in very different ways – struggled to revise and avoid and repudiate had re-emerged once again in full technicolour. The notion that the partition of Ireland was either 'settled' or 'over' was no longer tenable. If a metonym for the ongoing dialectic between empire and republic were needed, it was there in the incongruous and illogical international boundary meandering between Newry and Derry and Dundalk and Bundoran – separating people and communities for no good reason beyond the outworking of an unfinished decolonisation.

Thus, in our final three chapters we turn to ask what the reinvigorated tension between empire and republic means for Ireland and Irishness. Since Ireland remains locked into colonial structures in profound ways, what would it mean to renew the decolonisation project – diverted in the south, stymied in the north? What would it mean to finish the revolution? This is part of the broader question we raised in our introduction: is it possible to do anti-imperialism in the wake of 9-11? And in the wake of Covid-19? It is not only the Irish but the whole of the formerly colonised world that must engage with these questions. Moreover, asking questions about Irish reunification cannot but raise much broader international and transnational questions. Of course, this tension between a national project and internationalism has always been central to the theorists of anti-imperialism. As Franz Fanon (1961: 183) suggested:

> National consciousness, which is not nationalism, is the only thing that will give us an international dimension... Far from keeping aloof from other nations, therefore, it is national liberation which leads the nation to play its part on the stage of history. It is at the heart of national consciousness that international consciousness lives and grows.

Our final section, chapters 9 to 11, engages with the possibility – and promise – of decolonisation from this perspective and situates Ireland within this broader paradigm.

Padraig Pearse – leader of the 1916 uprising and author of the Proclamation

– captured the sense of a coming triumph over colonialism in his *Óró sé do Bheatha 'Bhaile*. Its chorus declares: 'Anois ar theacht an tSamhraidh!' – now the summer is coming![3] Pearse's *sluagh-ghairm* was both echoing centuries of Irish resistance and pre-echoing the powerful sense of the promise of liberation for other colonised peoples that followed through the twentieth century. Of course, the reality of post-colonialism often descended into a grubby compromise of unfulfilled dreams and broken promises – but the promise of liberation remains remarkably potent for people who have suffered under Empire. Moreover, for all the revisioning of Empire that plagues the academies and politics of the colonial powers, there are precious few former colonies or colonial subjects that ever hanker for a return to imperial dominion. Although it is rarely critiqued in this way, this urge to rehabilitate empire and re-evaluate colonialism is nearly always a white person's sport.

Situating Ireland within broader tropes of imperialism and anti-imperialism helps contextualise contemporary Irishness in several ways. Most obviously the obsession with violence[4] – particularly anti-colonial violence – appears misguided. Colonialism was a brutal process – it worked through the operation of 'merciless power' and the primacy of violence. Resistance to colonialism was often articulated in much the same way. At the colonial nexus 'both sides' routinely resort to massacre and genocide. On this count – *An Gorta Mór* excepted – Irish history appears less violent than most comparable struggles. Moreover, the space created for settler colonists in Ireland was – by and large – an unusually generous one.[5] The routine phenomenon of settler populations becoming 'more Irish than the Irish' was not replicated in many other places. So, it is necessary to recognise the virtues of Irish tradition alongside the specific challenges that this creates for any future framing of self-determination.

What we are arguing is that this commitment to inclusion and heterogeneity is more than simply a characteristic of Irish anti-imperialist politics – although this was remarkable in itself. Rather Ireland offers a wider exercise in *mestizaje* that offers a new,

---

[3] This phrase sees art oddly imitating life in the context of *Game of Thrones*. This epic series – much of it filmed in the north of Ireland and often posited as a phenomenon that might 'save' Northern Ireland through tourism and its growing associated filmmaking infrastructure, announces a whole series of ominous events with the phrase 'Winter is coming'.

[4] This came to the fore in the general election in the Republic in January 2020. The two parties which between them had dominated Irish politics since partition, Fianna Fáil and Fine Gael, were relentless in their attacks on Sinn Féin on the grounds of their past violence which was said to preclude their chances of ever being a proper democratic party – an irony at least, given the links between Fianna Fáil and Fine Gael and political violence of an earlier era. Despite the attacks, Sinn Féin, fighting on a programme of anti-austerity, topped the poll. Nevertheless, Fianna Fáil and Fine Gael went on to form a coalition government with the Green Party in June 2020.

[5] 'The nationalist attitude, republican and home rule alike, was a remarkable one. Almost alone among the peoples of Europe Irish nationalists aspired to integrate, rather than expel, the settler race. They offered the Ulster unionists a more generous federal solution than any emerging European nationality offered its settlers...' (Lee 2008: 171).

liberatory model of what Fanon identified as 'national consciousness'. Ireland's greatest modern writer James Joyce identified Irish history as a 'nightmare from which he was trying to awake'. But he also presented a macaronic vision of that which might replace the nightmare. As Cheng has argued, Joyce embodies these issues throughout his work. In particular:

> Ulysses, through the images revealed in its 'nicely polished looking-glass' of the cultural contact zone that was Dublin in 1904, advocates an acceptance simultaneously of heterogeneity and difference, on the one hand, and, on the other hand, of a potential sameness and solidarity of shared similar-in-difference – between Irish, Jewish, black, Oriental, Indian, English, Boer, paleface, redskin, jewgreek and greekjew – within a multivalent, inter-nationalist perspective, rather than within a binary polarisation that freezes essences into poles of absolute and unbridgeable difference. (Cheng 1995:248)

In the context of contemporary Ireland and its discontents, this suggests that the possibility of such heterogeneity remains one of the key promises of Irishness. It is, of course, important not to privilege the Irish perspective on this. The Irish have no more important perspective on colonialism than any other colonised people. But their experience is also as unique as anyone else's. And in this regard, there is a value in the specificity of the Irish gaze. Ireland's location – between Europe and the other continents, between the West and the rest, between whiteness and colour – lends a particular interest to the location. Furthermore, there is a specific connection to Americanness that further helps situate Ireland's post-colonial identity alongside the most powerful contemporary international actor of all. This was recently personified by the election of Joe Biden – following Kennedy, only the second Catholic ever to be US President. What does it mean that an Irish Catholic is now 'leader of the free world'?

It is from this complex location that sense is to be made of our own contemporary 'nightmare of history' – as well as any vision of a better, more inclusive Irish future. The unfinished nature of the Irish journey from colonialism means that Ireland is deeply embedded in the operation of contemporary dominion. In fact, the notion of dominion accurately captures the unfinished nature of decolonisation in most former colonies. This undermines any sense of self-determination and combines to allow colonial and racial privilege to prevail politically and culturally. In other words, the unfinished nature of the revolution in Ireland reflects the ongoing struggle for self-determination across the formerly colonised world. Ireland's contradictory location within colonialism is also a contradictory location within the contemporary world. In this sense, a focus on Ireland also offers a perspective on contemporary anti-imperialism. Thus, our final three chapters both situate Ireland within contemporary readings of colonialism and imperialism and offer an Irish perspective on those readings.

Before turning to the specificity of the Irish path to decolonisation, chapter 9 develops a general schema of decolonisation around the world. This is where the notion of an arc of decolonisation is directly considered. How did anti-imperialist, anti-colonial movements organise economically and politically? Was resistance primarily military or through non-violent struggles? How did colonial states disengage? There is a continuum from 'Winds of Change' reformism – in theory helping colonies to become 'independence-ready' – to the Yorktown/Saigon scenario where imperialist powers are military defeated and leave without any decolonisation process at all. And in what position are these former colonies now – what is the general state of decolonisation in 2020? Where are the models of good practice? And why did some of them go so wrong? Finally, continuing struggles – from Rhodes statues in South Africa and Oxford to the whole issue of reparations from India and the Caribbean to the US – indicate that the journey is far from complete anywhere in the formerly colonised world. The problematic might be focused starkly by the question, when might the UN Decolonisation Committee declare its work complete?

Chapter 10 turns to the specific experience of Ireland and situates Irish resistance to colonisation and imperialism within the broader analysis of anti-imperialism and self-determination. It traces a narrative across Irish resistance to colonisation from the arrival of the first English forces to the present. Ireland played a key role in anti-imperialism on at least two occasions. First, the emergence of the United Irish movement marks the first modern anti-imperialism – including an alliance between settler colonial and native forces that remains remarkable. Second, the declaration of the Republic in 1916 marked the first stage in the break-up of the British Empire. (Or at least the start of a definitive twentieth-century phase following the loss of the American colonies in 1776.) Here we trace the Irishness of this idea of the republic as well as some of its key attributes. Notable among these is its *mestizo* character – the notion that a new republic would replace the divisions embedded in the colonial process.

Chapter 11 turns towards Ireland in the coming times. It asks 'what is to be done' to complete this process of decolonisation in Ireland. It draws on the previous analyses to offer a trajectory towards completing the unfinished revolution. Rather than provide a blueprint or programme for decolonisation, we return to two themes which have threaded through this book: the notion of Ireland as a white dominion and the concept of *mestizaje*, mixedness. Of course, there are some practical pointers here, such as the urgency of ending partition. But more generally we argue that the path to the completion of the decolonisation project on the island is an abandonment of the real and putative privileges associated with the legacy of white dominion. This would require an embracing of the *mestizo* or mixed character of 'Irishness' which allows all – the planter, the Gael and the newcomer – to engage in the building of the new Ireland. And part of this process would possibly, as many times before, send a message to the world about how to resist imperial control.

Across these chapters, the analysis insists that the tension between empire and republic still matters. This truth holds for the most prosaic of issues: whether the union flag should really be flown to celebrate the birthday of Prince Andrew in the middle of a contemporary Belfast that is now only minority unionist; or whether the second city in the North is to be called 'Doire' or 'Derry' or 'Londonderry'. But it also holds for the most profound issues facing the Irish people as global citizens, in particular the growing recognition of climate emergency. On the one hand it is not unreasonable to ask what is the point of engaging with colonial history in Ireland if the whole world is only decades away from catastrophe. But even here the relevance of the tension between empire and republic is significant. Alongside the binaries already captured by our juxtaposition of empire and republic – English/Irish, European/Majority World, Black/white, settler/ native and coloniser/colonised – might be added *nature/anti-nature*. This is because the unresolved dialectic between imperialism and self-determination also frames the developing tension between the natural world and human agency that threatens the very life of the planet. The current climate emergency is beyond solution by any one nation state acting solely. In addition, there is no reason why a reunified Ireland should place the tackling of the climate catastrophe at the forefront of its programme for government. Our argument is simply that an as-yet decolonised Ireland has not got the political space to prioritise such a programme which it could have the other side of decolonisation.

Self-determination is a necessary condition for preventing climate catastrophe. This reality is as true in Ireland as anywhere else. In other words, the Irish environment has never been abstracted from the colonial process. Indeed, colonialism robbed Ireland of most of its natural environment. Even that which appears the most hackneyed caricature of Irishness – our peat bogs and our turf – is the product of an environmental holocaust. And if any one event were to symbolise the venality and dependency of the contemporary 26-county state, it was the rush to evict smallholders in Rossport to facilitate the crudest of exploitation of fossil fuels and contribute astronomically to the national carbon footprint (Storey and McCaughan 2009). In the North an even more profound powerlessness obtains. Here the recent idea which threatens the greatest environmental impact of all was the proposal that a bridge or tunnel should be constructed between Scotland and Ireland. Yet this remains a decision that is made by an English government without any reference to the government of either Scotland or Ireland – let alone any assessment of the environmental cost (BBC News 2020a, b). Of course, climate change is a global issue – a definitive example of why we can no longer think of any kind of meaningful self-determination in one country. But the path of resistance to climate emergency is also about national self-determination. Whatever coming struggles face the people of Ireland – from climate emergency to reunification to recovering from pandemic – these will remain framed by the dialectic between empire and republic.

Chapter 9

'They make a wasteland and call it peace': anti-imperialism and decolonisation – a genealogy

Dead, living, free, or in prison on the orders of the colonialists, it is not I who counts. It is the Congo, it is our people for whom independence has been transformed into a cage where we are regarded from the outside... History will one day have its say, but it will not be the history that Brussels, Paris, Washington, or the United Nations will teach, but that which they will teach in the countries emancipated from colonialism and its puppets... a history of glory and dignity. —Patrice Lumumba, 1960

The problem is not that we were once in charge, but that we are not in charge any more... The best fate for Africa would be if the old colonial powers, or their citizens, scrambled once again in her direction... —Boris Johnson, 2002

Calgach's speech at Mons Graupius (highlighted in our introduction) provides an ideal point of departure for any engagement with resistance to imperialism and colonialism. Our approach assumes that in order to resist, the colonised need to develop some appreciation of what they are resisting. In this sense, theory precedes practice. Calgach's thumbnail sketch on empire bears repetition: 'to ravage, to slaughter, to usurp under false titles, they call empire; and where they make a wasteland, they call it peace'. In other words, he turns the hubris and conceit of empire on its head from the first and identifies the naked greed and brutality that informs the process. 'Ravage, slaughter, false title' – what simpler or more apposite summary could there be of much that was to follow in the name of empire? With telling foresight, he also anticipates the ideological construction of 'peace' under empire. His subject was, of course, *Pax Romana* and the Roman Empire. But these defining characteristics of empire were equally emblematic of later colonialisms and imperialisms. Crucially, these involved a similar distortion of reality – reframing destruction as 'civilisation' and 'desolation' as 'peace'.

As we have already seen, Conradian 'horror' was to characterise much of what followed the Treaty of Tordesillas in 1494. Despite the catalogue of crimes against humanity that were to be committed in its name – including slavery and genocide – it took five centuries for the notion that colonisation was essentially a bad thing to become broadly accepted. Not surprisingly, those who had gained most from colonialism were least likely to accept any critique. Nevertheless, by the end of WWII decolonisation was regarded as both desirable and inevitable by most of the post-war world.[1] Delegates of 50 nations met in San Francisco in 1945 and agreed the UN Charter, the founding document of the United Nations. A commitment to decolonisation was integrated within this broad approach to international cooperation and peace. In particular, the decolonisation efforts of the UN derive from Article One of the Charter which envisages 'friendly relations among nations based on respect for the principle of equal rights and self-determination of peoples'. The Charter also included three further sections specifically devoted to the interests of dependent peoples: Chapter XI: Declaration regarding Non-Self-Governing Territories (NSGTs); Chapter XII: International Trusteeship System;[2] Chapter XIII: The Trusteeship Council.[3] In other words, while it took another twenty years for the British Empire to acknowledge this 'wind of change', world opinion had made it clear in 1945 that colonialism was no longer ideologically or politically acceptable in the post-war world.[4]

In 1960, to accelerate the progress of decolonisation, the General Assembly adopted the Declaration on the Granting of Independence to Colonial Countries and Peoples – the 'Declaration on Decolonisation' (United Nations 1960). This reaffirmed that all people have a right to self-determination and proclaimed that 'colonialism in all its forms and manifestations' should be brought 'to a speedy and unconditional end'. In 1962 the General Assembly established the Special Committee on Decolonisation to monitor implementation of the Declaration and to make recommendations on its application.[5] The Special Committee annually reviews the list of Territories to which the

---

[1] A key stage in the case of the United States was the formation of the Anti-Imperialist League on 15 June 1898, in Boston in opposition to the acquisition of the Philippines. The anti-imperialists opposed the expansion because they believed imperialism violated the principles of republicanism, especially the need for 'consent of the governed'. The League included famous citizens such as Andrew Carnegie, Henry James, and Mark Twain.

[2] The United Nations established the International Trusteeship System for the supervision of Trust Territories placed under it by individual agreements with the States administering them. Under Article 77 of the Charter, the Trusteeship System applied to: territories held under Mandates established by the League of Nations after the First World War; territories detached from 'enemy States' as a result of the Second World War; territories voluntarily placed under the System by states responsible for their administration. Today, all 11 territories have either become independent states or have 'voluntarily associated' themselves with a state. With no Territories left in its agenda, the Trusteeship System had completed its historic task.

[3] The Trusteeship Council was established under Chapter XIII of the Charter to supervise the administration of Trust Territories and to ensure that governments responsible for their administration took adequate steps to prepare them for the achievement of the Charter goals.

[4] The pattern of decolonisation differed between empires and within. The French departure from most of West Africa was relatively painless compared to what was 'an undeclared colonial war of unprecedented brutality' in Algeria (Thomas et al. 2008: 228). The British were more brutal in Kenya than in some other decolonising situations. The Portuguese held on to their empire longer than some others and as a result Angola and Mozambique 'witnessed some of the bloodiest wars of decolonisation not only in Africa but anywhere in the world' (Elkins 2005: 216). One element which defined different levels of brutality was the extent of settler privilege and control in specific societies.

[5] General Assembly Resolution establishing the Special Committee on Decolonisation.

Declaration is applicable and makes recommendations as to its implementation. It also hears statements from NSGT representatives, dispatches visiting missions, and organises seminars on the political, social and economic situation in the NSGTs.[6] Further, the Special Committee annually makes recommendations to mobilise public opinion in support of the decolonisation process and observes the Week of Solidarity with the peoples of NSGTs.

This specific UN commitment to decolonisation has continued over the years. In 1990, the General Assembly proclaimed 1990-2000 as the International Decade for the Eradication of Colonialism and adopted a plan of action. In 2001, the Second International Decade was proclaimed. Most recently, the Special Political and Decolonisation Committee had the General Assembly declare the period 2011-2020 as the Third International Decade for the Eradication of Colonialism, concluding its general debate on decolonisation. This also called upon member states to intensify their efforts to implement the plan of action for the Second International Decade and use those efforts as the basis for a plan of action for the Third Decade. This was approved by a recorded vote of 130 in favour and 3 against (United States, United Kingdom, Israel), with 20 abstentions. The Assembly similarly approved by a recorded vote of 150 in favour and 3 against (United States, United Kingdom, Israel) and no abstentions, the motion urging the administering powers and other member states to ensure that the activities of foreign economic and other interests in colonial territories did not run counter to the interests of the inhabitants of those territories and did not impede the implementation of the Declaration.

This episode suggested a certain deceleration in the decolonisation process. Twenty years before, the first international decade had been supported without a vote, and ten years before only two states had opposed the second decade – the UK and the USA. In 2010, the UK 'explained' its opposition to 'eradicating colonialism':

> The representative of the United Kingdom, explaining his delegation's opposition to both those texts, said the proposals for the Third International Decade and the Fiftieth anniversary of the Decolonisation Declaration were 'unacceptable', as the texts failed to recognize the progress that had been made in the relationship between the United Kingdom and its territories. With regard to the text relating to the Third International decade, his delegation strongly considered the 'Special Committee of 24' to be outdated and believed that the United Nations should devote its resources to more urgent issues. (United Nations 2010)

Given that the majority of territories remaining on the agenda of the committee 'belonged' to the UK, it might be assumed that the UK interest in focusing world attention on 'more urgent issues' had a motive other than concern regarding UN 'resources'.

Nevertheless, world opinion remains solidly anti-colonial – despite the opposition of Israel, the US and the UK. From this perspective, the legacies of colonialism and

---

[6] It also reviews the status of such territories in the context of the General Assembly Resolution defining the three options for self-determination – General Assembly Resolution 1541 (XV).

imperialism represent something to be 'eradicated' rather than cherished. In other words, considered world opinion has made it very clear that colonialism was not a 'good thing' and that colonial powers are under a direct moral and legal obligation to end their relationship with their 'territories' as quickly as possible. Moreover, this commitment to decolonisation – while still incomplete – has been largely operationalised. When the United Nations was established in 1945, some 750 million people – a third of the world's population – lived in territories that were defined as 'non-self-governing' and occupied by colonial powers. By 2020, fewer than two million people live in NSGTs. Since the creation of the United Nations more than 80 former colonies have gained their independence. Among them, all eleven UN Trust Territories have achieved self-determination through independence or free association with an independent State. Seventeen NSGTs remain. One of these, Western Sahara, remains disputed. Of the remainder: two 'belong' to France – New Caledonia and French Polynesia'; one 'belongs' to New Zealand – Tokelau; three to the United States – Guam, American Samoa and US Virgin Islands; and the other ten to the UK – Gibraltar, Pitcairn, Anguilla, Bermuda, British Virgin Islands, Cayman Islands, Falkland Islands/Malvinas, Montserrat, St Helena, and Turks and Caicos Islands. Despite these anachronisms, however, most of the colonial empires have been dismantled and most of the colonised world has been decolonised. For all the ongoing contradictions, self-determination for the peoples of the world has progressed.

The arc of decolonisation

In this chapter we trace the theory and practice of anti-colonialism and anti-imperialism leading towards decolonisation. Over time this would become one of the most theorised of all political ideologies – inspiring some of the greatest texts of world literature and political philosophy (Césaire 1955; Fanon 1961; Memmi 1990) alongside more direct exemplars of anti-imperialist praxis (Cabral 2016; Che Guevara 1967; Mao 1967).[7] But this belies the humble beginnings – arguably anti-imperialism started more prosaically. Since the first time that Europeans 'discovered' new peoples and territories, the dialectics of colonialism and resistance had been locked in place. For example, on 18 January 1788, the *Sirius*, the flagship of the British fleet carrying the first convoy of convicts to Australia, landed at Botany Bay. From the shore, some Dharawal men waved spears and shouted 'Warra! Warra!' 'These words, the first recorded ones spoken by a black to a white in Australia, meant "Go away!"' (Hughes 1987: 84). The nexus of 'contact' inevitably transformed people into 'natives' or 'indigenous' or 'Indians'. They were metamorphosed by the duality of coloniser/colonised that arrives with contact. From this defining moment, we can trace three broad stages across the arc of anti-

---

[7] The praxis might be summed up by Mao's formula for combating the Kuomintang: 'When the enemy advances, we retreat. When the enemy rests, we harass him. When the enemy avoids a battle, we attack. When the enemy retreats, we advance'.

colonialism. These develop at vastly different times in different countries, of course, but the sequencing is broadly comparable across colonial contexts.

First, the newly constructed 'natives' begin resisting the colonisation process itself. This first stage over which the colonial state pursues a process of effective control is often a long and bloody one. This is the time frame between 'contact' and the point at which the colonial state can claim a 'monopoly over the legitimate means of coercion'. While in the age of discovery it was routine for explorers to claim a piece of land in the name of their respective monarch, there was some distance between this claim and the point at which the people of a given land could be said to have been subjected.[8] This period traverses, therefore, the process of the formal construction of the colonial state. Over this period, people, land, and other property are expropriated – usually under the use or threat of vastly superior colonial military capacity. The whole period is usually characterised by notions of conquest, especially when there is an indigenous state *in situ*.

Second, once the colonial state formation is in place, the question arises of how the colonised can resist its imperium. This period is more clearly demarcated since the colonial state will usually be constitutionalised by the colonial power. Alongside its new monopoly over the legitimate means of coercion, the colonial state formation constructs a legal framework to codify its legitimacy. This completely transforms the agency of the colonised. Now their ability to resist is restricted by more than the expression of military power. Most significantly, resistance is criminalised, and any notion of self-determination is repudiated. The rights of the colonised – if they are recognised at all – are markedly unequal to those of the colonial settlers. This begs the question of how the colonised might self-determine in this context if they have restricted rights to political expression and representation. Nevertheless, the colonised do find ways to resist and dismantle the colonial state. For most former colonies, this phase has ended in some form of independence.

Third, following independence, the issue becomes one of how the new self-determined state should continue the process of decolonisation as well as how it should relate to remaining colonies. There were, of course, actually existing post-colonial formations in the US and Haiti by the start of the nineteenth century – from that point onwards, a template for a post-colonial world has been envisaged and every remaining colony can begin to engage practically with the question of how decolonisation should take place. Should it turn its attention to anti-colonialism in one country or see itself as part of a broader, continuing struggle to eradicate colonialism *per se*? This more general approach was normalised and legitimised by the UN after 1945, but the question of whether the post-colonial state should continue to resist wider processes of colonialism as an anti-imperialist state remained a radical and dangerous one. Most particularly, the question was particularly stark for post-independence African countries living in the shadow of apartheid; and it remains a defining one for neighbouring states engaging with their relationship with Israel.

---

[8] In the case of Ireland, the English themselves believed that this stage lasted 400 years.

Certainly, some post-colonial states became identified as anti-imperialist hubs – over the years these have included Algeria, Libya, and Cuba. But this question is writ large for all decolonised states – what role should they play in supporting decolonisation elsewhere? All these post-colonial formations confronted their own internal contradictions too, of course. The principle of *uti possidetis*[9] specified that boundaries imposed by colonialism could not be changed in the context of liberation; but these boundaries often bore little resemblance to anything approaching self-determination for different peoples – tribal and ethnic groups, linguistic communities and nationalities – within the new states.

It bears emphasis, of course, that this arc of decolonisation usually was – and remains – a slow process. Arguably it has not finished anywhere. (As will be seen, we argue that Ireland has the longest arc of all.) But the catastrophe of colonialism was often palpable and immediate. The most famous 'contact' of all – Columbus's 'discovery' of the Americas in 1492 – is still celebrated across both the 'old' and 'new' worlds (Cohen 1969).[10] But this event had immediately devastating consequences for the indigenous people he encountered. The society of the Taíno/Arawak people of Hispaniola deteriorated rapidly after contact with the Spanish. The natives of the island were systematically subjugated through the *encomienda* system implemented by Columbus. Spanish colonists under his rule began to buy and sell natives, including children, as slaves.

In fact, Columbus' soldiers killed and enslaved with impunity at every one of his four landings: stealing, killing, raping, and torturing natives, forcing them to reveal imagined sources of gold. Columbus organised his troops' efforts with military precision, forming a squadron of several hundred heavily armed men supplemented by attack dogs. Columbus' 'contact' immediately killed thousands of natives. Consequently, Columbus is viewed as a key agent of genocide among indigenous peoples, despite his valorisation across Europe and the Americas. Loewen (1995: 60) records that while 'Haiti under the Spanish is one of the primary instances of genocide in all human history' only one of twelve history texts he examined recorded Columbus' role in this.

The Spanish priest and defender of the Taíno/Arawak, Bartolomé de las Casas[11] (1989) wrote in his 1561 *History of the Indies*:

---

[9] The principle in customary international law which says that the boundaries of the colonial state remain unchanged when decolonisation occurs.

[10] Although opposition to this celebration is also common. Among people of Latin American descent in the US, for example, Columbus Day is reinterpreted as *El Dia de la Raza*. There is a graphic reproduced frequently in social media and elsewhere which shows a group of native Americans above the slogan: 'Fighting terrorism since 1492'.

[11] Las Casas was not without his own contradictions. He infamously supported African slavery for a time on the basis that it would avert the genocide of native Americans (Pruitt 2020). In a more critical reading of his life, Las Casas simply offered indigenous peoples a more liberal paternalistic, ecclesiastical imperialism rather than anything approaching anti-imperialism (Castro 2007).

There were 60,000 people living on this island [when I arrived in 1508], including the Indians; so that from 1494 to 1508, over three million people had perished from war, slavery and the mines. Who in future generations will believe this?

Other estimates for the pre-Columbian population of Hispaniola are lower – at around 300,000. Whatever the size of the population before 'discovery', the genocide was almost complete within a generation. The indigenous population in Hispaniola was further decimated by the first pandemic of European endemic diseases. The natives had no acquired immunity to unfamiliar diseases like smallpox. According to the contemporaneous historian Gonzalo Fernandez de Oviedo y Valdes, by 1548 – only 56 years after Columbus had 'discovered' them – fewer than 500 Taíno/Arawak were living on the island. From this perspective 'discovery' deserves no celebration and resistance to colonisation seems less an act of barbarism than a desperate attempt at survival.

Resisting the colonisation process

Given the genocidal implications of 'discovery', it was hardly surprising that resistance often began on day one of 'contact'. Nevertheless, in some contexts, the reception from indigenous peoples was often courteous and interested. This demonstrated the universal possibility of cross-cultural contact and human interfacing. However, once what was characterised in chapter 3 as the 'Powhatan truth' was recognised – that Europeans had come not only to explore and trade but also to 'invade and possess' – the dynamic changed. As soon as natives understood the nature of the colonial project, resistance began in earnest.

The price of resistance was considerable. When natives on Hispaniola began fighting back in 1495, Columbus' men captured 1,500 Taíno/Arawak men, women, and children in a single raid. The strongest were transported to Spain to be sold as slaves; nearly half of these enslaved people died *en route*. Loewen (1995: 60) suggests that 'Columbus not only sent the first slaves across the Atlantic, he probably sent more slaves – about five thousand – than any other individual'. According to Las Casas's contemporary *A Short Account of the Destruction of the Indies*, when slaves held in captivity began to die at high rates, Columbus ordered all natives over the age of thirteen to pay a 'hawk's bell' full of gold powder every three months. Natives who brought this amount to the Spanish were given a copper token to hang around their necks. The Spanish amputated the hands of those without tokens and left them to bleed to death. Not surprisingly the catastrophic changes that followed colonisation also created a spiritual desolation. Las Casas records how thousands of natives committed suicide by poison to escape their persecution.

The Taíno/Arawaks lacked the key technological resources available to the Spanish: armour, guns, swords, and horses. When taken prisoner, they were hanged or burned to death. Desperation led to mass suicides and infanticide among the natives. A combination of killing, disease and enslavement contributed to the depopulation. In just two years under Columbus' governorship, over half the natives in Hispaniola were dead, and in three decades 'virtually every member of the gentle race ... had been wiped out'. From the first it was clear that self-determination would neither be easy nor without cost. To this day, Las Casas' account can shock the reader:

> They laid Wagers among themselves, who should with a Sword at one blow cut, or divide a Man in two; or which of them should decollate or behead a Man, with the greatest dexterity; nay farther, which should sheath his Sword in the Bowels of a Man with the quickest dispatch and expedition. They snatcht young Babes from the Mothers Breasts, and then dasht out the brains of those innocents against the Rocks; others they cast into Rivers scoffing and jeering them, and call'd upon their Bodies when falling with derision, the true testimony of their Cruelty, to come to them, and inhumanely exposing others to their Merciless Swords, together with the Mothers that gave them Life. They erected certain Gibbets, large, but low made, so that their feet almost reacht the ground, every one of which was so order'd as to bear Thirteen Persons in Honour and Reverence (as they said blasphemously) of our Redeemer and his Twelve Apostles, under which they made a Fire to burn them to Ashes whilst hanging on them... (Las Casas 1689: 5)

He noted that even in terms of their own justification of conquest, the Spanish were failing. Claiming to bring the savages to the true religion, instead many people died without understanding 'the true Faith and Sacraments'. On occasion, they understood precisely, but not in the ways a missionary might desire. In Hispaniola an indigenous chief, or cacic, named Hathney was tied to a post and was about to be executed. A Franciscan monk

> discours'd with him concerning God and the Articles of our Faith, which he never heard of before, and which might be satisfactory and advantagious to him, considering the small time allow'd him by the Executioner, promising him Eternal Glory and Repose, if he truly believ'd them, or otherwise Everlasting Torments. After that Hathney had been silently pensive sometime, he askt the Monk whether the Spaniards also were admitted into Heaven, and he answering that the Gates of Heaven were open to all that were Good and Godly, the Cacic replied without further consideration, that he would rather go to Hell then Heaven, for fear he should cohabit in the same Mansion with so Sanguinary and Bloody a Nation. (Las Casas 1689: 9)

Similar acts of barbarity were repeated across the history of colonisation. This included biological warfare. Such tactics were employed during the siege of Fort Pitt in June and July 1763 in what is now Pittsburgh, Pennsylvania. This was a part of Pontiac's War, an effort by Native Americans to remove the British after they refused to honour their treaty commitments to leave voluntarily following the defeat of the French. The British gave clothing from the smallpox infirmary as gifts to Native Americans with the aim of spreading the disease to nearby tribes that had no natural resistance. Representatives from the Delaware tribe met with Fort Pitt officials to warn them of 'great numbers of Indians' coming to attack the fort and encourage them to leave the fort while there was still time. The commander of the fort refused to abandon the fort. Instead, the British gave them the 'gift' of smallpox. The trader and militia captain William Trent recorded the process in his diary: 'Out of our regard to them we gave them two Blankets and an Handkerchief out of the Small Pox Hospital. I hope it will have the desired effect' (Harpster 1938: 99). The smallpox epidemic spread through the territories of the Lenni Lenape (Delaware) and Shawnee villages, killing many Native Americans during and years after the war. Visiting Pittsburgh a few years later, David McClure (1899: 92) recorded:

> I was informed at Pittsburgh, that when the Delawares, Shawanese and others, laid siege suddenly and most traitorously to Fort Pitt, in 1764, in a time of peace, the people within, found means of conveying the small pox to them, which was far more destructive than the guns from the walls, or all the artillery of Colonel Boquet's army, which obliged them to abandon the enterprise.

This kind of genocidal barbarity was repeated time and again across the colonial process. The methodology was routinely brutally military in character – employing soldiers and armies of occupation. The primacy of violence in this dynamic saw massacre as a key tactic of both natives and colonists. Where there was an existing 'native' central state, the process also became one of conquest – there was a colonial campaign to defeat the military forces of the colonised state. The power imbalance was usually huge but there was still widespread resistance.

For example, the battle of Tenochtitlan in Mexico marked such a victory for the Spanish Empire in North America. In 1519 at the beginning of his conquest, the Conquistador Cortés entered Tenochtitlán, capital of the Aztec Empire which ruled some 500 small states with a total population of five to six million.[12] Whether through fear or courtesy, the Spanish were permitted to enter the city without resistance. They immediately took the Aztec ruler Moctezuma II hostage. The following spring – in a pre-echo of future colonial 'humanitarian' intervention – the Spanish agreed to allow the Tōxcatl festival on the condition that there would be no human sacrifice. Before the festival, however, they tortured some Aztecs and discovered that they were planning a revolt. The Spanish ordered the gates closed and initiated the killing of thousands of Aztec nobles, warriors, and priests. This triggered the Aztec revolt. During the Night of Sorrows in June 1520 the invading army of Spanish conquistadors and native allies were driven out of the Mexican capital. This anti-colonial victory was short-lived, however. Two years later, the Siege of Tenochtitlan became the decisive event in the Spanish conquest of Mexico. Its outcome was swayed by the effects of a smallpox epidemic which devastated the Aztec population. During the siege, around 100 Spaniards lost their lives compared to as many as 100,000 Aztecs. The city fell on 13 August 1521. This marked the end of the first phase of the Spanish conquest of the Aztec Empire. Ultimately, Spain conquered the whole of Mexico and thereby gained direct access to the Pacific Ocean, which meant that the Spanish Empire could achieve its original goal of reaching the Asian markets from Mexico's Pacific coast.

---

[12] Cortés acquired an enslaved indigenous woman known as Malinche, or Doña Marina, who became his interpreter. They had a son together – Martín – who is often regarded as the first ever *mestizo*.

In this manner colonisation was often characterised by decisive battles that mark the watershed between pre-colonial and colonial formations. In India, the Battle of Plassey in 1757 was a decisive victory of the British East India Company under Clive over the Nawab of Bengal and his French allies. The battle consolidated the Company's presence in Bengal, which later expanded to cover all of India over the next hundred years. A handful of conventional battles were won by indigenous American, Asian, and African forces employing numerical superiority or the element of surprise over colonial powers. For example, the Battle of Isandlwana in 1879 was the first major encounter in the Anglo–Zulu War between the British Empire and the Zulu Kingdom. Eleven days after the British commenced their invasion of Zululand in South Africa, a Zulu force of some 20,000 warriors attacked a portion of the British invasion force consisting of about 1,800 British, colonial, and native troops. The Zulu were equipped mainly with the traditional assegai iron spears and cowhide shields, but also had several rifles. The British troops were armed with state-of-the-art breech-loading rifles and field guns. Despite a vast disadvantage in weapons technology, the numerically superior Zulu ultimately overwhelmed the British, killing over 1,300 troops. The Zulu army suffered around 2,000 killed. The battle was a decisive victory for the Zulu and the army of the British Empire had suffered its worst defeat against an indigenous force with vastly inferior military technology.

Ultimately, however, Isandlwana resulted in the British taking an even more aggressive approach in the Anglo–Zulu War, leading to a heavily reinforced second invasion. King Cetshwayo's hopes of a negotiated peace ended with the final defeat of the Zulus at the hands of British forces at the Battle of Ulundi.[13] This was the last major battle of the Anglo-Zulu War as the British army broke the military power of the Zulu nation by capturing and razing the capital of Zululand, the royal kraal of Ulundi. After only half an hour of concentrated fire from the artillery, the Gatling Guns and thousands of British rifles, Zulu military power was broken. British casualties were ten killed and eighty-seven wounded, while nearly five hundred Zulus died with another 1,000 wounded.

Over time most indigenous forces faced similar staggering losses and discouraging defeats. Such trends were marked by the German suppression of the Maji Maji Rebellion. This armed rebellion against German colonial rule in German East Africa (modern-day Tanzania) was triggered by a German policy designed to force the indigenous population to grow cotton for export. It lasted from 1905 to 1907. The war resulted in up to 300,000 Tanzanian dead. Most of the dead were victims of famine (known as the *njaa* or 'Great Hunger'), caused by the scorched-earth policy of German Governor Gustav Adolf von Götzen. Von Götzen's troops lost 15 Europeans and 389 African soldiers.

---

[13] Half a world away, in Ireland, Charles Stewart Parnell addressed a gathering of 30,000 constituents in Navan in October 1879. The crowd spontaneously and repeatedly chanted the name of the Zulu king. As Townend (2007: 158) concludes, the war against the Zulu was 'used, over and over again at all levels of the emerging land movement, to rally support, and to catechise the Irish people about the true nature of their relationship to the British Empire'.

Arguably, however, this kind of coloniser/colonised power imbalance reached its nadir in the destruction of Mahdist cavalry by British Maxim machine guns at the Battle of Omdurman. In September 1898, an army commanded by the British General Kitchener defeated the army of Abdullah al-Taashi, the successor to the Mahdi, Muhammad Ahmad. The British regarded this venture as revenge for the 1885 death of General Gordon during the Mahdist uprising. The battle was a demonstration of the superiority of an industrialised army equipped with modern rifles, machine guns, and artillery over a force twice their size armed with older weapons. A key aspect of British technological superiority was that this was the first time that the 'Dum Dum' – an expanding bullet – was used in a major battle. It completed British efforts to re-conquer the Sudan. Around 12,000 Muslim fighters were killed, 13,000 wounded and 5,000 taken prisoner. Kitchener's force lost 47 men killed and 382 wounded. One eyewitness described the 'battle':

> They could never get near and they refused to hold back ... It was not a battle but an execution ... The bodies were not in heaps – bodies hardly ever are; but they spread evenly over acres and acres. Some lay very composedly with their slippers placed under their heads for a last pillow; some knelt, cut short in the middle of a last prayer. Others were torn to pieces. (Cited in Spielvogel 2018: 746)

Despite a controversy over the killing of the wounded after the battle, the episode was judged a remarkable imperial success.

Colonial invasion was sometimes more successfully challenged when an indigenous force used guerrilla warfare instead of committing to traditional pitched battles.[14] In this context, the Franco-Hova Wars (Madagascar 1883-1896) foreshadowed the later tactics of anti-imperialist struggle. Indigenous leaders such as Abdelkader ibn Muhieddine of Algeria, Mahmadu Lamine of Senegal, and Samori Ture of the Wassoulou Empire were able to resist European colonialism for years after disregarding traditional methods and using guerrilla tactics instead.

Despite the occasional reverse for imperialist forces, the broader scenario was a relentless advance of colonialism – supported by its vastly superior weaponry and resources – in the face of any military resistance. This did not, however, always entail a total defeat for the colonised. As colonisation progressed, the power dynamic between coloniser and colonised was often marked by treaties. These recognised the sovereignty of indigenous peoples in different ways – either explicitly or implicitly repudiating the notion of *terra nullius*. At the same time, the treaties frequently proved to be no protection to bloody military conquest. The archetypal example was the Treaty of Waitangi (Te Tiriti o Waitangi).[15] This was signed on 6 February 1840 by

---

[14] That said, the Mapuche people of the southern cone of South America claim to be the only indigenous group in the Americas which was never militarily conquered by the Spanish. Their success seems to have stemmed from two tactics: first, guerrilla warfare; second, adopting the invaders' tactics – fighting on horseback, massing large numbers of troops, building forts – all things they did not do previously. See Cruz 2010.

[15] Unlike the Māori, Aboriginal peoples in Australia were never offered a treaty by the British colonists. Some contemporary activists are demanding a treaty now with the (post-colonial) Australian government

representatives of the British Crown and Māori chiefs from the North Island of New Zealand. It continues to frame political relations between New Zealand's government and the Māori population. As part of establishing New Zealand as a British colony, the treaty recognised Māori ownership of their lands and other possessions and gave Māori the 'rights' of British subjects. The text of the Treaty includes a preamble and three articles. Article One of the English texts cedes 'all rights and powers of sovereignty' to the Crown. Article Two establishes the continued ownership of the Māori over their lands and establishes the exclusive right of pre-emption of the Crown. Article three gives Māori people full rights and protections as British subjects. It is bilingual, with the Māori text translated from the English – although the English text and the Māori text differ in meaning significantly, particularly in relation to the notion of 'sovereignty'. These differences led to disagreements in the decades following the signing, eventually culminating in the 'New Zealand Wars' (1845-72).

Armed conflict between Māori and European settlers broke out first in the South Island in June 1843 in the Wairau Valley. Settlers led by a representative of the New Zealand Company – which held a false title deed to a plot of land – attempted to clear Māori off the land in preparation for surveying. Fighting broke out and six Māori and 22 Europeans were killed. Several Europeans were subsequently killed after being captured. The Governor, Robert FitzRoy, investigated the incident and declared the settlers were at fault. Despite this, the war between the government and Māori spread to the North Island, culminating in the invasion of the Waikato in 1863–1864. The government also responded with legislation to imprison Māori and confiscate expansive areas of the North Island for sale to settlers, with the funds used to cover war expenses. These punitive measures provoked an intensification of Māori resistance. At the peak of hostilities in the 1860s, 18,000 British troops, supported by artillery, cavalry, and local militia, battled around 4,000 Māori warriors. The New Zealand government also developed its own army, including local militia, rifle volunteer groups, Forest Rangers and kūpapa (pro-government Māori). Despite the imbalance of soldiers and weaponry, the Māori used guerrilla tactics to great effect. During the wars over 2,000 Māori and 800 European lives were lost. In the aftermath, further Māori land was confiscated from both 'loyal' and 'rebel' tribes alike.

Following the Wars, the New Zealand government ignored the Treaty of Waitangi – a court case judgement in 1877 declared it 'a simple nullity'. Beginning in the 1950s, however, Māori increasingly sought to use the Treaty as a platform for reclaiming sovereignty and lost land. New Zealand governments in the 1960s and 1970s were more responsive to these arguments, giving the Treaty an increasingly central role in the

---

(Sovereign Union 2020). Others point out that as there are approximately 600 Aboriginal nations, it would take multiple treaties. Still others argue that the effect of such treaties would be that indigenous peoples recognise the legitimacy of the colonial government system that dispossessed them.

interpretation of land rights and relations between Māori people and the state. In 1975, the Waitangi Tribunal was established as a permanent commission of inquiry tasked with interpreting the Treaty, researching breaches of the Treaty, and suggesting redress. In most cases, recommendations of the Tribunal are not binding on the Crown and the Treaty has never been made part of New Zealand law. Nevertheless, settlements totalling almost $1 billion have been awarded in reparation. Legislation passed in the later part of the 20th century has also referenced the Treaty. Nowadays, the Treaty is widely regarded as the founding document of New Zealand. Waitangi Day – commemorating the signing of the Treaty – was established as a national holiday in 1974.

Many other treaties were signed in this process of colonial state formation. In Africa, the arch-imperialist Stanley simply forged them if he could not get native rulers to sign. They did sometimes have an effect in mediating aspects of the colonial process. The Maroons in Jamaica even managed to maintain their independence through a treaty with the British. More routinely, however, treaties were subsequently ignored or repudiated by the colonising powers. While they were mostly honoured in the breach, these formal agreements between the coloniser and the colonised continue to have significant reference for anti-imperialist struggle. Even the absence of a Treaty – such as in the *Mabo v Queensland* decision – can help to challenge and undermine some of the most egregious consequences of the application of *terra nullius*.[16] Most notoriously of all, treaties were routinely made and broken with Native American peoples across the history of the colonisation of North America – both before and after US independence.[17]

Between the Treaty of Tordesillas and the Berlin Conference most of the non-European world was absorbed into European empires. Arguably this European (and US) project reached its apogee at the turn of the twentieth century in the Eight-Nation Alliance invasion of China. This became what might be regarded as the antithesis of a fair fight. Towards the end of the Qing dynasty, between 1899 and 1901, there was a period of anti-foreign, anti-colonial, and anti-Christian resistance that was characterised as the 'Boxer rising'. The Eight-Nation Alliance – Japan, Russia, Britain, France, the United States, Germany, Italy and Austria-Hungary – was a multi-national military coalition set up in response. The Alliance brought 20,000 armed troops to China, defeated the Imperial Army, and occupied Beijing, relieving the siege of the Foreign Legations. This was followed by uncontrolled plunder of the capital and the surrounding countryside, along with the summary execution of those suspected of

---

[16] *Mabo v Queensland (No. 2)* (commonly known as Mabo decision) was a landmark High Court of Australia decision in 1992 recognising native title in Australia for the first time. The High Court held that the doctrine of *terra nullius*, which imported all laws of England to a new land, did not apply in circumstances where there were already inhabitants present – even if those inhabitants had been regarded at the time as 'uncivilised'.

[17] Wikipedia lists 570 separate treaties with Native American tribes between 1778 and 1904. Every single one was violated by the US government.

being Boxers. Much of the Chinese treasure that was looted was eventually repatriated to Europe and the US. The invasion ended with the signing of the Boxer Protocol. China was fined war reparations for the loss that it had allegedly caused. The reparation was to be paid within forty years. The sum of reparation was estimated by the Chinese population so that each Chinese person would pay one tael (forty grams of silver). One Irish journalist, George Lynch, who reported on the invasion summed it up: 'There are things that I must not write, and that may not be printed in England, which would seem to show that this Western civilisation of ours is merely a veneer over savagery' (Lynch 1903).

In this manner, nearly every inch of the world outside Europe had been colonised by the turn of the twentieth century. In this transformed context, resistance was now directed at the new colonial state formations which claimed sole legitimacy and were largely able to effect jurisdiction over the colonised.

Resisting the colonial state

The consolidation of the colonial state marked a new phase in anti-imperialist struggle. Now all the resources of the state were available to supplement the military arsenal of the colonising powers. The European empires were all committed to justifying their conquests as something other than criminal expropriation. Whether in terms of the American doctrine of 'manifest destiny' or the claim that Australia was a *terra nullius* (a land without people, a claim somewhat negated by the presence of aboriginal peoples), colonisation was represented as not simply rational but also legal and indeed altruistic. This was often coupled with a direct appeal to law. In Latin America, the conquistadors appealed to *res nullius*, a concept from Roman law, 'which 'allowed' them to take land from the indigenous people if they were simply claiming it but not using it effectively' (Elliot 2006: 12). This eventually developed into the Principle of Effectivity which emerged from the Berlin Conference of 1884-5. European powers, attempting to bring some agreed order to the scramble for Africa, decided that it was not enough for a colonial power simply to plant a flag on a territory. Until they sought to 'use' the territory effectively, it was open to another power to claim it instead.

The Spanish in South America employed a symbolic legal ritual to indicate 'possession'. When the conquistadors came to a new piece of territory they proposed to expropriate, 'they would read the *requerimiento*, drawn up in 1512 by jurist Juan Lopez de Palacios Rubio, to the inhabitants before then taking their land or slaughtering them. The Protestant English were never going to cite papal bulls but did justify seizing land in the name of the monarch, the 'Defender of the Faith' (Elliot 2006: 11). The British in North America insisted on a formal legal ceremony when taking possession of territory. For example, upon landing in Newfoundland in 1583, Sir Humphrey Gilbert 'had his commission under the great seal "solemnly read" to an assembled company of his own

men, together with a motley band of English and foreign merchants and fishermen'
(Elliot 2006: 31).

By this finesse almost any indigenous resistance had become 'rebellion'. The
formation of the new colonial state was, however, a moveable feast. In India it took two
hundred years of colonisation via the offices of the East India Company before the British
state assumed full responsibility for its colony in 1858. It was another twenty years
before it formally became an empire in 1877 – and even then, there were numerous
'princely states' with a semblance of autonomy that further complicated the colonial
model. In other words, the colonial state that emerged from the colonisation process
was often a complex and ambiguous entity. This meant that the target of anti-imperialism
was equally occluded at times. For example, in India there was an obvious question of
whether anti-colonialism in India was about the 'East India Company' or the 'Raj' – did
it include the whole territory including the 'Princely states' or only the areas of 'direct
rule'?[18] At one level anti-imperialism within the British Empire could only begin once
the empire had assumed a clear and fixed constitutional character.

Other colonial projects were of course more quickly formalised as unambiguous
colonial state formations – with laws and ideological and repressive state apparatuses
of different kinds. On this score, Leopold of Belgium's mission in the Congo provides a
paradigm case. As Leopold revealed to Stanley:

> It is a question of creating a new state, as big as possible, and of running it. It is clearly
> understood that in this project there is no question of granting the slightest political
> power to the negros. That would be absurd. (Cited in Gondola 2002: 51)

In this context, indigenous resistance was hardly unexpected. Since 'negros' or 'natives'
were to be excluded from political power and transformed into commodities and forms
of bonded labour, their opposition might be taken as a given. At least the target of anti-
imperialist resistance was clear – this 'new state' that expressly excluded any role for
indigenous peoples.

But this immediately raised the question of what forms of resistance were possible.
Once the colonial state was established, the first question in terms of self-determination
was what is the status of the colonised? This established the parameters around which
any form of self-determination would be constructed. It becomes misguided to read
this dynamic backwards. While contemporary perspectives cannot help but be grounded
in the 1948 United Nations provision of 'universal and equal suffrage' in the Universal
Declaration of Human Rights [Article 21(3)], this of course did not apply for most of the
colonial period. Moreover, it did not apply for most of the decolonisation process either.

---

[18] Thus, the Raj included colonial entities that had no cultural connection to India but were managed as
part of that imperial project for strategic or other reasons. From Aden to Australia, other bits of the empire
were integrated into the Raj at different times. But this immediately raised questions in terms of self-
determination. Where did these polities – or Ceylon or Burma – sit in terms of Indian self-determination?
These contradictions ultimately contributed to the partition of India.

Hong Kong was perhaps the most graphic example of this. It was transferred to China in 1997, after 156 years of British rule. The United Kingdom had been in possession of Hong Kong since the First Opium War in 1842, yet it held its first legislative elections in 1991 – only six years before decolonisation.[19] This kind of profoundly anti-democratic reality characterised almost the whole colonial experience.

Put simply, democracy was sometimes 'gifted' to the post-colonial regime by imperial powers at the point of decolonisation, but it was hardly ever a mechanism provided to determine policy within the colonial state. For almost the entire duration of colonial history, colonised peoples were offered nothing approaching either 'constitutional' or 'democratic' mechanisms to change their experience of colonialism. Colonialism was characterised for its duration by its anti-democratic character. This reality impacted most profoundly on indigenous peoples who were often disenfranchised even in the context of wider democratisation. They were generally provided no franchise at all; when they were provided with any franchise, they were usually minoritised in relation to white settlers.

In other words, there was no democratic road to self-determination for most colonised peoples. This meant that resistance was, by definition, unconstitutional – framed as 'rebellion' by the coloniser and 'uprising' by the colonised. This left two broad strategies of resistance – in Ireland these were neatly characterised as 'physical force' and 'moral force' nationalism. But it bears emphasis that both strategies were rendered unconstitutional and unlawful by the colonial state. This left no 'constitutional route' to self-determination. On the one hand, the physical force strategy quickly became defined by the colonial power as something far from a 'just war' – as 'rebellion' or 'mutiny', or 'terror'. But in the colonial context, the moral force tradition could be just as brutally repressed and just as contemptuously dismissed.

In this context, there is a broad sense across the whole colonised world of resistance followed by repression, uprising followed by subjugation. While there is a terrible sense of *déjà vu* across different uprisings, they ultimately 'worked' since decolonisation – sooner or later – occurred. It is, of course, impossible to detail all these uprisings – or, indeed, all the bloody reprisals that followed in their wake. Nevertheless, they are still at the core of anti-imperialism. Crucially, there comes a point at which the cost of colonial repression – economic, political and psychic – becomes unacceptable to the coloniser. This may not be a particularly edifying truth. But 'uprising' became a default resistance of colonised people because they had no alternatives. And, in the end, this methodology triumphed, albeit at terrible cost.

Paradigmatic cases of 'rising' emerge across the history of anti-imperialism in South America such as the Túpac Amaru uprising in Peru in 1780 and the Minas

---

[19] Half of the 70 representatives in the Legislative Council of Hong Kong are elected through universal suffrage, the other half through closed elections in the business sector. In 2014, there were protests demanding greater democracy, the so-called 'umbrella revolution'. Even greater protests developed in 2019, basically situating the protesters as pro-democracy in Hong Kong and therefore against mainland Chinese authoritarianism.

Conspiracy in Brazil in 1789.[20] The Túpac Amaru rebellion was an Inca revival and liberation movement that sought to improve the rights of indigenous Peruvians. Its leader, José Gabriel Condorcanqu, changed his name to Túpac Amaru II and declared his lineage to the last Inca ruler who had been executed by the Spanish in 1572. The uprising began with the capture and killing of the colonial governor, Antonio de Arriaga, in November 1780. Symbolically, Arriaga's slave Antonio Oblitas was tasked with executing his master. Releasing his first proclamation to all the inhabitants of the Spanish provinces, Tupac announced that 'there have been repeated outcries directed to me by the indigenous peoples of this and surrounding provinces, outcries against the abuses committed by European-born crown officials ... Justified outcries that have produced no remedy from the royal courts'. He went on to state: 'I have acted ... only against the mentioned abuses and to preserve the peace and well-being of Indians, mestizos, mambos, as well as native-born whites and blacks. I must now prepare for the consequences of these actions'. Túpac Amaru II assembled an army of 6,000 natives. As they marched towards Cuzco, the rebels occupied several provinces. By the time they had attacked Cuzco, however, the Spaniards had brought in reinforcements and were able to defeat the uprising. Túpac and his wife Micaela Bastidas were captured, and some 50,000 indigenous followers were repelled and dispersed (Walker 2016).[21]

Following the defeat of his rebellion, Túpac was sentenced to be tortured and executed after being forced to witness the execution of his wife and other family members, as well as some of his officers. His body was quartered and beheaded on the main plaza in Cuzco, in the same place his forebear Túpac Amaru I had been beheaded. His body parts were strewn across the towns loyal to him; his relatives declared 'infamous'; and all documents relating to his descent burnt. Following the defeat of the rising, Incan clothing, cultural traditions, and self-identification as 'Inca' were outlawed, along with other measures to forcibly assimilate the population to Spanish culture and government. This continued until Peru's independence as a republic in 1821.

---

[20] US independence provided the inspiration for the *Inconfidência Mineira* ('Minas Conspiracy') in Brazil in 1789. Led by Tiradentes – a soldier in a colonial regiment – it mobilised a hotch potch of different and contradictory ideologies: in theory, they wanted to create a democratic republic; however, the existing colonial race/class hierarchy – including the right to property and enslavement – would remain intact. The conspiracy was betrayed by informers. Tiradentes was hanged in 1792. Afterwards, his body was torn into pieces and displayed in the towns where he had propagated his revolutionary ideas. His conspiracy marked the beginning of the end for the Portuguese Empire in Brazil. Following the Brazilian War of Independence, the last Portuguese soldiers surrendered in 1824 and Portugal officially recognised Brazilian independence in 1825. The anniversary of Tiradentes' death is now celebrated as a national holiday in Brazil.

[21] Micaela Bastidas Puyucahua was possibly of mixed African and indigenous descent, identified as a 'Zamba' in the colonial-era racial hierarchy. She was fully involved in the revolt, telling her husband: 'I gave you plenty of warnings to march immediately on Cuzco, but you took them all lightly, giving the Spaniards time to prepare as they have done, placing cannon on Picchu Mountain, and devising other measures so dangerous that you are no longer in a position to attack them'. She added in a postscript: 'After I had finished this letter, a messenger arrived with the definite news that the enemy from Paruro is in Acos. I am going forward to attack them even if it costs me my life' (Keen 1955: 75).

Túpac Amaru II became an inspirational figure in both the Peruvian struggle for independence and the indigenous rights movement, as well as a talisman to wider anti-imperialist struggles in America and beyond. Although Túpac Amaru II's rebellion failed, it marked the first large-scale uprising in the Spanish colonies and inspired the revolt of many natives and *mestizo* people as across the Spanish Empire. The rebellion gave indigenous Peruvians a new anti-colonial nationalism that would determine the course of the country's future. They were now willing to join forces with others who opposed the Spanish. The multi-ethnic elements and utilisation of Incan history within the ideology of the uprising were also definitive. In contrast, however, Peruvian 'mixed race' creoles would prove to be South America's most conservative settler population. They remained vehemently pro-Royalist and pro-Spanish in the face of the independence movement due to the fear that independence would leave them disempowered by – and vulnerable to – indigenous populations.

Of course, anti-imperialist struggles did not always choose – and were not always forced – to adopt revolutionary violence as the primary means of liberation. While it also had its own history of violent uprising, India provides the paradigm case of 'moral force' organising. But even explicitly non-violent organisation could lead to brutal repression. In August 1917, in the context of India's contributions to the imperial war effort, the British Secretary of State for India, Edwin Montagu, announced the British commitment to 'increasing association of Indians in every branch of the administration, and the gradual development of self-governing institutions, with a view to the progressive realisation of responsible government in India as an integral part of the British Empire'. Although the plan envisioned limited self-government at first only in the provinces – with India locked within the British Empire – it represented the first British proposal for any form of representative government in a non-white colony. The Government of India Act 1919 followed and saw the expanded participation of Indians in different aspects of government through a diarchy. This Act represented the end of 'benevolent despotism' and saw the genesis of 'responsible government' in India. But these limited reforms failed to satisfy the growing independence movement.

On the wider liberation front, there were the stirrings of combined political organisation by Hindus, Muslims and Sikhs. The Punjab was experiencing a particular level of unrest: there was a separatist Sikh movement; returned soldiers were restless for social and political change; Gandhi was successfully organising opposition to British rule. The centre for much of the political upheaval was the Sikh holy city of Amritsar. One element of this lethal cocktail was that it displayed the intimate links between Ireland and empire. In military command of the Punjab was Reginald Dyer. Born in India, as a teenager he was sent to school in Middleton, Co. Cork. After finishing there, he began medical studies in Dublin, but did not last long. Instead, he went to Sandhurst and became a British army officer. His first posting was to Belfast in 1886 where there was widespread rioting in response to the first Home Rule bill. As unionists were the people doing the rioting, Dyer's job was to protect the nationalist population. He banned all meetings and gave his troops a relatively free hand to do what was necessary to maintain order. The unionists gave him the nickname 'Black Michael'. Thankfully, this was early in his career and his sojourn in Belfast was brief, so he didn't manage to reach the peak he later reached in India.

On 13 April 1919, thousands were gathered in Jallianwala Bagh, a public garden about six acres in size which was close to the Golden Temple. It was a Sikh holy day and the garden was full of worshippers and others, resting and eating. One month earlier, the Anarchical and Revolutionary Crimes Act had been passed which gave the military wide powers. Dyer took this as his cue to move into the garden and give orders to the Indian troops under his command to open fire on the unarmed and non-protesting crowd at close quarters. An official inquiry said 379 were killed; the Indian National Congress maintained the number of dead was closer to 1,000 (Collett 2005: 263).

The civilian lieutenant-governor of the Punjab was Sir Michael O'Dwyer from Tipperary. Although O'Dwyer had not authorised Dyer's action, he was quick to offer retrospective support to the action. He was also a relatively lone voice in doing so. Dyer's actions were condemned, not least by Winston Churchill and the British government. Dyer did not help matters by being bullish and unrepentant at an official inquiry. He said that his troops only ceased firing when they ran out of ammunition, otherwise he would have required them to keep going. In addition, the main entrance to the garden was through a narrow passageway and Dyer could not get his armoured vehicles through. He said that if he had managed to, he would have ordered the use of the mounted machine guns to fire on the crowd. He told the Hunter tribunal: 'I think it quite possible that I could have dispersed the crowd without firing but they would have come back again and laughed, and I would have made, what I consider, a fool of myself' (Collett 2005: 336). He was removed from his career on mental health grounds but was not prosecuted for his actions. He died in 1927.[22]

This moment – framed by its Irish participants – was to define the journey towards Indian independence.[23] The non-cooperation movement – led by Mahatma Gandhi – emerged as a direct response to the Jallianwala Bagh Massacre. It aimed to resist British rule in India through non-violent means, or 'Ahimsa'. Protesters refused to buy British goods, adopted the use of local handicrafts and picketed shops selling alcohol. The ideas of Ahimsa and non-violence, and Gandhi's ability to rally hundreds of thousands of

---

[22] In Jallianwala Bagh that day a young man was selling water. He was a Sikh named Udham Singh. Later he became a revolutionary and in a gesture of non-sectarianism changed his name to Ram Mohammed Singh Azad. Twenty-one years later in London he assassinated Michael O'Dwyer. He was hanged in Pentonville Prison. In 1974, the Indian government requested the return of his remains which are now interred in Jallianwala Bagh (Singh 1998).

[23] In October 1997, Queen Elizabeth II visited Jallianwala Bagh and in a masterpiece of understatement said: 'It is no secret that there have been some difficult episodes in our past – Jallianwala Bagh, which I shall visit tomorrow, is a distressing example. But history cannot be rewritten, however much we might sometimes wish otherwise. It has its moments of sadness, as well as gladness. We must learn from the sadness and build on the gladness' (Uday 2017).

common citizens towards the cause of Indian independence, were first seen on a large scale in this movement through the summer of 1920. The non-cooperation movement was launched on 1 January 1921.

The success of the campaign shocked the imperial authorities and was a massive boost to Indian nationalists. Unity in the country was strengthened and new political alliances forged across sectarian and ethnic lines. But in February 1922 a clash took place at Chauri Chaura, a small town in Uttar Pradesh. After a police officer attacked activists picketing a liquor shop, a crowd went to the police station. They set fire to the police station with some 22 police inside it. Mahatma Gandhi was disillusioned that the revolt had lost its non-violent nature. Gandhi appealed to the Indian public for all resistance to end, went on a fast lasting three weeks, and called off the non-cooperation movement.

Even though he had effectively stopped the national revolt single-handedly, Gandhi was arrested in March 1922. He was subsequently imprisoned for six years for publishing seditious materials. This led to suppression of the movement and was followed by the arrest of other leaders. Although most Congress leaders remained behind Gandhi, radicals and Islamists broke away, rejecting Gandhi's leadership. Many nationalists had felt that the non-cooperation movement should not have been stopped due to isolated incidents of violence, and most nationalists, while retaining confidence in Gandhi, were discouraged. Contemporary historians and critics suggest that the movement was successful enough to break the back of British rule and might have foreshortened the process that lead to independence in 1947. Other historians and Indian leaders of the time defended Gandhi's judgment.

The strategy was revived in 1930 – with Gandhi's blessing – as the civil disobedience movement. On 26th January 1930, the Indian National Congress made the *Purna Swaraj* declaration of sovereignty and self-rule. This was followed directly by the *Dandi Satyagraha* or 'Salt March'. This intervention continued the adherence to non-violence, but the strategic innovation was the introduction of a policy of violating the law. The non-violent civil disobedience was to produce salt from the seawater in the coastal village of Dandi – as was the practice of the local populace until British officials introduced taxation on salt production. Henceforth the British deemed their sea-salt reclamation activities illegal and then repeatedly used force to stop it. In 1930, the 24-day march launched a direct-action campaign of tax resistance and non-violent protest against the British salt monopoly. It gained worldwide attention which gave impetus to the Indian independence movement and started the nationwide Civil Disobedience Movement. The Satyagraha ended in success: the demands of Indians were met, and the Congress Party was recognised as a representative of the Indian people. The resulting Government of India Act 1935 also gave India its first taste of – albeit limited – self-governance.

This act – the longest Westminster ever enacted – included provision for the establishment of a 'Federation of India', to be made up of both British India and some or all of the 'princely states'. It also introduced direct elections – albeit only increasing the franchise from seven million to thirty-five million people. However, the degree of autonomy introduced at the provincial level was subject to profound limitations: the provincial governors retained important reserve powers, and the British authorities also retained a right to suspend responsible government. None of these measures was sufficient to meet Indian demands for 'complete spiritual and political independence'. British India was partitioned into the independent dominions of India and Pakistan by the Indian Independence Act 1947. In 1948 King George VI relinquished the title 'Emperor of India'. The Constitution of India was adopted by the Indian Constituent Assembly on 26 November 1949 and came into effect on 26 January 1950 with a democratic government system, completing the country's transition towards becoming an independent and democratic republic. The Republic day was chosen as 26 January as it was on this day, in 1930, that the Declaration of Indian Independence (*Purna Swaraj*) was proclaimed by the Indian National Congress in riposte to the dominion status offered by the British Empire. The British did not formally leave India until 1947 – and only after trying unsuccessfully to foist 'dominion' status on the former colony. In perhaps the paramount struggle between Empire and Republic of them all, the 'greatest empire' had been defeated by effective, non-violent anti-colonial organising.

A similar process of decolonisation followed with many French and British colonies in the 'winds of change' context of the 1950s and 1960s. Here there was a possibility of negotiated transfer of power. In this context, there was some movement towards democratisation towards the end of the colonial period. Thus, Sri Lanka provided universal suffrage for all irrespective of race, ethnicity, language, or gender in 1931 while still a part of the British Empire. In consequence, Sri Lanka is regarded as the oldest democracy in Asia. There the Constitution created by the colonial Donoughmore Commission was a significant development.[24] First, it was the only constitution in the British Empire (outside the white dominions of Australia, South Africa and Canada) enabling general elections with universal suffrage. For the first time, a dependent country-of-colour within the empires of Western Europe was given one-person, one-vote and the power to control domestic affairs. Here – in theory – was the pilot project whose success would ensure self-determination for whole swathes of Asia, Africa and the Caribbean. Second, it created a committee system of government specifically to address the complex ethnic cleavages across Sri Lanka which colonialism had generated. (Large Tamil and Muslim populations had been introduced as indentured labourers on plantations under British rule and remained distinct from the indigenous Buddhist Singhalese.) Under this system, no single ethnic community could dominate the political arena. Instead, every government

---

[24] The Donoughmore Commissioners had been appointed by the socialist Sydney Webb. Webb was briefly the Secretary of State for the Colonies in the Lib-Lab coalition government of 1927. Without any apparent sense of irony, he appointed Commissioners who shared his desire for an 'equitable and socialist' British empire. They developed a Constitutional arrangement for Sri Lanka which – in theory – would ensure that every community in the island had access to political power.

department was overseen by a committee of parliamentarians drawn from all the ethnic communities. This created a built-in series of checks and balances but also institutionalised ethnic division throughout the political system.

Under the same model Jamaica provided universal adult suffrage in 1944. Universal suffrage was granted in Ghana for the 1951 legislative election. This was the first election to be held in Africa under universal suffrage. But most other colonies only achieved universal adult suffrage *after* independence. In South America, this did not happen for the first time until the 1918 Uruguayan Constitution. Across Latin America, a literacy test was routinely used to disenfranchise indigenous populations even when 'democracy' had been instituted. In India – now 'the largest democracy in the world' – it was not until 1950 that the suffrage of all adult citizens was recognised by the Constitution, irrespective of race or gender or religion, on the founding of the Republic of India.

At this moment of transition between the colonial and postcolonial state, there was a core question on negotiation. Is the coloniser 'forced out' or do they leave voluntarily, their *mission civilisatrice* completed? In the absence of any such signal, other forms of resistance remained central to the transformation in brutal anti-colonial struggles across Asia and Africa and South America. Algeria, for example, witnessed one of the bloodiest decolonisations of all. The figures remain disputed but estimates of the number of casualties range from 90,000 to 300,000, including 27,000 French soldiers and perhaps 30,000 harkis, Muslim Algerian auxiliaries in the French army. After independence on 3 July 1962 650,000 settlers and 130,000 harkis moved to France (World Peace Foundation 2015). For all the ideological emphasis on the coloniser's sense of mission, the departure in even the most negotiated of contexts was hardly less shambolic that the 'Fall of Saigon'. This aspect of the colonial legacy was painfully captured by William James Fitzgerald, the last Chief Justice of Palestine: 'It is surely a new technique in our imperial mission to walk out and leave the pot we placed on the fire to boil over' (Brendon 2008: 478).

Decolonisation has, of course, seen a whole series of variations on this theme – from the ignominious French and US disengagements in Vietnam to the imperial pomp that accompanied the British departure from Hong Kong. This process could be generational or happen almost instantaneously. In two of Portugal's African colonies, Angola and Mozambique, it materialised almost overnight following the 'Carnation revolution' in 1974. But in much of Africa the process of decolonisation occurred over many years and was characterised by brutal racist and colonial violence. In places like Algeria, Vietnam, South Africa and Rhodesia there were long drawn-out struggles with decades of interim formations – apartheid in South Africa, UDI in Rhodesia – in which the decolonisation process was not simply stalled but reversed. Nevertheless, one way or another, the 'great' European empires – British, French, Dutch, Spanish and Portuguese – were defeated and forced to decolonise. In consequence, a host of newly independent states emerged in the aftermath of WWII. A useful marker for the end of this process is the point at which each of these newly self-determined countries was able to join the UN – this undoubtedly signals a key symbolic moment in the decolonisation process. At that moment, the anti-imperialist movement is immediately confronted by the question of how it is to reconfigure in the context of a post-colonial state.

Resisting as an anti-imperialist state

Once liberated, any post-colonial state is posed with two immediate questions: first, how should it stand in relation to other peoples that remain colonised?; second, how can it begin to dismantle the complex multiple racial hierarchies it inherited from colonisation? This tension around 'anti-colonial' solidarity existed from the very first instances of independence in the 'new world' – the US and Haiti. As both of these states began to take a post-colonial form, the paramount question remained: who should have dominion? There was an immediate challenge in terms of the tensions and contradictions of being an anti-imperialist movement in government. The issue was inextricably linked to the second question of how these emergent states might confront the continuing legacies of colonialism within their newly formed state formations. They all had to deliver against the neo-colonial odds. As Amilcar Cabral (1974: 72) pointed out:

> Always bear in mind that people are not fighting for ideas, for the things in anyone's head. They are fighting to win material benefits, to live better and in peace, to see their lives go forward, to guarantee the future of their children.

This prosaic reality put specific pressures on new states to do something transformative – to show that they were different to what had gone before under colonialism. But the means at their disposal had often been bled dry by the colonial process. One of the reasons for decolonisation was that colonial expropriation had already exhausted the immediate resources and surpluses within the colony – there was nothing left to give.

Despite the commitment to *uti possidetis*, new states were often also challenged by internal demands to self-determine. Colonialism had imposed a whole series of borders on colonial formations that bore little resemblance to pre-existing ethnic and other boundaries.[25] But the post-colonial state had to find some way of making these artificial polities 'work'. These tensions led to much bloodshed, such as when Katanga broke away from the Democratic Republic of the Congo in the early 1960s, Biafra seceded from Nigeria in the late 1960s, and Zimbabwe crushed secessionist moves in Matabeleland in 1983-84. In contrast, colonialism specifically partitioned a series of countries as part of the colonial and decolonising process. This was both a specific tactic of colonialism and a specific challenge for anti-colonialism. Thus, the question of anti-partitionism had to be engaged with as a general anti-imperialist strategy – in Haiti, Vietnam, Korea, India, Yemen – and, of course, Ireland.

---

[25] For example, in Nigeria, British colonialism left behind a newly liberated state whose borders contained over 250 separate ethnic groups.

These broad anti-imperialist challenges assumed prominence in the aftermath of WWII. Newly liberated states attempted an answer with two key colonial/post-colonial transnational organisations: the Non-Aligned Movement and the Tricontinental Conference. The Non-Aligned Movement (NAM) is a group of states not formally aligned with or against any major power bloc. As of 2020, the movement has 120 members. It was established in 1961 in Belgrade, Yugoslavia. An initiative of Yugoslav president Tito and Indian prime minister Nehru led to the first Conference of Heads of State or Government of Non-Aligned Countries. The term non-aligned movement appeared first in the fifth conference in 1976, where participating countries were denoted as 'members of the movement'. The organisation was characterised by Fidel Castro in his Havana Declaration of 1979 as pursuing 'the national independence, sovereignty, territorial integrity and security of non-aligned countries' in their 'struggle against imperialism, colonialism, neo-colonialism, racism, and all forms of foreign aggression, occupation, domination, interference or hegemony as well as against great power and bloc politics'. The countries of the Non-Aligned Movement represent nearly two-thirds of the United Nations' members and contain 55 per cent of the world population. Membership is particularly concentrated in countries considered to be part of the Majority World, though the Non-Aligned Movement also has a number of more developed states.

The contradictions of continued anti-colonial solidarity for the Non-Aligned Movement was brought into sharp focus immediately by its relationship to the Tricontinental Conference. While the non-aligned movement was made up of states, the Tricontinental Conference gathered liberation movements. Each of these aspired, of course, to establish additional post-colonial states. It was immediately clear that any further resistance to colonial states was a dangerous activity. Colonialism often sought to mediate resistance to colonialism through assassination. This took particular forms in attempts to control the type of transition that would occur with decolonisation. Perhaps most notoriously, the apartheid state in South Africa prepared for transition by executing Chris Hani, the most able and radical of all the liberation struggle leaders in South Africa.[26] But this pattern of late-colonial assassination was a much more general phenomenon (Brittain 2011). The list of anti-imperialist leaders executed or disappeared by imperialism and its allies is huge.[27] But we might regard the example of

---

[26] Chris Hani was an Umkhonto we Sizwe activist in Zimbabwe and later went on to head up the ANC's military wing in Zambia. With the unbanning of the ANC in 1990 he returned to South Africa where he replaced Joe Slovo as head of the South African Communist Party and fully supported the end of military actions. He was assassinated in April 1993.

[27] A non-exhaustive list of assassinated leaders includes: Ruben Um Nyobé, leader of the Union of the Peoples of Cameroon (UPC), killed by the French SDECE (French secret services); Barthélemy Boganda, leader of a nationalist Central African Republic movement, who died in a plane crash on March 29, 1959, eight days before the last elections of the colonial era; Félix-Roland Moumié, successor to Ruben Um Nyobe at the head of the Cameroon's People Union, assassinated in Geneva in 1960 by the SDECE; Patrice Lumumba, the first Prime Minister of the Democratic Republic of the Congo, assassinated on January 17, 1961; Burundi nationalist leader Louis Rwagasore, assassinated on October 13, 1961; Pierre Ngendandumwe, Burundi's

Ben Barka as definitive.[28] Exiled from Morocco, Ben Barka became a 'travelling salesman of the revolution'. He left for Algiers, where he met Che Guevara, Amílcar Cabral and Malcolm X. From there, he went to Cairo, Rome, Geneva and Havana, trying to unite the revolutionary movements of the Third World for the Tricontinental Conference meeting that was to be held in January 1966 in Havana. In a press conference, he claimed 'the two currents of the world revolution will be represented there: the current [that] emerged with the October Revolution and that of the national liberation revolution' (Umoja 2014).

As the leader of the Tricontinental Conference, Ben Barka was a major figure in the Third World movement and supported revolutionary anti-colonial action in various states. His activism provoked the anger of the United States and France, among others. Just before his disappearance, he was preparing the first meeting of the Tricontinental, scheduled to take place in Havana. The OSPAAAL (Organization for Solidarity with the People of Africa, Asia and Latin America) was founded on that occasion. Chairing the preparatory commission, he defined the objectives: assistance with the movements of liberation, support for Cuba during its subjection to the United States embargo, the liquidation of foreign military bases and ending apartheid in South Africa. Ben Barka was 'disappeared' in Paris in 1965 by Moroccan agents trained by the CIA and French police officers aided by the Israeli secret service (Brittain 2001). If we wanted a simple allegory for the clash of imperialism and anti-imperialism, it is there in the brutal murder of one of the most able and internationalist opponents of colonialism.

Perhaps the key challenge for anti-imperialism has been the question of strategic alliances. As we have seen imperialism was at its most obvious when it was manifest in pan-imperial projects – the Berlin conference that carved up Africa, the Eight-nation alliance that invaded and looted China, and the tawdry coalition of intelligence services that murdered Ben Barka. This immediately poses the question of how and why a similar alliance *against* colonialism and imperialism might be built and sustained. Sadly, this kind of broad solidarity movement now rests more in the minds of the most paranoid of US presidents and Hollywood film makers. There are, of course, regional organisations that provide levels of support and solidarity. Broadly, however, this broader alliance ended with the negotiated end of apartheid. Now even the most egregious of oppressions – from Palestine to Chiapas – find

---

first Hutu prime minister, also murdered on January 15, 1965; Sylvanus Olympio, the first president of Togo, assassinated on January 13, 1963; Nigerian leader Ahmadu Bello, assassinated in January 1966 during a coup which toppled Nigeria's post-independence government; Eduardo Mondlane, the leader of FRELIMO and the father of Mozambican independence, assassinated in 1969; Mohamed Bassiri, Sahrawi leader of the Movement for the Liberation of Saguia el Hamra and Wadi el Dhahab, 'disappeared' in El Aaiún in 1970, allegedly by the Spanish Legion; and Amílcar Cabral, killed on January 20, 1973 by Portuguese agents operating within the PAIGC.

[28] Mehdi Ben Barka (1920-1965) was born in Rabat, Morocco. He became a prominent member of the Moroccan opposition in the nationalist Istiqlal Party. He left Istiqlal in 1959 – after clashes with conservatives who supported a 'Greater Morocco' policy – to found the left-wing National Union of Popular Forces (UNFP). In 1962 he was accused of plotting against King Hassan II. He was exiled from Morocco, after calling upon Moroccan soldiers to refuse to fight Algeria in the 1963 Sand War.

contemporary states reluctant to undermine their relations with former colonial powers. Nevertheless, any people struggling with the legacy of colonialism and imperialism must necessarily engage with its relationship with these forces. As we shall see in the next chapter, this is one of the key challenges for Irish anti-imperialism.

To further complicate the challenges of post-colonial existence, a whole series of additional ethnic blocs had been introduced into these polities by the colonial process. Palestine was perhaps the ultimate example. Here Jewish migration to Palestine that had been facilitated by imperial policy suddenly became a core challenge to colonialism. Thus, Ze'ev Jabotinsky, the Zionist leader, suggested in 1931 that: 'The Jews might become the dynamite that will blow up the British Empire' (*Times*, 30 December 1931). And Zionism in Palestine was to produce its own peculiar anti-colonialism across the British mandate. But the Jewish presence there had only been possible because of imperial policy. And the new 'post-colonial' ethnic blocs – Arab and Jew – have been struggling profoundly with the consequences ever since. It was a defining characteristic of the colonial legacy that a whole series of ethnic tensions rooted in colonial policy – whether by accident or design – was embedded in almost every new polity that emerged from the end of empire. This dynamic assumed specific forms within the white dominions; these had their own peculiar relationship to both race and imperialism. As we have seen, some of these, such as Australia and New Zealand, even developed their own colonies. All of this suggested an odd and contradictory juxtaposition between white dominion and self-determination.

White dominion, Black liberation and decolonisation

The ethics and politics of colonisation generated a specific challenge for European settler populations. Where would they stand in terms of colonised peoples and colonised cultures? Their very identity was, of course, deeply embedded in the colonial process. Their material reality was based upon the initial and continuing expropriation of the colonised. Their relationship with the colonised – and other subjects of colour like enslaved and indentured labourers – was intimate. Yet they too were colonised subjects. So, when they came to resist, how would they relate to other colonised subjects? As we have seen – in the US, in most of Latin America, in the white dominions – they often made no common cause at all with either indigenous peoples or migrant labour. After decolonisation they renewed or intensified the racial hierarchies embedded in the colonial project. But this was not always the case. In different situations, from Tunisia to South Africa, liberation movements constructed a specific, albeit partial, space for their settler populations – and some at least played a key role in self-determination.

It helps to emphasise that the revolt of white settlers against metropolitan colonial masters did not of itself represent decolonisation. This category includes not only the British white dominions and the US outlier, but also the Spanish and Portuguese post-colonial states that emerged in particular in the 19th century. While they broke with empire – abruptly in the US case, more gradually in most of the others – they did almost nothing to eradicate the racialised power structures they inherited from colonialism. Rather these new dominions were constructed in the image of the coloniser in order to monopolise the benefits of colonisation and conquest for themselves. This argument has profound implications for the broader understanding of anti-imperialist theory and practice. The UN decolonisation committee, for example, has never engaged with any of these formations.

One of the first indications of this new direction was the failure of the US to recognise the independence of Haiti. Thus, less than thirty years after Americans achieved their freedom, the second republic in the 'New World' to achieve independence received no support from the first. 'Saint-Domingue' was a classically colonial formation under the French with an attendant racial hierarchy. According to the 1788 Census, Haiti's population consisted of around 25,000 Europeans, 22,000 'free coloureds' and perhaps 700,000 enslaved Africans. Toussaint L'Ouverture was the key figure in turning an anti-slavery insurgency into a revolutionary movement. L'Ouverture began his military career as a leader of the 1791 slave rebellion in the French colony; he was by then a free man and a Jacobin. Initially allied with the Spaniards of neighbouring Santo Domingo (now the Dominican Republic), L'Ouverture switched allegiance to the French when they abolished slavery.[29] He restored the plantation system using paid labour, negotiated trade treaties with the UK and the United States, and maintained a large and well-disciplined army. In 1801, he promulgated a new constitution – Constitution of Saint-Domingue – for the colony, with himself as Governor-General for Life. This Constitution put the abolition of slavery at the centre of its project:

> Art. 3. There cannot exist slaves on this territory, servitude is therein forever abolished. All men are born, live and die free and French.
>
> Art. 4. All men, regardless of color, are eligible to all employment.
>
> Art. 5. There shall exist no distinction other than those based on virtue and talent, and other superiority afforded by law in the exercise of a public function. The law is the same for all whether in punishment or in protection.

This revolution had turned Saint-Domingue – the most prosperous slave colony of the time – into the first free colonial society to have explicitly rejected race as the basis of social classification. Though L'Ouverture did not sever ties with France, he had created a separatist constitution. In response, Napoléon Bonaparte sent an expedition of 20,000 soldiers to retake the island and reimpose slavery.[30] The French lost two-thirds of these

---

[29] Revolutionary France under Robespierre abolished slavery in France's colonies in 1794.

[30] During the French Revolutionary Wars, French slave-owners actively supported the counter-revolution, and, through the Whitehall Accord, they threatened to transfer the French Caribbean colonies to British control since the British still allowed slavery. In this context Napoléon Bonaparte decided to re-establish slavery after becoming First Consul. He reintroduced slavery in 1802 and sent military governors and troops to the colonies to impose it.

forces; most died of yellow fever. They did, however, succeed in capturing L'Ouverture and transported him to France for trial where he died in 1803. His achievements, however, prepared the grounds for the Haitian army's absolute victory. Liberated slaves, along with free *gens de couleur* and allies, continued their fight for independence. Jean-Jacques Dessalines defeated French troops at the Battle of Vertières in November 1803 and France withdrew its remaining 7,000 troops from the island (James 2001).

The independence of Saint-Domingue was proclaimed by Dessalines on 1 January 1804. Haiti was thus the first ever nation to successfully gain independence through a slave revolt. Almost immediately, the 1804 'Haiti massacre' was carried out against the remaining white population of native French people and French Creoles (or Franco-Haitians) by Haitian soldiers under orders from Dessalines. He had decreed that all suspected of conspiring in the acts of the expelled army should be put to death. The massacre, which took place throughout Haiti, occurred from January until April 1804, and resulted in the death of 3,000 to 5,000 men, women, and children.

Despite this brutal backdrop, the 'Constitution of Hayti' of 1805 confirmed Toussaint's core principles:

> Article. 1. The people inhabiting the island formerly called St. Domingo, hereby agree to form themselves into a free state sovereign and independent of any other power in the universe, under the name of empire of Hayti.
>
> Article 2. Slavery is forever abolished.
>
> Article 3. The Citizens of Hayti are brothers at home; equality in the eyes of the law is incontestably acknowledged, and there cannot exist any titles, advantages, or privileges, other than those necessarily resulting from the consideration and reward of services rendered to liberty and independence.
>
> Article 4. The law is the same to all, whether it punishes, or whether it protects.

The new Constitution then proceeded to provide for a unique reframing of race in the new 'Empire'. Article 12 declared, 'No whiteman of whatever nation he may be, shall put his foot on this territory with the title of master or proprietor, neither shall he in future acquire any property therein'. Article 13 declared:

> The preceding article cannot in the smallest degree affect white women who have been naturalized Haytians by Government, nor does it extend to children already born, or that may be born of the said women. The Germans and Polanders naturalized by government are also comprized in the dispositions of the present article.

Article 14 declared:

> All acception of colour among the children of one and the same family, of whom the chief magistrate is the father, being necessarily to cease, the Haytians shall hence forward be known only by the generic appellation of Blacks.

This anti-enslavement constitution was immediately re-interpreted as 'anti-white'. Arguably, however, it was deconstructing 'whiteness' for the first time. Rather than signalling a racist – if understandable – disenfranchisement of white people, it was rather attempting to dismantle white privilege formally and constitutionally for the first time. It appears, of course, this took a brutal – if not genocidal form – but this took place in the context of an attempt to dismantle slavery. The crucial – if unanswerable – question was whether whites were killed because they were white or because they were enslavers.[31] There can be no doubting the political impact of the killings. Throughout the nineteenth century, these events were publicised in the United States as 'the horrors of Santo Domingo'. In addition, many white refugees went to the US from Haiti, settling in New Orleans, Charleston, New York, and other coastal cities and compounding opposition to abolition.

After Haiti gained its independence in 1804, the new state certainly faced incredible challenges and suffered profoundly in terms of the geopolitics of the region. Fearful of the influence of the revolution, US President Thomas Jefferson (who was himself a slave-owner) refused to recognise the new republic despite its being the second successful post-colonial state in the 'new world'. Most European nations – perhaps more expectedly – also refused recognition. French governments did not recognise the Haitian government until 1825. In a foretaste of what was to happen to some of its other colonies experiencing decolonisation in the 20th century, France further demanded payment for compensation to slaveholders who lost their 'property' and Haiti was saddled with unmanageable debt; it did not clear that debt to France until 1947.[32] Haiti became – and remains – one of the poorest countries in the Americas. After the Spanish portion of Hispaniola – Santo Domingo – declared its independence from Spain in 1821, Haitian forces took control

---

[31] CLR James comments thus on the events: 'The massacre of the whites was a tragedy; not for the whites. For these old slave-owners, those who burnt a little powder in the arse of a Negro, who buried him alive for insects to eat ... and who, as soon as they got the chance, began their old cruelties again; for these there is no need to waste one tear or one drop of ink. The tragedy was for the blacks and the Mulattoes. It was not policy but revenge, and revenge has no place in politics... such purposeless massacres degrade and brutalise a population, especially one which was just beginning as a nation and had had so bitter a past... Haiti suffered terribly from the resulting isolation. Whites were banished from Haiti for generations, and the unfortunate country, ruined economically, its population lacking in social culture, had its inevitable difficulties doubled by this massacre' (James 1989: 29).

[32] Haiti's total payments to France were £21 billion in current money. See Kushner 2019. The irony is that if UN guidelines had been followed payments would have flowed in the opposite direction. The UN World Conference against Racism, Racial Discrimination, Xenophobia and Related Intolerance, held in Durban, South Africa in 2001, committed the world to reparations, restitution, and other remedies for the descendants of slavery and the slave trade (Gutto 2013: 41). The mechanics of such reparations are highly problematic. In the US in 2014 Ta-Nehisi Coates published an essay in Atlantic magazine, 'The Case for Reparations', which ignited a contentious debate. When the House of Representatives judiciary subcommittee on the constitution, civil rights and civil liberties debated the matter of reparations in 2019, sides were taken which were sometimes counterintuitive. Thus, Coleman Hughes, an African-American writer, argued that they 'would insult many black Americans by putting a price on the suffering of their ancestors' (BBC News 2019c). In the same year, indigenous leaders in West Australia filed a claim for more than $290 billion for 'spiritual damage' caused by loss of their traditional land. This equated to almost a quarter of Australia's gross domestic product of $1.4 trillion and more than West Australia's gross state product of $259 billion (Higgins and Collard 2019).

of the entire island and ended slavery in Santo Domingo. In this sense Haiti remained a revolutionary, anti-colonial and anti-slavery state. In 1844, however, the Dominican Republic was partitioned from Haiti again. It became a client state of the US and gradually developed into the largest economy of Central America and the Caribbean.

The pro-slavery establishment in the US was – no doubt correctly – alarmed that the Haitian revolution could influence enslaved people across its newly independent states. The US refused to recognise Haiti's independence until 1862, after the start of the Civil War. Subsequently, President Andrew Johnson suggested annexing the island to secure influence over Europe in the Caribbean. The US Navy sent ships to Haiti numerous times between 1857 and 1915 to 'protect American lives and property'. During the Môle Saint-Nicolas affair in 1889 the US attempted to force Haiti to provide a naval base on the island. When the United States finally occupied Haiti in 1915, the world's first post-colonial state had effectively re-colonised its second.[33]

It is possible to juxtapose the US and Haiti as sides of the same coin of the toxic legacy of race and colonialism at the very start of the decolonisation process. They both offer a sobering portent of all the challenges that would face other colonised peoples as they struggled towards self-determination. Haiti – the first 'contact' in the 'new world' – had been reduced by genocide and the economics of slavery to a brutal poverty from which it still struggles to escape. While it attempted to construct a more inclusive, anti-racist post-colonial ideology, it remained trapped in profound poverty with ongoing ethnic tensions. But the US – the first white dominion – did not even pretend to embrace a more racially inclusive future. It internalised all the racial political economy it had learned from empire – most obviously in terms of native peoples and enslaved Africans – and reframed these as core principles of the newly self-determined state. It continued the polices of genocide towards indigenous people and the enslavement of Africans – and it fetishised the notion of whiteness to ever more ludicrous degrees with ever more destructive consequences.

Thus, the USA appears as an odd outlier across colonial and anti-colonial history. On the one hand it is the first act of successful anti-imperialist self-determination. On the other, it fails spectacularly to live up to its revolutionary principles. Ultimately it becomes accused of becoming the most powerful imperialist power of all. But our genealogy helps to make sense of this US exceptionalism. First, US independence was undoubtedly an anti-colonial moment. It marked the defeat of the first British Empire and the emergence of a post-colonial social formation from a violent and bitter fought anti-colonial war. But what it was replaced by was much closer to the white dominion model of the later British Empire than any more radically decolonised formation.

---

[33] This resulted in a little-remembered guerrilla war with the Cacos resistance. US forces were able to seize control of the cities, but the Cacos maintained stubborn resistance in the mountainous areas to the north. They almost defeated US Marines at the Battle of Fort Dipitie. Ultimately, the marines invaded the mountainous Cacos territory, defeating the guerrilla army at the Battle of Fort Rivière (see Tierney 1981).

This race dynamic was particularly acute among the British white dominions. Even here, however, there are stark contrasts. With the extension of voting rights to women – including Māori women – in 1893, New Zealand became the first permanently constituted jurisdiction in the world to grant universal adult suffrage. Suffrage had previously been universal for Māori men over 21 from 1867, and for white men from 1879 (Atkinson 2003; Joseph 2008). While Māori now constituted a minority in their own country, they were at least included in a broader democratic polity in this specific white dominion. This was, however, only in the context of the 'special representation' through the four 'Māori constituencies' which were established alongside some 72 white constituencies. Although this system is often compared to apartheid, it obtains to the present, supported by many Māori.

The record of the other white dominions was even less impressive on race. Canada, for example, enacted suffrage for federal elections for male and female citizens in 1920 – but with exceptions for Chinese Canadians and Aboriginal Canadians. Chinese Canadians were enfranchised in 1947, while Aboriginal Canadians were not allowed to vote until 1960, regardless of gender. Newfoundland – the former white dominion which joined Canada in 1949 – provided universal male suffrage in 1925. It had, however, wiped out its indigenous population by this point.

Australia followed a similarly racialised white dominion path. After Australia became a federation in 1901, the federal government passed the Immigration Restriction Act. This marked the commencement of the 'White Australia Policy' which did not formally end until 1973. Subsequent acts further strengthened the policy up to the start of WWII. In 1902, the new federal parliament legislated for voting rights for all white men and women. Indigenous people were, however, explicitly excluded. 'Non-racial' universal suffrage was not achieved until 1967 when the Commonwealth Electoral Act extended the right to vote to all Australians regardless of race. 'White Australia' policies effectively gave British migrants – as well as other northern European migrants – preference over all others through the first four decades of the 20th century. The strategy was designed to exclude Asians and Pacific Islanders in particular. During WWII, Prime Minister John Curtin reinforced the policy: 'This country shall remain forever the home of the descendants of those people who came here in peace in order to establish in the South Seas an outpost of the British race'.[34] This was particularly ironic in terms of our earlier discussion of NSGTs – Australia had been gifted 'Black colonies' in the region – including Papua New Guinea – in the aftermath of WWI.

The South African racial model became even more notorious, of course. But it bears emphasis that this was less an issue of principle than degree in comparison to the other white dominions. The political economy of whiteness did become singularly significant

---

[34] John Curtin (1885-1945) was Irish Australian. Both his parents had emigrated from County Cork. His later views appear to sit uneasily with his earlier anti-imperialism and anti-militarism. He began political life as a Marxist and was imprisoned for his opposition to conscription during WWI.

in this white dominion with its indigenous Black majority and substantial 'Coloured' and 'Asian' populations. The franchise was extended rapidly for whites in the context of dominion status: white women's suffrage was granted in 1930 and suffrage for all white adults regardless of property in 1931. Blacks and Coloureds were, however, denied the right to vote at the same time – well before the formal apartheid era (1948–1994). In this sense the empire and white dominion constructed the racial franchise in South Africa.

The US had a similarly protracted struggle for equal voting rights for African Americans and Native Americans. In the colonial era, there had been various restrictions on suffrage. Property restrictions on voting disenfranchised more than half of the white male population in most states. After the American Revolution, each state continued to determine who was eligible. In the early history of the US, most states allowed only white male adult property owners to vote. This was a tiny minority – perhaps 5 per cent of the population. Over subsequent decades, voting rights were extended and by 1856, after the period of Jacksonian democracy, all states had almost universal white adult male suffrage regardless of property ownership.[35] In 1868, the 14th Amendment counted all residents for apportionment including former slaves, overriding the calculation of the enslaved as representing three-fifths of a person. However, this was not enforced in practice. In 1870, the 15th Amendment granted suffrage to all males of any race, skin colour, and ethnicity, including former slaves (freedmen), meaning that male African Americans in theory had the right to vote throughout the United States. But Jim Crow legislation meant that African Americans in particular were disenfranchised. This only changed substantially in the South with the Voting Rights Act in 1965 – and ongoing *de facto* disenfranchisement continues for both African Americans and Native Americans (Anderson 2018; Newkirk 2008).

To repeat, Haiti and the US stand as ideal types of the two possibilities open to post-colonial societies.[36] When Haiti declared independence it became the first free colonial society to explicitly reject race as the basis of social status. This bears immediate contrast with the white dominion of US independence which had no place for native Americans and African Americans – despite the input of Paine and other radicals. It is not just an aberration of history that Washington and Jefferson were slave-owners and proponents of indigenous genocide. This was a cornerstone of political economy of the polity that they were creating. Their settler colonial demographic majority allowed them to imagine the first white dominion – a post-colonial formation in which whiteness (alongside gender of course) was established as the first principle of citizenship. It was to separate from empire without the blessing of empire. In this case, there was no ceremony marking the transition and lowering of the imperial flag. But what replaced the colonial state

---

[35] Although tax-paying requirements remained in five states, and two of these persisted into the 20th century.

[36] As we shall see in chapter 10, Ireland in the early days of the Free State presents an interesting example of a mid-range position. Unable to fully decolonise itself in the partitioned state in which it found itself, it was highly active on behalf of the decolonisation of others.

formation was an explicitly racist post-colonial formation. This new 'democracy' not only failed to address the colonial legacies for indigenous peoples and enslaved Africans but fetishised and codified their inequality in the novel form of a 'White Republic'.

The reality of this new form of white dominion was made even clearer in 1898, with the Spanish American War. In the Philippines, revolutionary leader Emilio Aguinaldo declared Philippine independence from Spain. He became the first president of a constitutional republic in Asia the following year with the establishment of the First Philippine Republic. The islands were, however, ceded by Spain to the United States at the end of the war. A compensation of $20 million was paid to Spain according to the terms of the 1898 Treaty of Paris. When the United States did not recognise the nascent First Philippine Republic, the Philippine–American War broke out (1899-1902). The war resulted in the deaths of tens of thousands of combatants as well as two hundred thousand civilians, mostly from a cholera epidemic. The First Republic was defeated, and the archipelago was administered by the US, first as a military government, then as 'The Insular Government of the Philippine Islands'. The title referred to the fact that the government operated under the authority of the US Bureau of Insular Affairs – a division of the United States Department of War that oversaw civil aspects of the administration of several 'unincorporated territories' from 1898. In 1935, the Commonwealth of the Philippines was established as a transitional government to prepare the country for independence from American control – a status it had already enjoyed before the Philippine-American war.

The Panama Canal Zone, Puerto Rico and Guam also had insular governments at this time and Cuba had a similar 'insular' status. The US Supreme Court wrestled with the constitutional status of people in these jurisdictions. To outsiders, they looked to all intents and purposes like colonies. In this context it bears emphasis that since 1953, the UN has been considering the political status of Puerto Rico and how to assist it in achieving 'independence' or 'decolonisation'. In 1978, the Special Committee determined that a 'colonial relationship' existed between the US and Puerto Rico. In a 2016 report, the Special Committee called for the United States to expedite the process to allow self-determination. And in 2020 its people narrowly voted for US statehood.

In our reading the notion of 'white dominion' is not a decolonised space. From this perspective, individual white dominions are – at best – at the start of a post-colonial journey. Unless and until they address their relationship to indigenous and subaltern colonised peoples within their polity – as well as any further colonies they have obtained – they remain white dominions. In this sense, 'dominion' represents less an emergence from colonisation and more the institutionalisation of colonial racial hierarchies in a new, 'independent' form. They continue to privilege colonial whiteness and to subalternise people of colour, formerly indigenous, enslaved or indentured as well as the citizens of their own colonies. In other words, while some of them became formally democratic, their legitimacy was grounded in their commitment to legitimising white privilege rather than democracy. And when democracy didn't work in the interests of this white privilege, they avoided or suspended democracy. We include the USA in this model.[37] Thus, when Kipling demanded that the US 'take up the white man's burden' in 1899, he missed the point.[38] The US had already assumed this mantle – albeit not as a racially-hierarchised empire but rather as an independent 'white republic' (Saxton 2003). In this sense the US is not an outlier at all but rather the template for every subsequent polity that did not want to decolonise. The implications of this new racially coded power were exemplified by William F. Buckley in 1957. Writing in opposition to the nascent civil rights movement, Buckley argued that 'the White community in the South is entitled to take such measures as are necessary to prevail, politically and culturally, in areas in which it does not predominate numerically' (Serwer 2019). Once 'such measures' are elevated to the level of statecraft, there could be no more concise definition of what we understand by white dominion. It is rooted in colonial relations and it is defined by the need of race privilege to prevail under the threat of decolonisation. In this reading, among all the white dominions states only South Africa – after 1994 – could be said to have made a transformative journey beyond the formal racial hierarchies imposed by colonisation.

Rather obviously even in South Africa the multiple racialised legacies of colonisation remain all too tangible. There – as elsewhere – the racial coding of colonisation remains deeply embedded in the post-colonial state. Thus, the dialectic between whiteness and otherness continues to define our contemporary world and each and every post-colonial state within it. In this regard our contemporary discontents around race and racism reflect very directly the unfinished business of decolonisation. Across a range of contexts, anti-imperialist ideology and practice was determined by relationships between race and resistance in the colonies.

Classically, resistance to the colonial power was conditioned by relations between three key ethnic blocs within the colonies – indigenous people, European settlers, and other subaltern migrants of colour. We see these racialised contradictions imprint across all resistance to colonialism. Moreover, they continue well into the dynamics of the post-colonial state whose characteristics are fundamentally defined by which of these identities is in the ascendant – both demographically and in terms of political and economic power. Thus, we see settler dominated polities emerging in much of south America,[39] former slave dominated polities emerging in places like Jamaica and Haiti,

---

[37] Although it is a somewhat provocative argument, Latin American countries may be included as white dominions also. They were colonised by white European states, their liberation struggles were led by descendants of colonists, their societies continue to be riven by the legacy of colonialism, including racism and genocide. Rather than redressing these legacies, the states have replicated them and continue to do so to this day. See Gott 2007.

[38] While it is also a broader celebration of imperial racism, Kipling wrote the poem in the context of the Philippine–American War (1899–1902), exhorting the US to assume colonial control of the Filipino people and their country.

[39] As in the British colonies of north America, the revolt against Spanish colonialisation was led by descendants of colonisers such as Simon Bolivar and Bernardo O'Higgins.

and indigenous dominated polities in places like India and Papua New Guinea. In other situations, the emergent post-colonial polities struggled to create a common identity out of their particular ethnic makeup – from Guyana to Sri Lanka to Fiji tensions between indigenous peoples and migrant worker populations of colour continue to dominate post-colonial politics.

Thus, colonisation also threw up additional new colonial ethnic blocs which sat in a complex relationship to native peoples. This most obviously assumed political form in the case of the white dominions, but there were many other contrasting examples. One obvious juxtaposition is of African Americans who were and are Black Africans in North America with Afrikaaners who were and are white Europeans in Africa. Alongside these settlers and colons emerged a whole series of 'mixed race' populations with varying degrees of power and influence within the colonised countries – *mestizos* and *mestizas* in Latin America, *metis* in North America, 'coloureds' in South Africa, 'Anglo-Indians' in India. Almost every colonial formation generated these kinds of new, complex multiethnic identities.

This constituting of race created new dynamics that fundamentally transformed the implication and operation of decolonisation. Sometimes the existence of these *mestizo* and *mestiza* populations underpinned ideological claims about the inclusiveness of the colonial societies involved which masked deep structural inequality. Thus, in many Latin American societies this ideology has helped to prevent an analysis of these societies as no less white dominions than their north American neighbours. The reality is that *mestizo* and *mestiza* populations tend to occupy a marginalised and liminal space in many colonial situations. Half-caste, half-breed, *chola*, *chabine*, *meti*, pikey, mulatto – all of these terms and others have often been labels of rejection and discrimination from Fiji to South Africa, from Australia to British Central Africa.

In many places, as in the United States, opposition to miscegenation rested on a fear of the 'problem' of 'mixed-race' offspring. For people in this position, the possibilities for individual resistance were often slim. And in terms of collective identity, mixing offered the *mestizaje* at least two possibilities in terms of belonging: with the oppressed and colonised, or with the coloniser. Of course, the latter bloc was reluctant to encourage such identification, but that did not prevent the aspiration. Take the case of Cape Verdean immigrants in the US. Inhabitants of the Cape Verde islands are of mixed African and European origins. Moreover, they are 'the only major group of Americans to have made the voyage from Africa to the United States voluntarily' (Halter 1993). Standing between the two major racial identities on offer in the US, it is not uncommon for many of them, despite being dark-skinned, to identify as white (Fisher and Model 2012).

At the same time, intermixing – *mestizaje* – was often the source of imaginative and exciting innovation globally. This has assumed a range of cultural forms as various as religion, cuisine and music. It is our argument, detailed at length in chapter 11, that *mestizaje* holds further and more directly political possibilities for the contribution to liberation and indeed decolonisation far from the negative consequences experienced by *mestizaje* at the height of colonialism. None of the complex new racial and ethnic encounters and identities generated by colonialism disappeared at the point of decolonisation. Unresolved tensions around race remain definitive of the post-colonial condition. Despite their many achievements, *every* post-colonial state continues to struggle profoundly with the legacies of colonial racism. The 'infinite distance' between white dominion and black liberation remains.

Towards complete spiritual and political independence?

If dominion was a creature of colonisation rather than decolonisation, what was the alternative? The colonised had to envisage a different post-colonial context. What would distinguish self-determination from the colonial formation or white dominion? As Prashad states:

> In 1950, Aimé Césaire, one of the clearest voices of the 20th century, looked back at the long history of colonialism that was coming to an end. He wanted to judge colonialism from the ashes of Nazism, an ideology that surprised the innocent in Europe but which had been fostered slowly in Europe's colonial experience. After all, the instruments of Nazism – racial superiority, as well as brutal, genocidal violence – had been cultivated in the colonial worlds of Africa, Asia, and Latin America. Césaire, the effervescent poet and communist, had no problem with the encounter between cultures. The entanglements of Europe's culture with that of Africa and Asia had forged the best of human history across the Mediterranean Sea. But colonialism was not cultural contact. It was brutality. (Prashad 2017b)

Césaire pulled no punches in this characterisation in his *Discourse on Colonialism* (1955: 2):

> Between colonialisation and civilisation there is an infinite distance; that out of all the colonial expeditions that have been undertaken, out of all the colonial statutes that have been drawn up, out of all the memoranda that have been dispatched by all the ministries, there could not come a single human value.

Césaire was adamant: colonialism had produced nothing that would earn it respect in the judgment of history. He was, of course, writing in the specific context of the post-WWII world. Some newly independent nations had just emerged from colonial rule, while many others were struggling to extricate themselves from colonial power. In this context, the Indian anti-imperialist movement defined the goal of self-determination as something beyond dominion status or home rule within the empire. This new status was powerfully characterised by the Indian National Congress as *Purna Swaraj* – 'complete spiritual and political independence'.

Seventy years later, in 2021 – the start of the Fourth International Decade for the Eradication of Colonialism – decolonisation is at an odd juncture. On the one hand, the formal project of decolonisation is almost complete. The remaining NSGTs are few and relatively small – both physically and in population. Moreover, as we have seen, only the UK, US and Israel dare to imply that eradicating colonialism is not a desirable goal for the world. On the other hand, the 'complete spiritual and political independence' of the formerly colonised world appears some distance from completion. Most particularly, the white dominions of British imperialism continue to dominate almost every sphere of influence around the world. These polities have hardly begun to address what eradicating colonialism might mean for them: neither addressing the legacies of genocide and slavery and indenture nor imagining a post-colonial formation in which their indigenous populations (those of them left) and other subaltern peoples of colour are offered citizenship comparable to that of their white European settler citizens.

Our earlier reference to the Roman Empire also reminds us of the importance of the power to name and frame the process of colonisation. Calgach identified this from the first: 'they create a wasteland and call it peace'. This aspect of dominion – the power to name – is ever-present in the designations of countries and cities across the colonised world: in their personal names; in their languages; in their very essence. Half of the world remains 'Indian' because that is way that European colonists constructed it: the 'riches of the Indies' were what drew them to the colonised world. But the focus of Calgach on 'peace' is, if anything, even more relevant. This signals an unfinished revolution in epistemology. Colonialism did not provide colonised peoples with 'peace' – it gave them genocide and enslavement and indenture and death. Whether in the US or Haiti it left a toxic legacy of racial hierarchy and inequality with associated poverty and misery. Yet, imperial memory remains heavily invested in the notion that it is on the side of 'peace' and 'civilisation' and opposed to 'terror' and 'barbarism'. The truth is, of course, somewhat different. What could be more 'savage' or 'barbaric' than quartering people in front of their families or killing them by tying them to the mouths of cannons so that their families have no possibility of finding a body for burial? What could be more monstrous than the 'passive' brutality of deliberately infecting whole peoples with infectious diseases or administering their starving to death? One of the key challenges for contemporary anti-imperialism is to capture this delusional aspect of imperialism – to find some way to challenge the false memory syndrome at the epicentre of European consciousness.[40] This would be a key first step in beginning to bridge Césaire's 'infinite distance' between colonialism and civilisation.

In this regard, the end of empire might also be experienced as a liberation by the colonising power – or at least by elements of its population. There has, however, been little evidence of any profound soul-searching across other former empires or the continuing

---

[40] In the British case, the limits of the questioning of colonialism are clear. Thus, when in 2019 Jeremy Corbyn proposed that British school children should be taught about the history of British imperialism and colonialism, Conservative MP Tom Loughton responded that Corbyn's proposals showed that he was 'ashamed' of his own country and was more interested in 'talking down' Britain rather than celebrating 'the immense amount of good we have done in the world over many centuries'. Jacob Rees Mogg agreed that while there were 'blots' on Britain's colonial history, it had some 'good bits' that were 'really wonderful'. Chief among these was Britain's abolition of the slave trade (Bradley 2018). This sanguine reading failed to acknowledge that Britain had previously negotiated a monopoly over the slave trade in the Treaty of Utrecht 1713.

white dominions. Moreover, despite the catalogue of crimes against humanity that have been documented as a core part of the colonial process, there was never any equivalent of 'denazification'. These empires committed genocide and crimes against humanity, routinely and prosaically. But they have never been called to account. Imperialism still awaits its Nuremberg moment. In this vein, Susan Nieman signals the lessons that other peoples might draw from the German process of *Vergangenheitsaufarbeitung* or 'working through the past' (2019). She addresses the wider lessons of this process in terms of ongoing debates around contested memory, reparations and controversies surrounding historical monuments. She argues that central to this process is the degree to which the Germans took responsibility for Nazism – in this sense they were 'liberated' rather than 'defeated' in 1945. This would be a novel perspective on disengagement from Ireland or India or Kenya for most English observers.

Of course, given the enormity of its crimes, there is also a temptation to blame everything that is wrong with the contemporary world on colonialism and imperialism. It becomes unhelpful, however, to label everything that happened subsequently as caused by colonialism – every drug- or alcohol-dependent first nation member, every act of violence against women in Latin America, every act of homophobia in Cuba or Uganda, the advent of ISIS in the Middle East – the list of contemporary discontents that might be rooted in the legacies of colonialism is endless. What is certain, however, is that all of these phenomena remain conditioned by colonialism. The capacity to resist and change and reform in any former colony emerges from underneath the long shadow of colonialism. The wider lesson is incontrovertible: the continuing struggle for agency among formerly colonised peoples and countries cannot be understood without close attention to the enduring legacies of colonialism and imperialism along the arc of decolonisation. Where Ireland sits on this arc – and what the Irish should take from this reading – is the subject of our next chapter.

Chapter 10

'Peoples endure; empires perish':
Irish anti-colonialism and anti-imperialism

Why should Ireland fight for Britain in this war? What has Britain ever done for our people? Whatever we got from her we wrested with struggle and sacrifice. No, men and women of the Irish race, we shall not fight for England. We shall fight for the destruction of the British Empire and the construction of an Irish republic. —James Larkin, 1914

Irish History is Divided into two Parts. Part One: the agents of British Rule make their presence known to the Irish; Part Two: The Irish People Defend Themselves. Part One is known as 'keeping the peace'; Part Two is of course terrorism. —Cormac, 1982

When in the 1980s Cormac presented his *A Quite Short History of Ireland* (see Curtis 1984b: 94), he cut to the quick of the colonial nexus in a way that more detailed and scholarly histories of Ireland – from Lecky (1892) to Roy Foster (1988) – have never quite managed to do.[1] He also nailed the significance of the imperial monopoly over the definition of the situation which we signalled in the previous chapter. In this context 'peace' had become a profoundly loaded term. It was always something that England brought to Ireland; often something that England *did* to Ireland. Likewise, the antonym of this civilising pacification was 'terrorism'. By the 1980s, all forms of Irish resistance to colonialism could be reduced, neutralised and dismissed by the application of this single toxic label. It is this aspect of the Irish story – the gulf between 'the Irish people defending themselves' and 'terrorism' – that frames our problematic for this chapter. The chapter considers the arc of decolonisation laid out clearly in the last chapter specifically in relation to Ireland. As elsewhere, there is no strict chronological narrative to this arc – different moments reflect a continuum between contact and liberation. Moreover, the unfinished nature of the Irish revolution means that partition left the two parts of Ireland in very different places on that arc: one state edging tentatively towards freedom from colonialism; the other further embedding colonial hierarchies in hyper-sectarian form. That said, the three phases of Irish anti-imperialism are broadly as follows: first, establishment and resistance – 12th to 17th centuries; second, resisting the established colonial state –

---

[1] Lecky's work also provides a neat metaphor for decolonising Irish historiography. His 'definitive' history of Ireland in the eighteenth century was extracted – or 'cabinetted' – from his *A History of England during the Eighteenth Century* (1878). His other publications included *The Empire, its Value and its Growth* (1893).

18th to 20th century, and beyond; third, anti-imperialism post-independence – 20th century to date.

We can also suggest that the Irish played a significant – and at least arguably *disproportionate* – role in developing the broader anti-colonialism sketched in the previous chapter. If nothing else, the *longevity* of the colonial nexus between England and Ireland allowed the considered development of different anti-imperialist tactics and strategies. In terms of Ireland itself, the Proclamation provides the classic summation of the principle of ongoing resistance:

> We declare the right of the people of Ireland to the ownership of Ireland and to the unfettered control of Irish destinies, to be sovereign and indefeasible. The long usurpation of that right by a foreign people and government has not extinguished the right, nor can it ever be extinguished except by the destruction of the Irish people. In every generation the Irish people have asserted their right to national freedom and sovereignty; six times during the past three hundred years they have asserted it in arms.

Jan Morris – in her critical but not unsympathetic overview of the British Empire – summarises a similar Irish disposition across the *diaspora*:

> Wherever they went, Irishmen remained the most virulent enemies of British rule. An Irish priest was one of Riel's closest advisers. An Irish labourer tried to kill Prince Alfred during his visit to Australia. The militant Governor of Montana during the worst period of Anglo-American rivalry in the west was an Irishman educated in the prisons of Tasmania. An Irish freelance, Alfred Aylward, alias Murphy, was an influential adviser to the Boer command in the Transvaal war. Far more than most emigrants, the Irish abroad retained their sense of nationhood and ancestral grievance. (1973: 468)[2]

As we saw in the previous chapter, resistance to colonialism was universal across empires. Nevertheless, this notion of a specifically Irish recalcitrance is widespread – 'Live Ireland, Perish the Empire' – suggesting a people uniquely unconvinced of the virtues of empire. This was especially galling to English imperialists. From the very beginning, for example – as emblemised in 'The English Flag' – Kipling's project was crucially informed by the defiance/insolence of Ireland and Irishness (Nagai 2006).[3]

But this notion also treads dangerously close to romanticism – implying that anti-colonial resistance had no cost in general and no cost in Ireland in particular. From

---

[2] She might well have added the remarkable Irish Australian Arthur Alfred Lynch (1861-1934) – polymath civil engineer, physician, journalist, author, soldier and anti-imperialist. Lynch raised the Second Irish Brigade which fought on the Boer side during the Boer War in South Africa. He was sentenced to death for treason for this but later pardoned. He served as MP at Westminster as member of the Irish Parliamentary Party, representing Galway from 1901 to 1902, and West Clare from 1909 to 1918. He supported the British war effort in the First World War, raising his own Irish battalion in Munster towards the end of the war.

[3] Kipling's poem makes little direct reference to Ireland but was responding to the burning of Cork Courthouse during the politically charged trial of five republicans in 1891. As the headnote to the poem records; 'Above the portico a flag-staff, bearing the Union Jack, remained fluttering in the flames for some time, but ultimately when it fell the crowds rent the air with shouts, and seemed to see significance in the incident'.

Captain MacMorris[4] in *Henry V* to Stephen of Ireland in *Braveheart*[5] there is a series of anti-Irish tropes exhibiting a pathological obsession to kill without compunction or apparent consequence. In truth, however, *any* resistance to colonisation entails life-changing effects for the colonised. There is always the lived experience of dispossession and injustice, but the crucial question is how the colonised process that experience. It would be reassuring to think, to quote a cliché, that repression breeds resistance. But the situation is much more complex than that. Sometimes it does, and sometimes it doesn't; sometimes that resistance is minimal, and sometimes more substantial but not necessarily easily visible. Sometimes the reaction of the colonised can be conformity, and sometimes it merely looks like that. And sometimes there are even signs of resistance in the most unlikely setting, namely among the colonisers.

For the colonised, at its most immediate, colonisation is an individual or family experience. But if one's neighbours, one's clan, one's region are living through the same experience, then there is no escaping the realisation that something fundamental and structural is at play. One does not need to have a sense of nationhood binding oneself to a vast population one has never met;[6] one simply has to acknowledge the evidence of one's experience, that this is a communal and not simply an individual experience. The question, however, is what can be done to push back against dispossession and injustice. Where is the space for resistance? At minimum, one can use the 'weapons of the weak', 'everyday forms of resistance' which include 'foot dragging, dissimulation, false compliance, pilfering, feigned ignorance, slander, arson, sabotage and so forth'. These forms of resistance 'stop well short of collective outright defiance'; they do not venture 'to contest the formal definitions of hierarchy and power' (Scott 1985: 29 and 33). Often, depending on the power of the coloniser and the severity of the blow delivered to native society and culture, the minimum may also be, in reality, the maximum. Collective resistance may be ruthlessly curtailed. Rebellion may be

---

[4] Shakespeare's Captain MacMorris is chiefly remembered for his notoriously anti-Irish attribution: 'Of my nation! What ish my nation? Ish a villain, and a bastard, and a knave, and a rascal. What ish my nation? Who talks of my nation?' But his more general predilection to violence reminds us of the continuity of such tropes across the most highbrow of English culture: Macmorris. 'It is no time to discourse, so Chrish save me: the day is hot, and the weather, and the wars, and the king, and the dukes: it is no time to discourse. The town is beseeched, and the trumpet call us to the breach; and we talk, and, be Chrish, do nothing: 'tis shame for us all: so God sa' me, 'tis shame to stand still; it is shame, by my hand: and there is throats to be cut, and works to be done; and there ish nothing done, so Chrish sa' me, la!' (Shapiro 2016).

[5] In *Braveheart*, the character of Stephen of Ireland is portrayed with an archetypical combination of lunacy and anti-Englishness:
Stephen: [to the sky as if addressing God] Alright, Father, I'll ask him.
Stephen: [turning to Wallace] If I risk my neck for you, will I get a chance to kill Englishmen?
Hamish: Is your father a ghost, or do you converse with the Almighty?
Stephen: In order to find his equal, an Irishman is forced to talk to God....
William Wallace: And the answer to your question is 'yes'. You fight for me, you get to kill the English.
Stephen: [grins] Excellent!

[6] Anderson (1991: 49) argues that nationalism involves an imagined community, an identification with others beyond the scope of one's daily life. '... the members of even the smallest nation will never know most of their fellow-members, meet them, or even hear of them, yet in the minds of each lives the image of their communion'.

doomed to failure. Actualising resistance can be severely restricted.

At the same time, the colonised come to realise that colonisation is quickly transforming almost every aspect of their society, obliterating the old and establishing a new order. Land ownership and use, taxation, legal sanctions, freedom of movement, symbols of authority and power are transformed. Towns appear where there were none before, or grow in size and importance, controlled and fortified to protect the coloniser. These changes quickly take on the substance of immutability. As such, by law or practice they become the only reality deemed to be acceptable. As a consequence, the colonised have little option but to conform, no matter how reluctantly – working for the incomer who stole the land, paying the taxes or rent to the stranger, bowing the knee or touching the peak of the cap to the passing noble. This does not necessarily mean acquiescence or conformity as such, but simply survival.

On the one hand the colonised have to perform as acquiescent no matter how difficult that charade may be. On the other hand, the natural and reasonable response to dispossession is resistance. The fundamental question is how to navigate that bifurcated reality. Some of the colonised may come to accept the colonial paradigm, their resistance being nothing more than seeking to acquire for themselves the greatest advantages possible within that curtailment. At the opposite pole, others may reject the colonial paradigm and seek to overturn it by any means possible. In this chapter we wish to focus mainly on the latter category. In looking synoptically at the history of Ireland we will seek to draw out a number of analytical points.

First, resistance can develop at different levels. At a basic level, it can involve one's personal rejection of colonialism and its effects and the attempts to undermine or transcend those effects. At a deeper level can be the realisation that the experience is not confined to oneself and one's immediate family, clan and neighbourhood. As a national consciousness and identity emerge, resistance can take on a society-wide articulated and organised form. Finally, this consciousness can become even more expansive, allowing the colonised to recognise that they share this experience with others who are not like them and whom they have never met, people elsewhere experiencing colonialism and with whom they feel a deep sense of resonance. At its most politically sophisticated, resistance can ultimately be articulated as anti-colonialist, anti-imperialist and internationalist. This will be examined specifically in the Irish context.

Second, the acceptance of the colonial paradigm by some of the colonised also can appear at different levels – from the individualistic and selfish attempt to get some of the crumbs from the colonisers' table, to a sophisticated politics which confronts colonisation in order to find some power and wealth, albeit subaltern, within the colonial system. This is not the same as the colonialism or imperialism of the coloniser, but a pro-colonialism and pro-imperialism with a native twist. This too, a common phenomenon in other colonial situations, will be examined specifically in the Irish context.

Third, these two strands of colonialism and anti-colonialism ebb and flow in different epochs, sometimes in response to each other, and sometimes coexisting within the same organisations and movements. We examine several examples of this in the Irish context below.

Fourth, resistance to colonialism by default is communal and collective. This is due, not least, to the fact that dispossession and repression are collective. The lands where the clan roamed with its cattle become privatised; the speaking of native languages or staying true to age-old native customs are criminalised, and so on. The result is that to continue those practices, even without any carefully articulated politics of resistance is in effect resistance. Colonialism thus gave rise to communities of resistance. In the 20th century this process was described by Sivanandan (1989: 25):

> They come together, too, over everyday cases of hardship to help out each other's families, setting up informal community centres to help them consolidate whatever gains they make. These are not great big things they do, but they are the sort of organic communities of resistance that, in a sense, were prefigured in the black struggles of the 1960s and 1970s and the insurrections of 1981 and 1985.

Similarly, in the North in the late 20th century what women did as neighbours and friends in a politicised situation often became politicised acts of resistance. Looking after a neighbour's children is one thing; looking after them when the parent is in prison lends an added level of significance. Putting up a neighbour's son or daughter for the night is one thing; putting them up when they are on the run from the British army is again of added significance. In the same vein, in the emergence and consolidation of colonialism the communal ways and practices of the native can become highly politicised.

Finally, as Memmi (1990) points out, there can be occasions when even the colonisers can break ranks. Confined and misunderstood by the metropolitan power they can become 'colonisers who refuse' and can even find enough common ground with sections of the colonised to unite in resistance. Given the unevenness of power and privilege involved, such combinations can be precarious and fraught. They hold out the promise of genuine revolutionary transformation, but, sadly, all too often they are short-lived. Arguably, however, Irish anti-imperialism has been characterised by a striking interplay between settler and native responses to colonialism. The earliest 'theorists' of colonialism – like Molyneux and Swift – emerged from the settler colonial community. Likewise, many of the greatest icons of Irish republicanism – like Wolfe Tone and Robert Emmet – and Irish nationalism – like Parnell – were Protestant. Equally, however, the locus of resistance was the 'people of no property' – poor, Catholic, Gaelic, and self-consciously *native*. This subaltern location is exemplified in the life and work of James Connolly, perhaps the most significant Irish anti-imperialist of all. In comparison to the wider context we traced in the previous chapter, we begin to locate an unusual 'balance' between these vastly different settler and native perspectives. Arguably this lends a dynamic – and sometimes salutary – *mestizo* quality to the theory and practice of Irish resistance to empire.

Resistance to colonisation

Resistance to English conquest began as soon as Strongbow and the other Norman knights arrived in Ireland. It was uneven and disjointed, organised along clan and regional lines. Thus, some clans aligned with the incomers, while others resisted. But even those who aligned often did so strategically rather than philosophically, using temporary peaceful coexistence as a springboard for organisation and resistance at a later date. Resistance occurred periodically up to and through the struggle of the northern clans under O'Neill against the Elizabethans four centuries later.

The political system of the island of Ireland was such that there were no overarching structures of power and governance. Despite the existence of a High King, power was decentralised and shifting. A sense of nationhood which might have given rise to a full-blooded anti-colonialism had not yet emerged. However, resistance existed, sometimes low key and even unintentional, such as the continued allegiance to native practices which were outlawed or sanctioned. And sometimes there were skirmishes and occasional rebellions. As in Munster in 1569–1573 and 1579–1583, not all the rebellions were staged solely by native Irish clans; the Old English, in this case the Desmonds, frequently displayed their differences with the colonial metropole in London.

By the time of Hugh O'Neill's 'War Aims' of 1599 (Aldous and Puirseil 2008: 30-4), an inchoate nationalist programme begins to emerge. His rebellion was couched in terms of a cocktail of Catholic and Irish and aristocratic rights and never implied a complete break with England. Nevertheless, in combination, this could be read by Mitchel and others as 'the grand thought of creating an Irish nation'. When the dispossessed themselves reacted again during the Confederation of Kilkenny between 1642 and 1649, this was the first stirring of a consolidated, united, proto-nationalist movement and therefore the first stirrings of articulated Irish anti-colonialism. The rebellion began in Ulster in October 1641 under the leadership of Phelim O'Neill. The rebels, claiming to act out of loyalty to King Charles I in his struggle with parliament, took up arms to seek an improvement of the position of the Gaelic clans under the Crown, a claim also made by the Scottish Covenanters at the same time (Canny 1988: 64).

Before long other natives seized the opportunity to turn their wrath on settlers, often close neighbours, and cruelty and atrocities were common. There was immediate and continuing dispute about the extent of such atrocities. Sir John Temple said 150,000 Protestant settlers died in two months, 300,000 in two years. At the trial of Lord Maguyre, it was stated that 152,000 settlers were killed. Clarendon put the number of casualties at 40,000. Sir William Petty said 37,000 (Froude 1969: 111). Hyperbole was rampant; the rebellion was 'so generally inhumane, barbarous and cruel as the like was never before heard of in any age or kingdom' (Borlase 1675: 233). Yet, fewer died than was frequently claimed. The fact that there were 'possibly up to 100,000 British settlers in Ireland when the rising occurred in 1641' (Canny 1988: 96) indicates that most of the figures given at the time were widely off the mark. Lenihan (2008: 100) concludes that 'the number of murdered settlers was wildly inflated'. He points out that the worst hit county was Armagh where at least 600 Protestants were killed. Multiplying this total by nine to account for all the planted counties would still fall far short of the wild estimates given then and since. At the same time, he adds, the Armagh dead constituted 17 per cent of the British population of the county, so the terror involved was real and significant.[7]

What further incensed many was the alleged manner of their deaths. Of central significance were the accounts of unborn babies being ripped from their mothers' wombs. It is difficult to assess the authenticity of such reports through the fog of propaganda. The basis of these accounts seems to consist of, 'two vague hearsay reports and a third more authentic-sounding report from County Donegal... Thus, what may have been a single ghoulish atrocity became, imperceptibly, commonplace fact' (Lenihan 2008: 100). There was undoubted cruelty involved. There was widespread destruction of Protestant religious property and artefacts, as well instances of exhumation and debasement of Protestant corpses. Displaced settlers were forced to travel naked to places of safety such as Drogheda and Dublin, and some died on the way (Canny 1988: 62).

The other issue which was central in the propaganda offensive related to the motivation of the perpetrators. Commentators such as Borlase (1680: 24) viewed the rebellion as being driven simply and solely by 'detestation of the English'. But it was more complex and indeed more rational than that. As even Borlase (1680: 23) himself acknowledges, their core demands related to land and religious toleration. Phelim O'Neill listed the rebels' demands: the posts of Lord Deputy, Justices of the Peace and others to be filled only by Irish men; no standing army; tithes paid by Catholics to go to Catholic priests rather than the established (Anglican) clergy; Catholic Church lands to be restored; all plantations since James I to be annulled and no new plantations to be undertaken; the abolition of debts to the British; all fortifications to be in the hands of the Irish who could freely add to them; British migrants to be restrained; all anti-Catholic laws and Poynings' Law to be repealed (Lenihan 2008: 93).

The allegation that the rebels were driven solely by Catholic prejudice was broadcast widely through the efforts of a number of Irish and English pamphleteers, in particular Henry Jones, Dean of Kilmore in Ireland, and Sir John Temple. Jones published a pamphlet – *A Remonstrance on Divers Remarkable Passages Concerning the Church and Kingdome of Ireland* (1642) – within months of the events which was widely read:

---

[7] Without striving for *post-hoc* justification, the atrocities committed by the colonised, from Ireland to Haiti (see James 1989: 373-4), must be seen in the context of the atrocities of colonialism. Todorov (1999: 133) estimates that 70 million indigenous people died in the Americas after the Spanish conquest, 90 percent of the population, the biggest genocide in history. Quijano (2007: 170) goes further: 'Between the Aztec-Maya-Caribbean and the Tawantinsuyana (or Inca) areas, about 65 million inhabitants were exterminated in a period of less than 50 years.' In 1798, 200 Protestants were burnt to death in a barn in Scullabogue in Wexford, while one sixth of the population of Wexford was massacred by British troops at the same time. By comparison, Russia lost one fifth of its population in World War II – some 27 million people.

> ... a most bloody and Antichristian combination and plot hatched, by well-nigh the
> whole Romish sect, by way of combination from parts foreign, with those at home,
> against this our Church and state; thereby intending the utter extirpation of the
> reformed Religion, and the possessors of it... (Jones, quoted in Elliott 2000: 105)

In the aftermath of the events, the Commission for the Despoiled Subject took witness testimonies from thousands of Protestants (Clarke 1986).[8] Having examined the depositions, Canny (2002) concluded that, as far as the victims were concerned, there was a range of motivations behind the actions of the rebels. The religious zeal of their attackers was only a partial explanation. Political and economic motivations were also prominent; rebels justified their actions by referring to the fact that plantation had resulted in their dispossession. Temple did not mention the non-theological rationale. As far as he was concerned, the Gaelic chieftains were 'pliant instruments of wily priests' (Canny 2002: 24). The rebellion was not represented as a revolt of the dispossessed against colonial expansion, but rather as a popish plot to exterminate Protestants. It was a war against Protestants, not against planters.

From the perspective of the colonised, however, the resistance of the rebels appeared not only comprehensible but reasonable. Had that interpretation been accepted by the government in England there was the real risk that concessions would be made to the rebels which would ultimately spell the death knell of plantation (Canny 1988: 65). The religious card was played by Temple, Jones and others to ensure that the English authorities did not accept the logic of the rebels' argument.[9]

Their writings thus threw an ideological lifeline to the settlers in Ireland at their lowest point. In the end, 1641 did not presage Armageddon for the settlers. They managed to suppress the insurrection largely though their own efforts, with some help from Scots soldiers. This gave them a great sense of confidence afterwards, a determination that they were here to stay (Canny 1988: 108). Before the rebellion the settlers constituted about 18 per cent of the population of Ireland; after it, despite the massacres, they made up about 27 per cent (Canny 1988: 110).[10] But there was a lasting cost: '... for the first time the main justification for dispossession' became religion (Elliott 2000: 102). The accusation of sectarianism against the rebels laid the basis for a sectarian mindset in the minds of the settlers and their supporters.

For their part, the rebels set out to establish the first experiment in a unified sovereign Irish state, the Confederation of Kilkenny. The Confederation brought together Irish chieftains and Old English lords, backed by the Papal Nuncio, and between 1642 and 1649 built up a General Assembly, or parliament, a Supreme Council, or

---

[8] These depositions are available online at Trinity College Dublin, TCD '1641 Depositions'.

[9] Temple's pamphlet went through more than ten editions between 1646 and 1812. No less than Cambrensis in a previous era, 'Temple managed to sear the English mind with an image of the Irish that would last for centuries' (Noonan 1998: 175).

[10] The fall in the native population which followed on Cromwell's actions in Ireland is a partial explanation for the increase in the settler population percentage.

executive, and an army. It effectively came to govern two-thirds of the island.[11] At
the core of the Confederates' demands were self-government, which meant the repeal
of Poynings' Law, freedom of religion, and the return of land confiscated during the
plantations. The demands were thus overwhelmingly secular and political rather than
sectarian and exclusivist. The goal of religious toleration of Catholicism was not a bid
for the suppression of Protestantism. In fact, their inclusive position was progressive
for its time:

> ... for he that is born in Ireland, though his parents and all his ancestors were aliens,
> nay if his parents are Indians or Turks, if converted to Christianity, is an Irishman
> as fully as if his ancestors were born here for thousands of years. (Quoted in Ó
> Siochrú 2008: 33)

As Ó Siochrú concludes: 'This remarkable statement of inclusiveness, although motivated
largely by self-interest, in an effort to preserve and extend the privileges of the Catholic
elite, contrasts starkly with the bigoted outpourings of the London news-sheets'.

Religion had been at the centre of the conquest of Ireland, dating back to Henry II's
mission to bring the Irish Catholic Church into the Roman mainstream. The Reformation
added a further level to the Protestant English denigration of the Irish who remained
obstinately Catholic. The pamphleteers of 1641, aided and abetted by the Puritan
revenge which was to follow on the rebellion, brought the religious motif to the fore in
English intervention in Ireland and judged it, wrongly, to be the main or only motivation
for native resistance and rebellion and therefore the justification for suppression.

Religion was, of course, part of the mix which led to resistance. Given the Europe-
wide schism resulting from the Reformation, it could hardly have been otherwise. At
the same time, the core of resistance rested on an emergent anti-colonialism. It was a
secular stance, related to disenfranchisement from land, wealth, culture and power. The
problems of the island of Ireland were now being seen as island-wide, and not simply
those of clans or regions. With the emergence of a national identity came a unified stance
against colonial conquest.

But this sense of Irishness was developing in the context of a series of catastrophic
defeats throughout the 17th century. The defeat of O'Neill, through the Cromwellian
Conquest to the Siege of Limerick, marked the relentless progress of colonial conquest.

---

[11] The period saw a confusing array of forces and often shifting allegiances in Ireland. This was not a simple
sectarian confrontation, nor indeed a straightforward clash between colonisers and colonised, given that
some of the old colonisers joined forces with the colonised against the new colonisers. The Confederates
swore allegiance to King Charles I, yet were at war with the Royalists, which included the Crown's
representative in Ireland, the Lord Deputy, Ormond. At the same time, Ormond was himself an Old English
Catholic. To confuse matters further, Owen Roe O'Neill, who had taken over the leadership of the powerful
Ulster clan, originally sided with the Royalists before switching to join the Confederates. And eventually
both Royalists and Confederates, on the basis of their shared declaration of loyalty to the King, joined forces
against the Parliamentarians. The Parliamentarians for their part had their base in Protestant-controlled areas
of the island, but not all Protestants were Parliamentarians. The Covenanters of Ulster, for example, in line
with the position of their Scottish co-religionists, backed the King and were among the most shocked at his
death at the hands of the Parliamentarians and Cromwell.

This was characterised by plantation and a massive transfer of land ownership from native Irish to English and Scots settlers. So now Irish anti-imperialism had to construct itself from a position of profound inequality. It also had to construct itself against the victorious 'Protestant Ascendancy' state in Ireland in which colonial conquest appeared absolute.

Coloniser and colonised: a brotherhood of affection?

The successive defeats of the 17th century and the subsequent destruction of the Gaelic social system allowed the settler colonists to reinvent their identity. In parallel with similar developments in north America, an inchoate settler anti-colonialism began to emerge. This development is often recognised as the first theorised Irish anti-colonialism. Of course, their very Irishness remained ambiguous. They 'called themselves the "Protestants of Ireland", the "English of this kingdom", even the "People of Ireland": any circumlocution except "Irish"' (Lenihan 2008: 197). As Jonathan Swift put it, 'I happened to be dropped here' (quoted in Lenihan 2008: 197).[12] Nevertheless, they began to see themselves as different from – and in opposition to – England and Englishness. Their argument was put most cogently by William Molyneux. As the Gaelic inhabitants and customs had more or less vanished, he argued, it was the Protestants of Ireland who now solely constituted the people of Ireland (Carty 1999: 72). They were not colonists but accepted English constitutional government and so deserved full representation in the English parliament:

> Previous to 1650 the settlers in Ireland, like the British settlers in seventeenth-century America, believed themselves engaged upon a colonial endeavor which involved them in asserting British authority over people and places that had not previously recognized that authority and in providing for the assimilation of those people and places into a civil order… they acknowledged themselves to be colonists because they were engaged upon specially designated ventures that enjoyed the approval of the English state and church… Once these programs have been fulfilled, or abandoned, and once the settlers were established in sufficient strength to be confident of controlling their destinies, they shifted their attention from the problems involved with their special mission to those deriving from their relationship with Britain. (Canny 1988: 125)

With the Gaelic threat diminished, this settler colonial class came to see England rather than the native Irish as their main problem. English-appointed officials 'did not have at heart the true interest of Protestantism' (Canny 1988: 121); all they were interested in was 'the plundering of the resources of the country for their own enrichment'. Molyneux and his class came to political conclusions similar to those reached by contemporary colonisers in North America. This critique came in two main forms: constitutionalist and revolutionary. Led by people like Henry Grattan in the move

---

[12] A similar statement credited to the Duke of Wellington, born on the island of island, is apocryphal: 'If a gentleman happens to be born in a stable, it does not follow that he should be called a horse'.

towards 'legislative independence', constitutionalism sought to remove the blockages to their development as an Irish bourgeoisie. They were facing a situation where English laws reminded them constantly of their subordinate economic status. Navigation laws to protect English industry and commerce ensured that no Irish business could legally trade internationally. Other laws prevented the development of industry, with the single exception of the linen industry, which was not thought to be a threat to English interests (Froude 1969: 264). There was a ban on the export of sheep and cattle from Ireland to Britain. '... the whole of Ireland was treated as a province or colony, whose interests were to be sacrificed to those of the mother-country' (Lewis 1977: 38).

The 'most persistent complaint of the settler community was that the English parliament had proceeded with legislation sponsored by interest groups in England without any regard to the well-being of the settler community in Ireland' (Canny 1988: 114). Consequently, they began to organise politically against the metropolitan power. They took on the trappings of physical force. They formed the Volunteer movement, ostensibly a home guard against a French invasion of Ireland. This organisation sent out a message of intent to the British government. In 1779, during celebrations for the birthday of King William III, the Volunteers paraded around William's statue outside Parliament House in Dublin. On a cannon they hung a placard: 'A free trade or this!' (Grattan 1839: 400).

They were never called upon to deliver on this threat. For all the rhetoric, they did not come close to acting like the American colonists whom they admired. While they made some political advances, ultimately, they posed little threat to the empire. In fact, incorporation in empire was at the core of their sabre rattling. And in as far as they could reveal themselves capable of 'responsible government', they presented empire with an innovative and smoother form of governance. They demanded the repeal of Poynings' Law and the Declaratory Act of 1719. The latter – popularly known as 'the Sixth of George I' – made Irish dependency explicit as *An Act for the better securing the dependency of the Kingdom of Ireland on the Crown of Great Britain* (6. Geo. I, c. 5). It declared that the British Parliament had the right to pass laws for the Kingdom of Ireland, and that the British House of Lords had appellate jurisdiction for Irish court cases. The Declaratory Act 1719 was repealed in its entirety by the Repeal of Act for Securing Dependence of Ireland Act 1782. This move towards 'legislative independence' was, however, a severely limited victory, as Theobald Wolfe Tone, noted:

> ... the revolution of 1782 was the most bungling, imperfect business that ever threw ridicule on a lofty epithet ... The power remained in the hands of our enemies ... with this difference, that formerly we had our distresses, our injuries, our insults gratis at the hands of England; but now we pay very dearly to receive the same with aggravation, through the hands of Irishmen – yet this we boast of and call a Revolution! (Quoted in Cronin 1963: 10 and 11)

At the same time, there was a section of the same Protestant bourgeois class which revealed what was possible if the colonists refused to play their expected part in colonisation and instead sought to combine with the natives in the interests of creating a sovereign republic. Theobald Wolfe Tone and the Society of United Irishmen had no difficulty continuing to view Ireland as a colony and pushed for liberation. Although their roots were in the Volunteer movement, their prognosis and diagnosis of Ireland's problems were much more radical than those of Grattan. They were at the forefront of anti-colonialism in Ireland. The Constitution of the United Irishmen stressed that they existed

> for the purpose of forwarding a brotherhood of affection, a communion of rights, and a union of power among Irishmen of every religious persuasion, and thereby to obtain a complete reform in the legislature, founded on the principle of civil, political, and religious liberty. (Quoted in Cronin 1963: 14)[13]

Tone summed up his own aspirations thus:

> To subvert the tyranny of our execrable government, to break the connection with England, the never-failing source of all our political evils, and to assert the independence of my country – these were my objects. To unite the whole people of Ireland, to abolish the memory of all past dissensions, and to substitute the common name of Irishman in place of the denominations of Protestant, Catholic, and Dissenter – these were my means. (Quoted in Cronin 1963: 8-9)

To that end, the United Irishmen, composed of Anglicans like Tone, some prominent northern Presbyterians and lower-class Catholics, staged an uprising in 1798. Although valiant efforts against British forces occurred in Wexford, Antrim and Down in particular, the rebellion failed. Tone had gone to the United States and France and had persuaded the French to aid the Irish republican revolutionaries. Commissioned as a adjutant general in the French army, he was instrumental in having a French expeditionary force sent to Ireland. It arrived in September 1798 after the rebellion had been suppressed. Tone was captured, tried, and sentenced to death. He died on 19 November 1798, seven days after an alleged suicide attempt.

Tone had moved in radical republican political circles in England, France and America. He was regularly in touch with Thomas Paine who was a prominent supporter of the United Irishmen (Thomson 1991). Tone dealt with key revolutionaries in France, persuading them to send military forces to Ireland. He also spent time in America, where he came to know well the politics of the radicals there. All of these influences are at the heart of his politics. His belief that the liberated Irish republic should be secular, for example, was strongly influenced by the French revolutionary policy of dechristianisation. At the same time, Tone was no mere mimic. He was less enamoured of the American revolutionaries, finding them as pompous as any European royal. He also profoundly disagreed with their

---

[13] With less political freedom, less education and less access to arms, Irish Catholics made up the *sans culottes* of Irish rebellion at the time. There were a few exceptions. Colonel John Kelly, immortalised in the song 'Kelly the Boy from Killane', was a Catholic leader of the rebellion in Wexford, as was Father John Murphy, the hero of the song 'Boolavogue'. In the North the leadership was definitely in Presbyterian hands, although Roddy McCorley, immortalised in the eponymous song, was probably a Catholic. See McLaughlin 2003: 57-75 and 97-107.

support for slavery. At the core of the United Irishmen agenda were Catholic emancipation and the abolition of slavery.[14] These aspirations were not universally shared in the Volunteer movement at the time, as Tone's encounter with Waddell Cunningham reveals. Cunningham was probably the most important of Belfast's business entrepreneurs, involved in banking, land and provisioning the slave colonies in the Caribbean. He was also a slave owner in Dominica. He was prominent in the Volunteers in Belfast, in which capacity he and Tone occasionally crossed paths. Cunningham was not in favour of either Catholic emancipation or the abolition of slavery. Tone was not impressed.

When he was in Belfast for the formation of the United Irishmen in October 1791, Tone had dinner at the home of Samuel and Martha McTier; another guest was Waddell Cunningham. Tone noted in his journal that he and Cunningham had 'a furious battle, which lasted two hours, on the Catholic question' (quoted in Chambers 1983: 45). The following year, Tone was again in Belfast for a meeting of Volunteer delegates. He records in his journal that at 1 am on 13 July 1792, he was awakened from his sleep by Samuel Neilsen, a local United Irishman. Neilsen was furious at Waddell Cunningham's behaviour, so he and Tone went to Cunningham's room where they found 'delegates from the country corp, with Waddell haranguing against the Catholics'. Tone concludes by giving his opinion of Cunningham: 'Waddell a lying old scoundrel' (Bartlett 1998: 133). In 1786, after the repeal of the Navigation Acts partially opened up international trade, Cunningham called a meeting with a view to establishing a slave-trading company in Belfast. The meeting ended without the company being established. The story circulated that the idea was scuttled by a radical, later member of the United Irishmen, Thomas McCabe, who is alleged to have written in the proposal book: 'May G__ eternally damn the soul of the man who subscribes the first guinea' (letter of William Drennan to his sister, Margaret McTier, 17 May 1806; quoted in Agnew 1999: 480). This episode anticipated many of the later tensions between a self-interested Irish nationalism and more principled anti-colonial internationalism.

The United Irishmen may not have had the successes of their French or American counterparts, but they gave the world an early and sophisticated lesson in anti-imperialism. The comparison with the American revolution could not be starker; Washington, Jefferson and the others were not calling for rights for native Americans, were not seeking the abolition of slavery. Their definition of 'liberty' was bourgeois, white and narrow, in both theory and practice a development of white dominion. Tone, Neilsen and the others in the United Irishmen produced a politics of liberty which was expansive and inclusive. For them, the liberation of their own class was not the end of the story. They used their own experience of injustice to identify with injustice more widely, not just on their own island but further afield. In this sense, the United Irish movement provided a powerful

---

[14] Leading United Irishman James Napper Tandy condemned the French counterrevolutionary actions against Toussaint L'Ouverture in Haiti. 'We are all of the same family, black and white...', he wrote. Another United Irishman, John Swiney, named one of his sons Toussaint. See Forsdick and Høgsbjerg (2017).

template for anti-imperialism not only in Ireland but around the world. Their notion of citizenship – grounded in the 'common name of Irish' – offered a vision of independence[15] that moved beyond the white settler republic model of the US and planted the seeds of an inclusive future defined by *mestizaje*. This was explicitly envisaged as a space in which *all* the religious and ethnic blocs generated by colonialism – Protestant, Catholic, Dissenter – would be integrated in a new, genuinely post-colonial Irish republic.

Union, Empire and the limits of solidarity

The Act of Union changed the terrain for Irish anti-imperialism. For the most part Presbyterians quickly became convinced unionists. Over the course of the next century, Catholics came to constitute the bulk of those in the forefront of nationalist struggle in Ireland.[16] But they had lost allies; the old ideal of unity of Protestant, Catholic and dissenter was now to all intents and purposes dead. When the escaped slave and abolitionist Frederick Douglass visited Belfast in 1845 he experienced the last vestige of radical northern Presbyterianism.[17] He was impressed by the radical stance of Belfast Presbyterians who supported the abolition of slavery and Catholic emancipation. He was particularly moved to encounter Protestants who took the bible as a basis of liberation rather than a handbook to justify enslavement. During a public address in Belfast, he spoke thus:

> … there is no greater calamity than being the slave of a Christian slave-holder. (Hear) … A man becomes the more cruel the more the religious element is perverted in him … if they are women-whippers, cradle-plunderers, and man-stealers before their conversion, they are women-whippers, cradle-plunderers, and man stealers after it – (hear) – and that 'religion' is to them but an additional stimulant to re-enact their atrocious deeds. (*Belfast Newsletter*, 26 December 1845, quoted in Rolston and Shannon 2002: 8)

To all intents and purposes Presbyterian radicalism in the north was to disappear almost completely. By the time of Douglass' visit the nationalist movement was in the hands of a Catholic leadership which was for the most part socially conservative. The leading example of this mentality was ironically Douglass' hero, the Liberator, Daniel

---

[15] The most immediate influence was on the Society of United Englishmen and the Society of United Scotsmen.

[16] At the same time Protestants continued to play key roles: Charles Stewart Parnell in the Irish Parliamentary Party; Isaac Butt, leader of the Home Rule League; Douglas Hyde, founder of the Gaelic League and first President of Ireland, Erskine Childers, Director of Publicity of the First Dáil.

[17] Frederick Douglass (1818-1895) was a slave in Maryland who escaped, aged 20. He quickly gained a reputation as a convincing orator in the abolitionist movement. His public profile was further enhanced when he published his autobiography in 1845, so he went on a speaking tour of Britain and Ireland to avoid possible recapture by his 'owner'. Returning to the United States, he became a noted writer and speaker, edited a popular newspaper, the *North Star,* acted as a recruiter for a Black regiment during the war with the Confederacy, was the only man present at the first women's rights convention in the US in 1878, was nominated by the Liberal Party as vice-presidential candidate in 1888, and towards the end of his life was US consul-general to Haiti. He was in fact *mestizo*, his father likely to have been his 'owner', although he was never able to establish that fact. As he observed: 'Genealogical trees do not flourish among slaves'.

O'Connell. When King George IV visited Ireland, O'Connell presented him with a laurel crown and pledged to donate money to build him a palace in Ireland (Curtis 1994: 25). Later he referred to Queen Victoria as 'the darling queen' (Curtis 1994: 27) when many of his contemporaries preferred the label 'the famine queen'.

The main rivals of Catholic O'Connell were the younger radicals gathered around *The Nation* newspaper, the Young Irelanders. They rejected his gradualist and constitutionalist approach to political change, urging a more radical and, if necessary, violent approach. To first appearances, their internationalism was as expansive as that of Tone. They aspired to instil a spirit of nationality, 'which may embrace Protestant, Catholic and Dissenter – Milesian and Cromwellian – the Irishman of a hundred generations, and the stranger who is within our gates...' (Davis 1945: 13). At the same time, unlike O'Connell, they could not find it in themselves to extend that same empathy to slaves. Writing in *The Nation,* they said:

> Notwithstanding the slavery of the negro, America is liberty's bulwark and Ireland's dearest ally ... Ireland knows that she has no Quixotic mission to hunt out and quarrel for (without being able to address) distant wrongs, when her own sufferings and thraldom require every exertion and every alliance ... we have really so very urgent affairs at home – so much abolition of white slavery to effect if we can ... that all our exertions will be needed in Ireland. Carolina planters never devoured our substance, nor drove away our sheep and oxen for a spoil ... Our enemies are nearer home than Carolina ... (Quoted in O'Connell 1990: 124 and 126)[18]

There were severe limits to the radical internationalism and anti-imperialism of most of the radicals gathered round *The Nation.* Thus, William Smith O'Brien's opposition to Britain was on the basis that: 'Ireland, instead of taking its place as an integral part of the great empire which the valour of her sons has contributed to win, has been treated as a dependent, tributary province' (quoted in Mitchel 1876: 43). The person who most fully followed the radical agenda through to logical conclusions was James Fintan Lalor.[19] He wrote that his goal was 'not to repeal the Union, but the conquest – not to disturb or dismantle the empire, but to abolish it utterly for ever...' (*Irish Felon*, 24 June, 1848; quoted in Lalor n.d.: 66). On another occasion he wrote: 'I trouble myself as little as

---

[18] Sentiments such as these led Frederick Douglass to side with O'Connell rather than the Young Irelanders. When O'Connell died, Douglass wrote that O'Connell 'was succeeded by the Duffys, Mitchells [sic] Meaghers, and others, men who loved liberty for themselves and their country but were utterly destitute of sympathy with the cause of liberty in countries other than their own' (Douglass 1962: 238).

[19] James Fintan Lalor (1807-1849) was born the first of twelve children into a relatively well-off family in Raheen, County Laois. His father was the first Catholic MP for the county. An accident in infancy left Fintan disabled and he suffered poor health all his life. His political involvement initially matched that of his father, namely opposition to tithes paid to the established Church of Ireland. Later, Fintan became involved with the Young Ireland movement where he became its most able writer and its most radical proponent of revolutionary change in Ireland. His watchword was: 'Ireland her own, and all therein, from the sod to the sky. The soil of Ireland for the people of Ireland'. He was arrested following the rebellion of 1848 and spent six months in prison before being released due to ill health. Just before he died, he was key organiser in a further insurrection in 1849.

anyone does about the "conquest" as taken abstractedly – as an affair that took place long ages ago. But that "conquest" is still in existence, with all its rights, claims, laws, relations, and results' (*The Irish Felon*, July 8, 1848; quoted in Lalor n.d.: 82).

Equally radical was Jemmy Hope, a northern Presbyterian who had fought in 1798 and 1803:

> It was my settled opinion that the condition of the labouring class was the fundamental question at issue between the rulers and the people, and there could be no solid foundation for liberty till measures were adopted that went to the root of the evil, and were specially directed to the restoration of the natural right of the people, the right of deriving a subsistence from the soil on which their labour was expended. (Hope 1972: 23)

Buoyed by the successes of revolution in Paris and political upheavals throughout western Europe in 1848, the Young Irelanders decided to stage an Irish rebellion. It was thwarted by a number of factors: unrealistic expectations of success based on the wider European experience, a misjudgement of the energy of the Irish peasantry, the negative intervention of the Catholic clergy and, significantly, the role of the government, in effect getting in its repressive reaction first. The most prominent of the Young Irelanders, John Mitchel, was transported to Van Diemen's Land for 14 years. The other leaders went ahead with the rebellion notwithstanding. It ended up being an inglorious affair, little more than a skirmish in Ballingarry, County Tipperary – 'a poor, extemporised abortion of a rising' (Mitchel 1913: 72). The other leaders were then transported.

There is any amount of scope in this tale to encourage mockery and denigration, but the event should not be written off. As Ó Cathaoir (1998) concludes: 'As revolution, the rising was a pathetic farce; as revolutionary theatre, however, it was a gesture against death and despair, evictions and emigration. Its political effects were profound and far-reaching'. In truth, there are few successes to point to in terms of military action by republicans in the last three centuries. 1798 was a much more major affair than 1848 but even it was destined to failure. At Vinegar Hill in Wexford, 16,000 or more rebels were engaged by a much smaller force of British soldiers. But the latter had artillery, while the former were armed with pikes and scythes; the outcome was a foregone conclusion.

The strength of state forces, spies and dissension among the rebels, the strength and tenacity of potential supporters among the peasantry and working class, state repression and coercion, Catholic Church denunciation – all of these in various permutations have been at the root of failure. One bishop, John Moriarty, was brutal in his condemnation. 'When we look down into the fathomless depths of the infamy of the heads of the Fenian conspiracy, we must acknowledge that eternity is not long enough nor hell hot enough for such miscreants' (quoted in *The Clare Champion* 2013). The Catholic Church position was deeply resented by Protestant Young Irelander William Smith O'Brien:

> He attributed his failure in great part to the behaviour (what shall I call it? – the cowardice, the treachery, the mere priestliness) of the priests. Priests hovered

round him everywhere; and on two or three occasions, when the people seemed to be gathering in force, they came whispering round, and melted off the crowd like a silent thaw. He described to me old, grey-haired men, coming up to him with tears streaming down their faces, telling him they would follow him so gladly to the world's end – that they had been long praying for that day – and God knows it was not life they valued; but there was his reverence, and he said that if they shed blood they would lose their immortal souls; and what could they do? God help them, where could they turn? And on their knees they entreated him to forgive them for deserting him. So they slunk home to take care of their paltry old souls and wait for the sheriff's bailiffs to hunt them in the poor-house. (Mitchel 1913: 267)

Despite such rhetoric, Mitchel was the radical who failed most spectacularly in terms of following the anti-imperialist logic through to its conclusion. He lambasted British imperial attitudes towards the Irish, on one occasion citing the prejudice of the British press as encapsulated in an editorial in the *Times* of London. 'Remove Irishmen to the banks of the Ganges, or the Indus – to Delhi, Benares, or Trincomalee, – and they would be far more in their element there than in the country to which an inexorable fate has confined them' (Mitchel 1876: 139). At the same time, he was quite capable of similar imperial prejudice himself. 'One is shocked to see either Irish peasants or English labourers ruled with the same rod of iron as Mahrattas or Belochees – with the same suspicious discipline as a mutinous man-of-war crew, or a black regiment at the Cape' (Mitchel 1876: 63). Transported to Tasmania in 1848, Mitchel later escaped and went to live in the United States. In 1857, now living in Tennessee, he wrote in the paper he had founded, the *Southern Citizen*:

I consider Negro slavery here the best state of existence for the Negro and the best for his master; and I consider that taking Negroes out of their brutal slavery in Africa and promoting them to a human and reasonable slavery here is good. (Quoted in MacCall 1938: 337)

Mitchel was eventually jailed for his outspoken support for the Confederacy.

If evidence were wanted for the all the contradictions of Irish anti-imperialism, it is to be found in the theory and practice of this one complex Irish Protestant Felon. The least that can be said about John Mitchel is that he is an enigma. Others go further and argue that, despite his keen analysis of Ireland's woes and his lifelong activism in relation to Irish freedom, he is a flawed hero and ought not to be adulated.[20] The reason for this rejection is his support for slavery. Not only did he support slavery in the US, and suffered a spell in prison accordingly, but he also supported the reopening of the African slave trade. He was totally consistent in arguing that the free Ireland he sought would include slavery. As he wrote in a private letter to Mary Thompson of Ravensdale, outside Dundalk:

---

[20] In the flurry of demands for the dismantling of statues by Black Lives Matter and other activists in 2020, there were calls for the prominent statue of Mitchel in Newry to be removed. See Hughes 2020.

> Be perfectly assured as I am that you (and the majority of the civilized nineteenth-century world) are altogether wrong on the whole question, and I absolutely right on it ... and when any of your taunting friends ask you (as you say they do) "What do you think of Ireland's emancipator now? Would you like an Irish Republic with an accompaniment of slave plantations?" – just answer quite simply – Yes, very much. At least I would answer so. (Quoted in *Irish Examiner* 2020)

Mitchel's republican credentials are beyond doubt. When he arrived in San Francisco after escaping from Van Diemen's land, thousands lined the streets to greet him. When he died, every major newspaper in Ireland, Britain and the USA carried the news. But, as Russell (2016) notes, he was no Wolfe Tone; not for him the rights of man nor the ideals of the French Revolution. His attitude was more patrician and classicist; if Greece and Rome could have slaves, why not Ireland?

The failures of 1798 and 1848 are clear. Still, Fintan Lalor attempted another rising in 1849 while the IRB rose in 1867 and this in turn anticipated the Easter Rising of 1916. This poses a broader anti-imperialist question: why should rebellion have continued to occur? This may seem a prime example of the wisdom attributed to Einstein: 'The definition of insanity is doing the same thing over and over again and expecting a different result'. More substantially, many writers and commentators on Irish republican history have concluded that, faced with insurmountable odds, republicans opted to idolise failure instead (Dudley Edwards 1977; Kearney 1980/1). This allows the rebels to draw on a deep well of Catholic doctrine and to mythologize themselves as Christ-like martyrs (Kearney 1978).

But the 1867 IRB Proclamation of an Irish Republic characterises itself in terms of *desperation* in the face of everyday realities of Ireland under empire as much as utopian sacrifice. Moreover, it embodies an internationalism and anti-sectarianism far removed from racist stereotyping of Irish resistance:

> We appealed in vain to the reason and sense of justice of the dominant powers. Our mildest remonstrances were met with sneers and contempt. Our appeals to arms were always unsuccessful. Today, having no honourable alternative left, we again appeal to force as our last resource. We accept the conditions of appeal, manfully deeming it better to die in the struggle for freedom than to continue an existence of utter serfdom. All men are born with equal rights, and in associating to protect one another and share public burdens, justice demands that such associations should rest upon a basis which maintains equality instead of destroying it. We therefore declare that, unable longer to endure the curse of Monarchical Government, we aim at founding a Republic based on universal suffrage, which shall secure to all the intrinsic value of their labour. The soil of Ireland, at present in the possession of an oligarchy, belongs to us, the Irish people, and to us it must be restored. We declare, also, in favour of absolute liberty of conscience, and complete separation of Church and State. We appeal to the Highest Tribunal for evidence of the justness of our cause. History bears testimony to the integrity of our sufferings, and we declare, in the face of our brethren, that we intend no war against the people of England – our war is against the aristocratic locusts, whether English or Irish, who have eaten the verdure of our fields – against the aristocratic leeches who drain alike our fields

and theirs. Republicans of the entire world, our cause is your cause... Herewith we proclaim the Irish Republic.

More generally, republicans themselves have frequently resorted to the rationalisation that failure is not as negative as it might appear. That is the base of the view that what is most important is to 'keep the flame lit', 'to strike a blow in this generation'. There is support for such a view in the canon of Irish republicanism; Terence MacSwiney stated that, 'it is not those who can inflict the most, but those that can suffer the most who will prevail'; Pádraig Pearse read aloud the Proclamation of Independence which contained the sentiment: 'In every generation the Irish people have asserted their right to national freedom and sovereignty; six times during the past three hundred years they have asserted it in arms'; a key symbol for the Fenians was the Phoenix, the bird that rises from its own ashes and can do so repeatedly. Such views could be dismissed as *post-hoc* rationalisation and self-delusion. But the incorporation of valiant failure can be a powerful resource for subaltern groups facing forces that are militarily and ideologically much more powerful. A rising can jump start a popular revolution, it can comfort the downtrodden and provide a chink of hope, it can attract the attention of more powerful external players who can bring pressure to bear on the ruling power. And sometimes, even at its most quixotic and foolhardy it can stand as a gesture, a symbol of the quest for liberty. So, not every rising has the same logic or the same effects, even if every attempt fails. If nothing else, the Irish displayed a commitment to this principle across empire. Thus, in both Australia[21] and Canada,[22] the Irish were central to insurrectionary moments that combined elements of Irish and colonial anti-imperialisms.

Despite the constant racialised accounts of an Irish predilection to violence, we insist that this was primarily an issue of tactics rather than principle. This was framed most coherently by Fintan Lalor. He did not pull any punches in this regard but was at pains to explain republican violence as responsive rather than due to philosophical commitment:

> As for the pledge of abstaining from the use of any but moral force, I am quite willing to take such pledge if, and provided, the English Government agree to take

---

[21] In 1804, there was a brief rising in Paramatta, near Melbourne, Australia, by transported United Irishmen. After the failure of Robert Emmet's rebellion in Dublin the previous year, this was in effect that last kick of the United Irishmen (O'Donnell 2004). Irish emigrants – led by Fintan Lalor's brother Peter – were also central to the uprising at Eureka in 1854 (Wright 2013). The complexity of the Irish diaspora is starkly revealed by the fact that Drummer Boy John Egan was the first military casualty at the Eureka gold fields where he was shot in the leg by a miner as the 1st Battalion of the East Suffolk Regiment entered the gold fields on the evening of the 28 November 1854 after a forced march of two days from Melbourne. He was born in Athlone in 1839 and enlisted as a boy in the regiment on 10 February 1852, aged 13.

[22] On at least six occasions between 1866 and 1870, Fenians in the United States invaded or attacked British military positions in Canada. The logic was to draw attention to British imperialism in Ireland, put pressure on the British to withdraw from Ireland, and perhaps, if enough successes were achieved, to draw troops from Britain thereby allowing for a rebellion in Ireland itself. The Battle of Ridgeway, Ontario, in which thousands of Fenians were involved and 18 Fenians (along with ten British soldiers) died, was the largest military battle undertaken by the Fenians (Doolin 2015). The policy was a failure, but it provided key military and organisational training for many who went on to build towards the Easter Rising of 1916. At the same time, there were an estimated 55,000 Fenians in the British army and navy (Foster 1988: 367).

it also; but 'if not, not'. Let England pledge not to argue the question by the prison, the convict-ship, or the halter; and I will readily pledge not to argue it in any form of physical logic. But dogs tied and stones loose is no bargain. Let the stones be given up; or unmuzzle the dog. (Lalor 1895: 6)

Thus, for Irish anti-imperialism the issue was always the question of the possibility of peaceful and democratic transformation under empire. Arguably in Ireland this issue had been settled definitively by what Terence MacSwiney called the 'shameless fiasco of Clontarf' (1921: 28). O'Connell and the Repeal Association had mobilised perhaps a million Irish people in a final mass demonstration in support of repeal of the Union in 1843. But the British banned the meeting and brought in troops to enforce the ban – despite its explicit commitments to peaceful and legal means. O'Connell submitted and called it off. Despite his abject surrender, his reward was a sentence of a year's imprisonment for conspiracy. As Ó Tuathaigh observes, 'the Clontarf show-down marks the effective end of the O'Connell Repeal campaign as a credible political movement' (1990: 190). The limitations of the strategy assumed a terrible poignancy only two years later with the onset of *An Gorta Mór* as the 'precious union' – unrepealed – administered the death by starvation of at least one million imperial subjects and the emigration of at least a further million.

This episode led many Irish people to conclude that physical force was the only methodology of anti-imperialism in Ireland. But this is not to suggest that this approach was without politics. The Fenians, sometimes dismissed as mindlessly committed to violence, had an anti-imperialist stance that allowed them to see the resonance between Ireland's condition and that of other colonised societies.

In 1878, John Devoy, the Irish Republican Brotherhood leader, wrote to Charles Stewart Parnell, leader of the Irish Parliamentary Party, saying that the IRB would support him if he agreed to a range of conditions, including: a declaration of self-government, land agitation, exclusion of sectarianism, energetic resistance to coercive legislation, and 'advocacy of all struggling nationalities in the British Empire or elsewhere' (quoted in Curtis 1994: 90).

In 1879 the IRB sought to send 20,000 dollars and a few military strategists to the Zulu to help them rise up against British rule. Their logic was that the English would find it much more difficult to fight one hundred thousand Africans

in their immense and practically unknown country than they would the same number of Irishmen in a little Island where every nook and corner is known and which is cut up in all directions by practicable roads... one million cartridges placed in the hands of the Zulus would help the Irish cause more than an equivalent amount of arms landed in Ireland. (Quoted in O'Brien and Ryan 1979: 410)

Michael Davitt, a member of the 11-man Supreme Council of the Irish Republican Brotherhood, actively worked to have Dadabhai Naoroji, an Indian resident in London, returned to the British parliament from an Irish constituency in order 'to give a direct voice in the house of commons to Indian nationalism...' (Moody 1981: 549). Actions such as these contributed to the reputation of Irish radicals as anti-colonialist and internationalist, a reputation not lost on those struggling against British rule in Africa and Asia.

That said, colonisation does not automatically breed native resistance, let alone any concerted opposition to empire. Many nationalists and home rulers were completely relaxed with the notion that a Home Rule Ireland would continue to have a place within the British Empire. In the everyday task of surviving, economically, socially and psychologically, colonisation also presents many opportunities for co-opting at least some of the natives. On the island itself, the incorporation of the colonised could involve acting as a rent collector for an absentee English landlord or joining the Royal Irish Constabulary. Beyond the island it often took the form of enrolment in the British army.

Military service was not the only way in which to embrace colonialism, as Irish immigrants to the United States learned. Ignatiev (1995: 41) points out that

> the first Congress of the United States voted in 1790 that only 'white' persons could be naturalized as citizens ... but ... it was by no means obvious who was 'white'. In the early years the Catholic Irish were shunned even more than the Scotch-Irish by WASP America and were frequently referred to as 'niggers turned inside out'...

As such, on occasion, they found common cause with African Americans. Slaves who escaped to the north not only were frequently helped by other Blacks (despite the potential penalties, including death), but also, 'some whites, among whom the Irish are most often mentioned, helped fugitives in their flight by forging passes for slaves' (Foner 1975: 503).

What changed is that part of the Irish population became 'white', 'came to boast the white skin as their highest prerogative' (Ignatiev 1995: 69). With the backing of the Democratic Party eager for their vote, Irish labourers organised to exclude black people from their trades and professions. Irish-American labour associations, 'denounced the abolitionists not for opposing slavery but for placing the cause of the slave ahead of the cause of the free worker' (Ignatiev 1995: 108). The Irish arrived at the politically empowering conclusion that they had to distance themselves as far as possible from slaves and Black people in order to become upwardly mobile:

> To be acknowledged as white it was not enough for the Irish to have a competitive advantage over Afro-Americans in the labor market; in order for them to avoid the taint of blackness it was necessary that no Negro be allowed to work in occupations where Irish were to be found. (Ignatiev 1995: 112)

They forced Black people out of numerous trades and occupations – house servant, cook, waiter, porter, longshoreman, labourer – and joined the white republic. As Frederick Douglass commented: 'Every hour sees the Black man elbowed out of employment by some newly-arrived immigrant whose hunger and whose colour are thought to give him a better title to the place' (quoted in Foner 1983: 214). One of the surest signs that they had arrived socially was when the first Irish policemen appeared on the streets – legally armed Irish Catholics in WASP America. The Irish had climbed the ladder by a rung or two, leaving the Blacks at the bottom and justifying the arrangements by racist attitudes which many Black commentators found remarkable for their intensity and apparent incongruity. Frederick Douglass (1962: 546) concluded:

> Perhaps no class of our fellow-citizens has carried this prejudice against color to a point more extreme and dangerous than have our Catholic Irish fellow-citizens, and yet no people on the face of the earth have been more relentlessly persecuted and oppressed on account of race and religion than have this same Irish people.

As the 'famine Irish' crowded into the cities of the East Coast and Midwest, they came face to face with Black labourers and saw them immediately as competitors for their low status jobs. Although the number of Blacks initially represented little real economic threat, the Irish quickly targeted Blacks as scapegoats. Many Irish immigrants saw the creation of 30 Black regiments within six months of the emancipation proclamation as tantamount to encouraging slave rebellions, while for others it was preferable that Black soldiers rather than white march off to be killed (Litwack 1961: 71).

The Irish community was not in favour of a war to coerce the South to abandon slavery; yet they came to be among the foremost supporters of that war. They solved the dilemma involved by making it clear that they were fighting for the Union, not for emancipation. The Irish proved loyal to the Union, volunteering in droves and forming 38 Union regiments with the word 'Irish' in their title (Shannon 1974: 59). Yet the attempt to draft New York Irish immigrants into the army led to severe riots in July 1863. Admittedly, the Irish had some reason for frustration; as poor labourers, they could not find the $200 which could have bought them out of donning the uniform. At the same time, the targets for the violence quickly became almost solely Black people and property (Wood 1970: 24). This anti-Black pogrom was only one of a number of the period in cities such as Milwaukee, Cincinnati (Wittke 1970: 126) and Detroit (Katzman 1973: 44). The riots represented the Irish working class' attempt to remove Black competition for their jobs, in the process gaining respectability in white America.

Despite their experience at the hands of the Irish, militarily or otherwise, many activists and radicals in other colonial situations looked to Ireland for inspiration. They also lent support to the cause of Irish liberation. Indian nationalists who founded the Congress Party in 1885 – such as Surendranath Banerjee – drew inspiration from the Irish Land League and in particular its tactic of boycotting (Kruger 1975: 305). There were close contacts between Irish and Indian nationalists. Indian nationalists identified with Ireland's independence struggle. The Irish American paper, *The Gaelic American*, frequently supported the Indian nationalist cause. Copies circulated widely in India itself, to the point that in October 1907, the British authorities banned its importation and sale (Kruger 1975: 308). Jawaharlal Nehru, later the first prime minister of India, recalled that as a student in England he had visited Ireland where he had been impressed by the ideas of Sinn Féin (Jeffery 1996a: 9). V.V. Giri, President of India from 1969 to 1974, studied law at University College Dublin between 1915 and 1925 and was deported to India because of his close links with Irish republicans.[23]

At the same moment, Patrick Ford's *Criminal History of the British Empire* provided an integrated anti-imperialist analysis.[24] This went well beyond any focus on Irish misfortune and offered an integrated critique of empire that dismayed imperialists – from William Gladstone at Westminster to James Craig at Stormont. Likewise, African Americans, and in particular their leading thinkers and activists, frequently displayed adulation of and support for the Irish struggle for freedom despite what some Irish Americans had done to them. Thus, after emancipation and the Civil War, Blacks met in each state of the Union to plan their future political progress. The State Convention meeting in California on 27 October 1865 adopted the following resolution:

> Resolved – That we sympathize with the Fenian movement to liberate Ireland from the yoke of British bondage, and when we have obtained our full citizenship in this country, we should be willing to assist our Irish brethren in their struggle for National Independence; and 40,000 colored troops could be raised to butt the horns off the hypocritical English bull. (Quoted in Foner and Walker, 1980: 178)

Two decades later, in a speech to the Colored National League of Boston in March 1886, Edward Everett Brown, who established the first Black law firm in Massachusetts, singled out the Irish anti-colonial struggle as the model to be followed by Black Americans seeking liberation (Foner and Branham, 1998: 680-2). A. Philip Randolph, the Black socialist, similarly saw the Irish struggle and that of African Americans as parallel (Moses 1978: 244-5).

Another Black American socialist, Claude McKay, lived in London during a key period in Anglo-Irish relations – from the end of 1919 to the beginning of 1921. At the socialist International Club in London he met many political activists from throughout Europe, including Ireland (Fryer 1984: 318-20). As Cooper (1987: 154) concludes, 'McKay loved the Irish. He considered them racially prejudiced, like other whites, but not hypocritical, like the Anglo-Saxons'. McKay wrote positively of the Irish revolution in articles such as 'How Black Sees Green and Red' in the *Liberator*, the socialist Afro-American periodical. At the same time, as a committed socialist, he was under no illusion

---

[23] Maud Gonne was involved in an attempt to rescue militant Indian nationalist Veer Savarleer from Brixton Jail in 1910 (Kapur 1997: 33).

[24] Patrick Ford (1837 – 1913) was an American Irish journalist. Born in Galway, he emigrated with his parents to Boston in 1845. He never returned to Ireland. He wrote: 'I might as well have been born in Boston. I know nothing of England. I brought nothing with me from Ireland – nothing tangible to make me what I am. I had consciously at least, only what I found and grew up with in here'. At 15, Ford went to work for William Lloyd Garrison's abolitionist newspaper, *The Liberator*. During the American Civil War (1861–1865) Ford served in Union forces. He spent four years after the war in Charleston, editing the *Southern Carolina Leader*, printed to support newly emancipated African Americans. He founded the *Irish World*, which became the principal newspaper of Irish America. It was later re-titled the *Irish World and American Industrial Liberator*. In 1880, Ford began to solicit donations through the *Irish World* to support Land League activities in Ireland. British Prime Minister William Gladstone suggested that without the funds from the *Irish World*, there would have been no agitation in Ireland.

about the socialist potential of Sinn Féin in 1921.

The identification of the Black radicals with the Irish was not confined to words. Cyril V. Briggs formed a secret society, the African Blood Brotherhood for African Liberation and Redemption, in 1919, modelled directly on the Irish Republican Brotherhood (Hill 1983: lxxii). S.A.G. Cox, the founder of the National Club of Jamaica, had been a law student in London in 1905, the year Arthur Griffith formed Sinn Féin. Later in Jamaica Cox named his newspaper *Our Own*, a reference to the translation of 'sinn féin' – 'ourselves' (Hill 1983: lxxiii).

The Assistant Secretary of the National Club of Jamaica at the time was Marcus Garvey, who later came to prominence through the United Negro Improvement Association (UNIA) in the United States and his 'Back to Africa' campaign. Garvey quite deliberately modelled his UNIA on similar developments by Irish activists. In 1919, he named the UNIA headquarters in New York Liberty Hall, in honour of the headquarters of James Connolly's Irish Citizen Army in Dublin (Hill 1983: lxxiv). In the same year he called for an 'International Convention of the Negro Peoples of the World', one week after 6,000 Irish Americans attended the third Irish Race Convention in Philadelphia (Hill 1983: lxxv). That Black Convention met in August 1920, and from it, Garvey sent a telegram to Eamon de Valera stating: 'We believe Ireland should be free even as Africa shall be free for the Negroes of the world' (Hill 1983: lxxviii). Shortly afterwards Garvey attended a meeting of Irish longshoremen in Liberty Hall, New York, to discuss a boycott of British ships in protest at the treatment of Terence MacSwiney, then on hunger strike in Britain. MacSwiney was the Sinn Féin Lord Mayor of Cork during the Tan War in 1920. He was arrested by the British on charges of sedition and imprisoned in Brixton Prison in England. His death there in October 1920 after 74 days on hunger strike brought the Irish struggle unprecedented international attention. He approached his hunger strike with remorseless dedication: 'I am confident that my death will do more to smash the British Empire than my release' (quoted in Ross 2010: 32).

When asked about the significance of the UNIA's tricolour, Garvey replied: 'The Red showed their sympathy with the "Reds" of the world, and the Green their sympathy for the Irish in their fight for freedom, and the Black – The Negro' (Hill 1983: lxxix). Garvey's admiration of and support for Irish liberation seems to have been rarely reciprocated. There is no record of de Valera having telegrammed Garvey urging Black liberation as being on a par with Irish independence. And Arthur Griffith, recipient of another telegram from Garvey congratulating him on the Treaty negotiations – 'your masterly achievement of partial independence for Ireland' (Hill 1983: lxxvii) – was not matched by anything approaching similar sentiments on Griffith's part. When writing the introduction to Mitchel's *Jail Journal* (1913), he condemned the fact that in every generation there was 'an inky tribe of small Irishmen' who sought to attack Mitchel. Griffith added:

> Even his views on Negro-slavery have been deprecatingly excused, as if excuse were
> needed for an Irish Nationalist declining to hold the Negro his peer in right. When
> the Irish Nation need explanation or apology for John Mitchel, the Irish nation will
> need its shroud. (Mitchel 1913: xiii-xiv)

The identification with politics in Ireland was not confined to Indian nationalists. Muhammed Ali Jinnah, leader of the Muslims and first President of Pakistan after partition, noted the similarities between his cause and that of the Ulster unionists. He argued that Indian Muslims deserved at least as much in terms of political concessions from the British as did the unionists in Ireland and was supported in the British parliament by leading Ulster unionist, Sir Edward Carson (Kapur 1997: 34). In the end, he was supported by the British government as well. From 1935, in the face of growing demands from the Congress Party, Britain was exploring giving greater autonomy to India. The two main players in this process were the Congress Party and the British government. When the Muslim League passed 'the Lahore Resolution' in 1940, committing themselves to working for a separate Muslim state to be called Pakistan, the Muslims and the British began to use Ireland as a comparator. In the speech launching the Lahore Resolution, Jinnah referred to Ireland:

> To yoke together two such nations under a single state, one as a numerical
> minority and the other as a majority, must lead to growing discontent and the final
> destruction of any fabric that may be built up for the government of such a state.
> History has presented to us many examples, such as the Union of Great Britain and
> Ireland, of Czechoslovakia and Poland.

L.S. Amery, British Secretary of State for India, believed that 'responsible government' for India merited conceding dominion status rather than any halfway measure. At the same time, he despised the Congress leaders, comparing Nehru to another colonial 'upstart' with whom the British had had substantial dealings in the previous decades:

> [Nehru is] a man who has spun himself into a cocoon of his own perversion of
> history and diatribes against the British which blind him to all real facts. The type
> is not unfamiliar among nationalist intellectuals in other countries – de Valera for
> instance.

The ghost of Irish negotiations also loomed large over the movement towards Indian independence. It was stated that there would be no transfer of power if the system of government planned was rejected by any major and powerful elements in India. In effect, as with the Ulster unionists, the Muslim League was presented with a veto over constitutional progress. Amery acknowledged this, stating that if the breakup of India occurred along the lines of the arrangement between 'Ulster and Éire' this would be 'a most disastrous solution'.

The British government then proposed that at the end of the war a constituent assembly would be elected from voters in all of the British Indian provinces. Any province could elect to opt out if it was unhappy with the new constitution, at which point the British would draft a constitution with such a province, thereby giving it the same status as the new Indian union. The South African prime minister, J.C. Smuts, who had advised the British government in relation to the Boundary Commission in Ireland, warned Churchill against using 'Irish tactics of partition'. Churchill's defence was that he had to negotiate with different 'sects and nations' in India and that the 'Moslems declare they will insist upon Pakistan, i.e. a sort of Ulster in the North'. Amery agreed:

> Nobody is going to work a constitution which has been imposed upon them against their will . . . The British constitution was pretty nearly wrecked by the Irish. If we had to force a majority constitution upon India I have no doubt the Moslems would probably wreck it in the parliamentary sense, if they did not wreck it in the military sense long before.

The antidote to violence, then, was to be partition which, in the British view, 'appeared to have provided a relatively painless way out of the Irish problem' (Fraser 1996: 92).

More broadly, therefore, in Ireland itself and across empire, we can trace countervailing tendencies within Irishness and Irish politics – some encouraging anti-imperialism and internationalism, others feeding racism and ethnic exclusivity. There were remarkable examples of shared learning and practice as well as clear indications of the limitations of such solidarity. These contradictions are not exclusive to Irishness. As was argued in the previous chapter, such contradictions are embedded in the ethnic interfaces that characterise *every* colonial situation and define *every* anti-imperialist politics. But in Ireland's relationship to colonialism, this grey area between empire and Republic has appeared *specifically* ambiguous. Throughout the history of Irish resistance to colonialism this has been epitomised by the contradictory location of 'Irish nationalism'.

Irish nationalism: which side are you on, boys?

The broader story of Irish attitudes towards and involvement in empire begs a specific question around Irish political identities and empire. How does nationalism – in many ways the *dominant* Irish political ideology from the Catholic Association through to the Irish Party and *Cumann na nGaedheal* and the SDLP – sit in terms of our reading of anti-colonialism and anti-imperialism in Ireland? This question becomes even more profound as we begin to realise that most political parties in contemporary 'Southern Ireland' are also nationalist rather than republican and anti-imperialist. In addition, both Fianna Fáil and Sinn Féin are 'fully constitutional' now. Yet the constitution that defines their contemporary politics continues to be framed by the unambiguously imperial Government of Ireland Act.

It bears emphasis that this notion of 'nationalism' was a wider colonial construction – it was the generic label that imperialism placed upon resistance to colonial rule. This should, of course, make us wary of the concept from the first. Nevertheless, what is broadly characterised as 'Irish nationalism' has carried the modal position in Irish political discourse from O'Connell onwards. It was clearly *nativist* – it represented the colonised, Catholic Irish. But what it wanted was never completely clear – this nationalism was defined by its opposition as much as its substance. Thus, it was often characterised by itself and its opponents as 'moral force' as against 'physical force'. In this sense, its constitutionalism and opposition to political violence were constants. In the context of 1801 and the Union, 'constitutionalism' implied both a commitment to empire and an acceptance of the anti-democratic basis of that particular constitutional settlement.

This acceptance of constitutionalism was, however, hardly a strategic principle of Irish organising in the Gandhian sense – at most it symbolised a tactical separation from anti-imperialist republicans and separatists of a more 'extreme' nature. O'Connell's two great projects – 'Catholic Emancipation' and 'Repeal of the Union' – provided the template for subsequent Irish nationalism. But these twin projects also signified the contradictions within the ideology. Catholic emancipation was a reformist, internal UK intervention which in practice had profoundly reactionary anti-democratic consequences. It might have gotten Catholic MPs back into the British parliament but it disenfranchised more than half of all Irish Catholics in the process. Repeal on the other hand was a separatist intervention that – whatever O'Connell's professed commitment to Crown and Empire – pointed inexorably towards Irish independence. In terms of the wider implications for imperialism, coupling Catholic emancipation and repeal constructed something that was much closer to self-determination than white dominion. (It was the equivalent, for example, in South Africa of enfranchising the 'natives' *alongside* the whites – something the British never contemplated, of course, in this comparable 'white dominion'.)

So, the simple dismissal of O'Connell as an imperialist lackey is both unfair and wrong in retrospect. O'Connell also deserves credit for other innovations. His greatest contribution was in terms of developing a model of mass mobilisation through the Catholic Association and the Repeal Association. He also modelled the resourcing of mass resistance; the 'Catholic rent' and 'Repeal Rent' that funded his mobilisations were ground-breaking mass populist political fundraising. Moreover, he was never the complete jackeen he is sometimes painted. On the abolition of slavery, for example, he was 'the single most important supporter that American anti-slavery had in Europe' (Riach 1976: 24). Moreover, he took a principled stand on slavery even at the cost of weakening the support for his Irish campaigns. He rejected the financial support of southern US slave-owners: 'I want no American aid if it comes across the Atlantic stained in Negro blood', he stated in 1845 (cited in O'Farrell 1991: 36). In 1839 he was one of the founders of the British India Society which sought to focus attention on the abuses carried out by the East India Company (Fraser 1996: 85). In this sense, his commitment to the principle of anti-imperialist solidarity appears much stronger than that of some more ideologically anti-imperial republicans.

Like Gandhi, O'Connell was sometimes perturbed by the consequences of the political forces he had mobilised. Unlike Gandhi, however, he failed to develop a philosophy that might allow an effective non-violent anti-imperialist approach to a colonial state that framed its response to anti-imperialist politics through coercion and violence. Nevertheless, the wider legacy of the innovative contributions of O'Connellism both in Ireland and beyond – a genuine mass movement capable of threatening empire – should not be underestimated. But his methods also formalised the tensions between his nationalism – constitutional, non-violent, reformist – and an established Irish anti-imperialist tradition – insurrectionary, revolutionary and republican.

These broad contradictions hardened after O'Connell's death and the huge social and political changes attendant on *An Gorta Mór*. They became particularly acute as the Irish Party developed into an effective parliamentary force at Westminster. This opportunity to resist empire *within* the imperial parliament was something which was denied every other colonised people. This was, of course, a huge anomaly. The Irish were sometimes regarded as the voice of the colonised inside the Westminster parliament. They also sometimes regarded themselves in this light.

But they also worked within self-imposed limits on separatism. Before Parnell the Irish parliamentary bloc was essentially a comfortably imperialist party. This helps explain the question of attitudes to empire among Irish nationalists in the latter half of the 19th century. A clear distinction was made between imperialism and colonialism:

> ... Irish nationalists saw no contradiction between rejecting the Union as an illegitimate tyranny and repudiating the idea that Ireland was a colony. Rather than seeing this as a contradiction, Irish nationalists made what they considered a vital distinction between nations that had come under imperial governance and colonized territories. This reflected contemporary usage of the term 'imperialism' ... they took a negative term associated with a despotic and foreign system of government and applied it to British government ... (Kelly 2009: 131)

So, 'Irish nationalists who comprehended the Anglo-Irish relationship as imperial did not necessarily hold that only full separation could produce a satisfactory status for Ireland: the government could be liberalized without severing the connection altogether' (Kelly 2009: 134). Without the dictatorial repression they were open to being happy with empire and sought to play their role in it. So, ranting against Britain did not necessarily mean siding with the colonised elsewhere. The closest that the Irish Party ever got to a separatist anti-imperialist position was the Parnell speech – which still declares its separatist principle beneath his memorial on O'Connell Street – that no-one can set the limits on a nationhood.[25] But this did reflect a wider mobilisation across Ireland for self-determination.

First, Parnell blurred the distinction between 'constitutional nationalism' and republicanism. This eventually produced the 'New Departure' of June 1879, signalling mutual support and a shared political agenda between Parnell and the Fenians. Second, Parnell was elected president of Michael Davitt's newly founded Irish National Land League in Dublin on 21 October 1879, forging a direct link between parliamentary action and Land League campaigning for land reform – this threatened the existing colonial land settlement so fundamentally that it became recognised as the 'Land War'. Tellingly, the word *boycott* entered the English language during the Land War (Davitt 1979: 274-279).[26] Crucially, the Land League inspired a new form of mass mobilisation. It was much more than a continuation of traditional forms of agrarian unrest; rather a sophisticated political intervention against the whole policy of coercion as well as a manifesto for non-violent direct action. As Fanny Parnell made clear (cited in Davitt 1979: 267):

Let the pike and rifle stand – we have found a better way, boys.
Hold the rent and hold the crops, boys.
Pass the word from town to town.
Pull away the props, boys.
So you'll pull coercion down.

Her brother Charles' new-found commitment to this kind of land agitation led to his imprisonment in Kilmainham Gaol in 1882. Following his release from prison with the Kilmainham Treaty, Parnell reinvented the Home Rule League as the Irish Parliamentary Party. This saw the emergence of the first disciplined democratic party at Westminster and the possibility of Irish self-determination being effected through parliamentary action.

---

[25] 'We cannot ask the British constitution for more than the restitution of Grattan's parliament, but no man has the right to fix the boundary of a nation. No man has the right to say to his country, "Thus far shalt thou go and no further", and we have never attempted to fix the "ne plus ultra" to the progress of Ireland's nationhood, and we never shall.'

[26] Davitt evokes this period powerfully in his *The Fall of Feudalism in Ireland* (1979: 268-285). Captain Charles Boycott was the land agent of an absentee landlord, Lord Erne, who lived in Lough Mask House, in County Mayo. In 1880, his tenants demanded a reduction in rents which Lord Erne refused. Boycott then attempted to evict eleven of these tenants. Parnell, in a speech in Ennis had proposed that when dealing with tenants who take farms where another tenant was evicted, rather than resorting to violence, everyone in the locality should shun them 'like the leper of old'. Despite the economic hardship to those undertaking this action, Boycott soon found himself isolated and most of his workforce withdrew their labour. Local businesspeople stopped trading with him. Boycott was unable to hire anyone for the harvest. Eventually 50 Orangemen from Cavan and Monaghan volunteered. They were escorted to and from Claremorris by one thousand police and soldiers, but the cost of this protection obviously far exceeded the value of the harvest. As Davitt observes: 'Some £350 worth of potatoes and other crops were eventually harvested by the "volunteers" during their stay at Lough Mask. This was the captain's own estimate of their value, and according to calculations made at the time it cost the sum of £3500 to the state and to the supporters of the expedition to have Boycott's potatoes dug' (1979: 277). The 'boycott' was successfully replicated elsewhere and boycotting became synonymous with non-violent direct action around the world.

This moment achieved radical results on land redistribution through the first of a series of land acts. The broader radical anti-imperialist alliance, however, collapsed definitively on 6 December 1890 in Committee Room 15 of the House of Commons. The combined moral outrage of Gladstone and the Irish Catholic Church at Parnell's relationship with Kitty O'Shea ensured that the IPP dissolved into Parnellite and anti-Parnellite factions. The notion that this defeat turns solely on Parnell and his personal life implies that there were no deeper contradictions between bourgeois nationalism, mass peasant direct action and revolutionary insurgency. Contradictions there were, of course, and such a pan-nationalist front was unable to sustain itself. (Parnell had already distanced himself from insurrectionary violence after his release from Kilmainham in 1882 and lost much Fenian support as a result.) Nevertheless, for a moment it looked as if the stars might align. After this, the nexus between parliamentary nationalism and separatism became increasingly ambiguous. After Parnell, if constitutional nationalism really implied 'independence by stealth', or the 'freedom to obtain freedom', almost nobody was in on the secret.

Neither, of course, could these overlapping tendencies be contained within any notion of a 'British Empire'. All this came to a head with WWI. As we have already seen, post-Parnell, the Irish Party positioned itself very specifically in terms of the Empire. Support for the imperial war effort would deliver Home Rule; and Home Rule would secure an appropriate place for Ireland *within* the Empire. Far from being anti-imperialist, the strategy was self-consciously imperialist. When unionists insisted that this innovation would signal the end of empire, nationalists could counter by insisting that Home Rule was in contrast a way of *saving* the empire. As the other white dominions moved from 'responsible government' to 'dominion status', Ireland could follow a similar path and guarantee the unity of the Empire. In the end, of course, the unionists were proved right and two thirds of Ireland left the Empire while there was still something to leave. But if this was really the nationalist strategy, it was never revealed to the Irish people. Like England with its Empire, Ireland was to become a republic in a 'fit of absence of mind' rather than through any ingenious nationalist strategy.

All this suggests that nationalism sits in a contradictory location between the Empire and the Republic. Accordingly, it would be silly to impose a simple pro- and anti-imperial politics on top of the existing Catholic/native and Protestant/settler dichotomy. From the nineteenth century onwards, there was rather a defining trichotomy involving unionism, nationalism and republicanism/separatism. It also bears emphasis, of course, that, so far as such a thing is measurable, a plurality of Irish people was probably within the Irish nationalism component of this division for much of the period. Certainly, most Irish people unambiguously supported O'Connell and his demands for both Catholic emancipation and repeal. But the shift in focus towards Home Rule also ensured later politics was 'constitutional' throughout the nineteenth century and up to the end of WWI. As we have seen, of course, the question of what most Irish people wanted politically was never tested in any democratic way until the 1918 election. But the accepted wisdom that most Irish were nationalists rather than republicans between 1847 and 1916 is probably accurate.[27] While anti-war activism increased as WWI progressed, when the Volunteer movement split, a much larger proportion went with the nationalist National Volunteers than the republican Irish Volunteers. Moreover, many of these nationalists joined the army of the British Empire beneath the 'fighting for Little Belgium' slogan – despite the fact that, as we have seen, 'Little Belgium' had the largest and most brutal colonial empire in Africa at the time. In other words, this was an Irish nationalism that was completely comfortable in terms of its location within empire – with all the compromises with imperialism that such a position entailed.

From this perspective, republicanism was only ever really in the political ascendant in Ireland for the years between 1918 and partition. After partition, nationalism assumed new forms. In the south the old Irish Party activists and structures did not simply disappear – many were absorbed into post-partition politics. Cumann na nGaedheal and later Fine Gael were 'Commonwealth' parties. And Fianna Fáil – which styled and styles itself as 'the Republican Party', never followed through on its commitment to declare the Republic. Arguably, therefore, all the southern parties of government are closer to traditional nationalist than republican politics. The Fianna Fáil notion of being 'slightly constitutional' conveys admirably just how odd and contradictory this space became in the context of the partitioned states.

Post-partition in the North, the votes of those broadly labelled as nationalists were split fairly evenly between republicans and nationalists, although most of the elected republican figures were from the South. Thus, the nationalist Joe Devlin remained by far the most iconic and popular northern politician after partition. He retained his Westminster seat into the 1930s. The rest of the Irish Party in the north reconstituted itself in multifarious manifestations of the 'Nationalist Party'. Northern nationalism trundled on in the face of an intense programme of gerrymandering which eventually saw most of its – already limited – political power removed in the six counties. Ironically, elections to the Westminster parliament remained the least vulnerable to gerrymandering and therefore the most open to nationalist 'victory'.[28] Throughout this period the nationalist label conveyed the otherness and marginalisation of northern Catholics. If their abstentionism was less principled than

---

[27] Although this is not true of the diaspora – particularly in the USA. There the Irish – and Clan na Gael and its leader John Devoy – remained determinedly insurrectionary and republican.

[28] Even here the notion that these contests were ever entirely democratic is slightly overstated. Until the 1990s the boundaries of the West Belfast constituency ran through the city centre and up through the docks. This had the effect of including the mostly unionist business vote within the West Belfast constituency which remained finely balanced between unionists and nationalists into the 1960s. And a continuing gerrymander in North Belfast kept this constituency unionist until the 2019 election – without attracting much opprobrium from Westminster (PRU 2013).

that of republicans, it was nearly as universal. Indeed, the Nationalist Party did not become the official opposition at Stormont until 1965, just as the state began to collapse.

This tendency was reinvigorated in the civil rights campaign with the formation of the SDLP, the Social Democratic and Labour Party. The name said it all. It was an attempt to merge the labourist tendencies of the Catholic working class with the social democratic tendencies of the Catholic middle class that had emerged from the welfare state in Northern Ireland. This had generated a new class of Catholic lawyers, teachers and health service staff – servicing the Catholic population in the context of the physical and social segregation that characterised Northern Ireland at the time.[29] The SDLP alliance held together right through 'the troubles' as the dominant political expression of the Catholic population. Despite the brutality of the conflict and its specific impact on Catholics, nationalism rather than republicanism remained dominant across the Catholic vote in the north for the duration of the conflict.

Arguably this nationalist hegemony only broke – and in ways that remain contested – with the election of Bobby Sands in 1981 while he was on hunger strike in prison. The SDLP brand of nationalism remained dominant until well into the post-GFA settlement. Indeed, it reached its symbolic apogee in the 1998 Assembly election in an understated moment of 'popish democracy' in Northern Ireland. With the DUP and UUP evenly split, the SDLP momentarily achieved the largest share of the vote of *all* parties in the state (22 per cent). It remained the largest nationalist party and retained the position of Deputy First Minister until the 2003 Assembly. Therefore, the St Andrews Agreement was the moment when northern republicanism *rather than nationalism* finally defined broad native/Catholic political relationships with the state. The principal political dynamic was now between the DUP and Sinn Féin – and this has remained the case ever since. Who was zooming who in this particular encounter remains, of course, the principal unresolved question in the history of the peace process.

It remains to be seen whether the dynamic around northern nationalism has completely run its course. In the context of the GFA, it remains difficult to see what the core project of SDLP might be. But the party has not disappeared. Presenting itself at once as more principled and more radical and more conservative than Sinn Féin, it has become more republican since it lost its majority of the nationalist vote. There are also periodic suggestions of a merger with one of the major southern parties; as of the time of writing, the party has reached an arrangement with Fianna Fáil which envisages future cooperation but falls short of a merger. This ongoing flirtation confirms that the SDLP remains the party of choice of the southern political establishment. They had, after all, spent years shoring up the SDLP in the north in the wake of the hunger strikes – so this under-focused aspect of southern 'interference' in northern

---

[29] It is still disconcerting to see the man who became Lord Fitt interviewed in the 1960s with a photograph of James Connolly in pride of place beside him.

politics may well continue. But in the specificity of Irish politics this is a dialectical process. If Sinn Féin looks much more nationalist than it did a generation ago given its reconciliation with constitutionalism, then the move toward all-Ireland organising by nationalist parties north and south of the border has generated a new, anti-partitionist *de facto* republicanism.

Nor should we underestimate the historical role of Irish nationalism. As we have already seen, the empire has a proven capacity for striking back. The British declaration of 'no selfish, strategic interest' was used effectively by the SDLP against Sinn Féin and the IRA in a critical phase of the peace process – it was emphasised by John Hume that, 'there can be no case for armed struggle in the context of that declaration'[30] From the perspective of 2021, however, this looks premature – on behalf of either the SDLP or the British government or both. Over recent years the notion of 'our precious union' dominated constructions of Brexit by the British government – without any reference to the neutrality asserted only a generation before. Understanding the critical role of Irish nationalism remains a task for the future as much as the past. The perennial question for Irish nationalism continues to be framed by the tension between empire and republic – which side are you on? In this regard, Ireland is no different from any other colonised county. It has to struggle unremittingly with the question of whether nationalism and anti-imperialism are complementary or contradictory forces.

The Easter Rising: 'to every generation its deed'

Mainstream Irish nationalism was caught unawares by the 1916 Easter Rising. The Irish political class which had negotiated the Home Rule bill and lent its support to WWI seemed unable to comprehend the 'incident' beyond a sense of 'misery' and 'heartbreak'. At Westminster, John Redmond was more concerned with the resignation of the reformist Chief Secretary Birrell, than the deaths in Ireland or their likely political consequences (Mitchell and O'Snodaigh 1985:21-2). In the same debate, however, Edward Carson unintentionally gave some sense of the developing extra-parliamentary dynamic:

> I think it is in the best interests of the country that this conspiracy of the Sinn Feiners, *which has nothing to do with either of the political parties in Ireland,* ought to be put down with courage and determination and with an example which would prevent a revival, yet it would be a mistake to suppose than any true Irishman calls for vengeance. (Mitchell and O'Snodaigh 1985:23, emphasis added)

---

[30] The Downing Street Declaration of 1993 stated: 'The Prime Minister, on behalf of the British Government, reaffirms that they will uphold the democratic wish of the greater number of the people of Northern Ireland on the issue of whether they prefer to support the Union or a sovereign united Ireland. On this basis, he reiterates, on behalf of the British Government, that they have no selfish strategic or economic interest in Northern Ireland. Their primary interest is to see peace, stability and reconciliation established by agreement among all the people who inhabit the island, and they will work together with the Irish Government to achieve such an agreement, which will embrace the totality of relationships' (British and Irish Governments 1993).

The significance, however, was not lost across the empire. After the Rising, Nehru wrote: 'But was that not true courage, which mocked at almost certain failure, and proclaimed to the world that no physical might could crush the invincible spirit of a nation' (quoted in Kapur 1997: 38). Nehru was correct in his analysis and the Rising proved perhaps they key moment in Ireland's long resistance to colonisation.

The received wisdom regarding the Easter Rising is often that it was a 'blood sacrifice' by a 'prophetic minority' that somehow kickstarted the more broad-based and popular anti-imperial resistance of 1918-22. We have suggested a slightly different reading. This relatively small act of anti-imperialist resistance took place in the context of a much greater imperial 'blood sacrifice' – the First World War. The reality of this war of empire and its slaughter on an industrial scale frames the politics of 1916.[31] Beyond this, however, we need to challenge two perspectives that have assumed the status of self-evident truths from the period. First that the uprising was hugely unpopular; second that it was a military fiasco. Since there had *never* been a democratic election in Ireland under colonialism, we have no way of knowing what the Irish people would have expressed regarding empire – or indeed anything else – in 1800 or 1900. Ascribing anti-democratic qualities to the Rising, invents a completely unwarranted democratic legitimacy to the state in Ireland and its political representatives at the time.

Clearly Ireland did not 'decide' to go to war in 1916; but neither did it decide in 1914 when thousands of Irish men and women were immediately plunged into war by pronouncement of a British monarch. An approximation of democracy was finally provided – post-war – in 1918, and Sinn Féin won a resounding victory on a resolutely anti-imperialist platform. In other words, it is misguided to read 1916 backwards through a 'democratic lens' from the perspective of 2020. Rather we need to understand the uprising in the context of a country than had been colonised for 800 years and never offered a democratic voice. In this context, the 'unpopularity' of the uprising remains a moot point.

The other received wisdom is that that it was a military failure. In other words, only the latest in a line of uprisings that had annoyed but not troubled the British empire. Here again we need to offer a different reading. It certainly threatened the British imperial war effort profoundly. The very brutality of its suppression is an indication of the seriousness with which it was approached by the military leadership of empire.

---

[31] James Connolly tackled this question head-on: 'We do not believe that war is glorious, inspiring, or regenerating. We believe it to be hateful, damnable, and damning. And the present war upon Germany we believe to be a hell-inspired outrage. Any person, whether English, German, or Irish, who sings the praises of war is, in our opinion, a blithering idiot. But when a nation has been robbed it should strike back to recover her lost property. Ireland has been robbed of her freedom, and to recover it should strike swiftly and relentlessly … But do not let us have any more maudlin trash about the "glories of war", or the "regenerative influence of war", or the "sacred mission of the soldier", or the "fertilising of all earth with the heroic blood of her children", etc, etc. We are sick of it, the world is sick of it.' ('Christmas Day, 1915', in the *Workers' Republic*. See Ó Cathasaigh 1997).

Connolly in particular did not go out to make a blood sacrifice – he went out to try to win a military encounter.

In reality, 1916 was a culmination of the hundreds of years of resistance that we have traced. More immediately it was the culmination of the work of thirty years engaging with the question of self-determination for the Irish people. Of course, this was carried out in the context of the ongoing intransigence of Westminster refusing to provide Home Rule. But it also went well beyond this reformist, nationalist political project. The work of the Gaelic League, the GAA, Irish-Ireland and a host of political organisations had framed the choice as one between empire and republic.

Moreover, as soon as Irish people were offered an opportunity to express their opinion politically after 1916, there was little ambiguity. From the election of Count Plunkett (father of 1916 leader Joseph Plunkett) in the North Roscommon by-election of February 1917, on an abstentionist platform, it was clear that the Irish Party – and its specific manifestation of Irish nationalism within the union – was finished as a political force. In this sense the Rising anticipates the 1918 election as much as causing it. As we have already seen, there was popular support for the uprising. No one would have expected either the *Irish Times* or the Irish colonial elite or the Irish Party to support the Rising, but neither is this evidence that it did not have widespread support. The moment at which Irish politics passed from determination by elite minority to the Irish people had arrived. As soon as Irish people were provided with a democratic mechanism, they made their views on empire and republic very clear.

Nations have a right to self-determination and part of that process is a right to resist – this is true for those that used some form of anti-imperialist violence. But this was true for all the great anti-imperialist struggles – from the US to India to South Africa. Most importantly, however, 1916 has to be read in context, not read backwards from contemporary norms. Of course, the uprising involved brutality and death on all sides. But this pales into insignificance when compared to the mountains of Irish dead across the Great War. These people died because of imperialist militarism – not for any great moral cause, not for 'liberty'. More specifically, the Irish were cynically duped into this carnage by the appeal to the fortunes of 'Little Belgium' – a colonising power that had genocided 80 per cent of the indigenous population of the Congo in the previous 50 years.

This sense of the profound immorality of the war on all sides of Irish nationalist and republican opinion was captured by the 'Unanimous Declaration' of the Mansion House Conference in April 1918:

> [W]e deny the right of the British Government or any external authority to impose compulsory military service in Ireland against the clearly expressed will of the Irish people. The passing of the Conscription Bill by the British House of Commons must be regarded as a declaration of war on the Irish nation.... It is in direct violation of the rights of small nationalities to self-determination.... The attempt to enforce it will be an unwarrantable aggression, which we call upon all Irishmen to resist by the most effective means at their disposal. (Mitchell and O'Snodaigh 1985: 42)

This declaration conveys some sense of the opposition to the war and conscription in Ireland: it was supported by all the key blocs in Ireland bar the unionists – republicans, nationalists, the labour movement – and the Catholic Church (Mitchell and O'Snodaigh 1985: 41-3). In this sense the greatest act of revisionism of all has been the rehabilitation of this imperialist war 100 years later. Participation in this slaughter was rightly resisted by most Irish people. It was simply the greatest and most grotesque human sacrifice in history – and all done on the altar of empire. In this context the implications are very simple: Irish people were right to do whatever they could to resist the industrialised slaughter of empire in 1916, and any that excuse it in 2021 are wrong to do so.

There is no stark epistemological break between 1916 and 1918. The Republic that was proclaimed in 1916 was endorsed in the general election of 1918. The Irish people did not suddenly 'convert' to anti-imperialism at some point in 1917. Rather, for the first – and, to date, last – time they were offered a democratic mechanism to make a choice on the Union and Empire. It bears emphasis that this was the only point at which the people of Ireland were ever able to exercise such an act of democratic will. Everything that followed in the revolutionary period 1916-22 – the establishment of the First Dáil, the Declaration of Independence and the War of Independence – remains rooted in the unambiguous anti-imperialism of the Rising. And the counter-revolutionary reaction that followed – partition and the dismantling of the Republic – was a countervailing imperial project. Once the dichotomy between empire and republic had crystallised, there was no excluded middle. The British Empire would do anything to prevent a republic and the partition strategy moved centre stage as the only means of maintaining the Union and shoring up the Empire. Ireland continues to fret in the shadow of this unfinished revolution and the imperial restraints it fashioned on Irish self-determination and decolonisation.

The uprising of 1916 remains the foundation moment of both contemporary states in Ireland. The Government of Ireland Act was only possible – or *necessary* – because of 1916. Despite all the froth of a 'decade of centenaries', however, it appears that the anti-imperialist significance of the event has been lost over the last 100 years. In other words, the colonial dynamics of the Rising and its aftermath needs to be reintegrated into the narrative of both states. From any perspective, the emergence of the Free State in 1922 must be regarded as the defining point on the Irish arc of decolonisation. At the same time, neither 1916 nor 1922 can be regarded as the *end* of anything – least of all the British Empire. The relationship of Ireland to union and empire had undoubtedly entered a new phase – and with that the challenge of finding an appropriate new response to colonialism and imperialism.

'Independence' and 'external relations'

Partition profoundly distorted the anti-imperialist impulse of Irish nationalism and republicanism. The Free State hit the ground running, as it were, in terms of asserting its (albeit limited) national independence. The Free State was admitted to the newly formed League of Nations on 10 September 1923 and quickly became recognised as one of the chief proponents for the full independence of smaller states. Although initially critical of the League, de Valera, when he came to power in 1932, switched to a policy of critical support of the League. He urged it to fulfil its obligations and criticised it when it failed to do so. For example, he argued strongly that the League should enforce international law during the Manchurian crisis of 1932 and the Abyssinian crisis of 1934-1936. De Valera was elected to the Presidency of the League Assembly in 1938, having already admitted to the Dáil two years earlier that the League 'does not command our confidence' (quoted in Carroll 2016).

The United Nations was formed in 1945. As far as the Irish were concerned, it was a 'victors' club'. As a state which had been neutral during the war, the Free State did not initially apply for membership. It did so the following year; the application was vetoed by the Soviet Union[32] but was supported by every other member of the United Nations. In December 1955 Ireland became one of 16 states to be admitted. As a small country, and a neutral one at that, its membership was particularly welcomed by many states in the Middle East, Asia and Latin America.

The central plank of this policy was a commitment to neutrality. This has been tested at different points over the last 100 years. Speaking at the end of the war, Winston Churchill praised Northern Ireland for its support of Britain and at the same time criticised de Valera and the Irish Free State for its stance of neutrality:

> This was indeed a deadly moment in our life, and if it had not been for the loyalty and friendship of Northern Ireland we should have been forced to come to close quarters with Mr. de Valera or perish forever from the earth. However, with a restraint and poise to which, I say, history will find few parallels, we never laid a violent hand upon them, which at times would have been quite easy and quite natural, and left the de Valera Government to frolic with the German and later with the Japanese representatives to their heart's content. (Mitchell and Ó Snodaigh 1985: 239)

---

[32] Irish attitudes toward the Soviet Union were mixed. The Russian revolution was welcomed in Ireland by Irish republicans hoping for a potential ally. De Valera supported Russian entry to the League of Nations and in 1927, Fianna Fáil proposed diplomatic and trade relations with the Soviet Union. But such moves ended when Fianna Fáil formed the government in 1932. One problem was that the vast majority of the Irish public, encouraged by the clergy, were antagonistic toward 'godless' Russia. In 1956 Liam Cosgrave – then foreign minister, later Taoiseach – stressed that Irish neutrality did not mean that Ireland was 'neutral in the conflict between the free world and the Godless East' (quoted in O'Corcora and Hill 1982: 261). When voting in favour of Russia's entry into the League of Nations in 1934, de Valera was careful to also call for religious freedom in the Soviet Union. After World War II Soviet influence in Eastern Europe led successive Irish administrations to view Russia as a colonial power. Moreover, the closer Ireland became aligned with other western governments, the US and eventually the EEC, the more it subscribed to cold war assessments of the Soviet Union. Rapprochement was enabled by two factors in the early 1970s: first, the opening up of the Soviet Union, politically and economically, and second, the realisation on the Irish side of the benefits of trade. Diplomatic ties between Ireland and Russia were agreed in 1973.

Three days later, on 16 May 1945, de Valera responded:

> Could he not find in his heart the generosity to acknowledge that there is a
> small nation that stood alone not for one year or two, but for several hundred
> years against aggression; that endured spoiliations, famines, massacres in endless
> succession; that was clubbed many times into insensibility, but that each time on
> returning consciousness took up the fight anew; a small nation that could never
> be got to accept defeat and has never surrendered her soul? Mr. Churchill is justly
> proud of his nation's perseverance against heavy odds. But we in this island are
> still prouder of our people's perseverance for freedom through all the centuries.
> (Mitchell and Ó Snodaigh 1985: 240-2)

During the Suez crisis of 1956, Ireland joined with other members in opposing the
Anglo-French invasion of Egypt. The Irish insisted that 'a small country like ours can only
exist if international obligations are respected' (Royal Irish Academy and the National
Archives of Ireland 2015), and consequently condemned the actions of Israel, Britain and
France in violating the UN Charter. It backed the US motion for an immediate ceasefire
and the Canadian motion for the establishment of a UN peace force. Also, in 1956 it
was one of a majority of members condemning the Soviet invasion of Hungary. Ireland's
representative to the United Nations, Fred Boland, stressed Hungary's right to self-
determination and Ireland's empathy for small states being invaded by more powerful
neighbours.

Ireland took a strong stance in relation to decolonisation in Algeria. Boland told the
French delegation that Ireland's past meant 'it was impossible for us not to sympathize
with the demands of the Algerian people for self-determination'(Royal Irish Academy
and the National Archives of Ireland 2015). In this, and in other ways, Ireland showed it
could take an independent line. In 1957 it took a minority stance of voting in favour of
discussing China's membership. This did not prevent it some years later co-sponsoring
resolutions on Tibet. Ireland was one of the first to advocate, in 1958, the non-
proliferation of nuclear weapons. In 1961, Ireland was the sole sponsor of a resolution
on the need to negotiate an international agreement on nuclear non-proliferation. By
1968 the Nuclear Non-Proliferation Treaty was agreed, and Ireland was invited to be the
first to sign the Treaty (Royal Irish Academy and the National Archives of Ireland 2015).
Finally, in the late 1970s, Ireland's anger over Israeli actions in Lebanon led to closer
support for the PLO. As a result, 'Ireland became the first EEC country to use the word
"state" in relation to Palestinian rights' (Miller 2006: 23).

There is a sense of historical justice involved where Ireland, given its own colonial
experience, supports decolonisation in two major forums, the League of Nations and
the United Nations. At the same time, there was at very least an irony involved in
Ireland supporting Algerian decolonisation or Palestinian statehood when, as a result of
partition, it was not itself decolonised. The seemingly impressive task of anti-imperialist
nation building was thwarted by its own incomplete revolution. It had been unable to

do for itself what it was trying to do for others. It also failed to use League of Nations and United Nations mechanisms to address partition and the unfinished nature of Irish decolonisation.[33]

Ireland has been neutral in international relations since the 1930s. The nature of Irish neutrality has varied over time and has been contested since the 1970s. Historically, the state was a non-belligerent in World War II – known in Ireland as the Emergency – and has never joined NATO, although during the Cold War it was anti-communist and distant from the Non-Aligned Movement. The compatibility of neutrality with Ireland's membership of the European Union has been a point of debate in EU treaty referendum campaigns since the 1990s. The Seville Declarations on the Treaty of Nice acknowledge Ireland's 'traditional policy of military neutrality', reflecting the narrow formulation of successive Irish governments. Others define Irish neutrality more broadly, as having, 'a strong normative focus, with a commitment to development, United Nations peacekeeping, human rights and disarmament' (World Heritage Encyclopedia).

As it disconnected from the British empire, the Irish state developed an idiosyncratic version of neutrality in international relations. Crucially, it has never joined the Non-Aligned Movement. It has also eschewed two of the defining aspects of neutrality – a comprehensive defence strategy and a resolute opposition to any foreign military activity within its territory. The Irish state was a 'non-belligerent' in the Second World War and did not join NATO – or the Warsaw Pact, of course – after the war. The Irish Defence Forces are allowed to be deployed in United Nations peacekeeping missions but this requires three forms of authorisation – the 'triple lock': first, a UN Security Council resolution or UN General Assembly resolution; second, a formal decision by the Irish government; third, approval by a resolution of Dáil Éireann. Irish Defence Forces have seen active service as part of United Nations peacekeeping activities – initially in the early 1960s Congo Crisis, and subsequently in Cyprus (UNFICYP) and the Lebanon (UNIFIL).

Ostensibly the commitment to neutrality obtains. The 2015 foreign policy Irish government defence review recognised that, 'military neutrality remains a core element of Irish foreign policy'. The 2015 defence white paper presupposed 'a policy of military neutrality which is characterised by non-membership of military alliances and non-participation in common or mutual defence arrangements'. Despite this, however, Irish neutrality has been incrementally undermined over the past fifty years. While Ireland did not join NATO, the transmission of information from the Irish government to the CIA started as early as 1955. Ireland has a long history of granting permission to foreign military aircraft to overfly or land in the state. Confirmation was required that the aircraft in question be unarmed, carry no arms, ammunition or explosives and that the

---

[33] Ironically, when the Free State declared itself a republic in 1949, a major concern of the British was that it would then join the United Nations where 'it would then be open to her to raise the question of partition in the General Assembly with the assurance of substantial support' (Fanning 1982: 100).

flights in question would not form part of military exercises or operations. After 9/11, however, these conditions were further diluted for different US military flights.

Moreover, the integration of the EU has further undermined the commitment to neutrality. The compatibility of neutrality with Ireland's membership of the European Union has been central to EU treaty referendum campaigns since the 1990s. The Seville Declarations on the Treaty of Nice acknowledge Ireland's 'traditional policy of military neutrality' and this is underlined in the Irish constitution: 'The State shall not adopt a decision taken by the European Council to establish a common defence pursuant to Article 42 of the Treaty on European Union where that common defence would include the State'. As was indicated in chapter 7, this was originally inserted by the 2002 amendment ratifying the Treaty of Nice and updated by the 2009 amendment ratifying the Treaty of Lisbon. Despite this, Ireland joined the EU's Permanent Structured Cooperation (PESCO), part of the EU's security and defence policy, at its establishment in December 2017. In other words, the Irish state is far from being 'non-aligned' and its *de facto* position is best characterised by the US perspective of being 'usefully neutral'. By now peacekeeping purposes have broadened to include cooperation with NATO as well as the EU.

In the meantime, of course, Northern Ireland remains fully integrated into UK – and NATO – defence institutions. Over the course of its history, Northern Ireland has played little autonomous role on the international stage. The Government of Ireland Act precluded any involvement in foreign affairs and this continued as an 'excluded matter' under the GFA settlement. If the people of Northern Ireland had any formal opinions on broader decolonisation, these were to be mediated through the Empire and Union. This did not, however, mean that Northern Ireland did not have a resonance on the international stage. We have seen this already in relation to Palestine. Ronald Storrs, the enthusiastically pro-Zionist British military governor of Jerusalem from 1920 to 1926, supported the movement of Jews to Palestine to form the state of Israel, thus forming for England 'a little loyal Jewish Ulster' in a sea of potentially hostile Arabism' (Storrs 1937: 364). And when John Vorster – as Minister for Justice in apartheid South Africa – introduced the Coercion Act in in the wake of the Sharpeville Massacre and the launch of the ANC's armed struggle, he went out of his way to signal the parallels: 'I would be willing to exchange all the legislation of this sort for one clause of the Northern Ireland Special Powers Act' (quoted in McVeigh 2006: 232). Since the GFA, the Northern Ireland state has been less of a model for reactionary regimes and more a template for peace processes. But there is little sense in which it intervenes internationally beyond periodic references to the peace process. There is certainly no sense in which it provides any kind of inspiration regarding outstanding questions around decolonisation.[34]

---

[34] Rather unionism has displayed a commitment to hyper-militarism. This has included proactive support for the location of nuclear weapons in the north and culminated in unionism being the only community in the UK to march *in favour* of the Gulf War.

Republicanism and anti-imperialism after partition

Following WWI and the Russian Revolution there was a wave of class revolt which swept Europe. Ireland was not left behind (Nielsen 2012). Soviets were formed in Limerick, Leitrim, Cork, Tipperary and elsewhere.[35] This was the period when Dáil Éireann was established in opposition to British plans for Ireland. It was also the period when the war of independence raged. In the midst of this, the Dáil regarded class actions as diversionary and used its police force, the IRA, to suppress them. Erskine Childers compiled and published two volumes of *The Constructive Work of Dáil Éireann*. Volume I was entitled *The National Police and the Courts of Justice* and commented somewhat gently about this phenomenon:

> While the IRA was establishing their authority as a national police, a grave danger threatened recrudescence in an acute form of an agrarian agitation for the breaking up of the great grazing ranches into tillage holdings for landless men ... The mind of the people was being diverted from the struggle for freedom by a class war ... But this crisis was surmounted, thanks to a patriotic public opinion, and the civic sense of justice expressed through the Arbitration Courts and enforced by the Republican police. (Quoted in Burns 1974: 50)

In the same vein, a Sinn Féin manifesto in 1920, signed by leading party members Piaras Béaslaí, Fionán Lynch and Austin Stack, condemned land seizures in Kerry:

> The present time – when the Irish people are locked in a life and death struggle for freedom... is ill-chosen for the stirring up of strife amongst our fellow countrymen... All our energies must be directed towards clearing out – not the occupier of this or that piece of land – but the foreigner who holds the Nation in his grip. (Quoted in Beatty 2016b: 64)

After the Treaty, the Free State government, faced with a civil war, finding its national feet and rebuilding a shattered and underdeveloped economy, likewise decided that there were certain priorities and therefore certain political no-go areas. Michael Collins stated the underlying position clearly: 'The Irish struggle has always been for freedom – freedom from English occupation, from English interference, from English domination – not for freedom with labels attached to it... it was freedom we sought, not the name of the government we should adopt when we got our freedom' (Collins 1968: 32-3). The Free State was certainly not going to be a union of soviets. And the policing of that restricted definition of the nation was to be in the hands of the IRA and later the national army of the state. Nor was the message any more radical from what was to be the other side of the Treaty divide. Speaking in Dundalk in December 1917, de Valera said that he was, 'not opposed to labour, but while they held in their hands the big question of Irish liberty they could not deal with labour problems. Once there was

---

[35] In addition, in January 1922, a group of 120 unemployed men briefly occupied Dublin's Rotunda. They were led by Liam O'Flaherty, later a well-known author of books such as *The Informer* (1925) and *Famine* (1937). See Ruxton 2019.

a national parliament and freedom, they would see what could be done to give practical effect to the aspirations of labour' (RTÉ 2019).

Thus, even before partition, republicanism's internationalist anti-imperialist streak was being severely curtailed; partition compounded this process. Half of the physical force movement was incorporated into the Free State as a respectable arm of the new polity. The other half was reduced to survival, the defence of northern nationalists, or symbolic armed struggle without the prospect of state capture. Anti-imperialism was an expensive luxury in such a situation.

Republicans struggled through the 20s and 30s to find a role. Losers in the Civil War, they could only watch as the governments of the Free State enthusiastically slipped into their dominion status. Anti-imperialism gave the losing republicans a sense of purpose and identity when they lost the battle for state capture. Cumann na mBan produced a newspaper in 1926 called *The Anti-Imperialist*. It and other republican newspapers such as *The Workers' Republic* (1923) and *An Phoblacht* (from 1926 to 1929) argued that, as their erstwhile republican friends in government worked to strengthen the British Empire, their role was to work to dismantle it. Another paper, *Saoirse – Irish Freedom* (1927 to the mid-1930s) argued that 'Britain must be isolated on the international scene if decolonisation was to occur' (Ní Bheacháin 2007: 62). Actions followed. Leading republicans Peadar O'Donnell and Frank Ryan were involved in establishing the Irish branch of the League Against Imperialism in 1927. They were also involved in the Indian-Irish Independence League from 1932. And they worked closely in campaigns with the Irish Communist Party. The high point, and yet the final stage of these developments, was the formation of the Republican Congress in the early 1930s. The Congress fell apart after a confrontation with more conservative republicans at the annual Wolfe Tone commemoration in Bodenstown in 1934. Many of the radical republicans, including a number of northern Protestants who had joined, then went to fight against Franco in Spain.[36] The leadership of the IRA, although containing some left-thinking people felt increasingly isolated as the Communist Party, following Moscow's orders, moved into its class-against-class phase and the Catholic Church and government used every opportunity to reference a 'red scare'. The opportunities for left-wing rhetoric and actions were closed down.

It was the 1960s before republicanism again espoused internationalism prominently. After the military failure of an IRA border campaign, the republican movement shifted to the left, espousing a Stalinist stages-theory approach to the republic and selling off its guns to the Free Wales Army. The sectarian attacks on working class nationalist areas

---

[36] 700 Blueshirts, members of former IRA chief Eoin O'Duffy's National Corporate Party, went to Spain to fight with Franco's forces, while 200 communists and left-wing republicans went to fight against Franco in the Connolly Column, named after James Connolly. The Irish fascists saw little action, their most spectacular encounter being a friendly fire incident which left four of them plus 13 of Franco's troops dead. They were quickly sent back to Ireland. The Connolly Column saw major action in 1936 and 1938 in battles at Jarama, Brunete, Teruel and the Ebro and lost almost one third of their contingent (See McGarry 2001; O'Riordan 1979).

in Belfast in 1969 led to a split and the emergence and growth of the Provisional IRA. The left-wing official republican movement declined rapidly from the mid-1970s. The Provisionals were in the first instance a defence group. They soon turned in a more offensive direction, but their anti-imperialism was defined solely in terms of military action against British occupation. Their manifesto of the early 1970s was narrow-minded, conservative and solipsistic. 'Import of capital would be controlled and foreign domination of any sector prevented. Foreign land purchase and export of capital by nationals would be forbidden' (Sinn Féin 1971: 15). 'There will be no need for foreign experts; our people are the experts in many foreign countries' (Sinn Féin 1971: 20). The term 'sinn féin' had never looked so insular. But transformation followed, especially in the jails where imprisoned republicans discussed Marxism, Third World liberation and feminism and built up an impressive library of books about international politics and revolution (McKeown 2001). The stage was set for republicanism not only to engage in wider social and economic issues on the island of Ireland but also to display its support for anti-imperialist struggles elsewhere. In many ways identification with Palestine, Cuba, South Africa and the like was gesture politics. But there is no denying the value of this shift. Colonialism and imperialism work through containing subaltern peoples. The knowledge that that containment has been breached and that solidarity has been expressed by outsiders can be a significant support for the colonised. In addition, in supporting anti-imperialist struggles elsewhere, Irish republicans were exploring a more sophisticated version of anti-imperialism in their own country beyond the slogan of 'Brits out'.

However, there was little republicans could do to actualise their internationalism. They were engaged in an armed struggle against a state whose main response was to attempt to contain that struggle not only within Ireland, not only within the North, but within a set number of ghettoes.[37] When republicans began to achieve political representation, the scope for internationalist action was confined in other ways. The end of the Cold War and the global shift after the 9-11 attacks not only made it increasingly difficult to engage in militant anti-imperialism worldwide but also to support this while participating in democratic politics. That said, republicans found a new outlet in terms of supporting peace processes and post-conflict transformation beyond their own shores.[38] At the same time, the Northern Ireland Assembly has no foreign policy brief

---

[37] There are many examples of how that containment in relation to the North of Ireland has been breached internationally. In Tehran the street on which the British embassy is situated was renamed 'Bobby Sands Street'. Streets have been named after Bobby Sands in a number of French cities, including Nantes, Saint-Étienne, Le Man, Vierzon and Saint-Denis. There are memorials to the Irish republican hunger strikers of 1981 in Havana; Hartford, Connecticut; and Sydney.

[38] One of Sinn Féin's chief negotiators in the Good Friday Agreement process, Gerry Kelly, travelled to the Philippines in 2009 for meetings with the government and rebels from the Moro Islamic Liberation Front (*An Phoblacht Republican News* 2009). Gerry Adams and Bertie Ahern, along with Tony Blair's advisor Jonathan Powell, were centrally involved in peace talks in the Basque Country in 2011. In 2006, Sinn Féin's Martin McGuinness went to Sri Lanka for peace talks (*Independent* 2006).

and Sinn Féin MPs do not take their seats in Westminster which does debate foreign policy. The only venue where they might have direct influence on foreign policy is in the Dáil.[39] Even that is significantly more than what the so-called dissident republicans have. Miniscule and constantly surveilled, they can do little beyond engage in gestures of solidarity with situations such as Palestine.

As we have already seen, references to Ireland abound in debates about Palestine during the 20th century. There were real imperial connections between Ireland and Palestine. Arthur Balfour, whose Declaration is at the root of the continuing conflict in the region, had previously served as Chief Secretary of Ireland. During a land protest in Mitchelstown, Co. Cork, in 1887, he had ordered police to open fire, resulting in the death of three people. In 1921, Winston Churchill, colonial secretary, decided that a 'picked force of white gendarmerie' was needed to police Palestine (Cronin 2017). That force was found among the Black and Tans and Auxiliaries who had recently proven their ruthlessness in Ireland. 800 of them were dispatched to Palestine. A legal adviser to the Colonial Office, Grattan Bushe, warned that 'repression by force is repeating the mistake which was made in Ireland'. But his advice had no effect in a situation where the British military were being told that they could take 'whatever measures are necessary'. They lived up to that by demolishing much of the old city of Jaffa, imposing collective punishment on villages and mass detention in labour camps. Later Menachem Begin, leader of the Irgun which later waged a guerrilla war against the British in Palestine, admired Michael Collins to the point that he used Collins' name as his own *nomme de guerre* (Begin 1951).

Across the history of the past 100 years, it is tempting to read this aspect of the post-war of independence Ireland in a negative and depressing light. Neither the Irish state nor its political parties or movements have played the key role in the deconstruction of empire that might have been anticipated in 1919 with the Declaration of Independence. But it is worth remembering that the task facing Ireland – the final transition to a postcolonial state – is one which few other former colonies have totally and successfully made. Of the former white dominions of the British Empire, only South Africa could be said to have made this full journey beyond dominion.[40] And in 2020, while no one could doubt the enormity of the South African struggle against colonialism and imperialism, most observers would still regard the

---

[39] In July 2018, the Irish senate agreed to a proposition from independent senator Frances Black, backed by Sinn Féin and other senators, that Ireland should boycott all goods produced in illegal Israeli settlements in Palestine. This is the first step towards having the policy become law (Holmes 2018).

[40] Ireland continued to serve as a beacon for activists in South Africa long after the events at the turn of the twentieth century. Thus: '[Walter] Sisulu had an intense interest in Ireland and particularly in the struggle for independence. Interviewed by the *Irish Times* in 1990 he expressed special admiration for Eamon de Valera. His support for the idea of a Truth and Reconciliation Commission stemmed to a very large extent from his knowledge of Irish affairs. Without a Commission he felt that South Africa could descend into the morass of bitterness that has characterised politics in Northern Ireland for so many decades' (*Irish Times*, 10 May 2003).

country as somewhere short of the 'glory and dignity' anticipated by Patrice Lumumba for independent African states (Lumumba 1961).

Conclusions – lessons in resistance from Ireland?

Perhaps the most important insight from Ireland's long struggle against colonialism was the sombre calculus invoked by Terence MacSwiney: in the metahistory of the colonial interface, it is not those who can inflict the most but those who can suffer the most who will overcome in the end. This lesson regarding anti-imperialist sacrifice has been reinforced time and again across colonial conflict. But it is perhaps most recently aggregated in terms of the experience of Vietnam. Famously, there is a terrible sense of the cost of war symbolised in Maya Lin's powerful Vietnam memorial in Washington to the 58,212 US combat troops who lost their lives. But this only tells a fraction of the story of Vietnam's struggle against imperialism – and only reflects a fraction of terrible loss of life across that story. Before the US intervened in Vietnam, the French colonial power lost some 55,000 troops and civilians. Moreover, the pro-French and pro-US Vietnamese forces lost perhaps four times this number. And the NVA (People's Army of Vietnam) and VC (Viet Cong) lost nearly ten times as many across years of resistance to the French and Americans. Civilian deaths were even higher across the liberation struggle – estimates suggest that perhaps 360,000 non-combatant Vietnamese died – and related deaths in Cambodia and Laos push the overall total into millions.[41]

MacSwiney's principle holds in the face of these grim statistics – arguably Vietnamese victory was predicated on the inability of first the French and then the US to sustain the level of casualties that Vietnamese anti-imperialist resistance inflicted. But the disproportionate Vietnamese suffering is starkly revealed in this juxtaposition. In other words, MacSwiney's observation is hardly a truth to be celebrated across anti-colonial struggle. We might observe that it would take an anti-imperialist of the moral turpitude of arch-imperialist General Haig in WWI to justify such human sacrifice as a military or philosophical principle.[42] Nevertheless, the observation holds in terms

---

[41] At the site of the My Lai massacre in Vietnam, where US troops killed around 400 villagers in March 1968, there is a memorial. 'Over its entrance are Ho Chi Minh's words, always inscribed at Vietnamese war cemeteries: "There is nothing compared to freedom and independence."' The site of the massacre is documented both by art and the famous photographs seen around the world after My Lai was discovered. The museum has in large letters over its front: "Never Forget Our Anger against the US Oppressive Imperialists." Sculpture groups are scattered throughout the site, all of them created by Thu Ho, whose wife, Vu Thi Lien, was a young girl who survived the massacre in the village and became its chief international witness after 1968 (Tatum 2003: 22-33).

[42] 'Butcher Haig' – Field Marshal The 1st Earl Haig (1861-1928), British commander at the Battle of the Somme and Passchendaele and a founder of the British Legion – was the chief architect of the war of attrition philosophy that saw the industrialised and strategically useless slaughter of WWI. He learned his trade in the militarism of empire, serving in India and at the Battle of Omdurman – which of course anticipated the level of slaughter of his later campaigns, albeit in a more one-sided fashion. The military historian John Keegan –

372 Ireland, Colonialism, and the Unfinished Revolution

of outcomes. Moreover, this point was made repeatedly throughout Irish history. MacSwiney articulated it best but he was not the first to adopt suffering as praxis. His own hunger strike followed the immediate example of Thomas Ashe in 1917. When subsequent Irish hunger strikers died – in the 1940s and 1970s and 1981– they made it clear that some Irish people were prepared to make sacrifices that other parties to the conflict – whether the British army or loyalists – were incapable of making.

This resonates with wider references from Mitchel onwards and culminates in what is often dismissed as the 'blood sacrifice' of 1916. This existential commitment to resistance in the face of an objective assessment of the inability of victory is a recurring motif. Arguably this is less a confirmation of a 'death principle' than a recognition of the profound nature of struggle that reappears in other contexts as diverse as the Tet Offensive and Huey P Newton's notion of 'revolutionary suicide'. In addition, sometimes simple *survival* – like the Falantil in the jungles of Timor or the 'Long March' in China or Che and Fidel in Cuba – in the face of overwhelming odds – is the key to long-term victory. In this context, the broader Irish absolutism outlined earlier also provides a kind of model – from Mitchel onwards a dogged commitment to resist simply for the sake of resisting also has wider implications.

Mitchel neatly characterised his own commitment to continued resistance as he contemplated suicide in the depths of political defeat incarcerated in Bermuda on route to the imperial penal colony of Tasmania:

> While I am known to be living in vile sinks of felony – and through such means – especially if other and better people follow through the same means, the mind of the young Irish generation will not easily settle down and acquiesce in the sway of the foreign enemy. But if I die, I, for one, will soon be forgotten. There will be one stimulus the less to Ireland's friends – one difficulty the less to her foes. And if I die by my own hand, I will be worse than forgotten – I will have confessed that England's brute power is resistless, and therefore righteous – at any rate that I for my part, am a beaten man. It will be my last speech and dying declaration, imploring my countrymen to avoid the terrible fangs of British law – my pupils

---

himself a supporter of western interventions in Vietnam, Kosovo and Iraq – was remorseless on Haig: 'On the Somme, he had sent the flower of British youth to death or mutilation; at Passchendaele he had tipped the survivors in the slough of despond' (Keegan 1999). Haig served as the President of The Royal British Legion until his death. The black plastic centre of the poppy was marked 'Haig Fund' until 1994. Scottish poppies are still made in the Lady Haig's Poppy Factory in Edinburgh. This gives some sense of the function of poppy-wearing as expiation for the most egregious of crimes against humanity – a tradition which still follows the precedent set by Haig. In August 2010, Tony Blair pledged the proceeds of his memoirs, *A Journey,* to the British Legion, 'as a way of marking the enormous sacrifice [the British armed forces] make for the security of our people and the world'. Reaction to the news was mixed. Some anti-war campaigners and families of soldiers killed during the wars in Iraq and in Afghanistan claimed the donation was 'blood money' and a public relations stunt. But there should be no underestimating of the totemic power of this imperial symbol. In Ireland, enormous ideological power continues to be brought to bear in order to enforce poppy-wearing – in formal commemoration of a war 'for Empire'. On Remembrance Day 2010 the SDLP's Margaret Ritchie was the first leader of a nationalist party to wear one. In 2017, Taoiseach Leo Varadkar wore a 'shamrock poppy' in the Dáil, the first Taoiseach and leader of Fine Gael to do so.

will hang their heads for shame; and, instead of an example, I shall have become a warning. (Mitchel 1913: 48)

In other words, whatever anyone made of the *content* of their programme, the existential commitment embedded in this strain of Irish resistance – from Mitchel to Bobby Sands – was remarkable. It marked the stark contrast between a 'tour of duty' and a 'long war'. This kind of commitment to endurance suggested that it could never be defeated – at least at the level of personal sacrifice. In short, the MacSwiney principle is both a sombre warning to any people of the cost of embarking on a struggle against colonialism and an empowering reminder of the continued *possibility* of victory for those who hold none of the objective or strategic advantages at the outset of resistance.[43]

This begs the question of what other contribution Irish resistance has made to wider anti-imperialist theory and practice. And, more directly, how these lessons might be applied to Ireland and its contemporary discontents. In terms of practice, there are several broader themes. These were routinely invoked and repeated across 'generations' in which 'the Irish people asserted their right to national freedom and sovereignty'. Here we might reference Maude Gonne's famous intervention in the midst of the Diamond Jubilee celebrations in Dublin – insisting that Ireland would never get justice from England until it was able to 'wrench it from her in some hour of danger or defeat, which, pray God, may come soon' (Morris 1968: 457-478). Thus, the notion that 'England's difficulty is Ireland's opportunity' is more widely generalisable – a key strategic decision is whether the colonial power is otherwise occupied.

Irish resistance also developed a key sense of the importance of diaspora communities. This was most obviously mobilised in terms of the Irish community in the US. But it happened in other ways. Irish Parliamentary Party MPs were elected in English constituencies; the IRA organised a brigade in Glasgow. We have already seen how significant the MacBride Principles were for equality in the North. When the peace process engaged, there is no doubt that US mediation of the British agenda was driven by the continuing importance of Irish American politicians.

Thus, in a myriad of ways, Irish history has provided broader lessons for anti-imperialist struggle as well as a more specific template for Ireland. We turn to the unresolved question of 'what is to be done?' in our next chapter. But we can already see some of the practical implications from this history. For example, if 'England's difficulty is Ireland's opportunity', there might be no better example post-WWII than the twin challenges of England's ongoing Brexit fiasco and reconstruction following the Covid-19 pandemic.

Beyond these kinds of tactical and strategic lessons, however, we root our analysis in Irish ideologies of anti-imperialist resistance. We can broadly trichotomise these broad

---

[43] This point was well captured in the title of the classic book on guerrilla warfare by Robert Taber, *The War of the Flea* (1965).

anti-imperialist tendencies in Ireland as *insurrectionary movement*, *mass movement* and *parliamentary intervention*. These movements rarely worked in synergy. But each provided lessons for Irish struggle as well as the wider anti-imperialist movement.

For example, O'Connell's two great mass movements – successful in terms of Catholic emancipation, unsuccessful in terms of the Repeal – offered a model for mass organisation across Europe and beyond. These were essentially democratising parliamentary interventions – or interventions to enable native Irish political leaders to make parliamentary interventions. No matter how unambitious and reformist and 'constitutional' the outcomes appear from this distance, the organising was revolutionary in impact. Moreover, it consciously provided a model for other, later mobilisation and resistance. Similarly, the boycott, a key tactic of resistance was widely adopted by other struggles. It was the one Irish tactic which assumed universal recognition. As this suggests, the Land League provided a model for mass mobilisation and direct action.

Most significantly of all, however, the United Irish movement provided an advanced programme of integrated settler/native anti-imperialism that transcended the dominant US revolutionary model and constructed an inclusive ideology for a post-colonial society. What they managed in 1795 has still arguably to be applied to any of the surviving white dominions more than 200 years later. The objectives of the United Irish movement still read as a manifesto for self-determination: *Subvert the tyranny of our execrable government; Break the connection with England; Assert the independence of our country*. The United Irish methodology retains its relevance too. This simple project remains both a strategy and a principle: to unite the whole people of Ireland, to abolish the memory of all past dissensions, and to substitute the common name 'Irish' in place of the denominations of Protestant, Catholic and Dissenter.[44] This was a remarkable moment of *mestizaje* – it insisted that an anti-imperialist future could be forged from all of the complex ethnic elements that colonialism had thrown together in Ireland.

But history never stands still. Such historical sensitivity to the complexity of the Irish imagined community, signals the need for a wider engagement with the question of how the 'whole people of Ireland' is currently constituted. Gender obviously must be central to this process in a way that it was not in 1798. How the diaspora is now to be connected to this process is also a core challenge. There may be a remarkable integrity to the *denominations* addressed by the United Irish movement but other ethnic cleavages also apply. Most obvious is the growing population of Irish people of colour – Black and migrant Irish – who need to feel an equal place within this project. We have argued that *Black Irishness* and Irishness of colour has to be recentered as a key element in this story. Likewise, sexuality has entered the dynamic in new

---

[44] The anachronistic gendered nature of this reading is obviously redundant. In 1795 Republican feminists were already signalling that the notion of 'Irishman' as excluding a majority of the Irish population. It is clear now that the Irish people should be the object of the appeal.

and transformative ways. In other words, any contemporary anti-imperialism has to begin by asking what place these emerged and emerging 'other' communities might find within the symbolism of the tricolour. We also might place less emphasis on abolishing past dissensions as if a single identity Irishness was possible and focus more on accommodating, respecting and celebrating such differences – a core element in our analysis is the need to remember rather than forget and to 'cherish equally' rather than to ignore difference. Nevertheless, both the means and the objectives of the United Irish movement remain remarkably relevant after more than 200 years. As we turn now to ask what is to be done in our final chapter, it would be difficult to over-estimate the importance of this revolutionary anti-imperialist *mestizaje* as a lodestone for *any* progressive politics in Ireland.

It also remains true, however, that we Irish have been very good at the rhetoric of resistance and generally less effective at the practicalities of self-determination. Of course, as we have seen, this tension defines the whole anti-imperialist movement – so there is nothing particularly Irish about any sense of postcolonial disillusionment. But Kevin O'Higgins had a point when he contrasted the 'poetry' of the aesthetics of struggle with the prosaic challenges of trying to make 'independence' work – as the anticipated promise of self-determination confronts the reality of post-colonial statehood. Arguably this holds across anti-imperialism – we are awesome until we actually overcome. But this reality should not undermine the real and practical organisational politics that Ireland brought to the struggle.

This practical, organisational anti-imperialist strategising reached its apogee in the 'popular front' of the 1880s. Here the great Irish mobilisations of the period – the Irish Party, the Land League and the IRB – synergised nationalism and social justice and anti-imperialism as never before or since. More specifically, this period saw the only effective alliance between the tendencies that we have characterised as republicanism and nationalism in Irish history. The New Departure deal in 1879 saw the IRB and the American republican organisation *Clan na Gael* support the Irish Party struggle for Home Rule. In exchange Parnell committed the Irish Party to mobilise on the land question and against coercive legislation. Thus, Parnell was dominant in constitutional politics – but his land war strategy was developed hand-in-hand with Davitt who brought a mass mobilisation that was determinedly radical and 'unconstitutional' and much closer to contemporary direct action. Davitt was in turn active in the IRB which drew on conspiratorial traditions of insurrection and an unambiguous commitment to revolution and a republic. But the contemporary IRB was also capable of seeing the advantages of such a broad front approach and the limitations of any unthinking commitment to militarism. At this one historical moment, these approaches appeared to be synergising towards a common end – certainly so to their imperialist opponents. With hindsight we might argue that the principle was self-determination and these contrasting tactics and strategies were at this stage complementary paths to the same destination. If we were looking to such a strategy again in 2020, we could suggest that any contemporary 'poetry' framing decolonisation and reunification would need to be wedded to an organisational strategy that was similarly disciplined and inclusive.

Chapter 11

Ireland in the coming times:
what is to be done?

When you understand British imperialism, it is an open window to all imperialism.
—Elizabeth Gurley Flynn, 1926

From little things big things grow. —Kevin Carmody and Paul Kelly, 1991

In this final chapter we turn towards the Irish future. In 1893, at the beginning of Ireland's last revolutionary period, Yeats characterised this kind of augury as a reflection on *Ireland in the coming times*. Our analysis engages our own coming times with determined optimism of the will – echoing Pearse's insistence that *summer is coming*. This approach assumes that Ireland sits at a further transformational juncture in 2020. In this regard we are particularly focused on the question of how the revolution begun in 1916 might be 'finished'. In consequence, our final chapter is less of a conclusion than a meditation on how to mobilise the history we have referenced to build a more just, peaceful and democratic Irish future. We can, however, draw various conclusions from our review of colonial history and Ireland's place within it.

First, the current global context is one in which the significance of colonialism remains essentially contested. The whole world is still wrestling with this legacy question. While the colonised continue to face its consequences, the colonisers and their inheritors – by and large – tend to downplay its significance or deny any responsibility whatsoever. In this sense *colonial privilege* is one of the most profound and the most denied senses of entitlement of all. Given the history of enslavement, genocide, and theft that has underwritten this privilege, the denial is hardly surprising. Rather, those who retain the profits of colonialism tend to reframe their advantages. Most obviously – repeating the best traditions of imperialism in its earlier Roman iteration – the West continues to position itself as liberal 'civilisation' facing down various formations of barbarism (Mishra 2020). Behind this façade, however, is an unanticipated triumph of 'know nothingism' across this western world – the 'free world' has rarely seemed less connected to learning or sophistication. Instead, 'dog whistle politics' prevail and a perpetual crisis around race – embedded in colonial hierarchies – has come to dominate the politics of the 'West'. As our review of imperialism makes clear, this has all been seen before – what is involved is simply the politics and practice of white dominion in novel forms.

In the British and US contexts – at the heart of the Anglosphere – at least the terrain is clear. Trumpism reconfigured the notion of a white republic in an innovative, consolidated form. As a people of colour majority promises to 'predominate numerically', William F. Buckley's prescription of the measures needed for the 'White community' to 'prevail, politically and culturally' has become writ large for the *whole* of the US. (In this regard, 21st-century America is curiously redolent of twentieth-century Stormont – characterised by gerrymandering and the perversion of democracy.) Likewise, in 2019 the English elected a Prime Minister with a remarkably unreconstructed approach to British colonial history. Alongside his gratuitous racist references to 'picanninies' and 'cannibals' and Muslim women as 'pillar boxes', his more considered analysis is that 'we can't blame colonialism'. His assessment of Barack Obama focused on 'the part-Kenyan president's ancestral dislike of the British Empire' (BBC News 2016). Post-Brexit the UK itself had finally become a white dominion in which race is the defining aspect of political life (Dorling and Tomlinson 2019; Ward and Rasch 2019). Empire 2.0 is regarded as a legitimate aspiration for the location of post-Brexit Britain in the world (Olusoga 2017). In this regard, the principle of empire remains a badge of honour rather than shame. 'Progressive patriotism' is now the watchword of the English left (Jones 2016) as much as the English right.[1] In terms of our own focus this matters profoundly of course. It is this novel British political formation – some distance from both Churchillian imperialism and the reformist social democracy of Lord Melchett – with which Ireland now must engage and disengage.

Our analysis suggests that the need for a more honest assessment of imperial debt has never been greater. Yet, the likelihood of any such critique has never been more distant. Running through this problematic is a constant theme of the profound racial, ethnic, religious and political differences generated by the colonial processes we have portrayed. This resonates with wider issues raised across colonial history, detailed time and again in our comparative examples. So how should we situate Ireland and Irishness in terms of the colonial story we have traced? Does this history matter in Ireland *at all*? And, if it does, how does it make sense of Ireland's place in the world? A generation ago it was still meaningful to ask if Ireland was a Third World country (Caherty et al. 1992. See also Coulter 1990). The country appeared trapped in circuits of dependency that were similar to the formerly colonised throughout South America, Asia and Africa. Thirty years later, post-Celtic Tiger, the question seems almost risible.

---

[1] This was riffing on a well-established theme. The post-war Atlee government was comfortable with the notion that 'The aim of Labour is to save the Empire' (Brendon 2008: 448). The speaker in this case was Patrick Gordon Walker – then junior minister, later Foreign Secretary. He persuaded the same Labour cabinet to agree to prevent Seretse Khama, the heir to the throne of the British protectorate of Bechuanaland, from becoming its king on the grounds that he had wed Ruth Williams – a white English woman – thus upsetting neighbouring apartheid South Africa. Despite this, Walker was eventually politically undone by the lurch towards a more explicitly racist white dominion in post-imperial Britain. He lost his Smethwick seat in Birmingham in 1964 in a contest in which the Tories notoriously campaigned on the slogan: 'If you want a nigger neighbour, vote Labour'.

For all the continuing dependency we have outlined, 'Ireland' now routinely appears on league tables of the richest nations in the world. The election of Joe Biden showed that some varieties of Irishness are as close to imperial power as it is possible to be. At this point the comparison with Bangladesh or South Sudan or Haiti seems cruelly inappropriate. But where in the world is Ireland in 2020? And where ought it to be? In this regard the apparent transition from colonial underdevelopment is only half the story. Ireland also must situate itself in terms of Europe and the UK state. Here the transition to premier league status is less obvious. If two-thirds of Ireland is now one of the richest nations in the world, the other third remains the UK's poorest region. Moreover, this is not simply an economic question but also a political and spiritual one. Even if Ireland now seems more at home among the ranks of the Europeans than the colonised, what kind of Europe does it want to belong to – a colonial or an anti-colonial one? It faces an equally challenging question in terms of its relationship to post-Brexit Britain: how should it sit in relation to Empire 2.0?

Irishness and white dominion

The question of the place of Ireland and Irishness in the world is powerfully symbolised by its relationship to whiteness. The contemporary situation is brought into sharp focus by the notion that the Irish 'have become white' and left their colonised past behind. By now this idea has almost achieved the status of self-evident truth. There is little resistance to the notion that the Irish have become white *everywhere*. Irishness and whiteness continue to be presented as an elective affinity. Immediate confirmation of this can be found in the British and Irish censuses. In the UK census, there is no recognition of Black Irishness *at all* – Irishness is only named as a subset of the white category.[2] In the southern Irish census there is at least a recognition of the *possibility* of Irishness of colour but this remains an asymmetrical oddity with the assumed naturalness of white Irishness. In the Northern Ireland census, the categories 'white' and 'Irish' are at least disaggregated but here ethnicity is constructed around colour. In a polity routinely – if somewhat hyperbolically – identified as 'the race hate capital of Europe', the state has no issue in defining ethnicity solely in terms of whiteness and non-whiteness. This imposes a stark racial divide upon all the cultural and ethnic complexity of contemporary Northern Ireland – *with 98 percent shoehorned into the white category*. More generally, there is a contemporary bureaucratic, social democratic variant of the process signalled by Ignatiev

---

[2] Thus, the 2011 English census asks, 'What is your ethnic group?' and offers a range of choices. But the category 'Irish' is restricted to whiteness – something that would, of course, be unthinkable in terms of 'Britishness' or 'Englishness' in the contemporary multicultural UK. Irishness is also separated from the white British categories: 'White English/Welsh/Scottish/Northern Irish/British' and framed as a specific category of whiteness: 'Irish' alongside 'Gypsy or Irish Traveller' and 'Any other White background'. In other words, the Irish – and Irish Travellers – are assumed by definition to be white. When the same census asks, 'What do you feel is your national identity?', Irish is not a named choice although 'Northern Irish' is. In this construction, Irishness assumes the quality of an 'ethnicity' defined solely by colour – again inescapably 'white'. Although the census forms are different, this formulation was the same in Scotland and Wales. In Northern Ireland, however, Irishness is permitted as a 'national identity' (Gov.uk 2020).

(2008) in 19th century United States – the recruitment of *some* Irish to whiteness as both a symbol of – and mechanism for – post-colonial transformation.

There is of course another side to this story. The embracing of whiteness by *some* sections of the Irish population involves simultaneously the complete denial of Irishness to other people of colour. This dialectic bears scrutiny. Ignatiev observed this process in nineteenth-century US. Thus, as some of the Irish 'became white' in the US, others simultaneously had their Irishness erased. A similar dynamic is now manifest across the Irish worldwide. As the possibilities of access to whiteness and Europeanness – and even Britishness – become possible for some Irish people; the other elements in Irish identity are repressed and denied. This confirms that whiteness is a process not a state – it remains an indication of location within a matrix of power rather than an indication of subtle gradations of skin tone.

It hardly requires emphasis that the equation of Irishness and whiteness is also, of course, palpably false. We have documented an alternative history of Irishness of colour across the colonial story. Of course, as our analysis has traced across the history of colonialism, Irishness and Blackness and indigeneity have interfaced in a whole series of ways that are far from unproblematic. Crucially, however, this history has also produced a whole community of people for whom Irishness and Blackness are both significant referents – people inhabiting what Ignatiev characterised as a 'common culture of the lowly'. In other words, despite what the census (and US nativists) say, *one does not have to be white to be Irish*. Moreover, in 2017 – without any great sense of either angst or achievement, Ireland elected a person of colour as *Taoiseach*. (If this seems a trivial gain, it should be compared with the inability of the British to integrate Megan Markle within its own more autocratic political hierarchies.) Post-Varadkar, the notion that there is any simple correlation between Irishness and whiteness *should* be difficult to sustain.[3]

Our argument, however, deconstructs the assumed affinity of whiteness and Irishness in a more profound way. We begin by insisting that the assumed whiteness of Irishness is empirically false. We also insist that it is politically dangerous because this 'commonsense' thesis situates Ireland and Irishness in a way that is toxic and racist. But we are proposing something beyond the bland observation that not all Irish people are white. Rather, we are insisting that – in the sense that it is a colonially and racially loaded term – *whiteness has no useful reference to Irishness at all*. We are suggesting that Irish people – *qua* Irish people – are *not white*. To that observation, we are also adding a prescription – Irish people should not think of themselves as white. This situates our conclusion within wider calls to 'abolish whiteness'.

---

[3] Lest we appear too sanguine on this point, witness the episode in which a Sinn Féin councillor suggested that a 'family man' should be running the country and that Leo Varadkar's Indian heritage meant he is 'separated' from the history of Ireland (RTÉ News 2020). The irony is that some of the leading figures of the republican movement from which the councillor emerges were also 'separated' from the history of Ireland while at the same time making that history in important ways. Additionally, in the aftermath of the killing of George Floyd in 2020, a number of Irish media outlets, including the *Irish Times* and the *Irish Examiner*, carried numerous stories of the racist experiences of Black Irish citizens. See for example Ryan 2020; Dabiri 2020. For a more general overview of Black Irish people, see the Facebook page 'Black and Irish'.

If 'treason to whiteness is loyalty to humanity', then one small act of fidelity is for the Irish to reclaim their Irishness removed of any aspiration to whiteness.[4] Noel Ignatiev (2002) explained how the repudiation of whiteness was rooted in his work on Irishness:

> My book on the Irish was the story of how people for whom whiteness had no meaning learned its rules and adapted their behavior to take advantage of them; *Race Traitor* was an attempt to run the film backwards, to explore how people who had been brought up as white might become unwhite.

From this perspective, whiteness is an essentially colonial, essentially racist concept which has no positive meaning in the context of Irishness. Insofar as other people subscribe to the reactionary imperialist and racist identity of whiteness, Irish people should distance themselves from it. Thus, to be Irish is to be 'not white'; to be Irish is to be 'of colour'.

This is not, however, a reworking of the old suggestion that the Irish should regard themselves as politically Black. There is no need – or indeed justification – for most Irish people to claim to be Black – not least because there were times in which this provided an easy defence for Irish racism: 'I can't be racist because I'm Irish'. Rather our proposal is to insist on the centrality of *mestizaje* to Irishness. We might start with St Patrick himself – who was, of course, not 'racially' Irish at all – but a Briton brought in chattel slavery to Ireland. But this racial and ethnic complexity holds through Irish history – Pearse was half-English, de Valera Spanish American. More recently, Ireland's greatest sporting (Paul McGrath) and musical (Phil Lynott) icons were both Black Irish. This provides some sense of the macaronic character of Irishness before even beginning to address the complex history of the construction of a political Irishness.[5] The 'Irish people' invoked in the declaration of the Republic in 1916 emerged out of the interface of Planter and Gael, native and settler, immigrants and emigrants, coloniser and colonised; all constituted by Ireland's experience of colonialism and imperialism.[6]

Recognising this racial and ethnic complexity should, of course, be a case of pushing at an open door. Culminating in the election of a Taoiseach of colour, the assumed equivalence of Irishness and whiteness has deconstructed in full view around the world. But the profusion of Irishness of colour – both in Ireland itself and abroad – has hardly encouraged any great unpacking of the central truth in Ignatiev's analysis. Ireland's

---

[4] 'Treason to whiteness is loyalty to humanity' is the tagline of the journal *Race Traitor*.

[5] In the macaronic song tradition, the song lyrics are in Irish and English, usually on alternate lines or verses. Examples include 'Siúil a Rúin' and 'By the Dawning of the Day', both sung by the Connemara singer Joe Heaney. The most interesting recent iteration of this tradition is the work of Kneecap – the rap act from West Belfast featuring two MCs, Móglaí Bap and Mo Chara, along with DJ Provaí. As Mullally (2019b) suggests: 'It is not unusual for tunes to be laced with stories of drug-fuelled nights out, but for these to be articulated in the Irish language is central to Kneecap's artistry. The results are dizzying, funny, surprising, cutting. Kneecap's latest track, H.O.O.D., qualifies one of its mid-song rallying calls ("Tiocfaidh ár lá, get the Brits out, lad") with the chorus, "I'm a hood, double-O-D, low-life scum that's what they say about me"'.

[6] In this regard it is worth remembering the important point made by Ó Ruairc (2020: 12), that the Irish language, 'has two terms denoting Irish identity – "Éireannach", a person from Ireland, and "Gael", any person who embraces Irish customs and culture'.

journey from colonisation towards liberation has been reified as a journey from non-whiteness to whiteness. If this had made the Irish 'free', of course, there might be a case for regarding this as a form of progress. But it has not. It has left the country locked in a relationship with its colonial master, profoundly partitioned both physically and spiritually, with its revolution 'unfinished'. In other words, the necessity of severing the connection between whiteness and Irishness obtains. Our thesis is that this act of deconstruction would return to Irishness a complexity which is much closer to the Gaeilge word *breac* – 'speckled' or 'multicoloured' – than white. In recognising the macaronic, *mestizo* and *mestiza* aspects of Irishness, we are simultaneously deconstructing Irish whiteness and helping to mitigate its toxic, racist implications.

The world of *mestizaje*

Each colonialism is different, and each colonised society has elements of uniqueness. Despite that, it is possible to see strong similarities between colonised societies. For example, in settler societies analytically the position and role of the colonised and coloniser can be laid out in stark duality, as has been done by Memmi. But beneath the analytical surface there is undoubted evidence of mixing. Where the mixing is most intimate is at the level of inter-relationships, whether abusive or consensual. For all the racist revulsion at the notion of miscegenation, it happened routinely – not least in those racialised formations which fetishised the taboo of inter-racial relationships. Thus, across the colonised world, the coloniser and the colonised had sexual relationships which led to mixed, *mestizo* and *mestiza* children. There is a spectrum in this regard. At one end are societies such as Paraguay where the amount of mixing was widespread[7] and at the other examples where it was minimal – this often reinforced by racist anti-miscegenation laws, of course. But even where this biological/genetic element was limited, there was widespread cultural exchange. The conclusion to be drawn is that settler colonial societies and their successor societies are defined by *mestizaje*.

This label has been most commonly used in relation to Latin America. Sometimes that use conveys a sense that, as a result of mixing, Latin American societies succeeded in avoiding the worst excesses of other settler societies, such as the United States which massacred the vast majority of indigenous people and enslaved millions of Africans. But the Spanish genocide of indigenous people was at least as widespread as that of the Anglo conquest of North America, and Black slaves in their millions also arrived in South America. Despite occasional pride in their mixed nature, colonised Latin American societies were and are exercises in white dominion, no less than the United States, South Africa or Australia (Gott 2007). For all the mixing of indigenous and incomer over the centuries, racism prevails in Latin America. This is most apparent in the persecution and

---

[7] In 1537 70 Spanish conquistadors travelled up the Paraguay river a thousand miles from the new port of Buenos Aires. Local Guarani Indians offered their daughters to them as wives, and they decided to settle there, founding what became Asunción. As a result, Paraguay is a unique, almost totally mestizo society (Elliott 2006: 83).

indeed attempted genocide of indigenous groups from the Maya of Guatemala to the Mapuche of Chile, both of which processes continue to the present day. And perhaps nothing is more indicative of these structures than the fact that, except for Morales in Bolivia, no Latin American country in modern times has had an indigenous president. There has been no Black president either, although there has been one president of Japanese descent in Peru as well as a president of Chinese descent in Guyana.[8]

Our operationalisation of these terms is novel. '*Mestizaje*' in relation to Ireland and 'white settler society' in relation to Latin American are not commonly used terms. Using them points in each case to a reality, albeit deeply hidden, and allows for a comparison that is analytically and, we would argue politically, valuable. Briefly put, '*mestizaje*' and 'white settler society' can coexist as descriptors of both sets of societies. If the notion of *mestizaje* or *métissage* were to be put in more contemporary terms the most likely word to be used would be one beloved of postmodernists, hybridity. To first appearances, this would seem to be a more suitable word to use in our analysis, the Spanish and French terms for 'mixing' not being commonplace in English nor specifically in analyses of Ireland. However, we hesitate to use this term. For a start, postmodernism offers little in our estimation to the understanding of the material reality of colonialism. Moreover, it is highly relativistic; there is no truth and no vantage point for judgement about right and wrong. Above all, postmodernism sees identity as akin to consumption – each of us can choose exactly who we are, what we want to be and how we want to act. There is no measure of objectivity which imposes an essentialist identity on each of us. Identity formation becomes a form of supermarket shopping. 'It rejoices in mongrelisation … Melange, hotch-potch, a bit of this and that, is how newness enters the world' (Rushdie 1991: 394). We are all free to choose identity and to play with identity. The obvious critique of this argument is to ask the question: what political space does the favela dweller in Buenos Aires or the Rohingya villager in Myanmar have in relation to choosing their identity? There are structures of confinement of individuals, especially the most marginalised individuals on the planet, which postmodernism can neither explain nor dismantle.

The concept of hybridity was popularised by Homi Bhabha when writing about indigenous Asian literature in the context of colonialism. In attempting to counter the hegemony of colonial discourse, Bhabha argued that it was impossible to view pure coloniser and colonised positions in colonial society. What existed was a hybrid culture, neither one nor the other but formed by the encounter of both. Everything happened in liminal space, in the interstices between both groups, in a 'third space'. This space was ultimately a revolutionary one because it deprives 'the imposed imperialist culture, not

---

[8] Alberto Fujimori was elected President of Peru in 1990 and reelected in 1995. He was the first person of Japanese descent, and the second person of Asian descent, to be elected president outside Asia. Arthur Chung became President of Guyana in 1970 – the first Caribbean republic in the Commonwealth. He was the first ethnic Chinese president of a non-Asian state. These examples are taken only from Latin America. There has only been one Black president in north America. The Caribbean, with its additional history of British, French and Dutch colonialism is somewhat more complicated. For example, Toussaint L'Ouverture was the first Black president of the first Black republic when it liberated itself from French colonial rule.

only of the authority that it has for so long imposed politically, often through violence, but even of its own claims to authenticity' (Bhabha 1994:23). The third space is the site of hybridity where 'subversion, displacement, newness, renegotiation of cultures and identities, and multiple positionality' becomes possible, where ultimately 'polarities are dissolved' (Acheraïou 2011: 91).

These grand claims made for hybridity are open to criticism. The focus is on culture, on writing, on discourse. Postmodernist/hybridity theories which locate resistance 'in the subversive counter-discursive practices implicit in the colonial ambivalence itself' (Ashcroft et al. 2007) are insufficient. In the material world there is anti-colonial struggle, resistance, state power, repression, the genocidal violence of the colonial system and the liberationist violence of the colonised. The focus on culture can point to countless examples of hybridity – from creole and pidgin languages to hybrid religious forms such as Santería in the Caribbean and musical forms such as salsa and jazz. But beyond this in the material world of colonial power relations it is much more difficult to point to a dilution or sharing of power and wealth or a lessening of the exploitation of the colonised which results solely from discursive practices.

We could attempt to retrieve the concept of hybridity, 'a slippery, ambiguous term, at once literal and metaphorical, descriptive and explanatory' (Burke 2009: 54), so that it can operate in a historical and materialist way. But rather than try to rehabilitate the term and drop its postmodernist baggage, we have chosen here instead to use the Spanish term for mixing, *mestizaje*. We believe it can be a useful concept to explain the broad sweep of ethnic mixing across empire. From that perspective we also believe it brings a new perspective to the specifics of Ireland in a fresh and meaningful way.

This is not to make overblown claims as to the extent or impact of *mestizaje*. For a start, 'the founding act and trope of mestizaje' is rape (Schiwy 2007: 276). Moreover, the power deficits, inequality and discrimination against indigenous peoples continue to be at the heart of settler colonialism *despite* mixing. Mixing exists, inequality exists: both of these statements are true. Equally, *mestizaje* is a description of an objective reality and does not of itself say anything about subjectivity. There is no inevitability that *mestizaje* leads to personal or societal liberation or equality. In fact, being *mestizo* or *mestiza* can be the occasion for even more sophisticated marginalisation and repression.

We are arguing, however, that it is more than a truism to suggest that in the world after colonialism, nearly everybody is *mestizo* or *mestiza*. Of course, as we have already seen, there remain a tiny number of 'pre-contact' people like the Sentinelese who remain 'protected' from colonial mixing. (It bears emphasis, that their very 'protection' is itself a colonial construction – their situation is not based on being 'undiscovered' but rather being 'discovered' and then 'protected' from the implications of that 'discovery'.) At the other end of this spectrum, there remains a huge range of political formations – the USA and EU included – that continue to operate along the principle of *white dominion*. In other words, despite formal decolonisation, they continue to erect walls and barriers to maintain the hierarchies of racial privilege first established by colonialism.

Apartheid South Africa was the classical example of this kind of dominion. But contemporary examples of this process of dominion are nearly as egregious. That the US under Donald Trump and the Israeli state have made a virtue of constructing physical walls in defence of such dominion makes this process easy to read. That these walls dissect Palestinian and Native American land without any regard for the existing spiritual and political contours of the people to whom the land belongs make them quintessentially colonial and racist.[9] But the very vulgarity of US and Israeli racism sometimes masks the more subtle machinations of other parallel projects in white dominion. Many other countries than the US and Israel invest hugely, politically and economically, in the project of *keeping people of colour out*. Brexit was constructed out of this simple aspiration. Most other European countries exhibit a similar commitment to exclusion. While this process is less commonly couched in terms of traditional racialised fears of 'swamping' and 'miscegenation', this betrays a pathological obsession with denying – and potentially reversing – existing hybridity and mixing. Thus, in both classical and contemporary forms we find white dominion sharing the discontents of settler colonialism.

But history shows that segregationist fantasies are continuously undermined by real social relations. Of course, the logic of colonial settlement is the displacement, marginalisation, denigration, and often genocide, of the native – to the point that contact is minimal and rigidly policed. Over time, however, intermixing, through marriage, concubinage, or sexual violence, leads to a growing section of society which is mixed. Settler colonialism sought to deny this in various ways. Miscegenation is seen as degeneracy. So, for some colonised populations this leads to the 'one drop' rule.[10] For African Americans, for example, descendants of slaves, there was a 'scientific' calculus which allowed for judgements on 'Africanness' – the mulatto (one white parent and one Black), the quadroon (three-quarters white, one-quarter Black), the octoroon (a person with one-eighth African 'blood'). In Saint Dominique the precision even extended to a *sang mêlè*, a person with one-sixty-fourth African 'blood'. This thrust to categorisation reached dizzy levels of Jesuitical casuistry. Take the observances of one traveller in New Spain in the 1770s:

> It is known that neither Indian nor Negro contends in dignity and esteem with the Spaniard; nor do any of the others envy the lot of the Negro, who is the 'most dispirited and despised'... If the mixed-blood is the offspring of a Spaniard and an Indian, the stigma disappears at the third step in descent because it is held

---

[9] A common expression by both Native Americans and Chicanos/Chicanas is: 'We didn't cross the border, it crossed us'.

[10] 'The nation's answer to the question "Who is black?" has long been that a black is any person with any known African black ancestry. This definition reflects the long experience with slavery and later with Jim Crow segregation. In the South it became known as the "one-drop rule," meaning that a single drop of "black blood" makes a person a black. It is also known as the "one black ancestor rule," some courts have called it the "traceable amount rule," and anthropologists call it the "hypo-descent rule," meaning that racially mixed persons are assigned the status of the subordinate group.' (Davis n.d.) In legal terms this 'rule' had major repercussions in issues such as ownership and inheritance.

as systematic that a Spaniard and an Indian produce a mestizo; a mestizo and a Spaniard, a castizo; and a castizo and a Spaniard, a Spaniard... Because it is agreed that from a Spaniard and a Negro a mulato is born; from a mulato and a Spaniard, a morisco; from a morisco and a Spaniard, a torna atrás [return-backward]; and from a torna atrás and a Spaniard, a tente en el aire [hold-yourself-in-mid-air], which is the same as mulato, it is said, and with reason, that a mulato can never leave his condition of mixed blood, but rather it is the Spanish element that is lost and absorbed into the condition of a Negro... The same thing happens from the union of a Negro and Indian, the descent begins as follows: Negro and Indian produce a lobo [wolf]; lobo and Indian, a chino; and chino and Indian, an albarazado [white spotted]; all of which incline towards the mulato. (Quoted in Loveman 2014: 63)[11]

On the other hand, a different strategy emerged for other colonised peoples. It was argued that, once the last 'pure' member of the 'race' had died – Truganini in Tasmania, for example – the colonised group ceases to exist. Thus, the label 'Native American is a racialisation that portrays contemporary Indigenous generations to be less authentic, less Indigenous than every prior generation in order to ultimately phase out Indigenous claims to land and usher in settler claims to property' (Tuck and Yang 2012: 12).

All these societies carry with them a fantasy of white dominion that is constantly undermined by the relentless logic of demographic transition towards a mestizo society. The most recent estimates suggest that the US – the paradigm case of white dominion – will have a non-white majority somewhere between 2040 and 2050 (Tavernise 2018). In other words, the days in which former colonies were reconstituted as gated communities for white settler populations are passing. The reality is that settler colonial societies create an in-between category: metis (people of mixed indigenous and Euro-American ancestry in Western Canada), mestizos and mestizas (people of mixed Spanish and indigenous ancestry in Latin America), creoles (resulting from the mixing between colonial-era emigrants from Europe with non-European peoples) or 'coloureds' (people of mixed European and African ancestry in South Africa). Some settler societies saw the emergence of such categories more easily than others. But the key point is that all, Ireland included, are on the spectrum. Despite the outliers, the world, for better or worse, is mestizo.

At the same time, we wish to emphasise the potential for liberation in terms of mestizaje. It begins with the recognition that mestizaje is a historical rather than biological fact. Liberation is thus a political choice. It enables what Acheraïou (2011: 7) refers to as 'resistive binarism'. It takes as given that the settler/native binary is real but can steer a way out of the dead-end politics which is often built on that fact. One such approach would be to argue that decolonisation ultimately requires the removal of the

---

[11] The traveller concerned was Pedro Alonso O'Crouley or O'Crowley (1740-1817). He was born in Cádiz into a family of Irish immigrants. His travel narrative, published in 1774, was titled *Idea compendiosa del Reyno de Nueva España*. See O'Crouley and Galvin (1974).

settler – 'one settler, one bullet' being its most stark form[12] – or the settlers' privilege.[13] Such an approach leads to a calculus no less rigid than that of colonial racism. Who are the settlers to be removed or dispossessed? Who are the natives who are to have their land returned? Does 'one drop' of 'blood' constitute the basis of either categorisation? And what of those who have 'drops' of both 'bloods'? Should there be DNA-testing of everyone in the colonial or postcolonial society? And what if mixing is so widespread that everyone tests positive as 'native'? Such approaches are not only impractical but also disturbingly essentialist. The alternative postmodernist route, leaving ethnicity to personal choice, is equally impractical, leading to countless Rachel Dolezals.[14]

What does the existence of *mestizos* and *mestizas* do to the essentialist approach which is at the heart of colonialism? Of itself, it does nothing necessarily. The 'half-breed' or 'half caste', to use the derogatory phrase for some children of *mestizaje* can be among the most marginalised person in colonial society. There is no necessary challenge to essentialism in his/her existence. At the level of analysis *mestizaje* challenges essentialism, but the real, living hybrid person may be the least well-placed to challenge the structures built on binary essentialism. In fact, such a person can end up unable to act because of shame of at least part of their hybrid heritage or because 'respectable' society has ostracised him/her. The much-vaunted liminal space of Bhabha can be a very lonely place.

At the same time, *mestizaje* does offer up the possibility of a different way, a third space. At the individual level the *mestizo* or *mestiza* may have opportunities to consider the dual aspects of their origin. In a way that is not so for someone who views him or herself as the 'pure' offspring of either side of the binary divide, the *mestizo* or *mestiza* can examine not simply the colonised without but the coloniser within. They can make choices as to what are the repressive and what are the liberating elements in their identity – and by extension, their society. And of course, *mestizaje* ensures that no mixed person is alone. Our argument is that there is no pure settler or native, especially centuries after the initial conquest. We thus agree with Bhabha in this regard, but not with his conclusion that thereby colonial hegemony is neutered. Elements of *mestizaje* pervade the whole society, whether they are

---

[12] This was a slogan of the Azanian People's Liberation Army in South Africa in the 1980s.

[13] 'Decolonising the Americas means all land is repatriated and all settlers become landless' (Tuck and Yang 2012: 27).

[14] Rachel Dolezal was a woman with no known African ancestry who passed herself off as Black and even managed to become president of the National Association for the Advancement of Colored People chapter in Spokane, Washington. Even though she resigned, she continued to insist that she identified as Black (BBC News 2015). The rationale of identification reached dizzy heights in April 2019 when the Hungarian State Opera decided to perform 'Porgy and Bess'. The composer George Gershwin had specified that the opera could only be performed by Black artists. The Hungarian State Opera got around this by requiring each member of its all-white cast to sign the following form: 'I, the undersigned, hereby state that African-American origin and identity are an inseparable part of my identity' (Walker 2019). In September 2020, Jessica Krug, an associate professor at George Washington University and an expert on Africa and its diaspora, admitted she had lied about being Black. She said her behaviour was 'the very epitome of violence, of thievery and appropriation, of the myriad ways in which non-Black people continue to use and abuse Black identities and cultures' (BBC News 2020e).

clearly seen or acknowledged. The potential for self-examination and choice is therefore available in colonised society. The hybrid society, like the *mestizo* or *mestiza* individual, can explore the elements of liberation and oppression within their common situation.

Mestizaje does not mean the end of difference or the bland conclusion that difference is what we have in common. Difference is real because, while *mestizaje* may challenge essentialism in the ideological sense, it does not automatically dismantle the structures which essentialism built. Difference matters because structures of privilege are erected on it. It may seem highly progressive to embrace difference, thereby rejecting the binary view of colonial or postcolonial society, but the fact is that the binary nature of that society continues and reproduces itself. Of itself, *mestizaje* is a factual observation; it does not dismantle power. What it does do is point to a space in which people may create the opportunities to examine the ways in which power may be dismantled. The third space is thus not a feelgood forum where difference is wished away; rather it is a potential political space where binary and essentialist reality can be challenged. In particular, in the colonial and postcolonial context it is the place where racism can be called out and battled.

Mestizaje is a potential tool of transformation. Like any tool, it does not use itself, nor does it transform just by existing; it must be used. And if used well, the end point can be that difference can become irrelevant, not by being ignored or wished away but because the structures that made it important have been dismantled. Until that time, *mestizaje* neither ignores difference nor sidelines it, but states that if it matters in structural terms, then it matters in political terms. At the heart of such an approach is not a wilful wishing away of binary and essentialist views, but an acknowledgement that where these hold sway, they must be confronted. Sides must be taken, choices made, and if they look binary, that is simply because the binary exists and cannot be ignored.

Ireland: 900 years of *mestizaje*?

We must continue deconstructing the synergy of Irishness and whiteness. In its place we posit the concept of a nation of *mestizaje*. This framing best describes the complex ethnic and racial mix that forms contemporary Ireland, north and south, as well as the diaspora. Moreover, it situates Ireland spiritually and politically in the correct place in the matrix of colonialism, that is in the anti-colonial camp. But it is also suggesting something beyond traditional notions of 'melting pot' or 'diversity'. Our thesis is that this is the fundamental building block of any new Ireland. This is who we Irish are, and it is from this complex, macaronic reality that we must construct an Irish future. More particularly, it is this mix that needs to be reflected in the task of finishing the revolution and building a state that embraces all of these aspects of contemporary Irishness.

At its simplest, this observation regarding the mixing of peoples seems neither revolutionary nor particularly profound. Our review has illustrated just how complicated the ethnic mixes and identities attendant upon colonialism have become. Moreover, we have confirmed that this post-imperial mosaic remains a huge challenge for all anti-imperialist/post-colonial societies. Unlike the other big challenges of decolonisation – from democratisation to electrification – this is a conundrum that has not really been resolved *anywhere*. Of course, there are examples of good and bad practice across the decolonised world. Nevertheless – despite the valiant attempts at a 'rainbow nation' in South Africa or complex multi-ethnic citizenship models in India and Indonesia and Latin America – forging a progressive, post-colonial polity out of the ashes of empire remains the single most intractable task of anti-imperialism. The promise of liberation has most often foundered on the inability to make *mestizaje* work in a transformative way. Rather communalism, sectarianism, racism, tribalism, and a host of more localised divisions undermine the inclusive vision of anti-imperialist struggle. So, this ethnic cleavage remains problematic for democrats and anti-imperialists *everywhere*. We have also shown that history provides a strong corrective to the notion that models of white dominion can ever resolve these issues. Rather, different forms of white dominion across the Americas and Africa and Asia have reified colonial forms of race in new and ever more entrenched postcolonial forms.

While this is a sobering conclusion, it is at one level reassuring to find that Ireland is not alone in struggling to come to terms with the specific form of *mestizaje* it inherited from 900 years of colonialism. Here too the promise of liberation – *anois ar theacht an tSamhraidh* – was profoundly compromised by the outworking of native/settler tensions. This was not simply because of an absence of forethought. Arguably, Irish anti-imperialism was cognisant of the challenge from the start. Thus, there was an attempt to replace division with the 'common name of Irishperson'.[15] The Proclamation was explicit in recognising its challenges in the face of 'divisions carefully fostered by an alien government'. But of course, recognising these differences – and the consequences of a sustained colonial strategy of divide and rule – is not the same as transcending them. As is obvious around the world, the categories 'native' and 'settler' represent a profound dichotomy that is not simply resolved by any verbal commitment to a plural post-colonial citizenship.

Partition was only the most concrete, constitutionalised manifestation of the profound differences that permeate Irishness, both in Ireland and around the world. Our argument is that the whole of Ireland, not just the north, is divided in this way. Understanding this complex reality is the key to our attempt to answer the question of 'what is to be done' in terms of 'finishing the revolution' in Ireland. *Mestizaje* is the key. Expressed as racism, as whiteness, the rejection of *mestizaje* is at the core of the post-colonial condition. If, however, *mestizaje* can be reconstituted as an opportunity rather than a burden, it can point to a way out of that condition. Exploring the liberating potential of *mestizaje* can be the beginning of the answer to the deceptively simple question: how is decolonisation to be completed?

---

[15] Of course, it was the Society of United Irishmen, not Irishpersons, but we are convinced that the radical thinkers in and around that Society, not least Mary Ann McCracken, would be happy to endorse this rewording.

In Ireland, this leads immediately back to the problematic of the extant state formations created by the Government of Ireland Act: 'Southern Ireland' and 'Northern Ireland'. 'Northern Ireland' has remained as it was framed; 'Southern Ireland' has — through several iterations — reinvented itself simply as 'Ireland'. Despite their expressly temporary status one hundred years ago, neither shows much capacity for engaging with questions of reunification or decolonisation. Nor is there much evidence of the 'poetic' vision of the first Dáil apparent in the politics of either of these formations in 2020. It is our thesis, however, that this less than inspiring reality is all about to change. The UK's Brexit debacle has forced the question of the Irish state — or states — back onto the agenda. This development has seen discussion of division in Ireland foregrounded for the first time in a generation. Moreover, the cultural reference to conflict in Ireland is now seen to have wider cachet. Cultural production like *Derry Girls*, *Milkman* and *Ulster American* is read as having a wider reference (both Irish and *British*) in the age of Brexit.[16] This time, however, international attention is focused not so much on the 'dreary steeples of Fermanagh and Tyrone' as on the extraordinary international border that tracks across the heart of Ulster. Like most of the borders across the colonised world, it is an artificial, imperial construct. Only one hundred years ago — before 1920 — there was effectively no difference — culturally, politically, economically — between Derry and Inishowen, West Tyrone and East Donegal, South Armagh and North Monaghan, or Newry and Dundalk. But there is a striking difference now. Alongside all the existing colonial dichotomies — native/settler, coloniser/colonised, planter/Gael — partition first constitutionalised and then progressively realised a further profound division between Irish people. Over the past 100 years these states have fashioned major differences in their populations — not least because they are *citizens* in one polity, *subjects* in the other. Differences that were insignificant in 1920 between the inhabitants of Belcoo and Blacklion or Strabane and Lifford or Culmore and Muff are now profound.

Partition completely reconstituted the Irish world. It divided three of the four Irish provinces from each other. Five of the six northern counties are now border counties, as are five of the 26 southern counties. With one cynical, anti-democratic, sectarian stroke of an imperial pen the British state reinvented Ireland and Irishness. In terms of sheer numbers of dead, the consequences were nothing like those of partition in India in 1947; but the implications for state formation were just as profound. Partition was the last significant act of colonisation in Ireland. This has not gone away. The state formations on the island remain those framed by the Government of Ireland Act 1920. Moreover, the

---

[16] *Derry Girls* is a sitcom written by Lisa McGee about four Derry schoolgirls (and their male English companion). Its two series were a major hit for Channel 4 in 2018 and 2019. Anna Burns' novel, *Milkman*, about a young North Belfast woman during 'the troubles' won the 2018 Man Booker Prize for Fiction, the first time a writer from Northern Ireland has been awarded the prize. *Ulster American*, a 2018 play by David Ireland, weaves together questions of 'the troubles', identity, and misogyny. Although only fully comprehensible through a knowledge of recent Irish history and conflict, all three cultural productions were successful beyond the confines of Northern Ireland.

artificial border that separates them threatens to become more marked, more contested, more militarised by Brexit.

Of course, these contemporary partitioned Irish states are significantly different from their 1920 iterations. The southern state journeyed through 'white dominion' to 'independence' to its current status as 'EU member state'; the northern state has attempted to shift its source of legitimacy even more radically from Protestant majoritarianism to 'good relations' peace enforcement. It now faces a uniquely uncertain future having been removed from the EU against its expressed political will. Neither state has ever been completely happy in its artificially constructed shell. Moreover, none of these changes has secured legitimacy in the current crisis; the post-Brexit northern state in particular is inherently unstable.

In this regard, there was a moment at the West Belfast Féile (Festival) in 2018 when this burgeoning crisis of state legitimacy emerged in emblematic form. As the Chief Constable and the Police Ombudsman clashed over dealing with the past, several other key actors looked on – including representatives of the police and the republican movement. This kind of dialogue was, of course, unthinkable before 1998. The Chief Constable couldn't and wouldn't have spoken at the West Belfast Féile. There was no Police Ombudsman – this is a human rights protection that emerged from the GFA. (Even if there had been, he or she would not have come from a Catholic background as the then Ombudsman did.) In other words what was striking about the event was less that the Chief Constable and Ombudsman were engaging with a republican audience – there has been a fair bit of that over the past twenty years – but rather that the state was now forced to engage *with itself* in this context. It had become clear that the state – the peculiar good relations state constructed out of the power matrix embedded in the Good Friday Agreement – was divided against itself. Crucially, despite the lashings of good relations syrup that accompanied the peace process, the centre of this formation has not held. Increasingly the repressive apparatus of the state – the criminal justice system, including policing and prisons – is in direct confrontation with the ideological good relations aspects.

In the early days of the post-1972 'community relations' intervention, these intrastate tensions were insignificant, David and Goliath confrontations. But increasingly as the model bedded down after 1998, these contradictions have become sharper and less resolvable. Moreover, they are increasingly located within the repressive state apparatus itself.[17] It was neither accidental nor insignificant that one of the first sectors of the Northern Ireland labour market to 'Catholicise' was the legal profession (FEC 1995: 31). Thus, by 2002 the Human Rights Commission was taking cases against the

---

[17] A prime example was when Michael Maguire, as Ombudsman, initiated legal action in 2014 against the Chief Constable, Matt Baggott, for withholding information which he needed to conduct his investigations. This was only 'solved' when Baggott's term of office ended and George Hamilton took over as Chief Constable and promised to comply with the Ombudsman's requests for documents. Incidentally, as human rights NGOs in the north point out, Hamilton did not manage to fully comply.

police on the policing of Ardoyne; and by 2011 the DPP was appointed from the firm of solicitors that had represented the Gibraltar Three.[18]

This ongoing transformation involved huge contradictions on all sides. On the republican side people were expected to learn to accept racism and oppression reinvented as 'cultural traditions'. This process negotiates a fine line between tragedy and farce – after the GFA embedded Ulster Scots language and culture as a constituent of peace, the 2020 deal added the concept of 'Ulster British' identity with who knows what further implications for ethno-racist mobilisation. On the other hand, the reformed post-GFA formation was expected to function with a sizeable portion of its population – right up to the Deputy First Minister – expressly committed to the dismantling of that same state. Behind this an even deeper paradox was building – the incompatibility of a sectarian apparatus that has traditionally functioned by Catholic exclusion confronting a good relations paradigm that can only work with Catholic inclusion. When the criminal justice system cannot resolve which model is to be dominant, the state is on the threshold of collapse. These increasing tensions are also manifest in – though less caused than *symbolised* by – the non-functioning of the power-sharing Executive itself. Until the settlement of January 2020 there had been no representative government in Northern Ireland for three years. In combination, all these contradictions leave post-GFA Northern Ireland perilously close to the notion of a 'failed state'.

In contrast, of course, the southern state looks an altogether more stable proposition. Despite the ignominious end of the Celtic Tiger, it has retained a degree of the self-confidence it developed in the 1980s. But all this hides a profound vulnerability in the southern polity. It cannot but be dragged into any crisis in the north. Conjoined since 1920, these 'Southern Ireland' and 'Northern Ireland' formations require each other to survive. Even if it wanted to, this southern state cannot survive the transformation of the north. It would require a wall of Trumpian proportions to reseal the border. Never mind the ties of politics and culture that still traverse and transcend the border, the very geography of the partition boundary makes it impossible to insulate or isolate the southern state from developments in the north. As Ireland's premier folksinger Christy Moore reminded us, whatever the latest crisis in the north, it occurs 'only ninety miles from Dublin'.

All this, of course, suggests that the GFA itself already appears less a solution to conflict in Ireland than a brief pause on the path towards a more permanent settlement. The key issue for us, however, is that these new post-GFA formations – north and south of the border – remain umbilically linked to the fact of partition. Both contemporary states remain determined by this historic, structural reality. Moreover, as we have illustrated, the politics that followed – and the politics that continues to characterise both states – was almost completely shaped by these novel, late-imperial state formations. Subsequent Irish politics – unionism, nationalism, and republicanism – have been determined by that same colonial act. It follows of course that neither of these entities has any simple right

---

[18] Three IRA members – Mairéad Farrell, Dan McCann and Sean Savage – on active service in Gibraltar in March 1988 were shot dead, although unarmed, by a British undercover SAS unit.

to self-determine – when Ireland finally exercises its right to self-determination, this can only be done by the Irish people as a whole.[19]

So, where do we go from here? The question logically breaks down into three elements: first, where is 'here', second, where is 'there', and third, how do we get from 'here' to 'there'? Superficially, the second of these questions is the easiest to answer in the abstract; the goal is decolonisation, which in the context of Ireland is the completion of the uncompleted revolution. This allows us to specify the starting point clearly: the failure of the revolutionary ideal of the republic. Despite a few brief flowerings – the 'common name of Irishperson' aspiration of the United Irish Movement, the Proclamation of the 1916 Rising, the 'poetic' ideals of the Democratic Programme of the First Dáil – the Republic was smothered at birth by a host of factors which ultimately derived from colonial dominion. We suggest that an appreciation of Irishness as *mestizaje* becomes the key to finally reaching the republic.

The politics of *mestizaje*: how the Irish might become '*breac*'

The concept of *mestizaje* helps reframe an understanding of contemporary Ireland. This conclusion is not negated by the fact that no one in common parlance or indeed political commentary has used the term in the Irish context; or, indeed, by the fact that, whatever it might be termed, the notion of mixing is not part of popular consciousness. Despite this, in the Irish context *mestizaje* was evident from the first. The Anglo-Normans took on Irish names and customs – indeed the Statutes of Kilkenny were introduced specifically to *prevent* mixing and creating what we might recognise retrospectively as English dominion. Anglican Wolfe Tone was secretary of the Catholic Association. Many of the leading lights of the Gaelic revival were Protestant. This biological and cultural interfacing continued down the centuries in both directions. In the North in particular, observers often comment on the similarities across the religious divide, especially in relation to aspects of popular culture.

This kind of cultural crossover and sharing finds definitive expression in the macaronic song tradition – with lyrics that combine Irish and English. This has implications that are much more profound that the simple observation of cultural diversity. It eschews monolingualism and demands a radically new epistemology – to fully understand these songs requires fluency in both English and Irish. From this perspective Ireland and

---

[19] This is, of course, yet another colonial legacy shared with other parts of the colonised world. The partition of India has been rightfully notorious. But other formations were also senselessly divided in the interest of late colonialism rather than decolonisation. One of the most egregious of all – the situation of the Chagos Islands – continues to attract opprobrium. These were divided from Mauritius two years before its independence in a cynical geopolitical land grab. Their population was subsequently evicted by the UK. On 22 May 2019, the UN passed a resolution demanding the UK return control of the Chagos Islands to Mauritius. British occupation of the islands was rendered unlawful by 116 votes to 6. The vote said something about the contemporary dynamics of white dominion – it was opposed by the U.S., Australia, Hungary, Israel and the Maldives as well as the UK of course. Ireland voted for the UK to relinquish the territory. There were 56 abstentions to the resolution, including from France, Germany and Portugal. (Organization for World Peace 2019)

Irishness present a classic example of *mestizo* culture. In tracing the specificity of this in terms of Irishness, the Irish language provides the notion of *breac*. This term captures the idea of being mixed – or 'speckled' or 'multi-coloured' – in many different forms – such as the colours of the trout or magpie or barmbrack (*bairín breac*). This helps give a specifically Irish inflection to *mestizaje*.[20]

Confronting the lived reality of mixing in contemporary Ireland, however, immediately raises the problem of how to refer to identity and division across the present situation of Ireland, centuries after colonial conquest and a century after partial decolonisation. Colonialism imposed a binary logic on Ireland; the division was starkly one of native versus settler. This was further compounded when nationalism emerged in Ireland. By the 19th century, Irish nationalism was challenging aspects of colonialism, and in the case of republicanism, was seeking to overthrow it. In many ways, however, nationalism reproduced the tropes of colonialism – whether in the military titles assumed by rebels, the 'high diction' of anti-English rhetoric, the opposition not to empire but to the failure to fully benefit from the spoils of empire and so on. Given that, there was nothing about this nationalist reaction which necessarily or inevitably challenged or dismantled the binary of settler and native. The few experiments at radical reimagining, such as the United Irish movement, were demolished by state repression. While colonialism was in the ascendant, there was little space to break ranks and transcend rigid labels.

At the same time, Ireland was no exception to the rule that few settler colonial societies succeeded in totally obliterating or assimilating their indigenous people, despite that being the fundamental logic of settler colonialism.[21] Consequently, the colonised and the colonisers continued to exist alongside each other. Despite the inequalities of power and wealth and the laws and policies commonly used to prevent interaction, they did not live in hermetically sealed blocs. This is not to conclude that there was an inherent thrust towards equality or reconciliation, nor that such societies became, to use the term dear to the hearts of assimilationists in the US in the 1960s and 1970s, melting pots. Rather, it is simply to state that, in living alongside each other on the same narrow ground, they interacted in cultural and other ways.

The concept of *mestizaje* enables valuable insights into the contemporary condition of Ireland. First, it helps determine what to call the social formation. Howe (2008: 146) is in no doubt that 'settler colonialism', if it ever was an applicable term in the Irish case, no longer is:

> Important aspects of the region's past can be 'captured' through use of concepts of the settler colony, and, of course, of the plantation, but whatever the perceptions and even self-perceptions of some actors, the distinctively settler-colonial features of Northern

[20] The notion also already has some traction. Thus, Notre Dame's journal of Irish Studies is *Breac* (Notre Dame 2019) while Hugo Hamilton's *The Speckled People* (2003) used this term in his reflection on the notion of 'half-Irishness'.

[21] '... the fundamental analytical difference between "colonisers" and "settler colonisers" is that they want different things; while the "coloniser" comes to the land of the colonised and tells them "you, work for me", the "settler coloniser" takes over the land of the colonised and tells them "you, go away"' (Smandych 2013: 93).

Irish society were largely eroded or dismantled during the nineteenth century. Thus, settler colonialism as usually conceived of has long ceased to explain much.

On the contrary, we wish to take as our starting point the insight of Wolfe (1999: 2) who argues that settler invasion is a structure, not an event. This means that what is established is a structure of power, a hierarchy and an ideology of privilege. These elements long outlast the original event and can be reproduced *ad infinitum*, even when the metropolitan centre modernises and moves on. The settler can be the staunchest supporter of colonial structure, power and ideology, even to the point of being prepared to go head to head with metropolitan authority to preserve these things – as in America 1776, Ireland 1782, Algeria 1961, Southern Rhodesia 1965.

A second issue, what to call the people of Ireland, can be approached through this question: when does the settler stop being a settler? In one sense, the answer is easy. By the second generation, it could be argued, the local-born children of the first wave of settlers are no longer settlers. But the answer is more complex than this and goes back once again to the question of structure. Do the inherent privileges in the structures continue to the next generation – and the next and the next? If so, the descendants of the original settlers continue to benefit from the structures of settlement and remain, in the politico-sociological sense, settlers. The label is even more apt if future generations continue to work tirelessly to preserve their privilege in perpetuity.

Arguably, then, it is only if and when the legacy of settlement, in terms of structure, power and ideology, disappears and a general egalitarianism exists that it becomes possible to see a society moving towards a post-settler state. At that point, with equality between the descendants of original natives and original settlers, it would be possible to say that the settler has stopped being a settler.

Connected to this is the further question: when does the native cease to be a native? To repeat, ultimately it is when equality is established. In the meantime, the descendants of the original natives can continue to experience the lack of power and the prejudice which were embedded in the structures of the society through the original conquest and which have been their legacy in terms of wealth, laws, policy and life chances. Being native is thus not simply a matter of birth; it too is a structural condition. This is caught in the statement of James Fintan Lalor which we have already quoted but bears repeating:

> I trouble myself as little as anyone does about the 'conquest' as taken abstractedly – as an affair that took place long ages ago. But that 'conquest' is still in existence, with all its rights, claims, laws, relations, and results. (*The Irish Felon*, July 8, 1848; quoted in Lalor n.d.: 82)[22]

At the same time, intermixing can allow descendants, especially those with minimal native progeny, to 'pass'. Take the case of the North of Ireland. When an IRA truce in West Belfast collapsed in 1974, the leader of the IRA on the republican side was Ivor

---

[22] It is also caught in the Palestinian slogan: 'Every day is nakba'.

Bell and the leader of the Ulster Defence Association on the loyalist side was Patrick Murphy (Ó Snodaigh 1995: 19). That the 'native' had a 'settler' name, and vice versa, would seem to reveal that a hybridity of sorts had taken place and that the structures of settlement were no longer particularly relevant. But although at a superficial level someone called Murphy was more likely to be stopped by state forces in their pursuit of counterinsurgency against republicans than someone called Bell, beyond the superficial, this indicates nothing about the wider reproduction of structures and privilege. In fact, it could be said that where such a superficial signifier as a name could be the trigger for state military attention is ample proof that the settler-originated structures remain intact and that *mestizaje* is having little impact.

There would be many in the North who would reject the validity of referring to 'settlers' and 'natives' four centuries after the initial settlement. This is where the value of emphasising settler colonialism as a structure again becomes apparent. It allows questions to be asked about the society rather than about people *per se*. Do the structures of power and privilege that derive from settler colonialism remain in the society? How are they reproduced? Which sections of the society seek to maintain those structures and which sections seek to remove them? How do the laws and policies of the society reproduce or undermine those structures? How, in the longer term, can equality be achieved? And can equality be achieved within the geographical and constitutional boundaries of the state as currently constructed? And finally, where, as individuals, do people in that society, whether ultimately descended from original natives or settlers or other migrants – or indeed of an intermixing of all of these – stand in relation to these questions?

This final question relates in a direct autobiographical sense to the authors of this book. As we have stated earlier, one has an Irish or Gàidhlig name but is descended from planters who came originally from Scotland to Antrim and was brought up in that tradition – Anglican, Presbyterian and unionist. The other has a surname which derives from English planters in Armagh and has Protestant great-grandfathers on both sides who married Catholics and whose children were brought up in that religion; he was thus born and raised in the nationalist tradition. But our argument is that, for us as for everyone in this society, the crucial political questions are not about accidents of birth or genealogy, but about politics and ideology.

In short, *mestizaje*/mixing is neither an aspiration nor a badge of postmodernist authenticity but simply a *description* of biological origins and cultural developments. Nor is it any *guarantee* of liberation or equality as postmodernists would contend. At the same time, if reconfigured, the term offers the possibility of considering roads to both equality and liberation. The *mestizo* or *mestiza* person, realising their mixed origins, has a choice: to pursue the agenda of the coloniser or the agenda of the colonised. This choice is political, not one determined by biology or provenance. Moreover 'Which side are you on?' is a question not about 'us' and 'them', but about the politics of 'us'. Do we work for the preservation of the white settler privilege that was open to part of our ancestral background, or for liberation, which was the goal of another part of that background? To repeat: the choice is political. But because it is a choice, already there is the potential of progressive and liberationist thinking in asking the question in this way. Our goal is to go beyond the feelgood notion of postmodernism, and its Northern Ireland equivalent of good relations, that it is enough that difference be respected and encouraged. It is to recognise differences of power and privilege, but to seek to overcome them.

Our argument regarding Ireland, which again goes against the grain of popular parlance and intellectual commentary, is that the North remains a settler colonial society, and as such is mixed. Given that, the political choice between privilege and liberation is the one facing all the people of the North. To work for liberation is a political act that does not derive from biology or even cultural tradition, much as the latter might make the political choice harder for some than for others. For these, the steep curve of political self-re-education involved may be daunting, but it is not impossible.

Moreover, as already intimated, *mestizaje* increases in Ireland with each passing day. Previously the possibilities of hyphenated identity were few and limited, but there now exist swathes of 'new Irish', children of first-generation immigrants from Poland, Lithuania, Nigeria and elsewhere. It is now much less unusual than in the time of Phil Lynott of Thin Lizzy to be Black Irish, in his case Guyanese Irish. The singer and actress Samantha Mumba is Zambian Irish, the singer Loah Sallay-Matu Garnett is Sierra Leonean rish, the footballer Paul McGrath is Nigerian Irish, the actress Ruth Negga is Ethiopian Irish. Rugby player Simon Zebo, soccer player Cyrus Christie, and footballer Rianna Jarrett are Black Irish. Not surprisingly, the diaspora throws up even more complex dimensions to this. For example, just as we have made sense of the Irishness of Ed Sheeran and Billy Eilish along comes Joy Crookes. Nominated as a 'rising star' at the 'Brits' awards, she sings in a South London accent about issues in contemporary London but her identity is 'Bangladeshi Irish' with 'a sound that combines the eclectic range of music her father played as he drove her to her weekly Irish dancing lessons' (BBC News 2020c).

And beyond these famous examples, there are Polish Irish bus drivers, Nigerian Irish civil servants, Lithuanian Irish shop assistants, Chinese Irish doctors, and so on. This development is specifically significant in the North; the children and grandchildren of immigrants are creating a third space of *mestizaje*. As such, they have no obvious political presence beyond *not necessarily* identifying in voting terms with either nationalism or unionism. But the increased mixing that they represent offers the possibility that they may come to challenge or infuse the traditional political blocs. They will have political choices to make about equality and liberation in what is now their homeland, no less than the people traditionally living here. Combining these new developments with the existing – but largely ignored and excluded – Black Irish diaspora, reveals that the assumed elective affinity between Irishness and whiteness is completely unsustainable. Ireland can only continue to see itself as a white dominion by engaging in the most egregious levels of historical and contemporary denial.

We have argued that the liberating insight of *mestizaje* is that political action derives from choice rather than biology. This allows all of us *mestizos* and *mestizas* to take sides, to choose. In the Irish context, north and south, the sides that must be taken, the choices that must be made relate, as for Tone, Mitchel, Pearse, Connolly, Markiewicz, Carney and others throughout Irish history, to one single binary: *empire versus republic*. To apply Memmi's insight: the ultimate choice for every citizen in the North, regardless of deep origins, is whether they accept or refuse the structures of settler colonialism and its legacy.

This choice is, of course, more complex across the diaspora. Regarding their position on Ireland itself, Irish people across the diaspora have the same choice: empire versus republic. (And across the years the Irish diaspora – from Patrick Ford to Bonar Law – has made this choice very explicitly.) More immediately, however, the Diaspora has a further choice in terms of its place of settlement – across the white dominions and beyond. In other words, Irish people in the US or Canada or Australia or South Africa must make the same decision about empire and republic *within* these polities as well. If decolonisation means anything at all, it should be expected to find Irishness at peace with itself not just in Ireland but also across the world. It hardly bears emphasis that this has often not been the case.

Most particularly, the Irish have a specific location within – and a particular challenge towards – white dominion. As Ignatiev suggested, Irishness and whiteness were synergised in this context. So, how to appropriately respond to this reality? One way is to juxtapose the cases of two children of the diaspora as ideal types: John Mitchel versus Paul Kelly. The first as we have already seen was a committed anti-imperialist. He – more than anyone else – framed the anti-imperialist reading of *An Gorta Mór* – 'God sent the blight but the English created the famine'. But he also notoriously took the Confederate side in the American Civil War and actively supported slavery. Moreover, when he was challenged on the contradictions between his Irish anti-imperialism and his racism, he remained characteristically unrepentant and unambiguously racist.

From Mitchel onwards there is little difficulty in finding Irish people who have been on the 'wrong side' in either the colonial process or the white dominions. Moreover, this isn't simply that they happen to be Irish; their Irishness is often mobilised in support of white dominion. But Irish people have just as significantly featured in speaking truth to power. Here, the singer Paul Kelly offers a contrasting approach, albeit in a different white dominion – a white Irish person who is recognised as having some specific engagement with racism and colonialism in Australia. His performance of 'From Little Things Big Things Grow' at Gough Whitlam's funeral offers a contrary take on the relationship with indigenous peoples and peoples of colour in a white dominion. But this performance also hints at a deeper more specifically Irish engagement – because the performance is a *duet* with Kevin Carmody – someone who is part of what we have identified as the Black Irish diaspora.[23] In other words, in combination Paul Kelly and Kev Carmody symbolise a very different relationship between Irishness and white dominion. This involves not just a repudiation of the offer of whiteness but also a reclaiming of Irishness of colour as a core part of that process.

Our approach posits a simple dichotomy between empire and republic. But we also imply the existence of an excluded middle with our constant reference to examples of white dominion. This notion frames those polities which emerged from the break-up of empire but, rather than decolonising, reframed colonial privilege in a new, entrenched autonomous forms. These include, obviously, those polities which were white dominions of the British Empire: Australia, Canada, Newfoundland, New Zealand, South Africa and, crucially for us, the Irish Free State. Historically at least they include offshoots of the British Empire which aspired to dominion status but were never provided it – these include Kenya and Zimbabwe. Other imperial offshoots like Palestine and Northern Ireland also flirted with variations on the theme. As we have noted, we also apply the term to many of the post-colonial Latin American polities. Thus, the notion of white dominion provides a general theorisation for the phenomenon across colonialisms. Dominion emerges from the unresolved dialectic between empire and republic. When empires – and crucially their settler colonial populations – refuse to recognise the independence of their colonies, they turn to the model of white dominion. The strategy was more or less universal. This strategy was tried in colonies with relatively few settlers like India; in colonies where settlers overwhelmingly dominated an indigenous population depleted by genocide, like Canada; and in colonies where settlers were a dominant, privileged minority population, like South Africa.

What does all this mean for Ireland in the coming times? Crucially for us, it helps Ireland make sense of its relationship to whiteness. Ignatiev brilliantly traced 'how the Irish became white' in the US – this analysis confirmed the arbitrariness of whiteness but also the benefits attendant on white privilege that were provided for *some* Irish people. But this process also negates Irishness of colour – all of those Irish *mestizos* and *mestizas* who were unable to 'pass' in the racial dynamics of the US. Moreover, this whitening process had no immediate or direct impact on the Irish in Ireland. Our thesis is that the

---

[23] Kev Carmody was born in 1946 in Cairns, Queensland. His father was second-generation Irish, his mother an indigenous Australian of the Murri people. He grew up on a cattle station in Queensland where his parents worked as drovers. When he was ten, Carmody and his brother were taken from their parents under the assimilation policy as part of the Stolen Generations and sent to a Catholic school in Toowoomba. He later returned to his roots and worked as an agricultural labourer. In the 1980s, Carmody developed a musical career producing multiple albums including *Eulogy (For a Black Person)* (1990). His work draws on both his Aboriginal and Irish heritage. In 1991 Carmody co-wrote the song, 'From Little Things Big Things Grow', with Paul Kelly. This was an account of the Gurindji tribe drovers' walkout led by Vincent Lingiari at Wave Hill station in the Northern Territory during the 1960s, the incident which sparked off the indigenous land rights movement. It was this song that Kelly and Carmody famously sang at the funeral of Gough Whitlam, the Australian Prime Minister who finally recognised native title and repudiated *terra nullius*.

Irish in Ireland had whiteness thrust upon them by the imposition of white dominion status in 1922. It has been confirmed by the integration of both Irish states within 'Fortress Europe' since 1973. Put simply, this is how the Irish in Ireland became white.

The key point in all this is that Irishness and whiteness were never an elective affinity. In imperial racial hierarchies the Irish were not white at all for most of their history. In other words, though counterintuitive, it is not nonsensical to suggest that the Irish 'changed colour' in 1922. Furthermore, this *volte face* has been undermined ever since. The Black Irish of the diaspora have come back to distort the conventional wisdom. Meanwhile the new Black Irish of the post-Celtic Tiger, post-GFA immigration have further undermined the notion that to be Irish is to be white. Only England continues to insist on the *identity* of Irishness and whiteness.

This is where our notion of *mestizaje* becomes important. It is our thesis that this enforced whitening of Irishness must be resisted. We have insisted that Irishness should not be colour-coded in this way: first, because it is empirically untrue; second, because its implications are racist and reactionary. More radically, we are stating that Irishness should be regarded as an alternative to whiteness, as *mestizaje*. In our configuration, to be Irish is to reject whiteness. This is a complex and counterintuitive reading, but it is profoundly significant to the question of where to go from here in the next stage of decolonisation.

It helps perhaps to illustrate what we mean by raising the question of where we might find Irish privilege as opposed to white privilege. As we have shown, we find multifarious varieties of Irishness across the different colonial formations that have illustrated our arguments. We can start to calibrate Irish privilege with the obvious – 'Southern Ireland'. Clearly, the 26-country state does privilege Irishness – there are obvious benefits attendant on Irish citizenship within that polity. Likewise, in the contemporary US Irishness often works in the ways that Ignatiev suggested – politically, formally and informally, as an ethnically-specific gateway to white privilege. From Tammany Hall to the election of Joe Biden, we find Irishness empowered in different ways across the US. This reality obtains perhaps now in the EU as well – broadly Irishness benefits more than it disempowers. But this is less clear in the other polities. It is not so obvious that Irishness conveys many favours in England or Scotland or Wales. Nor in the white dominions – in Australia they even made Irish people come on British passports if they wanted to be a part of its 'white Australia' policy – in that polity to be Irish was to be 'not white'. And in Northern Ireland – despite its very name – Irishness is still a mark of second-class citizenship – it invites discrimination rather than privilege. In the key metonym of our times, even after the peace process and the GFA, some people are denied the basic right to speak their own language.

In terms of where to go from here, we have suggested that our core project is to construct a decolonised state that can reflect the notion of the republic. It must be a decolonised state formation – one that expressly moves beyond the 'white dominion' model of 'Southern Ireland' and the 'Protestant dominion' model of 'Northern Ireland'.

Towards that end, we suggest it is valuable to frame Irishness as *mestizaje*. This helps avoid some of the essentialist binaries that have divided Ireland in the past – and corrupted the promise of postcolonialism across the decolonised world. It is around this understanding of Irishness as quintessentially macaronic– or *breac* – that the republic should be built.

Finishing the revolution

Our theorisation of this notion of *breac* in the context of our wider analysis of *mestizaje* reminds us that the whole world continues to grapple with issues deeply embedded in the legacies of colonialism. In this regard, the challenge of 'finishing the revolution' is not restricted to Ireland. Rather, it sits at the very heart of the measure of decolonisation across the colonised world. Arguably, this is the defining question that confronts *all* former colonies – have they excised all the negative impacts of colonisation? And, if they haven't, what should be done to continue – or renew – their own journey towards what the Indians called *Purna Swaraj* – 'complete independence'? This challenge raises a whole series of theoretical and philosophical questions. Arguably, the whole paradigm of postcolonialism was a meditation on this problematic. But this issue is also a question of *praxis*. In other words, it begs the question of political action as much as theory – most obviously framed by Lenin's classic revolutionary problematic: *what is to be done?*

Our review of the colonial process leaves little doubt as to the profoundly negative impacts of imperialism: addressing its legacy involves acknowledging *inter alia* genocide and slavery, indenture, and starvation. If this is what colonisation involved, what could be done to repair such catastrophic destruction and disruption of people's lives? There is no way to resurrect the dead peoples such as the Táino / Arawaks who committed mass suicide in the face of Spanish conquistadors and the Tasmanians who outlived colonial conquest by little more than a generation. Even if all the ill-gained wealth achieved by imperial nations through booty and forced labour could be calculated, how could it be realistically be returned without completely upending the economic and political structures of the contemporary world? The problem is a fundamental one: there is no going back to the *status quo ante*.

This is a profound and complex challenge for every people that survived colonialism – colonialism casts a long shadow and it remains embedded in the structural present – raising issues of neocolonialism, postcolonialism, and ongoing dependency. But the *first stage* in the decolonisation process is the formal removal of the dominion of the colonial power. This implies, of course, 'complete independence' rather than some form of 'dominion' within empire. In this regard, Ireland lags well behind most of the colonised world. In the Irish context the first steps towards such disengagement began promisingly enough one hundred years ago. But this happened only partially in 1922 – as we have seen, Ireland became a white dominion rather than a republic. Moreover, this faux decolonisation applied only to two-thirds of the island – Northern Ireland was ensnared more tightly than ever in both Union and Empire. In this regard, the unfinished nature of the Irish revolution is more palpable that in most other former colonies. In most of the colonised world, whatever the debates around postcolonialism and neocolonialism, at least the colonial flag has been lowered and the formal writ withdrawn. But Ireland has yet to complete this first hurdle.

So, how can the first stage of decolonisation be completed? We have argued already that Ireland is in a revolutionary moment in 2020. We have suggested that the context is uniquely propitious – better than is has been since the formation of the two states in 1920. The British state is deconstructing itself in the context of Brexit. The Northern Ireland state is profoundly undermined, not least by the demographic transition which is in the process of removing the unionist majority upon which it was erected. The southern state – while hardly leading the charge against imperialism around the world – is at least capable of resisting every British demand for compromise on the border. Its principles on this matter are, of course, now shored up by the EU.

Thus, whatever the tardiness of the Irish journey towards decolonisation – 900 years is a very long time in politics – our analysis suggests that Ireland now finds itself in a relatively fortuitous place. This is principally because of the structural realities of post-colonial location – Ireland is in a fortunate position in comparison to other decolonisation processes for several reasons. For example, Palestinians do not just need to 'try harder' – or indeed interpret their situation in new ways – to decolonise. Likewise, Native Americans or New Caledonians are both effectively trapped in white dominion contexts with no simple route towards decolonisation. In each of these situations the conditions for decolonisation are far poorer than they are in Ireland in 2020. In contrast, we Irish – as much by good luck as good judgement – are in an extremely opportune anti-colonial moment. The immediate reason for this is that partition did not work on its own terms – it has not created a permanent 'settler' majority in the north. In this regard, it is possible to see a 'democratic' and 'reformist' route to liberation.

More generally, it is possible to suggest that such a question should only set itself a task which it is possible to achieve in the current power matrix. For example, we could suggest from a decolonising perspective that 'what is to be done' in the US is to return the land to native title or in India to end partition between India and Pakistan (and Bangladesh); but neither of these perfectly reasonable options is likely to be achieved at least in the short term. Likewise, in the Irish context, even something as banal as Paul McCartney's request that England 'Give Ireland back to the Irish' might be similarly dismissed as utopian. But given what we said earlier about partition and the two states on the island, it *is* possible to frame an achievable decolonising objective. In the context of the specific forces at play in Ireland in 2020, there is an opportunity for genuine self-determination.

In Ireland, at this juncture, we can answer our own question directly. We can formulate an appropriately succinct answer to the question of what is to be done: *end partition*. This is the key to finishing the revolution. Most importantly, this is not somehow about ending the northern state and absorbing it into the 26 counties. While much positive and interesting work was done around the southern Irish 'Brexit and the Future of Ireland Uniting Ireland & Its People in Peace & Prosperity' report (Tithe an Oireachtas 2017), it still approached reunification from this profoundly unbalanced perspective. Rather ending partition is about dismantling the *two* partitionist states framed by the Government of Ireland Act 1920 and creating a Republic in their place. This process needs to be expedited; to end partition physically, end it politically, end it spiritually. This is Ireland's *purna swaraj*. In this phase of decolonisation, this is the target: everything else is tactical or strategic in relation to this goal.

Of course, this ending of partition is not just an outcome from a border poll – it is a process. In other words, the ending of partition and the reunification of Ireland must be framed as a decolonisation *project*. Its conclusion will mark the end of the first phase of decolonisation in Ireland – the point which India reached in 1947, South Africa in 1994 and Hong Kong in 1997. Crucially in terms of our earlier trialectic, the key elements of Irishness – north, south and diaspora – will each have a specific role to play in this project. Beyond these broad framing perspectives, however, it is a project in which every Irish person has her or his part of the play. It has political, economic, cultural dimensions. All of these intersect in much the same way as the same elements did before 1916-21 – across the IRB, the Gaelic League, the Volunteers, the GAA, the Abbey theatre, Cumann na mBan and so on.

In Ireland, our analysis on the outworking of colonialism has focused on the states that emerged from partial and interminable decolonisation. Craigavon famously awaited the judgment of history on the two states that emerged from partition – one 'Protestant' the other 'Catholic'. In this regard, the Catholic version – for all its deserved criticism appears considerably more successful. Northern Ireland has never worked for its Catholic population – indeed it was set up not to work for them. But increasingly it does not work for its Protestants – there is no starker metonym for this failure than the ongoing troubles of what remains of its totemic 'Protestant' firms – Harland and Wolff and Shorts. This is a reminder that there is a serious state-building project ahead in Ireland. A new state has to be built that reflects the idea of the Republic rather than the poor double dealing of the Southern and Northern Irelands created by partition and the Government of Ireland Act in 1920. Of course, this immediately presents a second-tier question to what is to be done – who is going to do it? Many of the Irish decolonising organisations are long gone – but the relevant question is how are their equivalent constituencies to be reenergised or reconstituted? And of course, there are other groups who were not obviously in the mix a century ago who could be mobilised now, such as those active on sexual politics and disability rights – including, of course, all the 'new Irish'.

This also provokes a focused political challenge. What kind of *politics* might end partition and re-envision a united Ireland? Traditionally, as we have seen, this political project reached its apogee in the late nineteenth century in the Parnellite 'popular front'.

At this point quite different strands of political action – insurrectionary movements, mass mobilisation and representative parliamentary intervention – worked in synergy. Of course, this optimistic template seems some distance from the reality of contemporary Irish politics, north and south of the border. As the tectonic shifts we have identified begin to impact, however, all three strands of Irish political discourse – unionism, nationalism, and republicanism – have been fundamentally unsettled.

This only hints at the real shift within contemporary republicanism. The most obvious revision for the republican movement is that it ditched insurrection as a core principle and practice along the way. Arguably the most traditional republican trope of all has been the commitment to armed struggle. Moreover, the use and principle of insurrectionary violence was obviously central to 1916 and the revolutionary surge that followed it. However, we argue that this too needs to be read as an issue of practice rather than principle. Our wider review of resistance to colonialism helps put this in context. If one truth emerges from the engagement with the history of colonialism and imperialism it is the ubiquity of political violence on all sides. Concomitantly there is little glory in the violence used on either side. In other words, from this perspective anti-imperialist political violence is a tactical question – does it work? We maintain that at this moment in Ireland, it does not, and it will not. But neither is it our job to join in a chorus of condemnation of other people's political choices. Our broader review of anti-imperialist strategy reminds us that opposition to anti-imperialist violence treads a fine line between principle and pacification.

We also would make a broader point on this. We spent some time in discussion of the MacSwiney principle. It bears emphasis that the colonised already bear an unequal share in the suffering attendant upon both colonial violence itself as well as resistance to colonialism. The recent Irish conflict was tiny compared to other colonial conflicts. But the period of the 'troubles' provides some terrible examples of the cost of war on all sides. Any accounting for this conflict needs to acknowledge this cost. Perhaps the relative size of the conflict makes this kind of accounting at least possible. Thus, from *Lost Lives* (Thornton et al. 2004) through *Children of the Revolution* (Rolston 2011) to *Children of the Troubles* (Duffy and McClements 2019) there exists a burgeoning literature that reminds us of the terrible price of war anywhere – and more particularly its profound consequences in Ireland. We remain personally convinced of the correctness of the strategy of non-violence in the coming times. We are therefore at pains to emphasise that our critical analysis of the continuing legacies of colonialism in Ireland should not be read as an endorsement of any return to armed struggle. For us, the key lesson of the Fenians was that it is sometimes sensible to forgo the principle of insurrection precisely because there are other paths to self-determination.

All this suggests that the coming times require something beyond a studied reference to the republican canon. In this regard, we suggest that any broader rejuvenated republicanism cannot depend on Sinn Féin alone. Indeed, the very notion of *ourselves alone* is no longer a progressive strategy – if it ever was. In other words, it requires a bolder popular front strategy to take us towards reunification. As we have suggested, the historical model for this is there in the Parnellite 'popular front'. This opens up the prospect of a whole new continuum of broader republican thinking from Fintan O'Toole to the politics of the 'dissidents'.[24] This should release a world of engagement with the question of what a new republic might – and should – look like. This sets the context for the *possibility* of a new popular front – a contemporary 'new departure'.

This approach presupposes that the 26 counties needs to decolonise as much as the six counties. The people of the 26 counties still must address the question of how it is to make the transition from Free State to Republic. It is this element that will meet most Free State/white dominion resistance – it will face the combined power of 'southern nationalism'. But it remains true that the republic abolished in 1921 has never been reinstated and its promise remains completely unfulfilled. Self-determination can only mean the self-determination of the Irish people *as a whole* – in other words, the 26-county state should disappear alongside the six-county state at the point of any future act of self-determination. Moreover, as we have insisted, the shape of the 26 counties is a colonial one not an anti-colonial one, its borders clearly defined by the Government of Ireland Act. More than this, the state formation itself was also shaped in more profound ways in just the same fashion. It was not an alternative to colonialism but rather the least that colonialism had to give to maintain white dominion – the minimum in area, the minimum in separation, the minimum in autonomy.

So, the focus should not be how to reform the political infrastructure of the 26-county state but rather, what is the model for the reunified state? And what best practice might be drawn from other post-colonial and formally partitioned polities? The broad parameters of this discussion can be immediately anticipated. Clearly the state would be reunified and republican. This starting point raises a series of challenges in terms of law, landownership and citizenship. There is an obvious question of whether this would be a centralised or federal state. Most immediately, however, is the question of a politics that both accepts and anticipates this endpoint. This notion of post-colonial *reconstruction* is a useful end by way of conclusion. While the Irish cannot and should not live as if colonialism had not happened, it is possible to aspire to a state which draws on this history to construct something better. It evokes a commitment to a politics of transformation. In terms of decolonisation, we might suggest that this prospect is simply but powerfully expressed by the late Alasdair Gray's maxim that we should, 'work as if we live in the early days of a better nation'.[25]

The first response to the question of what is to be done is to take Irish history

---

[24] Fintan O'Toole's *Enough is Enough* (2010) helps put some of this in perspective. His recent work provides a radical revision of the 26-county state but not the republic. Our point is, of course, that, while O'Toole's analysis provides plenty of food for thought for radical democratic renewal of this state formation, the 'Southern Ireland' state itself is part of the problem.

[25] Gray provided both a nationalist and an internationalist variant – later versions are rendered 'Work as if you live in the early days of a better *world*' (McGrath 2013).

seriously. We have suggested that the Irish revolution was unfinished in a way that was uniquely stultifying; that had profound and terrible consequences for the people of Ireland; that – as Connolly so accurately anticipated – partition created a context in which progressive forces in Ireland were specifically undermined and repressed. There is a range of other possible interventions which help with the broader process of coming to terms with Ireland's colonial history and contemporary legacies.[26] Alongside the need for a repositioning of Irishness within the diaspora, there is a broad need to interrogate Irishness within Ireland itself, north and south. The legacies of colonial expropriation and racism and sectarianism can be finally excised – or at least properly confronted as a prelude to their being excised.

Of course, it isn't just Ireland that has survived colonialism but most of the world. Thus, we need to end by reconnecting the question of Ireland in the coming times with the legacy of the broader injustices outlined at the start of our analysis. Any project for a decolonised Ireland has to ask how any new Ireland 'fits' in terms of the broader world. There can be no such thing as anti-imperialism in one country. Thus, the end of British colonisation in Ireland is part of a broader struggle. To put it simply, it is impossible to be on the 'right' side in Ireland and the 'wrong' side elsewhere. It is important to position any new Irish state – and the broader reality of Irishness – within a broader anti-imperialist worldview. Any new Ireland should be measured by whether it does right not just by Irish people but by the rest of the world, particularly in solidarity with other victims/survivors of colonialism.

This is also about rebuilding relationships *between* colonised people because, as we have already documented, empire operated routinely and definitively by divide and rule. From first to last, it mobilised different colonised peoples in different ways – Irish 'tommies' to conquer and repress Indians, Indian indentured workers to displace enslaved Africans, African 'Buffalo soldiers' to participate in the genocide of the Native Americans, Gurkhas to reclaim the Malvinas for the UK and so on and on. This deliberate strategy has left huge reservoirs of resentment and a need for reconciliation and reparation. Primo Levi provides a profound meditation on this dynamic, albeit out of another episode of European shame. As a Holocaust survivor, he conceptualised the 'grey zone' – the situation of those, 'who in some measure,

---

[26] One striking conclusion is that decolonisation helps to give England back to the English. In other words, Irish disengagement will help all of those trapped within the Union to deconstruct Britishness. Part of this process must be a recognition of how deeply embedded colonial tropes are within contemporary British – and more particularly English – society. Brexit has already helped to expose some of the more self-satisfied myths of British multiculturalism and liberalism. The appeal to racism that could be mobilised by the Tory 2005 election slogan, 'Are you thinking what we are thinking?', is at least easier to trace amid post-Brexit xenophobia. Still, basic truths regarding the British Empire remain unacknowledged: Gibraltar is not a colony; Winston Churchill was not racist or imperialist but 'the greatest Briton of all time'. The most immediate manifestation of this unionist/imperial rapprochement saw the DUP in government with the supposedly detoxified Tories. More generally, however, it emerges that Ulster unionism is much closer to British/English nationalism than most British would countenance. If the consequence of finishing the revolution is to break up the Union, then there will be the welcome – if also unintended – consequence of freeing other people, including the English, from its suffocating and reactionary embrace. In this context, the English need to experience something like the German denazification. The English need to confront their imperial legacy as much for their own sakes as for anyone else's.

perhaps with good intention, collaborated with … authority'. Levi drew on his own survivor status to theorise this painful location of people who were also victims and survivors:

> [This grey zone] constituted a phenomenon of fundamental importance for the historian, the psychologist, and the sociologist. There is not a prisoner who does not remember this and who does not remember his amazement at the time: the first threats, the first insults, the first blows came not from the SS but from other prisoners, from 'colleagues', from those mysterious personages who nevertheless wore the same striped tunic that they, the new arrivals, had just put on. (Levi 1989: 20)

A similar 'grey zone' runs through any moral accounting of empire. Whatever else can be taken from history, there should not be an expectation to find simple opportunities for virtue signalling. Irish people 'collaborated' with empire in a host of ways – with racism, antisemitism, gombeenism and corruption. In other words, Ireland – like the rest of the colonised world – must confront itself as much as its coloniser in any attempt to address the legacy of colonialism.

Most obviously of all, this raises the enduring question of economic justice. We have already traced the colonial legacy at the heart of contemporary capitalism. While colonialism carried with it a nihilist destructiveness – most terribly registered in the genocides we have traced – it was primarily interested in exploitation rather than destruction *per se*. In other words, it ordered the world in the interests of a tiny minority of the citizens of that world. This is perhaps its most continuing legacy. It is illustrative to note that *loot* is a Hindi word – one of the many things that was appropriated from India under the shadow of colonialism. Markets and commodities – from enslaved people to opium to guano – institutionalised inequality across empire, just as today the products are diamonds, palm oil and cadmium. Economic justice must unpack the capital logic of imperial accumulation. Reparations should, of course, play a part in this. But more profoundly – if the world is to become postcolonial it will have to correct the deep imbalances that still characterise the differences between 'north' and 'south', or 'the West' and the 'rest' – the differences between the rich and the poor across the world. These differences were fundamentally embedded by the colonial process.

Empire consummated the marriage of theft and violence. Furthermore, it perfected the representation of this abomination as both virtuous and inevitable. In this sense colonialism and imperialism did 'make' the modern world – and much of what is wrong with it. It is, of course, one final act of colonial hubris to claim that the British Empire did this all on its own. But, in concert, this *was* an 'achievement' of European power against the rest of the world. The European empires did make the world – not so much in their own image as into a system of dependency and inequality that endures.

Thus, a toxic combination of booty capitalism and militaristic bullying became normalised as both the way things are, and the way things should be. The collapse of the Soviet bloc appeared to 'end history' – at this point there was no alternative, and, to paraphrase Mitchel's (1913: 48) assessment of English colonialism, capitalism had become 'resistless and therefore righteous'. This is the broader world in which Ireland must attempt to finish the revolution. It is too easy, however, to characterise this reality simplistically as Trumpism because it is a wider and more complex phenomenon than simply boorishness and racism. Indeed, the brief interregnum between Suez in 1956 and US involvement in Vietnam signals the durability of empire in the post-WWII world. The same approach was evident with Bush and Blair in Afghanistan and continued in Iraq. While Obama undoubtedly gestured a shift in the optics – he became the first *mestizo* leader of a white dominion who *looked* like he might have emerged from the colonised world – the reality reflected more continuity than change.[27]

In other words, we must conclude by insisting that finishing the Irish revolution is a piece of a much bigger jigsaw. Transforming Ireland is only a small part of a much larger project. Any return to 'ourselves alone' places us on the wrong side of the internationalism that characterised the work of Connolly and the wider body of Irish anti-imperialism. Moreover, the resources to do this already exist. Irish America would seem to be the least likely source of such a deconstruction of imperial power alongside the commitment to justice for *all* colonised peoples. Nevertheless, as we have seen, it is named squarely in Patrick Ford's *Criminal History of the British Empire*. Here – out of the diaspora, out of Irish America – emerged an integrated analysis of empire that dismayed empire and imperialists – and spoke truth to power.

Moreover, despite the rush of speaking blarney to power that accompanied the recent election of the 'most Irish' of presidents, Joe Biden, others continue to offer an alternative positioning of contemporary Irishness, even in the US. Thus, Tom Hayden suggested: 'We have a unique role in reshaping American society to empathize with the world's poor, for their story is the genuine story of the Irish'.[28] Thus, Patrick Ford's analysis of the 'criminal history of empire' – written by an Irish person in the heart of the first 'white dominion' and at the apogee of imperialism – holds today: Ireland's struggle against colonialism will only be over when the world's is also finished. Ireland and the Irish people have once again their 'part to play' – but it is a small part in a much bigger picture. This is less of a denouement than an ongoing struggle. Despite all the determined revisionism that has taken place since the end of the first phase of decolonisation, neither colonialism nor imperialism can be rehabilitated. If our journey through Irish history teaches us anything at all, it confirms the simple observation that there is no acceptable face of colonialism – in Ireland or anywhere else – unless you can count its death mask as such.

---

[27] Thus, strikingly, when Obama was elected President, his consequent departure from the US Senate rendered this a completely white space once again (McVeigh 2010: 108).

[28] Tom Hayden (1939-2016) was a leading US anti-war and civil rights activist, authoring the seminal 'Port Huron Statement' of Students for a Democratic Society and standing trial as one of the 'Chicago Seven'. His *Irish on the Inside: In Search of the Soul of Irish America* (2001) is a radical rereading of contemporary Irishness in the US. Hayden also memorably provided his personal take on the notion of 'treason to whiteness'. In 2007, he greeted his son's marriage to his Black partner, as 'another step in a long-term goal of mine: the peaceful, non-violent disappearance of the white race'.

Section IV

Coda: the carnival is over

Partition would mean a carnival of reaction both North and South, would set back the wheels of progress, would destroy the oncoming unity of the Irish labour movement and paralyse all advanced movements while it lasted. —James Connolly, 1914

There is no future in England's Dreaming. —John Lydon, 1977

As we were completing this book in the first half of 2020, the Covid-19 pandemic began. The consequences affected the whole world, Ireland included, leading to the rethinking of old patterns and certainties. At the same time, the experience of the virus served to underline and emphasise many of the tropes and conclusions we articulate in the book.

There is a profusion of hyperbole around amid the Covid-19 pandemic. But it is probably fair to suggest that the advent of coronavirus has been a defining life experience for *everyone* who has lived through it. At one level it undoubtedly invoked the 'great chain of being' that is humanity. More so even than world wars, this experience has connected almost everybody on the planet. If nothing else, it has constituted a global social experiment. Thus the notion of 'social distancing' has become not just a means of reducing viral transmission but also a metaphor for the severing of the most basic networks of human relationships in ways that have been both sociologically fascinating and politically disquieting. Moreover, it seems inevitable that the whole world will have to live with the consequences of this experiment – economic, social, political, and legal – for generations. Definitively, the apparatus of repression was vastly increased globally – as lockdown metastasised seamlessly into curfew.

The pandemic, however, also *undermined* many of the traditional modalities of repression. Virus-laden aircraft carriers – formerly the advanced guard of contemporary imperialism, now latter-day coffin ships – have become a metaphor for something in these new times. Moreover, the barracks is now one of the prime spaces for a pandemic 'hotspot' – taking its place alongside the care home and the prison to constitute a Foucauldian trinity if ever there was one. So, there is no doubting that the virus took the wind out of the sails of much of the repressive state apparatus. Which begs the obvious question of 'What is the state going to do now?' If it cannot repress very effectively – and it can supply PPE (personal protection equipment) even less effectively – what is the role of the state post-pandemic? Of course, some states have proved more resilient than others. The worst of all were those that had seen any semblance of a welfare state hollowed out first by Reaganism and Thatcherism and confirmed by their sad echoes in Trumpism and Johnsonism. Here was the definitive example of tragedy repeated as farce. In recent decades there has been a partial 'withering away of the state,' not as a Marxist utopia but rather as capitalist dystopia. Thus, as we ponder Irish futures, there is little doubt that the whole world will have to come to a reckoning with the shortcomings of the contemporary state so ruthlessly exposed by the pandemic. Contrariwise, of course, the pandemic has also profoundly undermined traditional modalities of resistance – organisation, mobilisation, rallying and marching. Thus, it seems likely that *everyone* – privileged and subaltern, oppressor and oppressed – will have to recalibrate in the aftermath. Any meditation upon Ireland's future must now take place in the wider context of these new times.

If the coronavirus pandemic has an overriding lesson, however, it is that there is nothing 'natural' about catastrophe. It is not necessary to subscribe to any conspiracy theories about Bill Gates or laboratories in Wuhan to conclude that human agency created the context for the pandemic. This was most markedly evident in the broader relentless destruction of the planet that provides the backdrop to the whole affair. This was manifest immediately in the omnivorous wet markets that apparently generated the species-hopping virus and then compounded in the intensive fur farms that allowed it to mutate. But this is equally – and more broadly – evident in a globalised world that had lost any sense of distance – social, economic, and political. In this regard the moment represents the final triumph of the colonial project – every space has been occupied. Thus, globalisation ensured that this would be a truly worldwide phenomenon. Human agency also created the context for the *management* of the pandemic. It was not a contradiction that the same forces that so globalised and integrated the world created the context in which more people were more isolated than ever before in human history.

This issue of agency generated a haunting familiarity for Irish people. As was said of *An Gorta Mór*, 'God sent the blight but the English created the famine'. In other words, in the middle of all the contemporary – intensely ideological – efforts to insist of the pandemic that 'power is no protection from harm', there is an over-riding obligation to *sociologise* the context for our current catastrophe. Where did class, race and gender disappear to amid the appeals to universality? It helps to remember that the notion that 'we are all in it together' is the first refuge of the establishment in a crisis. If at first the virus seemed to speak truth to power in its exposure of the vulnerability of powerful men, it also reminded how other more traditional inequalities are reproduced through such a phenomenon. Thus, the old, the poor, the indigent, people of colour were all specifically vulnerable[1] – and its ongoing impact across the Majority World

---

[1] As of June 2020 a quarter of Covid-19 casualties in the US were African Americans, who make up 13 percent of the population. In the UK, Black people were twice as likely to catch the virus.

remains incalculable. In this regard, the advent of the virus was an historical moment that *accentuated* differences of entitlement and privilege much more than it dissolved them. It will leave behind it a world more rather than less unequal.

In this context, a focus on the contemporary lessons of *An Gorta Mór* is apposite. Amid all the horror of 2020 and 2021, it is sobering to remember that the Irish – along with many other colonised peoples, of course – have endured things far more terrible. As the English struggled to find a comparable experience – ultimately harking back to the Black Death – it was striking that the lessons from the Irish half of the 'precious union' were rarely evoked. This even though *An Gorta Mór* saw the 'disappearance' – through starvation, disease and emigration – of *half* the Irish population, upwards of four million people. Nor indeed was it remembered that the Irish population – approaching nine million in the 1840s – has *never* recovered from that catastrophe. This decimation took place within the 'precious union' and under the direct rule of 'the greatest empire ever': not on its doorstep but rather *inside* the constitutional formation created by union and empire. In other words, the Irish catastrophe played itself out at the centre of the richest, most powerful political formation on the earth at the time. This was a formation that had made the Irish people its *subjects* – against their expressed will – through the Act of Union a generation before.

Thus, *An Gorta Mór* must remain the moral and political compass in the task of making sense of – and reconstruction after – the Covid-19 pandemic. This encourages a further revaluation of the notion of the famine as genocide. This question can be approached from a slightly different vantage post-pandemic. In assessing the efficiency or otherwise of empires to deal with catastrophe, the focus should be less on their *intent* than on their *capacity* to address a natural disaster. From this perspective, the 'greatest empire in the world' had – unambiguously – the capacity to prevent the famine in Ireland between 1845-50 – *if it had wanted to*. It had the infrastructure to prevent starvation in place in 1845. It did this successfully for two years until a change of government policy saw relief withdrawn. The British response was initially relatively benign – programmes of work, soup kitchens, the importation of Indian meal all served to mediate the failure of one, albeit subsistence, crop. But political ideology replaced this intervention with colonial *laissez faire*. The decision was made that no relief from starvation would be resourced from imperial funds – this cost was to be placed solely on Irish taxpayers and the absentee landlord class. Moreover, the 'Gregory Clause' ensured that no relief would be provided for anyone holding more than a quarter of an acre of land. The abnegation of imperial responsibility was as absolute as it was brutal. And the consequences for Ireland and the Irish people were more terrible than the coronavirus pandemic. In this context the *intent* to wipe people out – to genocide – is neither here nor there for those people who are disappeared. In other words, from the perspective of those who starved and died of fever and emigrated, *laissez faire* is itself an intent.[2]

---

[2] The parallels with the pandemic are clear. Modelling by Imperial College concluded that, had lockdown in England and Wales occurred one week earlier, casualty figures would have been halved (BBC News 2020f).

Nevertheless, the Irish endured that catastrophe – often far from honourably – but they endured. In its aftermath, those who survived went on to envision a different and better future for Irishness. This helps put the current experience of pandemic in context. Of course, there has been a dangerous virus at the centre of it – but how society responded was a consequence of years of political and economic *agency*. The experience confirms that there is a price to pay if you hollow out the welfare state and deny even the existence of 'society'. There is also a counterfactual history to ponder. If all the resources that were spent on arms and wars and weapons of mass destruction since 1945 had been spent on a health infrastructure, the outcome would have been different for the whole world. In Ireland this time it is hardly fair to blame all of this on the English – imagine if the untold wealth generated in the Celtic Tiger had been ploughed into building a democratic and resilient national health and social care system across Ireland, north and south.

Thus, the contemporary resonance is plain enough. As with *An Gorta Mór*, the Covid-19 pandemic juxtaposed a natural phenomenon with a very human-made context. For all the ideological appeals to universality, the pandemic carried the brutal question, 'Who shall be saved?'. Now as human beings we face the task of reconstruction from a similar perspective – who should benefit? Of course, the pandemic has spotlighted the interconnectedness of all humanity – but the challenges of reconstruction for democratic structures on the island remain specific and national. Turning to the lessons of the Irish experience of colonialism, the framing narrative remains starkly unchanged since the 1840s. As we attempt to rebuild Irish society, do we want to be subjects or citizens? And what kind of political formation do we want to rebuild – empire or republic?

The wider context will also be different, of course. Around the world a massively ramped up emergency state apparatus has emerged.[3] The choice between the present imperial structures and a fairer, more democratic world remains the key one for us all.

In the more immediate context of Ireland and its relationship to the UK state, the whole management of the crisis has also a profoundly reactionary and unionist dimension to it – both locally and in terms of the whole British state. If it had not been so serious, the retreat of the BBC into censorship of 'bad news' and the desperate attempt to find compensating good news that would echo the demand of the British Queen for 'national self-discipline' – after she had left London for her second home in the suburbs. It was as if the criminal shortage of PPE could be disguised by a daily dose of appeals to British nationalism repackaged as 'commonsense'. Indeed, if the situation had not been so serious, the innumerable press briefings from members of the British royal family (hardly renowned for their scientific expertise) would have seemed more appropriate as a running gag in Monty Python.

There was also comic dimension to such loyalty in Northern Ireland. One poster in east Belfast in support of frontline workers reiterated widespread popular support

---

[3] See the revealing and disturbing statistics collected regularly by The Armed Conflict Location and Event Data Project's Covid-19 Disorder Tracker – https://acleddata.com/analysis/covid-19-disorder-tracker/

for the NHS, but added, without any hint of postmodernist irony: 'No surrender to Covid-19'. More problematically, there is a local version of the global phenomenon of the pandemic being used as a crude excuse for repression and authoritarianism (McBride 2020). Moreover, even Sinn Féin's participation in the power-sharing Northern Ireland Executive did not prevent the Department of Health (NI) aping Westminster policy – or lack of it. The island of Ireland offered a perfect experimental laboratory in relation to the pandemic. The government in the South moved more quickly on testing and tracing, as well as lockdown, than the government in the North. Despite the obvious opportunities for an organic, all-Ireland approach in relation to health, however, there has been a reinforcement of both partition and partitionism – particularly in the south. In this post-pandemic context, a meaningless and artificial border has assumed new and real qualities. It was striking – despite the Sinn Féin surge in the 2019 general election – that when a coalition government was finally cobbled together in June 2020, it had nothing to say about the six counties *at all*.

The notion, however, that the consequences of the pandemic would be *inherently* reactionary for the world all changed following the police murder of George Floyd in Minneapolis. Suddenly, people around the world felt compelled to resist once again; and the prism through which this resistance – and the pandemic itself – would be understood was racism and colonialism. This has been, of course, a complex and sometimes contradictory moment. Outside the US there has been a great deal of displacement going on under variations of the theme of 'Why is racism so much worse in the US?'. On the ground, however, – from Canada to Australia to Belgium – most people have been able to juxtapose police violence in the US with their own variant of institutional racism. Neither was this need to situate resistance lost on observers in the UK or Ireland. As traced across our narrative in some detail, it was the English variant of colonialism that constituted white dominion in the US in the first place. The vast bulk of African Americans exist in the US because of English colonial enslavement. In other words, it was unlikely that the attempts of the British establishment to frame the Black Lives Matter (BLM) protests as a reaction to something that happened in the US would be entirely successful. For all the bizarre contradictions – including the British police hierarchy expressing their solidarity with Black Lives Matter – a broader deconstruction of imperialism began to appear in both Britain and Ireland. This is a moment in which the broader history and legacy of colonialism that we frame in this book to help situate our Irish experience, is re-centred within broader, transnational progressive politics.

Thus, the focus of finishing the revolution in Ireland resonates with the wider zeitgeist. Moreover, this has a specific resonance in the north of Ireland. In this BLM moment, the multiple synergies in terms of Irish history should not escape notice. Given the hegemony of good relations approaches to Irish history, it is difficult to address any of the deaths in 'the troubles' without unleashing a depressing sequence of 'whataboutery'. Nevertheless, Irish history is peppered with the routine murder of unambiguously innocent Catholics by the state. Moreover, the Northern Ireland state was born out of the routine practice of killings by the Black and Tans and the RIC. The state was consolidated through police murder – most notoriously of the McMahon family in 1922. And as the whole of Ireland struggles with the outworking of its colonial history, it is salutary to remember how central police killing was to the most recent conflict. The 'troubles' began in 1969 with the police killing of Sammy Devenny, beaten by a police riot squad inside his own home in Derry. The first child killed in 'the troubles' was Patrick Rooney, shot dead in his own home by a police tracer bullet. More surprisingly, perhaps, the first British soldier to die was Hugh McCabe – shot by the police while on leave. In other words, in a world newly sensitised to racist, colonial policing, the positioning of Ireland assumes even greater relevance.

As we move towards reunification and finishing the revolution, it bears emphasis that this history remains unresolved. Families across Northern Ireland continue to live with the legacy of this form of dominion. We must insist – in solidarity with rather than opposition to the *zeitgeist* – that these lives too *mattered*. If nothing else, this confirms the importance of a northern perspective on any attempt to situate – and delimit – contemporary Irishness. This analysis has insisted that we have some distance to go to reach anything approaching a post-colonial condition. Now, we must approach this all from a markedly different position in 2021, in a moment constituted by the complex interfacing of Covid and BLM.

So, where do we go from here? Our most immediate conclusion has been that Ireland is on the cusp of epochal change and that every Irish person should begin to decide how to respond to this. Old certainties are collapsing. Most immediately the overlapping state formations that both frame and divide Ireland and Irishness – EU, UK and NI – are all either disintegrating or reconstituting. It appears inevitable that a new Irish post-partition state and social formation will emerge from this upheaval. This may evolve slowly over the coming times or it may progress very quickly as these old structures collapse precipitously. Either way, it is crucial for the democratic project that this becomes a liberatory rather than a reactionary process in Ireland. It must become an act of self-determination by the Irish people rather than one final imperial intervention by the British state. In other words, it must be about decolonisation rather than white dominion. At its core, our analysis seeks to repudiate the process of reconciliation with imperialism and reaction and replace this with the challenge of re-envisioning the project of a free, democratic, Irish Republic – to finish the revolution.

We have been at pains to emphasise that this is not a free choice. Our self-determination will always be framed and structured – and sometimes also determined – by wider social structures and processes. As with any other people, notions of Ireland and Irishness cannot but be constituted in the tension between that which is universal in humanity and that which is local and personal. To contradict one of our least favourite philosophers Margaret Thatcher, there is such a thing as society and it both permeates and transcends ideas of nationhood and statehood in ways that make essentialist discourse on these impossible. But this does not mean that either national identity or statehood disappear from broader discussions of self-determination. From this perspective, there needs to be an insistence that the kinds of questions that *are* addressed in terms of notions of nationhood and statehood have always been and will remain about *politics*.

Crucially, therefore, for Irish people – as for anyone else – the choice between Empire and Republic is a *political decision* not a national or racial imperative. On this there is no better example than the difference between siblings John and Charlotte French – arguably part of the diaspora, certainly scions of a leading Irish Ascendancy family who lived through the apogee of the British Empire. Despite their shared upbringing, their political biographies diverged starkly – albeit *both* siblings were ultimately intimidated from their homes in Ireland under the threat of violence. The brother became Field Marshal John French. He served in several colonial campaigns that have featured in our narrative – including the failed relief of Gordon in Khartoum and in the Boer war. He became Chief of the British Imperial Staff. He was, however, forced to resign following the Curragh Mutiny after promising that the army would not be used to coerce Ulster unionists into a Home Rule Ireland. He was commander of the British Expeditionary Force sent to Europe in August 1914 at the start of WWI. French returned to England to be appointed Commander in Chief of the British Home Forces in December 1915. In January 1916, he was ennobled as Viscount French of Ypres and of High Lake in the County of Roscommon.

At the end of WWI, French became Lord Lieutenant of Ireland, a position he held throughout much of the Tan War. His principal strategy in Ireland was to implement martial law as ruthlessly as possible and he was immediately responsible for the outrages and reprisals that characterised this stage of the conflict. French retired from the British Army in 1921. He had hoped to spend his retirement in Ireland, but his safety could not be guaranteed given that he was being actively targeted by the IRA. Following his death in 1925, thousands of people filed past his coffin as it lay in state at Westminster Abbey. French's remains were escorted by a military procession of six battalions of infantry, one battery of artillery, eight squadrons of cavalry and a detachment from the Royal Navy. In death as in life it would be difficult to find a more archetypal British imperialist – aristocratic, reactionary, militarist, and unionist. In a sense there is nothing particularly unexpected about this. French made his life choices and lived his life much as we might expect of anyone from his privileged class and colonial position (Holmes 2004).

And yet … French's sister Charlotte was Madame Despard: sometime Sinn Féiner, suffragist, novelist, vegetarian, anti-vivisectionist and communist (Linklater 1980; Mulvihill 1989). She was a delegate to the Second International and a leading member of the Women's Freedom League. Despard was also a committed Irish republican – although her support for revolutionary violence was mediated by her relationship with Gandhi. During the Tan War, she formed the Women Prisoners' Defence League with Maud Gonne to support republican prisoners. Her relationship with her brother ended abruptly – not unreasonably we might observe from the remove of a century – when in 1919 she applauded the IRA attempt on his life as Lord Lieutenant. As a member of Cumann na mBan she opposed the Anglo-Irish Treaty and was imprisoned by the Free State government during the Irish Civil War. After partition, she continued her radical activism. She was the bane of the Free State establishment and was burned out of her house in Dublin by Blue Shirts in the 1930s. She moved to Belfast, inspired by the Outdoor Relief strike, and later retired to her home *Nead na Gaoithe* in Whitehead, County Antrim. Charlotte Despard is buried in the Republican Plot at Glasnevin Cemetery.

The implication of this vignette for contemporary Ireland is simple. The politics of Empire and Republic are undoubtedly underpinned by gender, race and class – but they are also *choices*. As we enter a new period of political realignment in Ireland, north and south, *everyone* has a choice in terms of the side of history they want to be on. As Bobby Sands reminded us on his deathbed, everybody has his or her part to play. Of course, Marx was right when he said that people do not make history as they please. In the same vein Marx reminded us that the tradition of all dead generations weighs like a nightmare on the brains of the living. Put simply, it is impossible to simply *think* oneself out of one historical context and into another.

With a satisfying synchronicity, this notion of 'dead generations' is invoked in the first line of the Proclamation. Whether by accident or design, this suggests an antithetical role for the angel of history. In this context these dead generations provide the legitimacy of Irish nationhood. This invites us – like the Italian revolutionary Foscolo in the *Dei Sepolcri* – to invoke a pantheon of revolutionary icons in any hour of need. This is a superficially appealing prospect. Who among us would resist the offer of such help at this critical juncture? Imagine if the generation of 1916 could be mobilised in 2021 – what would James Connolly and Maude Gonne, Pádraig Pearse and Con Markiewicz bring to the resolution of our contemporary crisis? Imagine if a host of other activists – from Lalor and Speranza to the Parnell siblings to Bobby Sands and Betty Sinclair – were to return to provide counsel?

In a less elevated form, this is exactly what we have tried to do in our analysis – to draw on Irish history – and particularly those who made sense of that history in different ways – to build the Irish future. This acknowledged, we must remember that it is up to us – living, breathing Irish people, north and south and in the diaspora – to finish the revolution. At the end of the day, the Republic should be made for and by *daoine iseal* – ordinary people. In this context, we might turn Marx on his head and insist that, while people do not make history as they please or under self-selected circumstances, they *do* make their own history. If our analysis is broadly correct, Pearse's promise will finally be realised in the coming time – *Anois ar theacht an tSamhraidh*. But history can only do so much – it is up to us to build the Republic.

Bibliography

Acheraïou, Amar (2011) *Questioning Hybridity, Postcolonialism and Globalization*. New York: Springer

Agamben, Giorgio (2005) *States of Exception*. Chicago: University of Chicago Press

Agnew, Jean (1999) *Belfast Merchant Families in the 17th Century*. Dublin: Four Courts Press

Akenson, D.H. (1997) *If the Irish Ran the World*. Liverpool: Liverpool University Press

Aldous, Richard and Niamh Puirseil (2008) *We Declare: Landmark Documents in Ireland's History*. London: Quercus

An Phoblacht / Republican News (2009) 'Sinn Féin minister meets Government and guerrillas', 29 January

Anderson, Benedict (1991) *Imagined Communities: Reflections on the Origin and Spread of Nationalism*. London: Verso

Anderson, Carol (2018) 'Voting while black: the racial injustice that harms our democracy', *Guardian*, 7 June

Anderson, Carol (2019) 'Republicans Want a White Republic. They'll Destroy America to Get It', *Time*, July 17

Anderson, Mark (2013) 'Hanged on a comma: drafting can be a matter of life and death', 14 October; https://ipdraughts.wordpress.com/2013/10/14/hanged-on-a-comma-drafting-can-be-a-matter-of-life-and-death/

Anderson, Robert Nelson (1996) 'The Quilombo of Palmares: A New Overview of a Maroon State in Seventeenth-Century Brazil', *Journal of Latin American Studies* 29(3): 545-566

Arnold, Bruce (2019) 'Bought by Brussels, little Ireland's ridiculous leaders have landed it in a Brexit crisis', *Daily Telegraph*, 31 July

Ashcroft, Bill, Gareth Griffiths and Helen Tiffen (2007) *Post-colonial studies: the key concepts*. London: Routledge

Atkinson, Neill (2003) *Adventures in democracy: a history of the vote in New Zealand*. Dunedin: University of Otago Press in association with the Electoral Commission

Balibar, Etienne (2004) 'Etienne Balibar and Antonio Negri on the constitution of Europe; Notes from a seminar in Rome, June 2004', http://www.generation-online.org/p/fpbalibar3.htm

Balint, Jennifer, Julie Evans and Nesam McMillan (2014) 'Rethinking Transitional Justice, Redressing Indigenous Harm: A New Conceptual Approach', *International Journal of Transitional Justice* 8: 194–216

Bardon, Jonathan (2001) *A History of Ulster*. Belfast: Blackstaff Press

Barnard, Francis (1888) *Strongbow's Conquest of Ireland*. New York: David Nutt

Barry, John and Hiram Morgan (eds) (2013) *Great Deeds in Ireland: Richard Stanihurst's De Rebus in Hibernia Gestis*. Cork: Cork University Press

Bartlett, Thomas (ed) (1998) *Life of Theobald Wolfe Tone*. Dublin: Lilliput Press

Barton, Brian (2002) *From Behind a Closed Door*. Belfast: Blackstaff Press

BBC News (2011) 'Tom Elliott facing action over Ronan Kerr funeral', 3 June

BBC News (2014) 'Thatcher and Fitzgerald talks: redrawing of Northern Ireland border was discussed', 27 December

BBC News (2015), 'Race activist Rachel Dolezal: "I identify as black"', 16 June

BBC News (2016) 'Obama hits back at Boris Johnson's alleged smears', 22 April

BBC News (2018a) 'Grenfell Tower bonfire: Police search property', 6 November

BBC News (2018b) 'Lewes bonfire night effigies include "ghost train"', 6 November

BBC News (2018c) 'State papers: "Catholic majority"', 24 August

BBC News (2018d) 'Bombardier cuts 5000 jobs globally', 8 November

BBC News (2018e) 'New Caledonia: French Pacific territory rejects independence', 4 November

BBC News (2018f) 'Ian Paisley begins House of Commons suspension', 4 September

BBC News (2019a) 'Emma De Souza: Home Office appeal of case is upheld', 14 October

BBC News (2019b) 'Rory McIlroy: World number four 'more likely than not' to play at 2020 Olympics', 14 May

BBC News (2019c) 'Slavery reparations hearing ignites fiery debate in Congress', 19 June

BBC News (2019d) 'St Patrick's Day 2019 celebrated worldwide', 17 March

BBC News (2020a) 'Work 'under way' into Scotland-Northern Ireland bridge feasibility', 10 February

BBC News (2020b) 'Scotland-Northern Ireland bridge: Alister Jack backs tunnel plan', 5 March

BBC News (2020c) 'BBC Sound of 2020: Joy Crookes grabs fourth place', 6 January

BBC News (2020d) 'Apple has €13bn Irish tax bill overturned', 15 July

BBC News (2020e) 'Jessica Krug: George Washington University Professor says she lied about being black', 3 September

BBC News (2020f) 'Coronovirus: "Earlier lockdown would have halved death toll"', 10 June

Beatty, Aidan (2016) 'An Irish Revolution without a Revolution', *Journal of World Systems Research* 22(1): 54-76

Beckett, J.C. (1979) *A Short History of Ireland*. London: Hutchinson

Beckles, Hilary (1990) 'A "Riotous and Unruly Lot": Irish Indentured Servants and Freemen in the English West Indies 1644-1713', *William and Mary Quarterly* 47: 503-522

Begin, Menachem (1951) *The Revolt: Story of the Irgun*. London: W.H. Allen

Bell, Christine and Robbie McVeigh (2016) *A Fresh Start to Equality: the equality impacts of the Stormont House Agreement on the 'two main communities'*. Belfast: Equality Coalition

Bhabha, Homi (1994) *The Location of Culture*. London: Routledge

Blenerhasset, Sir Thomas (1972) *The Plantation of Ulster*. New York: De Capo Press (originally published London 1610)

Bolton, G.C. (1966) *The Passing of the Irish Act of Union: A Study in Parliamentary Politics*. Oxford: Oxford University Press

Booth, Robert (2020) '"Alarming" survey shows UK leading the world in yearning for an empire', *Guardian*, 11 March

Borlase, Edward (1675) *The Reduction of Ireland to the Crown of England*. London: Robert Clavel

Borlase, John (1680) *The History of the Execrable Irish Rebellion*. London: Robert Clavel.

Bowcott, Owen (2011) 'Ministry of Defence says sorry for killing of Majella O'Hare', *Guardian*, 28 March

Boyd, Andrew (1969) *Holy War in Belfast*. Tralee: Anvil Press

Boylan, Ciara (2006) 'Victorian ideologies of improvement: Sir Charles Trevelyan in India and Ireland', in Tadgh Foley and Maureen O'Connor (eds) *Ireland and India: Colonies, Culture and Empire*. Dublin: Irish Academic Press, 167-178

Bradley, Sorcha (2018) 'Rees Mogg passionately defends "WONDERFUL" achievements of British Empire', *Daily Express*, 15 October

Brannigan, Tim (2010) *Where are you Really from?* Belfast: Blackstaff Press

Breac: a digital journal of Irish Studies. University of Notre Dame; https://breac.nd.edu/about/

Brendon, Piers (2008) *The Decline and Fall of the British Empire, 1781-1997*. New York: Knopf

Brennan, Joe (2016) 'Leprechaun economics': EU mission to audit 26% GDP rise', *Irish Times*, 19 August

British and Irish Governments (1993) 'Joint Declaration on Peace: The Downing Street Declaration, Wednesday 15 December 1993'; http://cain.ulst.ac.uk/events/peace/docs/dsd151293.htm

Brittain, Victoria (2001) 'Ben Barka killed with French help', *Guardian*, 2 July

Brittain, Victoria (2011) 'Africa: a continent drenched in the blood of revolutionary heroes', *Guardian*, 17 January

Bueno-Hansen, Pascha (2015) *Feminist and Human Rights Struggles in Peru*. Urbana: University of Illinois Press

Burgess, Paul and Gareth Mulvenna (eds) (2015) *The Contested Identities of Ulster Protestants*. London: Palgrave Macmillan

Burke, Edmund (1834) *Works of Edmund Burke, with a Memoir*, volume 11. New York: George Dearborn

Burke, Peter (2009) *Cultural Hybridity*. Cambridge: Polity Press

Burns, Eleanor (1974) *British Imperialism in Ireland*. Cork: Cork Workers' Club (originally published 1931)

Butler, Hubert (1985) W*olfe Tone and the Common Name of Irishman*. Dublin: Lilliput Press

Cabral, Amilcar (1974) *Revolution in Guinea*. London: Stage 1

Cabral, Amilcar (2016) *Resistance and Decolonization*. Translated by Dan Wood. Lanham, MD: Rowman and Littlefield International

Caherty, Thérèse et al. (eds) (1992) *Is Ireland a Third World Country?* Belfast: Beyond the Pale Publications

Cameron Report (1969) *Disturbances in Northern Ireland*. London: HMSO

Campion, Edmund (1571) 'A History of Ireland', in James P. Myers (ed) (1983) *Elizabethan Ireland: A Selection of Writings by Elizabethan Writers on Ireland*. Hamden, Connecticut: Archon Books

Canny, Nicholas (1973) 'The ideology of English colonisation: from Ireland to America', *William and Mary Quarterly* 30(4): 575-598

Canny, Nicholas (1976) *The Elizabethan Conquest of Ireland: A Pattern Established 1565-76*. Hassocks, Sussex: Harvester Press

Canny, Nicholas (1988) *Kingdom and Colony: Ireland in the Atlantic World 1560-1800*. Baltimore: Johns Hopkins University Press

Canny, Nicholas (1998a) 'England's New World and the Old, 1480s-1630s', in Nicholas Canny (ed) *The Origins of Empire: British Overseas Enterprise to the Close of the Seventeenth Century*. Oxford: Oxford University Press, 148-169

Canny, Nicholas (1998b) *The Origins of Empire: British Overseas Enterprise to the Close of the Seventeeth Century*, Volume One. Oxford: Oxford University Press

Canny, Nicholas (2002) 'What really happened in Ireland in 1641?', in Jane Ohlmeyer (ed) *Ireland from Independence to Occupation*. Cambridge: Cambridge University Press

Carlin, Norah (1987) 'The Levellers and the Conquest of Ireland in 1649', *The Historical Journal* 30(2): 269-288

Carroll, Frances (2016) 'Ireland Among the Nations of the Earth: Ireland's Foreign Relations from 1923 to 1949', *Etudes Irlandaises* 41: 35-52

Carty, Anthony (1999) *Was Ireland Conquered? International Law and the Irish Question*. London: Pluto

Castro, Daniel (2007) *Another Face of Empire: Bartolomé de Las Casas, Indigenous Rights, and Ecclesiastical Imperialism*. Durham, NC: Duke University Press.

Cathcart, Brian (1993) 'South of the Border: What price would the people of the Irish Republic pay for peace?' *Independent*, 12 December

Césaire, Aimé (1955) *Discourse on Colonialism*. New York: Monthy Review Press

Chambers, George (1983) *Faces of Change: the Belfast and Northern Ireland Chambers of Commerce and Industry 1783-1983*. Belfast: Northern Ireland Chamber of Commerce and Industry

Cheng, Vincent J. (1995) *Joyce, Race, and Empire*. Cambridge: Cambridge University Press

Cheng, Vincent J. (2018) *Amnesia and the Nation: History, Forgetting, and James Joyce*. London: Palgrave McMillan

Chichester, Arthur and W.P. (1853) 'Original Documents Illustrative of Irish History. No. 1. Letter from the Lord Deputy, Sir Arthur Chichester, to the Earl of Northampton', *Ulster Journal of Archaeology*, First Series, Vol. 1: 180-183

Churchill, Ward (2004) *Kill the Indian, Save the Man*. San Francisco: City Lights Books

Clarke, Aidan (1986) 'The 1641 Depositions', in Peter Fox (ed) *Treasures of the Library, Trinity*

College Dublin. Dublin: Royal Irish Academy, 111-22

Clayton, Pamela (1996) *Enemies and Passing Friends: Settler Ideologies in Twentieth Century Ulster*. London: Pluto

Clissold, Stephen (1977) *The Barbary Slaves*. London: Elek Books

Coates, Sam (2018) 'Warning of food shortages in Ireland', *Times,* 7 December

Coffey, Thomas (1970) *Agony at Easter*. London: George Harrap and Co.

Cohen, J.M. (1969) *The Four Voyages of Christopher Columbus*. London: Penguin

Collett, Nigel (2005) *The Butcher of Amritsar*. London: Hambleton

Collins, Michael (1968) *The Path to Freedom*. Cork: Mercier Press

Colvin, Ian (1934) *The Life of Lord Carson*, volume two. London: Victor Gollancz Ltd.

Conn, David (2019) 'Three years on, we still need to be told: what does the EU do for us?' *Guardian*, 10 July

Connolly, James (1916) 'Last Statement', https://www.marxists.org/archive/connolly/1916/05/laststat.htm

Connolly, James (1972) *The Reconquest of Ireland*. Dublin: New Books (originally published 1915)

Coogan, Tim Pat (2012) *The Famine Plot: England's Role in Ireland's Greatest Tragedy*. London: St Martin's Press

Cooper, Wayne (1987) *Claude McKay: Rebel Sojourner in the Harlem Renaissance*. Baton Rouge: Louisiana State University Press

Coulter, Carol (1990) *Ireland: Between the First and Third Worlds*. Dublin: Attic Press

Critchley, Julian (1972) *Ireland: A New Partition*. London: Bow Publications

Cronin, David (2017) 'Winston Churchill sent the Black and Tans to Palestine', *Irish Times*, 19 May

Cronin, Sean (1963) *Wolfe Tone*. Dublin: Wolfe Tone Bicentenary

Crowley, John, William J. Smyth and Mike Murphy (eds) (2012) *Atlas of the Great Irish Famine*. New York: New York University Press

Cruz, Eduardo (2010) *The Grand Araucanian Wars (1541-1883) in the Kingdom of Chile*. Bloomington, Indiana: Xlibris

CSO (2016) *Census of Population 2016*. 'Profile 8: Irish Travellers, Ethnicity and Religion'

CSO (2020) *Vital Statistics Yearly Summary*. CSO statistical publication, 29 May

Cultural Studies – Critical Methodologies (2016) Special Issue: Gender, Nation, and Colonialism: Twenty-First Century Connections 16(4)

Curtis, Liz (1984a) *Ireland the Propaganda War*. London: Pluto

Curtis, Liz (1984b) *Nothing but the Same Old Story*. London: Information on Ireland

Curtis, Liz (1994) *The Cause of Ireland*. Belfast, Beyond the Pale Publications

Dabiri, Emma (2020) 'Ruth Negga: "People who say they don't consider skin colour ... are you f**king blind?"', *Irish Times*, 4 July

Dáil Éireann (1921) Volume T. No. 6. 19 December, 'Debate on Treaty'

Dáil Éireann (1928) Volume 22. No. 14. Wednesday, 21 March, 'Review of Prisoners' Cases'

Dáil Éireann (1937) Volume 66. No. 12. 27 April, 'Ceisteanna – Questions. Oral Answers. Representation at Imperial Conference'

Dáil Éireann (1949) Volume 115. 10 May, 'Protest against Partition – Motion'

Dáil Éireann (1972a) Dáil Debates, Volume 260. No. 11. 'Inter-Party Committee on the Implications of Irish Unity'

Dáil Éireann (1972b) Dáil Debates, Volume 267. No 6. 'All-Party Committee on Irish Relations'

Dáil Éireann (1999) Dáil Debate, Volume 50. No. 2, 30 September. 'Private Members' Business. – Ansbacher Accounts: Motion (Resumed)'

Dáil Éireann (2004a) Volume 583. 21 April, 'Twenty-seventh Amendment of the Constitution'

Dáil Éireann (2004b) Volume 588. 8 July, 'Written Answers: Citizenship Laws'

Dáil Éireann (2004c) Volume 591. 27 October, 'Irish Nationality and Citizenship Bill 2004: Second Stage'

Dáil Éireann (2004d) Volume 585. 19 May, Written Answers. – 'Citizenship Applications'

Dáil Éireann (2004e) Volume 586. 01 June, Written Answers. – 'Citizenship Rights'

Dáil Éireann (2004f) Volume 592. 09 November, 'Irish Nationality and Citizenship Bill 2004: Second Stage'

Dáil Éireann (2004g) Volume 584. No. 1, 'Twenty-seventh Amendment of the Constitution Bill 2004: Second Stage' Dáil Éireann debate – Thursday, 22 April

Dáil Éireann (2017) Volume 962. No. 2. 23 November, 'Finance Bill 2017: Report stage'

Daley, Paul (2015) 'Encounters exhibition: a stunning but troubling collection of colonial plunder', Guardian, 25 November

Dalrymple, William (2015a) 'The East India Company: The original corporate raiders', Guardian, 4 March

Dalrymple, William (2015b) 'The Great Divide: The violent legacy of Indian Partition'. New Yorker, 22 June

Dalrymple, William (2019) The Anarchy: How a Corporation Replaced the Mughal Empire, 1756-1803. London: Bloomsbury

Darby, John (1976) Conflict in Northern Ireland: The Development of a Polarised Community. Dublin: Gill and Macmillan

Davies, John (1969) Discovery of the True Causes why Ireland was never Entirely Subdued. Shannon: Irish University Press (originally published 1612)

Davies, John (1983) 'A discovery of the true causes why Ireland was never entirely subdued', in James P. Myers (ed) (1983) Elizabethan Ireland: A Selection of Writings by Elizabethan Writers on Ireland. Hamden, Connecticut: Archon Books (originally published 1612)

Davis, F. James (n.d.) 'Who is Black? One Nation's Definition', https://www.pbs.org/wgbh/pages/frontline/shows/jefferson/mixed/onedrop.html

Davis, Thomas (1945) Thomas Davis: Essays and Poems, with a Centenary Memoir 1845-1945. Dublin: M.H. Gill and Son

Davitt, Michael (1979) The Fall of Feudalism in Ireland. Shannon: Irish University Press 1979 (originally published 1904)

De Cesari, Chiari (2012) 'The paradoxes of colonial reparation: Foreclosing memory and the 2008 Italy-Libya Friendship Treaty', Memory Studies 5(3): 316-326

De las Casas, Bartolomé (1689) A Brief Account of the Destruction of the Indians by Bartolome de las Casas. London: R. Hewson. http://www.gutenberg.org/ebooks/20321

De Paor, Liam (1970) Divided Ulster. Harmondsworth: Penguin

De Silva Report (2012) Pat Finucane Review. London: The Stationary Office Limited

De Valera, Eamon (1932) 'Despatch from Eamon de Valera to J.H. Thomas (London), No. 59', 5 April

De Valera, Eamon (1945) 'Eamon de Valera's response to Winston Churchill', https://speakola.com/political/eamon-de-valera-churchill-criticism-1945

De Witte, Ludo (2001) The Assassination of Patrice Lumumba. London: Verso

Democratic Programme of Dáil Éireann (1919), https://www.oireachtas.ie/en/debates/debate/dail/1919-01-21/15/

Derricke, John (1883) The Image of Ireland with a Discoverie of Woodkarne. Edinburgh: Adam and Charles Black (originally published 1581)

Devenport, Mark (2018a) 'Fewer Northern Ireland people feel British than other UK regions – survey', BBC News online, 8 June

Devenport, Mark (2018b) 'Theresa May announces Festival of Great Britain and NI plan', BBC News online, 30 September

Dilke, Charles (1868) Greater Britain: A Record of Travel in English-Speaking Countries, volume 2. London: Macmillan

Dix, Dermot (2006) 'A Rough Guide to the British Empire: Charles Lord Cornwallis and his years in America, India and Ireland', in Tadhg Foley and Maureen O'Connor (eds) Ireland and India: Colonies, Culture and Empire. Dublin: Irish Academic Press, 200-213

Doherty, Charles (1980) 'Exchange and Trade in Early Medieval Ireland', *Journal of the Royal Society of Antiquaries of Ireland* 110: 67-89

Doolin, David (2015) *Transnational Revolutionaries:The Fenian Invasion of Canada, 1866*. Bern: Peter Lang

Dorling, Danny and Sally Tomlinson (2019) *Rule Britannia: Brexit and the End of Empire*. London: Biteback

Douglass, Frederick (1962) *Life and Times of Frederick Douglass*. New York: Collier Books (originally published 1892)

Driver, Ciaran (1975) 'Notes on the Economy of the North', *Bulletin of the Conference of Socialist Economists* 4(2)

Dudley Edwards, Ruth (1977) *Patrick Pearse:The Triumph of Failure*. London: Gollancz

Dudley Edwards, Ruth (2000) *The Faithful Tribe*. London: HarperCollins

Duffy, Joe and McClements, Freya (2019) *Children of the Troubles*. London: Hodder and Stoughton

Dunlop, John (1995) *A Precarious Belonging: Presbyterians and the Conflict in Ireland*. Belfast: Blackstaff Press

Dunlop, Robert (2015) *Daniel O'Connell*. Norwich: Palala Press

Dunn, Ken (2012) 'A short history of mixed marriage in Ireland', in *Mixed Emotions: Real Stories of Mixed Marriage*. Belfast: Northern Ireland Mixed Marriage Association

Durham, Lord (1912) *Lord Durham's Report on the Affairs of British North America*. Oxford: Clarendon Press, http://www.archive.org/stream/lorddurhamsrepor01durhiala/lorddurhamsrepor01durhiala_djvu.txt

Dwyer, Ryle (2011) 'A Royal Welcome', *Irish Examiner*, 5 March

ECNI (Equality Commission Northern Ireland) (2007) *Statement on Key Inequalities in Northern Ireland*, https://www.equalityni.org/KeyInequalities-Employment

ECNI (Equality Commission Northern Ireland((2016) *Fair Employment Monitoring Report 27*, https://www.equalityni.org/Delivering-Equality/Addressing-inequality/Employment/Monitoring-Report-27/Fair-Employment-Monitoring-Report-27

ECNI (Equality Commission Northern Ireland) (2020a) *Fair Employment Monitoring Report 29*. Annual Summary of Monitoring Returns 2018, https://www.equalityni.org/ECNI/media/ECNI/Publications/Delivering%20Equality/FETO%20Monitoring%20Reports/No29/MonReportNo29.pdf

ECNI (Equality Commission Northern Ireland) (2020b) Companies Data. Public Authorities 26+ employees (*2018 Monitoring Returns*), https://www.equalityni.org/ECNI/media/ECNI/Publications/Delivering%20Equality/FETO%20Monitoring%20Reports/No29/MonReport29-Public26Employees.pdf

ECNI (Equality Commission Northern Ireland) (2020c) Companies Data. Private Sector 26+ employees (*2018 Monitoring Returns*), https://www.equalityni.org/ECNI/media/ECNI/Publications/Delivering%20Equality/FETO%20Monitoring%20Reports/No29/MonReport29-Private26Employees.pdf

Economist (1988) 'Ireland: Poorest of the Rich: Special Report', 16 January

Economist (1997) 'Europe's Shining Light', 17 May

Economist (2004) 'The Luck of the Irish: Special Report', 16 October

Economist (2015) 'The Irish economy – Celtic phoenix', 19 November

Economist (2017) 'He's out, and he's in: Ireland looks set for a young, gay prime minister: Leo Varadkar is known for speaking his mind, not always wisely', 2 June

Elias, Norbert (2000) *The Civilizing Process: Sociogenetic and Psychogenetic Investigations*. Oxford, Basil Blackwell

Elkins, Caroline (2005) 'Race, Citizenship, and Governance: Settler Tyranny and the End of Empire', Introduction', in Caroline Elkins and Susan Pedersen (eds) *Settler Colonialism in the Twentieth Century: Projects, Practices, Legacies*. London: Routledge, 203-222

Elliott, J.H. (2006) *Empires of the Atlantic World: Britain and Spain in America 1492-1830*. New

Haven: Yale University Press

Elliott, Marianne (2000) *The Catholics of Ulster: A History*. London: Allen Lane

Equiano, Oloudah (1999) *The Life of Oloudah Equiano, or Gustavus Vassa, the African*. Mineola, NY: Dover Publications (originally published 1789)

European Commission, 'Representation in Ireland', https://ec.europa.eu/ireland/about-us/ireland-in-eu_en

European United Left, Nordic Green Left (2018) *Exposed: Apple's golden delicious tax deals. Is Ireland helping Apple pay less than 1% tax in the EU?*, https://www.guengl.eu/content/uploads/2018/06/Apple_report_final.pdf

Evans, E. Estyn (1969) 'The Scotch-Irish: Their Cultural Adaptation and Heritage in the American Old West', in E.R.R. Green (ed). *Essays in Scotch-Irish History*. London: Routledge and Kegan Paul, 69-86

Executive Office (2013) *Together: Building a United Community*. Belfast: Executive Office

Executive Office (2019) *Labour Force Survey Religion Report 2017*, Annual update. Belfast: NISRA/ONS

Fallon, Charlotte (1986) *Soul of Fire: A Biography of Mary MacSwiney*. Dublin: Mercier Press

Fallon, Donal (2015) *John MacBride*. Dublin: O'Brien Press

Fanon, Franz (2004) *Wretched of the Earth*. New York: Grove Press, 2004 (originally Présence Africaine, 1961)

Fanon, Franz (2007) *Black Skin, White Masks*. New York: Grove Press (originally Éditions du Seuil, 1952)

Fanning, Ronan (1982) 'The Response of the London and Belfast Governments to the Declaration of the Republic of Ireland, 1948-49', *International Affairs* 58(1): 95-114

Farrell, Michael (1980) *Northern Ireland: The Orange State*. London: Pluto

Farrell, Michael (1986) *The Apparatus of Repression*. Derry: Field Day Theatre Company

Ferguson, Niall (2012) *Empire: How Britain Made the World*. London: Penguin

Ferriter, Diarmaid (2015) *A Nation and Not a Rabble; The Irish Revolution 1913-1923*. London: Profile Books

Ferriter, Diarmaid (2018) 'Semantics and Ireland's tax status: Department of Finance persists in denying Ireland is world's biggest tax haven', *Irish Times*, 16 June

Ferriter, Diarmaid (2019) *The Border: The Legacy of a Century of Anglo-Irish Politics*. London: Profile Books

Ferry, Jules (1884) 'Jules François Camille Ferry's speech Before the French Chamber of Deputies on colonization of Africa in March 28, 1884', https://ejikeilodubablog.wordpress.com/2016/10/17/jules-francois-camille-ferrys-speech-before-the-french-chamber-of-deputies-on-colonization-of-africa-in-march-28-1884/

Fisher, Gene and Suzanne Model (2012) 'Cape Verdean identity in a land of Black and White', *Ethnicities* 12(3): 354-379

Fitzduff, Mari (1991) *Approaches to Community Relations Work*. Belfast: Community Relations Commission

FitzGerald, John (2017) 'John FitzGerald: the financial implications of Ireland leaving a union: After a Churchill and Cosgrave meeting, a deal was done for Ireland to pay £5m instead of £156m,' *Irish Times*, 1 December

FitzGerald, John and Sean Kenny (2017). *'Till Debt Do Us Part': Financial Implications of the Divorce of the Irish Free State from the UK, 1922-6* (Lund Papers in Economic History; No. 166). Department of Economic History, Lund University, https://portal.research.lu.se/portal/files/35344312/LUP_166_002_.pdf

Fitzgerald, Patrick (2001) 'A Sentence to Sail: The Transportation of Irish Convicts and Vagrants to Colonial America in the Eighteenth Century', in Patrick Fitzgerald and Steve Ickringill (eds) *Atlantic Crossroads: Historical connections between Scotland, Ulster and North America*. Newtownards: Colourpoint, 114-132

Fitzpatrick, Rory (1989) *God's Frontiersmen:The Scots-Irish Epic*. London:Weidenfeld and Nicolson

Foley-Fisher, Nathan and Eoin McLaughlin (2015) 'Sovereign Debt Guarantees and Default: Lessons from the UK and Ireland, 1920-1938'. University of St. Andrews, Discussion Papers in Environmental Economics. Paper 2015-11.

Foner, Philip (1975) *History of Black Americans: From Africa to the Emergence of the Cotton Kingdom*. Westport, Connecticut: Greenwood Press

Foner, Philip (1983) *History of Black Americans: from the Emergence of the Cotton Kingdom to the Eve of the Compromise of 1850*. Westport, Connecticut: Greenwood Press

Foner, Philip and Robert Branham (eds) (1998) *Lift Every Voice: African American Oratory, 1787-1900*. Tuscaloosa: University of Alabama Press

Foner, Philip and George Walker (eds) (1980) *Proceedings of the Black State Conventions, 1840-1865*, volume 2. Philadelphia:Temple University Press

Ford, Patrick (1915) *The Criminal History of the British Empire*. New York:The Irish World, https://archive.org/details/criminalhistoryo00ford/page/n4/mode/2up

Forsdick, Charles and Christian Høgsbjerg (2017) *Toussaint L'Ouveture:A Black Jacobin in the Age of Revolutions*. London: Pluto Press

Foster, Roy (1988) *Modern Ireland 1600–1972*. London: Allen Lane

Fowler, Naomi (2018) *New report: is Apple paying less than 1% tax in the EU?*, 25 June https://www.taxjustice.net/2018/06/25/new-report-is-apple-paying-less-than-1-tax-in-the-eu/

Frame, Robin (2012) *Colonial Ireland, 1169–1369*, 2nd edition. Dublin: Four Courts Press

Fraser,T.G. (1984) *Partition in Ireland, India and Palestine*. London: Macmillan

Fraser,T.G. (1996) 'Ireland and India', in Keith Jeffery (ed) *'An Irish Empire'? Aspects of Ireland and the British Empire*. Manchester, Manchester University Press: 77-93

Freeman-Molloy, Dan (2018) 'The international politics of settler self-governance: reflections on Zionism and "dominion" status within the British empire', *Settler Colonial Studies* 8(1): 80-95

Froude, James (1969) *The English in Ireland in the Eighteenth Century*, vol. 1. NewYork:AMS Press (first published 1881)

Fryer, Peter (1984) *Staying Power:The History of Black People in Britain*. London: Pluto Press

Furnivall, J. S. ([1948] 1956) *Colonial Policy and Practice*. Cambridge: Cambridge University Press

Galeano, Eduardo (2009) *Open Veins of Latin America*. London: Serpent'sTail

Gann, John and Kevin McNicholl (2015) *Understanding the 'Northern Irish' Identity*, http://www.niassembly.gov.uk/globalassets/documents/raise/knowledge_exchange/briefing_papers/series4/northern_ireland_identity_garry_mcnicholl_policy_document.pdf

Gann, Lewis and Peter Duignan (1979) *The Rulers of Belgian Africa, 1884–1914*. Princeton: Princeton University Press

Garry, John and Kevin McNicholl (2015) *Understanding the 'Northern Irish' Identity*. Briefing paper presented at the Knowledge Exchange Seminar Series, Stormont

Gerald of Wales (1988) *The History and Topography of Ireland*. Harmondsworth: Penguin

Ghosh, Durba (2004) 'Gender and Colonialism: Expansion or Marginalization?', *The Historical Journal* 47(3): 737-755

Gibbon, Edward (1996) *The History of the Decline and Fall of the Roman Empire*, volume 1. Harmondsworth: Penguin (first published 1776)

Gibbon, Peter (1975) *The Origins of Ulster Unionism*. Manchester: Manchester University Press

Gifford,Tony (1984) *Supergrasses:The Use of Accomplice Evidence in Northern Ireland*. London: Cobden Trust

Gilley, Bruce (2017) 'The case for colonialism', *ThirdWorld Quarterly*, DOI:10.1080/01436597.2017.1369037

Gilroy, Paul (2005) *Postcolonial Melancholia*. New York: Columbia University Press

Gondola, Didier (2002) *The History of the Congo*. London: Greenwood Press

Gordon, Gareth (2018) '"Catholic majority possible" in NI by 2021', BBC News, 19 April

Gosling, Paul and Pat McArt (2018) *A New Union, a New Society: Ireland 2050*. Derry: self-published

Gott, Richard (2007) 'Latin America as a White Settler Society', *Bulletin of Latin American Research* 26(2): 269–289

Gov.uk. 'List of Ethnic Groups', https://www.ethnicity-facts-figures.service.gov.uk/ethnic-groups

Graham, David (2017) 'The Strange Friendship of Martin McGuinness and Ian Paisley', *The Atlantic*, 21 March

Grant, A. (2012) *Irish Socialist Republicanism 1909-36*. Dublin: Four Courts Press

Grattan, Henry (1839) *A Memoir of the Life and Times of Henry Grattan*. London: Henry Colborn

Guardian (2016a) 'Apple and Ireland will fight the EU's €13bn tax ruling all the way', 19 December

Guardian (2016b) 'Ireland may not get Apple's €13bn back taxes in full, EU says' 19 December

Guardian (2017) Europe could allow a united Ireland to join EU after Brexit', 28 April

Guevara, Ernesto Che (1967) 'Message to the Tricontinental'.

Gurley Flynn, Elizabeth (1973) *The Rebel Girl*. New York: International Publishers

Guterl, Matthew Pratt (2016) 'The Irish Rebellion that Resonated in Harlem', *The New Republic*, 25 March

Gutto, Shadrack (2013) 'In search of real justice for Africa and Africans, and her/their descendants in a world of justice, injustices and impunity', *International Journal of African Renaissance Studies* 8(1): 30-45

Gwynn, Stephen (1919) *John Redmond's Last Years*. New York: Longmans, Green and Co.

Hall, Stuart (2016) *Stuart Hall: Selected Political Writings*. London: Lawrence and Wishart

Halpin, Hayley (2020) 'Verona Murphy elected in Wexford as Malcolm Byrne loses seat he won in November', *The Journal* 10 February

Halter, Marilyn (1993) *Between Race and Ethnicity: Cape Verdean American Immigrants, 1860-1965*. Champaign: University of Illinois Press

Hamill, Desmond (1986) *Pig in the Middle: Army in Northern Ireland, 1969-84*. London: Methuen Publishing

Hamilton, Hugo (2003) *The Speckled People*. Dublin: Fourth Estate

Harpster, John W. (1938) 'Journal of William Trent, 1763', in *Pen Pictures of Early Western Pennsylvania*. Pittsburgh: University of Pittsburgh Press

Hart, Bill (n.d.) 'Africans in 18th Century Ireland'. Coleraine: New University of Ulster, unpublished

Harvey, Dan (2015) *A Bloody Day: The Irish at Waterloo*. Cork: Drombeg Books

Hayden, Tom (2001) *Irish on the Inside: In Search of the Soul of Irish America*. New York: Verso

Heaney, Seamus (1995) Nobel Lecture.

Hechter, Michael (1975) *Internal Colonialism: The Celtic Fringe in British National Development, 1536-1966*. London: Routledge and Kegan Paul

Heffernan, Breda (2019) 'Surge in Irish passport applications from UK', *Irish Independent*, 20 May

Hepburn, A.C. (1980) *The Conflict of Nationality in Modern Ireland*. London: Edward Arnold

Hermon, John (1997) *Holding the Line: An Autobiography*. Dublin: Gill and Macmillan

Higgins, Isabella and Sarah Collard 2019. 'WA Indigenous group's $290 billion compensation claim could become one of world's biggest payouts', ABC News, 16 December, https://www.abc.net.au/news/2019-11-29/$290-billion-wa-native-title-claim-launched/11749206

Hill, Robert (ed) (1983) *The Marcus Garvey and Universal Negro Improvement Association Papers*, vol. 1: 1826-August 1919. Berkeley: University of California Press

Hocking, Bree (2015) *The Great Reimagining: Public Art, Urban Space and the Symbolic Landscapes of a 'New' Northern Ireland*. New York: Bergahn

Hoffman, Phillip T. (2015). *Why Did Europe Conquer the World?* Princeton, New Jersey: Princeton University Press

Holmes, Denis and Michael Holmes (1997) 'Ireland and India: a distant relationship', in Michael Holmes and Denis Holmes (eds) *Ireland and India: Connections, Comparisons, Contrasts*. Limerick: University of Limerick, Department of Government and Society, 1-11

Holmes, Oliver (2018) 'Irish senate approves ban on products from Israeli settlements', *Guardian*, 11 July

Holmes, Richard (2004) *The Little Field Marshal: A Life of Sir John French*. Weidenfeld & Nicolson.

Hope, Jemmy (1972) *The Memoirs of Jemmy Hope*. Belfast: Athol Books

House of Commons (1916) HC Deb 03 May 1916 vol 82 cc38

House of Commons (1920) HC Deb 29 March 1920 vol 127 cc990-1

House of Commons (1922a) HC Deb 28 March 1922 vol 152 cc1281-96 'Ireland', 1281, 1285

House of Commons (1922b) HC Deb 28 March 1922 vol 152 cc1281-96 'Ireland', 1284

House of Commons (1937) HC Deb 06 May 1937 vol 323 cc1237-8

House of Commons Library (2013) *The History of the Parliamentary Franchise*, Research Paper 13/14, 1 March

Howe, Stephen (2002) *Ireland and Empire: Colonial Legacies in Irish History and Culture*. Oxford: Oxford University Press

Howe, Stephen (2008) 'Questioning the (bad) question: "Was Ireland a colony?"' *Irish Historical Studies* 36(42): 138-152

Howell, Georgina (2015) *Queen of the Desert: The Extraordinary Life of Gertrude Bell*. London: Pan

Hughes, Brendan (2020) 'Petition urges removal of John Mitchel statue in Newry', *Irish News*, 20 June

Hughes, Robert (1987) *The Fatal Shore*. London: Pan Books

Hume, David (1773) *The History of England from the Invasion of Julius Caesar to the Revolution in 1688*, Vol. 2. London: A. Miller

Ignatieff, Michael (1996) 'Articles of Faith', *Index on Censorship* 25(5): 110-122

Ignatiev, Noel (1995) *How the Irish Became White*. New York: Routledge

Ignatiev, Noel (2002) 'Abolish the White Race', *Harvard Magazine* September/October

Imani Na Umoja (2014) 'Cabral: Exemplary light and guide for the pan-African and socialist revolution', January 22,

Irish Examiner (2020), 'We should not celebrate slavery icon', 9 June

Irish Unionist Alliance (1909) *Facts of Radical Misgovernment and the Home Rule Question Down to Date*. Dublin: Irish Unionist Alliance

Isles, K.S. and Norman Cuthbert (1957) *An Economic Survey of Northern Ireland*. Belfast: HMSO

Jackson, Alvin (2010) *Ireland 1798-1998: War, Peace and Beyond*. Hoboken, NJ: Wiley

Kapur, Narinder (1997) *The Irish Raj*. Antrim: Greystone Press

James, C L R (2001) *The Black Jacobins: Toussaint L'Ouverture and the San Domingo Revolution*. London: Penguin (originally published 1938)

Jeal, Tim (2001) *Baden-Powell*. New Haven, Connecticut: Yale University Press

Jeffery, Keith (1996a) 'Introduction', in Keith Jeffery (ed). *'An Irish Empire'? Aspects of Ireland and the British Empire*. Manchester: Manchester University Press, 1-24

Jeffery, Keith (1996b) 'The Irish Military Tradition and the British Empire', in Keith Jeffery (ed) *'An Irish Empire'? Aspects of Ireland and the British Empire*. Manchester: Manchester University Press, 94-122

Jennings, Louis (ed) (1889) *Speeches of the Right Honourable Lord Randolph Churchill M.P. 1880-1888*. London: Longmans, Green and Co.

Johnson, Boris (2002) 'Africa is a mess, but we can't blame colonialism', *The Spectator*, 2 February

Jones, Adam (2006) *Genocide: A Comprehensive Introduction*. London: Routledge

Jones, Maldwyn A. (1969) 'Ulster Emigration, 1783-1815', in E.R.R. Green (ed). *Essays in Scotch-Irish History*. London: Routledge and Kegan Paul, 46-68

Jones, Owen (2016) 'There's a fight over working-class voters. Labour must not lose it', *Guardian*, 6 October

Joseph, Philip A. (2008) *The Maori seats in Parliament*. Wellington: New Zealand Business Roundtable

Kapur, Narinder (1997) *The Irish Raj: Illustrated Stories about Irish in India and Indians in Ireland*.

Antrim: Greystone Press

Karsten, Peter (1983) 'Irish Soldiers in the British Army, 1792-1922: Suborned or Subordinate?', *Journal of Social History*, XVII: 31-64

Katzman, David (1973) *Before the Ghetto: Black Detroit in the Nineteenth Century*. Urbana: University of Illinois Press

Kearney, Richard (1978) 'Myth and Terror', *The Crane Bag* 2(1/2): 125-139

Kearney, Richard (1980/81) 'The IRA's Strategy of Failure ', *The Crane Bag* 4(2): 62-70

Kearney, Vincent (2020) 'Varadkar accepts Sinn Féin councillor apology over remarks', RTÉ News, 16 January

Keating, Geoffrey (2009) *The History of Ireland*. Translated into English by Edward Comyn and Patrick S. Dinneen, http://www.exclassics.com

Keegan, John (1999) *The First World War*. London: Pimlico

Keen, Benjamin (1955) *Readings in Latin-American Civilization: 1492 to the Present*. Boston: Houghton Mifflin.

Kelly, James (2001) 'Monitoring the Constitution: The Operation of Poynings' Law in the 1760s', *Parliamentary History* 20(1): 87-106

Kelly, Matthew (2009) 'Irish Nationalist Opinion and the British Empire in the 1850s and 1860s', *Past and Present* 204: 127-154

Kelly, Stephen (2017) *'A failed political entity': Charles Haughey and the Northern Ireland question, 1945–1992*. Dublin: Merrion Press

Kennedy, Liam (1986) *Two Ulsters: A Case for Repartition*. Belfast: Queen's University

Kiberd, Declan (1991) *Inventing Ireland: The Literature of the Modern Nation*. London: Vintage

Kiernan, Ben (2007) *Blood and Soil*. New Haven, Connecticut: Yale University Press

King, Thomas F. (2000) 'Gallagher of Nikumaroro: The Last Expansion of the British Empire'. Earhart Project Research Bulletin, https://vintageexpeditions.wordpress. com/2019/08/13/gallagher-of-nikumaroro-the-last-expansion-of-the-british-empire/

Kinsella, Ray (2017) 'Why Ireland should seriously consider Irexit', *Irish Times*, 30 August

Kitson, Frank (1971) *Low Intensity Operations*. London: Faber and Faber

Knickmeyer, Ellen (2006) 'The Woman who put Iraq on the map', *Washington Post*, 5 March

Koch, Alexander, Chris Brierley, Mark M. Maslin and Simon L. Lewis (2019) 'Earth system impacts of the European arrival and Great Dying in the Americas after 1492', *Quarternary Science Reviews* 207: 13-36

Kruger, H. (1975) 'India's Freedom Struggle and Beginnings of Solidarity between National Liberation Movements before World War 1 in Various Countries', in P.M. Joshi and M.A. Nareem (eds). *Studies in the Foreign Relations of India*. Hyderabad: State Archives, Government of Andra Pradesh: 292-323

Kushner, Jacob (2019) 'Haiti and the failed promise of US aid', *Guardian*, 11 October

Lalor, Fintan (n.d.) *Readings from Fintan Lalor*. Belfast Republican Press Centre

Lalor, Fintan (1895) *The Writings of James Fintan Lalor*. Dublin: T.G. O'Donoghue

Larkin, Emmet (1972) 'The Devotional Revolution in Ireland, 1850-75', *The American Historical Review* 77(3): 625-652

Lawton, Tim (2018) Facebook Post. 12 October, https://www.facebook.com/ TimLoughtonEWAS/posts/2235588636724230

Lee, Joseph (1989) *Ireland: 1912-1985: Politics and Society*. Cambridge: Cambridge University Press

Lee, Joseph (2008) *The Modernisation of Irish Society 1848-1918*. Dublin: Gill and Macmillan

Lenihan, Pádraig (2008) *Consolidating Conquest: Ireland 1603-1727*. Harlow: Pearson

Levi, Primo (1989) *The Drowned and the Saved*. New York: Vintage

Lewis, George Cornewall (1977) *Local Disturbances in Ireland*. Cork: Tower Books (originally published 1836)

Liberty Writers Africa (2019) 'How Cecil Rhodes Killed Millions of Southern Africans for

Diamonds and Lands', *LibertyWriters Africa*, April 12; https://libertywritersafrica.com/how-cecil-rhodes-killed-million-of-southern-africans-for-diamonds-and-lands/

Lindqvist, Sven (2002) *Exterminate the Brutes*. London: Granta

Lindqvist, Sven (2007) *Terra Nullius: A Journey through No One's Land*. London: Granta

Linklater, Andio (1980) *An Unhusbanded Life: Charlotte Despard, Suffragette, Socialist and Sinn Feiner.* London: Hutchinson

Litwack, Leon (1961) *North of Slavery: The Negro in the Free States, 1790-1860*. Chicago: University of Chicago Press

Lo, Anna (2016) *The Place I Call Home*. Belfast: Blackstaff Press

Loewen, James (1995) *Lies My Teacher Told Me: Everything your American History Textbook got Wrong*. Marden, Tennessee: Touchstone Books

Lorde, Audre (2018) *The Master's Tools Will Never Dismantle the Master's House*. London: Penguin Modern Classic (originally published 1979)

Loveman, Mara (2014) *National Colors – Racial Classification and the State in Latin America*. New York: Oxford University Press

Löytömäki, Stiina (2013) 'The Law and Collective Memory of Colonialism: France and the Case of "Belated" Transitional Justice', *International Journal of Transitional Justice* 7(2): 205–223

Lu, Catherine (2011) 'Colonialism as Structural Injustice: Historical Responsibility and Contemporary Redress', *The Journal of Political Philosophy* 19(3): 261–281

Lumumba, Patrice (1961) *The Truth about a Monstrous Crime of the Colonialists*. Moscow: Foreign Languages Publishing House

Lynch, George (1901) *The War of the Civilizations*. New York: Longmans, Green & Co

Lynch, George (1903) *Impressions of a war correspondent*. London: George Newnes

MacCall, Seamus (1938) *Irish Mitchel: A Biography*. London: Thomas Nelson

MacKenzie, F.A. (1916) *The Irish Rebellion: What Happened and Why*. London: C. Arthur Pearson

Macpherson, William (1999) *Report of the Stephen Lawrence Inquiry*. London: Home Office, Cm 4262

MacSwiney, Terence (1920) *Principles of Freedom*. Dublin: Talbot Press.

Maher, Eamon and Eugene O'Brien (eds) (2017) *Tracing the Cultural Legacy of Irish Catholicism: from Galway to Cloyne and Beyond*. Manchester: Manchester University Press

Manley, John (2018) 'DUP MLAs mock Ulster Unionist Robbie Butler for attending papal visit and label Pope "the antichrist"', *Irish News*, 22 October

Mansergh, Martin (ed) (1986) *The Spirit of the Nation: The Speeches and Statements of Charles J. Haughey (1957-1986)*. Cork: Mercier Press

Mao, Zedong (1967) *Quotations from Chairman Mao Zedong*. Beijing: Foreign Languages Press

Mark, Paul (2018) 'Ireland is the world's biggest corporate "tax haven", say academics: Study claims State shelters more multinational profits than the entire Caribbean', *Irish Times*, 13 June

Marx, Jenny (1870) *La Marseillaise*, 18 March; http://www.marxists.org/archive/marx/bio/family/jenny/1870-ire.htm

Marx, Karl (1979) 'The future results of British rule in India' (25 July 1853), in K. Marx and F. Engels. *Collected Works*, vol. 12. London: Lawrence and Wishart: 217-222

Marx, Karl (1980) 'History of the Opium Trade' (20 September 1858) in K. Marx and F. Engels. *Collected Works*, vol. 16. London: Lawrence and Wishart: 13-20

Maude, H. E. (1969) *Of Islands and Men: Studies in Pacific History*. Oxford: Oxford University Press.

Maxwell, William J. (2015) 'When Black Writers Were Public Enemy No. 1', *Politico Magazine*, 30 April, https://www.politico.com/magazine/story/2015/04/fbi-black-writers-117512

Mayo Ireland (2020) 'The Great Famine in Co. Mayo (1845-1849)', http://www.mayo-ireland.ie/en/about-mayo/history/the-great-irish-famine.html

McBride, Sam (2019) *Burned: The Inside Story of the 'Cash for Ash' Scandal and Northern Ireland's Secretive New Elite*. Dublin: Merrion Press

McBride, Sam (2020) 'The police's made-up Coronavirus law ought to unsettle anyone who understands democracy', *Newsletter* 18 April

McCafferty, Kate (2002) *Testimony of an Irish Slave Girl*. Harmondsworth: Penguin

McCann, Eamon (1974) *War and an Irish Town*. Harmondsworth: Penguin

McClements, Freya (2020) 'De Souzas receive donations of over £25,000 towards legal costs', *Irish Times*, 7 September

McClure, David (1899) *Diary of David McClure, Doctor of Divinity, 1748-1820*. New York: Knickerbocker Press

McCormack, W. J. (1989) 'Eighteenth-Century Ascendancy: Yeats and the Historians', *Eighteenth-century Ireland/Iris an dá chultúr* 4: 159-181

McDermott, Jim (2001) *Northern Divisions: The Old IRA and the Belfast Pogroms 1920-22*. Belfast: Beyond the Pale Publications

McDonald, Brian (2019) 'British fail to attend famine ceremony', *Independent*, 17 May

McDonald, Henry (2002) 'Punk Remembered', *Guardian*, 1 December

McDonald, Henry (2017) ' Northern Irish unionist parties alienating young Protestants, study says', *Guardian*, 4 August

McGarry, Fearghal (2001) 'Ireland and the Spanish Civil War', *History Ireland* 9(3): 35-40

McGovern, Mark (2019) *Counterinsurgency and Collusion in Northern Ireland*. London: Pluto

McGrath, Harry (2013) 'Early Days of a Better Nation', *Scottish Review of Books*, 28 March

McGregor, James (1836) 'Shaa-naan-dithit, or The Last of The Boëothics', *Fraser's Magazine for Town and Country* XIII (LXXV): 316–323

McGuffin, John (1973) *Internment*. Tralee: Anvil Books

McGuffin, John (1974) *The Guineapigs*. Harmondsworth: Penguin

McGuinness, Terry and Melanie Gower (2017) *The Common Travel Area, and the special status of Irish nationals in UK law*. House of Commons Library Briefing Paper Number 7661, 9 June

McKay, Susan (2000) *Northern Protestants: An Unsettled People*. Belfast: Blackstaff Press

McKeown, Laurence (2001) *Out of Time: Irish Republican Prisoners, Long Kesh 1972-2000*. Belfast: Beyond the Pale Publications

McLaughlin, John (2003) *One Green Hill: Journeys through Irish Songs*. Belfast: Beyond the Pale Publications

McLaughlin, Peter (2006) '…it's a United Ireland or Nothing'? John Hume and the Idea of Irish Unity, 1964-72', *Irish Political Studies* 21(2): 157-180

McNally, Frank (2016) 'Rudyard Kipling's "entertaining, if racist" short story about a red-haired Irishman', *Irish Times*, 16 March

McMahon, Aine (2020) 'Lack of testing in Northern Ireland putting whole island in jeopardy – expert', *Belfast Telegraph*, 13 May

McNamara, Kevin (2010) *The MacBride Principles: Irish America Strikes Back*. Liverpool: Liverpool University Press

McNeill, Ronald (1922) *Ulster's Stand for Union*. London: John Murray

McQuade, Joseph (2017) 'Stop glorifying colonialism. Have we already forgotten the starvation, plundering, and sheer brutality?' 29 September, https://qz.com/india/1090508/have-we-forgotten-the-starvation-plundering-and-sheer-brutality-of-colonialism/

McVeigh, Robbie (2006) '"Special Powers": Racism in a Permanent State of Exception', in A. Lentin and R. Lentin (eds) *Race and State*. Cambridge: Cambridge Scholars Press, 229-254

McVeigh, Robbie (2010) 'United in Whiteness? Irishness, Europeanness and the emergence of a "white europe" policy', *European Studies* 28: 251-278

McVeigh, Robbie (2019) *Sectarianism: The Key Facts*. Belfast: CAJ, Equality Coalition, UNISON.

McVeigh, Robbie (2020) 'Irishness and White Dominion: Reflections on Ignatiev', *Insurgent Notes*, 'Symposium: Noel Ignatiev 1940–2019', Issue 21, March, http://insurgentnotes.com/

McVeigh, Robbie and Bill Rolston (2007) 'From Good Friday to Good Relations: sectarianism, racism and the Northern Ireland state', *Race and Class* 48(4): 1-23

McVeigh, Robbie (2008) '"The Balance of Cruelty": Ireland, Britain and the Logic of

Genocide', *Journal of Genocide Research* 10(4): 541-561

McVeigh, Robbie and Bill Rolston (2009) 'Civilising the Irish', *Race and Class* 51(2): 2-28

Memmi, Albert (1990) *The Colonizer and the Colonized*. London: Earthscan

Meredith, Robbie (2018) 'Game of Thrones "will live on in Northern Ireland for a decade"', BBC News, 4 October

Miller, Rory (2006) 'Ireland and the Israeli-Palestinian Conflict: a Case Study in European-Israeli Relations', *Yale Israel Journal* 8

Mintz, Steven (n.d.) 'Historical Context: Facts about the Slave Trade and Slavery', *History Now*, http://www.gilderlehrman.org/history-by-era/slavery-and-anti-slavery/resources/facts-about-slave-trade-and-slavery

Mishra, Pankaj (2020) *Bland Fanatics: Liberals, Race and Empire*. London: Verso.

Mitchel, John (1876) *The Last Conquest of Ireland (Perhaps)*. Glasgow: Cameron and Ferguson

Mitchel, John (1913) *Jail Journal*. Dublin: M.H. Gill

Mitchell, Angus (2007) 'Roger Casement: the evolution of an enemy of empire', in Eóin Flannery and Angus Mitchell (eds) *Enemies of Empire: new perspectives on imperialism, literature and historiography*. Dublin: Four Courts Press, 40-57

Mitchell, Arthur and Padraig O'Snodaigh (1985) *Irish Political Documents 1916-49*. Dublin: Irish Academic Press

Moody, T.W. (1981) *Davitt and Irish Revolution 1846-82*. Oxford: Clarendon Press

Morgan, Austen (2011) *The Hand of History? Legal Essays on the Belfast Agreement*. Richmond, Surrey: Belfast Press Limited.

Morgan, Hiram (1993) *Tyrone's Rebellion: The Outbreak of the Nine Years War in Tudor Ireland*. Woodbridge, Sussex: Boydell Press

Morris, Jan (1968) *Pax Britannica: The Climax of Empire*. London: Faber and Faber

Morris, Jan (1973) *Heaven's Command: An Imperial Progress*. London: Faber and Faber

Morris, Jan (2004) *Farewell the Trumpets: An Imperial Retreat*. London: Faber and Faber

Mortimer, Caroline (2017) 'Former UK ambassador to Ireland is applying for Irish citizenship because of Brexit', *Independent,* 30 April

Moryson, Fynes (1617) 'An Itinerary', in James P. Myers (ed) (1983) *Elizabethan Ireland: A Selection of Writings by Elizabethan Writers on Ireland*. Hamden, Connecticut: Archon Books (originally published 1603)

Moses, Wilson (1978) *The Golden Age of Black Nationalism, 1850-1925*. New York: Oxford University Press

Moyo, Khanyisela (2015) 'Mimicry, Transitional Justice and the Land Question in Racially Divided Former Settler Colonies', *International Journal of Transitional Justice* 9: 70–89

Mulgrew, John (2019) 'Moy Park sales grow to £1.61bn', *Ulster Business,* 20 September

Mulholland, Marc (2004) 'Why Did Unionists Discriminate?' in Sabine Wichert (ed.) *From the United Irishmen to Twentieth-century Unionism: Essays in Honour of A.T.Q. Stewart*. Dublin: Four Courts Press

Mullally, Una (2019a) 'Brexit shows up our nonsensical approach to Irish citizenship: Easy access to Irish passports remains off limits to some sectors of our society', *Irish Times,* 21 October

Mullally, Una (2019b) 'Kneecap: "Low-life scum" of west Belfast rap whose day has come', *Irish Times,* 12 April

Mulloy, Eanna (1986) *Dynasties of Coercion*. Derry: Field Day Theatre Company

Mulvihill, Margaret (1989) *Charlotte Despard: a Biography*. Kings Lynn: Pandora

Munck, Ronnie and Bill Rolston (1987) *Belfast in the Thirties: An Oral History*. Belfast: Blackstaff Press

Murphy, Brian (2007) 'Erskine Childers: the evolution of an enemy of empire – 11', in Eóin Flannery and Angus Mitchell (eds) *Enemies of Empire: new perspectives on imperialism, literature and historiography*. Dublin: Four Courts Press, 72-100

Murtagh, Harman (1996) 'Irish Soldiers Abroad, 1600-1800', in Thomas Bartlett and Keith

Jeffery (eds) *A Military History of Ireland.* Cambridge: Cambridge University Press, 294-314

Muttarak, Ray, Heather Hamill, Anthony Heath and Chris McCrudden (2012) 'Does Affirmative Action Work? Evidence from the Operation of Fair Employment Legislation in Northern Ireland', *Sociology* 47(3): 560-579

Mutua, Makau (2001) 'Savages, Victims, and Saviors: The Metaphor of Human Rights', *Harvard International Law Journal* 42(1): 201-245

Myers, James (ed) (1983) *Eizabethan Ireland: A Selection of Writings by Elizabethan Writers on Ireland.* North Haven, Connecticut

Nagai, Kaori (2006) *Empire of Analogies: Kipling, India and Ireland.* Cork: Cork University Press

National Archives (2000) 'Statement by the Taoiseach, Jack Lynch, regarding events in Northern Ireland, Wednesday 13 August 1969', 2000/6/657

National Archives (2020) 'Vietnam War U.S. Military Fatal Casualty Statistics' https://www. archives.gov/research/military/vietnam-war/casualty-statistics#category

National Archives of Ireland and the Royal Irish Academy (2018) 'Ireland in the EU' Exhibition. Joint project of the National Archives of Ireland and the Royal Irish Academy, funded by the Department of Arts Heritage and the Gaeltacht.

NCCL (National Council of Civil Liberties) (1936) *Report of a Commission of Inquiry appointed to examine the purpose and effect of the Civil Authorities (Special Powers) Acts (Northern Ireland) 1922 & 1933.* London: NCCL

Nelson, Sarah (1984) *Ulster's Uncertain Defenders.* Belfast: Blackstaff Press

News Letter (2016) 'John Bruton: His full speech denouncing the Easter Rising', 29 March

Newkirk, Vann (2018) 'Voter Suppression Is Warping Democracy', *The Atlantic* and the Public Religion Research Institute, 17 July

Newsinger, John (2013) *The Blood Never Dried: A People's History of the British Empire.* London: Bookmarks

Ní Bheacháin, C. (2007) '"We are of necessity anti-imperialists": Irish republicans and empire, 1922-39', in E. Flannery and A. Mitchell (eds) *Enemies of Empire: new perspectives on imperialism, literature and historiography.* Dublin: Four Courts Press, 58-71

Nielsen, Robert (2012) 'Irish Soviets 1919-23', https://whistlinginthewind. org/2012/10/08/irish-soviets-1919-23/

Nieman, Susan (2019) *Learning from the Germans: Race and the Memory of Evil.* London: Allen Lane

Nietzsche, Friedrich (2001) 'On Truth and Lies in a Nonmoral Sense,' in Patricia Bizzell and Bruce Herzberg (eds) *The Rhetorical Tradition: Readings from Classical Times to the Present.* Boston: St. Martin's

NISRA (Northern Ireland Statistics and Research Agency) (2019a) *Equality Statistics for the Northern Ireland Civil Service: Based on staff in post at 1 January.* Belfast: NISRA

NISRA (Northern Ireland Statistics and Research Agency) (2019b) *Northern Ireland Composite Economic Index: Quarter 1 (January-March) 2019,* https://www.nisra.gov.uk/sites/nisra.gov. uk/files/publications/NI-Composite-Economic-Index-Statistical-Bulletin-Q1-2019.pdf

Nolan, Paul (2017) 'Two tribes: A divided Northern Ireland', *Irish Times,* 1 April

Nolan, Paul (2018) 'The cruel peace: killings in Northern Ireland since the Good Friday Agreement', *The Detail,* 23 April

Noonan, Kathleen (1998) '"The Cruell Pressure of an Enraged, Barbarous People": Irish and English Identity in Seventeenth-Century Policy and Propaganda', *The Historical Journal* 41(1): 151-177

Ó Cathaoir, Brendan (1998) 'The Rising of 1848', *History Ireland* 6(3), https://www. historyireland.com/18th-19th-century-history/the-rising-of-1848/

Ó Cathasaigh, Aindrias (ed) (1997) *The Lost Writings: James Connolly.* London: Pluto Press

Ó Corcora, Micheál and Ronald J. Hill (1982) 'The Soviet Union in Irish Foreign Policy', *International Affairs* 58(2): 254-270

Ó Ruairc, Pádraig. 2020. 'Take it down from the mast, Irish "Patriots"...', *History Ireland* 28(1)

2020: 12-13

Ó Siochrú, Micheál (2008) *God's Executioner: Oliver Cromwell and the Conquest of Ireland*. London: Faber and Faber

Ó Snodaigh, Padraig (1995) *Hidden Ulster: Protestants and the Irish Language*. Belfast: Lagan Press

Ó Tuathaigh, Gearoid (1992) *Ireland Before the Famine*. Dublin: Gill and MacMillan

O'Brien, Conor Cruise (1965) *Writers and Politics*. London: Chatto and Windus

O'Brien, Conor Cruise (1969) 'Holy War', *New York Review* 13(8) 1969: 11.

O'Brien, George (1919) *The Economic History of Ireland in the 17th Century*. Dubin: Maunsel and Co.

O'Brien, William and Desmond Ryan (eds) (1979) *Devoy's Post Bag*. Dublin: Academy Press,

O'Cahan, T.S. (1968) *Owen Roe O'Neill*. London: R. Joseph Keane and Co.

O'Callaghan, Sean (2000) *To Hell or Barbados*. Dingle: Brandon

O'Connell, Maurice (1990) *Daniel O'Connell: The Man and his Politics*. Blackrock: Irish Academic Press

O'Connor, Frank (1979) *Book of Ireland*. London: Collins

O'Crouley, Pedro Alonso and Seán Galvin (translator) (1974) *A Description of the Kingdom of New Spain by Sr. Dn. Pedro Alonso 1774*. Los Angeles: John Howell Books

O'Donnell, Ruan (2004) 'Castle Hill and Vinegar Hill: the Australian Rising of 1804', *History Ireland* 12(2), https://www.historyireland.com/18th-19th-century-history/castle-hill-and-vinegar-hill-the-australian-rising-of-1804/

O'Dowd, Liam (1980) 'Shaping and Reshaping the Orange State', in Liam O'Dowd, Bill Rolston and Mike Tomlinson, *Northern Ireland between Civil Rights and Civil War*. London: CSE Books: 1-29

O'Dowd, Liam, Bill Rolston and Mike Tomlinson (1980) *Northern Ireland Between Civil Rights and Civil War*. London: CSE Books

O'Dowd, Liam, Bill Rolston and Mike Tomlinson (1982) 'From Labour to the Tories: The Ideology of Containment in Northern Ireland', *Capital and Class* 18: 72-90

O'Dwyer, Peter (2018) 'Ireland named as world's biggest tax haven' *Times*, 14 June

O'Farrall, Fergus (1991) 'Liberty and Catholic Politics, 1710-1990', in Maurice O'Connell (ed) *Daniel O'Connell: Political Pioneer*. Dublin, IPA: 35-56

Brendan O'Leary (2019) *A treatise on Northern Ireland. Volume 1. Colonialism: The shackles of the state and hereditary animosities*. Oxford: Oxford University Press

O'Riordan, Michael (1979) *Connolly Column*. Dublin: New Books

O'Toole, Fintan (2009) 'Jedward are pure essence of an extinct culture', *Irish Times*, 3 November

O'Toole, Fintan (2010) *Enough is Enough: How to Build a new Republic*. London: Faber and Faber

O'Toole, Fintan (2018) *Heroic Failure: Brexit and the Politics of Pain*. London: Apollo

Old Currency Exchange (2014) 'Controversy follows 1927 Irish coin design competition results', 7 September, https://oldcurrencyexchange.com/2014/09/07/the-controversial-1927-irish-coin-design-competition/

Oliver, Ted and Michael White (2004) 'Ulster talks on track despite Paisley remark', *Guardian*, 1 December

Olusoga, David (2017) 'Empire 2.0 is dangerous nostalgia for something that never existed', *Guardian*, 19 March

Olusoga, David (2018a) *Civilisations: First Contact / The Cult of Progress*. London: Progress Books.

Olusoga, David (2018b) 'The Treasury's tweet shows slavery is still misunderstood', *Guardian*, 12 February

Organization for World Peace (2019) 'U.N. Demands U.K. Relinquishes Control Of Chagos Islands', http://theowp.org/u-n-demands-u-k-relinquishes-control-of-chagos-islands

Parnell, Anna (1986) *The Tale of a Great Sham*. Dublin: Arlen House

Parry, Benita (1998) *Delusions and Discoveries: India in the British Imagination 1880-1930*. London: Verso

Payne, Stanley (1984) *Spanish Catholicism: An Historical Overview*. Madison: University of

Wisconsin Press

Pearce, Roy (1998) *Savagism and Civilization: A Study of the Indian and the American Mind*. Berkeley: University of California Press

Peet, John (2004) 'The luck of the Irish', *Economist*, 16 October

Perera, Suvendrini (1996) 'Claiming Truganini: Australian National Narratives in the Year of Indigenous Peoples', *Cultural Studies* 10(3): 393-412

Petty, William (1687) *A Treatise of Ireland, 1687. The Elements of Ireland; and of its Religion, Trade & Policy. An Essay in Political Arithmetick concerning Ireland* https://www.taieb.net/auteurs/Petty/pastimes1.html

Pim, Herbert (1919) *Unconquerable Ulster*. Belfast: Carswell and Son

Prashad, Vijay (2017a) 'A Mighty Fall: Academic arguments backing white supremacy and colonialism are making an ominous comeback', *Quartz*, 22, September, https://qz.com/india/1083767/academic-arguments-backing-white-supremacy-and-colonialism-are-making-an-ominous-comeback/

Prashad, Vijay (2017b) 'Third World Quarterly row: Why some western intellectuals are trying to debrutalise colonialism', *MRonline*, 21 September, https://mronline.org/2017/09/25/third-world-quarterly-row/

Prendergast, John (1867) 'The Tory War of Ulster, with the history of the three Brennans of the County of Kilkenny; descriptive of Ireland from the Restoration to the Revolution', *The Journal of the Kilkenny and South-East of Ireland Archaeological Society*, https://archive.org/details/jstor-25502690/mode/2up

Pruitt, Adam (2020) 'Bartolome De Las Casas: Protector of the Indians', https://amplascasas.weebly.com/african-slave-trade.html

PSNI (2020) 'Workforce Composition Statistics', https://www.psni.police.uk/inside-psni/Statistics/workforce-composition-statistics/

Purdy, Martina (2007) '"Charming" ministers woo president', BBC News, 8 December

Quijano, Aníbal (2007) 'Coloniality and Modernity/Rationality', *Cultural Studies* 21(2-3): 168-178

Radharc (1964) 'Radharc in Derry', https://www.youtube.com/watch?v=LjhqP90uaro

Rankin, Jennifer (2018) 'The EU is too white and Brexit likely to make it worse, MEPs and staff say', *Guardian*, 29 August

Riach, Douglas (1976) 'Daniel O'Connell and American anti-slavery', *Irish Historical Studies*, XX(77): 3-25.

Rich, Barnabe (1610) 'A New Description of Ireland, together with the Manners, Customs and Dispositions of the People', in James P. Myers (ed) (1983) *Elizabethan Ireland: A Selection of Writings by Elizabethan Writers on Ireland*. Hamden, Connecticut: Archon Books

Richards, Frank (2003) *Old Soldier Sahib*. Unkfield, UK: Naval and Military Press

Robinson, Philip (1984) *The Plantation of Ulster: British Settlement in an Irish Landscape, 1600-1670*. Dublin: Gill and Macmillan

Rolston, Bill (1990) 'Political Vetting: An Overview' in *The Political Vetting of Community Work in Northern Ireland*. Belfast: Political Vetting of Community Work Group, 3-12

Rolston, Bill (1993) 'The Training Ground: Ireland, Colonisation and Decolonisation', *Race and Class* 34(4): 13-24

Rolston, Bill (2011) *Children of the Revolution: The Lives of Sons and Daughters of Activists in Northern Ireland*. Derry: Guildhall Press

Rolston, Bill and Michael Shannon (2002) *Encounters: How Racism Came to Ireland*. Belfast: Beyond the Pale Publications

Rolston, Bill with Mairead Gilmartin (2000) *Unfinished Business: State Killings and the Quest for Truth*. Belfast: Beyond the Pale Publications

Rose, Norman (1971) 'The Seventh Dominion', *The Historical Journal* 14(2): 397-416

Rowthorn, Bob and Naomi Wayne (1988) *Northern Ireland: The Political Economy of Conflict*. London: Polity Press

Royal Irish Academy and the National Archives of Ireland, in association with the Department of Foreign Affairs and Trade (2015) *Ireland: 60 Years at the United Nations*, https://www.dfa.ie/media/dfa/alldfawebsitemedia/aboutus/globalhorizonsyouthinitiative/Ireland – -60-Years-at-the-United-Nations.pdf

RTÉ News (2009) 'Irish vote good for Europe – Barroso', 3 October

RTÉ News (2013) 'Committee declines to call in multinationals over tax', 3 July

Rushdie, Salman (2010) *Imaginary Homelands: Essays and Criticism 1981-1991*. New York: Vintage

Russell, Anthony (2016) 'John Mitchel – Flawed Hero', *History Ireland* 24(1), https://www.historyireland.com/18th-19th-century-history/john-mitchel-flawed-hero/

Ruxton, Dean (2019) 'When "the unemployed" seized the Rotunda in protest', *Irish Times*, 18 January

Ryan, Larry (2020) '"It's not political. It's about racism. I was so angry." Antrim Ladies' footballer Dahunsi calls on GAA for support', *Irish Examiner*, 9 June

Said, Edward (1979) *Orientalism*. New York: Vintage

Saxton, Alexander (2003) *The Rise and Fall of the White Republic: Class Politics and Mass Culture in Nineteenth Century America*. London: Verso.

Scott, James (1985) *Weapons of the Weak: Everyday Forms of Peasant Resistance*. New Haven, Connecticut: Yale University Press

Schiwy, Freya (2007) 'Decolonization and the Question of Subjectivity', *Cultural Studies*, 21(2-3): 271-294

Scully, Marc (2018) 'Are Irish passport applicants in Britain becoming "more Irish"'? *Irish Times*, 4 May

Seanad Éireann (2004) Volume 178, 1 December, 'Irish Nationality and Citizenship Bill 2004: Second Stage'

Serwer, Adam (2019) 'A White Man's Republic, If They Can Keep It', *The Atlantic*, 4 June

Shannon, William (1974) *The American Irish: A Political and Social Portrait*. Amherst: University of Massachusetts Press

Shapiro, James (2016) 'What ish my nation?' Shakespeare's Irish connections', *Irish Times*, 23 April

Shearman, Hugh (1952) *Modern Ireland*. London: George Harrap

Sheehan, Bernard (1980) *Savagism and Civility: Indians and Englishmen in Colonial Virginia*. Cambridge: Cambridge University Press

Sheehan, John (1998) 'Early Viking age silver hoards from Ireland', in H.B. Clark et al. (eds) *Ireland and Scandanavia in the Early Viking Age*. Dublin: Four Courts Press, 166-202

Silvestri, Michael (2000) 'Sir Charles Tegart and Revolutionary Terrorism in Bengal', *History Ireland*, Winter: 40-44

Singh, Sikandar (1998) *Udham Singh*. Amritsar: B. Chatter Singh Jiwan Singh

Sinn Féin (1971) *Éire Nua*. Dublin: Sinn Féin

Sivanandan, A. (1983) 'Challenging Racism: Strategies for the '80s', *Race and Class* 25(2): 1-11

Sivanandan, A. (1985) 'RAT and the Degradation of Black Struggle', *Race and Class* 26(4): 1-33

Sivanandan, A. (1989) 'All that melts into air is solid: the hokum of New Times', *Race and Class* 31(3): 1-30

Slater, Eamonn and Terrence McDonough (2008) 'Marx on nineteenth-century colonial Ireland: analysing colonialism as a dynamic social process', *Irish Historical Studies* 36(142): 153-172

Smandych, Russell (2013) 'Colonialism, settler colonialism, and law: settler revolutions and the dispossession of Indigenous peoples through law in the long nineteenth century', *Settler Colonial Studies* 3(1): 82-101

Smith, Tony (1978) 'A Comparative Study of French and British Decolonization', *Comparative Studies in Society and History* 20(1): 70-102

Smyth, Patrick (2019) 'Explainer: Apple's €13 bn tax appeal has huge implications', *Irish Times*,

13 September

Sovereign Union (2020) Aboriginal Sovereign Manifesto of Demands from November 2014, http://nationalunitygovernment.org/content/aboriginal-sovereign-manifesto-demands

Spenser, Edmund (1596) 'A View of the Present State of Ireland, Discoursed by Way of a Dialogue between Eudoxus and Irenius', in James P. Myers (ed) (1983) *Elizabethan Ireland: A Selection of Writings by Elizabethan Writers on Ireland*. Hamden, Connecticut: Archon Books

Spielvogel, Jackson (2018) *Western Civilization*. Boston: Cengage Learning

Spivak, Gayatri Chakravory (1988) 'Can the Subaltern Speak?', in Cary Nelson and Laurence Grossberg (eds) *Marxism and the Interpretation of Culture*. London: Palgrave Macmillan

Stalker, John (1989) *The Stalker Affair*. London: Penguin

Stanley, Henry (1896) *The Story of the Abyssinian Campaign of 1866-7*. London: Sampson, Low, Mabston and Co., https://archive.org/details/magdalastoryaby00stangoog/page/n9

Stein, Robert Louis (1979) *The French Slave Trade in the 18th Century*. Madison: University of Wisconsin Press

Stephens, Philip (2019) 'Boris Johnson on Varadkar: "Why isn't he called Murphy like all the rest of them?"', *Irish Times*, 18 July

Stevens, Peter (2005) *The Rogue's March: John Riley and the St. Patrick's Battalion, 1846-48*. Washington D.C.: Potomac Books

Storey, Andy and Michael McCaughan (2009) *The Great Gas Giveaway: How the elites have gambled our health and wealth*. Dublin: Afri

Storrs, Ronald (1937) *The Memoirs of Sir Ronald Storrs*. New York: G.P. Putnam's Sons

Sunday Times Insight Team (1972) *Ulster*. Harmondsworth: Penguin

Survival International (2018) 'Survival International urges 'no recovery' of body in Sentinelese case'. 26 November, https://www.survivalinternational.org/news/12036

Swift, Jonathan (1985) *Gulliver's Travels*. Harmondsworth: Penguin (first published 1726)

Taber, Robert (1965) *War of the Flea: A Study of Guerrilla Warfare Theory and Practice*. New York: Citadel Press

Tacitus (2010) *Agricola and Germania* (translated by H. Mattingley). London: Penguin Classics

Tatum, James (2003) *The Mourner's Song: War and Remembrance from the Iliad to Vietnam*. Chicago: University of Chicago Press

Tavernise, Sabrina (2018) 'Why the Announcement of a Looming White Minority Makes Demographers Nervous', *New York Times*, 22 November

Taylor, Peter (1980) *Beating the Terrorists? Interrogation in Omagh, Gough and Castlereagh*. Harmondsworth: Penguin

TCD, *1641 Depositions*. http://1641.tcd.ie/

Tharoor, Shashi (2016) *Inglorious Empire: What the British Did to India*. London: Penguin

The Clare Champion 2013. 'The Bishop of Kerry and the Fenians', 21 February

The Honourable the Irish Society (2020) 'Our History', https://www.honourableirishsociety. org.uk/about-us/our-history/plantation-planned

The Journal (2018) 'Should Ireland leave the EU? New poll shows only 10% of voters would back "Irexit"', www.thejournal.ie/ireland-leave-eu-poll-february-2018-3836085-Feb2018/

Thomas, Martin, Bob Moore and L.J. Butler (2008) *Crises of Empire: Decolonization and Europe's Imperial States, 1918-1975*. London: Hodder Education

Thomson, Ann (1991) 'Thomas Paine and the United Irishmen', *Etudes Irlandaises* 16(1): 109-119

Thornton, Chris, Seamus Kelters, Brian Feeney and David McKittrick (2004) *Lost Lives: The Stories of the Men, Women and Children Who Died as a Result of the Northern Ireland Troubles*. Edinburgh: Mainstream Publishing

Tierney, John (1981) 'America's 'Black Vietnam': Haiti's Cacos vs. The Marine Corps, 1915-22', *Lincoln Review* 2(3)

Times of India (2018) 'Why the Sentinelese choose solitude even after 60,000 years', 26 November

Tithe na Oireachtas (2017) Joint Committee on the Implementation of the Good Friday Agreement Brexit and the Future of Ireland Uniting Ireland & Its People in Peace & Prosperity, August, https://senatormarkdaly.files.wordpress.com/2018/04/united-ireland-and-its-people-in-peace-and-prosperity-report-1-pager.pdf

Todorov, Tzvetan (1999) *The Conquest of America: The Question of the Other*. Norman, Oklahoma: University of Oklahoma Press

Tomlinson, Mike (2002) 'Reconstituting social policy: the case of Northern Ireland', *Social Policy Review* 14: 57-83

Tomlinson, Mike (2012) 'From Counter-terrorism to Criminal Justice: Transformation or Business as Usual?', *The Howard Journal*, 51(5): 442-457

Tomlinson, Mike (2020) 'Comparing Covid-19 on the island of Ireland: Impossible, undesirable or doable?' *Eolas Magazine*, Issue 40, June/July, 90-1

Townend, Paul (2007) 'Between Two Worlds: Irish Nationalists and Imperial Crisis 1878-1880', *Past and Present* 194: 139-174

Truxes, Thomas M. (1988) *Irish-American Trade, 1660-1783*. Cambridge: Cambridge University Press

Tuck, Eve and K. Wayne Yang (2012) 'Decolonization is not a metaphor', *Decolonization, Indegeneity, Education and Society* 1(1): 1-40

Uday, Singh Rana (2017) *When the Queen Paid Homage to Martyrs of Jallianwala Bagh Massacre*, 13 April, https://www.news18.com/news/india/when-the-queen-paid-homage-to-martyrs-of-jallianwala-bagh-1372767.html

Umoja, Imani Na (2014) 'Cabral – Exemplary Light and Guide for the Pan-African and Socialist Revolutions', *Pambazuka News*, 22 January

United Nations (1960a) United Nations Declaration on the Granting of Independence to Colonial Countries and Peoples. General Assembly resolution 1514 (XV) of 14 December 1960, https://www.ohchr.org/EN/ProfessionalInterest/Pages/Independence.aspx

United Nations (2010) 'Fourth Committee Sends 12 Draft Texts to General Assembly on Decolonization, Including Request for Third International Decade, Concludes Debate on Topic', A/SPD/455 11 October 2010 Sixty-fifth General Assembly Fourth Committee 7th Meeting (AM), https://www.un.org/press/en/2010/gaspd455.doc.htm

University of Ulster (2017) 'Ulster University research reveals attitudes to abortion in Northern Ireland', https://www.ulster.ac.uk/news/2017/june/ulster-university-research-reveals-attitudes-to-abortion-in-northern-ireland

Van Krieken, Robert (1999) 'The barbarism of civilization: cultural genocide and the "stolen generations"', *British Journal of Sociology* 50(2): 295-313

Walker, Charles F. (2016) *The Tupac Amaru Rebellion*. Cambridge, MA.: Harvard University Press

Walker, Peter (2018) 'No plans to intervene on Northern Ireland abortion law, says No 10', *Guardian*, 29 May

Walker, Sean (2019) 'White Porgy and Bess cast "asked to say they identify as African-American"', *Guardian*, 7 April

Ward, Margaret (1995) *Unmanageable Revolutionaries*. London: Pluto Press

Ward, Stuart James and Astrid Rasch (2019) *Embers of Empire in Brexit Britain*. London: Bloomsbury Academic

Warner, Jehlen and Michael Warner (1997) *The English Literatures of America 1500-1800*. New York: Routledge

Wikipedia (2019) 'List of the largest empires', https://en.wikipedia.org/wiki/List_of_largest_empiresthe_greatest_Empire_the_world_has_ever_known

Willacy, Mark (2018) 'Aboriginal man Daniel Love facing deportation to PNG, lawyers', *ABC*

News 19 September, https://www.abc.net.au/news/2018-09-19/aboriginal-man-facing-deportation-to-png-takes-case-high-court/10262952

Williams, Kam (2011) 'Interview with Dr. Cornel West: Prognosis For America', https://www.theaquarian.com/2011/01/19/interview-with-dr-cornel-west-prognosis-for-america/

Williams, Patrick (1994) *Colonial Discourse and Post-Colonial Theory: A Reader*. London: Routledge

Wilson, Robin (2017) *Northern Ireland Peace Monitoring Report 4*. Belfast: Community Relations Council

Wilson, Tom (ed) (1955) *Ulster Under Home Rule*. Oxford: Oxford University Press

Wittke, Carl (1970) *The Irish in America*. New York: Russell and Russell

Wolfe, Patrick (1999) *Settler Colonialism and the Transformation of Anthropology*. London: Cassell

Wood, Forrest (1970) *Black Scare: The Racist Response to Emancipation and Reconstruction*. Berkeley: University of California Press

Wood, Ian (2006) *Crimes of Loyalty: A History of the UDA*. Edinburgh: Edinburgh University Press 2006.

Woodham-Smith, Cecil (1962) *The Great Hunger*. London: Penguin

World Heritage Encyclopedia. 'Irish Neutrality'. Community.worldheritage.org/articles/eng/Irish-neutrality

World Peace Foundation (2015) 'Algeria: War of independence', 7 August, https://sites.tufts.edu/atrocityendings/2015/08/07/algeria-war-of-independence/#_edn8

Wright, Clare (2013) *The Forgotten Rebels of Eureka*. Melbourne: Text Publishing

Wyse, Thomas (1829) *Historical Sketch of the Catholic Association*. London: Henry Colburn, https://books.google.co.uk/books/about/Historical_sketch_of_the_late_Catholic_a.html?id=Xx69h95NX_cC

YouGov (2014) 'The British Empire is "something to be proud of"', https://yougov.co.uk/news/2014/07/26/britain-proud-its-empire/

Young, G.M. (1935) *Speeches by Lord Macaulay*. Oxford: Oxford University Press

Young, Robert (2001) *Postcolonialism: An Historical Introduction*. London: Blackwell

Index

Page numbers in italics relate to items cited in footnotes only.